Ford
Orion
Owners
Workshop
Manual

I M Coomber

Models covered
Ford Orion models with petrol engines, including
special/limited edition versions
1296 cc, 1297 cc, 1392 cc & 1597 cc

*Does not cover Diesel engine, CTX transmission or revised Orion
range introduced in September 1990*

(1009-9T8)

ABCDE
FGHIJ
KLMNO
PQR

2

Haynes Publishing Group
Sparkford Nr Yeovil
Somerset BA22 7JJ England

Haynes Publications, Inc
861 Lawrence Drive
Newbury Park
California 91320 USA

Acknowledgements

Thanks are due to the Champion Sparking Plug Company Limited, who supplied the illustrations showing spark plug conditions, to Holt Lloyd Limited who supplied the illustrations showing bodywork repair, and to Duckhams Oils, who provided lubrication data. Certain other illustrations are the copyright of the Ford Motor Company, and are used with their permission. Thanks are also due to Sykes-Pickavant, who supplied some of the workshop tools, and also to the staff at Sparkford who assisted in the production of this manual.

© **Haynes Publishing Group 1991**

A book in the **Haynes Owners Workshop Manual Series**

Printed by J. H. Haynes & Co. Ltd., Sparkford, Nr Yeovil, Somerset BA22 7JJ, England

ISBN 1 85010 842 0

British Library Cataloguing in Publication Data
A catalogue record for this book is available from the British Library

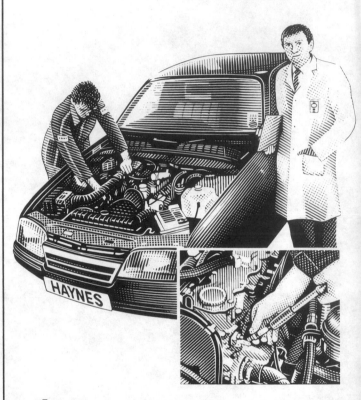

Contents

4

Ford Orion

About this manual

Its aim

The aim of this manual is to help you get the best value from your vehicle. It can do so in several ways. It can help you decide what work must be done (even should you choose to get it done by a garage), provide information on routine maintenance and servicing, and give a logical course of action and diagnosis when random faults occur. However, it is hoped that you will use the manual by tackling the work yourself. On simpler jobs it may even be quicker than booking the car into a garage and going there twice, to leave and collect it. Perhaps most important, a lot of money can be saved by avoiding the costs a garage must charge to cover its labour and overheads.

The manual has drawings and descriptions to show the function of the various components so that their layout can be understood. Then the tasks are described and photographed in a step-by-step sequence so that even a novice can do the work.

Its arrangement

The manual is divided into thirteen Chapters, each covering a logical sub-division of the vehicle. The Chapters are each divided into Sections, numbered with single figures, eg 5; and the Sections into paragraphs (or sub-sections), with decimal numbers following on from the Section they are in, eg 5.1, 5.2, 5.3 etc.

It is freely illustrated, especially in those parts where there is a detailed sequence of operations to be carried out. There are two forms of illustration: figures and photographs. The figures are numbered in sequence with decimal numbers, according to their position in the Chapter — eg Fig. 6.4 is the fourth drawing/illustration in Chapter 6. Photographs carry the same number (either individually or in related groups) as the Section or sub-section to which they relate.

There is an alphabetical index at the back of the manual as well as a contents list at the front. Each Chapter is also preceded by its own individual contents list.

References to the 'left' or 'right' of the vehicle are in the sense of a person in the driver's seat facing forwards.

Unless otherwise stated, nuts and bolts are removed by turning anti-clockwise, and tightened by turning clockwise.

Vehicle manufacturers continually make changes to specifications and recommendations, and these, when notified, are incorporated into our manuals at the earliest opportunity.

Whilst every care is taken to ensure that the information in this manual is correct, no liability can be accepted by the authors or publishers for loss, damage or injury caused by any errors in, or omissions from, the information given.

Introduction to the Ford Orion

The Ford Orion was introduced in late 1983, its traditional three-box styling filling the gap in the Ford range vacated by the demise of the Cortina. The Orion is available with the option of four engines and three transmissions. This manual covers the three CVH petrol variants of 1.3 and 1.6 litre capacity. The fourth option, the 1.6 litre diesel engine variant, is not covered.

The transmissions offered are four- or five-speed manual gearboxes or the new Ford ATX automatic transmission.

The mechanics, body and interior trim of the Orion have many similarities to the Escort, but particular emphasis has been made on providing a more spacious rear seat compartment. The split-fold rear seat provides additional luggage carrying capacity (when required) to the already large and well proportioned boot.

For the home mechanic the Orion is an ideal car to maintain and repair since design features have been incorporated to reduce the actual cost of ownership to a minimum, with the result that components requiring relatively frequent attention (eg the exhaust system) are easily removed.

Buying spare parts and vehicle identification numbers

Buying spare parts

Spare parts are available from many sources, for example Ford garages, other garages and accessory shops, and motor factors. Our advice regarding spare part sources is as follows:

Officially appointed Ford garages – This is the best source of parts which are peculiar to your vehicle and are otherwise not generally available (eg, complete cylinder heads, internal gearbox components, badges, interior trim etc). It is also the only place at which you should buy parts if your vehicle is still under warranty – non-Ford components may invalidate the warranty. To be sure of obtaining the correct parts it will always be necessary to give the storeman your vehicle's engine and chassis number, and if possible, to take the 'old' parts along for positive identification. Remember that some parts are available on a factory exchange scheme – any parts returned should always be clean! It obviously makes good sense to go straight to the specialists on your vehicle for this type of part for they are best equipped to supply you.

Other garages and accessory shops – These are often good places to buy materials and components needed for the maintenance of your vehicle (eg, spark plugs, bulbs, drivebelts, oils and greases, touch-up paint, filler paste, etc). They also sell general accessories, usually have convenient opening hours, charge lower prices and can often be found not far from home.

Motor factors – Good factors will stock all of the more important components which wear out relatively quickly (eg clutch components, pistons, valves, exhaust systems, brake cylinders/pipes/hoses/seals/shoes and pads etc). Motor factors will often provide new or reconditioned components on a part exchange basis – this can save a considerable amount of money.

Vehicle identification numbers

The *Vehicle Identification Number* is located on the plate found under the bonnet above the radiator. The plate also carries information concerning paint colour, final drive ratio, etc.

The *Vehicle Identification Number* is also stamped into the floor pan inside the car just to the right of the driver's seat. The carpet is cut to enable a flap of material to be slid out from under the scuff plate to reveal the number.

The engine number is located on the front right-hand side, next to the alternator bracket.

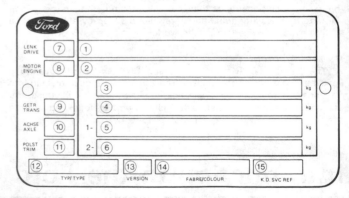

Vehicle identification (VIN) plate

1 Type approval number	9 Transmission
2 Vehicle identification number	10 Axle (final drive ratio)
3 Gross vehicle weight	11 Trim (interior)
4 Gross train weight	12 Body type
5 Permitted front axle loading	13 Special territory version
6 Permitted rear axle loading	14 Body colour
7 Steering (LHD/RHD)	15 KD reference (usually blank)
8 Engine	

Tools and working facilities

Introduction

A selection of good tools is a fundamental requirement for anyone contemplating the maintenance and repair of a motor vehicle. For the owner who does not possess any, their purchase will prove a considerable expense, offsetting some of the savings made by doing-it-yourself. However, provided that the tools purchased meet the relevant national safety standards and are of good quality, they will last for many years and prove an extremely worthwhile investment.

To help the average owner to decide which tools are needed to carry out the various tasks detailed in this manual, we have compiled three lists of tools under the following headings: *Maintenance and minor repair*, *Repair and overhaul*, and *Special*. The newcomer to practical mechanics should start off with the *Maintenance and minor repair* tool kit and confine himself to the simpler jobs around the vehicle. Then, as his confidence and experience grow, he can undertake more difficult tasks, buying extra tools as, and when, they are needed. In this way, a *Maintenance and minor repair* tool kit can be built-up into a *Repair and overhaul* tool kit over a considerable period of time without any major cash outlays. The experienced do-it-yourselfer will have a tool kit good enough for most repair and overhaul procedures and will add tools from the *Special* category when he feels the expense is justified by the amount of use to which these tools will be put.

It is obviously not possible to cover the subject of tools fully here. For those who wish to learn more about tools and their use there is a book entitled *How to Choose and Use Car Tools* available from the publishers of this manual.

Maintenance and minor repair tool kit

The tools given in this list should be considered as a minimum requirement if routine maintenance, servicing and minor repair operations are to be undertaken. We recommend the purchase of combination spanners (ring one end, open-ended the other); although more expensive than open-ended ones, they do give the advantages of both types of spanner.

Combination spanners - 10, 11, 12, 13, 14 & 17 mm
Adjustable spanner - 9 inch
Spark plug spanner (with rubber insert)
Spark plug gap adjustment tool
Set of feeler gauges
Brake bleed nipple spanner
Screwdriver - 4 in long x $\frac{1}{4}$ in dia (flat blade)
Screwdriver - 4 in long x $\frac{1}{4}$ in dia (cross blade)
Combination pliers - 6 inch
Hacksaw (junior)
Tyre pump
Tyre pressure gauge
Oil can
Fine emery cloth (1 sheet)
Wire brush (small)
Funnel (medium size)

Repair and overhaul tool kit

These tools are virtually essential for anyone undertaking any major repairs to a motor vehicle, and are additional to those given in the *Maintenance and minor repair* list. Included in this list is a comprehensive set of sockets. Although these are expensive they will be found invaluable as they are so versatile - particularly if various drives are included in the set. We recommend the $\frac{1}{2}$ in square-drive type, as this can be used with most proprietary torque wrenches. If you cannot afford a socket set, even bought piecemeal, then inexpensive tubular box spanners are a useful alternative.

The tools in this list will occasionally need to be supplemented by tools from the *Special* list.

Sockets (or box spanners) to cover range in previous list
Reversible ratchet drive (for use with sockets)
Extension piece, 10 inch (for use with sockets)
Universal joint (for use with sockets)
Torque wrench (for use with sockets)
'Mole' wrench - 8 inch
Ball pein hammer
Soft-faced hammer, plastic or rubber
Screwdriver - 6 in long x $\frac{5}{16}$ in dia (flat blade)
Screwdriver - 2 in long x $\frac{5}{16}$ in square (flat blade)
Screwdriver - 1$\frac{1}{2}$ in long x $\frac{1}{4}$ in dia (cross blade)
Screwdriver - 3 in long x $\frac{1}{8}$ in dia (electricians)
Pliers - electricians side cutters
Pliers - needle nosed
Pliers - circlip (internal and external)
Cold chisel - $\frac{1}{2}$ inch
Scriber
Scraper
Centre punch
Pin punch
Hacksaw
Valve grinding tool
Steel rule/straight-edge
Allen keys
Selection of files
Wire brush (large)
Axle-stands
Jack (strong scissor or hydraulic type)
Torx bits

Special tools

The tools in this list are those which are not used regularly, are expensive to buy, or which need to be used in accordance with their manufacturers' instructions. Unless relatively difficult mechanical jobs are undertaken frequently, it will not be economic to buy many of these tools. Where this is the case, you could consider clubbing together with friends (or joining a motorists' club) to make a joint purchase, or borrowing the tools against a deposit from a local garage or tool hire specialist.

The following list contains only those tools and instruments freely available to the public, and not those special tools produced by the vehicle manufacturer specifically for its dealer network. You will find occasional references to these manufacturers' special tools in the text of this manual. Generally, an alternative method of doing the job without the vehicle manufacturers' special tool is given. However, sometimes, there is no alternative to using them. Where this is the case and the relevant tool cannot be bought or borrowed, you will have to entrust the work to a franchised garage.

Valve spring compressor
Piston ring compressor
Balljoint separator
Universal hub/bearing puller
Impact screwdriver
Micrometer and/or vernier gauge
Dial gauge
Stroboscopic timing light
Tachometer
Universal electrical multi-meter
Cylinder compression gauge
Lifting tackle
Trolley jack
Light with extension lead

Buying tools

For practically all tools, a tool factor is the best source since he will have a very comprehensive range compared with the average garage or accessory shop. Having said that, accessory shops often offer excellent quality tools at discount prices, so it pays to shop around.

There are plenty of good tools around at reasonable prices, but always aim to purchase items which meet the relevant national safety standards. If in doubt, ask the proprietor or manager of the shop for advice before making a purchase.

Care and maintenance of tools

Having purchased a reasonable tool kit, it is necessary to keep the tools in a clean serviceable condition. After use, always wipe off any dirt, grease and metal particles using a clean, dry cloth, before putting the tools away. Never leave them lying around after they have been used. A simple tool rack on the garage or workshop wall, for items such as screwdrivers and pliers is a good idea. Store all normal wrenches and sockets in a metal box. Any measuring instruments, gauges, meters, etc, must be carefully stored where they cannot be damaged or become rusty.

Take a little care when tools are used. Hammer heads inevitably become marked and screwdrivers lose the keen edge on their blades from time to time. A little timely attention with emery cloth or a file will soon restore items like this to a good serviceable finish.

Working facilities

Not to be forgotten when discussing tools, is the workshop itself. If anything more than routine maintenance is to be carried out, some form of suitable working area becomes essential.

It is appreciated that many an owner mechanic is forced by circumstances to remove an engine or similar item, without the benefit of a garage or workshop. Having done this, any repairs should always be done under the cover of a roof.

Wherever possible, any dismantling should be done on a clean, flat workbench or table at a suitable working height.

Any workbench needs a vice: one with a jaw opening of 4 in (100 mm) is suitable for most jobs. As mentioned previously, some clean dry storage space is also required for tools, as well as for lubricants, cleaning fluids, touch-up paints and so on, which become necessary.

Another item which may be required, and which has a much more general usage, is an electric drill with a chuck capacity of at least $\frac{5}{16}$ in (8 mm). This, together with a good range of twist drills, is virtually essential for fitting accessories such as mirrors and reversing lights.

Last, but not least, always keep a supply of old newspapers and clean, lint-free rags available, and try to keep any working area as clean as possible.

Spanner jaw gap comparison table

Jaw gap (in)	Spanner size
0.250	$\frac{1}{4}$ in AF
0.276	7 mm
0.313	$\frac{5}{16}$ in AF
0.315	8 mm
0.344	$\frac{11}{32}$ in AF; $\frac{1}{8}$ in Whitworth
0.354	9 mm
0.375	$\frac{3}{8}$ in AF
0.394	10 mm
0.433	11 mm
0.438	$\frac{7}{16}$ in AF
0.445	$\frac{3}{16}$ in Whitworth; $\frac{1}{4}$ in BSF
0.472	12 mm
0.500	$\frac{1}{2}$ in AF
0.512	13 mm
0.525	$\frac{1}{4}$ in Whitworth; $\frac{5}{16}$ in BSF
0.551	14 mm
0.563	$\frac{9}{16}$ in AF
0.591	15 mm
0.600	$\frac{5}{16}$ in Whitworth; $\frac{3}{8}$ in BSF
0.625	$\frac{5}{8}$ in AF
0.630	16 mm
0.669	17 mm
0.686	$\frac{11}{16}$ in AF
0.709	18 mm
0.710	$\frac{3}{8}$ in Whitworth; $\frac{7}{16}$ in BSF
0.748	19 mm
0.750	$\frac{3}{4}$ in AF
0.813	$\frac{13}{16}$ in AF
0.820	$\frac{7}{16}$ in Whitworth; $\frac{1}{2}$ in BSF
0.866	22 mm
0.875	$\frac{7}{8}$ in AF
0.920	$\frac{1}{2}$ in Whitworth; $\frac{9}{16}$ in BSF
0.938	$\frac{15}{16}$ in AF
0.945	24 mm
1.000	1 in AF
1.010	$\frac{9}{16}$ in Whitworth; $\frac{5}{8}$ in BSF
1.024	26 mm
1.063	$1\frac{1}{16}$ in AF; 27 mm
1.100	$\frac{5}{8}$ in Whitworth; $\frac{11}{16}$ in BSF
1.125	$1\frac{1}{8}$ in AF
1.181	30 mm
1.200	$\frac{11}{16}$ in Whitworth; $\frac{3}{4}$ in BSF
1.250	$1\frac{1}{4}$ in AF
1.260	32 mm
1.300	$\frac{3}{4}$ in Whitworth; $\frac{7}{8}$ in BSF
1.313	$1\frac{5}{16}$ in AF
1.390	$\frac{13}{16}$ in Whitworth; $\frac{15}{16}$ in BSF
1.417	36 mm
1.438	$1\frac{7}{16}$ in AF
1.480	$\frac{7}{8}$ in Whitworth; 1 in BSF
1.500	$1\frac{1}{2}$ in AF
1.575	40 mm; $\frac{15}{16}$ in Whitworth
1.614	41 mm
1.625	$1\frac{5}{8}$ in AF
1.670	1 in Whitworth; $1\frac{1}{8}$ in BSF
1.688	$1\frac{11}{16}$ in AF
1.811	46 mm
1.813	$1\frac{13}{16}$ in AF
1.860	$1\frac{1}{8}$ in Whitworth; $1\frac{1}{4}$ in BSF
1.875	$1\frac{7}{8}$ in AF
1.969	50 mm
2.000	2 in AF
2.050	$1\frac{1}{4}$ in Whitworth; $1\frac{3}{8}$ in BSF
2.165	55 mm
2.362	60 mm

General repair procedures

Whenever servicing, repair or overhaul work is carried out on the car or its components, it is necessary to observe the following procedures and instructions. This will assist in carrying out the operation efficiently and to a professional standard of workmanship.

Joint mating faces and gaskets

Where a gasket is used between the mating faces of two components, ensure that it is renewed on reassembly, and fit it dry unless otherwise stated in the repair procedure. Make sure that the mating faces are clean and dry with all traces of old gasket removed. When cleaning a joint face, use a tool which is not likely to score or damage the face, and remove any burrs or nicks with an oilstone or fine file.

Make sure that tapped holes are cleaned with a pipe cleaner, and keep them free of jointing compound if this is being used unless specifically instructed otherwise.

Ensure that all orifices, channels or pipes are clear and blow through them, preferably using compressed air.

Oil seals

Whenever an oil seal is removed from its working location, either individually or as part of an assembly, it should be renewed.

The very fine sealing lip of the seal is easily damaged and will not seal if the surface it contacts is not completely clean and free from scratches, nicks or grooves. If the original sealing surface of the component cannot be restored, the component should be renewed.

Protect the lips of the seal from any surface which may damage them in the course of fitting. Use tape or a conical sleeve where possible. Lubricate the seal lips with oil before fitting and, on dual lipped seals, fill the space between the lips with grease.

Unless otherwise stated, oil seals must be fitted with their sealing lips toward the lubricant to be sealed.

Use a tubular drift or block of wood of the appropriate size to install the seal and, if the seal housing is shouldered, drive the seal down to the shoulder. If the seal housing is unshouldered, the seal should be fitted with its face flush with the housing top face.

Screw threads and fastenings

Always ensure that a blind tapped hole is completely free from oil, grease, water or other fluid before installing the bolt or stud. Failure to do this could cause the housing to crack due to the hydraulic action of the bolt or stud as it is screwed in.

When tightening a castellated nut to accept a split pin, tighten the nut to the specified torque, where applicable, and then tighten further to the next split pin hole. Never slacken the nut to align a split pin hole unless stated in the repair procedure.

When checking or retightening a nut or bolt to a specified torque setting, slacken the nut or bolt by a quarter of a turn, and then retighten to the specified setting.

Locknuts, locktabs and washers

Any fastening which will rotate against a component or housing in the course of tightening should always have a washer between it and the relevant component or housing.

Spring or split washers should always be renewed when they are used to lock a critical component such as a big-end bearing retaining nut or bolt.

Locktabs which are folded over to retain a nut or bolt should always be renewed.

Self-locking nuts can be reused in non-critical areas, providing resistance can be felt when the locking portion passes over the bolt or stud thread.

Split pins must always be replaced with new ones of the correct size for the hole.

Special tools

Some repair procedures in this manual entail the use of special tools such as a press, two or three-legged pullers, spring compressors etc. Wherever possible, suitable readily available alternatives to the manufacturer's special tools are described, and are shown in use. In some instances, where no alternative is possible, it has been necessary to resort to the use of a manufacturer's tool and this has been done for reasons of safety as well as the efficient completion of the repair operation. Unless you are highly skilled and have a thorough understanding of the procedure described, never attempt to bypass the use of any special tool when the procedure described specifies its use. Not only is there a very great risk of personal injury, but expensive damage could be caused to the components involved.

Jacking and towing

Jacking

The jack supplied in the vehicle tool kit should only be used for emergency roadside wheel changing, unless it is supplemented with axle stands.

The jack supplied is of half scissors type. Check that the handbrake is fully applied before using the jack.

Use the jack at the mounting points on either side of the vehicle just below the sill.

When using a trolley or other type of workshop jack, it can be placed under the front lower crossmember (provided a shaped block of wood is used as an insulator) to raise the front of the vehicle.

To raise the rear, place the jack under the right-hand suspension lower arm mounting bracket using a rubber pad as an insulator.

Axle stands should only be located under the double-skinned sections of the side-members at the front of the vehicle, or under the sill jacking points. At the rear of the vehicle place the stands under the

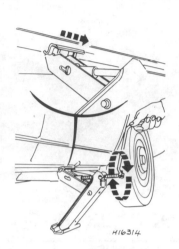

Engage vehicle jack as shown before winding up

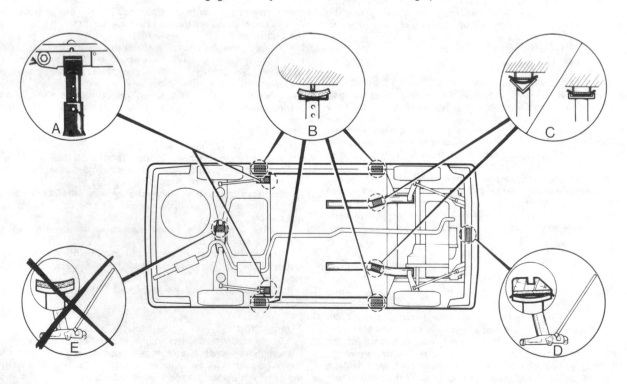

Jacking and support points on vehicle underside

A	Safety stands (rear)	
B	Safety stands (sills)	
C	Safety stands (front chassis runners)	
D	Trolley jack (front lower crossmember – use protector block)	
E	Trolley jack (centre at rear*)	
*	Not fuel injection models (injection pump location)	

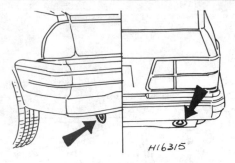

Vehicle towing eyes

member to which the trailing arms are attached.

Provided only one wheel at the rear of the vehicle is to be raised, the vehicle may be jacked up under the rear spring seat.

Towing

Towing eyes are fitted to the front and the rear of the vehicle for attachment of a tow rope.

Always unlock the steering column if being towed by another vehicle. If servo-assisted brakes are fitted, remember that the servo is inoperative if the engine is not running.

If the vehicle being towed has automatic transmission reference should be made to the precautionary notes in Section 18 of Chapter 6.

General dimensions, weights and capacities

For modifications, and information applicable to later models, see Supplement at end of manual

Dimensions
Overall length	4228 mm (166.5 in)
Overall height:	
Max	1408 mm (55.4 in)
Min	1385 mm (54.5 in)
Overall width	1640 mm (64.6 in)
Wheelbase	2400 mm (94.5 in)
Turning circle:	
Between kerbs	10.0 m (32.8 ft)
Between walls	10.6 m (34.8 ft)

Weights
Gross vehicle weight:	
1.3	1300 kg (2866 lb)
1.6 Manual (carburettor model)	1325 kg (2921 lb)
1.6 Automatic	1350 kg (2976 lb)
1.6 Manual (fuel injection)	1350 kg (2976 lb)
Basic kerb weight:	
1.3	895 kg (1973 lb)
1.6 Manual (carburettor model)	905 kg (1994 lb)
1.6 Manual (fuel injection)	935 kg (2061 lb)
1.6 Automatic	945 kg (2083 lb)
Maximum towing limit – all models	900 kg (1984 lb)
Maximum roof rack load – all models	75 kg (165 lb)

Capacities
Engine oil with filter change	3.50 litres (6.16 Imp pints)
Engine oil without filter change	3.25 litres (5.72 Imp pints)
Fuel tank	48 litres (10.6 Imp galls)
Cooling system capacity:	
1.3 engine	7.1 litres (12.5 Imp pints)
1.6 engine	6.9 litres (12.1 Imp pints)
Transmission:	
Four-speed manual	2.8 litres (4.9 Imp pints)
Five-speed manual	3.1 litres (5.5 Imp pints)
Three-speed automatic	7.9 litres (13.9 Imp pints)

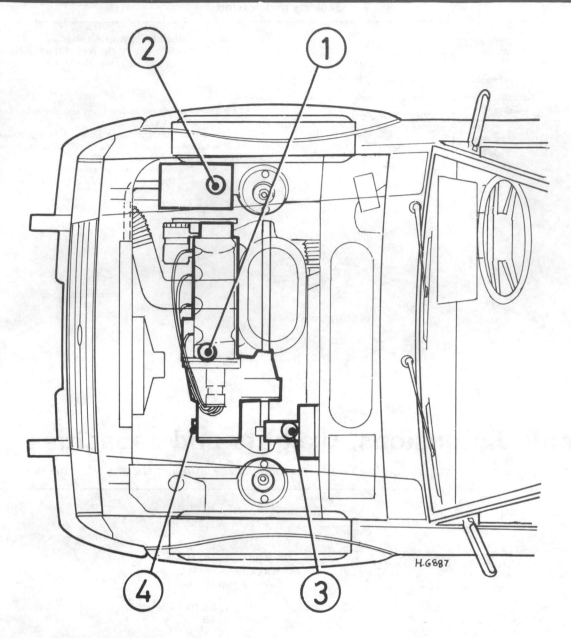

H.G887

Recommended lubricants and fluids

For information applicable to later models, see Supplement at end of manual

Component or system	Lubricant type/specification	Duckhams recommendation
Engine (1)	Multigrade engine oil, viscosity SAE 10W/30, to API SF/CC	Duckhams QXR, Hypergrade, or 10W/40 Motor Oil
Cooling system (2)	Antifreeze to Ford spec SSM-97B 9103-A	Duckhams Universal Antifreeze and Summer Coolant
Braking system (3)	Brake fluid to Ford spec SAM-6C 9103-A	Duckhams Universal Brake and Clutch Fluid
Manual gearbox (4)	Hypoid gear oil, viscosity SAE 80 EP, to Ford spec SQM-2C 9008-A	Duckhams Hypoid 80
Automatic transmission:		
Early models	ATF to Ford spec SQM-2C 9010-A or ESP-M2C 138-CJ	Duckhams Uni-Matic or D-Matic
Later models (black dipstick)	ATF to Ford spec ESP-M2C 166H	Duckhams Uni-Matic or Q-Matic

Safety first!

Professional motor mechanics are trained in safe working procedures. However enthusiastic you may be about getting on with the job in hand, do take the time to ensure that your safety is not put at risk. A moment's lack of attention can result in an accident, as can failure to observe certain elementary precautions.

There will always be new ways of having accidents, and the following points do not pretend to be a comprehensive list of all dangers; they are intended rather to make you aware of the risks and to encourage a safety-conscious approach to all work you carry out on your vehicle.

Essential DOs and DON'Ts

DON'T rely on a single jack when working underneath the vehicle. Always use reliable additional means of support, such as axle stands, securely placed under a part of the vehicle that you know will not give way.

DON'T attempt to loosen or tighten high-torque nuts (e.g. wheel hub nuts) while the vehicle is on a jack; it may be pulled off.

DON'T start the engine without first ascertaining that the transmission is in neutral (or 'Park' where applicable) and the parking brake applied.

DON'T suddenly remove the filler cap from a hot cooling system – cover it with a cloth and release the pressure gradually first, or you may get scalded by escaping coolant.

DON'T attempt to drain oil until you are sure it has cooled sufficiently to avoid scalding you.

DON'T grasp any part of the engine, exhaust or catalytic converter without first ascertaining that it is sufficiently cool to avoid burning you.

DON'T allow brake fluid or antifreeze to contact vehicle paintwork.

DON'T syphon toxic liquids such as fuel, brake fluid or antifreeze by mouth, or allow them to remain on your skin.

DON'T inhale dust – it may be injurious to health (see *Asbestos* below).

DON'T allow any spilt oil or grease to remain on the floor – wipe it up straight away, before someone slips on it.

DON'T use ill-fitting spanners or other tools which may slip and cause injury.

DON'T attempt to lift a heavy component which may be beyond your capability – get assistance.

DON'T rush to finish a job, or take unverified short cuts.

DON'T allow children or animals in or around an unattended vehicle.

DO wear eye protection when using power tools such as drill, sander, bench grinder etc, and when working under the vehicle.

DO use a barrier cream on your hands prior to undertaking dirty jobs – it will protect your skin from infection as well as making the dirt easier to remove afterwards; but make sure your hands aren't left slippery. Note that long-term contact with used engine oil can be a health hazard.

DO keep loose clothing (cuffs, tie etc) and long hair well out of the way of moving mechanical parts.

DO remove rings, wristwatch etc, before working on the vehicle – especially the electrical system.

DO ensure that any lifting tackle used has a safe working load rating adequate for the job.

DO keep your work area tidy – it is only too easy to fall over articles left lying around.

DO get someone to check periodically that all is well, when working alone on the vehicle.

DO carry out work in a logical sequence and check that everything is correctly assembled and tightened afterwards.

DO remember that your vehicle's safety affects that of yourself and others. If in doubt on any point, get specialist advice.

IF, in spite of following these precautions, you are unfortunate enough to injure yourself, seek medical attention as soon as possible.

Asbestos

Certain friction, insulating, sealing, and other products – such as brake linings, brake bands, clutch linings, torque converters, gaskets, etc – contain asbestos. *Extreme care must be taken to avoid inhalation of dust from such products since it is hazardous to health.* If in doubt, assume that they *do* contain asbestos.

Fire

Remember at all times that petrol (gasoline) is highly flammable. Never smoke, or have any kind of naked flame around, when working on the vehicle. But the risk does not end there – a spark caused by an electrical short-circuit, by two metal surfaces contacting each other, by careless use of tools, or even by static electricity built up in your body under certain conditions, can ignite petrol vapour, which in a confined space is highly explosive.

Always disconnect the battery earth (ground) terminal before working on any part of the fuel or electrical system, and never risk spilling fuel on to a hot engine or exhaust.

It is recommended that a fire extinguisher of a type suitable for fuel and electrical fires is kept handy in the garage or workplace at all times. Never try to extinguish a fuel or electrical fire with water.

Note: *Any reference to a 'torch' appearing in this manual should always be taken to mean a hand-held battery-operated electric lamp or flashlight. It does NOT mean a welding/gas torch or blowlamp.*

Fumes

Certain fumes are highly toxic and can quickly cause unconsciousness and even death if inhaled to any extent. Petrol (gasoline) vapour comes into this category, as do the vapours from certain solvents such as trichloroethylene. Any draining or pouring of such volatile fluids should be done in a well ventilated area.

When using cleaning fluids and solvents, read the instructions carefully. Never use materials from unmarked containers – they may give off poisonous vapours.

Never run the engine of a motor vehicle in an enclosed space such as a garage. Exhaust fumes contain carbon monoxide which is extremely poisonous; if you need to run the engine, always do so in the open air or at least have the rear of the vehicle outside the workplace.

If you are fortunate enough to have the use of an inspection pit, never drain or pour petrol, and never run the engine, while the vehicle is standing over it; the fumes, being heavier than air, will concentrate in the pit with possibly lethal results.

The battery

Never cause a spark, or allow a naked light, near the vehicle's battery. It will normally be giving off a certain amount of hydrogen gas, which is highly explosive.

Always disconnect the battery earth (ground) terminal before working on the fuel or electrical systems.

If possible, loosen the filler plugs or cover when charging the battery from an external source. Do not charge at an excessive rate or the battery may burst.

Take care when topping up and when carrying the battery. The acid electrolyte, even when diluted, is very corrosive and should not be allowed to contact the eyes or skin.

If you ever need to prepare electrolyte yourself, always add the acid slowly to the water, and never the other way round. Protect against splashes by wearing rubber gloves and goggles.

When jump starting a car using a booster battery, for negative earth (ground) vehicles, connect the jump leads in the following sequence: First connect one jump lead between the positive (+) terminals of the two batteries. Then connect the other jump lead first to the negative (–) terminal of the booster battery, and then to a good earthing (ground) point on the vehicle to be started, at least 18 in (45 cm) from the battery if possible. Ensure that hands and jump leads are clear of any moving parts, and that the two vehicles do not touch. Disconnect the leads in the reverse order.

Mains electricity and electrical equipment

When using an electric power tool, inspection light etc, always ensure that the appliance is correctly connected to its plug and that, where necessary, it is properly earthed (grounded). Do not use such appliances in damp conditions and, again, beware of creating a spark or applying excessive heat in the vicinity of fuel or fuel vapour. Also ensure that the appliances meet the relevant national safety standards.

Ignition HT voltage

A severe electric shock can result from touching certain parts of the ignition system, such as the HT leads, when the engine is running or being cranked, particularly if components are damp or the insulation is defective. Where an electronic ignition system is fitted, the HT voltage is much higher and could prove fatal.

Routine maintenance

For modifications, and further information, see Supplement at end of manual

Maintenance is essential for ensuring safety, and desirable for the purpose of getting the best in terms of performance and economy from the vehicle. Over the years the need for periodic lubrication – oiling, greasing and so on – has been drastically reduced, if not totally eliminated. This has unfortunately tended to lead some owners to think that because no such action is required the items either no longer exist or will last for ever. This is a serious delusion. It follows therefore that the largest initial element of maintenance is visual examination. This may lead to repairs or renewals.

Weekly or every 400 km (250 miles)

Check the engine oil level and top up if necessary (photos)
Check the coolant level in the expansion tank and top up if necessary
Check the battery electrolyte level and top up if necessary (where applicable – see Chapter 11)
Top up the fluid level in the washer reservoirs (photo) adding a screenwash such as Turtle Wax High Tech Screen Wash
Check brake fluid level, investigate any sudden fall in level (photo)
Check the operation of all lights
Check the operation of the horn
Check the operation of washers and wipers
Check tyre pressures, including the spare
Check the tyres for wear or damage

At the first 2500 km (1500 miles) – new vehicles

Check the alternator drivebelt tension (see Chapter 11)
Check torque of intake and exhaust manifold bolts (cold)

Check brake hydraulic system connectors for leaks
Check idle speed, CO% (mixture) and choke adjustment (see Chapter 3)
Check emission control system components and hoses for condition and security (as applicable) as given in Chapter 3.

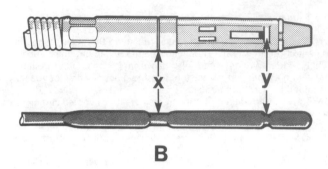

Engine oil dipstick level markings

A   Dipstick with warning system   X   Maximum oil level
B   Standard dipstick   Y   Minimum oil level

Engine oil dipstick

Topping-up the engine oil

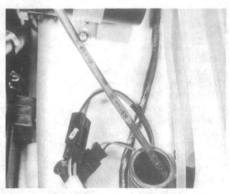

Check level of windscreen washer fluid in reservoir (wing-mounted type)

Brake fluid reservoir

Sump drain plug

Engine oil filter

Every 10 000 km (6000 miles)

Drain and renew the engine oil and oil filter (photos)
Check for oil, fuel and water leaks
Clean the fuel pump filter
Check the brake disc pads (front) and shoe linings (rear) for excessive wear (see Chapter 8)
Check steering and suspension joints for wear and gaiters for deterioration (see Chapter 9)
Check tightness of roadwheel bolts

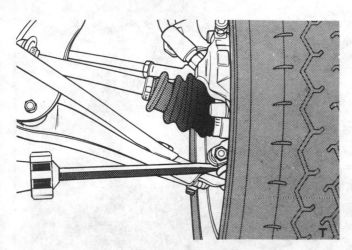

Suspension balljoint being checked for wear

Every 20 000 km (12 000 miles)

Remove and renew the spark plugs
Check HT leads and connections for security. Clean the leads and also the distributor cap (see Chapter 4)
Lubricate the controls, hinges and locks
Check security and condition of the exhaust system
Check the transmission oil level and top up if necessary (see Chapter 6)
Check the driveshaft gaiters for deterioration or damage
Check the rear hub bearing adjustment (see Chapter 10)
Check the car underbody and floorpans for signs of serious corrosion, particularly near to the suspension mountings

Check windscreen wiper blades and operation of washers
Check the seat belts for condition, operation and security at mountings

Every 40 000 km (24 000 miles)

Remove and renew the air cleaner element (see Chapter 3)
Check the air cleaner temperature control (see Chapter 3)
Renew the crankcase emission control filter (photo)

Every 2 years

Drain and renew the engine coolant together with the specified antifreeze/inhibitor (see Chapter 2)

Every 3 years

Make a thorough inspection of all brake components for signs of leaks, general deterioration and wear in mechanical parts
Drain and renew the hydraulic fluid (see Chapter 8)

Crankcase emission control filter (fuel injection engine)

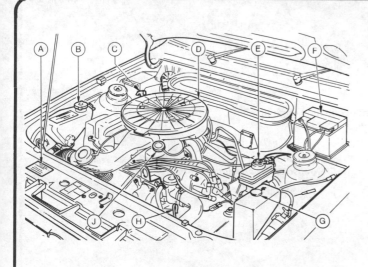

Engine compartment – automatic transmission model

A   Vehicle identification plate
B   Coolant expansion tank reservoir
C   Engine oil dipstick
D   Air cleaner unit
E   Brake fluid reservoir
F   Battery
G   Windscreen washer reservoir
H   Automatic transmission fluid dipstick
J   Engine oil filler cap

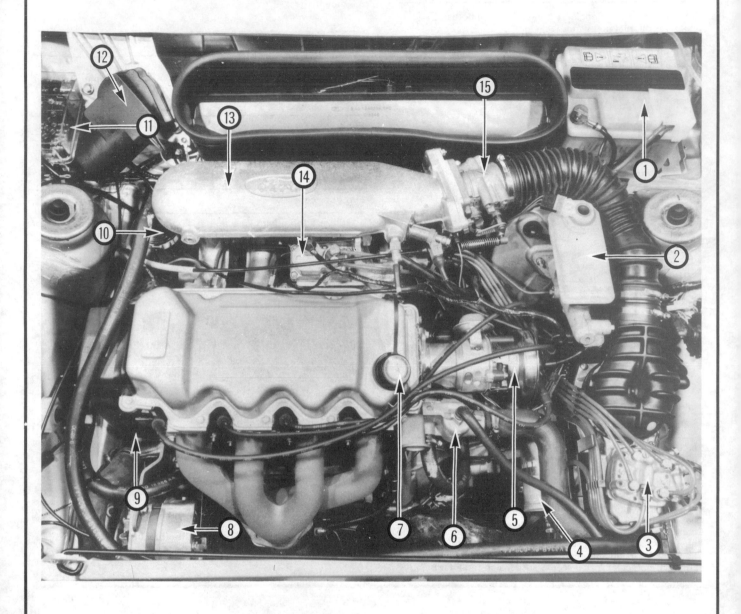

Engine compartment (fuel injection engine)

1 Battery	4 Fuel filter	9 Water pump	12 Windscreen wiper motor
2 Brake master cylinder and fluid reservoir	5 Distributor	10 Crankcase emission control filter	13 Plenum chamber
3 Fuel mixture control unit and air cleaner (underneath)	6 Thermostat	11 Fuse and relay box	14 Warm-up regulator
	7 Oil filler cap		15 Throttle housing
	8 Alternator		

Underside view of car at front

1	Steering unit	4	Anti-roll bar	7	Disc brake unit	10	Gear selector rod
2	Driveshaft	5	Exhaust system	8	Suspension arm	11	Gear selector unit
3	Sump	6	Transmission	9	Track (tie) rod		

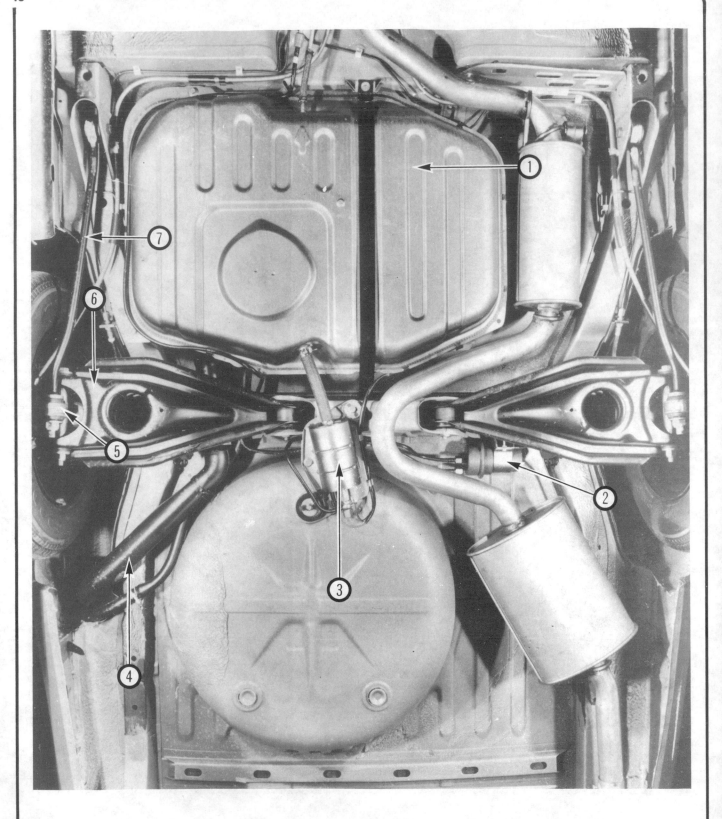

Underside view of car at rear (fuel injection model)

1 Fuel tank   3 Fuel pump   5 Tie-bar mounting   7 Tie-arm
2 Fuel accumulator   4 Fuel filler hose   6 Suspension arm

Fault diagnosis

Introduction

The vehicle owner who does his or her own maintenance according to the recommended schedules should not have to use this section of the manual very often. Modern component reliability is such that, provided those items subject to wear or deterioration are inspected or renewed at the specified intervals, sudden failure is comparatively rare. Faults do not usually just happen as a result of sudden failure, but develop over a period of time. Major mechanical failures in particular are usually preceded by characteristic symptoms over hundreds or even thousands of miles. Those components which do occasionally fail without warning are often small and easily carried in the vehicle.

With any fault finding, the first step is to decide where to begin investigations. Sometimes this is obvious, but on other occasions a little detective work will be necessary. The owner who makes half a dozen haphazard adjustments or replacements may be successful in curing a fault (or its symptoms), but he will be none the wiser if the fault recurs and he may well have spent more time and money than was necessary. A calm and logical approach will be found to be more satisfactory in the long run. Always take into account any warning signs or abnormalities that may have been noticed in the period preceding the fault – power loss, high or low gauge readings, unusual noises or smells, etc – and remember that failure of components such as fuses or spark plugs may only be pointers to some underlying fault.

The pages which follow here are intended to help in cases of failure to start or breakdown on the road. There is also a Fault Diagnosis Section at the end of each Chapter which should be consulted if the preliminary checks prove unfruitful. Whatever the fault, certain basic principles apply. These are as follows:

Verify the fault. This is simply a matter of being sure that you know what the symptoms are before starting work. This is particularly important if you are investigating a fault for someone else who may not have described it very accurately.

Don't overlook the obvious. For example, if the vehicle won't start, is there petrol in the tank? (Don't take anyone else's word on this particular point, and don't trust the fuel gauge either!) If an electrical fault is indicated, look for loose or broken wires before digging out the test gear.

Cure the disease, not the symptom. Substituting a flat battery with a fully charged one will get you off the hard shoulder, but if the underlying cause is not attended to, the new battery will go the same way. Similarly, changing oil-fouled spark plugs for a new set will get you moving again, but remember that the reason for the fouling (if it wasn't simply an incorrect grade of plug) will have to be established and corrected.

Don't take anything for granted. Particularly, don't forget that a 'new' component may itself be defective (especially if it's been rattling round in the boot for months), and don't leave components out of a fault diagnosis sequence just because they are new or recently fitted. When you do finally diagnose a difficult fault, you'll probably realise that all the evidence was there from the start.

Electrical faults

Electrical faults can be more puzzling than straightforward mechanical failures, but they are no less susceptible to logical analysis if the basic principles of operation are understood. Vehicle electrical wiring exists in extremely unfavourable conditions – heat, vibration and chemical attack – and the first things to look for are loose or corroded connections and broken or chafed wires, especially where the wires pass through holes in the bodywork or are subject to vibration.

All metal-bodied vehicles in current production have one pole of the battery 'earthed', ie connected to the vehicle bodywork, and in nearly all modern vehicles it is the negative (–) terminal. The various electrical components – motors, bulb holders etc – are also connected to earth, either by means of a lead or directly by their mountings. Electric current flows through the component and then back to the battery via the bodywork. If the component mounting is loose or corroded, or if a good path back to the battery is not available, the circuit will be incomplete and malfunction will result. The engine and/or gearbox are also earthed by means of flexible metal straps to the body or subframe; if these straps are loose or missing, starter motor, generator and ignition trouble may result.

Assuming the earth return to be satisfactory, electrical faults will be due either to component malfunction or to defects in the current supply. Individual components are dealt with in Chapter 11. If supply wires are broken or cracked internally this results in an open-circuit, and the easiest way to check for this is to bypass the suspect wire temporarily with a length of wire having a crocodile clip or suitable connector at each end. Alternatively, a 12V test lamp can be used to verify the presence of supply voltage at various points along the wire and the break can be thus isolated.

If a bare portion of a live wire touches the bodywork or other earthed metal part, the electricity will take the low-resistance path thus formed back to the battery: this is known as a short-circuit. Hopefully a short-circuit will blow a fuse, but otherwise it may cause burning of the insulation (and possibly further short-circuits) or even a fire. This is why it is inadvisable to bypass persistently blowing fuses with silver foil or wire.

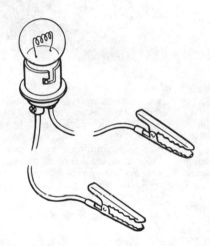

A simple test light is useful for tracing electrical faults

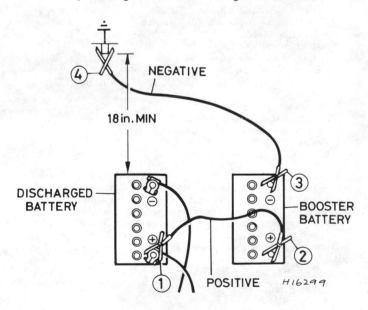

Jump start lead connections for negative earth vehicles – connect leads in the order shown

Carrying a few spare parts can save you a long walk!

Spares and tool kit

Most vehicles are supplied only with sufficient tools for wheel changing; the *Maintenance and minor repair* tool kit detailed in *Tools and working facilities*, with the addition of a hammer, is probably sufficient for those repairs that most motorists would consider attempting at the roadside. In addition a few items which can be fitted without too much trouble in the event of a breakdown should be carried. Experience and available space will modify the list below, but the following may save having to call on professional assistance:

> *Spark plugs, clean and correctly gapped*
> *HT lead and plug cap – long enough to reach the plug furthest from the distributor*
> *Distributor rotor*
> *Drivebelt – emergency type may suffice*
> *Spare fuses*
> *Set of principal light bulbs*
> *Tin of radiator sealer and hose bandage*
> *Exhaust bandage*
> *Roll of insulating tape*
> *Length of soft iron wire*
> *Length of electrical flex*
> *Torch or inspection lamp (can double as test lamp)*
> *Battery jump leads*
> *Tow-rope*
> *Ignition water dispersant aerosol*
> *Litre of engine oil*
> *Sealed can of hydraulic fluid*
> *Worm drive clips*

If spare fuel is carried, a can designed for the purpose should be used to minimise risks of leakage and collision damage. A first aid kit and a warning triangle, whilst not at present compulsory in the UK, are obviously sensible items to carry in addition to the above.

When touring abroad it may be advisable to carry additional spares which, even if you cannot fit them yourself, could save having to wait while parts are obtained. The items below may be worth considering:

> *Clutch and throttle cables*
> *Cylinder head gasket*
> *Alternator brushes*
> *Fuel pump repair kit*
> *Tyre valve core*

One of the motoring organisations will be able to advise on availability of fuel etc in foreign countries.

Engine will not start

Engine fails to turn when starter operated
Flat battery (recharge, use jump leads, or push start)
Battery terminals loose or corroded
Battery earth to body defective
Engine earth strap loose or broken
Starter motor (or solenoid) wiring loose or broken
Automatic transmission selector in wrong position, or inhibitor switch faulty
Ignition/starter switch faulty
Major mechanical failure (seizure)
Starter or solenoid internal fault (see Chapter 11)

Starter motor turns engine slowly
Partially discharged battery (recharge, use jump leads, or push start)
Battery terminals loose or corroded
Battery earth to body defective
Engine earth strap loose
Starter motor (or solenoid) wiring loose
Starter motor internal fault (see Chapter 11)

Starter motor spins without turning engine
Flat battery
Starter motor pinion sticking on sleeve
Flywheel gear teeth damaged or worn
Starter motor mounting bolts loose

Engine turns normally but fails to start
Damp or dirty HT leads and distributor cap (crank engine and check for spark)
No fuel in tank – also check for delivery
Excessive choke (hot engine) or insufficient choke (cold engine)
Fouled or incorrectly gapped spark plugs (remove, clean and regap)
Other ignition system fault (see Chapter 4)
Other fuel system fault (see Chapter 3)
Poor compression (see Chapter 1)
Major mechanical failure (eg camshaft drive)

Engine fires but will not run
Insufficient choke (cold engine)
Air leaks at carburettor or intake manifold

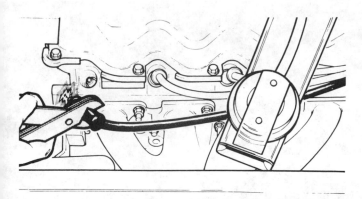

Insert a nail or similar item into plug cap, crank engine with ignition on and check for spark. Note use of insulated tool. End of nail must be within 5 mm (1/5 in) of block

Fuel starvation (see Chapter 3)
Ballast resistor defective, or other ignition fault (see Chapter 4)

Engine cuts out and will not restart

Engine cuts out suddenly – ignition fault
Loose or disconnected LT wires
Wet HT leads or distributor cap (after traversing water splash)
Coil or condenser failure (check for spark)
Other ignition fault (see Chapter 4)

Engine misfires before cutting out – fuel fault
Fuel tank empty
Fuel pump defective or filter blocked (check for delivery)
Fuel tank filler vent blocked (suction will be evident on releasing cap)
Carburettor needle valve sticking
Carburettor jets blocked (fuel contaminated)
Other fuel system fault (see Chapter 3)

Engine cuts out – other causes
Serious overheating
Major mechanical failure (eg camshaft drive)

Engine overheats

Ignition (no-charge) warning light illuminated
Slack or broken drivebelt – retension or renew (Chapter 11)

Ignition warning light not illuminated
Coolant loss due to internal or external leakage (see Chapter 2)
Thermostat defective

Low oil level
Brakes binding
Radiator clogged externally or internally
Electric cooling fan not operating correctly
Engine waterways clogged
Ignition timing incorrect or automatic advance malfunctioning
Mixture too weak

Note: *Do not add cold water to an overheated engine or damage may result*

Low engine oil pressure

Gauge reads low or warning light illuminated with engine running
Oil level low or incorrect grade
Defective gauge or sender unit
Wire to sender unit earthed
Engine overheating
Oil filter clogged or bypass valve defective
Oil pressure relief valve defective
Oil pick-up strainer clogged
Oil pump worn or mountings loose
Worn main or big-end bearings

Note: *Low oil pressure in a high-mileage engine at tickover is not necessarily a cause for concern. Sudden pressure loss at speed is far more significant. In any event, check the gauge or warning light sender before condemning the engine.*

Engine noises

Pre-ignition (pinking) on acceleration
Incorrect grade of fuel
Ignition timing incorrect
Distributor faulty or worn
Worn or maladjusted carburettor
Excessive carbon build-up in engine

Whistling or wheezing noises
Leaking vacuum hose
Leaking carburettor or manifold gasket
Blowing head gasket

Tapping or rattling
Worn valve gear
Worn timing chain or belt
Broken piston ring (ticking noise)

Knocking or thumping
Unintentional mechanical contact (eg fan blades)
Worn alternator drivebelt
Peripheral component fault (generator, water pump etc)
Worn big-end bearings (regular heavy knocking, perhaps less under load)
Worn main bearings (rumbling and knocking, perhaps worsening under load)
Piston slap (most noticeable when cold)

Chapter 1 Engine

For modifications, and information applicable to later models, see Supplement at end of manual

Contents

Specifications

General

Engine type .... Four cylinder, in-line, overhead camshaft, water cooled, transverse
mounting

Engine code:
    1.3 HC .... JPA
    1.6 HC .... LPA
    1.6 HC (fuel injection) .... LRA

Power output (DIN):
    1.3 HC .... 69 PS (51 kW) at 6000 rpm
    1.6 HC .... 79 PS (58 kW) at 5800 rpm
    1.6 HC (fuel injection) .... 105 PS (77 kW) at 6000 rpm

Maximum torque (DIN):
    1.3 HC .... 74 lbf ft (100 Nm) at 3500 rpm
    1.6 HC .... 92 lbf ft (125 Nm) at 3000 rpm
    1.6 HC (fuel injection) .... 102 lbf ft (138 Nm) at 4800 rpm

Bore:
    All engines .... 79.96 mm (3.15 in)

Stroke:
    1.3 engines .... 64.52 mm (2.54 in)
    1.6 engines .... 79.52 mm (3.13 in)

Cubic capacity:
    1.3 engines .... 1296 cc
    1.6 engines .... 1597 cc

Compression ratio .... 9.5 : 1

Cylinder block

Material	Cast iron
Number of main bearings	5
Cylinder bore (diameter):	
Standard (1)	79.94 to 79.95 mm (3.1472 to 3.1476 in)
Standard (2)	79.95 to 79.96 mm (3.1476 to 3.1480 in)
Standard (3)	79.96 to 79.97 mm (3.1480 to 3.1484 in)
Standard (4)	79.97 to 79.98 mm (3.1484 to 3.1488 in)
Oversize (A)	80.23 to 80.24 mm (3.1587 to 3.1590 in)
Oversize (B)	80.24 to 80.25 mm (3.1590 to 3.1594 in)
Oversize (C)	80.25 to 80.26 mm (3.1594 to 3.1598 in)
Main bearing shell inner diameter:	
Standard	58.011 to 58.038 mm (2.2839 to 2.2850 in)
Undersize 0.25 mm	57.761 to 57.788 mm (2.2740 to 2.2751 in)
Undersize 0.50 mm	57.511 to 57.538 mm (2.2642 to 2.2653 in)
Undersize 0.75 mm	57.261 to 57.288 mm (2.2544 to 2.2554 in)

Crankshaft

Main bearing journal diameter:	
Standard	57.98 to 58.00 mm (2.2827 to 2.2835 in)
Undersize 0.25 mm	57.73 to 57.75 mm (2.2728 to 2.2736 in)
Undersize 0.50 mm	57.48 to 57.50 mm (2.2630 to 2.2638 in)
Undersize 0.75 mm	57.23 to 57.25 mm (2.2531 to 2.2539 in)
Main bearing running clearance	0.011 to 0.058 mm (0.0004 to 0.0023 in)
Thrust washer thickness:	
Standard	2.301 to 2.351 mm (0.0906 to 0.0926 in)
Oversize	2.491 to 2.541 mm (0.0981 to 0.1000 in)
Crankshaft endfloat	0.09 to 0.30 mm (0.0035 to 0.0118 in)
Crankpin (big-end) diameter:	
Standard	47.89 to 47.91 mm (1.8854 to 1.8862 in)
Undersize 0.25 mm	47.64 to 47.66 mm (1.8756 to 1.8764 in)
Undersize 0.50 mm	47.39 to 47.41 mm (1.8657 to 1.8665 in)
Undersize 0.75 mm	47.14 to 47.16 mm (1.8559 to 1.8567 in)
Undersize 1.00 mm	46.89 to 46.91 mm (1.8461 to 1.8468 in)
Big-end bearing running clearance	0.006 to 0.060 mm (0.0002 to 0.0024 in)

Camshaft

Number of bearings	5
Drive	Toothed belt
Camshaft thrustplate thickness	4.99 to 5.01 mm (0.1965 to 0.1972 in)
Camlift (inlet and exhaust):	
1.3 and 1.6 HC	5.79 mm (0.2280 in)
1.6 HC fuel injection	6.09 mm (0.2398 in)
Cam length – inlet (heel to toe):	
1.3 and 1.6 HC	38.305 mm (1.5081 in)
1.6 HC fuel injection	38.606 mm (1.5199 in)
Cam length – exhaust (heel to toe):	
1.3 and 1.6 HC	37.289 mm (1.4681 in)
1.6 HC fuel injection	37.590 mm (1.4799 in)
Camshaft bearing diameter:	
1	44.75 mm (1.7618 in)
2	45.00 mm (1.7717 in)
3	45.25 mm (1.7815 in)
4	45.50 mm (1.7913 in)
5	45.75 mm (1.8012 in)
Camshaft endfloat	0.05 to 0.15 mm (0.0020 to 0.0059 in)
Camshaft belt pulley identification – 1.6 engine	Suffix and groove on front face

Pistons and rings

Diameter:	
Standard 1	79.910 to 79.920 mm (3.1461 to 3.1465 in)
Standard 2	79.920 to 79.930 mm (3.1465 to 3.1468 in)
Standard 3	79.930 to 79.940 mm (3.1468 to 3.1472 in)
Standard 4	79.940 to 79.950 mm (3.1472 to 3.1476 in)
Standard service	79.930 to 79.955 mm (3.1468 to 3.1478 in)
Oversize 0.29 mm	80.210 to 80.235 mm (3.1579 to 3.1589 in)
Oversize 0.50 mm	80.430 to 80.455 mm (3.1665 to 3.1675 in)
Piston-to-bore clearance:	
Production	0.020 to 0.040 mm (0.00079 to 0.0016 in)
Service	0.010 to 0.045 mm (0.00039 to 0.0018 in)
Piston ring gap:	
Compression	0.30 to 0.50 mm (0.0118 to 0.0197 in)
Oil control	0.4 to 1.4 mm (0.0157 to 0.0551 in)

Gudgeon pin
Pin length .... 66.20 to 67.00 mm (2.606 to 2.638 in)

Pin diameter:
    White .... 20.622 to 20.625 mm (0.8119 to 0.8120 in)
    Red .... 20.625 to 20.628 mm (0.8120 to 0.8121 in)
    Blue .... 20.628 to 20.631 mm (0.8121 to 0.8122 in)
    Yellow .... 20.631 to 20.634 mm (0.8122 to 0.8124 in)
Play in piston .... 0.005 to 0.011 mm (0.0002 to 0.0004 in)
Interference fit in piston .... 0.013 to 0.045 mm (0.0005 to 0.0018 in)

Connecting rod
Big-end bore diameter .... 50.890 to 50.910 mm (2.0035 to 2.0043 in)
Small-end bore diameter .... 20.589 to 20.609 mm (0.8106 to 0.8114 in)
Big-end bearing shell inside diameter:
    Standard .... 47.916 to 47.950 mm (1.8865 to 1.8878 in)
    Undersize 0.25 mm .... 47.666 to 47.700 mm (1.8766 to 1.8779 in)
    Undersize 0.50 mm .... 47.416 to 47.450 mm (1.8668 to 1.8681 in)
    Undersize 0.75 mm .... 47.166 to 47.200 mm (1.8569 to 1.8583 in)
    Undersize 1.00 mm .... 46.916 to 46.950 mm (1.8471 to 1.8484 in)
Big-end bearing running clearance .... 0.006 to 0.060 mm (0.0002 to 0.0024 in)

Cylinder head
Material .... Light alloy
Valve seat angle .... 45°
Valve seat width .... 1.75 to 2.32 mm (0.0689 to 0.0913 in)
Upper correction angle – inlet/exhaust:
    Production .... 30°
    Service cutter .... 15°
Lower correction angle – inlet/exhaust:
    Production .... 77°/70°
    Service cutter .... 75°/70°
Valve guide bore diameter – inlet/exhaust:
    Standard .... 8.063 to 8.094 mm (0.3174 to 0.3187 in)
    Oversize 0.2 mm .... 8.263 to 8.294 mm (0.3253 to 0.3265 in)
    Oversize 0.4 mm .... 8.463 to 8.494 mm (0.3332 to 0.3340 in)
Camshaft bearing bore in head:
    1 .... 44.783 to 44.808 mm (1.7631 to 1.7639 in)
    2 .... 45.033 to 45.058 mm (1.7729 to 1.7739 in)
    3 .... 45.283 to 45.308 mm (1.7828 to 1.7838 in)
    4 .... 45.533 to 45.558 mm (1.7926 to 1.7936 in)
    5 .... 45.783 to 45.808 mm (1.8025 to 1.8034 in)
Valve lifter bore in head (standard) .... 22.235 to 22.265 mm (0.8754 to 0.8766 in)
Maximum allowable cylinder head distortion (over full length
of head) .... 0.15 mm (0.0059 in)
Minimum allowable combustion chamber depth (after refacing) .... 19.60 mm (0.7717 in)

Valves (general)

	1.3 and 1.6 engines	1.6 fuel injection engine
Inlet valve opens	13° ATDC	8° ATDC
Inlet valve closes	28° ABDC	36° ABDC
Exhaust valve opens	30° BBDC	34° BBDC
Exhaust valve closes	15° BTDC	6° BTDC
Valve lift:		
Inlet	9.56 mm (0.3764 in)	10.09 mm (0.3972 in)
Exhaust	9.52 mm (0.3748 in)	10.06 mm (0.3961 in)
Valve spring free length	47.2 mm (1.8583 in)	47.2 mm (1.8583 in)

Inlet valve
Length .... 134.54 to 135.00 mm (5.297 to 5.315 in)
Head diameter .... 41.9 to 42.1 mm (1.650 to 1.657 in)
Stem diameter:
    Standard .... 8.025 to 8.043 mm (0.3159 to 0.3167 in)
    Oversize 0.2 mm .... 8.225 to 8.243 mm (0.3238 to 0.3245 in)
    Oversize 0.4 mm .... 8.425 to 8.443 mm (0.3317 to 0.3324 in)
Valve stem-to-guide clearance .... 0.020 to 0.063 mm (0.0008 to 0.0025 in)

Exhaust valve
Length:
    1.3 engines .... 131.17 to 131.63 mm (5.1642 to 5.1823 in)
    1.6 engines .... 131.57 to 132.03 mm (5.1799 to 5.1980 in)
Head diameter:
    1.3 engines .... 33.9 to 34.1 mm (1.3346 to 1.3425 in)
    1.6 engines .... 36.9 to 37.1 mm (1.4528 to 1.4606 in)
Valve stem diameter:
    Standard .... 7.999 to 8.017 mm (0.3149 to 0.3156 in)
    Oversize 0.2 mm .... 8.199 to 8.217 mm (0.3228 to 0.3235 in)
    Oversize 0.4 mm .... 8.399 to 8.417 mm (0.3307 to 0.3314 in)
Valve stem-to-guide clearance .... 0.046 to 0.089 mm (0.0018 to 0.0035 in)

Lubrication

Oil pump type	Gear, driven by crankshaft
Minimum oil pressure at 80°C (176°F):	
At 750 rpm	1.0 Kgf/cm² (14.2 lbf/in²)
At 2000 rpm	2.8 Kgf/cm² (39.8 lbf/in²)
Engine oil capacity:	
Without filter change	3.25 litre (5.7 Imp pint)
With filter change	3.50 litre (6.2 Imp pint)
Engine oil type/specification..	Multigrade engine oil, viscosity SAE 10W/30, to API SF/CC (Duckhams QXR, Hypergrade, or 10W/40 Motor Oil)
Oil filter...	Champion C104

Torque wrench settings

	Nm	lbf ft
Main bearing cap bolts	95	70
Big-end bearing cap bolts	30	22
Oil pump mounting bolts	10	7
Oil pump pick-up tube bolt to block	20	15
Oil pump pick-up to pump	10	7
Rear oil seal carrier bolts	10	7
Sump bolts	10	7
Flywheel	85	63
Crankshaft pulley bolt	110	81
Cylinder head bolts:		
Stage 1	25	18
Stage 2	55	41
Stage 3	¼ turn from stage 2	
Stage 4	¼ turn from stage 3	
Camshaft thrustplate bolts	12	9
Camshaft sprocket bolt	55	41
Belt tensioner bolts	18	13
Coolant pump bolts	8	6
Rocker arm studs in head	21	16
Rocker arm nuts (nylon insert)	27	20
Rocker cover screws	8	6
Timing cover screws	8	6
Exhaust manifold bolts	16	12
Intake manifold bolts	18	13
Carburettor mounting bolts	20	15
Thermostat housing bolts	8	6
Clutch pressure plate bolts	10	7
Spark plugs	31	23
Transmission oil filler plug	25	18
Timing belt tensioning torque (new belt):		
1.3 engines (blue)	62	46
1.6 engines (yellow)	47	35
Engine/transmission mountings:		
Bolt to apron panel	47	35
Nut to side-member	57	42
Gearbox bracket	57	42
Engine-to-transmission bolts	41	30
Oil pressure switch	20	15

1 General description

The Ford CVH type engine is used in all models in the Orion range, being of 1.3 or 1.6 litre capacity. The CVH (Compound Valve angle, Hemispherical combustion chambers) engine is of four-cylinder, in-line, overhead camshaft (ohc) design.

The engine is mounted, together with the transmission, transversely at the front of the vehicle and transmits power through open driveshafts to the front roadwheels.

The crankshaft is supported in five main bearings within a cast iron crankcase.

The cylinder head is of light alloy construction, supporting the overhead camshaft in five bearings. These bearings cannot be renewed and in the event of wear occurring, the complete cylinder head must be changed. The fuel pump is mounted on the side of the cylinder head and is driven by a pushrod from an eccentric cam on the camshaft. The distributor is driven from the rear (flywheel) end of the camshaft by means of an offset dog.

The cam followers are of hydraulic type, which eliminates the need for valve clearance adjustment. The cam followers operate in the following way. When the valve is closed, pressurised engine oil passes through a port in the body of the cam followers and four grooves in the plunger and into the cylinder feed chamber. From this chamber, oil flows through a ball type non-return valve into the pressure chamber. The tension of the coil spring causes the plunger to press the rocker arm against the valve and to eliminate any free play.

As the cam lifts the cam follower, the oil pressure in the pressure chamber increases and causes the non-return valve to close the port feed chamber. As oil cannot be compressed, it forms a rigid link between the body of the cam follower, the cylinder and the plunger which then rise as one component to open the valve.

The clearance between the body of the cam follower and the cylinder is accurately designed to meter a specific quantity of oil as it escapes from the pressure chamber. Oil will only pass along the cylinder bore when pressure is high during the moment of valve opening. Once the valve has closed, the escape of oil will produce a small amount of free play and no pressure will exist in the pressure chamber. Oil from the feed chamber can then flow through the non-return valve into the pressure chamber so that the cam follower cylinder can be raised by the pressure of the coil spring, thus eliminating any play in the arrangement until the valve is operated again.

As wear occurs between rocker arm and valve stem, the quantity of oil which flows into the pressure chamber will be slightly more than the quantity lost during the expansion cycle of the cam follower. Conversely, when the cam follower is compressed by the expansion of the valve, a slightly smaller quantity of oil will flow into the pressure chamber than was lost.

If the engine has been standing idle for a period of time, or after overhaul, when the engine is started up, valve clatter may be heard. This is a normal condition and will gradually disappear within a few

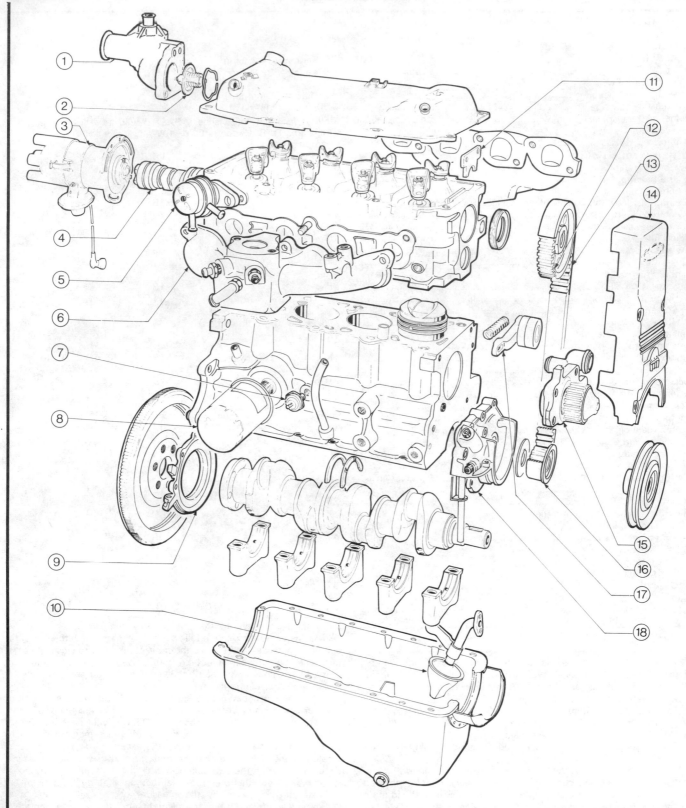

Fig. 1.1 Exploded view of the Ford CVH engine (Sec 1)

1 Thermostat housing	6 Intake manifold (carburettor engine)	10 Oil pump strainer and intake pipe	14 Timing belt cover
2 Thermostat			15 Water pump
3 Distributor	7 Oil pressure switch	11 Thrustplate (camshaft)	16 Belt pulley (crankshaft)
4 Camshaft	8 Oil filter	12 Belt pulley (camshaft)	17 Timing belt tensioner
5 Fuel pump (carburettor engine)	9 Crankshaft oil seal carrier	13 Timing belt	18 Oil pump

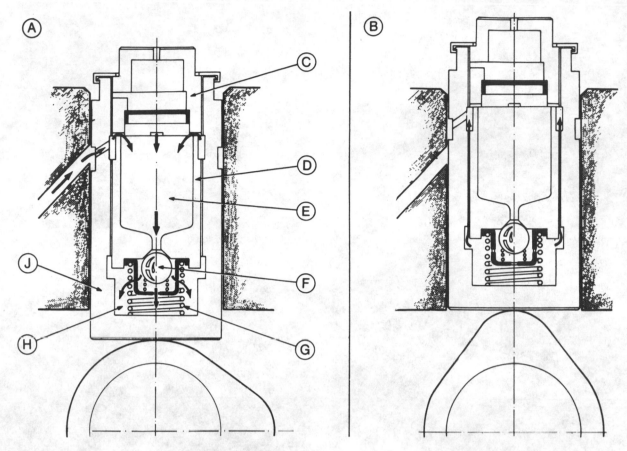

Fig. 1.2 Sectional views showing operation of hydraulic cam followers (Sec 1)

A   Valve closed   D   Cylinder   F   Non-return valve   H   Pressure chamber
B   Valve open   E   Feed chamber   G   Coil spring   J   Body
C   Plunger

minutes of starting up as the cam followers are pressurised with oil.

The coolant pump is mounted on the timing belt end of the cylinder block and is driven by the toothed belt.

A gear type oil pump is mounted on the timing belt end of the cylinder block and is driven by a gear on the front end of the crankshaft.

A full-flow oil filter of throw-away type is located on the side of the crankcase.

2   Operations possible without removing engine from the vehicle

The following work can be carried out without having to remove the engine:

(a)   Timing belt – renewal
(b)   Camshaft oil seal – renewal
(c)   Camshaft – removal and refitting
(d)   Cylinder head – removal and refitting
(e)   Crankshaft front oil seal – renewal
(f)   Sump – removal and refitting
(g)   Piston/connecting rod – removal and refitting
(h)   Engine/transmission mountings – removal and refitting
(j)   Intake (inlet) and exhaust manifolds – removal and refitting

3   Operations only possible with engine removed from the vehicle

1   The following work should be carried out only after the engine has been removed:

(a)   Crankshaft main bearings – renewal
(b)   Crankshaft – removal and refitting
(c)   * Flywheel – removal and refitting
(d)   ** Crankshaft rear oil seal – renewal
(e)   * Oil pump – removal and refitting

2   Although it is possible to undertake those operations marked * without removing the engine, and those marked ** by removing the transmission (see Chapter 6), such work is not recommended and is unlikely to save much time over that required to withdraw the complete engine/transmission.

4   Timing belt – removal, refitting and adjustment (engine in car)

1   Renewal of the timing belt is a routine operation on all CVH engines, and should be carried out at 36 000 mile (60 000 km) intervals.
2   Disconnect the battery earth lead.
3   Release the alternator mounting and adjuster link bolts, push the alternator in towards the engine and slip the drivebelt from the pulleys.
4   Unscrew the four bolts and remove the timing belt cover (photo).
5   Using a ring spanner on the crankshaft pulley bolt, turn the crankshaft until the timing mark on the camshaft sprocket is opposite the tdc mark on the cylinder head and the small projection on the crankshaft belt sprocket front flange is in alignment with the tdc mark on the oil pump casing. Remove the timing belt lower guard. Remove the starter motor or the transmission bellhousing lower cover plate and jam the starter ring gear with a cold chisel or similar item. As the engine is in the car the crankshaft may be held against rotation by engaging a gear and applying the handbrake or foot-brake hard. There is very little space between the crankshaft pulley bolt and the body side-member so use a ring spanner to unscrew the bolt. Remove the pulley (photos).

4.4 Timing belt cover removal

4.5A Camshaft sprocket timing mark

4.5B Crankshaft sprocket timing marks

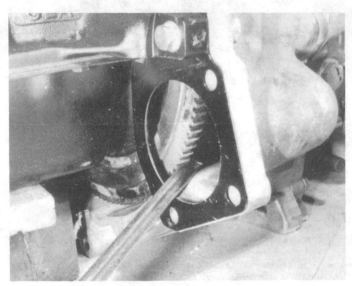
4.5C Jam the flywheel ring gear

4.8 Removing the timing belt

4.11 Timing belt correctly located

6   Slacken the bolts which secure the belt tensioner and, using a
large screwdriver, prise the tensioner to one side to relieve spring
tension on the belt. (Some tensioners do not incorporate a spring).
Temporarily retighten the bolts.
7   If the original belt is to be refitted, which we do not recommend,
mark it for direction of travel and also the exact tooth positons on all
three sprockets.
8   Slip the timing belt from its sprockets (photo).
9   Refit by reversing the removal operations, but before engaging the
belt to the camshaft and crankshaft sprockets, check that they are set
to tdc as previously described. Adjust the position of the sprockets
slightly if necessary, but avoid any excessive movement of the
sprockets while the belt is off, as the piston crowns and valve heads
may make contact with consequent damage to both components.
10   Engage the timing belt with the teeth of the crankshaft sprocket
(slip the sprocket off the crankshaft if necessary to avoid kinking the
belt), and then pull the belt vertically upright on its right-hand run.
Keep it taut and engage it with the teeth of the camshaft sprocket.
Check that the positons of the crankshaft and camshaft sprockets have
not altered.
11   Wind the belt around the camshaft sprocket, around and under the
tensioner idler pulley and over the coolant pump sprocket (no set
position for this) (photo).

Timing belt tension adjustment – old belt
12   Release the timing belt tensioner bolts so that the tensioner pulley
recoils against the belt, then rotate the crankshaft in a clockwise
direction two full turns and align the camshaft sprocket mark with the
one on the cylinder head (tdc). Now tighten the belt tensioner pulley
retaining bolts to the specified torque setting, tightening the right-
hand bolt first.

Timing belt tension adjustment – new belt
13   Release the timing belt tensioner bolts allowing the tensioner to act
against the belt, then lock the crankshaft with number one piston at
top dead centre. Fit a 41 mm socket to the raised hexagon casting on
the camshaft and using a torque wrench turn the camshaft
anti-clockwise to the specified tensioning torque, according to engine
type. Maintain the applied torque and tighten the tensioner retaining
bolts to their specified torque, tightening the right-hand bolt first.

General
14   Always carry out belt adjustment on a cold engine.
15   Refit the belt cover, refit and adjust the vee belt and reconnect the
battery. It is recommended that the belt tension is finally checked by
your Ford dealer using the official belt tensioning gauge.

5   Camshaft oil seal – renewal (engine in car)

1   Disconnect the battery earth lead.
2   Release the timing belt from the camshaft sprocket, as described
in the preceding Section.
3   Pass a bar through one of the holes in the camshaft sprocket to
anchor the sprocket while the retaining bolt is unscrewed. Remove the
sprocket.
4   Using a suitable tool, hooked at its end, prise out the oil seal.
5   Apply a little grease to the lips of the new seal and draw it into
position using the sprocket bolt and a suitable distance piece.
6   Refit the sprocket, tightening the bolt to the specified torque
wrench setting. Thread locking compound should be applied to the
threads of the bolt.
7   Refit and tension the timing belt, as described in the preceding
Section.
8   Reconnect the battery.

6   Camshaft – removal and refitting (engine in car)

1   Disconnect the battery earth lead.
2   **Carburettor engine models:** Disconnect the crankcase
ventilation hose from the intake manifold and the rocker cover.
Remove the air cleaner unit (Chapter 3).
3   **Fuel injection models:** Disconnect the air hose at the fuel
distributor and throttle valve unit.

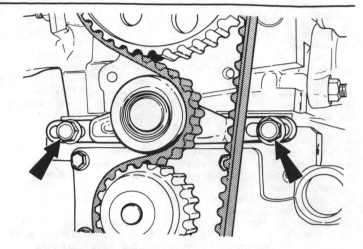
Fig. 1.3 Timing belt tensioner bolts (Sec 4)

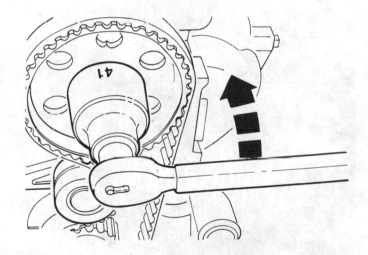
Fig. 1.4 Tensioning a new timing belt (Sec 4)

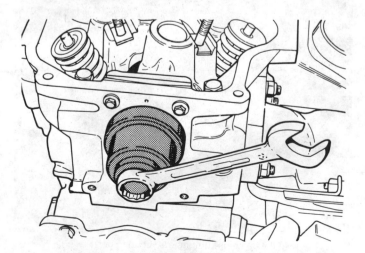
Fig. 1.5 Installing the camshaft oil seal (Sec 5)

4   Disconnect the HT leads from the spark plugs, then remove the distributor cap and secure it to the left-hand side of the engine compartment.

5   Unscrew the three bolts and withdraw the distributor from the cylinder head. Note that the distributor body is marked in relation to the cylinder head.

6   **Carburettor engine models:** Unbolt and remove the fuel pump, insulating spacer and operating pushrod. Unbolt the throttle cable bracket at the carburettor and then disconnect the cable by sliding back the spring clip.

7   Remove the rocker cover.

8   Unscrew the securing nuts and remove the rocker arms and guides. Keep the components in their originally installed sequence by marking them with a piece of numbered tape or by using a suitably sub-divided box.

9   Withdraw the hydraulic cam followers, again keeping them in their originally fitted sequence.

10   Slacken the alternator mounting and adjuster link bolts, push the alternator in towards the engine and slip the drivebelt from the pulleys.

11   Unbolt and remove the timing belt cover and turn the crankshaft to align the timing mark on the camshaft sprocket with the one on the cylinder head.

12   Slacken the bolts on the timing belt tensioner, lever the tensioner against the tension of its coil spring (if fitted) and retighten the bolts. With the belt now slack, slip it from the camshaft sprocket.

13   Pass a rod or large screwdriver through one of the holes in the camshaft sprocket to lock it and unscrew the sprocket bolt. Remove the sprocket (photos).

14   Extract the two bolts and pull out the camshaft thrustplate (photos).

15   Carefully withdraw the camshaft from the distributor end of the cylinder head (photo).

16   Refitting the camshaft is a reversal of removal, but observe the following points.

17   Lubricate the camshaft bearings before inserting the camshaft into the cylinder head.

18   It is recommended that a new oil seal is always fitted after the camshaft has been installed (see preceding Section). Apply thread locking compound to the sprocket bolt threads. Tighten the bolt to the specified torque.

19   Fit and tension the timing belt, as described in Section 4.

20   Oil the hydraulic cam followers with hypoid type transmission oil before inserting them into their original bores.

21   Refit the rocker arms and guides in their original sequence, use new nuts and tighten to the specified torque. It is essential that before each rocker arm is installed and its nut tightened, the respective cam follower is positioned at its lowest point (in contact with cam base circle). Turn the camshaft (by means of the crankshaft pulley bolt) as necessary to achieve this.

22   Use a new rocker cover gasket and, to ensure that a good seal is

6.13A Camshaft sprocket bolt removal

6.13B Remove the camshaft sprocket

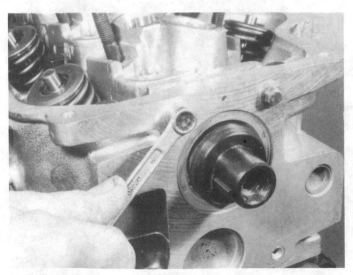

6.14A Remove the camshaft thrustplate securing bolts ...

6.14B ... and lift out the thrustplate

6.15 Withdraw the camshaft

made, check that its location groove is clear of oil, grease and any portions of the old gasket. A length of sealant should be applied to the gasket recess where the cover engages under the timing belt cover. When in position tighten the cover retaining screws to the specified torque setting.

7   Cylinder head – removal and refitting (engine in car)

1   Disconnect the battery earth lead.
2   **Carburettor engine models:** Remove the air cleaner and detach the connecting hoses.
3   **Fuel injection models:** Disconnect the fuel distributor-to-throttle valve air hose and then detach the wires from the thermotime switch, the warm-up regulator, the cold start valve, the auxiliary air valve and the earth lead from the deceleration fuel cut-off valve at the throttle valve stop. Reference to the fuel injection system layout in Chapter 3 will assist in identification of these components where necessary.
4   **Fuel injection models:** Detach the fuel pipes from the cold start valve and from the fuel distributor and the vacuum hose from the deceleration fuel cut-off valve.
5   Drain the cooling system (Chapter 2).
6   Disconnect the coolant hoses from the thermostat housing.
7   **Carburettor engine models:** Disconnect the coolant hoses from the automatic choke.
8   **Fuel injection engines:** Disconnect the crankcase breather hoses from the intake manifold and the rocker cover. Disconnect the coolant hoses from the injection valve intermediate flange and the thermostat housing.
9   Disconnect the throttle cable and location bracket from the carburettor or throttle housing (fuel injection engines).
10   **Carburettor engine models:** Disconnect the fuel pipe from the fuel pump.
11   Disconnect the vacuum servo pipe from the intake manifold.
12   **Carburettor engine models:** Disconnect the leads from the coolant temperature gauge sender unit, the ignition coil, the cooling fan temperature sensor and the anti run-on solenoid valve at the carburettor.
13   **Fuel injection engines:** Detach the leads from the coolant gauge sender unit and the distributor.
14   Unbolt the exhaust downpipe from the manifold by unscrewing the flange nuts. Support the exhaust pipe by tying it up with wire.
15   Release the alternator mounting and adjuster link bolts, push the alternator in towards the engine and slip the drivebelt from the pulleys.
16   Unbolt and remove the timing belt cover.
17   Slacken the belt tensioner bolts, lever the tensioner to one side against the pressure of the coil spring (if fitted) and retighten the bolts.
18   With the timing belt now slack, slip it from the camshaft sprocket.
19   Disconnect the leads from the spark plugs and unscrew and remove the spark plugs.
20   Remove the rocker cover.
21   Unscrew the cylinder head bolts, progressively and in the reverse

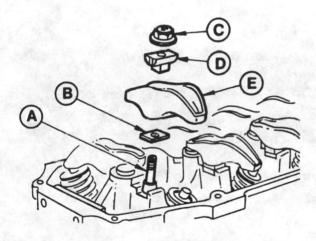

Fig. 1.6 Rocker arm components (Sec 6)

A	Rocker stud	D	Rocker guide
B	Spacer plate	E	Rocker arm
C	Nut		

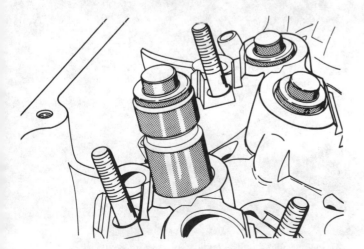

Fig. 1.7 Cam follower removal (Sec 6)

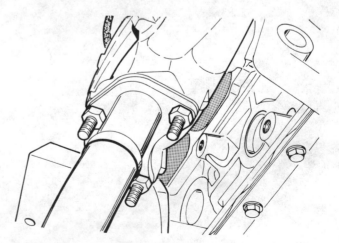

Fig. 1.8 Exhaust downpipe to manifold connection (Sec 7)

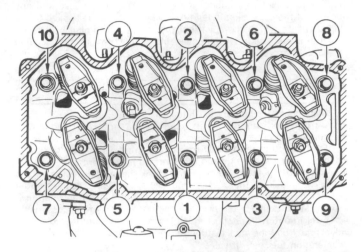

Fig. 1.9 Cylinder head bolt tightening sequence (Secs 7 and 18)

sequence to that given for tightening (Fig. 1.9). Discard the bolts, as new ones must be used at reassembly.

22 Remove the cylinder head complete with manifolds. Use the manifolds if necessary as levers to rock the head from the block. Do not attempt to tap the head sideways off the block as it is located on dowels, and do not attempt to lever between the head and the block or damage will result.

23 Dismantling and overhaul of the cylinder head is described in Sections 20 and 21.

24 Before installing the cylinder head, make sure that the mating surfaces of head and block are perfectly clean with the head locating dowels in position. Clean the bolt holes free from oil. In extreme cases it is possible for oil left in the holes to crack the block.

25 Turn the crankshaft to position No 1 piston about 20 mm (0.8 in) before it reaches tdc.

26 Place a new gasket on the cylinder block and then locate the cylinder head on its dowels. The upper surface of the gasket is marked OBEN-TOP (photos).

27 Install and tighten the **new** cylinder head bolts, tightening them in four stages (see Specifications). After the first two stages, the bolt heads should be marked with a spot of quick-drying paint so that the paint spots all face the same direction. Now tighten the bolts (Stage 3) through 90° (quarter turn) followed by a further 90° (Stage 4).

7.26A Locate the new cylinder head gasket into position

7.26B Cylinder head gasket marking (note belt tensioner spring)

7.26C Refit the cylinder head

7.27 Cylinder head bolt alignment marks (arrowed)

Tighten the bolts at each stage only in the sequence shown before going on to the next stage. If all the bolts have been tightened equally, the paint spots should now all be pointing in the same direction (photo).
28 Fit the timing belt, as described in Section 4.
29 Refitting and reconnection of all other components is a reversal of dismantling.
30 Refill the cooling system.

8 Crankshaft front oil seal – renewal (engine in car)

1 Disconnect the battery earth lead.
2 Release the alternator mounting and adjuster link bolts, push the alternator in towards the engine and slip the drivebelt from the pulleys.
3 Unbolt and remove the timing belt cover.
4 Locate a spanner or socket onto the crankshaft pulley bolt and turn the crankshaft over in its normal direction of travel until the timing marks of the camshaft sprocket and cylinder head are in alignment.
5 You will now need to remove the crankshaft pulley. To prevent the crankshaft turning, place the vehicle in gear and have an assistant apply the brakes or unbolt and remove the starter motor so that the flywheel ring gear can be jammed with a cold chisel or suitable implement. Unbolt the crankshaft pulley and remove it with its thrust washer.
6 Slacken the belt tensioner bolts, lever the tensioner to one side and retighten the bolts. With the belt slack, it can now be slipped from the sprockets. Before removing the belt note its original position on the sprockets (mark the teeth with quick-drying paint), also its direction of travel.
7 Withdraw the crankshaft sprocket. If it is tight you will need to use a special extractor, but due to the confined space available you may need to lower the engine from its mounting on that side. Before resorting to this, try levering the sprocket free using screwdrivers. If the mounting is to be disconnected proceed as described in Section 11.
8 Remove the dished washer from the crankshaft, noting that the concave side is against the oil seal.
9 Using a suitably hooked tool, prise out the oil seal from the oil pump housing.
10 Grease the lips of the new seal and press it into position using the pulley bolt and a suitable distance piece made from a piece of tubing.
11 Fit the thrust washer (concave side to oil seal), the belt sprocket and the pulley to the crankshaft.
12 Fit and tension the timing belt by the method described in Section 4.
13 Fit the timing belt cover.
14 Refit and tension the alternator drivebelt.
15 Remove the starter ring gear jamming device (if fitted), refit the starter motor and reconnect the battery.

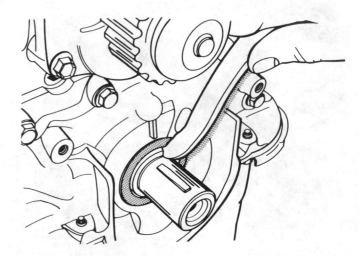

Fig. 1.10 Extracting the oil seal from the oil pump casing (Sec 8)

9 Sump – removal and refitting (engine in car)

1 Disconnect the battery earth lead.
2 Drain the engine oil.
3 Unbolt and remove the starter motor.
4 Unbolt and remove the cover plate from the clutch housing.
5 Unscrew the plastic timing belt guard from the front end of the engine (two bolts).
6 Unscrew the sump securing bolts progressively and remove them.
7 Remove the sump and peel away the gaskets and sealing strips.
8 Make sure that the mating surfaces of the sump and block are clean, then fit new end sealing strips into their grooves and stick new side gaskets into position using thick grease. The ends of the side gaskets should overlap the seals (photos).
9 Offer up the sump, taking care not to displace the gaskets and insert the securing bolts (photo). Tighten the bolts in two stages to the final torque given in the Specifications (photo). Fit the timing belt guard (photo).
10 Refit the cover plate to the flywheel housing (photo).
11 Refit the starter motor.
12 Fill the engine with oil and reconnect the battery.

9.8A Locating the sump rear sealing strip

9.8B Sump gasket to overlap seal strip

9.9A Fitting the sump

9.9B Tightening the sump bolts

9.9C Refit the timing belt lower guard

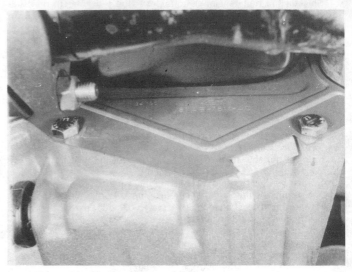

9.10 Refit the flywheel housing cover plate

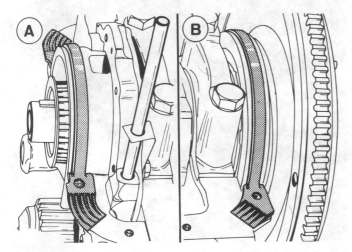

Fig. 1.11 Sump sealing strip locations at the front (A) and rear (B)
(Sec 9)

10 Piston and connecting rods – removal and refitting (engine in car)

1   Remove the sump, as described in the preceding Section, and the cylinder head, as described in Section 7.

2   Check that the connecting rod and cap have adjacent numbers at their big-end to indicate their position in the cylinder block (No 1 nearest timing cover end of engine) (photo).

3   Bring the first piston to the lowest point of its throw by turning the crankshaft pulley bolt and then check if there is a wear ring at the top of the bore. If there is, it should be removed using a scraper, but do not damage the cylinder bore.

4   Unscrew the big-end bolts and remove them.

5   Tap off the cap. If the bearing shell is to be used again, make sure that it is retained with the cap. Note the two cap positioning roll pins.

6   Push the piston/rod out of the top of the block, again keeping the bearing shell with the rod if the shell is to be used again.

7   Repeat the removal operations on the remaining piston/rod assemblies.

8   Dismantling a piston/connecting rod is covered in Section 19.

9   To refit a piston/rod assembly, have the piston ring gaps staggered

---

10.2 Connecting rod and cap numbers

10.11 Locating bearing shell in connecting rod

10.13 Installing a piston and connecting rod

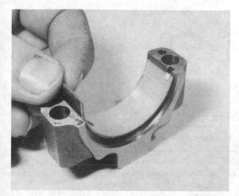
10.15 Locate bearing shells in the big-end caps

10.16A Fitting a big-end cap

10.16B Tighten big-end cap bolts to specified torque

as shown in the diagram (Fig. 1.12). Oil the rings and apply a piston ring compressor. Compress the piston rings.

10 Oil the cylinder bores.

11 Wipe clean the bearing shell seat in the connecting rod and insert the shell (photo).

12 Insert the piston/rod assembly into the cylinder bore until the base of the piston ring compressor stands squarely on the top of the block.

13 Check that the directional arrow on the piston crown faces towards the timing cover end of the engine, then apply the wooden handle of a hammer to the piston crown. Strike the head of the hammer sharply to drive the piston into the cylinder bore and release the ring compressor (photo).

14 Oil the crankpin and draw the connecting rod down to engage with the crankshaft. Make sure the bearing shell is still in position.

15 Wipe the bearing shell seat in the big-end cap clean and insert the bearing shell (photo).

16 Lubricate the bearing shell with oil then fit the cap, aligning the numbers on the cap and the rod, screw in the bolts and tighten them to the specified torque setting (photos).

17 Repeat the operations on the remaining pistons/connecting rods.

18 Refit the sump (Section 9) and the cylinder head (Section 7). Refill the engine with oil and coolant.

11 Engine/transmission mountings – removal and refitting

1 The engine mountings can be removed if the weight of the engine/transmission is first taken by one of the three following methods.

2 Either support the engine under the sump using a jack and a block of wood, or attach a hoist to the engine lifting lugs. A third method is to make up a bar with end pieces which will engage in the water channels at the sides of the bonnet lid aperture. Using an adjustable hook and chain connected to the engine lifting lugs, the weight of the engine can be taken off the mountings.

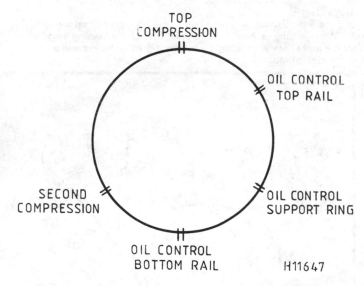
Fig. 1.12 Piston ring gap orientation when fitted to piston (Sec 10)

TOP COMPRESSION
OIL CONTROL TOP RAIL
OIL CONTROL SUPPORT RING
OIL CONTROL BOTTOM RAIL
SECOND COMPRESSION
H11647

Rear mountings

3 Unbolt the mounting, according to type from the body member or panel, also from the engine or transmission. With the mounting withdrawn, the centre bolt can be unscrewed and the flexible component detached (photos).

11.3A Rear mounting – left-hand side

11.3B Rear mounting – right-hand side

11.4 Front left-hand mounting to transmission

Front left-hand mounting

4   Removal of the front mounting on the transmission requires a different removal procedure. Remove the centre bolt from the mounting and then, using one of the methods described, raise the transmission just enough to be able to unbolt and remove the four mounting-to-transmission bolts. Raise and withdraw the mounting and insulator from the front corner plate (photo).

All mountings

5   Refitting of all mountings is a reversal of removal. Make sure that the original sequence of assembly of washers and plates is maintained.

12 Oil filter – removal and refitting

1   The oil filter is of the disposable cartridge type and is mounted on the rear (bulkhead) side of the crankcase. Access to the filter on fuel injection models is from underneath only, so run the car onto ramps or raise and support the car at the front end and chock the rear roadwheels.
2   The filter should be unscrewed using a strap or chain wrench.
3   When fitting a new filter, smear the rubber sealing ring with grease and screw it on as tightly as possible using hand pressure only, not a tool (photo).

4   After starting the engine, the oil pressure warning light will stay on for a few seconds while the filter fills with oil. This is normal after fitting a new filter.
5   Check for any signs of oil leakage around the filter seal.
6   On fuel injection models remove the rear wheel chocks and lower the vehicle.

13 Lubrication system – description

1   The oil pump draws oil from the sump through a pick-up pipe and then supplies pressurised oil through an oilway on the right-hand side of the engine into a full-flow oil filter. A pressure relief valve is incorporated inside the pump casing (photo).
2   Filtered oil passes out of the filter casing through the central threaded mounting stud into the main oil gallery.
3   Oil from the main gallery lubricates the main bearings, and the big-end bearings are lubricated from oilways in the crankshaft.
4   The connecting rods have an oil hole in the big-end on the side towards the exhaust manifold. Oil is ejected from this hole onto the gudgeon pins and cylinder bores.
5   The oil pressure warning switch is located next to the oil filter and connected by an internal passage to the main oil gallery. Oil from this passage is supplied to the centre camshaft bearing.

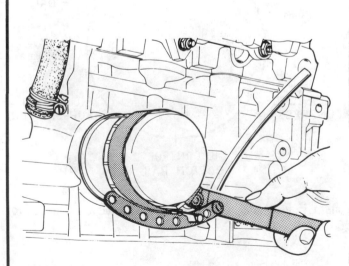

Fig. 1.13 Oil filter removal using a strap wrench (Sec 12)

12.3 Screwing a new oil filter into position
Use hand pressure only

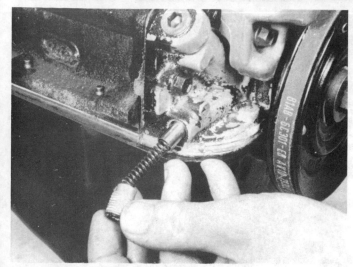

13.1 Oil pressure relief valve location

6   Oil is provided to the other camshaft bearings by means of a longitudinal drilling within the camshaft.
7   The hydraulic cam followers (tappets) are supplied with oil through the grooves in the camshaft bearing journals and oilways in the cylinder head.
8   The contact face of the rocker arm is lubricated from ports in the tappet guides, while the end faces of the valve stems are splash lubricated.
9   An engine oil cooler is located under the oil filter on fuel injection and automatic transmission models.

14 Crankcase ventilation system – description

1   The system is of closed type, in which oil and blow-by fumes are extracted from the crankcase and passed into the intake manifold, after which they are burnt during the normal combustion cycle.

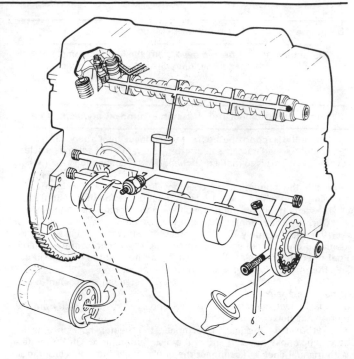

Fig. 1.14 The engine lubrication circuit (Sec 13)

2   At light throttle openings, the emissions are drawn out of the rocker cover, through a control orifice in the crankcase ventilation filter and into the intake manifold. Under full throttle conditions the gas flow routing is still as just described, but in addition the gases are drawn through a filter and pass into the air cleaner.
3   This arrangement offsets any tendency for the fuel/air ratio to be adversely affected at full throttle.
4   Models intended for operation in countries with strict emission control laws also have an exhaust gas recirculation system. This is considered in Chapter 3.

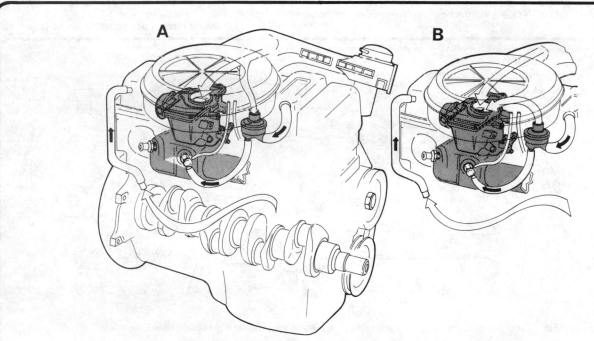

Fig. 1.15 Typical crankcase ventilation system – carburettor engine (Sec 14)

A   Ventilation up to half throttle   B   Ventilation under high throttle

15 Engine – method of removal

The engine should be removed from the vehicle complete with transmission (gearbox and final drive) in a **downward** direction.

16 Engine and manual transmission – removal and separation

1   Open and support the bonnet. Disconnect the battery earth lead.
2   On four-speed models select 4th gear, on five-speed models select reverse gear. This is to make gearchange rod reconnection easier when refitting.
3   Mark the bonnet hinge positions in relation to the bonnet by outlining them with a pencil on the bonnet underside then, with the aid of an assistant, unbolt the hinges and lift the bonnet from the vehicle.
4   **Carburettor models:** Unscrew the two air cleaner retaining bolts, then lift the assembly until the breather and vacuum hoses can be identified and disconnected. Remove the air cleaner from the engine.
Fuel injection models: Disconnect the air hose at the fuel distributor and the intake manifold and remove the hose.
5   Drain the cooling system (Chapter 2), retaining the coolant if it is to be used again.
6   Disconnect the radiator top hose and overflow tank pipe from the thermostat housing.
7   **Carburettor models:** Disconnect the heater hoses from the automatic choke housing and at the distribution piece. On 1.3 models with manual choke, disconnect the choke cable from the carburettor.
Fuel injection models: Disconnect the coolant hoses from the thermostat housing, The water pump and oil cooler three-way connector (photo).
8   **Carburettor models:** Slide the clip back and disconnect the end of the throttle cable from the carburettor throttle lever. Unbolt the cable support bracket and tie the cable assembly to one side of the engine compartment. **Fuel injection models:** Detach the leads from the cold start valve, the warm-up regulator, the thermotime switch and the auxiliary air valve. Disconnect the earth lead from the throttle valve stop.
9   **Carburettor models:** Disconnect the fuel pipe from the fuel pump and plug the pipe. **Fuel injection models:** Disconnect the fuel lines from the warm-up regulator, the cold start valve and the fuel distributor. To avoid the possibility of confusion when reconnecting, label or colour code the hoses with tape. Plug the hoses to prevent the ingress of dirt.

16.7 Three-way connector and hoses (fuel injection models)

10   Disconnect the brake servo vacuum hose from the intake manifold or pipe.
11   **Fuel injection models:** Disconnect the fuel cut-off valve vacuum hose and detach the engine ventilation valve hose by pulling it free.
12   Disconnect the leads from the following electrical components:

    (a)   *Alternator and electric fan*
    (b)   *Oil pressure sender*
    (c)   *Coolant temperature sender*
    (d)   *Reversing lamp switch*
    (e)   *Anti run-on solenoid valve (carburettor engines only)*
    (f)   *Oil dipstick (where applicable)*

13   Disconnect the HT and LT (distributor) wires from the coil terminals.
14   Unscrew the speedometer drive cable from the transmission and release the breather hose.
15   Disconnect the clutch cable from the release lever and from its transmission support (manual transmission only).
16   If the vehicle is not over an inspection pit, it should be jacked up

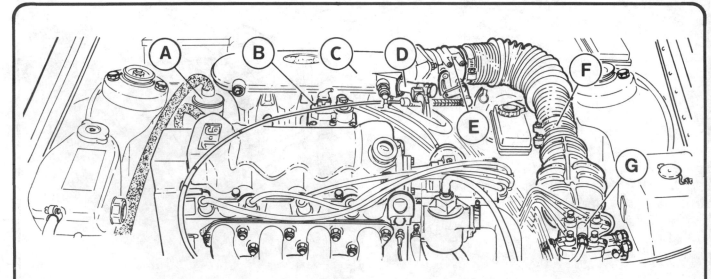

Fig. 1.16 Fuel injection engine layout showing ancillary equipment locations (Sec 16)

A Crankcase breather valve	C Intake manifold	E Throttle valve unit	G Fuel distributor
B Warm-up regulator	D Cold start valve	F Air hose	

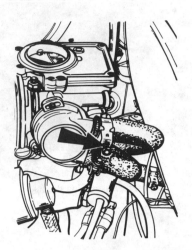

Fig. 1.17 Disconnect the carburettor auto-choke hoses (Sec 16)

Fig. 1.18 Engine lifting lug positions (Sec 16)

and safety stands fitted to provide sufficient clearance beneath it to be able to remove the engine/transmission from below. A distance of approximately 686 mm (27.0 in) is recommended between the floor and the bottom edge of the front panel.

17 Disconnect the exhaust downpipe from the manifold flange connection by unscrewing the securing nuts, then disconnect the exhaust system from its flexible mountings and remove the system complete (to prevent straining the mountings).

18 Disconnect the starter motor leads and the engine earth strap.

19 Disconnect the gearchange rod from the gearbox selector shaft. Do this by releasing the clamp rod and withdrawing the rod. Tie the rod to the stabiliser and then unhook the tension spring (where fitted).

20 Unscrew the single bolt and disconnect the stabiliser from the gearbox. Note the washer which is located between the stabiliser trunnion and the gearbox casing.

21 Drain the gearbox. As no drain plug is fitted, this is carried out by unscrewing the cap nut on the selector shaft locking assembly. Take care not to lose the locking pin and spring.

22 Unscrew and remove the pivot bolt and nut from the inboard end of the front suspension lower arm, then remove the bolt which secures the balljoint at the outboard end of the lower arm to the stub axle carrier. A Torx bit can be used to prevent the bolt turning while the nut is unscrewed.

23 The right-hand driveshaft must now be released from the transmission. Do this by inserting a lever between the inboard constant velocity (CV) joint and the transmission. With an assistant pulling the roadwheel outwards, strike the lever hard with the hand.

24 Tie the driveshaft up to the steering rack housing to prevent strain to the CV joints.

25 Restrain the differential pinion cage to prevent the cage from turning, using a plastic plug or similar. Failure to do this may make reconnection of the driveshafts difficult.

26 Release the inboard and outboard ends of the front suspension lower arm on the left-hand side of the vehicle, as described for the right-hand side.

27 Disconnect the left-hand driveshaft, as previously described for the right-hand one.

28 Connect a suitable hoist to the engine, preferably using a spreader bar and connecting lifting hooks to the engine; lifting lugs provided.

29 With the weight of the engine and transmission just supported, disconnect the engine and transmission mountings (see Section 11).

30 Release the anti-roll (stabiliser) bar at each side of the front suspension (four bolts) and lower the bar together with the suspension lower arms.

31 Unbolt the engine mounting (complete with coolant hose support bracket) from the side-member and from the wing apron panel. Place a protective board over the rear face of the radiator.

32 Carefully lower the engine/transmission and withdraw it from under the car. To ease the withdrawal operation, lower the engine/transmission onto a crawler board or a sheet of substantial plywood placed on rollers or lengths of pipe.

Separation

33 Unscrew and remove the starter motor bolts and remove the starter.

34 Unbolt and remove the clutch cover plate from the lower part of the clutch bellhousing.

35 Unscrew and remove the bolts from the clutch bellhousing to engine mating flange.

36 Withdraw the transmission from the engine. Support its weight so that the clutch assembly is not distorted while the input shaft is still in engagment with the splined hub of the clutch driven plate.

17 Engine and automatic transmission – removal and separation

1 Proceed as described in Section 16, but ignore references to the manual transmission. Disconnect the starter inhibitor switch leads and the downshift cable and speed selector linkage. Disconnect and plug the transmission fluid cooler pipes.

2 To disconnect the automatic transmission refer to Chapter 6, Section 24 and complete the instructions given in paragraphs 8 to 18 inclusive. Ignore paragraph 12 if the engine and transmission are not to be separated on removal.

3 To separate the engine from the transmission, first unscrew and remove the starter motor retaining bolts and withdraw the starter motor.

4 Working through the driveplate cover aperture, unscrew and remove the four nuts securing the driveplate to the torque converter. For this to be accomplished it will be necessary to progressively turn the crankshaft for access to each nut in turn. Unscrew the nuts in a progressive manner, one turn at a time until removed.

5 Unscrew and remove the engine-to-transmission flange bolts and then separate the two units, but take care not to catch the torque converter on the driveplate bolt. The torque converter is only loosely attached, so keep it in position in the transmission housing during and after removal of the transmission.

18 Engine – complete dismantling

1 The need for dismantling will have been dictated by wear or noise in most cases. Although there is no reason why only partial dismantling cannot be carried out to renew such items as the oil pump or crankshaft rear oil seal, when the main bearings or big-end bearings have been knocking and especially if the vehicle has covered a high mileage, then it is recommended that a complete strip-down is carried out and every engine component examined, as described in Section 19.

2 Position the engine so that it is upright and safely chocked on a bench or other convenient working surface. If the exterior of the engine is very dirty it should be cleaned before dismantling, using paraffin and a stiff brush or a water-soluble solvent.

18.3A Remove alternator mounting bolt

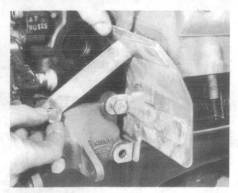

18.3B Alternator heat shield

18.25 Unscrewing the oil pressure switch

3   Remove the alternator, the mounting bracket and exhaust heat shield, and the adjuster link (photos).
4   Disconnect the heater hose from the coolant pump.
5   Drain the engine oil and remove the filter. On automatic transmission and fuel injection models, also remove the oil cooler and gasket by unscrewing the retaining sleeve onto which the filter is screwed.
6   Jam the flywheel starter ring gear to prevent the crankshaft turning and unscrew the crankshaft pulley bolt. Remove the pulley.
7   Unbolt and remove the timing belt cover (4 bolts).
8   Slacken the two bolts on the timing belt tensioner, lever the tensioner against its spring pressure and tighten the bolts to lock it in position.
9   With the belt now slack, note its running direction and mark the mating belt and sprocket teeth with a spot of quick-drying paint. This is not necessary if the belt is being renewed.
10 Disconnect the spark plug leads and remove the distributor cap complete with HT leads.
11 Unscrew and remove the spark plugs.
12 Disconnect the crankcase ventilation hose from its connector on the crankcase.
13 Remove the rocker cover.
14 Unscrew the cylinder head bolts in the reverse order to tightening (Fig. 1.9) and discard them. New bolts must be used at reassembly.
15 Remove the cylinder head complete with manifolds.

16 Turn the engine on its side. Do not invert it, as sludge in the sump may enter the oilways. Remove the sump bolts, withdraw the sump and peel off the gaskets and sealing strips.
17 On manual transmission models release the bolts from the clutch pressure plate in a progressive manner until the pressure of the assembly is relieved and then remove the cover, taking care not to allow the driven plate (friction disc) to fall to the floor.
18 Unbolt and remove the flywheel or driveplate. The bolt holes are offset so it will only fit one way.
19 Remove the engine adaptor plate.
20 Unbolt and remove the crankshaft rear oil seal retainer.
21 Unbolt and remove the timing belt tensioner and take out the coil spring. (This spring is not used on all models).
22 Unbolt and remove the coolant pump.
23 Remove the belt sprocket from the crankshaft using the hands or if tight, a two-legged puller. Take off the thrust washer.
24 Unbolt the oil pump and pick-up tube and remove them as an assembly.
25 Unscrew and remove the oil pressure switch (photo).
26 Turn the crankshaft so that all the pistons are half-way down the bores, and feel if a wear ridge exists at the top of the bores. If so, scrape the ridge away, taking care not to damage the bores.
27 Inspect the big-end and main bearing caps for markings. The main bearings should be marked 1 to 5 with a directional arrow pointing to the timing belt end. The big-end caps and connecting rods should have

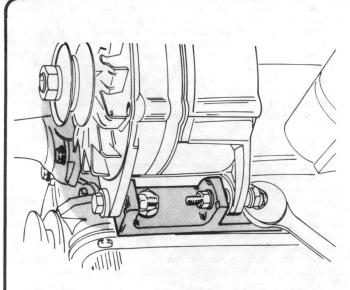

Fig. 1.19 Alternator mounting bracket (Sec 18)

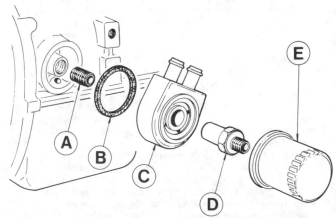

Fig. 1.20 Remove the oil filter (E) and, where applicable, the sleeve (D), oil cooler (C), gasket (B) and threaded bush (A) (Sec 18)

Fig. 1.21 Remove the coolant pump bolts (Sec 18)

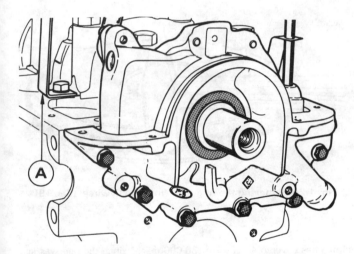

Fig. 1.22 Oil pump unit showing the pick up tube/filter bracket attachment (A) to the crankcase (Sec 18)

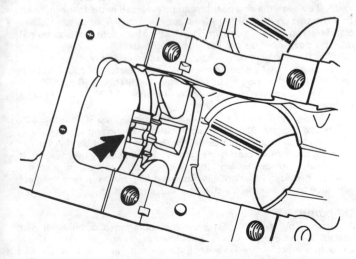

Fig. 1.23 Crankcase ventilation baffle (Sec 18)

adjacent matching numbers. Number 1 is at the timing belt end of the engine. Make your own marks if necessary.

28 Unscrew the bolts from the first big-end cap and remove the cap. The cap is located on two roll pins, so if the cap requires tapping off make sure that it is not tapped in a sideways direction.

29 Retain the bearing shell with the cap if the shell is to be used again.

30 Push the piston/connecting rod out of the top of the cylinder block, again retaining the bearing shell with the rod if the shell is to be used again.

31 Remove the remaining pistons/rods in a similar way.

32 Remove the main bearing caps, keeping the shells with their respective caps if the shells are to be used again. Lift out the crankshaft.

33 Take out the bearing shells from the crankcase, noting the semi-circular thrust washers on either side of the centre bearing. Keep the shells identified as to position in the crankcase if they are to be used again.

34 Prise down the spring arms of the crankcase ventilation baffle and remove it from inside the crankcase just below the ventilation hose connection.

35 The engine is now completely dismantled and each component should be cleaned and examined, as described in the following Section.

19 Engine components – examination and renovation

1 Clean all components using paraffin and a stiff brush, except the crankshaft, which should be wiped clean and the oil passages cleaned out with a length of wire.

2 Never assume that a component is unworn simply because it looks all right. After all the effort which has gone into dismantling the engine, refitting worn components will make the overhaul a waste of time and money. Depending on the degree of wear, the overhauler's budget and the anticipated life of the vehicle, components which are only slightly worn may be refitted, but if in doubt it is always best to renew.

Crankshaft, main and big-end bearings

3 The need to renew the main bearing shells or to have the crankshaft reground will usually have been determined during the last few miles of operation when perhaps a heavy knocking has developed from within the crankcase or the oil pressure warning lamp has stayed on, denoting a low oil pressure probably caused by excessive wear in the bearings.

4 Even without these symptoms, the journals and crankpins on a high mileage engine should be checked for out-of-round (ovality) and taper. For this a micrometer will be needed to check the diameter of the journals and crankpins at several different points around them. A motor factor or engineer can do this for you. If the average of the readings shows that either out-of-round or taper is outside permitted tolerance (see Specifications), then the crankshaft should be reground by your dealer or engine reconditioning company to accept the undersize main and big-end shell bearings which are available. Normally, the company doing the regrinding will supply the necessary undersize shells.

5 If the crankshaft is in good condition, it is wise to renew the bearing shells as it is almost certain that the original ones will have worn. This is often indicated by scoring of the bearing surface or by the top layer of the bearing metal having worn through to expose the metal underneath.

6 Each shell is marked on its back with the part number. Undersize shells will have the undersize stamped additionally on their backs.

7 Crankshafts with standard size journal diameters are not marked, but if a green spot is seen on the crankshaft then this indicates that 0.025 mm (0.00098 in) undersize big-end bearings are used.

Cylinder bores, pistons, rings and connecting rods

8 Cylinder bore wear will usually have been evident from the smoke emitted from the exhaust during recent operation of the vehicle on the road, coupled with excessive oil consumption and fouling of spark plugs.

9 Engine life can be extended by fitting special oil control rings to

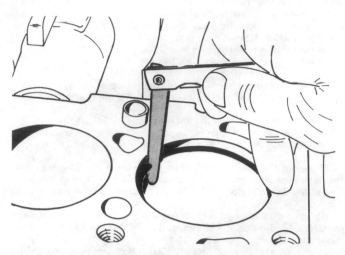

Fig. 1.24 Check the end gap of each piston ring before assembly (Sec 19)

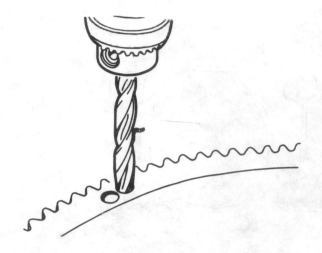

Fig. 1.25 Drilling the flywheel starter ring for removal (Sec 19)

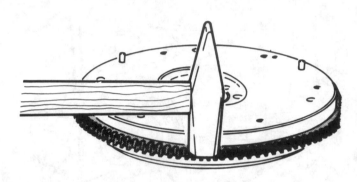

Fig. 1.26 Removing the ring gear from the flywheel (Sec 19)

the pistons. These are widely advertised and will give many more thousands of useful mileage without the need for a rebore, although this will be inevitable eventually. If this remedy is decided upon, remove the piston/connecting rods as described in Section 10 and fit the proprietary rings in accordance with the manufacturer's instructions.

10 Where a more permanent solution is decided upon, the cylinder block can be rebored by your dealer or engineering works, or by one of the mobile workshops which now undertake such work. The cylinder bore will be measured both for out-of-round and for taper to decide how much the bores should be bored out. A set of matching pistons will be supplied in a suitable oversize to suit the new bores.

11 Due to the need for special heating and installing equipment for removal and refitting of the interference type gudgeon pin, the removal and refitting of pistons to the connecting rods is definitely a specialist job, preferably for your Ford dealer. If the pistons are to be separated from their rods, have the rods checked for alignment before assembly.

12 The removal and refitting of piston rings is, however, well within the scope of the home mechanic. Do this by sliding two or three old feeler blades round behind the top compression ring so that they are at equidistant points. The ring can now be slid up the blades and removed. Repeat the removal operations on the second compression ring and then the oil control ring. This method will not only prevent the rings dropping onto empty grooves as they are withdrawn, but it will also avoid ring breakage.

13 Even when new piston rings have been supplied to match the pistons, always check that they are not tight in their grooves and also check their end gaps by pushing them squarely down their particular cylinder bore and measuring with a feeler blade. Adjustment of the end gap can be made by careful grinding to bring it within the specified tolerance.

14 If new rings are being fitted to an old piston, always remove any carbon from the grooves beforehand. The best tool for this job is the end of a broken piston ring. Take care not to cut your fingers, piston rings are sharp. The cylinder bores should be roughened with fine glass paper to assist the bedding-in of the new rings.

15 The top rings are coated with molybdenum. Avoid damaging the coating when fitting the rings to the pistons.

16 The lower (oil control) ring must be fitted so that the manufacturer's mark is towards the piston crown, or the groove towards the gudgeon pin. Take care that the rails of the oil control ring abut without overlapping.

Timing sprockets and belt

17 It is very rare for the teeth of the sprockets to wear, but attention should be given to the tensioner idler pulley. It must turn freely and smoothly, be ungrooved and without any shake in its bearing. Otherwise renew it.

18 Always renew the coil spring (if fitted) in the tensioner. If the

engine has covered 48 000 km (30 000 miles) since the belt was last changed, then it is recommended that a new belt is fitted, even if the original one appears in good condition.

Flywheel

19 Inspect the starter ring gear on the flywheel for wear or broken teeth. If evident, the ring gear should be renewed in the following way. Drill the ring gear with two holes, approximately 7 or 8 mm (0.3 in) diameter and offset as shown (Fig. 1.25). Make sure that you do not drill too deeply or you will damage the flywheel.

20 Tap the ring gear downward off its register and remove it.

21 Place the flywheel in the household refrigerator for about an hour and then heat the new ring gear to between 260 and 280°C (500 and 536°F) in a domestic oven. Do not heat it above 290°C (554°F) or its hardness will be lost.

22 Slip the ring onto the flywheel and gently tap it into position against its register. Allow it to cool without quenching.

23 The clutch friction surface on the flywheel should be checked for grooving or tiny hair cracks, the latter being caused by overheating. If these conditions are evident, it may be possible to surface grind the flywheel provided its balance is not upset. Otherwise, a new flywheel will have to be fitted – consult your dealer about this.

Oil pump

24 The oil pump is of gear type, incorporating a crescent-shaped spacer. Although no wear limit tolerances are specified, if on inspection there is obvious wear between the gears, or between the driven gear and the pump casing, the pump should be renewed. Similarly if a high mileage engine is being reconditioned, it is recommended that a new pump is fitted.

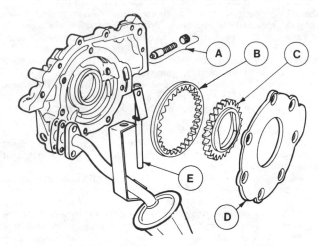

Fig. 1.27 Oil pump components (Sec 19)

A   Relief valve   D   Cover plate
B   Driven gear   E   Oil return pipe
C   Driving gear

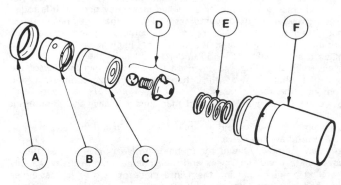

Fig. 1.28 Exploded view of hydraulic cam follower (Sec 19)

A   Crimped retainer   D   Non-return valve
B   Plunger   E   Coil spring
C   Cylinder   F   Body

Crankcase

25 Clean out the oilways with a length of wire or by using compressed air. Similarly clean the coolant passages. This is best done by flushing through with a cold water hose. Examine the crankcase and block for stripped threads in bolt holes; if evident, thread inserts can be fitted.
26 Renew any core plugs which appear to be leaking or which are excessively rusty.
27 Cracks in the casting may be rectified by specialist welding, or by one of the cold metal key interlocking processes available.

Oil seals and gaskets

28 Renew the oil seals in the oil pump and in the crankshaft rear oil seal retainer as a matter of routine at time of major overhaul. It is recommended that the new seals are drawn into these components using a nut and bolt and distance pieces, rather than tapping them into position, to avoid distortion of the light alloy castings.
29 Renew the camshaft oil seal after the camshaft has been installed.
30 Always smear the lips of a new oil seal with grease, and check that the small tensioner spring in the oil seal has not been displaced during installation.
31 Renew all gaskets by purchasing the appropriate engine set, which usually includes the necessary oil seals.

Camshaft and bearings

32 Examine the camshaft gear and lobes for damage or wear. If evident, a new camshaft must be purchased, or one which has been built-up, such as are advertised by firms specialising in exchange components.
33 The bearing internal diameters in the cylinder head should be checked against the Specifications if a suitable gauge is available, otherwise check for movement between the camshaft journal and the bearing. If the bearings are proved to be worn, then a new cylinder head is the only answer as the bearings are machined directly in the cylinder head.
34 Check the camshaft endfloat by temporarily refitting the camshaft and thrustplate. If the endfloat exceeds the specified tolerance, renew the thrustplate.

Cam followers

35 It is seldom that the hydraulic type cam followers (tappets) wear in their cylinder head bores. If the bores are worn then a new cylinder head is called for.
36 If the cam lobe contact surface shows signs of a depression or grooving, grinding out the wear surface will not only remove the hardened surface of the follower but may also reduce its overall length to a point where the self-adjusting capability of the cam follower is

exceeded and valve clearances are not taken up, with consequent noisy operation.
37 Cam followers cannot be dismantled so if they become worn after high mileage, they must be renewed. On refitting, it is only necessary to smear the outside surfaces with clean engine oil, as they are self priming and will fill with engine oil once the engine is running, although initial operation may be noisy until primed.

20 Cylinder head – dismantling, examination and renovation

1 The usual reason for dismantling the cylinder head is to decarbonise and to grind in the valves. Reference should therefore be made to the next Section in addition to the dismantling operations described here.
2 Remove the intake and exhaust manifolds and their gaskets, also the thermostat housing (Chapter 2).
3 Unscrew the nuts from the rocker arms and discard the nuts. New ones must be fitted at reassembly.
4 Remove the rocker arms and the hydraulic cam followers, keeping them in their originally fitted sequence. Keep the rocker guide and spacer plates in order.
5 The camshaft need not be withdrawn but if it is wished to do so, first remove the thrustplate and take the camshaft out from the rear of the cylinder head.
6 The valve springs should now be compressed. A standard type of compressor will normally do the job, but a forked tool (Part No 21-097) can be purchased or made up to engage on the rocker stud using a nut and distance piece to compress it.

Fig. 1.29 Special valve spring compressing tool (Sec 20)

7   Compress the valve spring and extract the split collets. Do not overcompress the spring, or the valve stem may bend. If it is found when screwing down the compressor tool that the spring retainer does not release from the collets, remove the compressor and place a piece of tubing on the retainer so that it does not impinge on the collets and place a small block of wood under the head of the valve. With the cylinder head resting flat down on the bench, strike the end of the tubing a sharp blow with a hammer. Refit the compressor and compress the spring.
8   Extract the split collets and then gently release the compressor and remove it.
9   Remove the valve spring retainer, the spring and the valve stem oil seal. Withdraw the valve.
10 Valve removal should commence with No 1 valve (nearest timing cover end). Keep the valves and their components in their originally installed order by placing them in a piece of card which has holes punched in it and numbered 1 to 8.
11 To check for wear in the valve guides, place each valve in turn in its guide so that approximately one third of its length enters the guide. Rock the valve from side to side. If any more than the slightest movement is possible the guides will have to be reamed (working from the valve seat end) and oversize stemmed valves fitted. If you do not have the necessary reamer (Tool No 21-071 to 21-074), leave this work to your Ford dealer.
12 Examine the valve seats. Normally the seats do not deteriorate, but the valve heads are more likely to burn away, in which case new valves can be ground in, as described in the next Section. If the seats require recutting, use a standard cutter, available from most accessory or tool stores.
13 Renewal of any valve seat which is cracked or beyond recutting is definitely a job for your dealer or motor engineering works.
14 If the rocker arm studs have to be removed for any reason ensure that the stud hole(s) are clean by blowing out with compressed air before fitting a new stud and tightening it to the specified torque setting. Ford recommend the replacement of the rocker arm, guide, spacer plate and nut whenever a rocker stud is renewed. If a rocker arm is damaged, renew all eight rocker arms.
15 Check the rocker arm contact surfaces for wear. Renew the valve springs if they have been in service for 80 000 km (50 000 miles) or more.
16 If the cylinder head mating surface is suspected of being distorted, it can be checked and surface ground by your dealer or motor engineering works. Distortion is possible with this type of light alloy head if the bolt tightening method is not followed exactly, or if severe overheating has taken place.

21 Cylinder head and pistons – decarbonising

1   With the cylinder head removed as described in Section 7, the carbon deposits should be removed from the combustion surfaces using a blunt scraper. Take great care as the head is of light alloy construction and avoid the use of a rotary (power-driven) wire brush.
2   Where a more thorough job is to be carried out, the cylinder head should be dismantled, as described in the preceding Section, so that the valves may be ground in, and the ports and combustion spaces

cleaned and blown out after the manifolds have been removed.
3   Before grinding in a valve, remove the carbon and deposits completely from its head and stem. With an inlet valve this is usually quite easy, simply a case of scraping off the soft carbon with a blunt knife and finishing with a wire brush. With an exhaust valve, the deposits are very much harder and those on the valve head may need a rub on coarse emery cloth to remove them. An old woodworking chisel is a useful tool to remove the worst of the valve head deposits.
4   Make sure that the valve heads are really clean, otherwise the rubber suction cup grinding tool will not stick during the grinding-in operations.
5   Before starting to grind in a valve, support the cylinder head so that there is sufficient clearance under it for the valve stem to project fully without being obstructed, otherwise the valve will not seat properly during grinding.
6   Take the first valve and apply a little coarse grinding paste to the bevelled edge of the valve head. Insert the valve into its guide and apply the suction grinding tool to its head. Rotate the tool between the palms of the hands in a back-and-forth rotary movement until the gritty action of the grinding-in process disappears. Repeat the operation with fine paste and then wipe away all trace of grinding paste and examine the seat and bevelled edge of the valve. A matt silver mating band should be observed on both components, without any sign of black spots. If some spots do remain, repeat the grinding-in process until they have disappeared. A drop or two of paraffin, if applied to the contact surfaces, will speed the grinding process, but do not allow any paste to run down into the valve guide. On completion, wipe away every trace of grinding paste using a paraffin-moistened cloth.
7   Repeat the operations on the remaining valves, taking care not to mix up their originally fitted sequence.
8   An important part of the decarbonising operation is to remove the carbon deposits from the piston crowns. To do this (engine in vehicle), turn the crankshaft so that two pistons are at the top of their stroke and press some grease between the pistons and the cylinder walls. This will prevent carbon particles falling down into the piston ring grooves. Plug the other two bores with rag.
9   Cover the oilways and coolant passages with masking tape and then, using a blunt scraper, remove all the carbon from the piston crowns. Take great care not to score the soft alloy of the crown or the surface of the cylinder bore.
10 Rotate the crankshaft to bring the other two pistons to tdc and repeat the operations.
11 Wipe away the circles of grease and carbon from the cylinder bores.
12 Clean the top surface of the cylinder block by careful scraping.

22 Cylinder head – reassembly

1   Before starting to reassemble the cylinder head, check that all surfaces are clean of grinding paste, carbon deposits and dirty oil, paying particular attention to the intake parts, the valve seat faces and the valve guide bores.
2   Commence reassembly of the cylinder head by fitting new valve stem oil seals (photos).

22.2A Using a socket to install a valve stem oil seal

22.2B Valve stem oil seal installed

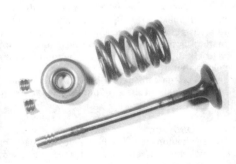

22.2C Valve components

22.3 Locate valve into guide ...

22.4A ... fit valve spring and ...

22.4B ... valve spring retainer

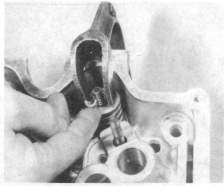
22.5 Inserting a split collet

22.9 Inserting a hydraulic cam follower

22.10A Fitting a rocker arm spacer plate

22.10B Fitting a rocker arm and guide

22.10C Tightening a rocker arm nut

23.1 Crankcase ventilation baffle

3   Oil No 1 valve stem and insert the valve into its guide (photo).
4   Fit the valve spring (closer coils to cylinder head), then the spring retainer (photos).
5   Compress the spring and engage the split collets in the cut-out in the valve stem. Hold them in position while the compressor is gently released and removed (photo).
6   Repeat the operations on the remaining valves, making sure that each valve is returned to its original guide, or new valves have been fitted into the seat into which it was ground.
7   Once all the valves have been fitted, support the ends of the cylinder head on two wooden blocks and strike the end of each valve stem with a plastic or copper-faced hammer, just a light blow to settle the components.
8   Fit the camshaft (if removed) and a new oil seal, as described in Section 8.

9   Smear the hydraulic cam followers with hypoid type transmission oil and insert them into their original bores (photo).
10 Fit the rocker arms with their guides and spacer plates, use new nuts and tighten to the specified torque. It is important that each rocker arm is installed only when its particular cam follower is at its lowest point (in contact with the cam base circle) (photos).
11 Refit the exhaust and intake manifolds and the thermostat housing, using all new gaskets.

23 Engine – reassembly

1   With everything clean and parts renewed where necessary, commence reassembly by inserting the ventilation baffle into the crankcase. Make sure that the spring arms engage securely (photo).

2   Insert the bearing half shells into their seats in the crankcase, making sure that the seats are perfectly clean (photo).

3   Stick the semi-circular thrust washers on either side of the centre bearing with thick grease. Make sure that the oil channels face outwards (photo).

4   Oil the bearing shells and carefully lower the crankshaft into position (photos).

5   Insert the bearing shells into the main bearing caps, making sure that their seats are perfectly clean. Oil the bearings and install the caps to their correct numbered location and with the directional arrow pointing towards the timing belt end of the engine (photos).

6   Tighten the main bearing cap bolts to the specified torque (photo).

7   Check the crankshaft endfloat. Ideally a dial gauge should be used, but feeler blades are an alternative if inserted between the face of the thrust washer and the machined surface of the crankshaft balance web, having first prised the crankshaft in one direction and then the other (photo). Provided the thrust washers at the centre bearing have been renewed, the endfloat should be within specified tolerance. If it is not, oversize thrust washers are available (see Specifications).

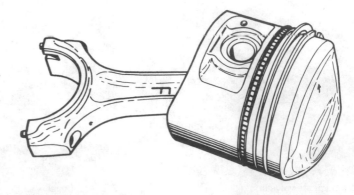

Fig. 1.30 Piston/connecting rod alignment (Sec 23)

23.2 Inserting a main bearing shell into the crankcase

23.3 Crankshaft thrust washer

23.4A Lubricate the main bearing shells

23.4B Refit the crankshaft

23.5A Locating a main bearing shell in its cap

23.5B Fitting a main bearing cap

23.5C Main bearing cap markings

23.6 Tightening a main bearing cap bolt

23.7 Checking crankshaft endfloat with a feeler blade

8   The pistons/connecting rods should now be installed. Although new pistons will have been fitted to the rods by your dealer or supplier due to the special tools needed, it is worth checking to ensure that with the piston crown arrow or cast nipple in the piston oil cut-out pointing towards the timing belt end of the engine, the F mark on the connecting rod or the oil ejection hole in the rod big-end is as shown (Fig. 1.30).

9   Oil the cylinder bores and install the pistons/connecting rods as described in Section 10, paragraphs 9 to 17 inclusive.

10 Fit the oil pressure switch and tighten to the specified torque.

11 Before fitting the oil pump, action must be taken to prevent damage to the pump oil seal from the step on the front end of the crankshaft. First remove the Woodruff key and then build up the front end of the crankshaft using adhesive tape to form a smooth inclined surface to permit the pump seal to slide over the step without its lip turning back or the seal spring being displaced during installation (photo).

12 If the oil pump is new, pour some oil into it before installation in order to prime it and rotate its driving gear a few turns (photo).

13 Align the pump gear flats with those on the crankshaft and install the oil pump complete with new gasket. Tighten the bolts to the specified torque (photos).

14 Remove the adhesive tape and tap the Woodruff key into its groove (photo).

15 Bolt the oil pump pick-up tube into position (photos).

16 To the front end of the crankshaft, fit the thrust washer (belt guide) so that its concave side is towards the pump (photo).

17 Fit the crankshaft belt sprocket. If it is tight, draw it into position using the pulley bolt and a distance piece. Make sure that the belt retaining flange on the sprocket is towards the front of the crankshaft and the nose of the shaft has been smeared with a little grease before fitting (photo).

18 Install the coolant pump using a new gasket and tightening the bolts to the specified torque (photos).

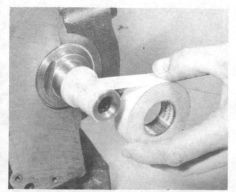
23.11 Building up the crankshaft front end with tape

23.12 Prime the oil pump before fitting

23.13A Oil pump ready for fitting

23.13B Tightening the oil pump securing bolts

23.14 Locate the crankshaft Woodruff key

23.15A Oil pump pick-up tube location

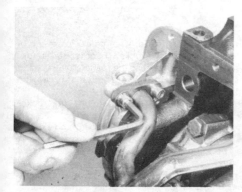
23.15B Tighten the oil pickup tube securing bolt

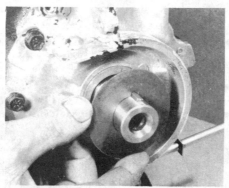
23.16 Crankshaft timing belt guide

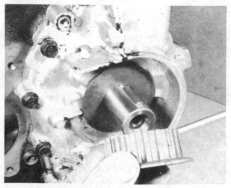
23.17 Fit crankshaft timing belt sprocket

23.18A Fit the coolant pump ...

23.18B ... and tighten the securing bolts

23.20 Locate the crankshaft rear oil seal and retainer

23.21A Fit the engine adapter plate into position ...

23.21B ... followed by the flywheel

23.21C Use new flywheel bolts which are ready-coated with thread sealant ...

23.21D ... and tighten them to the specified torque

23.24A Locate the intake manifold gasket ...

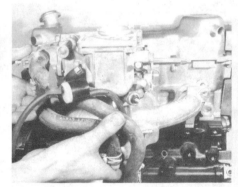

23.24B ... then fit the manifold

19 Fit the timing belt tensioner and its coil spring (where fitted). Lever the tensioner fully against spring pressure and temporarily tighten the bolts.

20 Using a new gasket, bolt on the rear oil seal retainer, which will have been fitted with a new oil seal and the seal lips greased (photo).

21 Engage the engine adaptor plate on its locating dowels and then offer up the flywheel. It will only go on in one position as it has offset holes. Insert **new** bolts and tighten to the specified torque. The bolts are pre-coated with thread sealant (photos).

22 Fit the clutch and centralise it (refer to Chapter 5).

23. With the engine resting on its side (not inverted unless you are quite sure that the pistons are not projecting from the block), fit the sump, gaskets and sealing strips, as described in Section 9.

24 Fit the cylinder head, as described in Section 7, using **new** bolts. Refit the manifolds (photos).

25 Install and tension the timing belt, as described in Section 4.

26 Before refitting the rocker cover smear a 40 mm (1.6 in) length of sealant across the gasket recess where the rocker cover is fitted under the timing belt cover. Using a new gasket, refit the rocker cover, taking care not to dislodge the gasket. Tighten the retaining screws to the specified torque setting.

27 Reconnect the crankcase ventilation hoses between the rocker cover and the crankcase.

28 Screw in a new set of spark plugs, correctly gapped, and tighten to the specified torque – this is important. If the specified torque is exceeded, the plugs may be impossible to remove.

29 Fit the timing belt cover.

30 Fit the crankshaft pulley and tighten the bolt to the specified torque while the flywheel ring gear is locked to prevent it turning.

31 Smear the sealing ring of a new oil filter with a little grease, and screw it into position using hand pressure only.

32 Install the engine mounting brackets, if removed.

33 Refit the ancillaries. The alternator bracket and alternator (Chapter 11), the fuel pump (Chapter 3), the thermostat housing (Chapter 2), and the distributor (Chapter 4).
34 Fit the distributor cap and reconnect the HT leads.
35 Check the tightness of the oil drain plug and insert the dipstick.

24 Engine and manual transmission – reconnection and refitting

1 This is a direct reversal of removal and separation of the engine from the transmission. Take care not to damage the radiator or front wings during installation.

Reconnection

2 Check that the clutch driven plate has been centralised, as described in Chapter 5.
3 Make sure that the engine adaptor plate is correctly located on its positioning dowels.
4 Smear the splines of the transmission input shaft with a little grease and then, supporting the weight of the transmission, connect it to the engine by passing the input shaft through the splined hub of the clutch plate until the transmission locates on the dowels (photo).
5 Screw in the flange bolts and tighten to the specified torque.

Installation

6 First check that the engine sump drain plug is tight and that the gearbox cap nut (removed to drain the oil) has been refitted with its locking pin and spring (photos).
7 Manoeuvre the engine/transmission under the vehicle and attach a lifting hoist to the engine lugs.
8 Raise the engine/transmission carefully until the engine front left mounting bolt can be located. Fit the insulator and cup to the underside of the mounting bracket and screw on the nut.
9 Fit the left-hand rear mounting.
10 Fit the right-hand rear mounting. Make sure that the sequence of mounting washers and plates is as originally located, and don't forget the wing inner panel bolt which secures the rear mounting (photo).
11 Release the lifting hoist and remove it.
12 If some sort of plug was used to prevent the differential pinion cage from turning, extract it now. If a plug was not used, insert the finger into the driveshaft hole in the transmission and align the cage ready to receive the driveshaft.
13 Using a new snap-ring, reconnect the left-hand driveshaft to the transmission by applying pressure inwards on the roadwheel. Check that the snap-ring has locked securely in position. It is sometimes difficult to fully engage the driveshaft and its snap-ring in the differential unless the driveshaft is raised to a horizontal attitude. In this case, the hub assembly should be raised and it will be easier to do if the roadwheel is first removed to reduce its weight.

24.4 Connecting the transmission to the engine

24.6A Gearbox cap nut, spring and plunger

24.6B Fitting the gearbox cap nut assembly

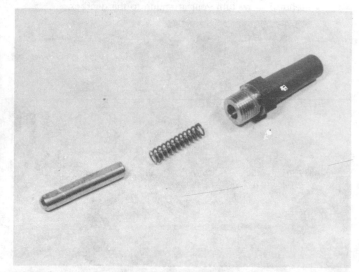
24.10 Engine mounting wing inner panel bolt (right-hand rear)

14 Reconnect the left-hand lower arm of the front suspension. Tighten the bolts to the specified torque. When tightening the balljoint pinch-bolt, the bolt head can be prevented from turning by inserting an Allen key into its socket head. Although this is not the correct tool, it will serve as an alternative. Where the socket is rounded through abuse, mole grips can be used.

15 Refit the driveshaft and suspension lower arm to the opposite side in a similar way to that just described. Reconnect the anti-roll bar.

16 Reconnect the transmission stabiliser rod, making sure to insert the washer between the rod and the transmission casing (photo).

17 Check that the gearchange control lever is still in 4th gear position, (or reverse gear on five-speed models). On four-speed models hook the gearchange rod tension spring to the longitudinal body side-member.

18 The selector mechanism must now be reconnected and adjusted according to gearbox type as given below:

Four-speed manual transmission

(a) Pull downwards on the gearchange rod and slip it onto the selector shaft which projects from the transmission. The clamp should be loose on the gearchange rod (photo).

(b) Using a 3.5 mm (0.14 in) diameter rod or pin, insert it as shown and pull the gear lever downwards to lock it in the selector slide. When inserting the rod, point it upward to 'feel' the cut-out in the gear lever before prising it downwards (photo). Now turn your attention to the gearbox.

(c) Using a pin or rod, inserted into the hole in the end of the projecting selector shaft, turn the shaft clockwise viewed from the rear of the car to its stop and retain it in this position with a strong rubber band. Now tighten the clamp pinch-bolt (photo).

(d) Remove the locking pins and connect the gearchange rod tension spring.

Five-speed manual transmission

(a) Using a drift inserted into the drilling in the selector shaft, turn the shaft as far as it will go in a clockwise direction and push it right in. This will ensure reverse gear is engaged.

(b) Refit the gearchange rod to the selector shaft, but do not tighten the pinch-bolt at this stage.

(c) Taking care not to disengage the gearchange rod from the selector shaft, place the gear lever in the reverse position.

(d) Push down on the gear lever and move it back and forth very slightly until the holes in the selector housing and gearchange rod are aligned. Insert a 3.5 mm (0.14 in) diameter pin or rod through the aligned holes to lock the mechanism.

(e) Now turn the gearbox selector shaft clockwise viewed from the rear of the car to take up any free play, then tighten the gearchange rod pinch-bolt.

(f) Finally remove the alignment pin or rod from the hole in the selector housing.

24.16 Connect the transmission stabiliser rod

24.18A Sliding the clamp onto the transmission selector shaft

24.18B Locking the gear lever into the selector slide

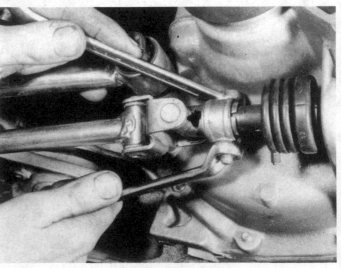

24.18C Tightening the gearchange rod clamp bolt

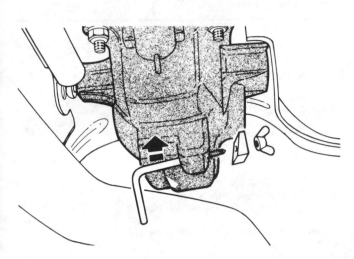

Fig. 1.31 Hold gear lever in position with lock tool (Sec 24)

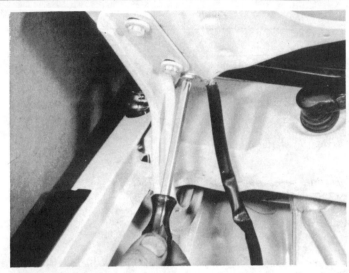

24.32 Bonnet bonding strap screw

19 Reconnect the starter motor and the engine earth leads. Fit the drivebelt plastic cover to the front end of the sump.
20 Refit the exhaust system and connect the exhaust downpipe to the manifold.
21 Reconnect the speedometer drive cable.
22 Reconnect the clutch cable to the release lever and transmission support (Chapter 5).
23 Reconnect the leads listed in paragraphs 12 and 13 of Section 16.
24 Reattach the brake vacuum servo hose to the intake manifold and the distributor advance vacuum pipe.
25 **Fuel injection models:** Reconnect the crankcase breather valve hose and also the deceleration fuel cut-off valve hose. Connect the fuel lines to the fuel distributor, the cold start valve and the warm-up regulator.
26 **Carburettor engine models:** Reconnect the throttle cable and bracket to the carburettor and the fuel pipe to the pump.
27 **Fuel injection models:** Reconnect the leads to the cold start valve, the warm-up regulator, the thermotime switch and the auxiliary air valve. Attach the air valve stop earth lead.
28 **Carburettor engine models:** Attach the automatic choke heater hoses to the thermostat housing and the distribution piece.
29 **Fuel injection models:** Reattach the hoses to the thermostat housing, the water pump and three-way connector of the oil cooler.
30 Reconnect the respective overflow tank and radiator top hose to the thermostat housing and reconnect the radiator bottom hose to the water pump.
31 Fill up with engine oil, transmission oil and coolant, reconnect the battery.
32 Install the bonnet, bolting the hinges to their originally marked positions. Reconnect the bonding strap (for radio interference suppression) (photo).
33 Reconnect the windscreen washer pipe.
34 Fit the air cleaner and reconnect its hoses and air intake spout.
35 **Fuel injection models:** Refit the air hose to the fuel distributor and throttle valve assembly.
36 Once the engine is running, check the timing, idle speed and mixture adjustment (refer to Chapters 3 and 4).
37 If a number of new internal components have been installed, run the vehicle at a restricted speed for the first few hundred miles to allow time for the new components to bed in. It is also recommended that with a new or rebuilt engine, the engine oil and filter are changed at the end of the running-in period.

25 Engine and automatic transmission – reconnection and refitting

1 Reconnecting and refitting of the engine and automatic transmission is basically a reversal of the removal procedure. Before attaching the transmission to the engine check that the torque converter is fully seated in the transmission housing and engaged at three points. If it was removed, fit the adaptor plate into position on its guide bushes on the engine flange before refitting the transmission.
2 Tighten the engine and transmission bolts and nuts to their respective torque settings.
3 Reinstall the engine and transmission, as given in Section 24 of this Chapter, but ignore the manual transmission references.
4 When refitting is completed refer to Chapter 6, Section 24, paragraphs 24 to 28 inclusive, for details on the selector and linkage engagement and adjustment.

26 Engine – initial start-up after major overhaul

1 Make sure that the battery is fully charged and that all lubricants, coolant and fuel are replenished.
2 Double check all fittings and electrical connections. Ensure that the distributor is correctly fitted and that the ignition timing setting is correct. If in doubt refer to Chapter 4.
3 Remove the spark plugs and the '–' connection from the ignition coil. Turn the engine over on the starter motor until the oil pressure warning light is extinguished or until oil pressure is recorded on the gauge. This will ensure that the engine is not starved of oil during the critical few minutes running after initial start-up. The fuel system will also be primed during this operation.
4 Reconnect the '–' connection on the ignition coil and refit the spark plugs and leads if they are still disconnected. Start the engine.
5 As soon as the engine fires and runs, keep it going at a fast tickover only (no faster) and bring it up to normal working temperature.
6 As the engine warms up there will be odd smells and some smoke from parts getting hot and burning off oil deposits. The signs to look for are leaks of water or oil, which will be obvious if serious. Check also the exhaust pipe and manifold connections, as these do not always find their exact gastight position until the warmth and vibration have acted on them, and it is almost certain that they will need tightening further. This should be done, of course, with the engine stopped.
7 When normal running temperature has been reached, adjust the engine idle speed, as described in Chapter 3.
8 Stop the engine and wait a few minutes to see if any lubricant or coolant is dripping out when the engine is stationary.
9 After the engine has run for 20 minutes check the tightness of all the easily accessible bolts. **Do not** re-torque the cylinder head bolts.
10 Road test the car to check that the timing is correct and that the engine is giving the necessary smoothness and power. Do not race the engine – if new bearings and/or pistons have been fitted it should be treated as a new engine and run in at a reduced speed for the first 1000 miles (1600 km).

27 Fault diagnosis – engine

Symptom	Reason(s)
Engine fails to turn over when starter operated	
No current at starter motor	Flat or defective battery
	Loose battery leads
	Defective starter solenoid or switch, or broken wiring
	Engine earth strap disconnected
Current at starter motor	Jammed starter motor drive pinion
	Defective starter motor or solenoid
Engine turns over but will not start	
No spark at spark plug	Ignition damp or wet
	Ignition leads to spark plugs loose
	Shorted or disconnected low tension leads
	Defective ignition switch
	Ignition leads connected wrong way round
	Faulty coil
Excess of petrol in cylinder or carburettor flooding	Too much choke allowing too rich a mixture to wet plugs
	Float damaged or leaking or needle not seating
	Float lever incorrectly adjusted
Engine stalls and will not start	
No spark at spark plug	Ignition failure
No fuel getting to engine	No petrol in petrol tank
	Petrol tank breather choked
	Obstruction in carburettor
	Water in fuel system
	Fuel injection system fault
Engine misfires or idles unevenly	
Intermittent spark at spark plugs	Ignition leads loose
	Battery leads loose on terminals
	Battery earth strap loose on body attachment point
	Engine earth lead loose
	Low tension leads to SW (+) and CB (–) terminals on coil loose
	Low tension lead from CB (–) terminal side to distributor loose
	Dirty, or incorrectly gapped plugs
	Tracking across inside of distributor cover
	Ignition too retarded
	Faulty coil
No fuel at carburettor or fuel injection system	No petrol in petrol tank
	Vapour lock in fuel line (in hot conditions or at high altitude)
	Blocked float chamber needle valve
	Fuel pump filter blocked
	Choked or blocked carburettor jets
	Faulty fuel pump
Fuel shortage at engine	Mixture too weak
	Air leak in carburettor
	Air leak at intake manifold to cylinder head, or intake manifold to carburettor
Mechanical wear	Burnt out exhaust valves
	Sticking or leaking valves
	Weak or broken valve springs
	Worn valve guides or stems
	Worn pistons and piston rings
Lack of power and poor compression	
Fuel/air mixture leaking from cylinder	Burnt out exhaust valves
	Sticking or leaking valves
	Worn valve guides and stems
	Weak or broken valve springs
	Blown cylinder head gasket (accompanied by increase in noise)
	Worn pistons and piston rings
	Worn or scored cylinder bores
Incorrect adjustments	Ignition timing wrongly set. Too advanced or retarded
	Incorrectly set spark plugs

Symptom	Reason(s)
Carburation and ignition faults	Distributor automatic balance weights or vacuum advance and retard mechanisms not functioning correctly Faulty fuel pump giving top end fuel starvation

Excessive oil consumption

Oil being burnt by engine	Badly worn, perished or missing valve stem oil seals Excessively worn valve stems and valve guides Worn piston rings Worn pistons and cylinder bores Excessive piston ring gap allowing blow-by Piston oil return holes choked
Oil being lost due to leaks	Leaking oil filter gasket Leaking sump gasket Loose sump plug

Unusual noises from engine

Excessive clearances due to mechanical wear	Worn valve gear (noisy tapping from rocker box) Worn big-end bearing (regular heavy knocking) Worn timing belt and gears (rattling from front of engine) Worn main bearings (rumbling and vibration) Worn crankshaft (knocking, rumbling and vibration)

Chapter 2 Cooling system

For modifications, and information applicable to later models, see Supplement at end of manual

Contents

Specifications

System type
Fully pressurized with belt-driven water pump, a radiator, thermostatically-controlled fan, thermostat and expansion (degas) tank

Coolant capacity
1.3 engine .... 7.1 litre (12.5 Imp pint)
1.6 engine .... 6.9 litre (12.1 Imp pint)

Antifreeze
Antifreeze type .... Antifreeze to Ford specification SSM-97B 9103-A (Duckhams Universal Antifreeze and Summer Coolant)
Antifreeze mixture (ratio) .... 45% antifreeze (by volume)
Antifreeze/water mixture specific gravity 1.069

Radiator
Type .... Corrugated, fin on tube
Pressure cap rating .... 0.85 to 1.10 bar (12.3 to 16.0 lbf/in^2)

Thermostat
Type .... Wax
Opening temperature .... 85 to 89°C (185 to 192°F)
Temperature when fully open .... 99 to 107°C (210 to 225°F)
Allow ± 3°C (5°F) for a used thermostat

Water pump
Type .... Belt-driven, centrifugal

Torque wrench settings

	Nm	lbf ft
Radiator mounting bolts	7 to 9	5 to 7
Thermostat housing bolts	7 to 9	5 to 7
Fan shroud bolts (to radiator)	7 to 9	5 to 7
Fan motor (to shroud)	8 to 10	6 to 7
Water pump bolts	7 to 9	5 to 7

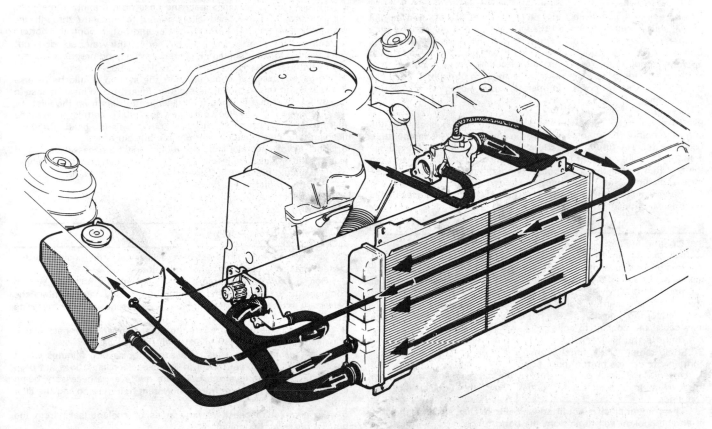

Fig. 2.1 Cooling system (Sec 1)

1 General description

The cooling system on all models comprises a radiator, a coolant pump, a thermostat and an electrically-operated radiator fan. The system is pressurised and incorporates an overflow container (expansion tank).

The cooling system operates in the following way. When the coolant is cold, the thermostat is shut and coolant flow is restricted to the cylinder block, cylinder head, intake manifold and the vehicle interior heater matrix.

As the temperature of the coolant rises the thermostat opens, allowing initially partial and then full circulation of the coolant through the radiator.

If the vehicle is in forward motion then the rush of air cools the coolant as it passes across the radiator. If the coolant temperature rises beyond a predetermined level, due for example to ascending a gradient or being held up in a traffic jam, then the electric fan will cut in to supplement normal cooling.

The expansion tank is of the degas type and the necessary pressure/vacuum relief valve is incorporated in the tank cap.

On models fitted with an oil cooler, engine coolant is circulated to a cooler unit which is fitted between the oil filter unit and the crankcase.

Cars with automatic transmission have a fluid cooler built into the radiator side tank.

2 Cooling system – maintenance

1 At the intervals recommended in Routine Maintenance at the beginning of this manual, visually check the coolant level in the expansion tank. If topping-up is required, use antifreeze mixture of the same strength as the original coolant used for filling the system.

2 Topping-up or refilling the cooling system is made through the expansion tank. If the addition of coolant is required and the engine is hot, *remove the pressure cap from the expansion tank very carefully,*

2.2 Remove expansion tank pressure cap (with care if hot) for topping-up coolant level

having first covered it with a cloth to prevent any possibility of scalding (photo).

3 Top up to between the marks on the tank.

4 Regularly inspect all coolant hoses for security of clips and for evidence of deterioration of the hoses.

5 Frequent topping-up of the system will indicate a leak, as under normal conditions the addition of coolant is a rare occurrence.

6 If a leak is not easily detectable, have the system pressure tested by your Ford dealer. In most instances this will indicate the leak in the system.

7 No attention will be needed to the coolant pump drive alone as on these engines the pump is driven by the toothed timing belt.

8   If the electric radiator cooling fan has not been heard to operate for some time, a simple test can be carried out to check that the fan motor is serviceable. Switch on the ignition and pull the lead from the temperature sensor which is screwed into the thermostat housing. Bridge the two contacts of the lead connecting plug and the fan should operate. Although this test does not, of course, prove the function of the temperature switch, the switch is unlikely to be faulty if there has been an indication of normal temperature during the preceding period of motoring.

Safety note

9   Take particular care when working under the bonnet with the engine running or ignition switched on. As the coolant temperature rises the temperature-controlled radiator cooling fan may suddenly actuate, so make sure that ties, clothing, hair and hands are away from the fan. Remember that the coolant temperature will continue to rise for a short time after the engine is switched off.

10 Renew the coolant (antifreeze) mixture at the intervals specified in Routine Maintenance.

3   Cooling system – draining

1   It is preferable to drain the cooling system with the engine cold. If this is not possible, place a thick cloth over the expansion tank filler cap and turn it slowly 90° in an anti-clockwise direction until the first step is reached, then wait until all the pressure has been released. Be prepared for the emission of very hot steam, as the release of pressure may cause the coolant to boil.

2   Remove the filler cap.

3   Some radiators are fitted with a drain plug, otherwise place a container under the bottom hose.

4   Unscrew the drain plug, or loosen the clip and ease the bottom hose away from the radiator outlet. Drain the coolant into the container.

5   The cylinder block is not fitted with a drain plug, since the majority of engine coolant will drain from the bottom hose.

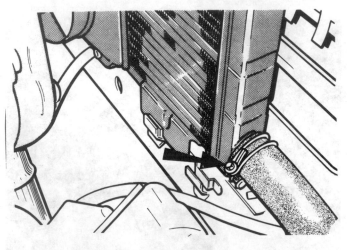

Fig. 2.2 Radiator bottom hose clip – arrowed (Sec 3)

4   Cooling system – flushing

1   After some time the radiator and engine waterways may become restricted or even blocked with scale or sediment, which reduces the efficiency of the cooling system. When this occurs, the coolant will appear rusty and dark in colour and the system should then be flushed. In severe cases, reverse flushing may be required, as described later.

2   First drain the cooling system, as described in the previous Section.

3   Disconnect the top hose from the radiator, then insert a hosepipe and allow water to circulate through the radiator until it runs clear from the outlet.

4   Insert the hosepipe in the expansion tank filler neck and allow water to run out of the bottom hose until clear.

5   Where applicable, disconnect the hose from the intake manifold, connect the hosepipe, and allow water to circulate through the manifold, automatic choke (1.6) heater and out through the bottom hose until clear. If, after a reasonable period, the water still does not run clear, the radiator should be flushed with a good proprietary cleaning system such as Holts Radflush or Holts Speedflush.

6   In severe cases of contamination the system should be reverse flushed. To do this, remove the radiator, invert it, and insert a hose in the outlet. Continue flushing until clear water runs from the inlet.

7   The engine should also be reverse flushed. To do this, remove the thermostat and insert the hose into the cylinder head. Continue flushing until clear water runs from the bottom hose.

8   The use of chemical cleaners should only be necessary as a last resort, and regular renewal of the antifreeze/corrosion inhibitor solution should prevent the contamination of the system.

9   Refit the radiator and thermostat (if removed).

10 Reconnect the hose(s).

5   Cooling system – filling

1   The radiator itself does not have a filler neck, the coolant for the system must be poured into the expansion tank.

2   Before refilling the system first check that any hoses or system components are secure. The coolant to be used must contain the necessary antifreeze/corrosion inhibitor, as described in the following Section.

3   Pour the coolant mixture into the expansion tank filler neck until it reaches the maximum level mark, then refit the cap.

4   Run the engine at a fast idle speed for several minutes whilst checking that the coolant level in the expansion tank does not drop below the minimum level mark. Top up the level as necessary, being careful to release pressure from the system before removing the filler cap.

5   On completion check for any signs of coolant leaks from the bottom hoses and connections.

6   Antifreeze/corrosion inhibitor mixture – general

Note: *The antifreeze/corrosion inhibitor is toxic and must not be allowed to contact the skin. Precautions must also be taken to prevent the mixture contacting the bodywork and clothing.*

1   The antifreeze/corrosion inhibitor should be renewed at regular intervals (see routine Maintenance). This is necessary not only to maintain the antifreeze properties (although the antifreeze content does not deteriorate), but mostly to prevent corrosion which would otherwise occur as the properties of the inhibitors become progressively less effective.

2   Always use the antifreeze recommended in the Specifications, as this has been tested by the manufacturers.

3   Before adding the mixture, the cooling system should be completely drained and flushed, and all hose connections checked for tightness.

4   The mixture consists of 45% antifreeze and 55% water. Mix the required quantity in a clean container then fill the cooling system, with reference to Section 5.

5   Never operate the vehicle with plain water in the cooling system. Apart from the danger of freezing during winter conditions, an important secondary purpose of antifreeze is to inhibit the formation of rust and to reduce corrosion.

7   Thermostat – removal, testing and refitting

1   Drain the cooling system, as described in Section 3.

2   Disconnect the three hoses from the thermostat housing (photo).

3   Disconnect the lead from the fan thermal switch on the thermostat housing.

4   Unscrew and remove the three bolts and remove the thermostat housing from the cylinder head. If it is stuck, tap it off gently with a plastic-faced hammer.

5   Extract the spring retaining ring and remove the thermostat, followed by its sealing ring.

6   To test the thermostat suspend it with a piece of string in a container of water. Gradually heat the water and note the temperature

7.2 Thermostat housing and hose connections

Fig. 2.3 Checking the thermostat (Sec 7)

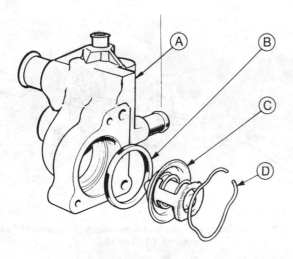

Fig. 2.4 Thermostat fitting components (Sec 7)

A	Housing	C	Thermostat
B	Sealing ring	D	Retaining clip

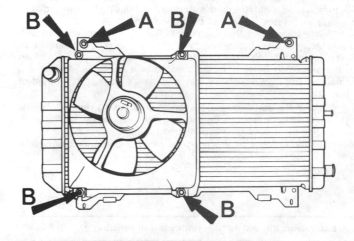

Fig. 2.5 Fan cowl and radiator mounting bolts (Sec 8)

A	Radiator bolts	B	Fan cowl bolts

at which the thermostat starts to open. Remove the thermostat from the water and check that it is fully closed when cold.

7   Renew the thermostat if the opening temperature is not as given in the Specifications or if the unit does not fully close when cold.

8   Clean the housing and the mating face of the cylinder head. Check the thermostat sealing ring for condition and renew it, if necessary.

9   Refitting is a reversal of removal, but use a new gasket.

10 On completion refill the cooling system, as given in Section 5, restart the engine and run it until its normal operating temperature is reached, then check for leaks around the thermostat housing and coolant hose connections.

---

8   Radiator fan unit – removal and refitting

1   Disconnect the battery earth lead.

2   Detach the fan motor wiring connector plug from the rear face of the motor and unclip the wire from the fan unit cowling.

3   Unscrew and remove the two upper bolts which secure the cowling to the radiator.

4   Loosen off the two lower bolts securing the cowling to the radiator

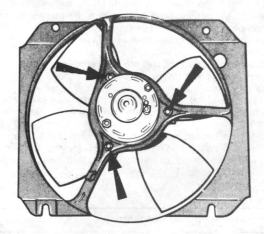

Fig. 2.6 Fan motor mounting bolts – arrowed (Sec 8)

at the bottom, then lift the fan and cowl unit clear, taking care not to damage the radiator.
5   Extract the retaining clip and remove the fan from the motor shaft.
6   Unscrew and remove the three securing nuts and separate the fan motor from the cowling.
7   Reassembly is a reversal of the removal procedure. When refitting the fan unit into position take care not to damage the radiator and check that the wiring connections are securely made. Run the engine on completion and check that the fan cuts in once the normal operating temperature is reached. **Note**: *Another method of testing the fan motor for satisfactory operation is given in Section 2, paragraph 8.*

9 Radiator – removal and refitting

1   Drain the cooling system, as described in Section 3. Retain the coolant if it is fit for further service.
2   Release the retaining clips and disconnect all the hoses from the radiator. On cars equipped with automatic transmission, disconnect the fluid cooling hoses from the radiator and plug the hoses.
3   Disconnect the wiring plug from the rear of the radiator fan motor.
4   Unscrew and remove the two mounting bolts and carefully lift the radiator, complete with cowl and fan, from the engine compartment. The base of the radiator is held in place by lugs (photo).
5   If the purpose of removal was to thoroughly clean the radiator, first reverse flush it with a cold water hose. The normal coolant flow is from left to right (from the thermostat housing to the radiator) through the matrix and out of the opposite side.
6   If the radiator fins are clogged with flies or dirt, remove them with a soft brush or blow compressed air from the rear face of the radiator. It is recommended that the fan assembly is first removed, as described in the preceding Section. In the absence of a compressed air line, a strong jet from a water hose may provide an alternative method of cleaning.
7   Minor leaks from the radiator can be cured using Holts Radweld. Extensive damage should be repaired by a specialist or the unit exchanged for a new or reconditioned radiator.
8   Refit the radiator by reversing the removal operations, but make sure that the rubber lug insulators at its base are in position.
9   Fill the system as described in Section 5.

10 Expansion (degas) tank – removal and refitting

1   Remove the expansion tank filler cap, taking care to release any pressure from the system before fully removing it.
2   Disconnect the level indicator wire at its connector (photo).
3   Remove the two screws which secure the tank lower retaining clamp, then slide the tank from its upper clamp and support it at a height to prevent coolant flow into it from the hoses.
4   Invert the tank and drain its contents into a suitable container.
5   Disconnect the intake hose at the tank (from the thermostat housing) and plug or clamp the hose to prevent leakage.
6   Disconnect the lower outlet hose at the tank (to the radiator) and plug or clamp the hose.
7   The expansion/degas tank can now be removed.
8   To remove the level warning indicator switch unit from the tank unscrew its retainer and withdraw it.
9   Refitting is a reversal of the removal procedure. On completion top up the coolant level to the maximum mark using the recommended antifreeze/corrosion inhibitor mixture. Refit the filler cap and run the engine at a fast idle speed for several minutes and check for any signs of coolant leaks. Stop the engine and, if necessary, top up the coolant level, taking the necessary precautions to avoid being scalded by escaping coolant.

11 Water pump – removal and refitting

1   Disconnect the battery earth lead.
2   Drain the cooling system, as described in Section 3.

9.4 Radiator location lug (viewed from underneath)

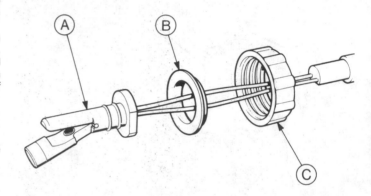

Fig. 2.7 Expansion tank level warning switch (A) spacer (B) and retainer (C) (Sec 10)

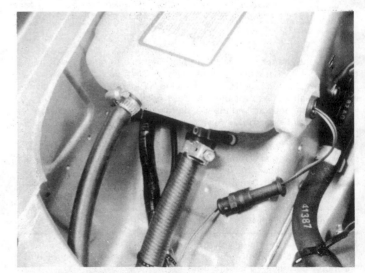

10.2 Level indicator warning wire connector and expansion tank hose connections

11.3 Alternator adjuster strap and coolant pump hose connection

11.5 Unbolt and remove the timing belt cover (4 bolts)

3 Release the alternator mountings and adjuster strap bolt, push the alternator in towards the engine and slip the drivebelt from the pulley (photo).
4 Apply a spanner to the crankshaft pulley bolt and turn the crankshaft until the notch on the pulley is opposite the tdc mark on the belt cover scale.
5 Remove the timing belt cover (photo) and check that the camshaft and the crankshaft sprockets are aligned with their timing marks (see Chapter 1). This will prove that No 1 piston is at tdc, not No 4 piston. If the marks are not aligned, turn the crankshaft through another complete turn.
6 Using a spot of quick-drying paint, mark the teeth of the belt and their notches on the sprockets so that the belt can be re-engaged in its original position in relation to the sprocket teeth.
7 Slacken the belt tensioner bolts (see Fig. 1.3 in Chapter 1) and slide the tensioner to relieve the tautness of the belt, then slip the belt from the crankshaft sprocket, tensioner pulley and the coolant pump sprocket.
8 Release the clamps and disconnect the hoses from the coolant pump.
9 Remove the timing belt tensioner.
10 Unscrew the four bolts and remove the coolant pump from the engine cylinder block.

11 Clean away the old gasket and ensure that the mating surfaces of the pump and block are perfectly clean.
12 Position a new gasket (on the cylinder block) which has been smeared both sides with jointing compound. Offer up the coolant pump, screw in the bolts and tighten to the specified torque.
13 Fit the belt tensioner, but with the mounting bolts only screwed in loosely.
14 Reconnect and tension the timing belt as described in Chapter 1 Section 4.
15 Refit the timing belt cover.
16 Fit the alternator drivebelt and tension it, as described in Chapter 11, Section 6.
17 Reconnect the coolant hoses to the pump and the bottom hose to the radiator.
18 Fill the cooling system, as described in Section 5.

12 Heating and ventilation system – description

The heater is of the type which utilises waste heat from the engine coolant. The coolant is pumped through the matrix in the heater casing where air, force-fed by a duplex radial fan, disperses the heat into the vehicle interior.

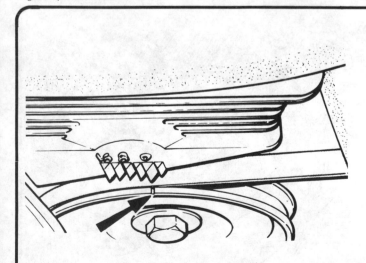

Fig. 2.8 Align pulley notch (arrowed) with TDC mark (Sec 11)

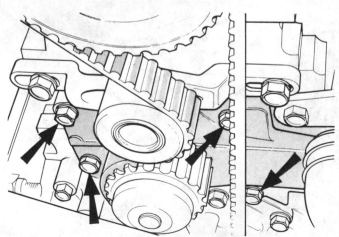

Fig. 2.9 Coolant pump retaining bolts (Sec 11)

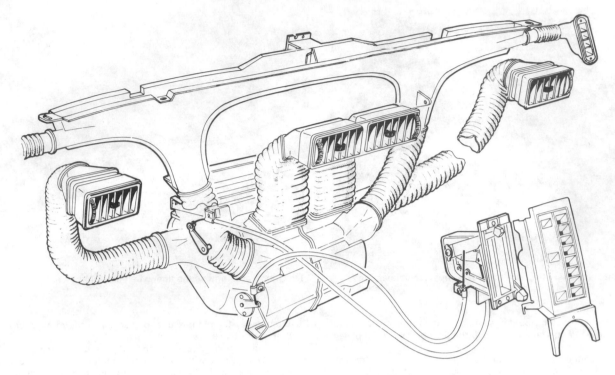

Fig. 2.10 Heater/ventilation system (Sec 12)

Fresh air enters the heater or the ventilator ducts through the grille at the rear of the bonnet lid. Air is extracted from the interior of the vehicle through outlets at the rear edges of the doors.

The heater/ventilator controls are of lever type, operating through cables to flap valves which deflect the air flowing through the heater both to vary the temperature and to distribute the air between the footwell and demister outlets.

13 Heater controls – adjustment

1   Incorrect airflow direction is most likely to be due to the control cables being out of adjustment. Adjust the cables as follows.
2   Set both the control levers at about 2.0 mm (0.08 in) up from their lowest setting.

3   Release the securing bolts on the cable clamps and pull the temperature control and air direction flap valve arms to the COLD and CLOSED positions respectively. Check to see that the setting of the levers on the control panel has not changed and retighten the cable clamps.

14 Heater controls – removal and refitting

1   Working inside the vehicle, remove the dash lower trim panel from the right-hand side. The panel is secured by two metal tags and two clips.
2   Detach the air ducts from the right-hand side of the heater casing and swivel them to clear the control cables.
3   Disconnect the control cables from the heater casing.

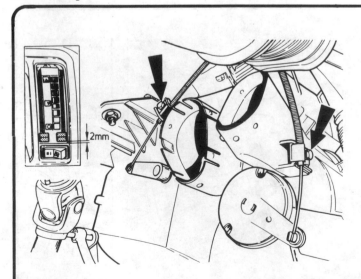

Fig. 2.11 Heater control cable connections (Sec 13)

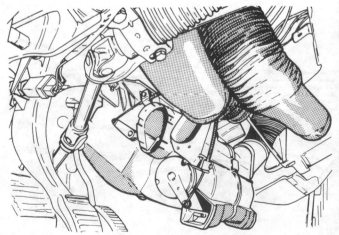

Fig. 2.12 Heater air ducts disconnected – LH drive version (Sec 14)

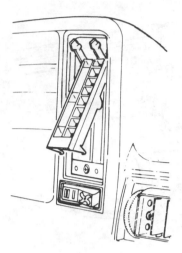

Fig. 2.13 Heater control panel plate removal (Sec 14)

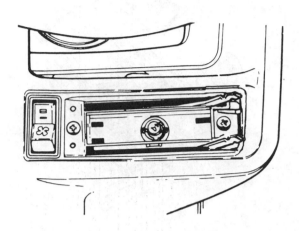

Fig. 2.14 Heater control unit securing screws (Sec 14)

4   Giving a sharp jerk, pull the knobs from the control levers on the facia panel, then press the control indicator plate downwards and remove it.
5   Unscrew and remove the two screws which are now exposed and which hold the control lever assembly in position.
6   Carefully withdraw the control unit with the cables from the facia and disconnect the wire from the illumination lamp.
7   Refitting is a reversal of removal. On completion, adjust as described in the preceding Section.

15 Heater – removal and refitting

1   Disconnect the battery earth lead.
2   Working within the engine compartment, disconnect the coolant hoses from the heater pipe stubs at the rear bulkhead. Raise the ends of the hoses to minimise loss of coolant.
3   The heater matrix will contain coolant and should be drained by blowing into the upper heater pipe stub and catching the coolant which will be ejected from the lower one (approximately 0.5 litres/1 pint).
4   Remove the cover plate and gasket from around the heater pipe stubs. This is held to the bulkhead by two self-tapping screws.
5   Working inside the vehicle, remove the dash lower trim panels from both sides. The panels are held in position by clips and tags.
6   Pull the air distribution ducts from the heater casing and swivel them as necessary to clear the control cables.
7   Disconnect the control cables from the heater casing and the flap arms (photo).
8   Remove the two heater mounting nuts and lift the heater assembly out of the vehicle, taking care not to spill any remaining coolant on the carpet.
9   Refitting is a reversal of removal. Check that the heater casing seal to the cowl is in good order, otherwise renew it. Adjust the heater controls on completion, as described in Section 13.
10 Top up the cooling system (Section 5) and reconnect the battery.

16 Heater casing – dismantling and reassembly

1   With the heater removed from the vehicle, as previously described, extract the two securing screws and slide the matrix out of the heater casing.
2   If further dismantling is necessary, cut the casing seal at the casing joint, prise off any securing clips and separate the two halves of the casing.
3   Remove the air flap valves. It should be noted that the lever for the air distribution valve can only be removed when the mark on the lever is in alignment with the one on the gearwheel.

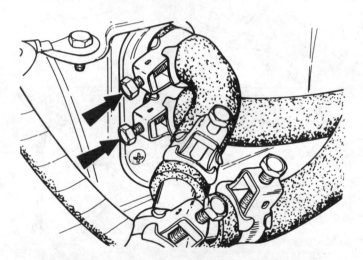

Fig. 2.15 Heater hose connections at bulkhead (Sec 15)

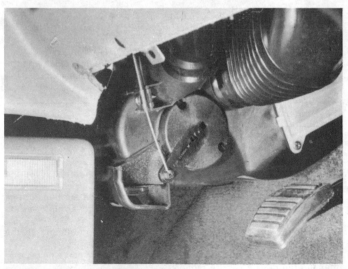

15.7 Detach air valve control cable

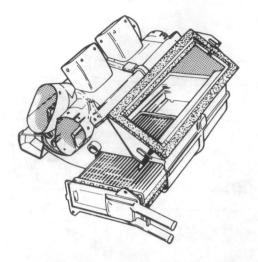

Fig. 2.16 Withdraw the heater matrix from the casing (Sec 16)

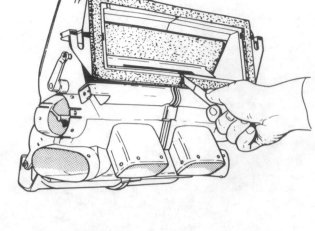

Fig. 2.17 Cutting the heater casing seal (Sec 16)

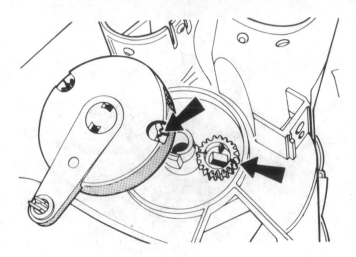

Fig. 2.18 Air distribution valve lever and gear marks – arrowed
(Sec 16)

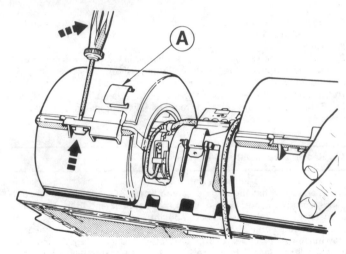

Fig. 2.19 Heater motor fan cover and clip (A) (Sec 17)

4   If the heater matrix is leaking, it is best to obtain a new or
reconditioned unit. Home repairs are seldom successful. A blocked
matrix can sometimes be cleared using a cold water hose and reverse
flushing, but avoid the use of searching chemical cleaners.
5   Reassembly is a reversal of removal. Take care not to damage the
fins or tubes of the matrix when inserting it into the casing.

17 Heater motor/fan – removal and refitting

1   Open the bonnet, disconnect the battery and pull off the rubber
seal which seals the air intake duct to the bonnet lid when the lid is
closed.
2   Prise off the five spring clips from the plenum chamber cover and
detach the cover at the front.
3   Disconnect the wiring harness multi-plug and the earth lead at its
body connection adjacent to the heater pipe stub cover plate on the
engine compartment bulkhead (photo).
4   Unscrew and remove the fan housing mounting nuts and lift the
housing from the engine compartment.
5   Insert the blade of a screwdriver and prise off the securing clips so
that the fan covers can be removed.
6   Remove the resistor and lift out the motor/fan assembly.
7   Reassembly and refitting are reversals of dismantling and removal.

17.3 Heater motor unit showing wiring connector (A) and securing
nuts (B)

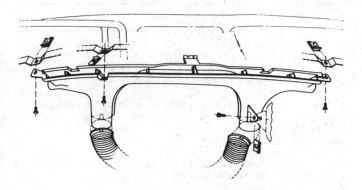

Fig. 2.20 Demister nozzle fixing screw locations (Sec 18)

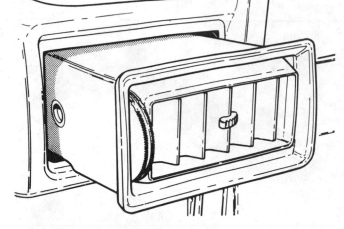

Fig. 2.21 Face level side vent nozzle removal (Sec 19)

18 Demister nozzle – removal and refitting

1 Disconnect the battery earth lead.
2 Remove the dash lower trim panels.
3 Remove the shrouds from the upper part of the steering column. The upper section of the shroud is secured by one screw while the lower one is held by three screws.
4 Remove the instrument cluster cowl and the instrument cluster, as described in Chapter 11.
5 Pull the hoses from the demister nozzles and then detach the hose from the right-hand side vent.
6 Unscrew and remove the four fixing screws from the demister nozzle assembly.
7 As the upper fixing screw of the crash pad also secures the demister nozzle, the crash pad must be removed by extracting four screws. One screw is located under the ashtray, one screw at each windscreen pillar and after pulling the crash pad forward the last screw may be extracted, also releasing the demister nozzle.
8 Remove the demister by drawing it downward and to the side with the front door wide open.
9 Refitting is a reversal of the removal procedure.

19 Face level vent (right- or left-hand) – removal and refitting

1 Remove the dash lower trim panels.
2 Reach up behind the facia panel and pull the hose from the vent nozzle.
3 Apply pressure to the rear of the nozzle to eject it from the front of the facia.
4 Refit by reversing the removal operations.

20 Face level vent (centre) – removal and refitting

1 Prise up the loudspeaker grille and remove it from its spring clips. Extract the speaker mounting screws and withdraw the speaker (if

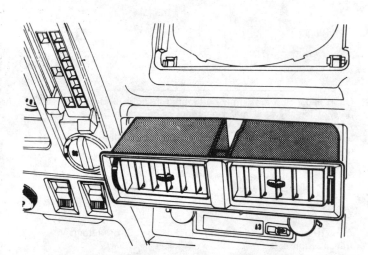

Fig. 2.22 Face level centre vent removal (Sec 20)

fitted) until the leads can be disconnected and the speaker removed.
2 Pull the hoses from the centre vent assembly by inserting the hand into the aperture left by removal of the loudspeaker grille.
3 Extract the screw which secures the rear of the centre vent and push the vent out of the front of the facia panel.
4 Refitting is the reverse of the removal procedure.

Fault diagnosis appears overleaf

21 Fault diagnosis – cooling system

Symptom	Reason(s)
Overheating	Insufficient coolant in system Faulty thermo-electric cooling fan Radiator core blocked or radiator grille restricted Bottom coolant hose collapsed, impeding flow Thermostat not opening properly Ignition timing incorrect or automatic advance malfunctioning (accompanied by loss of power and perhaps misfiring) Carburettor incorrectly adjusted (mixture too weak) Exhaust system partially blocked Oil level in sump too low Blown cylinder head gasket (water/steam being forced down the expansion tank overflow pipe under pressure) Engine not yet run-in Brakes binding
Engine runs too cool	Thermostat jammed open Incorrect grade of thermostat fitted allowing premature opening of valve Thermostat missing
Loss of coolant from system	Loose clips on water hoses Top or bottom coolant hoses perished and leaking Radiator core leaking Thermostat gasket leaking Pressure cap spring worn or seal ineffective Blown cylinder head gasket (pressure in system forcing water/steam down expansion tank pipe) Cylinder wall or head cracked
Oil in expansion tank (may be ignored if slight oil deposit present initially after major overhaul or decarbonising)	Blown cylinder head gasket Cracked head or block
Lack of heat in vehicle interior, poor air distribution or demisting/ defrosting capability	Thermostat faulty or of incorrect type Heater matrix blocked Incorrectly adjusted heater controls Blower motor inoperative due to blown fuse or other fault Disconnected ducts or hoses for air distribution Overcooling in cold weather by continuously running radiator fan Deteriorated seal at bonnet lid-to-air intake
Coolant in transmission fluid or fluid in coolant on automatic transmission cars	Perforated fluid cooler in radiator

Chapter 3 Fuel and exhaust systems

For modifications, and information applicable to later models, see Supplement at end of manual

Contents

Specifications

Carburettor engines
Carburettor
Type .... Ford variable venturi (VV)
Part number:
   1.3 litre (all markets) 84SF-9510-KAA
   1.6 litre with manual transmission (all markets but Sweden) 81SF-9510-KFA
   1.6 litre with manual transmission (Sweden) 81SF-9510-KHB
   1.6 litre with automatic transmission (all markets) 82SF-9510-KAA
Choke type:
   1.3 litre .... Manual
   1.6 litre .... Automatic
Idle speed settings:
   Manual transmission (cooling fan on) .... 750 to 850 rpm
   Automatic transmission (cooling fan on) .... 800 to 900 rpm
Idle CO content .... 1.0 to 2.0%

Air cleaner
Type .... Disposable paper element
Application:
    1.3 CVH .... Champion W127
    1.6 CVH .... Champion W169
    1.6 CVH injection .... Champion U502

Ported vacuum switches
Operating temperatures:
    Two port valve .... 52 to 55°C (126 to 131°F)
    Three port valve .... 52 to 55°C (126 to 131°F)

Fuel system
Pump type .... Mechanical diaphragm
Tank capacity .... 48 litres (10.6 gallons)
Fuel grade .... Four star (minimum 97 octane)

Torque wrench settings

	Nm	lbf ft
Carburettor flange nuts	14 to 18	10 to 13
Fuel pump mounting bolts	18	13
Exhaust manifold-to-downpipe nuts	38 to 45	28 to 33
Exhaust joint U-bolts	38 to 45	28 to 33
Exhaust downpipe-to-system coupling	38 to 45	28 to 33

Fuel injection engines
General
Type .... Bosch K-Jetronic
Idle speed (cooling fan on) .... 750 to 850 rpm
Idle CO content .... 1.00 to 1.50%
Fuel filter .... Champion L204

Torque wrench settings

	Nm	lbf ft
Air cleaner securing screws	4.5 to 5.0	3.3 to 3.7
Fuel distributor-to-sensor plate screws	32 to 38	24 to 28
Sensor plate-to-air cleaner screws	8.5 to 10.5	6.3 to 7.7
Main system pressure regulator	20 to 25	15 to 18
Start valve securing bolts	3.5 to 5.0	2.6 to 3.7
Warm-up regulator securing bolts	3.5 to 5.0	2.6 to 3.7
Auxiliary air device retaining bolts	3.5 to 5.0	2.6 to 3.7
Banjo bolts:		
Distributor fuel inlet and return	16 to 20	12 to 15
Distributor injector pipes	5 to 8	4 to 6
Distributor start valve feed pipe	5 to 8	4 to 6
Distributor warm-up regulator feed	5 to 8	4 to 6
Distributor warm-up regulator return	5 to 8	4 to 6
Warm-up regulator – inlet (M10)	11 to 15	8 to 11
Warm-up regulator – outlet (M8)	5 to 8	4 to 6
Fuel pump, filter and accumulator	16 to 20	12 to 15

PART A: CARBURETTOR AND ASSOCIATED FUEL SYSTEM COMPONENTS

1 General description

The fuel system on all models (except petrol injection models) is composed of a rear-mounted fuel tank, a fuel pump, a carburettor and an air cleaner.

The fuel tank is mounted under the floorpan beneath the rear seat. The tank is ventilated, has a simple filler pipe and a fuel gauge sender unit.

The fuel pump is a mechanical diaphragm type actuated by means of a pushrod bearing on an eccentric cam on the camshaft. The pump is a sealed unit and, if defective, must be renewed.

The carburettor is a Ford variable venturi type which will have a manual or automatic choke mechanism fitted, depending on model.

The air cleaner has a thermostatically controlled air intake, supplying either hot air from the exhaust manifold heat box or cold air from the front end of the engine compartment. A flap valve within the cleaner unit regulates the air intake temperature according to operating conditions in conjunction with a vacuum diaphragm unit and a heat sensor unit.

A detailed explanation of the carburettor and its operating functions is given in Section 12.

2 Air cleaner and checking of the thermostatic control

1 The air cleaner is of renewable paper element type, and is thermostatically controlled to provide air at the most suitable temperature for combustion with minimum emission levels.

2 This is accomplished by drawing in both cold and hot air (from the exhaust manifold box) and mixing them. The proportion of hot and cold air is varied by the position of a deflector flap which itself is controlled by a vacuum diaphragm. The vacuum pressure is monitored by a heat sensor within the air cleaner casing to ensure that according to the temperature requirements of the carburettor, the appropriate degree of intake manifold vacuum is applied to the air deflector flap to alter the volume of hot or cold air being admitted.

3 To check the thermostatic control of the air cleaner the engine must be cold. First observe the position of the air cleaner control flap which should be fully closed prior to starting the engine.

4 Now start the engine and check that the control flap opens fully at idle speed to allow warm air to be channelled from the exhaust manifold into the air cleaner.

5 Should the flap remain in the closed position once the engine is started, then the diaphragm unit or the heat sensor is at fault and should be tested to find which is defective.

6 Check that all vacuum lines are secure and free from leaks as a final check.

7 Detach the diaphragm-to-heat sensor vacuum pipe (at the sensor

end) and connect up a vacuum pump to the diaphragm. Pump and apply a vacuum up to 100 mm (4.0 in) of mercury and retain this whilst checking the air flap.

8 If the flap opens, the heat sensor is defective and must be renewed, but if it remains shut then the diaphragm or control flap is faulty.

9 Disconnect the vacuum pump and reconnect the vacuum pipe to the sensor unit.

3 Air cleaner element – renewal

1 To remove the air cleaner lid unscrew and remove the retaining screws from the top face and lift the lid clear (photo).

2 Remove and discard the paper element and wipe out the air cleaner casing (photo). Place the new element in position and refit the lid.

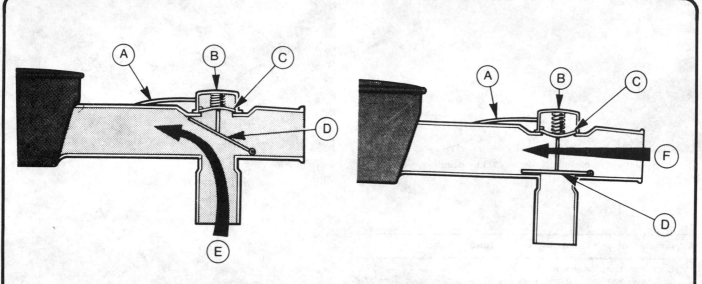

Fig. 3.1 Air cleaner flap valve under high vacuum conditions (Sec 2)

A	Vacuum pipe to heat sensor	D	Flap valve
B	Diaphragm unit	E	Hot air flow
C	Diaphragm		

Fig. 3.2 Air cleaner valve under low vacuum conditions (Sec 2)

A	Vacuum pipe to heat sensor	D	Flap valve
B	Diaphragm unit	F	Cool air flow
C	Diaphragm		

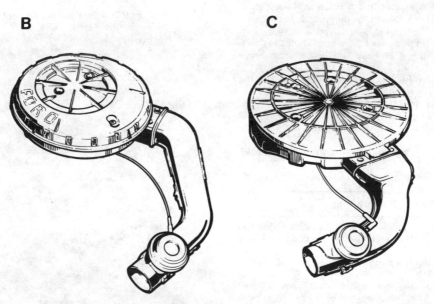

Fig. 3.3 Air cleaner unit (Sec 3)

B   1.3 engine   C   1.6 engine

3.1 Removing the air cleaner lid screws (1.3 models)

3.2 Withdraw the element

4 Air cleaner unit – removal and refitting

1   Disconnect the battery earth lead.
2   Unscrew and remove the two larger headed screws from the cover.
3   The air cleaner assembly can now be lifted off the carburettor sufficiently far to be able to disconnect the vacuum hose, the crankcase (flame trap) emission hose and the cold air intake duct.
4   Refitting is a reversal of the removal procedure.

5 Fuel pump – cleaning

1   Most fuel pumps are sealed units so that the internal filter cannot be cleaned. On pumps which have a detachable cover, clean the filter in the following way at the intervals specified in Routine Maintenance.
2   To do this, place a piece of rag around the pump body to catch the fuel which will drain out when the cover is removed.
3   Unscrew and remove the single cover screw and lift off the cover.
4   Take out the rubber sealing ring and the filter screen from inside the cover.
5   Clean the screen by brushing it in clean fuel, then fit it into the cover, noting the projections on some screens which centralise it.
6   Fit the sealing ring. If it is not in good order, renew it.
7   Locate the cover on the pump body. On some pumps, the cover is correctly installed when the notch in the cover engages in the groove in the pump body.
8   Screw in the retaining screw, but do not overtighten it provided it is making a good seal.

6 Fuel pump – testing, removal and refitting

1   The fuel pump may be quite simply tested by disconnecting the fuel inlet pipe from the carburettor and placing its open end in a container.
2   Disconnect the LT lead from the negative terminal of the ignition coil, to prevent the engine firing.
3   Actuate the starter motor. Regular well-defined spurts of fuel should be seen being ejected from the open end of the fuel inlet pipe.
4   Where this is not evident and yet there is fuel in the tank, the pump is in need of renewal. The pump is a sealed unit and cannot be dismantled or repaired.
5   The pump is mounted on the cylinder head and is actuated by a pushrod from an eccentric cam on the camshaft.
6   To remove the pump, disconnect and plug the fuel inlet and outlet hoses at the pump and then unbolt it from the engine (photo).

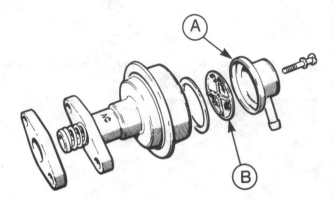

Fig. 3.4 Fuel pump assembly (Sec 5)

A   Cover   B   Filter screen

6.6 Fuel pump removal

6.8 Withdrawing the fuel pump operating rod

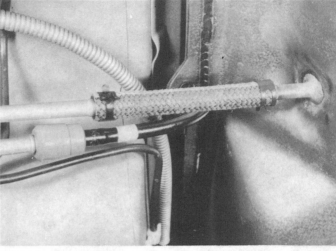

7.3 Fuel tank flexible hose connections (at front)

7   Retain any insulating spacers and remove and discard the flange gaskets.

8   Withdraw the pushrod with coil spring (photo).

9   Where oil leakage is noticeable from the pump-to-cylinder head mating flange, clean the flange faces of old gaskets and dirt, then refit the pump into position **without** fitting the pushrod and gasket. Now check the pump to cylinder head flange clearance which should be within 0.25 mm (0.01 in). A feeler gauge can be used for this check. If the clearance is greater than the figure specified, the pump must be renewed.

10   Refitting is a reversal of removal, but use new flange gaskets. If crimped type hose clips were used originally, these will have been destroyed when disconnecting the fuel hoses. Renew them with conventional nut and screw or plastic ratchet type clips.

7   Fuel tank – removal and refitting

1   The fuel tank will normally only need to be removed if it is severely contaminated with sediment or other substance, or requires repair.

2   As there is no drain plug incorporated in the tank, the best time to remove it is when it is nearly empty. If this is not possible, syphon as much fuel as possible from the tank into a container which can be sealed, but before doing so, observe the following precautions:

   (a)   Disconnect the battery
   (b)   Do not smoke or bring naked lights near
   (c)   Avoid placing the vehicle over an inspection pit as the fuel vapour is heavier than air

3   With the rear of the vehicle raised and supported securely, disconnect the flexible hose connection between the sections of rigid fuel line at the front face of the tank (photo). On some models dual pipelines are used, the second one being a fuel return line which returns excess fuel from the carburettor.

4   Disconnect the electrical leads from the tank sender unit.

5   Brush away all adhering dirt and disconnect the tank filler pipe and vent pipes from the tank pipe-stubs. Some models may be fitted with a single filler pipe which is a push fit into a seal on the fuel tank.

6   Support the tank and unscrew the tank securing bolts and the tank strap bolt (photos).

7   Lower the tank until the fuel hoses can be detached from the sender unit and from their retaining clips.

8   If the tank is to be cleaned out, repaired or renewed, remove the sender unit. To do this, unscrew the unit in an anti-clockwise direction using the special tool (23-014) or a suitable lever engaged behind the tabs.

9   If the tank contains sediment or water, clean it out by shaking vigorously using paraffin as a solvent. After several changes, rinse out finally with petrol.

10   If the tank is leaking, leave repair to a specialist company.

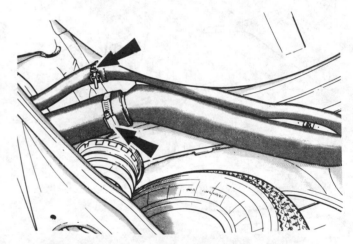

Fig. 3.5 Fuel tank filler and vent pipe connections (Sec 7)

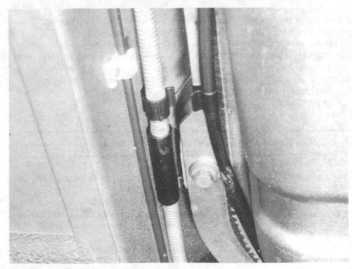

7.6A Fuel tank flange bolt – note pipe and clip

7.6B Fuel tank retaining strap bolt

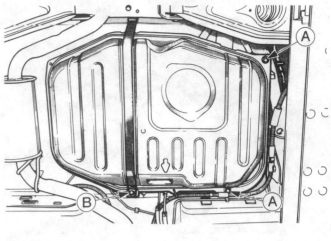

Fig. 3.6 Fuel tank retaining bolts and strap positions (Sec 7)

A   *Tank bolts*   B   *Strap bolt*

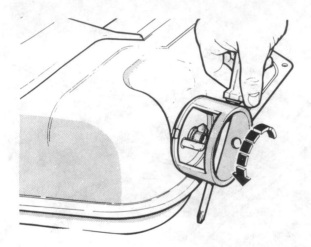

Fig. 3.7 Fuel tank sender unit removal using special tool 23-014 (Sec 7)

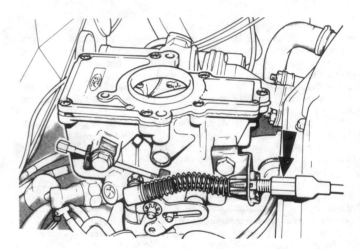

Fig. 3.8 Accelerator cable adjusting screw – manual transmission type (Sec 8)

Attempting to weld or solder the tank without it first having been steamed out for several hours is extremely dangerous.

11 Refit the sender unit using a new sealing ring.

12 Refit the tank into the vehicle by reversing the removal operations. When reconnecting the pipelines check that the coloured clips are correctly positioned, green for return, blue for outlet.

13 Check all connections for leaks after the tank has been partly filled with fuel.

8 Accelerator cable – adjustment

1 Disconnect the battery earth lead.

2 On manual transmission models remove the air cleaner unit, as given in Section 4 (carburettor models only).

3 Get an assistant to sit in the driving seat and fully depress the accelerator pedal, then whilst it is depressed turn the cable adjuster at the carburettor/throttle housing connection to the point at which the linkage is just fully open.

4 Release the accelerator pedal then fully depress and release it again and check that when depressed the throttle is fully opened. Readjust if necessary.

5 On completion refit the air cleaner and reconnect the battery earth lead.

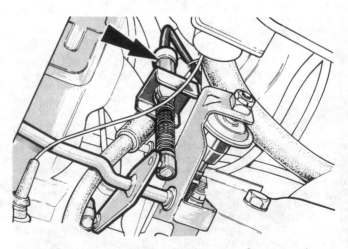

Fig. 3.9 Accelerator cable adjusting screw for automatic transmission models – viewed from underneath (Sec 8)

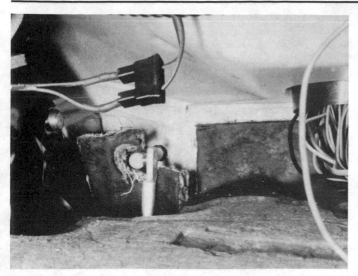

9.3 Accelerator cable connection under dash

9.6 Accelerator cable connection to throttle housing on fuel injection models

9 Accelerator cable – removal and refitting

1 Disconnect the battery earth lead.
2 Working within the vehicle, remove the dash lower insulation panel.
3 Disconnect the cable from the upper end of the accelerator pedal arm. Do this by sliding off the spring clip to release the cable end from the ball-stud (photo).
4 Working under the bonnet, release the cable from the bulkhead. This is probably more easily carried out if an assistant can punch the cable grommet out from inside the vehicle.
5 Remove the air cleaner (manual transmission carburettor models only).
6 The cable must now be detached from its bracket on the carburettor (throttle housing on fuel injection models). Prise out the clip and then depress the four lugs on the retainer simultaneously so that the retainer can be slid out of the bracket. Take care not to damage the outer cable (photo).

7 Disconnect the end of the cable from the ball-stud on the throttle lever by sliding back the spring retaining clip.
8 Fit the new cable by reversing the removal procedure then adjust, as described in the preceding Section.

10 Choke control cable – removal, refitting and adjustment

1 Disconnect the battery earth lead.
2 For improved access, remove the air cleaner unit (Section 4).
3 At the carburettor end of the cable, loosen the cable clamp bolt, detach the outer cable securing clip at the choke control bracket and disconnect the cable.
4 Working inside the car, remove the coin box from the lower dash panel (beneath the choke control knob).
5 Remove the clip retaining the cable control knob and withdraw the knob from the switch lever.
6 Remove the control switch bezel and then, reaching up

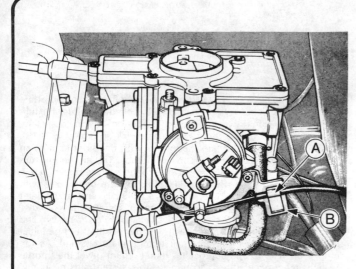

Fig. 3.10 Choke cable attachment to carburettor (Sec 10)

A   Outer cable securing clip   C   Inner cable clamp bolt
B   Support bracket

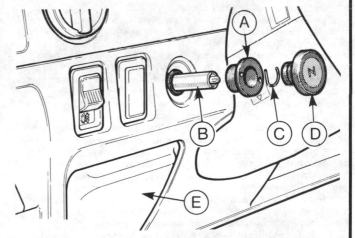

Fig. 3.11 Choke control knob assembly (Sec 10)

A   Bezel   D   Knob
B   Switch lever   E   Coin box
C   Clip

underneath the dash panel, withdraw the switch from the underside of the dash panel (through the coin box aperture).

7   The choke cable can now be pulled through the engine bulkhead and the switch removed.

8   Refit in the reverse order of removal. Check that the switch knob retaining clip is fully engaged when reassembling and adjust the cable at the carburettor before fully tightening the clamp bolt.

9   Pull the choke lever out to give a clearance of 34 mm (1.3 in) between the inner face of the knob and the bezel face (Fig. 3.12).

10   Now reclamp the outer cable to the retaining bracket on the choke control bracket so that its end is within 4.5 mm (0.177 in) of the clip.

11   Engage the inner cable into the swivel nut and, holding the choke actuation lever in the maximum choke position, tighten the cable clamp bolt.

12   A clearance of 1 mm (0.039 in) must exist between the lever and stop when the choke is off.

13   Refit the air cleaner and reconnect the battery earth lead.

11   Accelerator pedal – removal and refitting

1   The accelerator pedal can be removed once the cable has been disconnected from it as described in Section 9.

2   Unbolt the pedal support bracket. On LHD models two nuts are accessible from inside the engine compartment and one from the interior of the vehicle; on RHD models the two bolts are accessible from inside the vehicle.

3   Refitting is the reverse of the removal procedure. Adjust the accelerator cable linkage, if necessary, as described in Section 18.

12   Carburettor – description

1   Due to the anti-pollution regulations being introduced in various countries, Ford developed a variable choke carburettor of their own design in order to comply with such regulations. The unit, known as the Ford VV (variable venturi) carburettor, provides improved fuel atomisation and air/fuel mixture ratio under normal operating conditions. It operates in the following manner.

2   Fuel is supplied to the carburettor via a needle valve which is actuated by the float. When the fuel level is low in the float chamber in the carburettor, the float drops and opens the needle valve. When the correct fuel level is reached the float will close the valve and shut off the fuel supply.

3   The float level on this type of carburettor is not adjustable since minor variations in the fuel level do not affect the performance of the carburettor. The valve needle is prevented from vibrating by means of a ball and light spring. To further ensure that the needle seals correctly it is coated in a rubber-like coating of Viton.

4   The float chamber is vented internally via the main jet body and carburettor air inlet, thus avoiding the possibility of petrol vapour escaping into the atmosphere.

5   The air/fuel mixture intake is controlled by the air valve which is opened or closed according to the operating demands of the engine. The valve is actuated by a diaphragm which in turns opens or closes according to the vacuum supplied through the venturi between the air valve and the throttle butterfly. As the air valve and diaphragm are connected they open or close correspondingly.

6   When the engine is idling the air intake requirement is low and therefore the valve is closed, causing a high air speed over the main jet exit. However, as the throttle plate is opened, the control vacuum (depression within the venturi) increases and is diverted to the diaphragm which then releases the air valve to balance the control spring and control vacuum.

7   When the throttle is opened further this equality of balance is maintained as the air is progressively opened to equalise the control spring and control vacuum forces throughout the speed range.

8   Fuel from the float chamber is drawn up the pick-up tube and then regulated through two jets and the tapered needle and into the engine. The vacuum within the venturi draws the fuel. At low engine speeds the needle taper enters the main jet to restrict the fuel demand. On acceleration and at higher engine speeds the needle is withdrawn through the main jet by the action of the air valve to which it is attached. As the needle is tapered, the amount by which it is moved regulates the amount of fuel passing through the main jet.

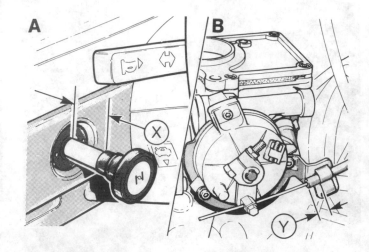

Fig. 3.12 Choke cable adjustment (Sec 10)

A   X = 34 mm (1.3 in)   B   Y = 4.5 mm (0.177 in)

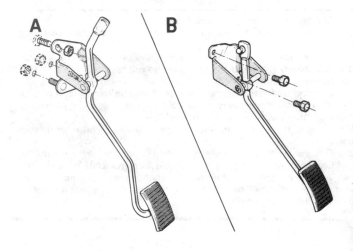

Fig. 3.13 Accelerator pedal (Sec 11)

A   LHD models   B   RHD models

9   The sonic idle system as used on other Ford fixed jet carburettors is also employed in the VV type, with 70% of the idle fuel mixture supplied via the sonic idle system and 30% from the main system. When idling, fuel is drawn through the main pick-up tube (Fig. 3.19), passes through the idle jet and then mixes with the air stream being supplied from the air bleed in the main jet body. The air/fuel mixture then passes on through the inner galleries to the mixture control screw which regulates the fuel supply at idle. This mixture then mixes with the air from the by-pass idle channel and finally enters the inlet manifold via the sonic discharge tube at an accelerated rate of flow.

10   Throttle actuation is via a progressive linkage which has a cam and roller mechanism. The advantage of this system is that a large initial throttle pressure allows only a small throttle plate opening. As the throttle is opened up and approaches its maximum travel the throttle plate movement accelerates accordingly. This system aids economy, and gives a good engine response through the operating range.

11   To counterbalance the drop in vacuum when initially accelerating, a restrictor is fitted into the air passage located between the control vacuum areas and the control diaphragm. This restrictor causes the valve to open slowly when an increase in air flow is made which in turn causes a higher vacuum for a brief moment in the main jet, caused by

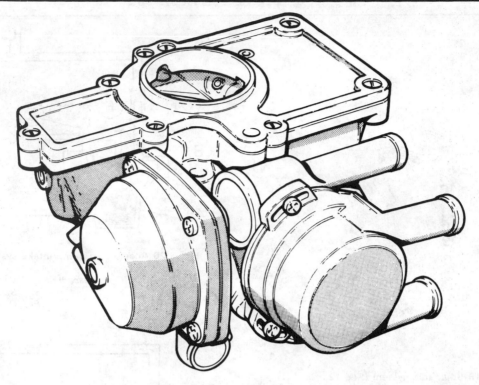

Fig. 3.14 Ford variable venturi (VV) carburettor (Sec 12)

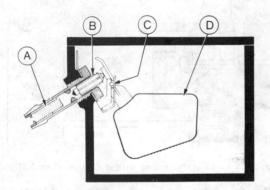

Fig. 3.15 The fuel intake components (Sec 12)

A   Intake filter   C   Float pivot
B   Needle valve   D   Float

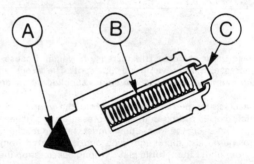

Fig. 3.16 Fuel intake needle valve (Sec 12)

A   Viton tip   C   Plunger
B   Spring

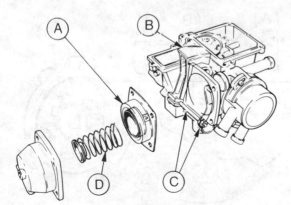

Fig. 3.17 The air valve unit (Sec 12)

A   Vacuum diaphragm   C   Operating linkage
B   Air valve   D   Return spring

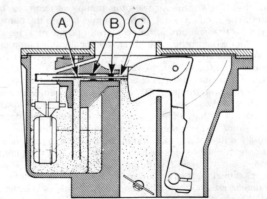

Fig. 3.18 Main jet system (Sec 12)

A   Tapered needle (metering rod)   C   Main fuel outlet
B   Main and secondary jets

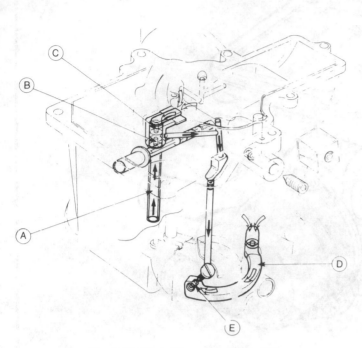

Fig. 3.19 Sonic idle system (Sec 12)

A   Main pick up tube   D   By-pass gallery
B   Idle fuel jet   E   Sonic discharge tube
C   Idle air jet

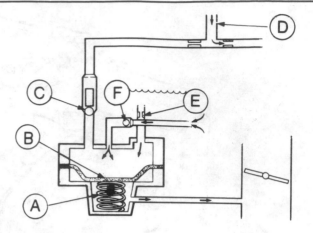

Fig. 3.20 Accelerator pump intake system (Sec 12)

A   Return spring (compressed)   D   Vacuum break air hole
B   Diaphragm   E   Back bleed
C   One-way valve   F   One-way valve

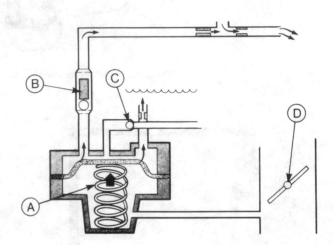

Fig. 3.21 Accelerator pump outlet system (Sec 12)

A   Return spring   C   Intake valve (closed)
    (uncompressed)   D   Throttle plate (open)
B   Outlet valve (open)

the increase in air velocity. This increase in vacuum causes the fuel
flow to increase, thus preventing a 'flat spot'. The larger amounts of
fuel required under heavy acceleration are supplied by the accelerator
pump.

12 The accelerator pump injects fuel into the venturi direct when
acceleration causes a drop in manifold pressure. This richening of the
mixture prevents engine hesitation under heavy acceleration. The
accelerator pump is a diaphragm type and is actuated from vacuum
obtained from under the throttle plate. During acceleration the vacuum
under the throttle plate drops, the diaphragm return spring closes the
diaphragm and the fuel in the pump is fed via the inner galleries
through the one-way valve and into the venturi. The system incorporates a back bleeder and vacuum break air hole. Briefly explained,
the back bleed allows any excess fuel vapour to return to the float
chamber when prolonged idling causes the carburettor temperature to
rise and the fuel in the accelerator pump reservoir to become
overheated. The vacuum break air hole allows air into the pump outlet
pipe to reduce the vacuum at the accelerator pump jet at high speed.
Too much fuel would otherwise enter the accelerator pump system.

13 A manual or automatic choke are fitted to the VV carburettor,
depending on model. Whilst the choke system itself is the same on
both types, the manual choke is operated by means of a cable attached
to the lever housing, the lever of which is spring-loaded and engages
with the choke linkage. As with the automatic type choke system, the
manual choke type has a choke pull-down system which deactivates
the choke when it is not required ie under heavy load.

14 The fully automatic choke system operates in accordance with a
bi-metal spring which opens or closes depending on the temperature
of engine coolant passing through the choke housing. The spring
movement activates the choke mechanism, which consists of a
variable needle jet and a variable supply of air. Fuel to the choke jet is
fed from the main pick-up tube via the internal galleries within the
main jet body. When the bi-metal spring is contracted (engine cold), it
pulls the tapered needle from the jet to increase the fuel delivery rate.
The spring expands as the engine warms up and the needle reduces
the fuel supply as it re-enters the jet. The choke air supply is supplied
via the venturi just above the throttle plate. The fuel mixes with the air
in the choke air valve, whence it is delivered to the engine.

Fig. 3.22 Manual choke unit (Sec 12)

A   Linkage   C   Pull-down piston
B   Needle valve   D   Spring-loaded lever

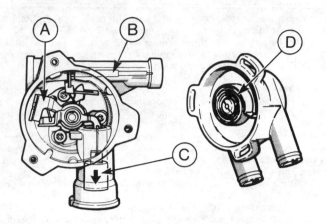

Fig. 3.23 Automatic choke unit (Sec 12)

A   Linkage   C   Pull-down piston
B   Needle valve   D   Bi-metal coil and housing

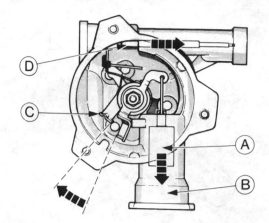

Fig. 3.24 Manual choke pull-down system (Sec 12)

A   Pull-down piston movement   C   Choke lever (fully
B   High vacuum   anti-clockwise
                                D   Needle valve closing

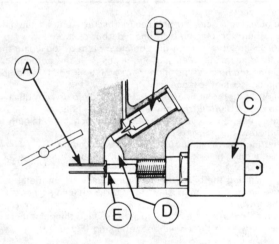

Fig. 3.25 Anti-run-on valve arrangement (Sec 12)

A   Sonic discharge tube   D   Bypass air channel
B   Mixture screw   E   Viton tip
C   Anti-run-on valve

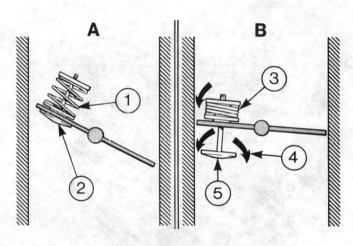

Fig. 3.26 Deceleration valve operation (Sec 12)

A   Closed for normal operation   3   Spring compressed
B   Open for deceleration   4   Air and fuel mixture
1   Control spring   5   Valve open
2   Valve closed

15 A choke pull-down system is employed whereby, if the engine is under choke, but is only cruising, ie not under heavy load, the choke is released. This is operated by the vacuum piston which is connected to the choke spindle by levers.

16 An anti-dieseling valve is fitted, being visible on the outside of the body of the carburettor. This valve shuts off the fuel supply to the idle system when the engine is turned off and so prevents the engine running on or 'dieseling'. The solenoid valve is actuated electrically. When the ignition is turned off, it allows a plunger to enter and block the sonic discharge tube to stop the supply of fuel into the idle system. When the ignition is switched on the solenoid is actuated and the plunger is withdrawn from the tube.

17 A deceleration valve is fitted to the throttle butterfly (plate) valve and its purpose is to further regulate the air and fuel mixture supply to the intake manifold. The valve is normally held shut by a return spring, but during deceleration the higher manifold vacuum overrides the effect of the spring and opens the valve to allow an increase of air and fuel into the manifold. The valve is set during manufacture and **must not** be tampered with.

13 Carburettor – adjustment

1   Run the engine to normal operating temperature then stop it.
2   Connect a tachometer and, if available, an exhaust gas analyser to the engine.
3   On automatic transmission models loosen off the downshift linkage adjuster screw on the downshift/throttle valve shaft lever so that there is a clearance of 2 to 3 mm (0.08 to 0.12 in) between the end of the screw and the stop.
4   Run the engine at 3000 rpm for 30 seconds, then allow it to idle and note the idle speed. If using an exhaust gas analyser it should be noted that initially the CO% reading will rise, but then fall and stabilise after a period of 5 to 25 seconds. The CO reading should then be as specified (with the cooling fan on).
5   If necessary, adjust the idle speed screw to give the specified idle speed.
6   Adjustment of the CO content (mixture) is not normally required during routine maintenance, but if the reading noted in paragraph 4 is

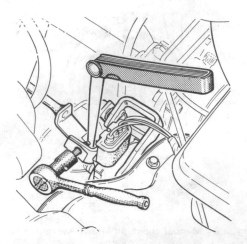

Fig. 3.27 Idle speed adjustment check – automatic transmission models (Sec 13)

Set downshift/throttle valve shaft lever clearance as specified during check

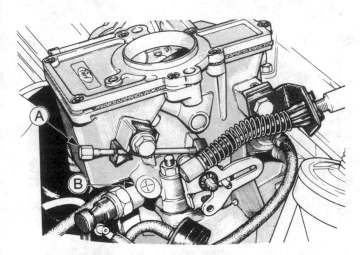

Fig. 3.28 Idle adjuster screw (A) and mixture screw (B) (Sec 13)

not as given in the Specifications first remove the tamperproof plug, prising it free using a small screwdriver.
7   Run the engine at 3000 rpm for 30 seconds then allow it to idle. Adjust the mixture screw within 10 to 30 seconds. If more time is required run the engine at 3000 rpm again for 30 seconds.
8   Adjust the idle speed if necessary and recheck the CO content.
9   Fit a new tamperproof plug to the mixture adjuster screw on completion. It should be noted that mixture adjustment without a CO analyser is not accurate and therefore not recommended.
10 On automatic transmission models readjust the downshift linkage, as given in Section 22 of Chapter 6.

14 Manual choke unit – removal and refitting

1   Disconnect the battery earth lead.
2   Remove the air cleaner unit securing screws, lift the unit clear of the carburettor and place it to one side.
3   Loosen the choke cable retaining screw, unclip the outer cable-to-location bracket clamp and detach the cable from the choke lever.

4   Unscrew and remove the lever housing retaining screws and withdraw the lever housing, together with the cable location bracket, from the choke housing.
5   Carefully remove the three screws which secure the main choke unit to the carburettor and withdraw the choke unit from the carburettor, together with the gasket.
6   If necessary, the choke unit and the lever housing assembly must both be renewed.
7   To refit the choke unit first position a new gasket onto the carburettor mating face, locate the choke unit and fit the retaining screws.
8   When refitting the choke lever housing assembly, align the new gasket with the screw holes and the lever actuation arc slot. With the lever at its mid-travel position, fit the lever housing so that the spring-loaded arm engages with the linkage lever.
9   Refit the choke cable support bracket and lever housing retaining screws.
10 Reconnect the choke cable and adjust it, as given in Section 10.
11 Relocate and make secure the air cleaner unit, ensuring that the vacuum hose is not distorted and the crankcase emission control filter is secure in the underside of the filter body.
12 On restarting the engine check the actuation of the choke and, when the normal operating temperature has been reached, check the idle and mixture speed settings, as given in Section 13.

15 Automatic choke bi-metal housing – removal and refitting

1   Disconnect the battery earth lead.
2   Remove the air cleaner unit securing screws and lift the unit clear of the carburettor, placing it to one side out of the way.
3   Release any pressure in the cooling system by loosening the filler cap, then detach the inlet and outlet hoses at the automatic choke unit. Clamp the hoses or position them with their ends facing upwards to minimise coolant leakage.
4   Mark the bi-metal housing-to-choke body joint with quick-drying paint to ensure correct realignment on reassembly.
5   Unscrew and remove the three bi-metal housing retaining screws and withdraw the housing and gasket.
6   Refitting is a reversal of the removal procedure.
7   Use a new gasket between the main body and the bi-metal housing.
8   When fitting the bi-metal housing, engage the bi-metal coil with the choke lever slot then loosely fit the three retaining screws, starting with the lower one.
9   Before tightening the retaining screws, align the paint mark on the bi-metal body with the choke body marking (Fig. 3.33).

16 Automatic choke unit – removal and refitting

1   Proceed as given in paragraphs 1 to 5 inclusive in the previous Section.
2   Carefully remove the three screws within the choke housing body and withdraw the unit from the carburettor, together with the gasket.
3   If a new choke unit is to be fitted, it will first be necessary to tap out the securing screw holes for the bi-metal housing. The thread can be tapped out using the retaining screws which are of the thread-cutting type. **Do not** cut the threads with a standard tap.
4   Refit the choke unit to the carburettor using a new mating gasket between the two. If the bi-metal housing has been removed, this must be refitted, as described in the previous Section.
5   On completion check the carburettor adjustments, as given in Section 13.

17 Carburettor – removal and refitting

1   Disconnect the battery earth lead.
2   Remove the air cleaner unit as given in Section 4.
3   On automatic choke carburettors, if the engine is still hot, depressurise the cooling system by carefully releasing the pressure cap on the expansion tank (see Chapter 2). Disconnect the coolant hoses from the automatic choke housing and clamp or plug them to prevent coolant loss.

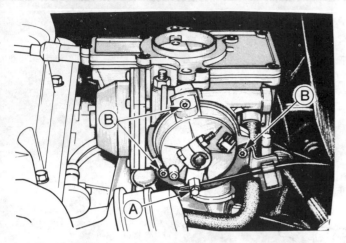

Fig. 3.29 Manual choke unit connections (Sec 14)

A   Cable
B   Lever housing securing
    screws

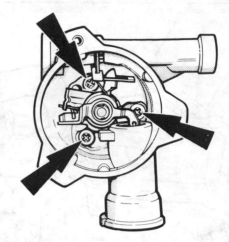

Fig. 3.30 Manual choke unit retaining screw positions (Sec 14)

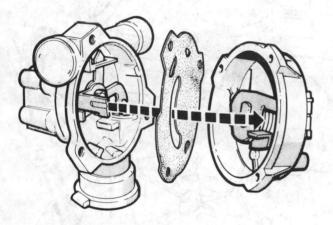

Fig. 3.31 Gasket location for lever housing refitting (Sec 14)

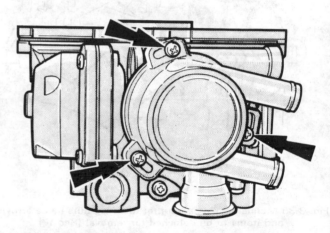

Fig. 3.32 Automatic choke housing retaining screws (Sec 5)

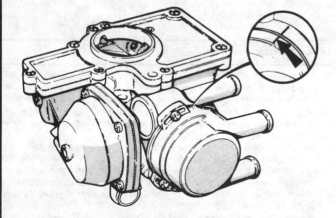

Fig. 3.33 Align auto-choke bi-metal housing and body marks
(Sec 15)

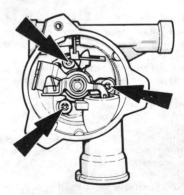

Fig. 3.34 Automatic choke unit retaining screw positions
(Sec 16)

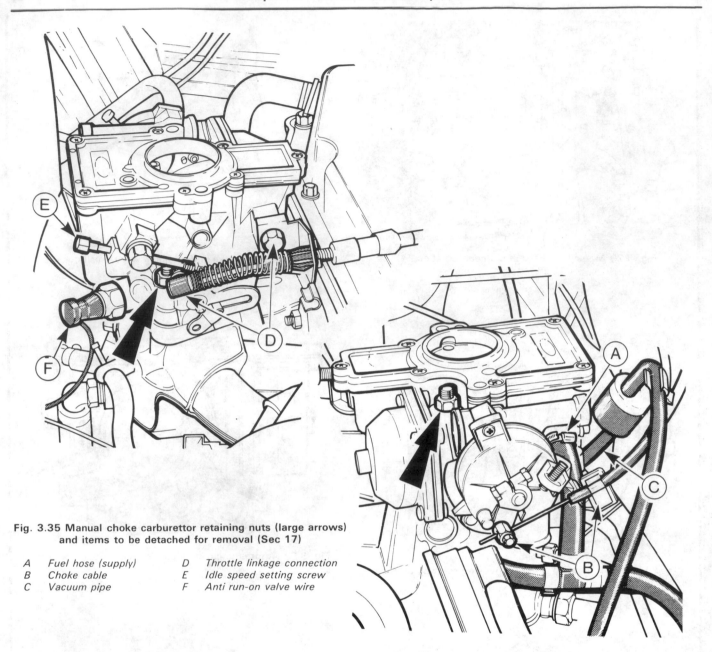

Fig. 3.35 Manual choke carburettor retaining nuts (large arrows) and items to be detached for removal (Sec 17)

A   Fuel hose (supply)   D   Throttle linkage connection
B   Choke cable   E   Idle speed setting screw
C   Vacuum pipe   F   Anti run-on valve wire

4   Detach the anti-run-on valve lead at the carburettor end.
5   On manual choke models disconnect the choke cable from the lever and the outer cable from its clamp on the support bracket.
6   Disconnect the distributor vacuum pipe.
7   Disconnect the throttle cable by pulling the spring clip to release the end fitting from the ball-stud and then unscrewing the cable bracket fixing bolt.
8   Disconnect and plug the fuel inlet hose from the carburettor. If crimped type hose clips are used, cut them off and fit screw type clips at reassembly.
9   Unscrew the two carburettor mounting flange nuts and lift the carburettor from the intake manifold. Remove the idle speed screw if necessary for access to the nut.
10 Refitting is a reversal of removal, but make sure that a new flange gasket is used on perfectly clean mating surfaces.
11 On manual choke models readjust the choke cable on reconnection, as given in Section 10.
12 When reconnecting the vacuum pipe make sure that the fuel trap is correctly positioned.
13 On automatic choke models recheck the coolant level.
14 On completion restart the engine and check the idle speed and mixture adjustments, as given in Section 13.

18 Carburettor – overhaul

1   Complete overhaul of the carburettor is seldom required. It will usually be found sufficient to remove the top cover and mop out fuel, dirt and water from the fuel bowl and then blow through the accessible jets with air from a tyre pump or compressed air line. Do not direct air pressure into the accelerator pump air bleed or outlet, or the air valve vent, as diaphragm damage may occur.
2   To completely dismantle a carburettor, carry out the following operations, but remember that for a unit which has been in service for a high mileage it may be more economical to purchase a new or reconditioned one rather than to renew several individual components.
3   Remove the carburettor from the engine, as described in Section 17 and clean away external dirt.
4   Extract the seven screws and lift off the top cover and gasket.
5   Drain the fuel from the float bowl.
6   Using a thin-bladed screwdriver, prise out the metering rod tamperproof plug.
7   Unscrew and withdraw the main metering rod, making sure to keep the air valve closed during the process.
8   Extract the four cross-head screws and detach the main jet body

Fig. 3.36 Exploded view of Ford VV carburettor (Sec 18)

A	Top cover	E	Auto-choke	J	Accelerator pump
B	Manual choke	F	Bi-metal housing		diaphragm
C	Lever housing	G	Control diaphragm cover	K	Accelerator pump cover
D	Choke cable bracket	H	Control diaphragm	L	Progressive throttle cam

M	Mixture screw
N	Solenoid
P	Idle speed screw
Q	Needle valve
R	Float bracket

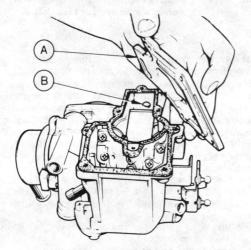

Fig. 3.37 Removing top cover from carburettor (Sec 18)

A   Top cover   B   Metering rod tamperproof
                           plug

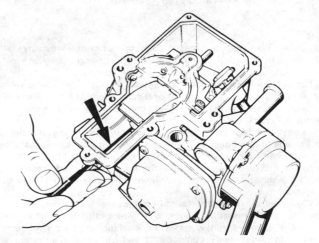

Fig. 3.38 Removing main metering rod (arrowed) from carburettor (Sec 18)

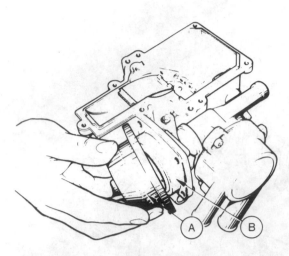

Fig. 3.39 Removing air valve control diaphragm from
carburettor (Sec 18)

A   Housing   B   Diaphragm

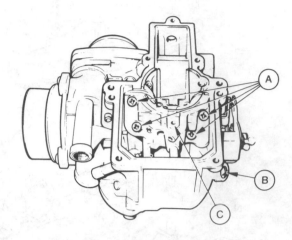

Fig. 3.40 Main jet body fixing screws (Sec 18)

A   Screws   C   Main jet body
B   Mixture screw tamperproof
    plug

Fig. 3.41 Removing accelerator pump housing (arrowed) from
carburettor (Sec 18)

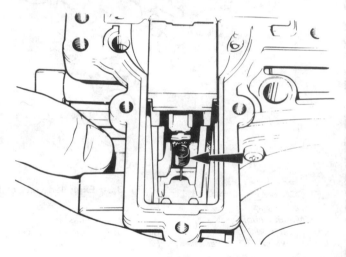

Fig. 3.42 Metering rod bias spring (arrowed) correctly located on
air valve of carburettor (Sec 18)

and gasket. Take out the accelerator pump outlet one-way valve ball
and weight by inverting the carburettor and allowing the components
to drop out.

9   Lift out the float, the float spindle and the fuel inlet needle valve.

10   Use a thin-bladed screwdriver and carefully prise free the mixture
adjustment screw tamperproof plug, then unscrew and remove the
mixture adjuster.

11   Extract the four cross-head screws and remove the air control
vacuum diaphragm housing, the return spring and the spring seat. The
diaphagm can be removed after the circlip is extracted.

12   Invert the carburettor, remove the three cross-head screws and
detach the accelerator pump diaphragm, taking care not to lose the
return spring.

13   Clean out all drillings, jets and passages in the carburettor with
compressed air – never by probing with wire. Examine all components
for wear or damage; renew gaskets and diaphragms as a matter of
routine. Many necessary components will be supplied in repair kit
form. The throttle linkage and air valve mechanism are particularly
subject to wear, as are the diaphragm return springs to compression.
Renew as necessary.

14   Commence reassembly by making sure that the metering rod bias
spring is correctly installed to the air valve.

15   Fit the accelerator pump assembly, making sure that the gasket-
faced side of the diaphragm is towards the cover.

16   Reconnect and refit the air valve control vacuum diaphragm
housing, making sure that the vacuum hole in the diaphragm is in
alignment with the gallery in the carburettor body and the housing.

17   Relocate the mixture adjuster screw. Screw the adjuster in fully,
then unscrew it by three full turns to provide the initial setting. Do not
overtighten the screw when fitting and leave fitment of the new
tamperproof plug until after the engine is running and any adjustments
have been made.

18   Fit the fuel inlet needle valve, the float and the float pivot pin. The
needle valve should be so installed that the spring-loaded plunger on
the valve will be in contact with the float once the fuel has entered the
float bowl.

19   Insert the accelerator pump ball and weight into the pump
discharge passage (in that order).

20   Use a new gasket and fit the main jet body.

21   Very carefully slide the metering rod into position, hold the air
valve closed and screw in the rod until its shoulder is aligned with the
vertical face of the main jet body. If the rod binds when screwing it in,
do not force it, but check the reason. Do not overtighten it.

22   Fit a new tamperproof plug to the metering rod hole.

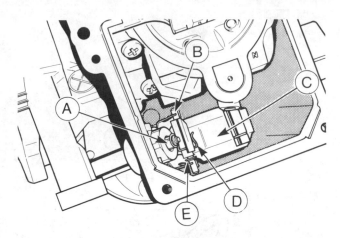

Fig. 3.43 Needle valve detail on the carburettor (Sec 18)

A   Needle valve   D   Spring clip
B   Float pin   E   Spacer washer
C   Float

23   Fit the top cover with a new gasket.
24   Once the carburettor has been fitted to the engine, the idle speed and mixture must be checked and adjusted as described in Section 13.

19 Manifolds

Removal and refitting of the manifolds is covered in Chapter 1.

Intake

1   The intake manifold is of light alloy construction and is coolant-heated to improve the atomisation of the fuel/air mixture.

Exhaust

2   The exhaust manifold is of cast iron construction (photo) and, on carburettor models, incorporates a heated air box as part of the air intake system for the thermostatically controlled air cleaner.

20 Exhaust system

1   The exhaust system is a two-section type with a coupling between the dual downpipe and the main system.
2   All systems incorporate a silencer and an expansion box, and the system is suspended on rubber mountings (photo).

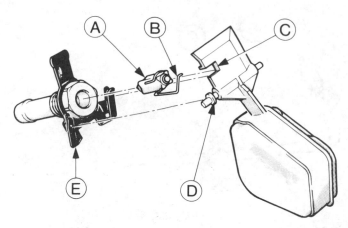

Fig. 3.44 Arrange needle valve clip and float cut-out (Sec 18)

A   Needle valve   D   Spacer washer
B   Valve clip   E   Pivot pin bracket
C   Float cut-out

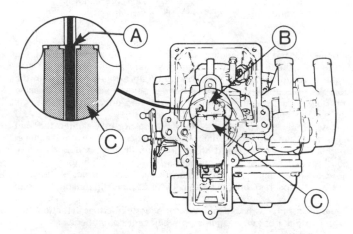

Fig. 3.45 Main metering rod adjustment on carburettor (Sec 18)

A   Shoulder on rod   C   Air valve
B   Main jet body

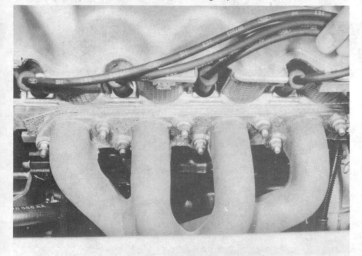

19.2 Exhaust manifold – fuel injection models

20.2 Exhaust system rubber mounting

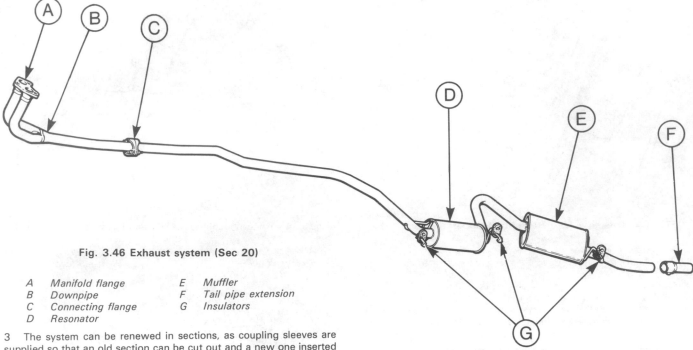

Fig. 3.46 Exhaust system (Sec 20)

A   Manifold flange   E   Muffler
B   Downpipe   F   Tail pipe extension
C   Connecting flange   G   Insulators
D   Resonator

3   The system can be renewed in sections, as coupling sleeves are supplied so that an old section can be cut out and a new one inserted without the need to renew the entire system at the same time.

4   It is recommended when working on an exhaust system that the complete assembly be removed from under the vehicle by releasing the downpipe from the manifold (photo) and unhooking the flexible suspension hangers.

5   Assemble the complete system, but do not fully tighten the joint clips until the system is back in the vehicle. Use a new exhaust manifold/flange gasket and check that the flexible mountings are in good order, also check the connecting flange joint (photo).

6   Set the silencer and expansion box in their correct attitudes in relation to the rest of the system before finally tightening the joint clips.

7   Check that with reasonable deflection in either direction, the exhaust does not knock against any adjacent components.

8   Holts Flexiwrap and Holts Gun Gum exhaust repair systems can be used for effective repairs to exhaust pipes and silencer boxes, including ends and bends. Holts Flexiwrap is an MOT approved permanent exhaust repair. Holts Firegum is suitable for the assembly of all exhaust system joints.

PART B: EMISSION CONTROL SYSTEMS

21 Emission control system (UK models) – description and component renewal

An emission control system is fitted in order to reduce the noxious gases that would otherwise be emitted from the vehicle exhaust. The system fitted can vary according to model, but whatever system is used it should be realised that for optimum reduction of exhaust gas CO level, the good tune of the engine (carburettor and ignition) and efficiency of the temperature-controlled air cleaner are essential requirements.

To improve driveability, particularly during warm-up conditions and to keep exhaust emission levels to a minimum a vacuum-operated

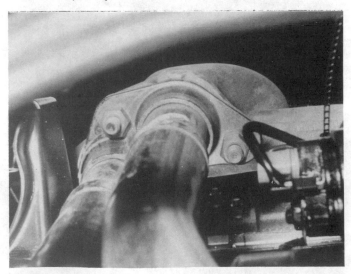

20.4 Exhaust downpipe flange connection to manifold

20.5 Exhaust system connecting flange joint

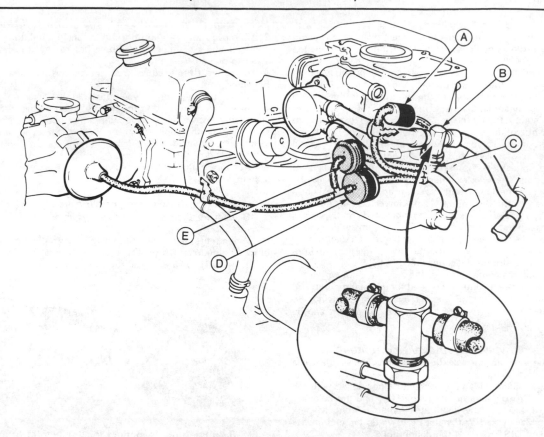

**Fig. 3.47 Emission control system fitted to UK market models
(Sec 21)**

A	Fuel trap	C	Ported vacuum switch
B	Ported vacuum switch	D	Spark sustain valve
	adaptor	E	Spark delay valve

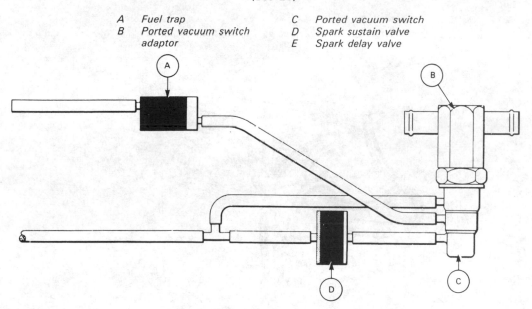

Fig. 3.48 Emission control system (UK models) showing alternative vacuum hose connections to the sustain valve (Sec 21)

A	Fuel trap	B	Ported vacuum switch adaptor	C	Ported vacuum switch	D	Spark sustain valve

temperature-sensitive emission control system is fitted. The system is designed to ensure that the rate of distributor vacuum advance is compatible with the change in fuel/air mixture flow under all throttle conditions, thus resulting in more complete combustion and reduced exhaust emissions.

Under part throttle cruising conditions, distributor vacuum advance is required to allow time for the fuel/air mixture in the cylinders to burn. When returning to a part throttle opening after accelerating or decelerating, the distributor vacuum increases before the fuel/air mixture has stabilised. This can lead to short periods of incomplete combustion and high exhaust emission. To reduce this condition a spark delay valve is incorporated in the vacuum line between the carburettor and distributor to reduce the rate at which the distributor advances. Under certain conditions, particularly during the period of engine warm-up, some models may suffer from a lack of throttle response. To overcome this problem a spark sustain valve may be fitted in the vacuum line either individually or in conjunction with the spark delay valve. This valve is used to maintain distributor vacuum under transient throttle conditions, thus stabilising the combustion process

The operation of the valves is controlled by a ported vacuum switch (PVS) which has the vacuum lines connected to it. The PVS operates in a similar manner to that of the thermostat in the cooling system. A wax-filled sensor is attached to the plunger which operates a valve. The PVS is actuated by the engine coolant and is sensitive to changes in engine operating temperature. When the engine is cold the sensor moves the plunger to open the upper and middle ports of the PVS. Therefore vacuum applied to the middle port is directed to the distributor via the upper port. As the engine warms up and coolant temperature increases, the wax expands and the plunger closes the upper port and opens the lower port. Vacuum applied to the centre port is now directed to the distributor via the lower port. In this way the spark sustain or delay valves can be activated, or bypassed, according to engine operating temperature. The vacuum applied to the middle port of the PVS is taken from a connection on the carburettor through a fuel trap. The fuel trap prevents fuel or fuel vapour from being drawn into the distributor vacuum unit.

Testing of the various components of the system is not within the scope of the home mechanic, due to the need for a vacuum pump and gauge, but if a fault has been diagnosed by a garage having the necessary equipment, the renewal of a defective component can be carried out in the following way.

Spark delay/sustain valve – removal and refitting
1   Disconnect the vacuum lines at the valve and remove the valve from the engine.
2   When refitting a spark delay valve it must be positioned with the black side (marked CARB) towards the carburettor and the coloured side (marked DIST) towards the distributor. When refitting a spark sustain valve the side marked VAC must be towards the carburettor and the side marked DIST towards the distributor.

Ported vacuum switch – removal and refitting
3   Remove the filler cap from the expansion tank to reduce pressure in the cooling system. If the engine is hot, remove the cap slowly using a rag to prevent scalding.
4   Disconnect the vacuum lines and the water hoses, then unscrew the valve.
5   When refitting the valve, note that the vacuum line from the carburettor is connected to the middle outlet on the PVS, the vacuum line from the spark delay valve (where fitted) is connected to the outlet nearest to the threaded end of the PVS, and the vacuum line from the spark sustain valve is connected to the outlet furthest from the threaded end of the PVS.
6   Reconnect the water hoses and if necessary top up the cooling system.

Fuel trap – removal and refitting
7   Disconnect the vacuum lines and remove the fuel trap from the engine.
8   When refitting, make sure that the fuel trap is positioned with the black side (marked CARB) towards the carburettor and the white side (marked DIST) towards the PVS.

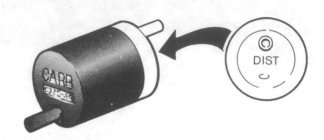

Fig. 3.49 Fuel trap is marked for direction of fitting (Sec 21)

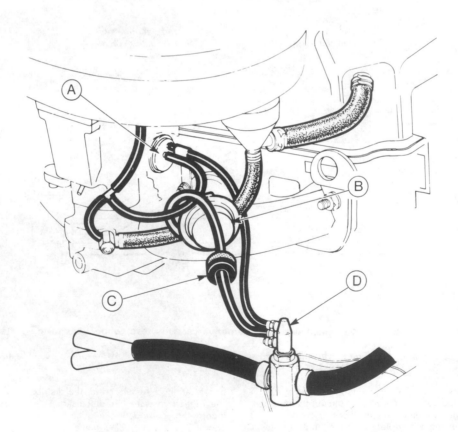

Fig. 3.50 Carburettor speed control system layout (Sec 22)

A   Temperature vacuum switch   B   Carburettor speed control   C   Spark delay valve   D   Three-port vacuum switch
                                     valve   (PVS) and adaptor

22 Carburettor speed control system – description and component renewal

The carburettor speed control system is an integral part of the emission control system on some UK models as well as for some overseas market models.

The system's function is to improve the air and fuel mixture when the engine is cold in low ambient temperatures. It achieves this by increasing the air volume into the intake manifold in order to weaken the mixture ratio which has been enriched by choke operation.

The carburettor speed control valve is fitted to a vacuum hose which is located between the air cleaner unit and the intake manifold on UK models.

Testing of the system components should be entrusted to a Ford garage. The renewal of a defective system component can be carried out as given in Sections 21 or 23, according to the component concerned.

23 Emission control system (Sweden and Switzerland) – description and component renewal

On vehicles destined for operation in Sweden and Switzerland, an emission control system is fitted in order to reduce the level of noxious gases being emitted from the vehicle exhaust.

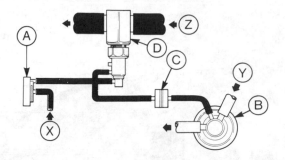

Fig. 3.51 Carburettor speed control system operation (Sec 22)

A   Temperature vacuum switch
B   Carburettor speed control valve
C   Spark delay valve
D   PVS and adaptor
X   Manifold vacuum
Y   Air (from air cleaner)
Z   Engine coolant

The arrangement used is an Exhaust Gas Recirculation (EGR) system which redirects a small quantity of exhaust gas back into the intake manifold in order to reduce peak combustion temperatures and pressures. In turn, this has the effect of reducing the emissions of noxious gases by up to 60%.

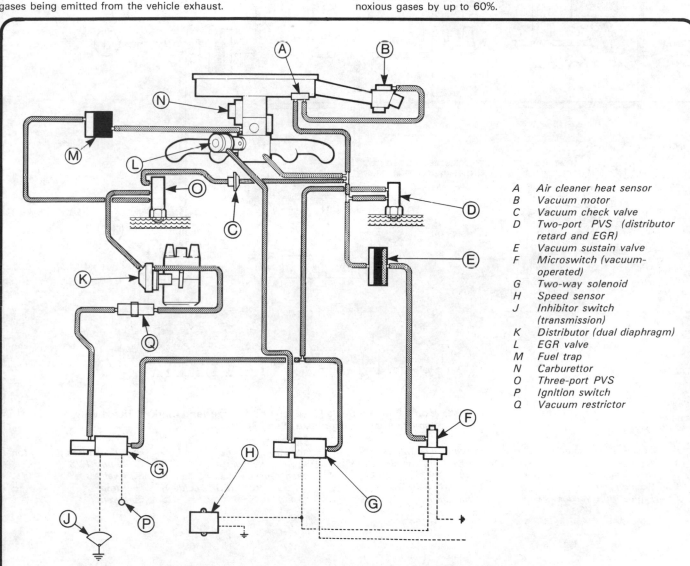

A   Air cleaner heat sensor
B   Vacuum motor
C   Vacuum check valve
D   Two-port PVS (distributor retard and EGR)
E   Vacuum sustain valve
F   Microswitch (vacuum-operated)
G   Two-way solenoid
H   Speed sensor
J   Inhibitor switch (transmission)
K   Distributor (dual diaphragm)
L   EGR valve
M   Fuel trap
N   Carburettor
O   Three-port PVS
P   Ignition switch
Q   Vacuum restrictor

Fig. 3.52 Emission control system layout – for 1.6 litre – Sweden and Switzerland market models – with automatic transmission and automatic choke (Sec 23)

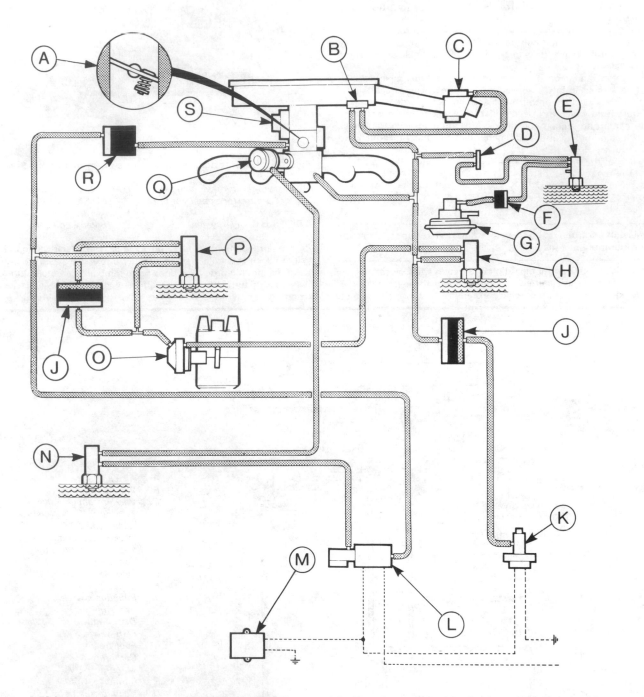

Fig. 3.53 Layout of emission control system on 1.6 litre models (Sweden and Switzerland market) fitted with manual transmission and auto-choke (Sec 23)

A	Deceleration valve (in venturi)	F	Vacuum delay valve	K	Vacuum microswitch	O	Dual diaphragm distributor
B	Heat sensor (in air cleaner)	G	Carburettor speed control	L	Two-way solenoid	P	Three-port PVS
C	Vacuum motor		valve	M	Speed sensor	Q	EGR valve
D	Temperature vacuum switch	H	Two-port PVS (distributor	N	Two-port PVS (EGR cold	R	Fuel trap
E	Three-port PVS		retard cut-out)		cut-out)	S	Carburettor
		J	Vacuum sustain valve				

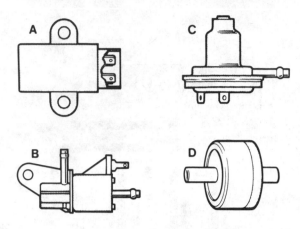

Fig. 3.54 EGR system control components (Sec 23)

A   Speed sensor
B   Solenoid vacuum switch

C   Vacuum-operated microswitch
D   Vacuum sustain valve

The main components of the system comprise the following:

(a) The EGR valve, vacuum-operated with diaphragms, to prevent EGR operating during cranking or full throttle

(b) Ported Vacuum Switch (PVS), used to prevent the injection of exhaust gases at cold starting. The valve is responsive to coolant temperature and cuts off vacuum to the EGR valve when the engine is cold

(c) Speed sensor, solenoid vacuum switch, microswitch and vacuum sustain valve. These are components of the EGR control system which prevent the system becoming operational at low engine speeds and at light throttle cruising when the formation of noxious gases is not a problem

In addition to the foregoing components, a dual diaphragm distributor is fitted, also a fuel trap to prevent fuel passing down the vacuum hose and damaging the distributor diaphragm.

For optimum reduction of the exhaust gas CO level, the general condition of the engine must be good and the carburettor and ignition system adjusted correctly.

Testing of the various components of the system is not within the scope of the home mechanic, due to the need for a vacuum pump and gauge, but if a fault has been diagnosed by a service station having the necessary equipment, the renewal of a defective component can be carried out in the following way.

EGR valve

1   Disconnect the hoses from the valve. Unbolt the two mounting bolts and remove the valve.

Speed sensor

2   This is located on the left-hand side of the engine compartment rear bulkhead. Disconnect the wiring from the sensor and extract its two self-tapping mounting screws.

PVS

3   Check that the cooling system is not under pressure by removing the pressure cap (see Chapter 2). Disconnect the vacuum hoses from the switch and unscrew the switch. Plug the tapped hole in the intake manifold to prevent loss of coolant.

Solenoid valve

4   This is located adjacent to the Speed Sensor. Disconnect the vacuum hoses and the electrical lead from the switch and remove the single self-tapping mounting screw.

Microswitch

5   This is located adjacent to the Speed Sensor. Disconnect the vacuum hose and electrical leads from the switch and then extract the two self-tapping mounting screws.

PART C: FUEL INJECTION SYSTEM

24 General description and principle of operation

The fuel injection system fitted is of the continuous injection type and supplies a precisely controlled quantity of atomized fuel to each cylinder under all operating conditions.

This system, when compared with conventional carburettor arrangements, achieves a more accurate control of the air/fuel mixture resulting in reduced emission levels and improved performance.

The main components of the fuel injection system fall into two groups:

A   Fuel tank
     Fuel pump
     Fuel accumulator
     Fuel filter
     Fuel distributor/mixture control assembly
     Throttle valve (plate)
     Injector valves
     Air box (plenum chamber)
     Warm-up regulator
     Auxiliary air device
     Fuel start valve
B   Thermotime switch
     Safety module
     Fuel shut-off valve
     Speed sensor module
     Wiring

The fuel tank is similar to the one described in Section 7 for carburettor type vehicles except that before removing it, the pipes to the fuel pump and accumulator and the pipe from the pressure regulator must be disconnected and plugged.

The fuel pump is of electrically-operated, roller cell type. A pressure relief valve is incorporated in the pump to prevent excessive pressure build-up in the event of a restriction in the pipelines.

The fuel accumulator has two functions, (i) to dampen the pulsation of the fuel flow, generated by the pump and (ii) to maintain fuel pressure after the engine has been switched off. This prevents a vapour lock developing with consequent hot starting problems.

The fuel filter incorporates two paper filter elements to ensure that the fuel reaching the injection system components is completely free from dirt.

The fuel distributor/mixture control assembly. The fuel distributor controls the quantity of fuel being delivered to the engine, ensuring that each cylinder receives the same amount. The mixture control assembly incorporates an air sensor plate and control plunger. The air sensor plate is located in the main airstream between the air cleaner and the throttle butterfly. During idling, the airflow lifts the sensor plate which in turn raises a control plunger which allows fuel to flow past the plunger and out of the metering slits to the injector valves. Increases in engine speed cause increased airflow which raises the control plunger and so admits more fuel.

It is important to note that each injection supply pipe connection in the distributor head has a screw adjacent to it. These four screws are **not** for adjustment and must not be removed or have their settings altered.

The throttle valve assembly is mounted in the main air intake between the mixture control assembly and the air box. The throttle valve plate is controlled by a cable connected to the accelerator pedal.

During manufacture the throttle plate is adjusted so that it is fractionally open, to avoid the possibility of it jamming shut, and it **must not** be repositioned. Idle speed adjustment is provided for by means of a screw which, according to its setting, restricts the airflow through the air bypass channel in the throttle housing.

The injector valves are located in the intake manifold and are designed to open at a fuel pressure of 3.5 bar (50.8 lbf/in^2).

The air box is mounted on the top of the engine and functions as an auxiliary intake manifold directing air from the sensor plate to each individual cylinder.

The warm-up regulator is located on the intake manifold and incorporates two coil springs, a bi-metal strip and a control pressure valve. The regulator controls the fuel supplied to the control circuit which provides pressure variations to the fuel distributor control

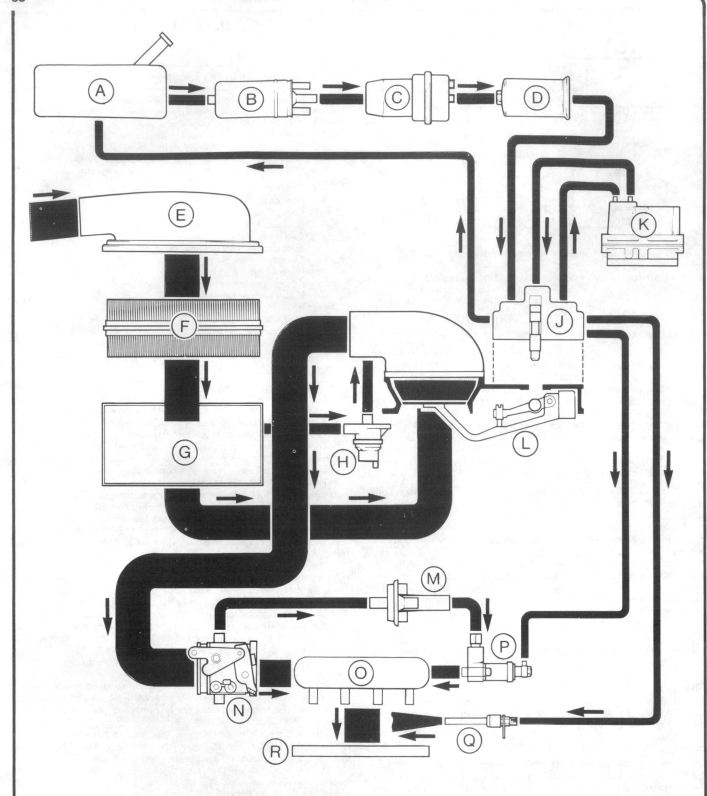

Fig. 3.55 Fuel injection system layout and components (Sec 24)

A	Fuel tank	F	Air filter	K	Warm up regulator	O	Plenum chamber
B	Pump	G	Cleaner body	L	Sensor plate	P	Start valve
C	Accumulator	H	Shut-off valve	M	Auxiliary air device	Q	Injectors
D	Filter	J	Fuel distributor	N	Throttle housing	R	Intake manifold
E	Air intake						

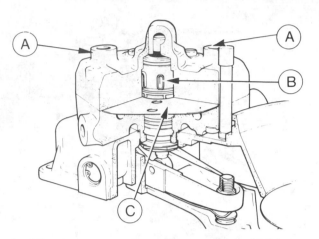

Fig. 3.56 The fuel distributor unit; cutaway view showing the fuel outlet connections (A), control plunger and barrel (B) and steel diaphragm (C) (Sec 24)

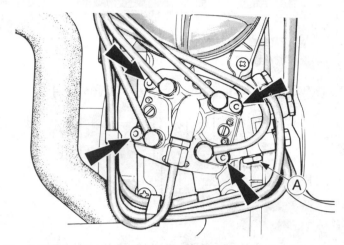

Fig. 3.57 Top view of distributor head showing the regulator screw (A) (Sec 24)

Do not remove or tamper with the four screws arrowed

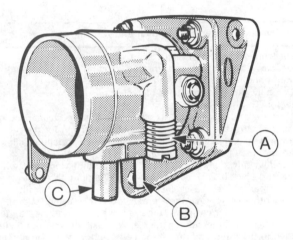

Fig. 3.58 Idle speed adjustment screw (A), distributor vacuum pipe connection (B) and auxiliary air hose connector (C) (Sec 24)

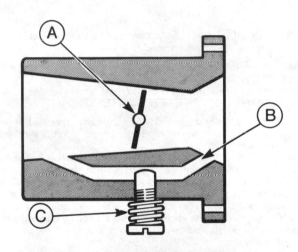

Fig. 3.59 Sectional view of the throttle housing (Sec 24)

A   Throttle plate   C   Idle speed adjustment screw
B   Bypass air channel

plunger. When the coil springs are pushing against the control pressure valve there is a high control pressure and this gives a weak mixture. The coil spring pressure application is controlled by the bi-metal strip which in turn is activated in accordance with engine temperature and an electrical heat coil.

The **auxiliary air device** is located on the intake manifold. It consists of a pivoted plate, bi-metal strip and heater coil. The purpose of this device is to supply an increased volume of fuel/air mixture during cold idling rather similar to the fast idle system on carburettor layouts.

The **fuel start valve** system consists of an electrical injector and a **thermotime switch.** Its purpose is to spray fuel into the air box to assist cold starting, the thermotime switch regulating the amount of fuel injected.

The **safety module** is located under the facia panel on the driver's side and is coloured purple. Its purpose is to shut off the power supply to the fuel pump should the engine stall or the vehicle be involved in an accident. The module is basically a sensor which senses the ignition low tension circuit pulses. When the pulses stop the module is deactivated and power to the fuel pump is cut.

The **fuel shut-off valve** system is an economy device whereby air is drawn from within the air cleaner unit through the shut-off valve and directed into the ducting chamber above the air sensor plate and causing a depression. This then causes the sensor plate to drop which,

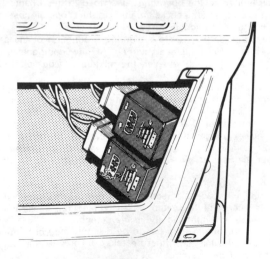

Fig. 3.60 Speed sensing module and fuel pump safety module (Sec 24)

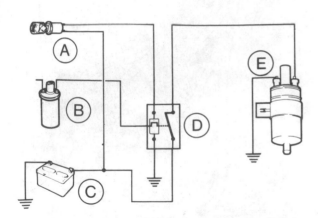

Fig. 3.61 The safety control circuit (Sec 24)

A	Ignition key	D	Safety module
B	Coil	E	Fuel pump
C	Battery		

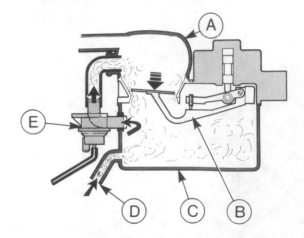

Fig. 3.62 Shut-off valve system components (Sec 24)

A	Air ducting	D	Air intake
B	Sensor plate	E	Shut-off valve (open)
C	Air cleaner body		

in turn, shuts off the fuel supply. The shut-off valve will only operate under the following circumstances:-

(a) When the engine coolant temperature is at or above 35°C (95°F)

(b) When the throttle is closed and with the engine speed decelerating from speeds above 1600 rpm

The coolant temperature must be above that specified to ensure that the valve does not shut off the fuel supply during the initial engine warm-up period.

When the throttle is released to the closed position it contacts an electrical switch which will only operate once the specified coolant temperature is reached. This switch will activate the shut-off valve when the throttle is fully released and the engine speed is over 1600 rpm, but once the engine speed drops below 1400 rpm the switch and valve are deactivated. The engine speed is sensed by a **speed sensing module** which is coloured black and located beneath the facia panel on the driver's side.

25 Maintenance, adjustments and precautions – general

1   Due to the complexity of the fuel injection system, any work should be limited to the operations described in this Chapter. Other adjustments and system checks are beyond the scope of most readers and should be left to your Ford dealer.
2   The mixture setting is pre-set during production of the car and should not normally require adjustment. If new components of the system have been fitted however, the mixture can be adjusted after reference to Section 27.
3   The only adjustment which may be needed is to vary the engine idle speed by means of the screw mounted in the throttle housing. Use the screw to set the engine speed to that specified when the engine is at the normal operating temperature.
4   Routine servicing of the fuel injection system consists of checking the system components for condition and security, and renewing the air cleaner element at the specified intervals (see Routine Maintenance).
5   In the event of a malfunction in the system, reference should be made to the Fault diagnosis Section at the end of this Chapter, but first make a basic check of the system hoses, connections, fuses and relays for any obvious and immediately visible defects.
6   If any part of the system has to be disconnected or removed for any reason, particular care must be taken to ensure that no dirt is allowed to enter the system.
7   The system is normally pressurised, irrespective of engine temperature, and care must therefore be taken when disconnecting fuel lines; the ignition must also be off and the battery disconnected.

26 Air cleaner element – removal and refitting

1   Disconnect the battery earth lead.
2   Unscrew and loosen off the air ducting-to-sensor plate unit securing band, then separate the two (photos).
3   Carefully pull free the shut-off valve hose from the air ducting connector. The hose is a press fit (photo).
4   Unscrew and remove the six air sensor plate-to-cleaner top cover retaining screws, but leave the plate unit in position for the moment.
5   Prise free and release the air cleaner cover retaining clips and detach the hose from the cover at the front (photo).
6   Carefully lift the sensor plate clear (photo), together with its gasket, and pivot it back out of the way. Withdraw the shut-off valve from the rear end of the cleaner case cover (photo) then lift out the cover (photo) and remove the element from the casing (photo).
7   If the air cleaner casing is to be removed you will need to detach the fuel filter from the side of the cleaner casing (leave the fuel lines attached to the filter) and the air intake hose from the front end of the case. Unscrew and remove the casing retaining nuts from the inner wing panel and lift out the casing.
8   Refitting is the reversal of the removal procedure. Wipe the casing clean before inserting the new element. When fitting the sensor plate unit into position on the top cover check that the gasket is in good condition and aligned correctly (photo).
9   Check that all connections are secure on completion.

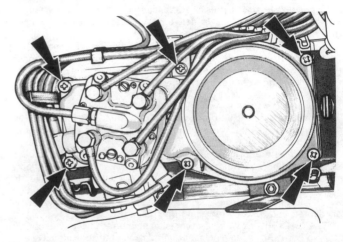

Fig. 3.63 Air sensor plate-to-air cleaner retaining screws (Sec 26)

26.2A Loosen the securing band screw ...

26.2B ... lift the air duct away from the sensor plate unit

26.3 Detach the shut-off valve hose

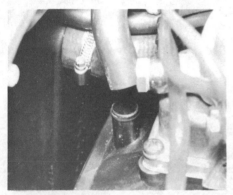
26.5 Detach the hose from the cleaner casing cover at the front end

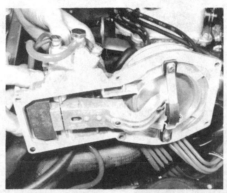
26.6A Lift sensor plate unit clear ...

26.6B ... detach shut-off valve from cleaner case cover ...

26.6C ... lift out the cover ...

26.6D ... and withdraw the element

26.8 Locating the sensor unit gasket

27 Idle speed and fuel mixture – adjustment

1   The idle speed and fuel mixture adjustments will normally only be required after the installation of new components.

2   The idle speed screw is located at the rear of the throttle housing (photo) and access is severely limited unless the front section of the heater air intake scoop is removed, as described in Section 17 of Chapter 2.

3   The idle is best checked and, if necessary, adjusted using an externally attached tachometer connected in accordance with the manufacturer's instructions.

4   Run the engine up to its normal operating temperature before making any checks and adjustments.

5   With the engine warmed up run the engine at 3000 rpm and hold it at this speed for 30 seconds, then allow the engine to idle and check the tachometer reading. If idle speed adjustment is necessary, turn the adjuster screw to set the speed at that specified.

6   To check the mixture adjustment an exhaust gas analyser is needed and should be connected according to the manufacturer's instructions. A 3 mm Allen key will also be required to make any adjustments.

7   Before checking the mixture adjustment the idle speed must be correct.

8   Break off the tamperproof cap from the mixture control screw on top of the fuel distributor (photo).

9   Stabilise the exhaust gases, as described in paragraph 5.

10   Insert a 3 mm Allen key into the head of the mixture screw and turn the screw until the correct CO reading is obtained. Readjust the idle speed screw.

11   If the mixture adjustment cannot be finalised within 30 seconds

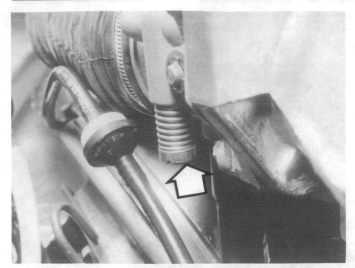

27.2 Idle speed setting screw (arrowed)

27.8 Tamperproof cap on mixture control screw (arrowed)

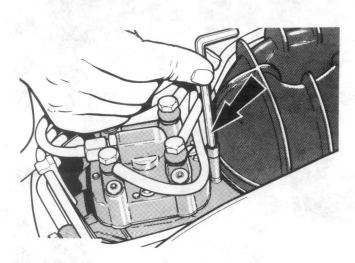

Fig. 3.64 Mixure setting adjustment using 3 mm Allen key
(Sec 27)

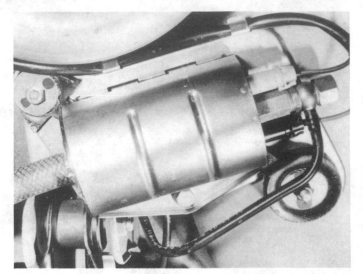

28.1 Fuel pump

from the moment of stabilising the exhaust gases, repeat the operations described in paragraph 5 before continuing the adjustment procedure.

12 On completion fit a new tamperproof plug and disconnect the tachometer and CO meter.

13 **Do not** under any circumstances touch the screws adjacent to each injector pipe on the fuel distributor head, see Fig. 3.57.

28 Fuel pump – removal and refitting

1   The fuel pump is bolted to the underside of the car just to the rear of the fuel tank to the right of the fuel accumulator (photo). For access raise and support the car at the rear.

2   Disconnect the battery earth lead.

3   To relieve the system pressure, slowly loosen the fuel feed pipe at the warm-up regulator and absorb fuel leakage in a cloth (photo).

4   Clamp the fuel inlet hose midway between the tank and the pump using a brake hose clamp, self-locking grips or similar. If the fuel level in the tank is low you may prefer to drain the fuel from the tank into a suitable container once the inlet hose is disconnected.

5   Disconnect the fuel inlet and outlet pipes from the pump, catching fuel spillage in a suitable container. Once disconnected do not allow dirt to enter the pipes, temporarily plug or seal them if necessary.

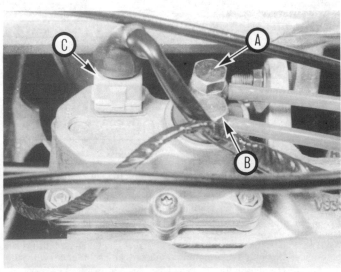

28.3 Warm-up regulator feed pipe (A), outlet pipe (B) and electric connector plug (C)

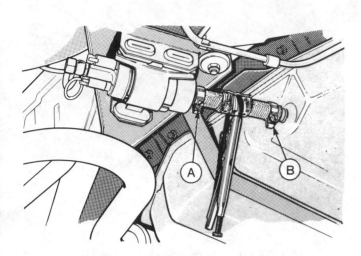

Fig. 3.65 Clamp the fuel inlet hose between the pump (A) and tank connections (B) (Sec 28)

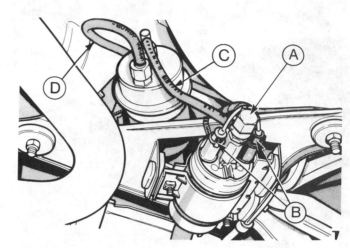

Fig. 3.66 Fuel pump and accumulator connections (Sec 28)

A   Outlet union   D   Outlet pipe from
B   Wiring connections   accumulator
C   Inlet pipe to accumulator

6   Note the electrical connections to the pump and disconnect them.
7   Loosen the pump bracket retaining bolt and then withdraw the pump unit with rubber protector sleeve.
8   Refitting of the fuel pump is a reversal of the removal procedure. Renew the feed pipe from the tank if it is damaged or defective.
9   Check that the rubber protector sleeve is correctly positioned round the pump before tightening the clamp nut.
10   On completion retighten the warm-up regulator fuel inlet connector, reconnect the battery earth lead, restart the engine and check for any signs of leaks from the pump and warm up regulator hoses.

29 Fuel accumulator – removal and refitting

1   The fuel accumulator is mounted adjacent to the fuel pump, above the rear left-hand suspension arm.
2   Disconnect the battery.
3   Raise the rear of the car on ramps or axle-stands.
4   Relieve the system pressure by slowly loosening the fuel feed pipe at the warm-up regulator. Absorb fuel leakage in a cloth.
5   Disconnect the fuel pipes from the fuel accumulator and catch the small quantity of fuel which will be released.

6   Remove the clamp screw (photo) and remove the accumulator.
7   Refitting is a reversal of removal. Check for leaks on completion (with the engine restarted).

30 Fuel filter – removal and refitting

1   Disconnect the battery earth lead.
2   To relieve the system pressure, slowly loosen the fuel feed pipe at the warm-up regulator and absorb the fuel leakage in a cloth.
3   Position a suitable container beneath the filter pipe connections and disconnect the fuel inlet and outlet pipes from the filter (photo).
4   Loosen the filter clamp bracket screw and withdraw the filter from the bracket.
5   Refit in the reverse order of removal. On completion restart the engine and check the filter hoses and warm-up regulator feed pipe connections for any signs of leaks.

31 Fuel injectors and injector delivery pipes – removal and refitting

1   Disconnect the battery earth lead.
2   Detach the four supply pipes from the injectors.

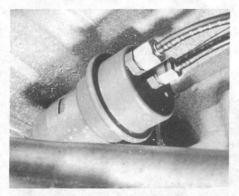

29.5 Fuel accumulator and pipe connections

29.6 Fuel accumulator clamp screw

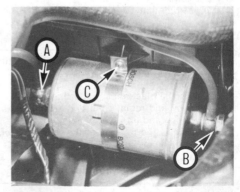

30.3 Fuel filter inlet pipe (A), outlet pipe (B) and clamp bracket screw (C)

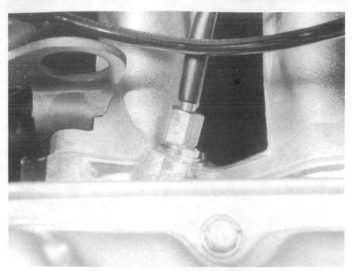

31.3 Injector connection to intake manifold

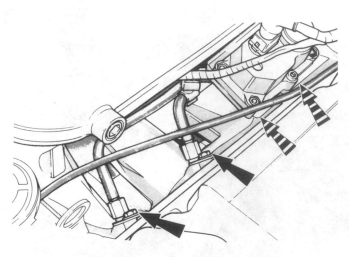

Fig. 3.67 Injector retaining bolts (Sec 31)

3   Unscrew and remove the respective injector retaining bracket bolts then withdraw the injectors and their O-ring seals (photo).
4   The injector fuel delivery pipes can be removed by unscrewing and removing the four banjo bolts at the distributor head. Note the respective pipe connections as they are detached and remove the pipes complete with the plastic hoses and the injector harness. **Do not** separate the pipes or hoses from the injector harness.
5   Before reassembling the fuel delivery pipes, or the injectors, clean all pipe connections thoroughly and use new O-ring seals on the injectors. Use new seal washers on the banjo connections fitting two washers (one each side) per union. Do not overtighten the banjo bolts, or the washers may fracture.
6   Refitting of the injectors and the fuel delivery pipes is otherwise a reversal of the removal procedure. On completion check that the pipes and hoses are not distorted and when the engine is restarted check for any signs of leaks.

32 Fuel start valve – removal and refitting

1   Disconnect the battery earth lead connection.
2   Detach the electrical lead connector from the valve (photo).
3   Slowly unscrew and remove the fuel supply pipe banjo bolt. Take care on removal, as the system will be under pressure. Soak up fuel spillage with a cloth.
4   Unscrew and remove the two socket-head mounting bolts using an Allen key and remove the valve.
5   Refitting is a reversal of the removal procedure. Do not overtighten the banjo bolt or the washers may fracture (use a new one each side of the union).
6   On completion restart the engine and check for signs of fuel leakage.

33 Auxiliary air device – removal and refitting

1   Disconnect the battery earth lead.
2   Detach the electric plug and the two air hoses from the device.
3   Unscrew and remove the two socket-head mounting bolts using a Torx wrench and lift the unit away.
4   Refitting is the reversal of the removal procedure.

34 Warm-up regulator – removal and refitting

1   Disconnect the battery earth lead.
2   Detach the electric plug from the regulator.
3   Unscrew and remove the fuel inlet and outlet pipe banjo bolts,

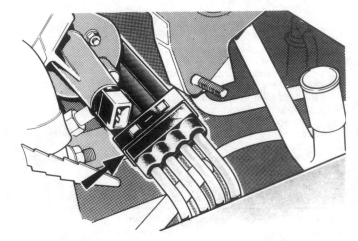

Fig. 3.68 Injector pipes and hoses harness (Sec 31)

32.2 Detach lead connector from fuel start valve

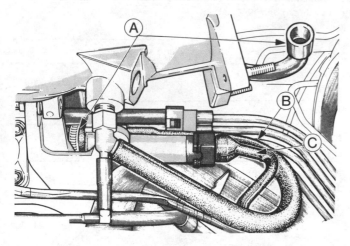

Fig. 3.69 Auxiliary air device connections (Sec 33)

A   Throttle housing hose   C   Electric plug
B   Start valve hose

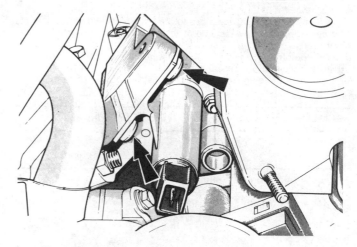

Fig. 3.70 Auxiliary air device retaining bolts (Sec 33)

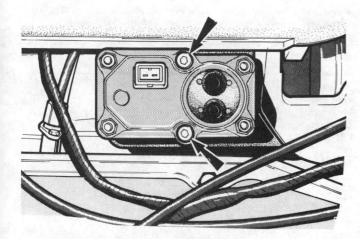

Fig. 3.71 Warm-up regulator showing Torx retaining screws –
arrowed (Sec 34)

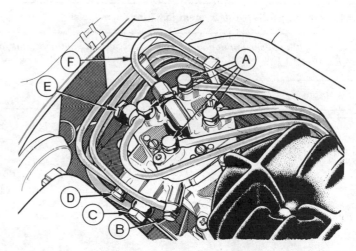

Fig. 3.72 Fuel distributor pipe connections (Sec 35)

A   To injectors   D   From regulator
B   To start valve   E   Fuel inlet
C   Fuel return   F   To warm-up regulator

taking care to unscrew the first one slowly to relieve any pressure in
the system. Soak up any fuel spillage with a cloth.
4   Unscrew and remove the two socket-head bolts which secure the
regulator unit in position then withdraw the unit.
5   Refitting is a reversal of the removal procedure. Use a locking
compound on the threads of the unit securing bolts. When
reconnecting the fuel lines use new banjo bolt washers (one each side
of the union) and take care not to overtighten the bolts.
6   On completion check the fuel pump connections for any sign of
leakage with the engine running.

35 Fuel distributor – removal and refitting

1   Disconnect the battery earth lead.
2   Slowly unscrew and disconnect the warm-up regulator feed pipe
connection at the distributor, catching any fuel spillage in a cloth.
3   Disconnect the injector feed pipes from the distributor, also the
fuel inlet and return pipes. Note the sealing washers which must be
renewed on reconnection of the pipes. Take care not to let dirt enter
the pipes or their connection points.
4   Unscrew and remove the three retaining screws from the top face
and remove the distributor and O-ring.
5   Refitting is a reversal of the removal process. Ensure that the air

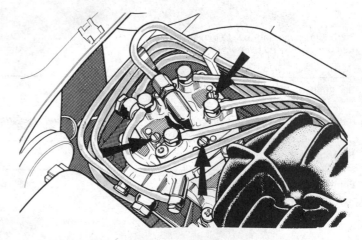

Fig. 3.73 Fuel distributor retaining screws (Sec 35)

sensor plate and distributor mating faces are clean before reassembly. Use a new O-ring seal.

6   When reconnecting the pipes to their distributor connection points fit a new seal washer each side of the unions. Do not overtighten the union bolts.

7   On completion check for any signs of leaks and have the system pressure checked by your dealer.

8   Adjust the idle speed and mixture, as described in Section 27.

36 Accelerator cable – removal, refitting and adjustment

Refer to Sections 8 and 9.

37 Fuel tank – removal and refitting

Refer to Section 7. Note that the pipes to the fuel pump and

accumulator, and the pipe from the pressure regulator must all be disconnected and plugged.

38 Accelerator pedal – removal and refitting

Refer to Section 11.

39 Manifolds

Refer to Section 19.

40 Exhaust system

Refer to Section 20.

PART D: FAULT DIAGNOSIS

41 Fault diagnosis – fuel system (carburettor models)

Note: *High fuel consumption and poor performance are not necessarily due to carburettor faults. Make sure that the ignition system is properly adjusted, that the brakes are not binding and that the engine is in good mechanical condition before tampering with the carburettor.*

Symptom	Reason(s)
Fuel consumption excessive	Air cleaner choked, giving rich mixture Leak from tank, pump or fuel lines Float chamber flooding due to incorrect level or worn needle valve Carburettor incorrectly adjusted Idle speed too high Choke faulty (sticks on) Excessively worn carburettor
Lack of power, stalling or difficult starting	Faulty fuel pump Leak on suction side of pump or in fuel line Intake manifold or carburettor flange gaskets leaking Carburettor incorrectly adjusted Faulty choke Emission control system defect
Poor or erratic idling	Weak mixture (screw tampered with) Leak in intake manifold Leak in distributor vacuum pipe Leak in crankcase extractor hose Leak in brake servo hose
High idle speed and low CO level (cannot be corrected by adjustment)	Renew crankcase vent filter (flame trap) in air cleaner (where fitted)

42 Fault diagnosis – fuel system (fuel injection models)

Before assuming that a malfunction is caused by the fuel system, check the items mentioned in the special note at the start of the previous Section

Symptom	Reason(s)
Engine will not start (cold)	Faulty fuel pump or fuel injection relay Auxiliary air device not opening Start valve not operating Start valve leak Sensor plate rest position incorrect Sensor plate and/or control plunger sticking Vacuum system leak Fuel system leak Thermotime switch remains open

Symptom	Reason(s)
Engine will not start (hot)	Faulty fuel pump or fuel injection relay
	Warm control pressure low
	Sensor plate rest position incorrect
	Sensor plate and/or control plunger sticking
	Vacuum system leak
	Fuel system leak
	Leaky injector valve(s) or low opening pressure
	Incorrect mixture adjustment
Engine difficult to start (cold)	Cold control pressure incorrect
	Auxiliary air device not opening
	Faulty start valve
	Sensor plate rest position faulty
	Sensor plate and/or control plunger sticking
	Fuel system leak
	Thermotime switch not closing
Engine difficult to start (hot)	Warm control pressure too high or too low
	Auxiliary air device faulty
	Sensor plate/control plunger faulty
	Fuel or vacuum leak in system
	Leaky injector valve(s) or low opening pressure
	Incorrect mixture adjustment
Rough idling (during warm-up period)	Incorrect cold control pressure
	Auxiliary air device not closing (or opening)
	Start valve leak
	Fuel or vacuum leak in system
	Leaky injector (valve(s), or low opening pressure
Rough idling (engine warm)	Warm control pressure incorrect
	Auxiliary air device not closing
	Start valve leaking
	Sensor plate and/or control plunger sticking
	Fuel or vacuum leak in system
	Injector(s) leaking or low opening pressure
	Incorrect mixture adjustment
Engine backfiring into intake manifold	Warm control pressure high
	Vacuum system leak
Engine backfiring into exhaust manifold	Warm control pressure high
	Start valve leak
	Fuel system leak
	Incorrect mixture adjustment
Engine misfires (on road)	Fuel system leak
Engine 'runs on'	Sensor plate and or control plunger sticking
	Injector valve(s) leaking or low opening pressure
Excessive petrol consumption	Fuel system leak
	Mixture adjustment incorrect
	Low warm control pressure
High CO level at idle	Low warm control pressure
	Mixture adjustment incorrect
	Fuel system leak
	Sensor plate and/or control plunger sticking
	Start valve leak
Low CO level at idle	High warm control pressure
	Mixture adjustment incorrect
	Start valve leak
	Vacuum system leak
Idle speed adjustment difficult (too high)	Auxiliary air device not closing

Chapter 4 Ignition system

For modifications, and information applicable to later models, see Supplement at end of manual

Contents

Specifications

System type .... Battery, coil, electronic breakerless distributor with magnetic reluctance trigger system

Coil
Output (minimum) .... 30.0 kilovolt
Primary resistance .... 0.72 to 0.88 ohms
Secondary resistance .... 4500 to 7000 ohms

Distributor
Type .... Breakerless with mechanical and vacuum automatic advance control
Drive method .... By offset dog on rear of camshaft
Rotation direction .... Anti-clockwise (viewed from transmission)
Advance (initial) .... 12° BTDC at 800 rpm
Dwell angle .... Governed by module (no check requirement)
Advance characteristics at 2000 rpm, no load:
Crankshaft degrees; initial advance not included

	Mechanical	Vacuum	Total
Lucas:			
1.3	2.4° to 8.4°	14.0° to 22.0°	16.4° to 30.4°
1.6	0.8° to 6.8°	18.0° to 26.0°	18.8° to 32.8°
Bosch:			
1.3	2.8° to 8.8°	14.0° to 22.0°	16.8° to 30.8°
1.6	0.5° to 6.5°	18.0° to 26.0°	18.5° to 32.5°

Spark plugs
Type:
1.3 and 1.6 .... Champion RC7YCC or RC7YC
1.6 injection .... Champion C6YCC or RC6YC
Gap:
RC7YCC and C6YCC .... 0.8 mm (0.032 in)
RC7YC and RC6YC .... 0.7 mm (0.028 in)

HT leads
Maximum resistance per lead .... 17 500 ohms
Type .... Champion CLS 9 boxed set

Firing order .... 1-3-4-2 (No 1 cylinder at timing belt end)

Torque wrench settings
	Nm	lbf ft
Distributor mounting bolts	5.0 to 7.0	3.7 to 5.2
Distributor cap screws:		
Bosch	2.5 to 4.0	1.8 to 3.0
Lucas	1.8 to 2.3	1.3 to 1.7
Module retaining screws	1.0 to 1.4	0.7 to 1.0
Spark plugs	31	23

Are your plugs trying to tell you something?

Normal.
Grey-brown deposits, lightly coated core nose. Plugs ideally suited to engine, and engine in good condition.

Heavy Deposits.
A build up of crusty deposits, light-grey sandy colour in appearance.
Fault: Often caused by worn valve guides, excessive use of upper cylinder lubricant, or idling for long periods.

Lead Glazing.
Plug insulator firing tip appears yellow or green/yellow and shiny in appearance.
Fault: Often caused by incorrect carburation, excessive idling followed by sharp acceleration. Also check ignition timing.

Carbon fouling.
Dry, black, sooty deposits.
Fault: over-rich fuel mixture.
Check: carburettor mixture settings, float level, choke operation, air filter.

Oil fouling.
Wet, oily deposits. Fault: worn bores/piston rings or valve guides; sometimes occurs (temporarily) during running-in period.

Overheating.
Electrodes have glazed appearance, core nose very white – few deposits. Fault: plug overheating. Check: plug value, ignition timing, fuel octane rating (too low) and fuel mixture (too weak).

Electrode damage.
Electrodes burned away; core nose has burned, glazed appearance. Fault: pre-ignition. Check: for correct heat range and as for 'overheating'.

Split core nose.
(May appear initially as a crack). Fault: detonation or wrong gap-setting technique. Check: ignition timing, cooling system, fuel mixture (too weak).

WHY DOUBLE COPPER IS BETTER FOR YOUR ENGINE.

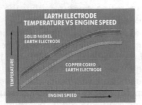

Unique Trapezoidal Copper Cored Earth Electrode —
— 50% Larger Spark Area
— Copper Cored Centre Electrode

Champion Double Copper plugs are the first in the world to have copper core in both centre <u>and</u> earth electrode. This innovative design means that they run cooler by up to 100°C – giving greater efficiency and longer life. These double copper cores transfer heat away from the tip of the plug faster and more efficiently. Therefore, Double Copper runs at cooler temperatures than conventional plugs giving improved acceleration response and high speed performance with no fear of pre-ignition.

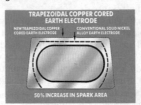

Champion Double Copper plugs also feature a unique trapezoidal earth electrode giving a 50% increase in spark area. This, together with the double copper cores, offers greatly reduced electrode wear, so the spark stays stronger for longer.

 FASTER COLD STARTING

 FOR UNLEADED OR LEADED FUEL

 ELECTRODES UP TO 100°C COOLER

 BETTER ACCELERATION RESPONSE

 LOWER EMISSIONS

 50% BIGGER SPARK AREA

 THE LONGER LIFE PLUG

Plug Tips/Hot and Cold.
Spark plugs must operate within well-defined temperature limits to avoid cold fouling at one extreme and overheating at the other.
Champion and the car manufacturers work out the best plugs for an engine to give optimum performance under all conditions, from freezing cold starts to sustained high speed motorway cruising.
Plugs are often referred to as hot or cold. With Champion, the higher the number on its body, the hotter the plug, and the lower the number the cooler the plug. For the correct plug for your car refer to the specifications at the beginning of this chapter.

Plug Cleaning
Modern plug design and materials mean that Champion no longer recommends periodic plug cleaning. Certainly don't clean your plugs with a wire brush as this can cause metal conductive paths across the nose of the insulator so impairing its performance and resulting in loss of acceleration and reduced m.p.g.
However, if plugs are removed, always carefully clean the area where the plug seats in the cylinder head as grit and dirt can sometimes cause gas leakage.
Also wipe any traces of oil or grease from plug leads as this may lead to arcing.

1 Description and maintenance

One of two systems may be fitted, Bosch or Lucas. Interchanging of alternative makes of component should not be done, except for the coil. **Never** fit a coil from a conventional mechanical breaker system.

The system includes a breakerless distributor driven from the flywheel end of the camshaft.

The electronic module, which is usually remotely-sited on these systems, is integrated in the distributor on the Ford Orion.

A high output type ignition coil is located on the side of the engine compartment.

Ignition adjustments (dwell angle and timing) have been eliminated from routine service operations.

The breakerless distributor has no mechanical contact breaker or condenser, these components being replaced by a trigger wheel, a trigger plate and a pick-up coil. The rotor arm is driven at half engine speed and rotates in an anti-clockwise direction when viewed from the transmission.

The electronic amplifier module may be one of two different makes – Bosch or AC Delco (used on the Lucas distributor). The module is a sealed unit, which should be treated with care, and is connected to the distributor body by a multi-plug.

The action of the distributor is to provide a pulse to the electronic module, which in turn triggers the ignition to fire the fuel/air mixture through the spark plug electrodes. This pulse is created by a magnetic signal generating system within the distributor.

Spark advance and distribution is carried out in an identical way to that used in conventional mechanical breaker systems. A dual diaphragm type distributor is fitted to emission control models supplied to Sweden and Switzerland.

Maintenance consists of keeping all electrical connections secure, the HT leads and distributor cap clean. Inspect the distributor cap and rotor arm for cracks if misfiring occurs (refer to Section 7).

Repair and overhaul operations should be limited to those described in this Chapter as the supply of spare parts is restricted to the distributor cap, the rotor arm, electronic module, drive dog and vacuum diaphragm unit.

Safety note

The voltage produced from the HT circuit on an electronic ignition system is considerably greater than that from a conventional system. In consequence, take extra precautions when handling the HT leads with the engine running. Although not lethal, the shock experienced could be severe.

Care should be taken not to knock the distributor when the ignition is switched on and the engine not running. It is possible for the engine to fire on one cylinder under these conditions, with resultant injury to the hands if engaged in overhaul or adjustment operations.

2 Ignition timing – adjustment

1   Ignition timing adjustment is normally only necessary if a new distributor is being fitted or if the original setting has been disturbed for any reason.

2   The ignition timing position was originally marked on the distributor mounting flange and the cylinder head. It should not be necessary to alter the distributor from this setting if the original distributor (and cylinder head) are fitted.

3   To check and, if necessary, adjust the distributor timing on a car with the original distributor and cylinder head, first check that the timing marks made during manufacture are in alignment (photo). If they are not, loosen off the three distributor clamp bolts, align the marks and retighten the bolts.

4   Where a new distributor or cylinder head have been fitted, position the distributor so that the clamp bolts are central within the distributor flange slots.

5   Disconnect and plug the distributor vacuum pipe(s).

6   Using a little quick-drying white paint, increase the contrast of the timing notch in the crankshaft pulley and the appropriate mark (see Specifications) on the timing belt cover scale (photo).

7   Connect a timing light (stroboscope) in accordance with the manufacturer's instructions.

8   Start the engine, allow it to idle and point the timing light at the

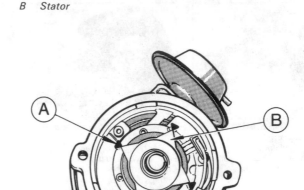

Fig. 4.1 Lucas distributor pulse triggering device (Sec 1)

A   Trigger coil   C   Trigger wheel
B   Stator

Fig. 4.2 Bosch distributor pulse triggering device (Sec 1)

A   Stator   B   Trigger wheel

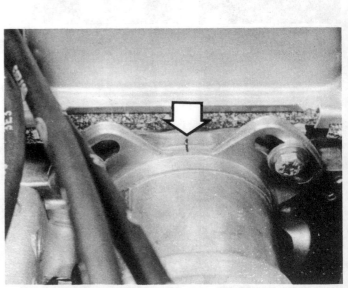

2.3 Distributor and cylinder head flanges showing timing alignment marking (arrowed)

2.6 Ignition timing marks on timing belt cover and notch on crankshaft pulley (arrowed)

timing marks. They should appear stationary and in alignment. If they are not, rotate the distributor as necessary to bring them into line and then tighten one of the distributor bolts.

9 Switch off the engine, and then tighten all the distributor mounting bolts to the specified torque. Recheck the timing.

10 Punch mark the distributor flange at a point exactly opposite the mark on the cylinder head to give the new timing reference marks for any future repair and ignition timing checks.

11 Disconnect the timing light and reconnect the vacuum pipe(s).

12 If the advance characteristics of the distributor are to be checked proceed as given in Section 3.

3 Distributor advance – checking

1 A secondary use of the timing light is to check that the centrifugal and vacuum advance functions of the distributor are working.

2 The tests are not precise, as would be the case if sophisticated equipment were used, but will at least indicate the serviceability of the unit.

3 With the engine idling, timing light connected and vacuum pipe(s) disconnected and plugged, as described in the preceding Section, increase the engine speed to 2000 rpm and note the approximate

distance which the pulley mark moves out of alignment with the mark on the scale.

4 Reconnect the vacuum pipe to the distributor and repeat the test when for the same increase in engine speed, the alignment differential of the timing marks should be greater than previously observed. Refer to the Specifications for typical figures.

5 A further check of the vacuum advance can be made by removing the distributor cap after the engine has been switched off, disconnecting the distributor vacuum pipe at its suction end, and sucking the pipe. The suction should be sufficient to move the distributor baseplate slightly.

6 If these tests do not prove positive, renew the vacuum unit, as described in Section 6.

7 Some models are equipped with a spark delay/sustain valve in the vacuum line from carburettor to distributor, the purpose of which is to delay vacuum advance under certain part throttle conditions. If such a valve is suspected of malfunctioning, it should be tested by substitution, or taken to a Ford dealer for specialised checking. The main effect of the valve is to reduce exhaust emission levels and it is unlikely that malfunction would have a noticeable effect on engine performance.

8 If a ported vacuum switch (PVS) is fitted in the vacuum line, its purpose is to bypass the spark sustain valve when normal engine operating temperature (as sensed by the temperature of the coolant flowing round the intake manifold) has been reached.

9 For further information on the spark delay/sustain valve and ported vacuum switch refer to the emission control information in Chapter 3.

4 Distributor – removal and refitting

Original unit

1 The original distributor is precisely positioned for optimum ignition timing during production and marked accordingly with a punch mark on the distributor mounting flange and the cylinder head.

2 Disconnect the HT leads from the distributor cap (photo).

3 Unclip and remove the distributor cap shield.

4 Extract the distributor cap screws (photo), lift off the cap and position it with the leads to one side.

5 Disconnect the wiring harness multi-plug from the distributor. Disconnect the vacuum pipe.

6 Unscrew and remove the three distributor flange mounting bolts (photo) and withdraw the distributor from the cylinder head.

7 Before refitting the distributor, check the condition of the oil seal and renew it if necessary (photo).

8 Hold the distributor so that the punch marks on the distributor body and the offset drive dog are in approximate alignment, then insert the distributor into its recess.

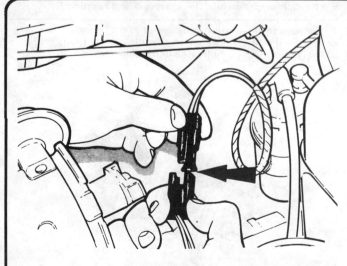

Fig. 4.3 Distributor multi-plug LT connections (Sec 4)

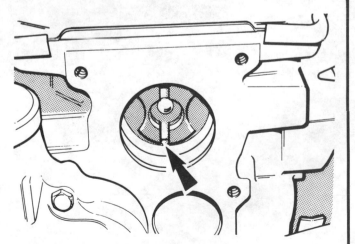

Fig. 4.4 Distributor drive dog engagement slot in camshaft (Sec 4)

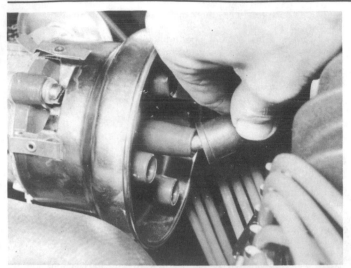

4.2 Detach HT leads from distributor cap (cap shield fitted)

4.4 Removing a distributor cap screw

4.6 Distributor retaining bolts (arrowed)
The third bolt is not visible

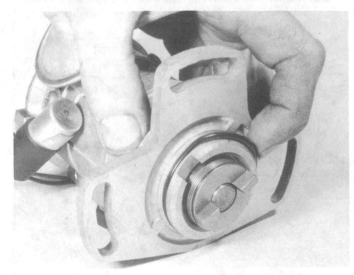

4.7 Check the condition of the oil seal

9   Check that the drive components have engaged and then rotate the distributor until the punch marks on the flange and head are in alignment. Insert the bolts and tighten to the specified torque.
10   Reconnect all the disconnected components.

New unit
11   Where a new distributor is being installed, its flange will obviously not have a punch mark and it must therefore be fitted in the following way.
12   Hold the distributor in approximately its fitted position, making sure that the vacuum unit is horizontal and towards the right-hand side when viewed from the roadwheel. Also ensure that the drive dog is in approximately the correct alignment to engage with the offset segments of the camshaft dog.
13   Locate the distributor on the cylinder head. When you are sure that the drive dogs are fully engaged, screw in the flange bolts so that they are hand tight and then adjust the distributor fitted position so that its retaining bolts are central in the flange slots.
14   Reconnect the distributor cap, shield and high and low tension leads, but leave the vacuum pipe detached.
15   Plug the end of the vacuum pipe and then check and adjust the distributor timing, as given in Sections 2 and 3.

5   Ignition amplifier module – removal and refitting

1   Remove the distributor as described in the preceding Section.
2   Extract the two screws which hold the module to the distributor body and pull the module from its multi-plug.

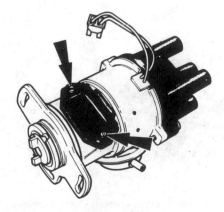

Fig. 4.5 Module securing screws – arrowed (Sec 5)

3   Before refitting, check that the rubber grommet is in good condition. If not, renew it.

4   Coat the metal rear face of the module with special heat sink compound available from your dealer. This is to ensure good earthing contact.

5   Refit the distributor, as described in Section 4.

6   Distributor – overhaul

1   As noted in Section 1, distributor spare parts are not generally available. In the event of malfunction or mechanical wear occurring in the distributor itself, a new unit must be obtained.

2   The rotor arm is simply pulled off the shaft once the cap has been withdrawn (two screws) from the distributor.

3   Access to the trigger wheel and associated components is gained by removing the plastic shield (where fitted).

4   The trigger wheel on both Lucas and Bosch distributors is secured to the shaft by a circlip.

5   If it is wished to remove the distributor baseplate to gain access to the vacuum unit, **do not** slacken the screws which hold the

permanent magnet in position on the Lucas distributor, or the air gap will be altered. The baseplate is secured by three screws.

6   As the baseplate is lifted away, the vacuum unit operating lever can be disconnected. The vacuum unit is secured to the distributor body by two screws.

7   Do not drop or strike the distributor or its components, some of which are both mechanically and electrically fragile.

7   Spark plugs, HT leads and distributor cap – general

Spark plugs

1   The correct functioning of the spark plugs is vital for the correct running and efficiency of the engine. It is essential that the plugs fitted are appropriate for the engine, and the suitable type is specified at the beginning of this chapter. If this type is used and the engine is in good condition, the spark plugs should not need attention between scheduled replacement intervals. Spark plug cleaning is rarely necessary and should not be attempted unless specialised equipment is available as damage can easily be caused to the firing ends.

2   The spark plugs normally only need to be removed when renewed.

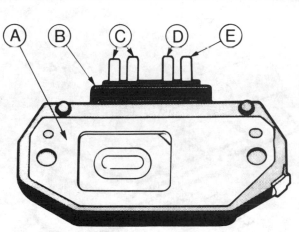

Fig. 4.6 Base of electronic amplifier module (Sec 5)

A   Module
B   Flexible seal
C   To distributor trigger coil
D   Feed from ignition switch
E   To coil LT terminal

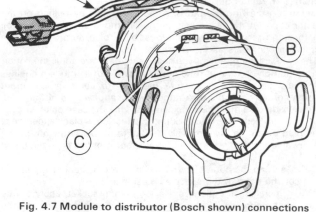

Fig. 4.7 Module to distributor (Bosch shown) connections (Sec 5)

A   Coil and ignition 12 volt feed LT wires
B   Module/trigger coil socket
C   Module/LT wires socket

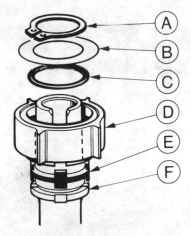

Fig. 4.8 Trigger wheel components – Lucas (Sec 6)

A   Circlip
B   Washer
C   O-ring
D   Trigger wheel
E   Toothed collar
F   Shaft slots

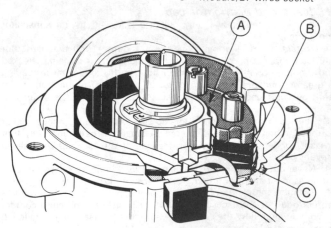

Fig. 4.9 Distributor signal operating system – Lucas (Sec 6)

A   Stator
B   Permanent magnets
C   Baseplate (upper)

Note: Do not remove slotted collar screws each side of A

2   Maintenance is minimal, but nevertheless important. Make sure that the HT and LT lead connections are secure and that the HT tower is kept clean and dry. If removing the HT lead from the coil at any time, pull on the insulator connector, not the lead.
3   One of two types of coil will be fitted, being of either Bosch or Lucas manufacture. The Bosch one differs in appearance by having a black protector cap fitted which *should not be removed*.
4   Should you ever need to renew the ignition coil **never** fit a

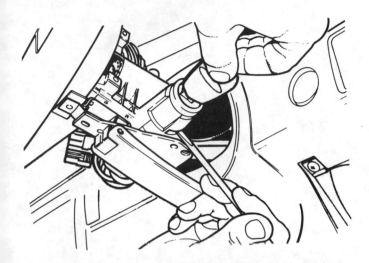

Fig. 4.11 Removing the ignition lock cylinder (Sec 9)

conventional ignition system coil or the result could well mean a damaged electronic module.
5   Both the Bosch and the Lucas type coil fitted have similar output characteristics and are therefore interchangeable.

9   Ignition lock cylinder – removal and refitting

1   Disconnect the battery earth terminal, then remove the steering column lower shroud.
2   Insert the ignition key into the lock and turn to position I.
3   Using a screwdriver, depress the cylinder retaining clip and withdraw the lock cylinder by pulling on the key.
4   Refit by simply pushing the cylinder into position with the key held in position I.
5   Refer to Chapter 9, for details of steering column lock removal.

Fig. 4.12 Ignition key positions (Sec 9)

O Off	*III Start engine (repeat*
I Ignition off, radio on,	*operation only after*
* steering unlocked*	*returning key to position I)*
II Ignition on	

10 Fault diagnosis – ignition system

Symptom	Reason(s)
Engine fails to start	Discharged battery Loose battery connections Disconnected ignition leads Crack in distributor cap or rotor Faulty amplifier module
Engine starts and runs but misfires	Faulty spark plug Crack in distributor cap Cracked rotor arm Worn advance mechanism Faulty coil Poor earth connections
Engine overheats and lacks power	Perforated or disconnected vacuum pipe Faulty centrifugal or advance mechanism
Engine pinks	Advance mechanism stuck Low fuel octane rating

Note: *Any of the foregoing symptoms could be caused by incorrect timing, but unless the distributor mounting bolts have become slack this is unlikely, as the timing is preset during production with the distributor flange and cylinder head punch marks aligned.*

Chapter 5 Clutch

Contents

Specifications

General

Type	Single dry plate, diaphragm spring
Actuation	Cable with automatic adjuster

Driven plate

Diameter:

1.3 engine	190 mm (7.5 in)
1.6 engine	200 mm (7.9 in)
Lining thickness	3.20 mm (0.126 in)
Number of torsion springs	4

Pedal stroke .... 155 mm (6.1 in)

Torque wrench settings

	Nm	lbf ft
Pressure plate cover to flywheel	18	13
Clutch release fork bolt	34	25

1 General description

The clutch is of single dry plate with a diaphragm spring pressure plate.

Actuation is by cable and the pendant mounted pedal incorporates a self-adjusting mechanism.

The release bearing is of ball type and is kept in constant contact with the fingers of the diaphragm spring by the action of the pedal self-adjusting mechanism. In consequence, there is no pedal free movement adjustment required.

When the clutch pedal is released, the adjustment pawl is no longer engaged with the teeth on the pedal quadrant, the cable being tensioned, however, by the spring which is located between the pedal and the quadrant. When the pedal is depressed the pawl engages in the nearest vee between the teeth. The particular tooth engagement position will gradually change as the components move to compensate for wear in the clutch driven plate and stretch in the cable.

The size of the clutch varies according to engine capacity (see Specifications).

2 Clutch pedal − removal and refitting

1 If difficulty in engaging gears and/or noisy reverse gear selection has been a problem, a new clutch pedal quadrant, pawl and pawl

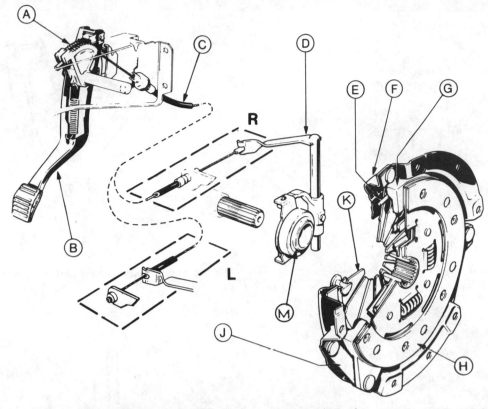

Fig. 5.1 Clutch assembly components (Sec 1)

A	Automatic adjuster	E	Fulcrum ring	H	Driven plate	L	LHD cable arrangement
B	Clutch pedal	F	Cover	J	Steel straps	M	Release bearing
C	Clutch cable	G	Pressure plate	K	Diaphragm spring	R	RHD cable arrangement
D	Release assembly						

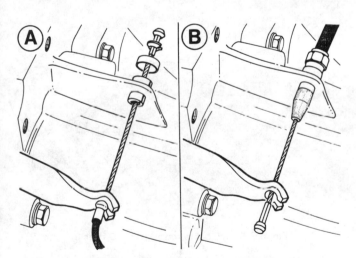

Fig. 5.2 Clutch cable and release lever on left-hand drive (A) and right-hand drive (B) models (Sec 2)

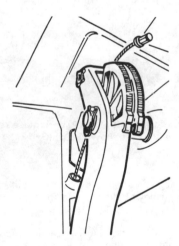

Fig. 5.3 Disconnect the cable from the pedal segment (Sec 2)

spring should be fitted. This later type assembly can be identified by the pawl spring being blue in colour.

2 Working inside the car, remove the lower insulation panel adjacent to the pedals. The panel is secured by clips. Disconnect the clutch cable from the release lever on the transmission housing.

3 Inside the vehicle, release the clutch cable from the quadrant at the top of the clutch pedal.

4 Remove the retaining clip securing the brake pedal to the master cylinder or brake servo linkage pushrod.

5 Make a note of the spacers and wave washers fitted between the pedals and pedal bracket. To remove the pedals the shaft itself must be removed. Start by removing the circlip on the pivot shaft on the outside of the brake pedal and slide the shaft sideways to release the clutch and brake pedals.

6 The clutch pedal can now be dismantled in order to renew the bushes, or the quadrant and adjuster mechanism.

7 Before refitting the assembly, grease the pivot shaft with molybdenum disulphide grease, and set the pawl so that it is in contact with the smooth part of the quadrant (see Fig 5.6).

8 Position the pedals in the pedal bracket then fit the pivot shaft,

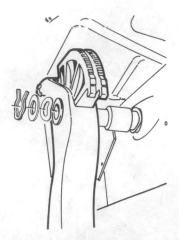

Fig. 5.4 Pedal shaft retaining clip and washers (Sec 2)

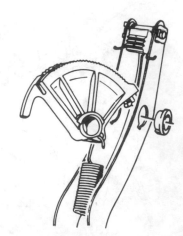

Fig. 5.5 Adjuster segment and clutch pedal shaft bushes (Sec 2)

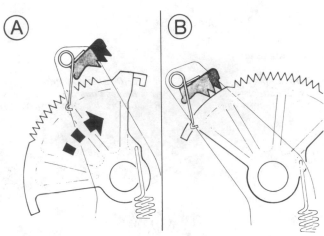

Fig. 5.6 Segment refitting: lift pawl (A) and rotate segment to position pawl as shown in (B) (Sec 2)

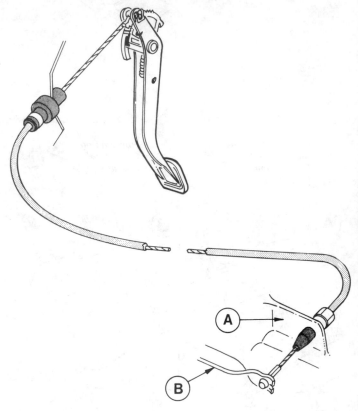

Fig. 5.7 Clutch cable routing – RHD (Sec 3)

A   Clutch housing   B   Release lever

ensuring the spacers and wave washers are fitted in the same position from which they were removed. Refit the circlip to the pivot shaft.
9   Reconnect the brake pedal to the master cylinder or brake servo linkage.
10 Connect the clutch cable to the adjuster quadrant and to the clutch release lever on the transmission housing.
11 Operate the clutch pedal several times to set the adjuster mechanism.
12 Refit the dash lower insulating panel to complete, then check that the clutch operation is satisfactory.

3   Clutch operating cable – renewal

1   The cable is released from the release lever and the pedal, as described in the preceding Section.
2   On LHD vehicles, draw the cable towards the engine compartment rear bulkhead and remove the cable retainer and its bush.
3   On RHD vehicles, remove the plastic clip which secures the cable to the steering rack housing.

4   Refit the cable by reversing the appropriate removal operations. On RHD vehicles, align the white band on the cable with the paint spot on the steering rack housing before fitting the cable securing clip.

4   Clutch – method of access

1   The usual method of access to the clutch assembly is by removing the transmission, as described in Chapter 6.
2   If the engine is also being removed for major overhaul then the engine/transmission will be removed as a combined unit and separated later.

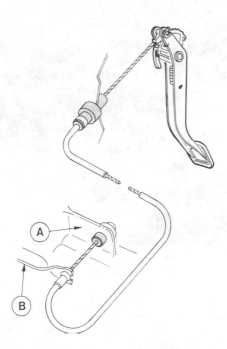

Fig. 5.8 Clutch cable routing – LHD (Sec 3)

A   *Clutch housing*   B   *Release lever*

5   Clutch – removal

1   With the flywheel exposed, unbolt the clutch pressure plate. Unscrew the retaining bolts in a diagonal sequence a turn at a time until the pressure of the diaphragm spring is relieved. Remove the bolts completely.

2   Carefully prise the pressure plate from its locating dowels and remove it. Take care not to allow the driven plate to fall, as will certainly happen as the pressure of the plate is withdrawn.

6   Clutch – inspection and renovation

1   The most likely reason for dismantling the clutch will be due to the occurrence of faults described in Section 8.

2   Unless the vehicle has been used under conditions of very low traffic density and in fairly flat terrain, then clutch driven plate will certainly require renewal any time after 80 000 km (50 000 miles) have been covered.

3   Under dense traffic driving conditions, in hilly country or if the driver is heavy footed and seldom matches the speed of the engine to that of the transmission when changing gear, the clutch renewal may be required at half the mileage just mentioned, or even earlier.

4   Examine the friction linings of the driven plate. If they are worn down to the rivet heads then renew the plate. Don't attempt to re-line the plate with new linings yourself, it is seldom satisfactory.

5   If the friction linings appear oil-stained, renew the driven plate and before fitting it, rectify the oil leak. This will probably mean renewal of the crankshaft rear oil seal or the transmission input shaft oil seal.

6   It is difficult to decide whether to renew the clutch pressure plate at the same time as the driven plate is renewed. If a really good mileage has been covered by the old components then it is recommended that all the components are renewed at the same time. If the driven plate has had a short life, however, due to adverse operating conditions, then the pressure plate assembly will probably give further service until the next driven plate renewal stage is reached.

7   If the pressure plate is not renewed as a routine measure examine it very closely for scoring of the pressure plate face, cracking of the diaphragm spring fingers or rust or corrosion. If any of these conditions are evident, renew the assembly.

8   Now check the contact surface of the flywheel. If it is grooved or deeply scored, the flywheel must be renewed or refinished. Refer to Chapter 1, Section 19. Hair cracks are usually a sign of overheating due to excessive clutch slip.

9   A pilot bearing is not used in the centre of the flywheel/crankshaft rear flange as the input shaft is supported independently on two bearings within the transmission housing.

10   Finally, check the condition of the clutch release bearing. If it is noisy when turned with the fingers or is obviously worn, it must be renewed. It is always best to renew it at a time of clutch overhaul as it has a hard life and failure at a later date will mean removing the transmission again for this one component to be changed.

7   Clutch – refitting and centralising

1   Check that the contact surfaces of the flywheel and pressure plate are clean and free from oil or grease.

2   Offer up the driven plate to the flywheel. Make sure that the projecting hub of the driven plate is **not** against the flywheel. The plate is usually marked FLYWHEEL SIDE (photo).

3   Hold the driven plate in position and then locate the pressure plate/cover assembly on its positioning dowels on the flywheel, so trapping the driven plate (photo).

7.2 Clutch driven plate marking

7.3 Locate the driven plate and fit the pressure plate/cover assembly

7.7 Tightening the pressure plate cover bolts to the specified torque
Note the driven plate centralising tool

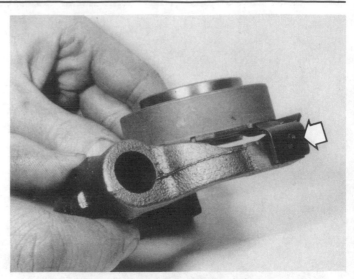

7.10 The clutch release bearing attachment to fork
Roll pin arrowed

4   Insert the retaining bolts, but only screw them in finger tight.
5   The clutch driven plate must now be centralised in order to facilitate mating of the transmission to the engine. To do this, a clutch alignment tool is needed. Either purchase one of the several multi-purpose types available from motor accessory stores, or the official tool (21-103), or use an old input shaft or make up something by winding tape around a rod until suitable diameters are achieved.
6   The tool should be passed through the splined hub of the driven plate and its end engaged in the centre hole in the flywheel. The action of engaging the end of the tool in the flywheel will move the driven plate so as to centralise it.

7   Without moving the driven plate or tool, tighten the pressure plate cover bolts to the specified torque in a diagonal sequence and in a progressive manner (photo).
8   Withdraw the alignment tool.
9   Smear the splines of the input shaft and the release bearing hub sliding surfaces with molybdenum disulphide grease.
10 Connect the release bearing to the fork, noting that it is only retained at its upper point by being hooked over a roll pin (photo).
11 The transmission can now be reconnected to the engine, as described in Chapter 6.

8 Fault diagnosis – clutch

Symptom	Reason(s)
Judder when taking up drive	Loose engine/transmission mountings Worn friction linings Oil saturated linings Worn splines on input shaft or clutch driven plate
Clutch spin (failure to disengage) so that gears cannot be meshed	Driven plate sticking on input shaft splines due to rust. May occur after standing idle for long periods* Damaged or misaligned pressure plate assembly
Clutch slip (increase in engine speed does not result in comparable increase in road speed – particularly on gradients)	Friction surfaces worn or oil contaminated Weak clutch engagement due to fault in automatic cable adjuster or weak diaphragm spring
Noise evident on depressing clutch pedal	Dry, worn or damaged release bearing Play between driven plate and input shaft splines
Noise evident as clutch pedal released	Distorted driven plate Weak or broken driven plate torsion springs Distorted or worn input shaft Release bearing loose on mounting hub

*This condition may also be due to the driven plate being rusted to the flywheel or pressure plate. It is possible to free it by applying the handbrake, engaging top gear and operating the starter motor. If really badly corroded, then the engine will not turn over, but in the majority of cases the driven plate will free. Once the engine starts, rev it up and slip the clutch several times to clear the rust deposits.

Chapter 6 Transmission

For modifications, and information applicable to later models, see Supplement at end of manual

Contents

Specifications

Manual transmission

Type .... Four-speed (1.3 models) and five-speed (1.3 model option and 1.6 models). Synchromesh on all forward gears

Ratios(:1)

	1.3 (four-speed)	1.3 (five-speed)	1.6
1st	3.58	3.58	3.15
2nd	2.04	2.04	1.91
3rd	1.35	1.35	1.28
4th	0.95	0.95	0.95
5th	–	0.76	0.76
Reverse	3.77	3.61	3.62
Final drive	3.84	3.84	3.58*

Final drive on fuel injection models = 3.84:1

Lubrication

Lubricant capacity:	
Four-speed	2.8 litres (4.9 pints)
Five-speed	3.1 litres (5.5 pints)
Lubricant type/specification	Hypoid gear oil, viscosity SAE 80 EP, to Ford spec SQM-2C 9008-A (Duckhams Hypoid 80)
Grease type (assembly only – see text):	
Four-speed	To Ford specification SM1C-1020-B
Five-speed:	
Gears, contact and thrust faces	Molybdenum Disulphide paste to Ford spec SM1C-4505-A
Synchroniser cones and mainshaft assemblies	Colloidal Molybdenum Disulphide in oil to Ford spec SM1C-4504-A
5th gear on input shaft	Ford grease type ESEA-M1C-1014-A
Selector shaft locking assembly sealer	Anaerobic retaining and sealing compound to Ford spec SM4G-4645-AA or AB

Snap-ring thicknesses (mainshaft and input shaft) ....   1.86 to 1.89 mm (0.0732 to 0.0745 in)
                                                              1.94 to 1.97 mm (0.0763 to 0.0776 in)
                                                              2.01 to 2.04 mm (0.0791 to 0.0803 in)

Automatic transmission
Type ....   Ford ATX (automatic transaxle)

Torque converter ....   Hydraulic and mechanical

Oil cooler ....   Twin tube in radiator water tank

Ratios (:1)
1st 2.79
2nd 1.61
3rd 1.00
Reverse 1.97
Axle ratio 3.31:1
Converter ratio 2.35:1

Lubricant
Type/specification ....   ATF to Ford spec SQM-2C 9010-A or ESP-M2C 138-CJ
                                                              (Duckhams Uni-Matic or D-Matic)
Capacity (including converter and oil cooler) ....   7.9 litres (13.9 pints)

All transmission types
Torque wrench settings

	Nm	lbf ft
Four-speed manual transmission		
Transmission-to-engine flange bolts	35 to 45	26 to 33
Cover – clutch housing	35 to 45	26 to 33
Starter motor bolts	35 to 45	26 to 33
Gearbox-to-front mounting bolts	41 to 51	30 to 38
Gearbox mounting bolts front and rear	52 to 64	38 to 47
Spindle carrier to balljoint	70 to 90	52 to 66
Gearshift stabiliser (to gearbox)	50 to 60	37 to 44
Shift rod-to-gearbox clamp bolts	14 to 17	10 to 13
Cap nut (selector shaft lock mechanism)	30	22
Gearshift housing to floor pan	13 to 17	10 to 13
Oil filler plug	23 to 30	17 to 22
Five-speed manual transmission		
Where different to or not included in four-speed transmission settings		
Clutch housing to support bracket	19 to 25	14 to 18
Selector block to main selector shaft	12 to 15	9 to 11
Gearshift housing to floorpan	15 to 22	11 to 16
Reverse light switch	23 to 30	17 to 22
5th gear housing to gearbox	12 to 15	9 to 11
5th gear selector pin clamp bolt	14 to 20	10 to 15
5th gear selector plate to housing	27 to 34	20 to 25
5th gear housing cover	8 to 11	6 to 8
Automatic transmission		
Transmission-to-engine bolts	30 to 50	22 to 37
Torque converter to driveplate	35 to 40	26 to 30
Driveplate to crankshaft	80 to 88	59 to 65
Converter housing cover plate	7 to 10	5 to 7
Oil lines to cooler	18 to 22	13 to 16
Oil lines to transmission	22 to 44	16 to 32
Oil pan to transmission	20 to 26	15 to 19
Starter inhibitor switch screws	9 to 12	7 to 9
Shift shaft nut	43 to 65	32 to 48
Transmission mounting to body	52 to 64	38 to 47
Shift cable bracket	40 to 45	30 to 33
Downshift linkage to engine bracket	20 to 25	15 to 18
Downshift linkage control lever-to-damper clamp nut	5 to 7	4 to 5
Damper locknut	5 to 8	4 to 6
Downshift/throttle valve shaft lever nut	13 to 15	10 to 11
Selector mechanism to floor	9 to 10	6 to 7
Selector lever-to-lever guide nut	20 to 23	15 to 17

1 Manual transmission – description

A four- or five-speed manual transmission is fitted to the Orion, the five-speed transmission being fitted as standard on 1.6 litre models and available as an option on the 1.3 litre version.

The gearbox and differential are housed in a two section light alloy casting which is bolted to the transversely-mounted engine.

Drive from the engine/transmission is transmitted to the front roadwheels through open driveshafts.

The engine torque is transmitted to the gearbox input shaft. Once a gear is selected, power is then transmitted to the main (output) shaft. The helically cut forward speed gears on the output shaft are in constant mesh with the corresponding gears on the input shaft.

All forward gears have synchromesh gear selection.

When the clutch pedal is depressed and the gearchange lever is moved to select a higher gear, the synchro baulk ring is pressed onto the gear cone. The friction generated causes the faster rotating gear on the input shaft to slow until its speed matches that of the gear on the output shaft. The gears can then be smoothly engaged.

When changing to a lower gear, the principle of operation is similar except that the speed of the slower rotating gear is increased by the action of the baulk ring on the cone.

Reverse gear is of the straight-cut tooth type and is part of the 1st/2nd synchro unit. A sliding type reverse idler gear is used.

The torque from the gearbox output shaft is transmitted to the crownwheel which is bolted to the differential cage and thence through the differential gears to the driveshafts.

All adjustment to the differential and its bearings has been obviated by the inclusion of two diaphragm springs which are located in the smaller half of the transmission housing. Any tolerances which may exist are taken up by the sliding fit of the outer bearing ring in the smaller section of the housing.

Gear selection is obtained by rotary and axial movements of the main selector shaft (transmitted through a selector dog bolted to the selector shaft) and two guide levers to the guide shaft which also carries a selector dog.

Rotary movement of the main selector shaft engages a cam on the guide shaft selector dog either in the cut-out of the 1st/2nd or 3rd/4th gear selector fork or in the aperture in the reverse gear guide lever.

Axial movement of the selector shaft moves the appropriate selector fork on the guide shaft or reverse idler gear through the medium of the guide lever, so engaging the gear.

The selected gear is locked in engagement by a shift locking plate which is carried on the guide shaft selector dog and a spring-loaded interlock pin located in the smaller housing section.

The five-speed transmission is basically the same as the four-speed version with the exception of a modified selector mechanism, and an additional gear and synchro-hub contained in a housing attached to the side of the main transmission casing.

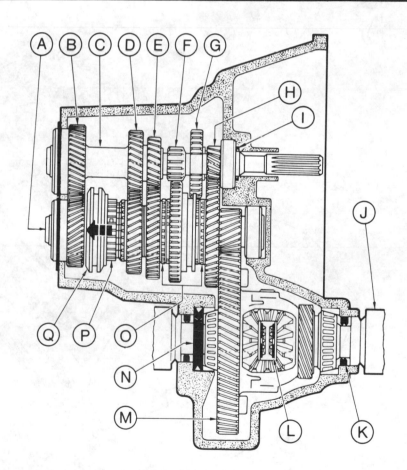

Fig. 6.1 Cutaway view of the four-speed transmission (Sec 1)

A	Mainshaft	H	1st gear	N	Diaphragm springs
B	4th gear	I	Input shaft oil seal	O	1st/2nd synchro with
C	Input shaft	J	Driveshaft inboard		reverse gear
D	3rd gear		CV joint	P	3rd/4th synchro
E	2nd gear	K	Oil seal	Q	3rd/4th synchro sleeve
F	Reverse gear	L	Driveshaft snap-ring		(4th gear engaged)
G	Reverse idler gear	M	Crownwheel		

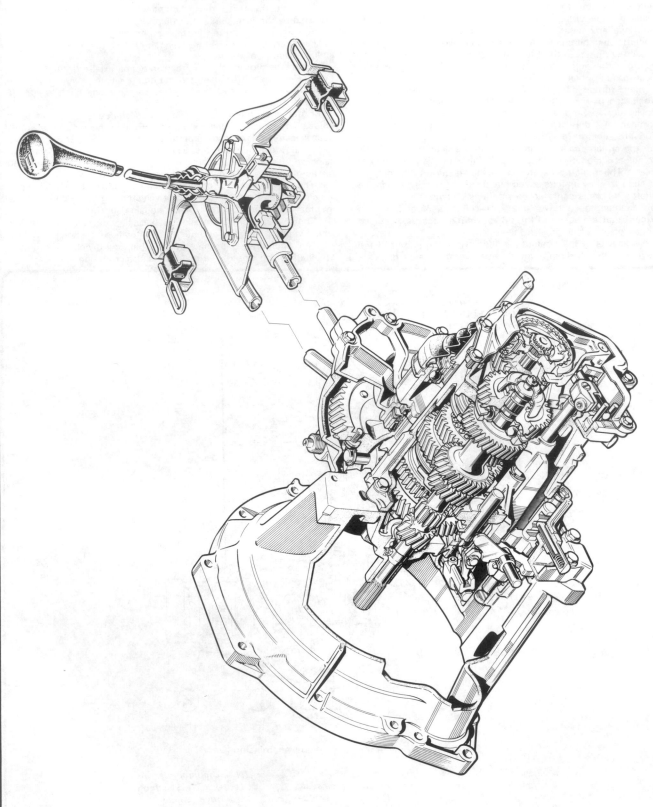

Fig. 6.2 Cutaway view of the five-speed transmission unit and selector mechanism (Sec 1)

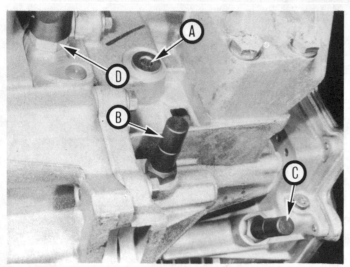

2.2 Filler/level plug position (A) – five-speed transmission shown
Also shown are the lock cap positions for the 1st/4th/reverse (B) and 5th (C) gear selector shaft mechanisms, and the reversing light switch (D)

2 Manual transmission – maintenance

1 The only maintenance required is to check and top up, if necessary, the oil level in the transmission at the intervals specified in Routine Maintenance at the beginning of this manual.

2 A combined level/filler plug is fitted and the correct oil level is established when the oil is 5.0 mm below the bottom edge of the plug hole when the vehicle is on level ground (photo).
3 Regular oil changing is not specified by the manufacturers, but the oil can be drained if necessary (prior to removal of the unit or after transversing a flooded road for example) by removing the selector shaft locking mechanism (Fig. 6.3).

3 Gearchange mechanism – adjustment

1 This is not a routine operation and will normally only be required after dismantling, to compensate for wear or to overcome any 'notchiness' evident during gear selection.
2 To set the linkage correctly, refer to Chapter 1, Section 24.

4 Gearchange mechanism (four-speed transmission) – removal, overhaul and refitting

1 Before commencing removal operations, engage 4th gear.
2 Unscrew the gear lever knob, slide the rubber gaiter up to the lever and remove it.
3 If the vehicle is not over an inspection pit, jack it up and fit axle stands.
4 Unhook the tension spring which runs between the gearchange rod and the side-member.
5 Slacken the clamp bolt and pull the gearchange rod from the selector shaft which projects from the transmission.
6 Unbolt the end of the stabiliser from the transmission housing. Note the washer between the stabiliser trunnion and the transmission.
7 Still working under the vehicle, unbolt the gearchange housing from the floor. Withdraw the housing/stabiliser from the vehicle.
8 To dismantle, unbolt the housing from the stabiliser and detach

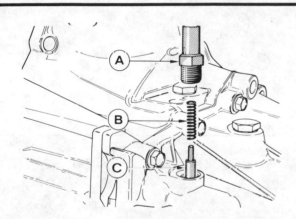

Fig. 6.3 Selector shaft cap nut (A), spring (B) and interlock pin (C) (Secs 2 and 5)

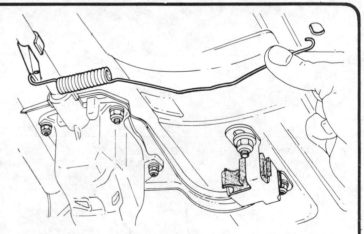

Fig. 6.4 Gearchange rod tension spring (Secs 4 and 5)

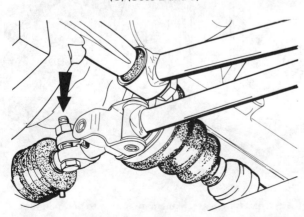

Fig. 6.5 Gearchange rod clamp bolt – arrowed (Secs 4 and 5)

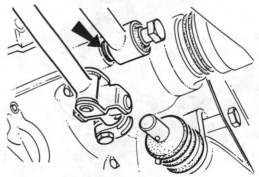

Fig. 6.6 Gearchange rod and stabiliser bar disconnected (Secs 4 and 5)

Note washer (arrowed)

the gearchange lever with plastic cover and the stabiliser from the slide block.

9   Detach the gearchange rod from the slide block. This is done by unclipping the upper guide shell and withdrawing the rod.

10 The gear lever can be removed by prising off the rubber spring retaining clip and withdrawing the spring, and plastic cover.

11 Renew any worn components and reassemble by reversing the dismantling procedure, but observe the following points.

12 Make sure that the cut-out at the edge of the plastic cover is aligned with the curve in the gearchange lever as shown (Fig. 6.8).

13 The gear lever must locate in the shift rod cut-out.

14 To install the gearchange mechanism to the vehicle, offer it up from below and loosely attach it to the floorpan.

15 Reconnect the stabiliser to the gearbox, remembering to fit the washer between the trunnion and the gearbox.

16 The mechanism should now be secured to the floor pan by tightening the nuts to the specified torque.

17 Reconnect the gearchange rod to the shaft at the gearbox, as described in Chapter 1, Section 24.

18 Working inside the vehicle, refit the gaiter and the knob to the gear lever.

19 Lower the vehicle to the ground.

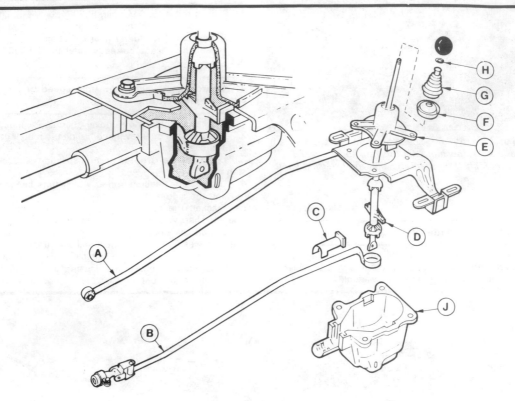

Fig. 6.7 Gearchange mechanism components (four-speed) (Sec 4)

A	Stabiliser	D	Gear lever	F	Spring carrier	H	Circlip
B	Gearchange rod	E	Housing	G	Rubber spring	J	Slide block
C	Guide shell						

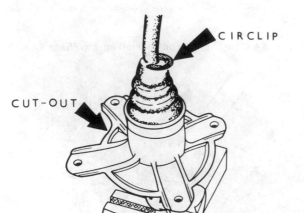

Fig. 6.8 Circlip location and cut-out section of cover (Sec 4)

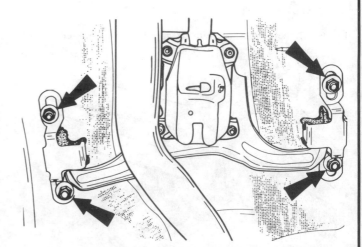

Fig. 6.9 Gearchange mechanism mounting to floorpan (Sec 4)

5 Manual transmission – removal and refitting

1 Disconnect the battery earth lead connector.
2 To ensure correct engagement of the selector mechanism during later operations, engage 4th gear on four-speed models or reverse gear on five-speed models.
3 Support the weight of the engine either by using a jack and block of wood under the sump or by attaching a hoist (refer to Chapter 1, Section 11).
4 Disconnect the speedometer cable from the transmission after unscrewing the retaining nut (photo).

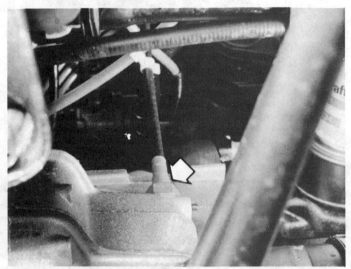

5.4 Speedometer cable to engine connection viewed from underneath (five-speed transmission shown)

5 Unhook the clutch cable from the release lever, as described in Chapter 5.
6 Unscrew and remove the top four bolts which hold the gearbox flange to the engine.
7 Release the gearbox breather tube from the side rail.
8 Move the heater hose which runs between the thermostat housing and the heater to one side of the engine compartment and retain it with a piece of wire. This will prevent it obstructing the transmission during removal.
9 If the vehicle is not over an inspection pit, raise its front end and fit axle stands.
10 Working under the vehicle, disconnect the leads from the starter motor and the reversing lamp switch.
11 Unbolt and remove the starter motor.
12 Unbolt and remove the cover plate from the lower face of the clutch housing.
13 Disconnect the gearchange rod from the gearbox selector shaft by releasing the clamp pinch-bolt and pulling the rod towards the rear of the vehicle. On four-speed models, unhook the tension spring from the gearchange rod (Figs. 6.4 and 6.5).
14 Unbolt the stabiliser rod from the side of the transmission, noting that there is a washer between the trunnion of the rod and the transmission casing (Fig. 6.6).
15 Tie the gearchange rod and the stabiliser rod to the steering rack using a piece of wire.
16 Drain the oil from the transmission into a suitable container. As a drain plug is not fitted, unscrew the selector shaft locking assembly which includes the nut, cap, spring and interlock pin (Fig. 6.3).
17 Unscrew and remove the balljoint retaining bolt from the outboard end of the right-hand suspension arm. The bolt is of Torx type, having a socket head, and in the absence of the correct tool, an Allen key may be used to stop the bolt turning while the nut is unscrewed. Unbolt and detach the suspension arm from its body mounting.
18 Disconnect the right-hand driveshaft from the transmission. Do this by inserting a lever between the constant velocity joint and the transmission. With an assistant pulling the roadwheel outwards, strike the end of the lever to release the joint from the differential. In order

to prevent the differential pinions from turning and obstructing the driveshaft holes, insert a plastic plug or similar. Refer to Chapter 7 for full details.
19 Tie up the disconnected driveshaft to avoid putting any strain on the joints. The maximum permissible angles to which the joints may be bent without straining them is 20° for the inner joint and 45° for the outer joint.
20 Disconnect the suspension arm and the driveshaft from the left-hand side in a similar manner.
21 Check that the engine/transmission is still securely supported and unbolt the front left-hand mounting from the transmission.
22 Unscrew and remove the centre bolt from the mounting flexible component.
23 Unscrew and remove the centre nut from the left-hand rear mounting and then remove the three bolts which hold the mounting bearer plate.
24 Unscrew and remove the two remaining bolts from the lower part of the clutch housing/engine flange.
25 Detach the anti-roll bar from the crossmember on the left-hand side.
26 With the engine securely supported, withdraw the transmission towards the side of the engine compartment until the input shaft clears the clutch driven plate splined hub and then lower the transmission and remove it from under the vehicle.
27 Before refitting the transmission, lightly smear the splined part of the input shaft with a little grease, also the thrust bearing guide sleeve.
28 If the clutch has been dismantled, make sure that the driven plate has been centralised, as described in Chapter 5.
29 Check that the engine adaptor plate is correctly located on its dowels (Fig. 6.11).

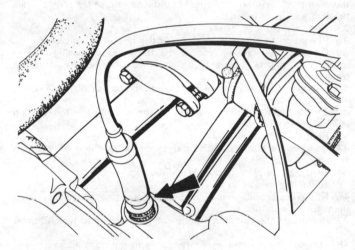

Fig. 6.10 Speedometer drive cable connection to gearbox housing (Sec 5)

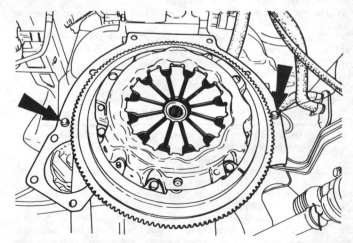

Fig. 6.11 Position engine adaptor plate on dowels – arrowed (Sec 5)

30 With the transmission positioned on the floor below the vehicle, lift it up and engage the input shaft in the splined hub of the clutch driven plate. Obtain the help of an assistant for this work as the weight of the gearbox must not hang upon the input shaft while it is engaged in the driven plate.

31 Push the transmission into full engagement with the engine and check that the unit sits on its locating dowels and that the adaptor plate has not been displaced. Any reluctance for the transmission to mate with the engine may be due to the splines of the input shaft and clutch driven plate not engaging. Try swivelling the transmission slightly, or have your assistant rotate the crankshaft by applying a spanner to the crankshaft pulley bolt.

32 Once the transmission is fully engaged, screw in the two lower retaining bolts to hold it to the engine.

33 Refit the front and rear mountings to the transmission and to the body side member. Refit the anti-roll bar left-hand mounting. Remove the engine hoist or support device.

34 Insert the selector shaft interlock pin, spring and cap bolt, having smeared the threads of the bolt with jointing compound.

35 Remove the temporary plastic plugs used to prevent displacement of the pinion gears in the differential. If plugs were not used, insert the finger into each driveshaft hole and align the pinion gear splined hole ready to accept the driveshaft. A mirror will assist in correct alignment (photo).

36 Fit a new snap-ring to the splined end of the left-hand driveshaft and insert the shaft into the transmission. Turn the shaft as necessary to engage the splines with those on the pinion gear. Once engaged, have an assistant push hard on the roadwheel until the snap-ring engages, with the shaft fully home. Any reluctance to engage may be due to the driveshaft not being in a sufficiently horizontal attitude. In this event, remove the roadwheel in order to reduce the weight while the hub assembly is lifted.

37 Reconnect the suspension track control arm

38 Repeat all the operations and refit the right-hand driveshaft.

39 Connect the stabiliser rod to the transmission making sure to insert the washer between the trunnion of the rod and the transmission casing.

40 Reconnect and adjust the gearchange rod as described in Chapter 1, Section 24.

41 On four-speed models reconnect the gearchange rod tension spring.

42 Refit the starter motor.

43 Connect the leads to the starter motor and to the reversing lamp switch.

44 Fit the cover plate to the clutch housing.

45 Lower the vehicle to the ground.

46 Fit the upper bolts to the clutch housing/engine flange and tighten them to the specified torque.

47 Reconnect the clutch operating cable according to type (Chapter 5).

48 Connect the speedometer drive cable to the transmission.

49 Fill the unit with the correct quantity and grade of oil (refer to Section 2).

50 Reconnect the battery earth lead.

51 Locate the transmission breather hose in the aperture in the longitudinal member.

52 Check the selection of all gears, and check the torque wrench settings of all nuts and bolts which were removed now that the weight of the vehicle is again on the roadwheels.

6   Manual transmission – removal of major assemblies

1   With the gearbox removed from the vehicle, clean away external dirt and grease using paraffin and a stiff brush or a water-soluble solvent. Take care not to allow water to enter the transmission.

2   Unscrew the lockbolt which holds the clutch release fork to the shaft and remove the shaft, followed by the fork and release bearing.

3   If not removed for draining, unscrew the selector shaft cap nut, spring and interlock pin.

4   Unbolt and remove the transmission housing cover.

5   Remove the snap-rings from the main and input shaft bearings.

6   Unscrew and remove the connecting bolts and lift the smaller housing from the transmission. If it is stuck, tap it off carefully with a plastic-headed mallet.

5.35 Pinion gear displaced in differential

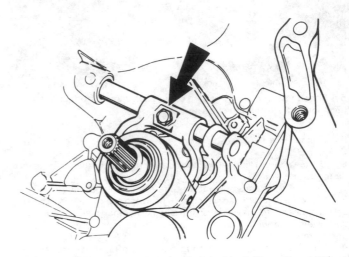

Fig. 6.12 Clutch release bearing fork lockbolt (Secs 6 and 16)

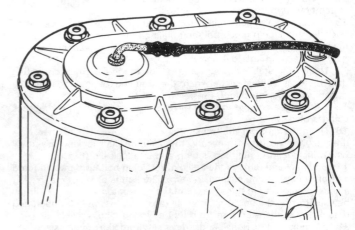

Fig. 6.13 Transmission cover plate (Sec 6)

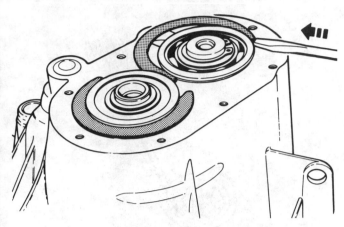

Fig. 6.14 Main and input shaft bearing snap-ring removal

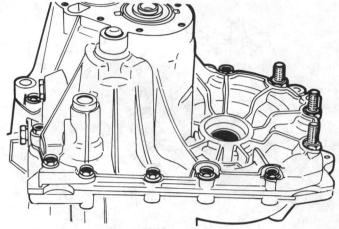

Fig. 6.15 Smaller transmission housing section (Sec 6)

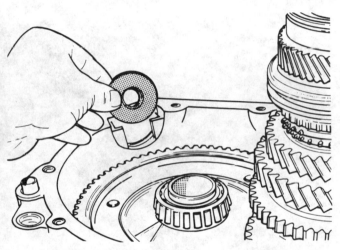

Fig. 6.16 Remove the magnetic swarf collector (Sec 6)

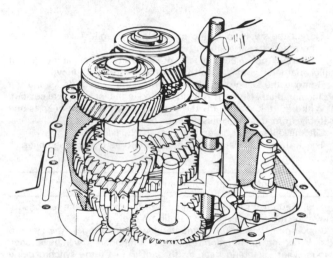

Fig. 6.17 Withdraw the selector shaft (Sec 6)

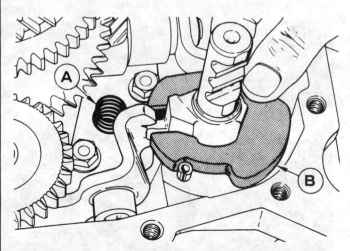

Fig. 6.18 Selector shaft coil spring (A) and shift lockplate (B)
(Sec 6)

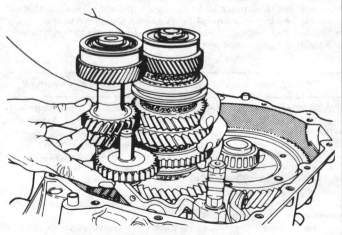

Fig. 6.19 Withdrawing the gear trains (Sec 6)

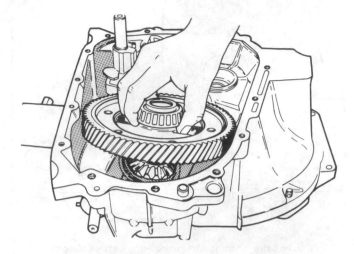

Fig. 6.20 Withdrawing the differential unit (Sec 6)

Fig. 6.21 Breaking the mainshaft bearing plastic cage (Sec 8)

7   Extract the swarf collecting magnet and clean it. Take care not to drop the magnet or it will shatter.
8   Withdraw the selector shaft, noting that the longer portion of smaller diameter is at the bottom as the shaft is withdrawn.
9   Remove the selector shaft coil spring, the selector forks and the shift locking plate. Note the roll pin located in the locking plate cut-out.
10 Withdraw the mainshaft, the input shaft and reverse gear as one assembly from the transmission housing.
11 Lift the differential assembly from the housing.
12 The transmission is now dismantled into its major assemblies.

7   Manual transmission – dismantling (general)

1   The need for further dismantling will depend upon the reasons for removal of the transmission in the first place.
2   A common reason for dismantling will be to renew the synchro units. Wear or malfunction in these components will have been obvious when changing gear by the noise, or by the synchro being easily beaten.
3   The renewal of oil seals may be required as evident by pools of oil under the vehicle when stationary.
4   Jumping out of gear may mean renewal of the selector mechanism, forks or synchro sleeves.
5   General noise during operation on the road may be due to worn bearings, shafts or gears and when such general wear occurs, it will probably be more economical to renew the transmission complete.
6   When dismantling the geartrains, always keep the components strictly in their originally installed order.

8.3A Transmission housing oil seal location

8   Transmission housing and selector mechanism – overhaul

1   To remove the mainshaft bearing, break the plastic roller cage with a screwdriver. Extract the rollers and the cage, the oil slinger and retainers. Remove the bearing outer track.
2   When fitting the new bearing, also renew the oil slinger.
3   When renewing the input shaft oil seal, drive the oil seal out by applying the drift inside the bellhousing (photos).
4   The constant velocity (CV) joint oil seals should be renewed at time of major overhaul.
5   The differential bearing tracks can be removed, using a drift inserted from the large housing section.
6   The differential bearing outer track and the diaphragm adjustment springs can be driven out of the smaller housing section using a suitable drift such as a piece of tubing.
7   Refit the input shaft oil seal so that its lips are as shown (Fig. 6.23). Apply grease to all the oil seal lips and check that the lip retaining spring has not been displaced during installation of the seal.
8   When installing the differential diaphragm springs and bearing

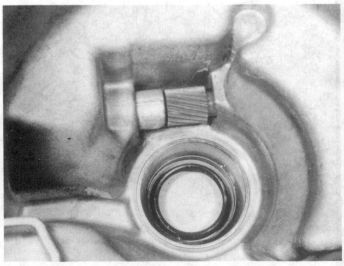

8.3B Transmission housing oil seal and speedometer driven gear

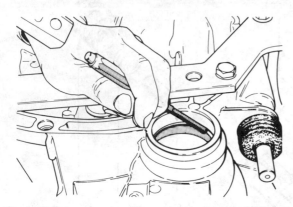

Fig. 6.22 Removing the differential bearing track (Sec 8)

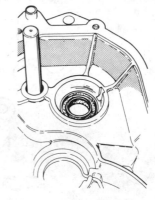

Fig. 6.23 Input shaft oil seal correctly installed (Sec 8)

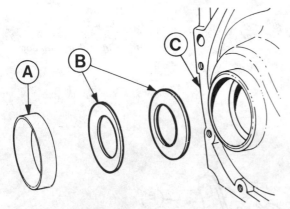

Fig. 6.24 Differential bearing preload diaphragm springs (Sec 8)

A   Bearing track   C   Small housing section
B   Diaphragm springs

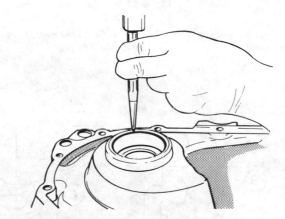

Fig. 6.25 Staking the differential bearing track in the small housing section (Sec 8)

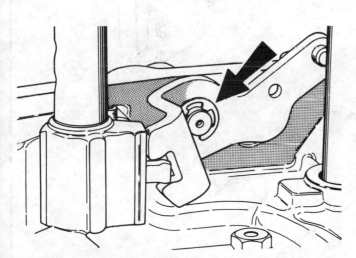

Fig. 6.26 Reverse selector lever retaining clip (arrowed) (Sec 8)

8.9 Selector mechanism (four-speed transmission)

track to the smaller housing section, note that the spring convex faces are towards each other. Stake the track with a light blow from a punch. This is only to hold the track during assembly of the remainder of the transmission.

9   If the selector mechanism is worn, sloppy or damaged, dismantle it by extracting the circlip and taking off the reverse selector lever (photo).

10   Remove the guide lever retaining plate and the guide shaft. Two bolts hold these components in place.

11   Extract the two circlips and detach the guide lever from the retaining plate.

12   To remove the main selector shaft, pull the rubber gaiter up the shaft and then extract the single socket screw which secures the selector dog. Withdraw the shaft.

13   The selector shaft plastic bushes and oil seal should be renewed.

14   Reassembly is a reversal of dismantling, but when fitting the rubber gaiter make sure that its drain tube will point downwards when installed in the vehicle. Use new circlips at reassembly.

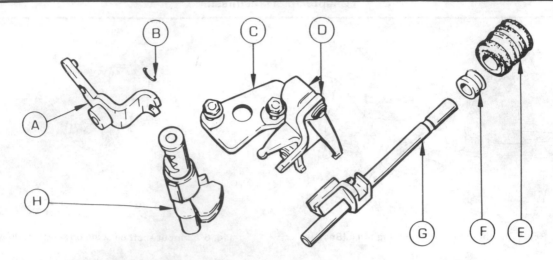

Fig. 6.27 Exploded view of the four-speed gearbox selector mechanism (Sec 8)

A	Reverse selector lever	C	Guide lever retaining plate
B	Circlip	D	Guide levers
		E	Flexible gaiter

F	Oil seal
G	Selector shaft with dog
H	Guide shaft with dog

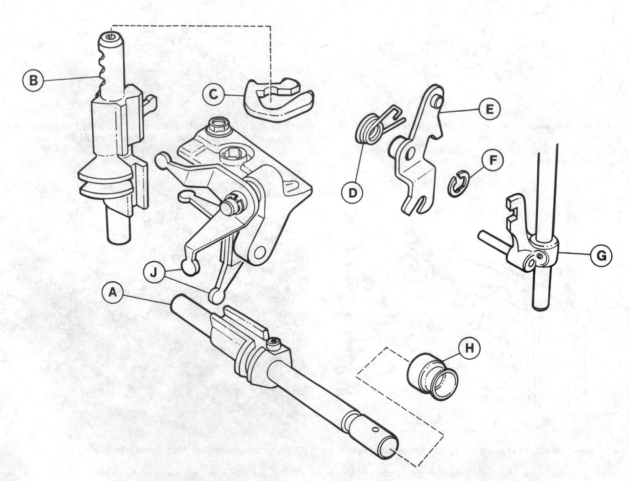

Fig. 6.28 Exploded view of the five-speed gearbox selector mechanism (Sec 8)

A	Main selector shaft (with selector block)	D	Spring – reverse gear selector lever
B	Guide shaft	E	Reverse gear selector lever
C	Shift locking plate		

F	Circlip
G	Reverse and 5th gear shift rod
H	Oil seal
J	Retaining plate (with guide levers)

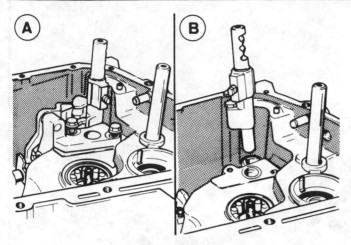

Fig. 6.29 Selector mechanism dismantling (Sec 8)

A   Retaining plate removal   B   Guide shaft removal

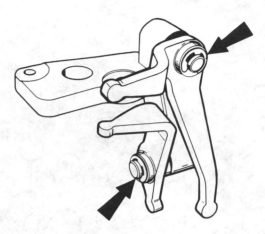

Fig. 6.30 Guide lever retaining circlips – arrowed (Sec 8)

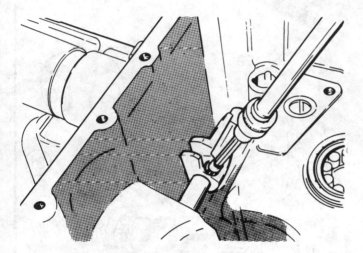

Fig. 6.31 Extracting the lockscrew securing the dog to the selector shaft (Sec 8)

9 Mainshaft – overhaul

Dismantling

1   Extract the circlip which holds the bearing to the shaft.
2   Using a puller, engaged behind 4th speed gear, draw off the gear and the bearing from the end of the mainshaft (photo).
3   Discard the bearing.
4   Extract the circlip and remove the 3rd/4th synchro with 3rd gear, using hand pressure only.
5   Remove the anchor ring and the two thrust semi-circular segments, then take 2nd gear from the mainshaft.
6   Extract the circlip and take off 1st/2nd synchro unit with 1st gear.
7   The mainshaft is now completely dismantled (photo). Do not attempt to remove the drive pinion gear.

Synchronisers

8   The synchro units can be dismantled and new components fitted after extracting the circular retaining springs.
9   When reassembling the hub and sleeve, align them so that the cut-outs in the components are in alignment, ready to receive the sliding keys.
10   The two springs should have their hooked ends engaged in the

9.2 4th gear and bearing removal from mainshaft (four-speed transmission)

9.7 Mainshaft stripped (four-speed transmission)

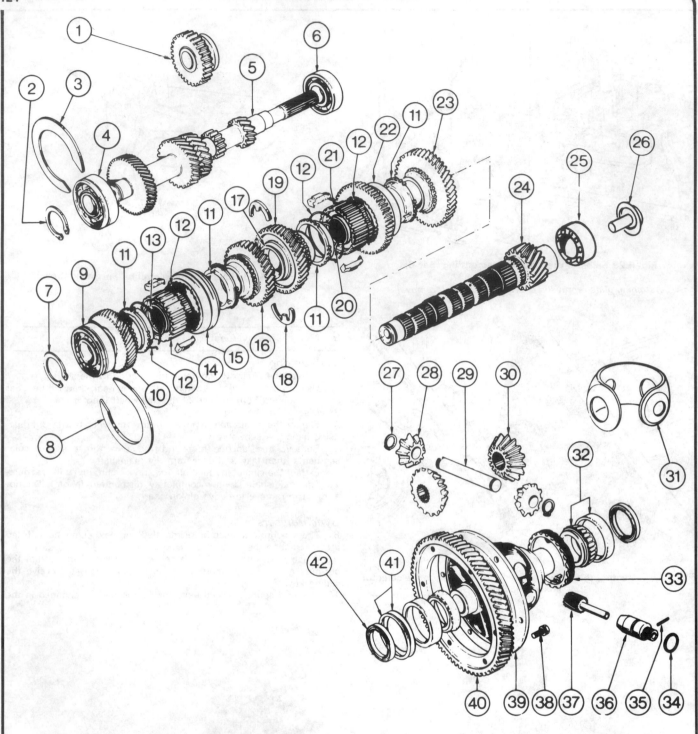

Fig. 6.32 Transmission gear assemblies and associate components (four-speed transmission) (Sec 9)

1 Reverse idler gear	12 Spring	22 1st/2nd synchro sleeve	32 Tapered roller bearing
2 Circlip	13 Circlip	with reverse gear	33 Speedometer drivegear
3 Bearing snap-ring	14 3rd/4th synchro	23 1st gear	34 O-ring
4 Bearing	15 Synchro sleeve	24 Mainshaft	35 Roll pin
5 Input shaft	16 3rd gear	25 Bearing	36 Speedo drive pinion
6 Bearing	17 Segment anchor ring	26 Oil slinger	bearing
7 Circlip	18 Semi-circular thrust	27 Circlip	37 Speedo drive pinion
8 Bearing snap-ring	segment	28 Differential pinion	38 Crownwheel bolts
9 Bearing	19 2nd speed gear	29 Differential shaft	39 Differential case
10 4th gear	20 Circlip	30 Pinion gear (driveshaft)	40 Crownwheel
11 Baulk ring	21 1st/2nd synchro-hub	31 Thrust cage	41 Diaphragm springs
			42 Oil seal

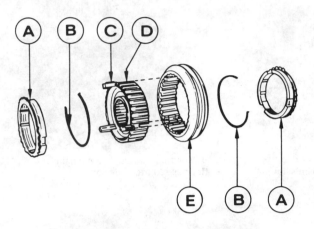

Fig. 6.33 Synchroniser dismantled (Sec 9)

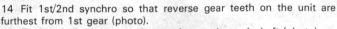

Fig. 6.34 Fitting direction of synchro ring springs (Sec 9)

A Baulk ring
B Key retaining spring
C Sliding key
D Hub
E Sleeve

same sliding key, but must run in opposing directions as shown in Fig. 6.34.

11 The baulk rings should be renewed if they do not 'stick' when pressed and turned onto the gear covers, or if a clearance no longer exists between the baulk ring and the gear when pressed onto its cone.

Reassembly

12 With all worn or damaged components renewed, commence reassembly by oiling the shaft and then sliding 1st gear onto the shaft so that the gear teeth are next to the pinion drivegear (photo).

13 Fit 1st/2nd synchro baulk ring (photo).

14 Fit 1st/2nd synchro so that reverse gear teeth on the unit are furthest from 1st gear (photo).

15 Fit the circlip to secure the synchro to the mainshaft (photo).

16 Slide on the synchro baulk ring (photo).

17 Slide on 2nd speed gear (photo).

18 Fit 2nd gear so that the cone is towards the baulk ring.

19 Fit the thrust semi-circular segments and their anchor ring (photos).

20 To the shaft fit 3rd gear so that its teeth are towards 2nd gear (photo).

21 Fit the baulk ring (photo).

9.12 Fitting 1st gear to mainshaft (four-speed transmission)

9.13 Fitting 1st/2nd baulk ring (four-speed transmission)

9.14 Fitting 1st/2nd synchro with reverse gear (four-speed transmission)

9.15 Fitting synchro securing circlip to mainshaft (four-speed transmission)

9.16 Fitting 1st/2nd synchro baulk ring (four-speed transmission)

9.17 Fitting 2nd gear to mainshaft (four-speed transmission)

9.19A Thrust segments installed (four-speed transmission)

9.19B Thrust segment anchor ring installation (four-speed transmission)

9.20 Fitting 3rd gear to mainshaft (four-speed transmission)

9.21 Fitting 3rd/4th synchro baulk ring (four-speed transmission)

9.22 Fitting 3rd/4th synchro to mainshaft (four-speed transmission) *Note that serrated edge is downwards*

9.23 Securing 3rd/4th synchro with circlip (four-speed transmission)

9.24 Fitting last (4th) synchro baulk ring to the mainshaft (four-speed transmission)

9.25 Fitting 4th gear to the mainshaft (four-speed transmission)

9.26A Locate the mainshaft bearing (four-speed transmission)

9.26B Using tube to drive on mainshaft bearing (four-speed transmission)

9.27A Fitting mainshaft bearing circlip (four-speed transmission)

9.27B Mainshaft fully assembled (four-speed transmission)

22 Slide on 3rd/4th synchro so that its serrated edge is towards the shaft drive pinion gear (photo).
23 Secure the synchro to the mainshaft with the circlip (photo).
24 Fit the baulk ring (photo).
25 Fit 4th gear (photo).
26 Fit the bearing so that its circlip groove is nearer the end of the shaft. Apply pressure only to the bearing centre track, using a press or a hammer and a piece of suitable diameter tubing (photos).
27 Fit the circlip to secure the bearing to the shaft. The mainshaft is now fully assembled (photos).

10 Input shaft – overhaul

1 The only components which can be renewed are the two ball-bearing races (photo).
2 Remove the securing circlip from the larger one and extract both bearings with a two-legged extractor or a press (photos).
3 When fitting the new bearings, apply pressure to the centre track only, using a press or a piece of suitable diameter tubing and a hammer. When installing the larger bearing, make sure that the circlip groove is nearer the end of the shaft.

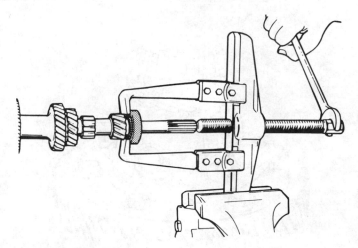

Fig. 6.35 Input shaft small bearing removal (Sec 10)

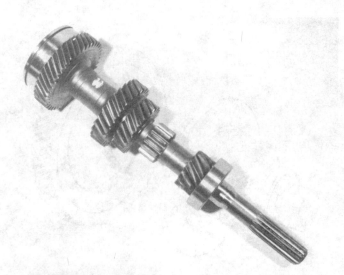

10.1 Input shaft (four-speed transmission)

10.2A Input shaft large bearing and retaining circlip (four-speed transmission)

10.2B Input shaft smaller bearing (four-speed transmission)

11 Differential – overhaul

1 With the differential removed from the transmission housing, twist both drive pinions out of the differential case.
2 Extract one of the circlips from the end of the differential shaft, press the shaft out of the differential case and extract the pinions and the cage.
3 The differential tapered roller bearings can be drawn off using a two-legged extractor.
4 The crownwheel can be separated from the differential case after removing the six securing bolts. Tap the components apart, using a plastic mallet.
5 If the crownwheel is to be renewed, then the gearbox mainshaft should be renewed at the same time, as the gear teeth are matched and renewal of only one component will give rise to an increase in noise during operation on the road.
6 Reassembly is a reversal of dismantling, but make sure that the deeply chamfered edge of the inside diameter is against the differential case. Tighten all bolts to the specified torque.
7 The pinion gears should be held in position by inserting plastic plugs or similar so that they will be in correct alignment for eventual installation of the driveshafts, refer to Section 5 of this Chapter.

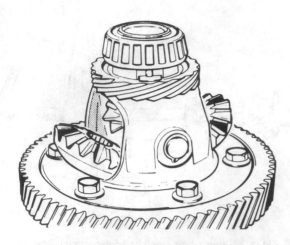

Fig. 6.36 Sliding drive pinions from the differential unit (Sec 11)

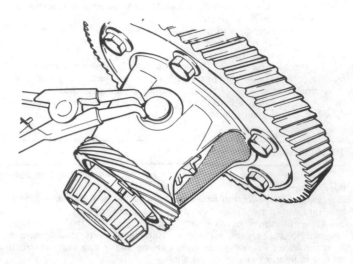

Fig. 6.37 Differential shaft circlip removal (Sec 11)

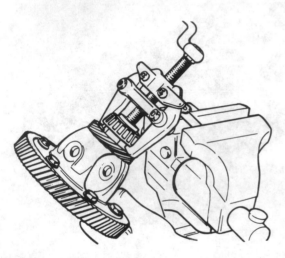

Fig. 6.38 Differential bearing removal (Sec 11)

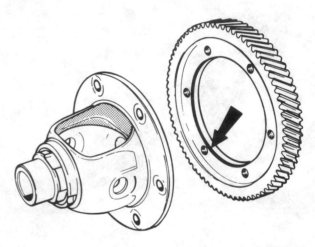

Fig. 6.39 Crownwheel chamfered edge – arrowed (Sec 11)

12 Four-speed manual transmission – reassembly

1   With the larger housing section on the bench, lubricate the differential bearings with gear oil and insert the differential assembly into the housing (photos).
2   Slide reverse idler gear onto its shaft, at the same time engaging the selector lever in the groove of the gear which should be pointing downwards (photo).
3   In order to make installation of the mainshaft and input shaft easier, lift the reverse idler gear so that its selector lever is held by the reversing lamp switch spring-loaded ball (photo).
4   Mesh the gears of the mainshaft and the input shaft and install both geartrains into the transmission housing simultaneously (photo).
5   Lower the reverse idler gear and its selector lever.
6   Fit the shift locking plate (photo).
7   Engage 1st/2nd selector fork with the groove in the mainshaft synchro sleeve. This fork has the shorter actuating lever (photo).
8   Engage 3rd/4th selector fork with the groove in its synchro sleeve. Make sure that the end of this fork actuating lever is engaged with the shift locking plate (photo).
9   Insert the coil spring in the selector shaft hole and pass the shaft downwards through the holes in the forks, make sure that the longer section of the reduced diameter of the rod is pointing downwards (photos).
10 Actuate the appropriate selector fork to engage 4th gear. Do this by inserting a rod in the hole in the end of the selector shaft which

projects from the transmission casing and turning the shaft fully clockwise to its stop, then pushing the shaft inwards (photo).
11 Insert the magnetic swarf collector in its recess, taking care not to drop it (photo).
12 Locate a new gasket on the housing flange, install the smaller housing section and screw in and tighten the bolts to the specified torque (photos).
13 Fit the snap-rings to the ends of the main and input shafts. Cutouts are provided in the casing so that the bearings can be levered upwards to expose the snap-ring grooves (photos). Snap-rings are available in three thicknesses and the thickest possible ring should be used which will fit into the groove. If any difficulty is experienced in levering up the bearing on the input shaft, push the end of the shaft from within the bellhousing.
14 Tap the snap-rings to rotate them so that they will locate correctly in the cut-outs in the cover gasket which should now be positioned on the end of the housing (photo). Fit a new gasket.
15 Fit the cover plate, screw in the bolts and tighten them to the specified torque (photos).
16 Fit the interlock pin, spring and cap nut for the selector shaft locking mechanism. The threads should be coated with jointing compound before installation.
17 Refit the clutch release shaft, lever and bearing into the bellhousing (photos).
18 The transmission is now ready for installation in the vehicle. Wait until it is installed before filling with oil.

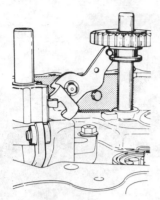

Fig. 6.40 Reverse selector lever supported on reversing lamp switch plunger ball (Sec 12)

12.1A Interior of transmission larger housing (four-speed transmission)

12.1B Fitting the differential (four-speed transmission)

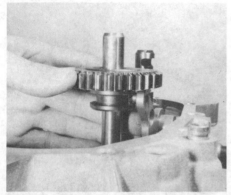

12.2 Fitting reverse idler gear (four-speed transmission)

12.3 Reverse idler gear supported in raised position (four-speed transmission)

12.4 Installing the geartrains (four-speed transmission)

12.6 Fitting shift locking plate (four-speed transmission)

12.7 Fitting 1st/2nd selector fork (four-speed transmission)

12.8 Fitting 3rd/4th selector fork (four-speed transmission)

12.9A Inserting selector shaft coil springs (four-speed transmission)

12.9B Fitting the selector shaft (four-speed transmission)

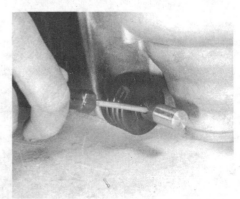

12.10 Turning the selector shaft to stop (four-speed transmission)

12.11 Magnetic swarf collector (four-speed transmission)

12.12A Locate the housing flange gasket (four-speed transmission)

12.12B Fit the transmission smaller housing (four-speed transmission)

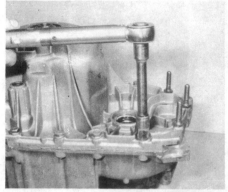

12.12C Tighten the housing connecting bolts (four-speed transmission)

12.13A Raising bearing for snap-ring installation (four-speed transmission)

12.13B Fitting bearing snap-ring (four-speed transmission)

12.14 Bearing snap-rings and gasket in position (four-speed transmission)

12.15A Fitting transmission cover plate and gasket (four-speed transmission)

12.15B Tightening cover plate bolts (four-speed transmission) – note breather tube

12.17A Inserting clutch release shaft

12.17B Tightening clutch release fork bolt

13 Speedometer driven gear – removal and refitting

1   This work may be done without having to remove the transmission from the vehicle.
2   Using a pair of side cutting pliers, lever out the roll pin which secures the speedometer drive pinion bearing in the transmission housing.
3   Withdraw the pinion bearing, together with the speedometer drive cable. Separate the cable from the pinion by unscrewing the knurled ring or nut.
4   Slide the pinion out of the bearing.

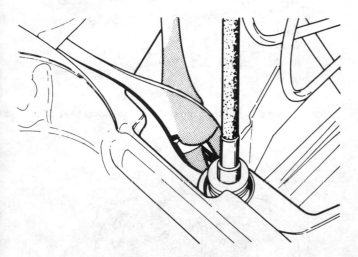

Fig. 6.41 Extracting speedometer pinion retaining roll pin (Sec 13)

5   Always renew the O-ring on the pinion bearing before refitting.
6   Insert the pinion and bearing into the transmission housing using a back-and-forth twisting motion to mesh the pinion teeth with those of the drivegear. Secure with the roll pin.
7   Reconnect the speedometer cable.

14 Five-speed manual transmission – general

As mentioned in the introduction of this Chapter, the five-speed transmission is virtually the same as the four-speed type, the main differences being the additional gear and synchro-hub and a modified selector mechanism.

The overhaul procedures described previously for the four-speed gearbox are therefore also applicable to the five-speed unit, the exceptions being described in the following Sections.

It is important to note that during the assembly of the five-speed transmission the sub-assembly components should be lubricated with grease, as given in the Specifications.

When referring to previous Sections for overhaul procedures, it should be noted that all photos, except where indicated, are of the four-speed transmission. Due to the close resemblance of the two transmissions, the photos shown can also be used in most instances for pictorial guidance when working on the five-speed transmission.

15 Gearchange mechanism (five-speed transmission) – removal, overhaul and refitting

1   Proceed as described in paragraphs 1, 2 and 3 of Section 4, but engage reverse gear instead of 4th.
2   Disconnect the exhaust pipe from the rubber mountings at the rear.
3   Proceed as given in paragraphs 5, 6 and 7 of Section 4.
4   To dismantle, unscrew and remove the three guide element spring

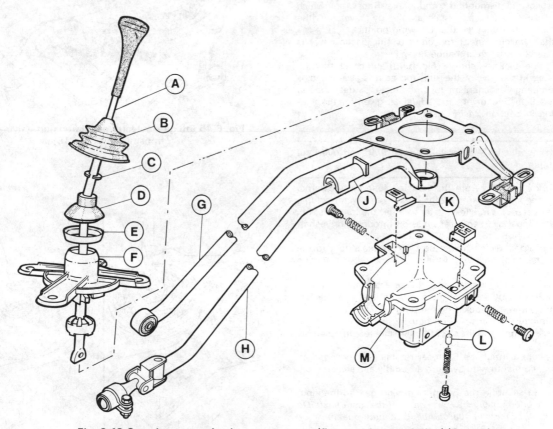

Fig. 6.42 Gearchange mechanism components (five-speed transmission) (Sec 15)

A Gear lever	D Rubber spring	G Stabiliser	K Guide elements
B Gaiter	E Spring carrier	H Shift rod	L Locking pin
C Circlip	F Housing cover	J Guide shell	M Selector housing

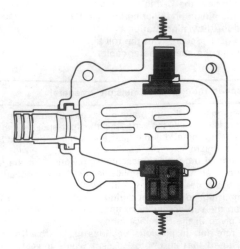

Fig. 6.43 Refit the guides and springs (Sec 15)

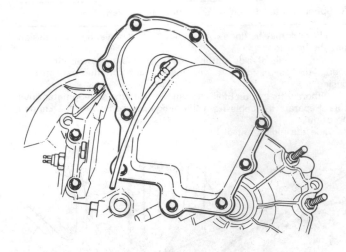

Fig. 6.44 Five-speed transmission housing cover (Sec 16)

retaining screws, one from each side of the selector housing, and one underneath (which also holds a lockpin). Extract the three springs and the lockpin.

5   Unscrew and remove the four selector housing-to-stabiliser/mounting frame and gear lever housing cover bolts. Lift the gearlever and cover away.

6   Unclip the upper guide shell and lift the shift rod out of the selector housing.

7   To dismantle the gear lever prise off the rubber spring securing ring using a screwdriver and withdraw the rubber spring, the spring carrier and the housing cover.

8   Clean and inspect the dismantled components. Renew any which show signs of excessive wear. Reassemble by reversing the dismantling procedure, but observe the following points.

9   Make sure that the cut-out at the edge of the plastic cover is aligned with the curve in the gearchange lever.

10 Position the guide shells as shown (Fig. 6.43) and check that the gear lever is located in the ring of the shift rod as it is assembled.

11 Refit the gearchange mechanism to the vehicle, as described in paragraphs 14 to 19 in Section 4, and adjust as given for the five-speed transmission in Section 24 in Chapter 1.

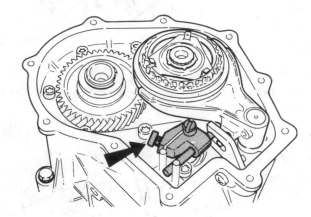

Fig. 6.45 5th gear selector pin clamp bolt – five-speed transmission (Sec 16)

16 Five-speed transmission – removal, dismantling and overhaul of major assemblies

1   With the gearbox removed from the vehicle, clean away external dirt and grease using paraffin and a stiff brush, or a water-soluble grease solvent. Take care not to allow water to enter the transmission.

2   Drain off any residual oil in the transmission through a driveshaft opening.

3   Unscrew the lockbolt which holds the clutch release fork to the shaft and remove the shaft, followed by the fork and release bearing (see Fig. 6.12).

4   If not removed for draining, unscrew the selector shaft cap nut, spring and interlock pin. Now remove the additional 5th gear selector shaft cap nut, spring and interlock pin (see photo 2.2).

5   Unbolt and remove the transmission housing cover.

6   Unscrew the clamp bolt and lift the 5th gear selector pin assembly off the shift rod.

7   Using circlip pliers, extract the 5th gear retaining snap-ring, then lift off the 5th gear, complete with synchro assembly and selector fork from the mainshaft.

8   Extract the circlip securing the 5th gear driving gear to the input shaft. Using a two-legged puller, draw the gear off the input shaft. *Do not re-use the old circlip when reassembling; a new one must be obtained.*

9   Unscrew the nine socket-headed bolts securing the 5th gear casing to the main casing and carefully lift it off.

10 Remove the snap-rings from the main and input shaft bearings.

11 Unscrew and remove the connecting bolts and gearbox mounting

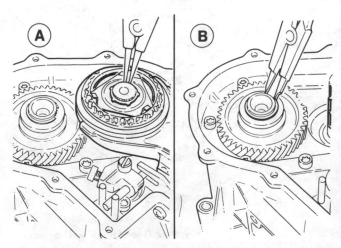

Fig. 6.46 5th gear retaining snap-ring (A) and input shaft circlip (B) locations – five-speed transmission (Sec 16)

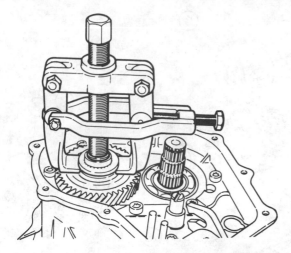

Fig. 6.47 Removal of 5th gear from input shaft with puller –
five-speed transmission (Sec 16)

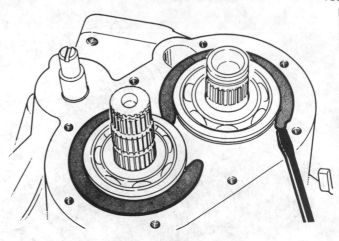

Fig. 6.48 Bearing snap-ring removal – five-speed transmission
(Sec 16)

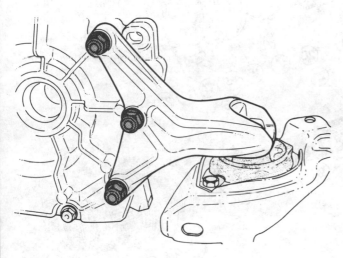

Fig. 6.49 Gearbox mounting retaining bolt locations – five-
speed transmission (Sec 16)

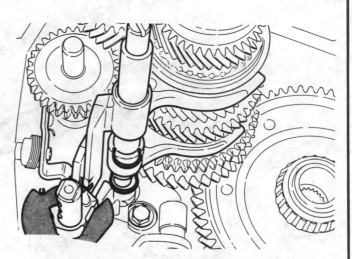

Fig. 6.50 Selector shaft guide sleeve and 1st/2nd gear selector
fork circlip locations – five-speed transmission (Sec 16)

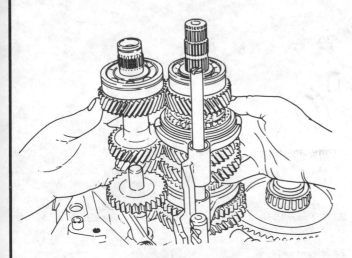

Fig. 6.51 Removal of mainshaft and input shaft as a complete
assembly – five-speed transmission (Sec 16)

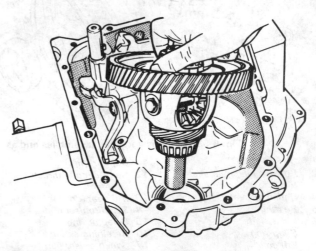

Fig. 6.52 Differential unit removal – five-speed transmission
(Sec 16)

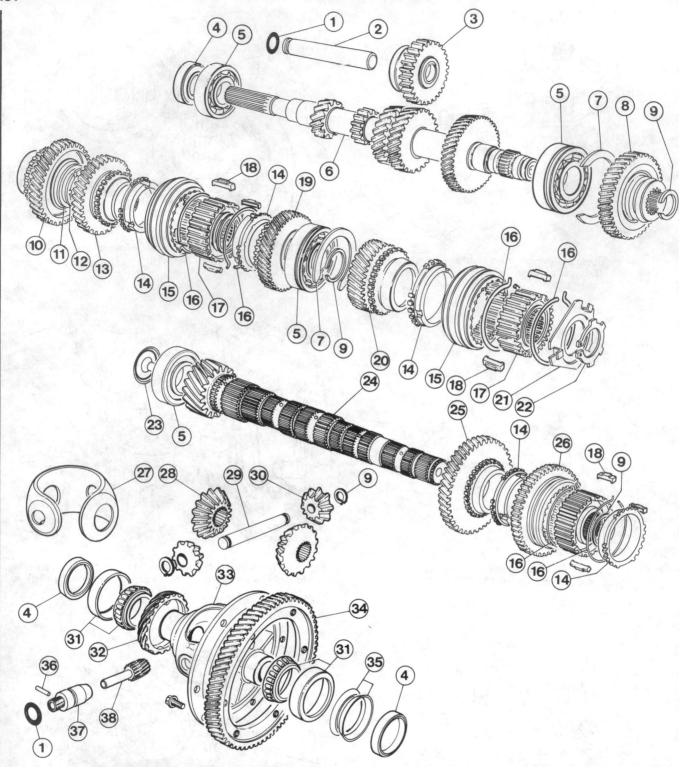

Fig. 6.53 Transmission gear assemblies and associate components (five-speed transmission) (Sec 16)

1	O-ring	11	Supporting ring	21	Retaining plate	31 Taper roller bearing
2	Reverse idler gear shaft	12	Semi-circular thrust	22	Circlip	32 Speedometer drive worm
3	Reverse idler gear		segment	23	Oil slinger	33 Differential housing
4	Radial oil seal	13	3rd gear (driven)	24	Mainshaft	34 Final drivegear
5	Bearing	14	Synchroniser ring	25	1st gear (driven)	35 Spring washers (2)
6	Input shaft	15	Selector ring	26	Selector ring with	36 Locking pin
7	Snap-ring	16	Retaining spring		reverse gear	37 Speedometer drive pinion
8	5th gear	17	Synchroniser hub	27	Thrust cage	bearing
9	Circlip	18	Blocker bar	28	Axleshaft pinion	38 Speedometer drive pinion
10	2nd gear (driven)	19	4th gear (driven)	29	Differential shaft	
		20	5th gear (driven)	30	Differential pinion	

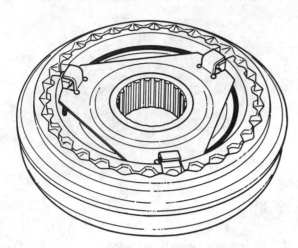

Fig. 6.54 5th gear synchroniser unit (Sec 16)

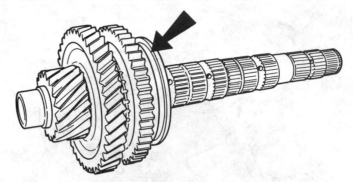

Fig. 6.55 Locate 1st/2nd synchro with selector groove (arrowed) positioned as shown (Sec 16)

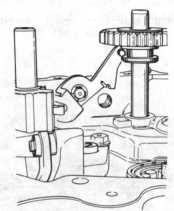

Fig. 6.56 Engage reverse selector lever into groove of idler gear (Sec 17)

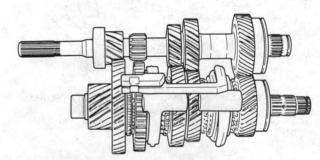

Fig. 6.57 Mainshaft meshed with input shaft and selector forks fitted (Sec 17)

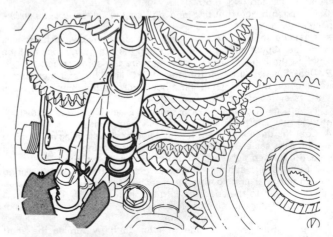

Fig. 6.58 Locate 1st/2nd gear selector fork using new circlips (Sec 17)

bolts, then lift the smaller housing from the transmission casing. If it is stuck, tap it off carefully with a plastic-headed mallet.

12 Extract the swarf-collecting magnet and clean it. Take care not to drop the magnet or it will shatter.

13 Release the circlips from the selector shaft guide sleeve and 1st/2nd gear selector fork. Carefully withdraw the guide sleeve.

14 Lift out the complete mainshaft assembly together with the input shaft, selector forks and reverse gear as a complete unit from the transmission housing.

15 Remove the selector shaft and the shift locking plate.

16 Finally lift the differential assembly from the housing.

17 The transmission is now dismantled into its major assemblies, which can be further dismantled if necessary, as described in Sections 7, 8, 9 and 10, but note the following differences when overhauling the mainshaft.

18 If overhauling the 5th gear synchronizer unit, note that the blocker bars are secured by means of a retaining plate. When assembling the unit proceed as described for the other synchro units (Section 9), but ensure that the retaining spring located between the hub and the retaining plate is pressing against the blocker bars (Fig. 6.54).

19 When reassembling the mainshaft, fit the 1/2nd synchro so that the reverse gear teeth on the unit are positioned towards 1st gear, with the selector groove facing 2nd gear (Fig. 6.55).

17 Five-speed transmission – reassembly

1 With the larger housing section on the bench, lubricate the differential bearings with gear oil and insert the differential assembly into the housing.

2 Slide the reverse idler gear onto its shaft, at the same time engaging the selector lever in the groove of the gear which should be pointing downwards.

3 Refit the selector shaft and shift locking plate.

4 Refit the mainshaft and input shaft as an assembly complete with selector forks. Guide the selector forks past the shift locking plate, noting that the plate must be turned clockwise to bear against the dowel.

5 Install the selector shaft guide sleeve and secure the 1st/2nd gear selector fork on the guide sleeve using new circlips.

6 Refit the swarf-collecting magnet to its location in the housing.

7 Locate a new gasket on the housing flange and place the small housing section in position. Refit and tighten the retaining bolts to the specified torque. Refit the gearbox mounting bracket.

8 Fit the snap-rings to the ends of the main and input shafts. Cut-outs are provided in the casing so that the bearings can be levered upwards to expose the snap-ring grooves. Snap-rings are available in three thicknesses, and the thickest possible ring should be used which will fit into the groove. If any difficulty is experienced in levering up the bearing on the input shaft, push the end of the shaft from within the bellhousing.

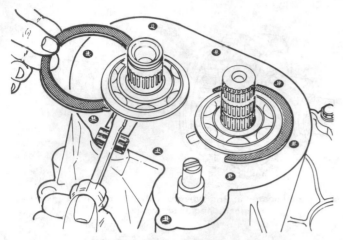

Fig. 6.59 Lever up the bearings to engage snap-rings in bearing grooves (Sec 17)

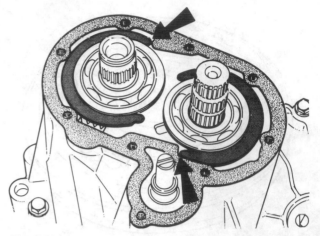

Fig. 6.60 Locate snap-rings correctly when fitted (Sec 17)

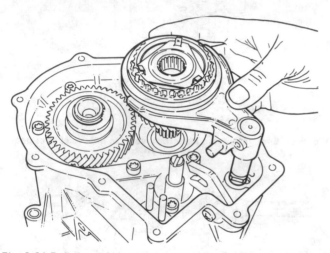

Fig. 6.61 Refitting 5th gear synchro assembly and selector fork – five-speed transmission (Sec 17)

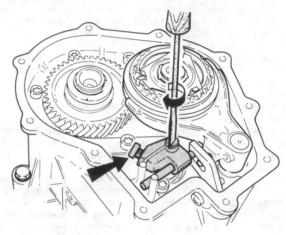

Fig. 6.62 Turning the shift rod clockwise with a screwdriver prior to tightening selector pin clamp bolt – five-speed transmission (Sec 17)

9   Tap the snap-rings to rotate them so that they will locate correctly in the cut-outs in the 5th gear housing gasket, which should now be placed in position (Fig. 6.60).

10 Fit the 5th gear housing and tighten the retaining bolts to the specified torque.

11 Coat the splines of 5th gear and the input shaft with the special grease (see Specifications). Before fitting the 5th gear, check that the marks on the input shaft and gear web are the same colour.

12 Heat 5th gear to approximately 80°C (176°F), and then drift it into place on the input shaft. Fit a new circlip to the input shaft using a tube of suitable diameter as a drift.

13 Fit 5th gear, complete with synchro assembly and selector fork, onto the mainshaft and secure with the snap-ring.

14 Coat the threads of the 5th gear selector shaft locking mechanism cap nut with sealer (see Specifications). Fit the interlock pin, spring and cap nut, then tighten the nut to the specified torque.

15 Fit the 1st-4th and reverse gear selector shaft interlock pin, spring and cap nut after first coating the threads of the cap nut with sealer. Tighten the nut to the specified torque (photo 2.2).

16 Refit the 5th gear selector pin assembly to the shift rod, but do not tighten the clamp bolt at this stage.

17 Engage 5th gear with the selector shaft by turning the shaft clockwise as far as it will go from the neutral position, and then pulling it fully out.

18 Slide the selector ring and selector fork onto 5th gear.

19 Rotate the shift rod clockwise viewed from the rear of the car as far as the stop, using a screwdriver, and retain it in this position. Smear the threads of the clamp bolt with thread locking compound, then fit it and tighten to the specified torque setting.

20 Place a new gasket in position and refit the housing cover, tightening the retaining bolts to the specified torque.

21 At this stage check the operation of the selector mechanism by engaging all the gears with the selector shaft.

22 Refit the clutch release shaft, lever and bearing into the bellhousing.

23 The transmission is now ready for installation in the vehicle. Wait until it is installed before filling with oil.

---

18 Automatic transmission – description and safety precautions

The Ford ATX (automatic transaxle) transmission has three forward and one reverse gear. It is mounted transversely, in line with the engine, and incorporates an integral final drive assembly. The drive to the axle shafts is transmitted by an axle driving gear from the gearbox through an intermediate gear to the driven (differential drive) gear.

The ATX transmission is a split torque type whereby engine torque

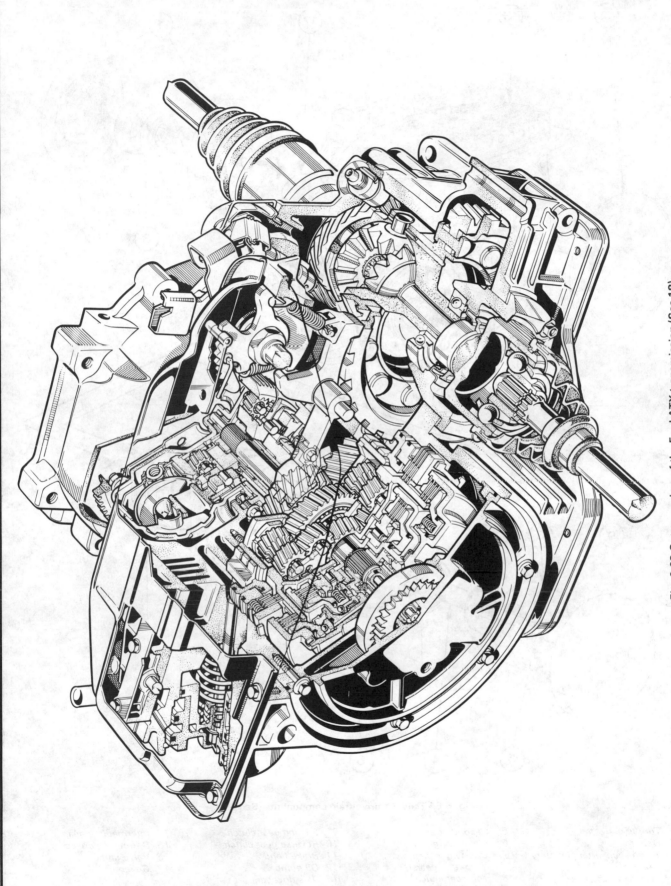

Fig. 6.63 Cutaway view of the Ford ATX transmission (Sec 18)

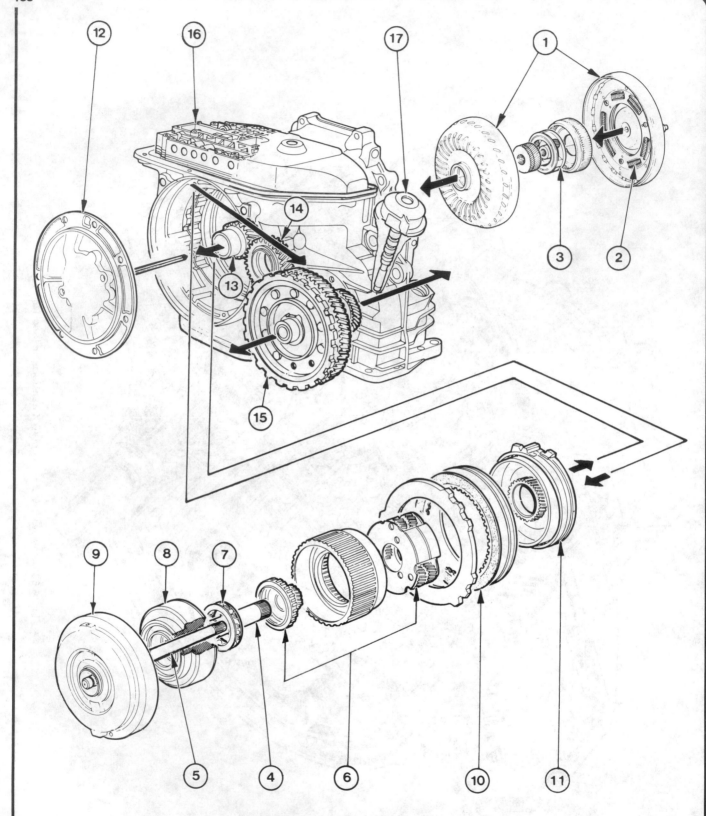

Fig. 6.64 The ATX drive train components (Sec 18)

1	Torque converter	5	Second gear shaft	9	Second gear clutch	14	Intermediate gear
2	Damper	6	Planetary gears	10	Reverse gear clutch	15	Differential drivegear
3	Torque converter planetary gears	7	One-way clutch (planetary gears)	11	Brake band	16	Valve unit
4	Turbine shaft	8	Top gear clutch	12	Oil pump	17	Governor
				13	Axle drivegear		

is transmitted to the gearbox by mechanical or hydraulic means in accordance with the gear selected and the road speed. This system provides for improved efficiency and fuel economy when compared with the C3 type automatic transmission fitted to other Ford models.

The mechanical torque transference is by a planetary gear set attached to the torque converter unit. A damper assembly reduces the engine to transmission vibrations when operating under 'mechanical drive' conditions. The main components of the transmission are shown in Fig. 6.64.

Due to the complexity of the automatic transmission unit, if performance is not up to standard, or overhaul is necessary, it is imperative that this be left to the local main agents who will have the special equipment for fault diagnosis and rectification.

The content of the following sections is therefore confined to supplying general information and any service information and instruction that can be used by the owner.

Safety precautions

The following safety precautions must be noted and adhered to where an automatic transmission is fitted.

Whenever the vehicle is parked or is being serviced or repaired, ensure that the handbrake is fully applied and the selector lever is in position P.

Never exceed an engine speed of 4500 rpm when stationary.

If the vehicle is to be towed at any time the selector lever must be set in the N position. The maximum towing distance should not exceed 20 km (12 miles) and the towing speed must be kept down to a maximum speed of 30 to 40 kph (19 to 25 mph).

19 Automatic transmission – fluid level checking

1   The automatic transmission fluid level should be checked every 10 000 km (6000 miles). A level dipstick is provided for this purpose.
2   Before making the fluid level check the transmission fluid must be at its normal operating temperature. Therefore this check is best made directly after a journey in the car or, failing this, run the vehicle on the road for a distance of approximately 8 km (5 miles) to warm it up.
3   Park the car on level ground, then fully apply the handbrake.
4   With the engine running at its normal idle speed, apply the footbrake and simultaneously move the selector lever through the full range of positions three times then move it back to P. Allow the engine to run at idle for a further period of one minute.
5   With the engine still idling, extract the transmission fluid level dipstick and wipe it clean with a non-fluffy cloth. Fully reinsert the dipstick and then extract it again and check the fluid level mark, which must be between the MAX and MIN markings.
6   If topping-up is necessary, use only the specified fluid type and pour it through the dipstick tube, but take care not to overfill. *The level must not exceed the MAX mark.*
7   If the fluid level was below the minimum mark when checked or is in need of frequent topping-up, check around the transmission unit and the oil cooler for any signs of excessive oil leaks, if present they must be rectified without delay.
8   If the colour of the fluid is dark brown or black this denotes the sign of a worn brake band or transmission clutches, in which case have your Ford dealer check the transmission at the earliest opportunity.

20 Automatic transmission gear selector – removal, overhaul and refitting

1   Move the selector lever to its D position.
2   Raise and support the bonnet, then loosen off the shift cable nut (see Fig. 6.66).
3   Unscrew and remove the gear selector lever knob, then carefully prise up and remove the selector gate cover from the console.
4   Remove the console unit which is secured in position by two screws at the rear and screws on each side at the front.
5   Remove the selector gate and stop plate which are secured by two screws one on each corner at the front.
6   Disconnect the shift cable from the selector lever and housing by removing the securing clips.
7   Disconnect the escutcheon light holder from the lever housing, then unscrew and remove the four housing retaining screws. Lift the housing clear.

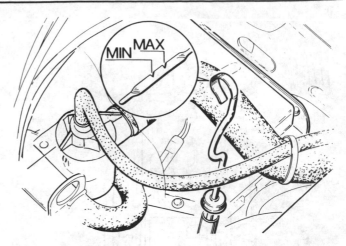

Fig. 6.65 ATX transmission fluid level dipstick location and level markings (Sec 19)

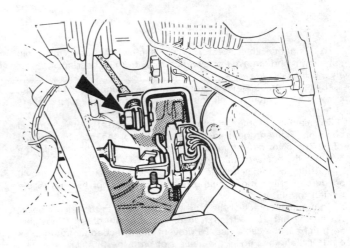

Fig. 6.66 Shift cable nut – arrowed (Sec 20)

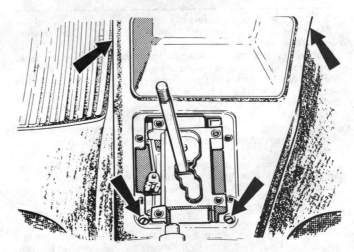

Fig. 6.67 Console securing screw positions (Sec 20)

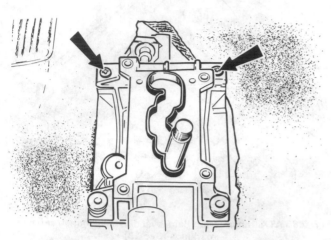

Fig. 6.68 Selector gate and stop plate retaining screws (Sec 20)

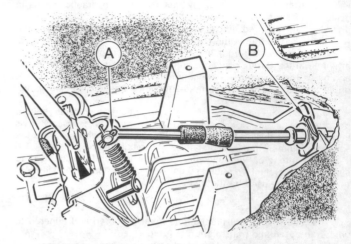

Fig. 6.69 Shift cable attachment to selector lever (A) and housing (B) (Sec 20)

8   To dismantle the selector unit, unscrew the lever pivot pin retaining nut and remove the lever assembly from its housing, together with the bushes.
9   The lever can be removed from the guide by unhooking the spring, unscrewing the retaining pin nut and withdrawing the pin, washers and lever.
10 Reassembly of the selector unit is a reversal of the removal procedure. Tighten the selector lever nut to the specified torque setting. The pivot pin nut must be tightened so that the lever can be moved easily, but without slackness.
11 Refitting of the gear selector unit is a reversal of the removal procedure. Tighten the retaining screws of the lever housing to the specified torque.
12 On completion adjust the shift cable by moving the selector lever to D, check that the shift shaft lever is still in the preset D position, then retighten the cable nut. To prevent the threaded pin rotating as the nut is tightened press the cable slot onto the thread.

21 Automatic transmission downshift linkage – removal and refitting

1   Raise and support the bonnet.
2   Disconnect the downshift linkage from the transmission downshift/throttle valve shaft.
3   Disconnect the throttle linkage from the linkage pivot lever beneath the intake manifold by removing the securing clip.
4   Unscrew and remove the two nuts which secure the downshift cable mounting bracket (on the right-hand side of the engine). Withdraw the linkage and bracket.
5   Disconnect the throttle linkage from the downshift linkage pivot lever by extracting the clips, then remove the clamp bolt and nut to separate the downshift linkage from the control lever. Remove the downshift linkage.
6   To refit, insert the linkage into the bracket and tighten the clamping bolt nut. Check that lever movement is possible.
7   Reattach the throttle linkage to the pivot lever, then refit the downshift linkage and bracket. Slide the linkage onto the downshift/throttle valve shaft of the transmission, fitting the stepped washer between the lever and linkage on the valve shaft. The bracket securing screws should be tightened to the specified torque setting.
8   Secure the throttle linkage to the downshift linkage pivot lever by refitting the retaining clip. Refit and tighten the downshift/throttle valve shaft nut.
9   Adjust the downshift linkage (Section 22).

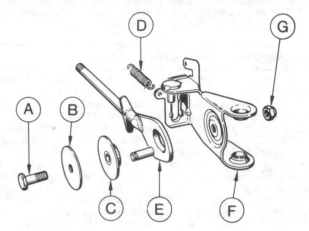

Fig. 6.70 Selector lever components (Sec 20)

A   Pin   E   Lever
B   Steel washer   F   Lever guide
C   Spacer (plastic)   G   Nut
D   Spring

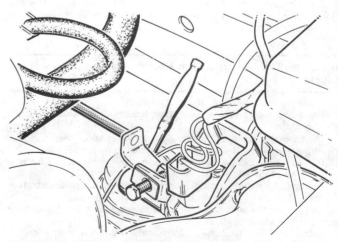

Fig. 6.71 Downshift linkage to transmission connection (Sec 21)

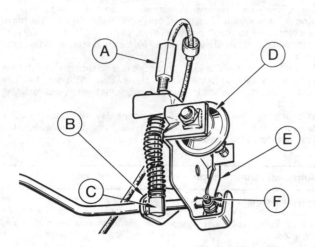

Fig. 6.72 Throttle/downshift linkage components (Sec 21)

A   Throttle cable
B   Downshift linkage
C   Clip
D   Damper
E   Control lever
F   Clamp nut and bolt

Fig. 6.73 Downshift linkage adjuster screw (A) (Sec 22)

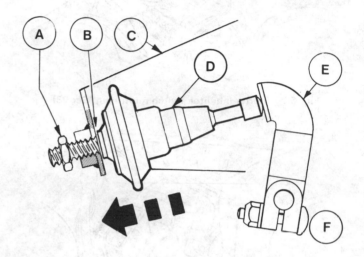

Fig. 6.75 Set downshift linkage (Sec 22)

A   Locknut
B   Bracket-to-damper
    clearance
C   Damper bracket
D   Damper
E   Downshift linkage
    control lever
F   Clamp bolt

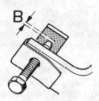

Fig. 6.74 Adjuster screw-to-end face clearance (B) (Sec 22)

22 Automatic transmission downshift linkage – adjustment

1   Before making any adjustments the engine and transmission must be at normal operating temperature, with the correct transmission fluid level and with carburettor and ignition system adjustments as specified (Chapters 3 and 4).
2   Slacken the adjuster screw on the throttle valve shaft lever to give a clearance of 2 to 3 mm (0.079 to 0.118 in) between the stop end face and the adjuster screw (Fig. 6.74). Use a feeler gauge to set this clearance.
3   With the handbrake fully applied, start the engine and check that the idle speed is correct, then tighten the adjuster screw to reduce the stop end face-to-adjuster screw clearance to 0.1 to 0.3 mm (0.004 to 0.012 in).
4   The following additional adjustment should be carried out if the downshift linkage has been removed and refitted, or if the position of the damper has been disturbed.
5   Slacken the locknut and screw in the damper to give a clearance of 1 mm (0.04 in) between the damper body and the bracket (Fig. 6.75). Use a feeler gauge or drill bit of suitable diameter to check this.
6   Slacken the linkage control lever clamp bolt, move the lever so that it just contacts the plastic cap of the damper rod and tighten the clamp bolt.
7   Make a reference mark on the damper body then turn the damper so that the damper body-to-bracket dimension is now 7 mm (0.28 in).
8   Hold the damper in this position and tighten the locknut.

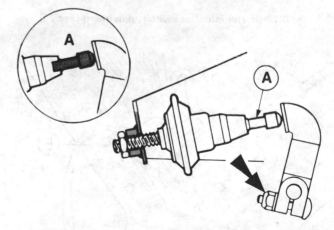

Fig. 6.76 Damper rod (A) to control lever setting – clamp bolt arrowed (Sec 22)

23 Starter inhibitor switch – removal, refitting and adjustment

1   Disconnect the multi-plug connector from the switch.
2   Remove the retaining nut and disconnect the linkage from the throttle valve shaft on the transmission.
3   To remove the downshift linkage from the transmission, unscrew

and remove the two securing screws from the location bracket on the right-hand side of the engine and pull the linkage free.
4   Remove the downshift/throttle valve shaft lever together with the stepped washer and disconnect the return spring.
5   Unscrew the two retaining screws and remove the starter inhibitor switch.
6   The switch must be renewed if it is known to be defective.

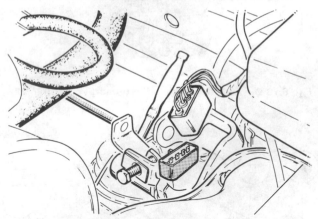

Fig. 6.77 Starter inhibitor switch multi-plug (Sec 23)

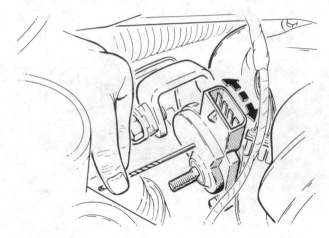

Fig. 6.78 Starter inhibitor switch adjustment (Sec 23)

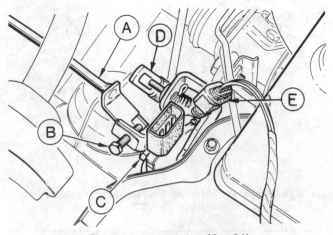

Fig. 6.79 General view (Sec 24)

A   Downshift linkage
B   Adjuster screw
C   Linkage to downshift/
     throttle valve
D   Shift cable (detached)
E   Inhibitor switch
     multi-plug (detached)

7   On refitting the starter inhibitor switch do not fully tighten the securing screws until it is adjusted for position. To do this first move the selector lever to the D position, then, using a 2.3 mm (0.091 in) diameter drill shank, as shown (Fig. 6.78), locate it into the hole in the switch body.
8   Move the switch whilst pushing on the drill so that the switch case aligns with the inner location hole in the switch. With the drill fully inserted so that the switch is immobilised, fully tighten the retaining screws to the specified torque.
9   With the switch in position, refitting of the downshift/throttle valve shaft lever and linkage is a reversal of the removal procedure, but readjust the downshift linkage, as given in Section 22.

24 Automatic transmission – removal and refitting

Any suspected faults must be referred to the main agent before unit removal, as with this type of transmission the fault must be confirmed, using specialist equipment, before it has been removed from the car.
1   Raise and support the bonnet.
2   Disconnect the battery earth lead connector.
3   Disconnect the starter inhibitor switch lead multi-plug connector, then, with the selector lever in the D position, unscrew the shift cable-to-lever retaining nut on the shift shaft.
4   Loosen off the downshift linkage adjuster screw and disconnect the linkage from the downshift/throttle valve shaft which is secured by a single nut. To allow the disconnection of the downshift linkage from the shaft (and eventual refitting) you will also need to remove the downshift linkage mounting support bracket on the right-hand side of the engine compartment. This is secured by two bolts.
5   Unscrew and remove the two upper gearbox-to-engine flange securing bolts.
6   Jack up and securely support the front end of the vehicle. It will need to be raised sufficiently to allow you to work underneath and also to allow the transmission to be removed from underneath when fully disconnected.
7   The weight of the engine must now be supported. Either support the engine under the sump using a jack and block of wood or attach a hoist to the engine lifting lugs. A third method is to make up a bar with end pieces spaced to engage in the water channel each side of the bonnet lid aperture. Using an adjustable hook and chain suspended from the bar and attached to the engine lifting lugs, the weight of the engine can be taken off the mountings. With this method take care not to damage the wing panels with the support bar. *If the drain channels are rusty do not use this method.*
8   Unscrew and detach the speedometer drive cable from the transmission.
9   Unscrew and remove the two shift cable bracket securing bolts from the transmission.
10 Detach the starter motor leads and then unbolt and remove the starter motor which is secured by three bolts.

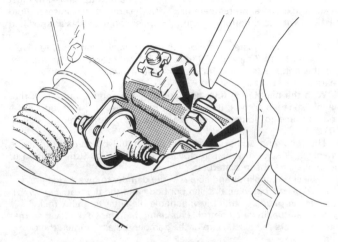

Fig. 6.80 Downshift linkage mounting bracket bolts (Sec 24)

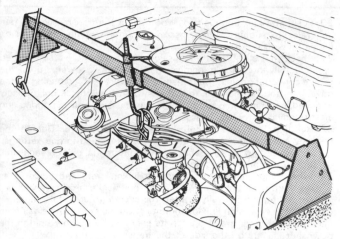

Fig. 6.81 Engine support bar in position – Ford tool 21-060 (Sec 24)

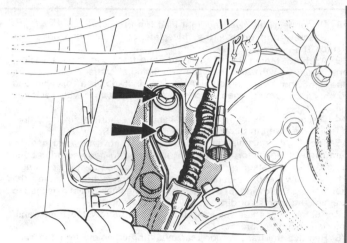

Fig. 6.82 Shift cable bracket bolts (Sec 24)

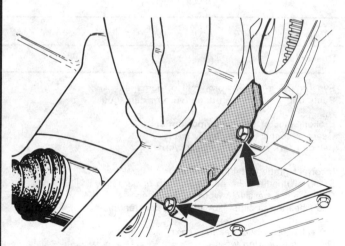

Fig. 6.83 Drive plate cover and retaining bolts – arrowed (Sec 24)

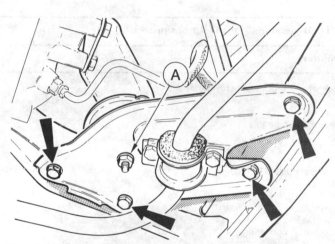

Fig. 6.84 Front transmission mounting retaining bolts (arrowed) and insulator nut (A) (Sec 24)

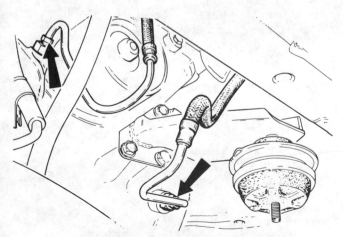

Fig. 6.85 Oil cooler hose connections – arrowed (Sec 24)

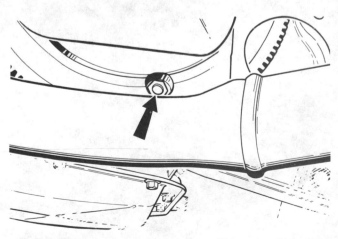

Fig. 6.86 Drive plate-to-torque converter retaining nut (Sec 24)

11 Disconnect the reversing light lead from the switch.
12 Unscrew and remove the driveplate cover securing bolts and detach the cover.
13 At the outboard end of the right-hand track control (suspension) arm, disengage the arm from the hub (spindle) carrier by unscrewing and removing the pinch-bolt and nut. The pinch-bolt is a Torx type, and to prevent it turning when unscrewing the nut retain it with a suitable bit.
14 Disconnect the right- and left-hand driveshafts from the transmission, as given in Section 5, paragraphs 18, 19 and 20.
15 The front transmission mounting must now be detached by removing the insulator nut and four mounting-to-body securing bolts (Fig. 6.84). The stabiliser bar can remain attached to the mounting.
16 Unscrew and disconnect the oil cooler hoses from the transmission, allowing for oil leakage. Plug the lines whilst detached to prevent the ingress of dirt.
17 Remove the three retaining bolts and withdraw the front transmission mounting bracket.
18 Remove the transmission rear mounting complete from the body and transmission by unscrewing the five retaining bolts (and two nuts).
19 Working through the driveplate cover aperture, unscrew and remove the four nuts securing the driveplate to the torque converter. For this to be accomplished it will be necessary to turn the crankshaft for access to each nut in turn. Remove the nuts in a progressive manner, one turn at a time.

20 Position a jack and piece of wood under the transmission oil pan and raise to support. Now unscrew and remove the transmission flange bolts at the front.
21 Check that all of the transmission attachments are disconnected then carefully lower the transmission. As it is being lowered press the torque converter against the transmission to prevent it catching on the driveplate bolt. Remember that the torque converter is only loosely attached, so keep it in position in the transmission housing during and after removal of the transmission.
22 Refitting is a reversal of the removal procedure. Tighten the respective retaining nuts and bolts to their specified torque settings.
23 When refitting the driveshafts to the differential unit on each side, be sure to use new snap-rings.
24 When reconnecting the downshift linkage refit and adjust it as follows. First slide the linkage onto the downshift/throttle valve shaft and locate, but do not fully tighten the securing nut at this stage.
25 Refit the downshift linkage mounting (on the right-hand side of the engine compartment) and tighten its securing bolts. Now tighten the downshift linkage on the side of the transmission housing.
26 With the selector lever (inside the car) and the lever on the shift shaft still in the D position attach the shift cable to the shift shaft lever.
27 Reconnect the starter inhibitor switch multiplug.
28 When the battery earth lead is reconnected and the transmission oil at the level specified, adjust the downshift linkage, as given in Section 22.

25 Fault diagnosis – manual transmission

Symptom	Reason(s)
Weak or ineffective synchromesh	Synchronising cones worn, split or damaged Baulk ring synchromesh dogs worn or damaged
Jumps out of gear	Broken selector shaft interlock spring Gearbox coupling dogs badly worn Selector fork rod groove badly worn
Excessive noise	Incorrect grade of oil in gearbox or oil level too low Brush or needle roller bearings worn or damaged Gear teeth excessively worn or damaged Shaft bearing circlips allowing excessive endplay
Noise when cornering	Driveshaft or wheel bearing worn Differential bearing worn

26 Fault diagnosis – automatic transmission

Faults in these units are nearly always the result of low fluid level or incorrect adjustment of the selector linkage or downshift cable. Internal faults should be diagnosed by your main Ford dealer who has the necessary equipment to carry out the work.

Chapter 7 Driveshafts

For modifications, and information applicable to later models, see Supplement at end of manual

Contents

Specifications

Type
Right-hand .... Tubular, three-section with two constant velocity (CV) joints
Left-hand .... Solid, three-section with two CV joints

Driveshaft identification marks
All models .... Blue

Lubrication
Lubricant capacity (each joint) .... 40g (1.4 oz)
Lubricant type .... Grease to S-MIC-75-A/SQM-1C-9004-A

Torque wrench settings

	Nm	lbf ft
Lower track control arm balljoint pinch-bolt	48 to 60	35 to 44
Lower track control arm pivot bolt	51 to 64	38 to 47
Lower arm balljoint to lower arm	75 to 90	55 to 66
Anti-roll bar to lower track control	90 to 110	66 to 81
Caliper mounting bolts	51 to 61	38 to 45
Roadwheel bolts	70 to 100	52 to 74
Driveshaft/hub nut	205 to 235	151 to 173

1 Description and maintenance

1   The two open driveshafts are of unequal length with the longer (hollow) one having a greater diameter than the shorter (solid) one.

2   Each driveshaft consists of three sections: the inboard end, namely a splined output shaft and constant velocity joint, the outboard end, being the splined front hub spindle and constant velocity joint, and a centre shaft with splined ends.

3   The inboard ends of the driveshaft are retained in the differential gears by the engagement of snap-rings. The outboard ends are secured to the hub by a nut which is staked after tightening.

4   The constant velocity joints are lubricated and sealed by flexible gaiters. The only maintenance required is a visual inspection for splits in the gaiter or an oil leak from the inboard oil seal. A leakage of grease from the hub seal will indicate that the hub bearing oil seal is in need of renewal and this is described in Section 3 of Chapter 10.

5   Where a driveshaft gaiter is split, it must be renewed immediately to avoid the entry of dirt and grit (see Section 3 or 4).

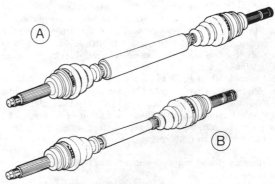

Fig. 7.1 The driveshafts (Sec 1)

A   Right-hand (tubular)   B   Left-hand (solid)

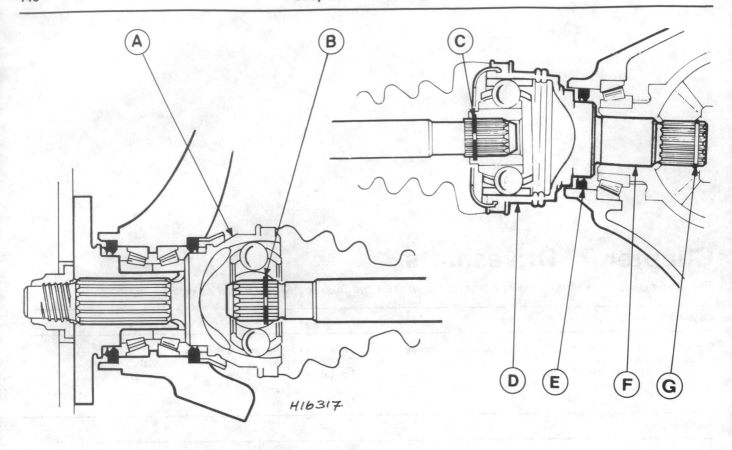

Fig. 7.2 Sectional view of driveshaft constant velocity (CV) joints (Sec 1)

A	Outboard joint	C	Circlip	E	Oil seal	G	Snap-ring
B	Circlip	D	Inboard joint	F	Inboard driveshaft	

2   Driveshaft inboard oil seal – renewal

1   Raise the front end of the vehicle and support on stands placed under the jacking points on the side members.

2   Drain the transmission oil by unscrewing and removing the cap nut from the selector shaft locking mechanism. Take care not to lose the spring and interlock pin which will be ejected – see Chapter 6.

3   Unscrew and remove the pinch-bolt and nut and disconnect the suspension lower track control arm from the hub carrier.

4   Disconnect the track control arm from the body at its inboard end by removing the pivot bolt. A Torx bit will be required.

5   With an assistant pulling the roadwheel, insert a lever between the inboard constant velocity joint and the transmission. Strike the end of the lever, so prising the driveshaft out of the transmission. Tie the driveshaft to the steering rack housing to avoid strain on the CV joints caused by excessive deflection of the driveshaft. The maximum allowable angle of deflection must not exceed 45° for the outer joint, 20° for the inner joint.

6   Using a tool with a hook at its end, prise out the oil seal from the differential housing. Take care not to damage the seal housing.

7   Wipe out the oil seal seat, apply grease to the lips of a new oil seal and tap it into position using a piece of tubing or similar as a drift.

8   Using a mirror, check that the pinion gear within the differential is in correct alignment to receive the driveshaft. If not, insert the finger to align it.

9   Fit a new snap-ring to the driveshaft and then offer it up to engage it in the transmission.

10   Have your assistant push inwards on the roadwheel until the snap-ring is fully engaged. If any difficulty is experienced in pushing the driveshaft fully home, remove the roadwheel to reduce weight and lift the hub assembly until the driveshaft is in a more horizontal attitude.

11   Reconnect the suspension track control arm and lower the vehicle to the ground. Tighten nuts and bolts to the specified torque when the weight of the vehicle is again on its roadwheels.

12   Fill the transmission with oil after having refitted the selector cap nut assembly.

Fig. 7.3 Disconnect the lower suspension arm balljoint from the hub carrier (Sec 2)

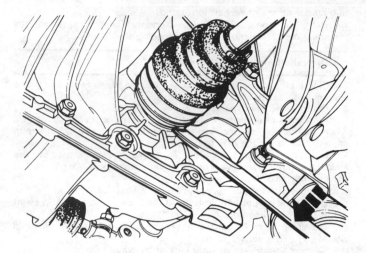

Fig. 7.4 Driveshaft removal from transmission (Sec 2)

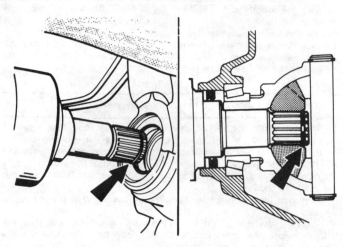

Fig. 7.5 Inserting driveshaft into transmission (left) and driveshaft snap-ring fully engaged with differential pinion gear (arrowed, right) (Sec 2)

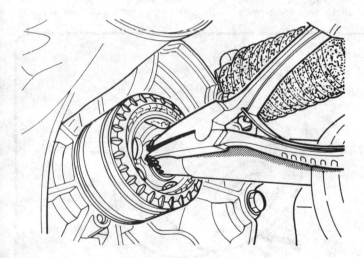

Fig. 7.6 Releasing joint circlip (Sec 3)

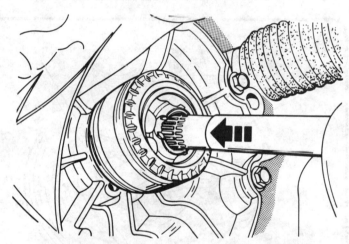

Fig. 7.7 Engaging driveshaft with CV joint (Sec 3)

3 Driveshaft inboard joint bellows – renewal

1   Jack up the front of the vehicle and support securely. Wipe the driveshaft free from dirt and grease.

2   Disconnect the front suspension track control arm balljoint from the hub carrier by removing the pinch-bolt and nut. The bolt is of socket headed (Torx) type and can be prevented from rotating in the absence of a special tool by using an Allen key.

3   Disconnect the track control arm from the body at its inboard end by removing the pivot bolt.

4   Disconnect both clamps from the bellows on the inboard driveshaft joint and slide the bellows off the CV joint and along the shaft.

5   Wipe enough grease from the joint to expose the circlip which secures it to the shaft. Using a pair of circlip pliers, extract the circlip.

6   Pull the driveshaft out of the joint and slide the bellows off the end of the shaft.

7   To fit the new bellows, slide them onto the shaft and then connect the driveshaft to the CV joint. The circlip should be engaged in its groove in the joint and the shaft slid through it until the circlip snaps into its groove in the shaft.

8   Replenish the joint with grease of the specified type and then pull the bellows over the joint.

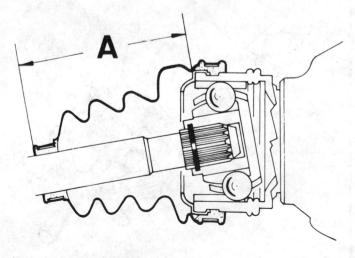

Fig. 7.8 Driveshaft inboard joint bellows setting diagram (Sec 3)

A = 132 mm (5.20 in)

9   Set the length of the bellows (A in Fig. 7.8) to the appropriate dimension.
10 Fit the bellows clamps and tighten.
11 Reconnect the track control arm, tighten all bolts and lower the vehicle. Finally tighten all fastenings to the specified torque when the weight of the vehicle is again on its wheels.

4   Driveshaft outboard joint bellows – renewal

1   The following method of driveshaft renewal avoids the need to disconnect the driveshaft from the hub carrier. If working on the right-hand driveshaft however, some difficulty may be experienced in sliding the bellows over the large tubular section of the shaft. If this is the case, remove the driveshaft as described in Section 5, and carry out the work on the bench.
2   Remove the inboard joint bellows, as described in the preceding Section.
3   Release the clamps on the outboard joint bellows and slide the bellows along the driveshaft until they can be removed from the inboard end of the shaft.
4   Thoroughly clean the driveshaft before sliding on the new bellows. Replenish the outboard joint with specified lubricant and slide the bellows over the joints, setting its overall length to the appropriate dimension of 82 mm (3.23 in).
5   Fit and tighten the bellows clamps, but make sure that the crimped part of the clamp nearest the hub does not interfere with the

hub carrier as the driveshaft is rotated.
6   Refit the inboard bellows and connect the driveshaft to the transmission, as described in the preceding Section.

5   Driveshaft – removal and refitting

1   Slacken the roadwheel bolts, then raise the front of the vehicle and support with safety stands.
2   Remove the roadwheel.
3   Refit two of the roadwheel bolts as a means of anchoring the disc when the hub nut is unscrewed (the disc retaining screw is not strong enough to prevent the disc from rotating).
4   Have an assistant apply the footbrake and then unscrew the staked hub nut and remove it together with the plain washer. Note that the hub nut must be renewed.
5   Remove the temporary wheel bolts.
6   Unbolt the caliper and tie it up to the suspension strut to prevent strain on the flexible hose.
7   Disconnect the inboard end of the driveshaft as described in Section 2, paragraphs 2 to 5.
8   Support the driveshaft on a jack or by tying it up.
9   Extract the small retaining screw and withdraw the brake disc from the hub.
10 It may now be possible to pull the hub from the driveshaft. If it does not come off easily, use a two-legged puller.
11 Withdraw the driveshaft complete with CV joints. If both driveshafts are being removed at the same time then the differential pinion

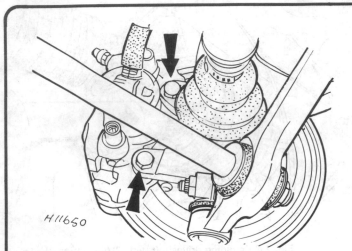

Fig. 7.9 Brake caliper mounting bolts (Sec 5)

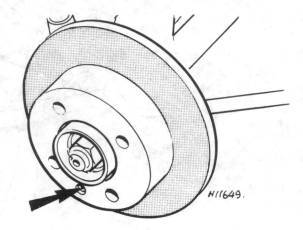

Fig. 7.10 Brake disc securing screw (Sec 5)

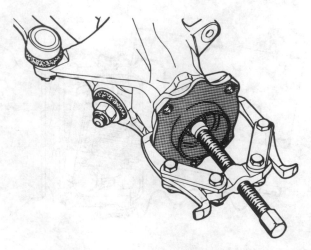

Fig. 7.11 Hub withdrawal from driveshaft using a puller (Sec 5)

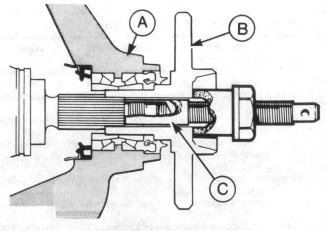

Fig. 7.12 Hub refitting method – Ford special tool 14-022 shown (Sec 5)

A   Hub carrier   C   Special tool
B   Hub

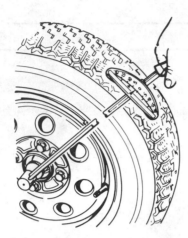

Fig. 7.13 Tighten hub nut to specified torque setting (Sec 5)

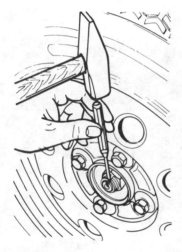

Fig. 7.14 Staking hub retaining nut for security (Sec 5)

gears must be retained in alignment with their transmission casing holes by inserting pieces of plastic tubing or dowel rods.

12 To refit the driveshaft, first engage it in the splines of the hub carrier while supporting the shaft in a horizontal attitude to avoid strain on the CV joints.

13 Using the original nut and distance pieces of varying lengths, draw the driveshaft into the hub carrier. A special tool is available, see Fig. 7.12.

14 Remove the old nut and distance pieces and fit the washer and a new nut, but only finger tight at this stage.

15 Fit the brake disc and caliper.

16 Connect the inboard end of the driveshaft and the suspension components as described in Section 2.

17 Temporarily screw in two wheel bolts and then have an assistant apply the footbrake.

18 Tighten the new hub nut to the specified torque. In the absence of a suitable torque wrench with a high enough range, full hand pressure on a knuckle bar or pipe extension about 457 mm (18 in) in length should give approximately the correct torque. Once tight, stake the nut into the shaft groove. Fit the roadwheel and lower the vehicle.

19 Tighten the roadwheel bolts and then check the torque wrench settings of the other front suspension attachments now that the weight of the vehicle is on the roadwheels.

6 Driveshaft – overhaul

1   Remove the driveshaft, as described in the preceding Section.

2   Clean away external dirt and grease, release the bellows clamps and slide the bellows from the CV joint.

3   Wipe away enough lubricant to be able to extract the circlip and then separate the CV joint with its splined shaft section from the main member of the driveshaft.

4   Thoroughly clean the joint components and examine for wear or damage to the balls, cage, socket or splines. A repair kit may provide a solution to the problem, but if the socket requires renewal, this will of course include the splined section of shaft and will prove expensive. If both joints require renewal of major components, then a new driveshaft or one which has been professionally reconditioned may prove to be more economical.

5   Reassemble the joint by reversing the dismantling operations. Use a new circlip and pack the joint with the specified quantity of lubricant. When fitting the bellows, set their length in accordance with the information given in Section 3 or 4 according to which joint (inboard or outboard) is being worked upon.

6   Refit the driveshaft, as described in Section 5.

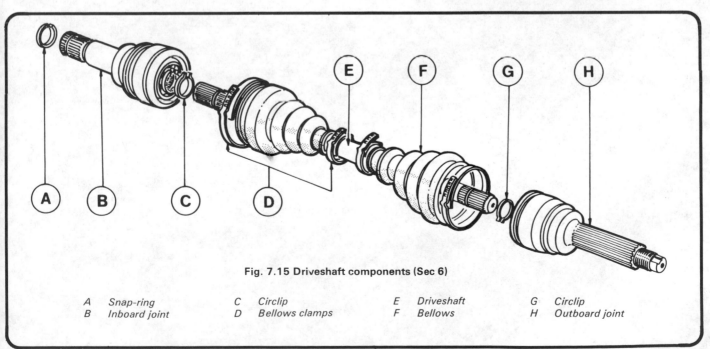

Fig. 7.15 Driveshaft components (Sec 6)

| A | Snap-ring | C | Circlip | E | Driveshaft | G | Circlip |
| B | Inboard joint | D | Bellows clamps | F | Bellows | H | Outboard joint |

7　Fault diagnosis – driveshafts

Symptom	Reason(s)
Knock when taking up drive or on overrun	Wear in joint Wear in shaft splines Loose roadwheel bolts
Noise, especially on turns	Lack of lubrication Wear in joint Loose hub retaining nut
Leakage of lubricant	Split bellows or loose retaining clamp Faulty oil seal at differential end of shaft Faulty oil seal at roadwheel end of shaft (refer to Chapter 10)

Chapter 8 Braking system

For modifications, and information applicable to later models, see Supplement at end of manual

Contents

Specifications

System type .... Hydraulic, dual-circuit, discs front, drums rear. Servo standard. Handbrake mechanical to rear wheels only

Disc brakes
Caliper type .... Single piston, sliding type
Disc diameter .... 239.45 mm (9.43 in)
Disc thickness:
    1.3 (solid) .... 10.0 mm (0.39 in)
    1.6 (ventilated) .... 24.0 mm (0.95 in)
Minimum disc thickness (after refinishing):
    1.3 (solid) .... 8.7 mm (0.34 in)
    1.6 (ventilated) .... 22.7 mm (0.89 in)
Maximum disc run-out .... 0.15 mm (0.006 in)
Caliper cylinder diameter .... 54.0 mm (2.12 in)
Minimum pad friction material thickness .... 1.5 mm (0.06 in)

Drum brakes
Drum diameter:
    1.6 Fuel injection .... 203 mm (8.0 in)
    Other models .... 180 mm (7.1 in)
Shoe width:
    Except fuel injection models .... 30.0 mm (1.18 in)
    Fuel injection models .... 38.0 mm (1.5 in)
Wheel cylinder diameter .... 19.05 mm (0.75 in)
Minimum shoe friction lining thickness .... 1.5 mm (0.06 in)

Master cylinder
Type .... Tandem
Cylinder diameter .... 20.64 mm (0.813 in)

Servo diameter .... 200 mm (7.87 in)

Brake fluid
Type/specification .... Brake fluid to Ford specification SAM-6C 9103-A (Duckhams Universal Brake and Clutch Fluid)

Torque wrench settings

	Nm	lbf ft
Caliper piston housing to anchor bracket	24	17
Caliper anchor bracket to hub carrier	60	44
Rear backplate fixing bolts	50	37
Hydraulic unions	15	11
Brake pressure regulating valve bolts	24	17

1 General description

The braking system is of four-wheeled hydraulic type, with discs at the front and drums at the rear.

The hydraulic system is of dual-circuit type, each circuit controls one front brake and one rear brake linked diagonally.

The calipers are of single piston, sliding piston housing type. The discs are of solid on 1.3 models, but of ventilated type on 1.6 versions.

The rear brakes are of leading and trailing shoe design with a self-adjusting mechanism. To compensate for the greater lining wear of the leading shoe, its friction lining is thicker than that on the trailing shoe.

The master cylinder incorporates a reservoir cap which has a fluid level switch connected to a warning lamp on the instrument panel.

A vacuum servo is standard on all models. When fitted to RHD versions, because of the location of the servo/master cylinder on the left-hand side of the engine compartment the brake pedal is operated through a transverse rod on the engine compartment rear bulkhead.

A brake pressure regulating control valve is fitted into the hydraulic circuit to prevent rear wheel locking under conditions of heavy braking.

The floor-mounted handbrake control lever operates through cables to the rear wheels only.

2 Maintenance

1 At weekly intervals, check the fluid level in the translucent reservoir on the master cylinder. The fluid will drop very slowly indeed over a period of time to compensate for lining wear, but any sudden drop in level, or the need for frequent topping-up should be investigated immediately.

2 Always top up with hydraulic fluid which meets the specified standard and has been left in an airtight container. Hydraulic fluid is hygroscopic (absorbs moisture from the atmosphere) and must not be stored in an open container. Do not shake the tin prior to topping-up. Fluids of different makes can be intermixed provided they all meet the specification.

3 Inspect the thickness of the friction linings on the disc pads and brake shoes as described in the following Sections, at the intervals specified in Routine Maintenance.

4 The rigid and flexible hydraulic pipes and hoses should be inspected for leaks or damage regularly. Although the rigid lines are

plastic-coated in order to preserve them against corrosion, check for damage which may have occurred through flying stones, careless jacking or the traversing of rough ground.

5 Bend the hydraulic flexible hoses sharply with the fingers and examine the surface of the hose for signs of cracking or perishing of the rubber. Renew if evident.

6 Renew the brake fluid at the specified intervals and examine all rubber components (including master cylinder and piston seals) with a critical eye, renewing where necessary.

3 Disc pads – inspection and renewal

1 At the intervals specified in Routine Maintenance, place a mirror between the roadwheel and the caliper and check the thickness of the friction material of the disc pads. If the material has worn down to 1.5 mm (0.060 in) or less, the pads must be renewed as an axle set (four pads).

2 Slacken the roadwheel bolts, raise the front of the vehicle, support with safety stands and remove the roadwheel(s).

3 Disengage the brake pad wear sensor from its retaining clip (beneath the bleed nipple) and disconnect the lead connector (photo).

4 Using a screwdriver as shown, prise free the retaining clip from the caliper (photo).

5 Using a 7 mm Allen key, unscrew the bolts until they can be withdrawn from the caliper anchor brackets (photo).

6 Withdraw the piston housing and tie it up with a length of wire to prevent strain on the flexible hose (photo).

7 Withdraw the inboard pad from the piston housing.

8 Withdraw the outboard pad from the anchor bracket.

9 Clean away all residual dust or dirt, **taking care not to inhale the dust** as, being asbestos based, it is injurious to health.

10 Using a piece of flat wood, a tyre lever or similar, push the piston squarely into its bore. This is necessary in order to accommodate the new thicker pads when they are fitted.

11 Depressing the piston will cause the fluid level in the master cylinder reservoir to rise, so anticipate this by syphoning out some fluid using an old hydrometer or poultry baster. Take care not to drip hydraulic fluid onto the paintwork, it acts as an effective paint stripper.

12 Commence reassembly by fitting the inboard pad into the piston housing. Make sure that the spring on the back of the pad fits into the piston (photo).

3.3 Detach disc pad wear sensor lead at connector

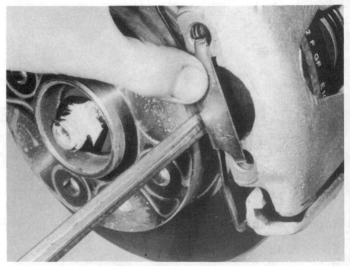

3.4 Prise free the retaining clip from caliper

3.5 Unscrew the caliper piston housing bolts

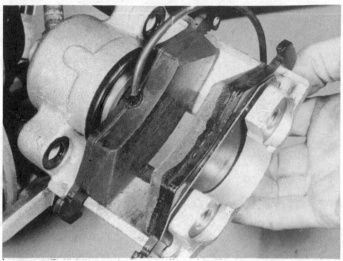

3.6 Caliper piston housing removed giving access to pads

13 Feed the wear sensor wire through the opening in the caliper and then reattach it to the bleed nipple clip.

14 Where the cable has become unwound, loosely coil the surplus wire so that slack is taken out yet enough flexibility (25 mm/1 in) is still allowed for pad wear. The coiled wire must on no account be stretched.

15 Peel back the protective paper covering (if fitted) from the surface of the new outboard pad and locate it in the jaws of the caliper anchor bracket.

16 Locate the caliper piston housing and screw in the Allen bolts to the specified torque.

17 Fit the retaining clip.

18 Repeat the operations on the opposite brake.

19 Apply the footbrake hard several times to position the pads against the disc and then check and top up the fluid in the master cylinder reservoir.

20 Fit the roadwheel(s) and lower the vehicle.

21 Avoid heavy braking (if possible) for the first hundred miles or so when new pads have been fitted. This is to allow them to bed in and reach full efficiency.

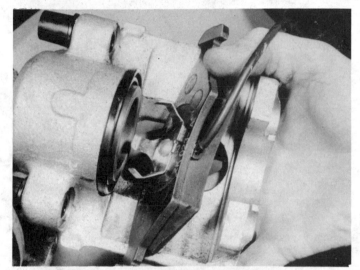

3.12 Fitting the inboard piston into position

4 Caliper piston assembly – removal, overhaul and refitting

1 Proceed as described in paragraphs 2 to 9 in the previous Section.

2 Disconnect the brake flexible hose from the caliper. This can be carried out in one of two ways. Either disconnect the flexible hose from the rigid hydraulic pipeline at the support bracket by unscrewing the union, or, once the caliper is detached, hold the end fitting of the hose in an open-ended spanner and unscrew the caliper from the hose. Do not allow the hose to twist.

3 Brush away all external dirt and pull off the piston dust-excluding cover.

4 Apply air pressure to the fluid inlet hole and eject the piston. Only low air pressure is needed for this, such as is produced by a foot-operated tyre pump.

5 Using a sharp pointed instrument, pick out the piston seal from the groove in the cylinder bore. Do not scratch the surface of the bore.

6 Examine the surfaces of the piston and the cylinder bore. If they are scored or show evidence of metal-to-metal rubbing, then a new piston housing will be required. Where the components are in good condition, discard the seal and obtain a repair kit.

7 Wash the internal components in clean brake hydraulic fluid or methylated spirit only, nothing else.

8 Using the fingers, manipulate the new seal into its groove in the cylinder bore.

9 Dip the piston in clean hydraulic fluid and insert it squarely into its bore.

10 Connect the rubber dust excluder between the piston and the piston housing (photo) and then depress the piston fully.

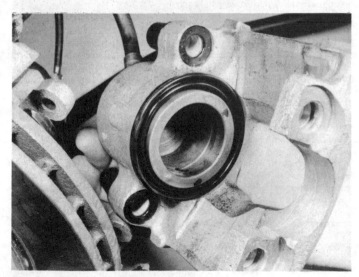

4.10 Piston and dust excluder in position in housing

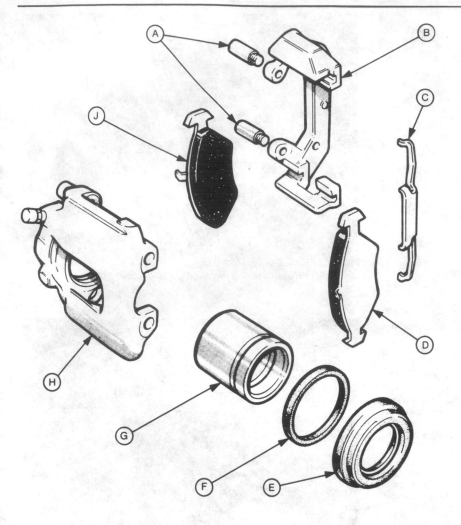

Fig. 8.1 Exploded view of the disc caliper (Sec 4)

A   Caliper piston housing bolts
B   Anchor bracket
C   Retaining clip
D   Disc pad
E   Dust excluder
F   Piston seal
G   Piston
H   Piston housing
J   Disc pad

11 Refit the caliper by reversing the removal operations, referring to paragraphs 12 to 17 in the previous Section.
12 Reconnect the brake hose to the caliper, taking care not to distort it. When secured it must not interfere with any of the adjacent steering or suspension components.
13 Bleed the brake hydraulic circuit as given in Section 12, then refit the roadwheel(s) and lower the vehicle.

5 Brake disc – examination, removal and refitting

1   Fully apply the handbrake then loosen off the front roadwheel bolts. Raise and support the front of the vehicle on safety stands and remove the roadwheel(s).
2   Examine the surface of the disc. If it is deeply grooved or scored or if any small cracks are evident, it must either be refinished or renewed. Any refinishing must not reduce the thickness of the disc to below a certain minimum (see Specifications). Light scoring on a brake disc is normal and should be ignored.
3   If disc distortion is suspected (refer to Fault Diagnosis, Section 19), the disc can be checked for run-out using a dial gauge or feeler blades located between its face and a fixed point as the disc is rotated.
4   Where the run-out exceeds the specified figure, renew the disc.
5   To remove a disc, unbolt the caliper, withdraw it and tie it up to the suspension strut to avoid strain on the flexible hose (see Section 3).
6   Extract the small disc retaining screw and pull the disc from the hub.
7   If a new disc is being installed, clean its surface free from preservative.
8   Refit the caliper and the roadwheel and lower the vehicle to the floor.

6 Rear brake linings – inspection and renewal

Drum combined with hub

1   Due to the fact that the rear brake drums are combined with the hubs, which makes removal of the drums more complicated than is the case with detachable drums, inspection of the shoe linings can be carried out at the specified intervals by prising out the small inspection plug from the brake backplate and observing the linings through the hole using a mirror (photo).
2   A minimum thickness of friction material must always be observed on the shoes (see Specifications); if it is worn down to this level, renew the shoes.
3   Do not attempt to reline shoes yourself but always obtain factory relined shoes.
4   Renew the shoes in an axle set (four shoes), even if only one is worn to the minimum.
5   Slacken the roadwheel bolts, raise the rear of the vehicle and support it securely. Remove the roadwheels.
6   Release the handbrake fully.
7   Tap off the hub dust cap, remove the split pin, nut lock, nut and thrust washer (photos).
8   Pull the hub/drum towards you and then push it back enough to be able to take the outer bearing from the spindle (photo).
9   Remove the hub/drum and brush out any dust, **taking care not to inhale it** (photo).
10 Remove the shoe hold-down spring from the leading shoe (photo). Do this by gripping the dished washer with a pair of pliers, depressing it and turning it through 90°. Remove the washer, spring and the hold-down post. Note the locations of the leading and trailing shoes and the cut-back of the linings at the leading ends.
11 Pull the leading shoe outwards and upwards away from the

Fig. 8.2 Brake disc retaining screw location (Sec 5)

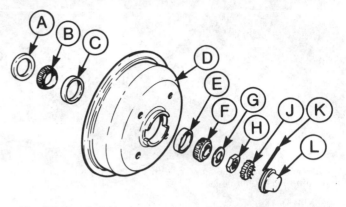

Fig. 8.3 Rear hub/drum components (non-injection models)
(Sec 6)

A   Oil seal
B   Tapered roller bearing
    (inner)
C   Bearing track
D   Hub/drum
E   Bearing track

F   Taper roller bearing
    (outer)
G   Thrust washer
H   Nut
J   Nut lock
K   Split pin
L   Dust cap

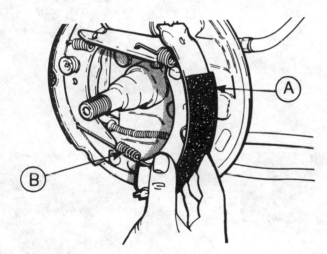

Fig. 8.4 Withdrawing leading shoe (non-injection models)
(Sec 6)

A   Shoe   B   Spring

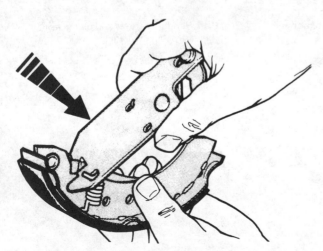

Fig. 8.6 Separating trailing shoe from adjuster strut (arrowed)
(Sec 6)

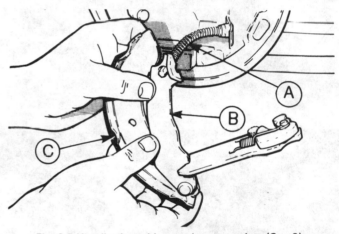

Fig. 8.5 Handbrake cable attachment to shoe (Sec 6)

A   Cable   C   Shoe
B   Lever

backplate.

12 Twist the shoe to unhook it from its return springs. If you have any doubt about remembering into which holes the springs engage, mark or sketch them.

12 Remove the trailing shoe in a similar way, at the same time withdrawing the adjuster strut.

14 Release the end of the handbrake cable from the lever on the shoe.

15 Disconnect the trailing shoe from the adjuster strut by pulling the shoe outwards and twisting the shoe spring.

16 Commence reassembly by installing the trailing shoe. Do this by engaging the handbrake lever return spring to the shoe. Hook the strut onto the spring and lever it into position . Set the strut self-adjusting mechanism to its contracted position.

17 Locate the webs of the trailing shoe on the wheel cylinder and the fixed abutment, making sure that the lower end of the handbrake lever is correctly located on the face of the plastic plunger and not trapped behind it (photo).

18 Fit the trailing shoe hold-down post and spring. Hold the leading shoe in position.

19 Connect the larger shoe return spring at the lower (abutment) position between both shoes.

20 Holding the leading shoe almost at right-angles to the backplate, connect the spring between it and the strut and then engage the bottom end of the shoe behind the abutment retainer plate.

21 Swivel the shoe towards the backplate so that the cut-out in its

6.1 Checking rear brake lining wear with a mirror (non-injection models)

6.7A Removing rear hub dust cap

6.7B Extracting rear hub split pin

6.7C Unscrewing rear hub nut

6.7D Removing rear hub thrust washer

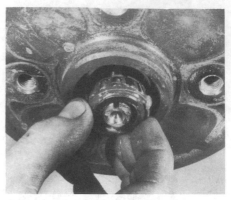
6.8 Removing rear hub outer bearing

6.9 Rear hub/drum removed

6.10 Releasing brake shoe hold-down washer

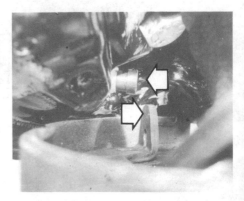
6.17 Handbrake lever and plunger – check they are positioned against each other

6.27 Remove the drum retaining screw

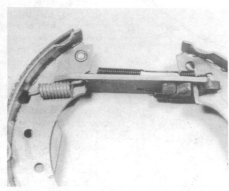
6.31A Note orientation and locations of the springs, spacer strut and automatic adjuster before dismantling

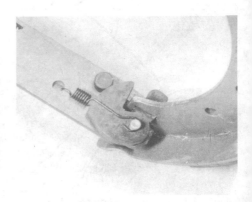
6.31B Automatic adjuster assembly

web passes over the quadrant lever. Fit the shoe hold-down post, spring and washer.

22 Centralise the shoes within the backplate by tapping them if necessary with the hand, then fit the hub/drum and slide the outer bearing onto the spindle.

23 Fit the thrust washer and nut and whilst rotating the drum, tighten the nut to a torque of 24 Nm (17 lbf ft). Unscrew the nut one half a turn and then screw the nut up again, but this time only finger tight.

24 Without altering the position of the nut, fit the nut lock so that suitable cut-outs align with the split pin hole. Insert a new split pin and bend the ends **around** the spindle, **not** over the end of it or the pin may rub on the inside of the dust cap.

25 Depress the brake pedal hard several times to actuate the self-actuating mechanism and to bring the shoes up close to the drum.

26 Refit the roadwheel and lower the vehicle to the floor.

Drum separate from hub

27 On certain models the brake drum is separate from the hub and can be removed after undoing the retaining screw for inspection of the shoes without the need to remove the hub as well (photo). The bearings will therefore not need to be reset during reassembly.

28 The brake shoe removal procedure is very similar to that described for non-injection models, but note the following differences.

29 Disconnect the lower shoe return spring which bridges the shoes and then disconnect the handbrake cable from the lever.

30 Prise the shoes away from the lower pivot, twist them from the wheel cylinder and remove as an assembly.

31 With the shoes removed they can be separated from the strut. Note how the components are positioned before dismantling (photos).

32 Refitting is a reversal of the removal procedure; complete as described for non-injection models.

7 Rear wheel cylinder – removal, overhaul and refitting

1 Remove the rear brake shoes, as described in the preceding Section.

2 Disconnect the fluid pipeline from the wheel cylinder and cap the end of the pipe to prevent loss of fluid. A bleed screw rubber dust cap is useful for this.

3 Unscrew the two bolts which hold the wheel cylinder to the brake backplate and remove the cylinder with sealing gasket.

4 Clean away external dirt and then pull off the dust-excluding covers.

5 The pistons will probably shake out. If they do not, apply air pressure (from a tyre pump) at the inlet hole to eject them.

6 Examine the surfaces of the pistons and the cylinder bores for scoring or metal-to-metal rubbing areas. If evident, renew the complete cylinder assembly.

7 Where the components are in good condition, discard the rubber seals and dust excluders and obtain a repair kit.

8 Any cleaning should be done using hydraulic fluid or methylated spirit – nothing else.

9 Reassemble by dipping the first piston in clean hydraulic fluid and inserting it into the cylinder. Fit a dust excluder to it.

10 From the opposite end of the cylinder body, insert a new seal, spring, a second new seal, the second piston and the remaining dust excluder. Use only the fingers to manipulate the seals into position and

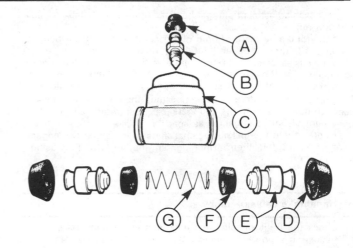

Fig. 8.7 Rear wheel cylinder components (Sec 7)

A	Dust cap	E	Piston
B	Bleed nipple	F	Piston seal
C	Wheel cylinder	G	Spring
D	Dust cover		

make quite sure that the lips of the seals are the correct way round.

11 Bolt the wheel cylinder to the backplate (photo), reconnect the fluid line and refit the shoes (Section 6).

12 Refit the brake drum and roadwheel and lower the vehicle to the floor.

13 Bleed the hydraulic circuit (Section 12).

8 Brake drum – inspection and renewal

1 Whenever a brake drum is removed, brush out dust from it, **taking care not to inhale it** as it contains asbestos and is injurious to health.

2 Examine the internal friction surface of the drum. If deeply scored, or so worn that the drum has become pocketed to the width of the shoes, then the drums must be renewed.

3 Regrinding is not recommended as the internal diameter will no longer be compatible with the shoe lining contact diameter.

9 Handbrake – adjustment

1 Adjustment of the handbrake is normally automatic by means of the self-adjusting mechanism working on the rear brake shoes.

2 However, due to cable stretch, occasional inspection of the handbrake adjusters is recommended. Adjustment must be carried out if the movement of the control lever becomes excessive.

3 Chock the front wheels then fully release the handbrake.

4 Raise and support the vehicle at the rear with safety stands.

7.11 Wheel cylinder in position on brake backplate

9.5 Handbrake adjustment check plunger (arrowed)

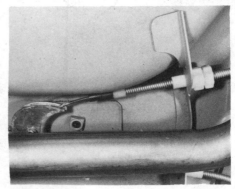

9.7 Handbrake cable locknut, adjuster sleeve and equaliser

5 Grip each adjustment plunger between finger and thumb and move it in and out.

6 If the total movement of both plungers added together is between 0.5 and 1.0 mm (0.02 and 0.04 in) then the adjustment of the handbrake is satisfactory. In this condition, the handbrake lever should be pulled over three to six 'clicks' to fully apply the brakes. If the plunger movement is incorrect, carry out the following operations.

7 Loosen the handbrake cable locknut, then rotate the adjuster sleeve (photo) so that the plungers can just rotate and the total movement of both plungers is as specified above.

8 Hand tighten the locknut against the sleeve so that two engagement clicks are felt, then further tighten another two clicks using a suitable wrench.

10 Handbrake cables – renewal

1 Chock the front wheels, then fully release the handbrake.
2 Raise and support the vehicle at the rear with safety stands.

Primary cable

3 Extract the spring clip and clevis pin and disconnect the primary cable from the equaliser.

4 Working inside the vehicle, disconnect the cable from the handbrake control lever, again by removal of clip and pin. Drift out the cable guide to the rear and withdraw the cable through the floorpan.

5 Refitting is a reversal of removal. Adjust the handbrake, if necessary, as described in Section 9.

Secondary cable

6 Loosen the cable adjuster locknut and then rotate the sleeve so that it can be disengaged from its location bracket.

7 Release the cable connector from its body guide by extracting the spring clip and passing the inner cable through the slit in the guide.

8 Now disconnect the cable from its body guide on the right-hand side of the vehicle.

9 Separate the cable assembly/equaliser from the primary cable by extracting the spring clip and clevis pin.

10 Release the cable from the body guides.

11 Remove the rear roadwheels and the brake drums.

12 Release the shoe hold-down spring so that the shoe can be swivelled and the handbrake lever unclipped from the relay lever.

13 Remove the cable ends through the brake backplate and withdraw the complete cable assembly from the vehicle.

14 Refitting is a reversal of removal. Grease the cable groove in the equaliser and adjust the handbrake, as described in Section 9.

11 Handbrake lever – removal and refitting

1 Chock the front wheels, raise and support the vehicle at the rear using safety stands. Release the handbrake.

2 Working underneath the vehicle, extract the lever-to-equaliser cable retaining clip, remove the pin and separate the cable from the equaliser.

3 Remove the front seats (Chapter 12) and the long console, if fitted (Chapter 12). It may also be necessary to remove the carpet.

4 Detach the handbrake warning switch.

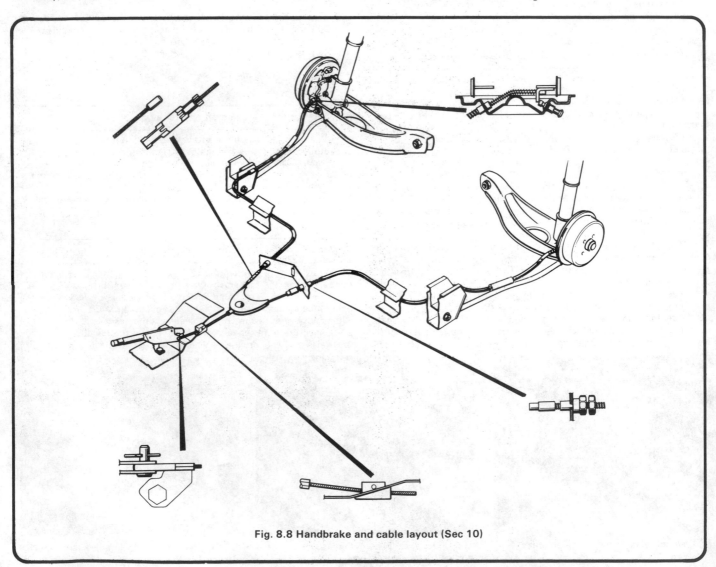

Fig. 8.8 Handbrake and cable layout (Sec 10)

5   Disconnect the cable from the handbrake lever by extracting the clip and pin.
6   Unscrew the lever securing bolts and remove the lever.
7   Refit in the reverse order of removal. On completion, check the handbrake adjustment, as given in Section 9.

12 Hydraulic system – bleeding

1   This is not a routine operation, but will be required after any component in the system has been removed and refitted or any part of the hydraulic system has been 'broken'. When an operation has only affected one circuit of the hydraulic system, then bleeding will normally only be required to that circuit (front and rear diagonally opposite). If the master cylinder or the pressure regulating valve have been disconnected and reconnected, then the complete system must be bled.
2   One of three methods can be used to bleed the system.

Bleeding – two-man method
3   Gather together a clean jar and a length of rubber or plastic bleed tubing which will fit the bleed screw tightly. The help of an assistant will be required.
4   Take great care not to spill fluid onto the paintwork as it will act as a paint stripper. If any is spilled, wash it off at once with cold water.
5   Clean around the bleed screw on the front right-hand caliper and attach the bleed tube to the screw.
6   Check that the master cylinder reservoir is topped up and then destroy the vacuum in the brake servo (where fitted) by giving several applications of the brake foot pedal.
7   Immerse the open end of the bleed tube in the jar, which should contain 50 to 76 mm (2 to 3 in) of hydraulic fluid. The jar should be positioned about 300 mm (12.0 in) above the bleed nipple to prevent any possibility of air entering the system down the threads of the bleed screw when it is slackened.
8   Open the bleed screw half a turn and have your assistant depress the brake pedal slowly to the floor and then quickly remove his foot to allow the pedal to return unimpeded. Tighten the bleed screw at the end of each downstroke to prevent expelled air and fluid being drawn back into the system.
9   Observe the submerged end of the tube in the jar. When air bubbles cease to appear, fully tighten the bleed screw when the pedal is being held down by your assistant.
10 Top up the fluid reservoir. It must be kept topped up throughout the bleeding operations. If the connecting holes to the master cylinder

are exposed at any time due to low fluid level, then air will be drawn into the system and work will have to start all over again.
11 Repeat the operations on the left-hand rear brake, the left-hand front and the right-hand rear brake in that order (assuming that the whole system is being bled).
12 On completion, remove the bleed tube. Discard the fluid which has been bled from the system unless it is required for bleed jar purposes, never use it for filling the system.

Bleeding – with one-way valve
13 There are a number of one-man brake bleeding kits currently available from motor accessory shops. It is recommended that one of these kits should be used whenever possible as they greatly simplify the bleeding operation and also reduce the risk of expelled air or fluid being drawn back into the system.
14 Connect the outlet tube of the bleeder device to the bleed screw and then open the screw half a turn. Depress the brake pedal to the floor and slowly release it. The one-way valve in the device will prevent expelled air from returning to the system at the completion of each stroke. Repeat this operation until clean hydraulic fluid, free from air bubbles, can be seen coming through the tube. Tighten the bleed screw and remove the tube.
15 Repeat the procedure on the remaining bleed nipples in the order described in paragraph 11. Remember to keep the master cylinder reservoir full.

Bleeding – with pressure bleeding kit
16 These are available from motor accessory shops and are usually operated by air pressure from the spare tyre.
17 By connecting a pressurised container to the master cylinder fluid reservoir, bleeding is then carried out by simply opening each bleed screw in turn and allowing the fluid to run out, rather like turning on a tap, until no air bubbles are visible in the fluid being expelled.
18 Using this system, the large reserve of fluid provides a safeguard against air being drawn into the master cylinder during the bleeding operations.
19 This method is particularly effective when bleeding 'difficult' systems or when bleeding the entire system at time of routine fluid renewal.

All systems
20 On completion of bleeding, top up the fluid level to the mark. Check the feel of the brake pedal, which should be firm and free from any 'sponginess' which would indicate air still being present in the system.

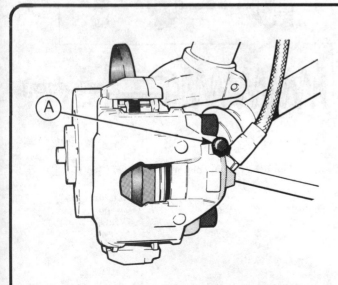

Fig. 8.9 Bleed nipple location (A) (Sec 12)

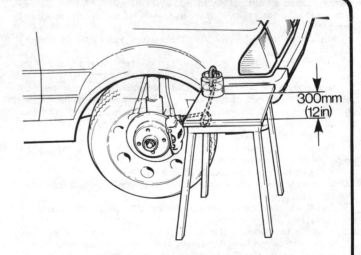

Fig. 8.10 Arrangement for brake bleeding (Sec 12)

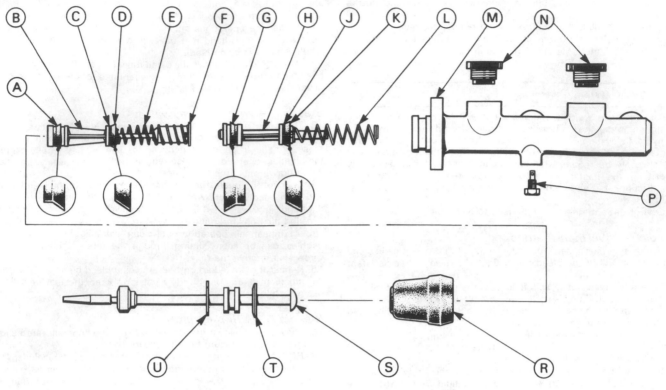

Fig. 8.11 Exploded view of master cylinder (Sec 13)

A	Seal	F	Retainer
B	Primary piston	G	Seal
C	Shim	H	Secondary piston
D	Seal	J	Shim
E	Spring	K	Seal
L	Spring	R	Dust excluder
M	Cylinder body	S	Pushrod
N	Reservoir seals	T	Washer
P	Piston stop bolt	U	Circlip

13 Master cylinder – removal, overhaul and refitting

1   Disconnect the leads from the level warning switch in the reservoir cap. Remove the cap.

2   Syphon out as much fluid as possible from the master cylinder reservoir using an old battery hydrometer or a poultry baster. Do not drip the fluid onto the paintwork as it will act as an effective paint stripper.

3   Disconnect the pipelines from the master cylinder by unscrewing the unions.

4   Unbolt the master cylinder unit from the servo unit and withdraw it.

5   Clean away external dirt and then detach the fluid reservoir by tilting it sideways and gently pulling. Remove the two rubber seals.

6   Secure the master cylinder carefully in a vice fitted with jaw protectors.

7   Unscrew and remove the piston stop bolt.

8   Pull the dust excluder back and, using circlip pliers, extract the circlip which is now exposed.

9   Remove the pushrod, dust excluder and washer.

10   Withdraw the primary piston assembly, which will already have been partially ejected.

11   Tap the end of the master cylinder on a block of wood and eject the secondary piston assembly.

12   Examine the piston and cylinder bore surface for scoring or signs of metal-to-metal rubbing. If evident, renew the cylinder complete.

13   Where the components are in good condition, dismantle the primary piston by unscrewing the screw and removing the sleeve. Remove the spring, retainer, seal and shim. Prise the second seal from the piston.

14   Dismantle the secondary piston in a similar way.

15   Discard all seals and obtain a repair kit.

16   Cleaning of components should be done in brake hydraulic fluid or methylated spirit – nothing else.

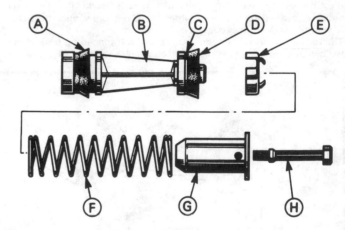

Fig. 8.12 Primary piston dismantled (Sec 13)

A	Seal	E	Retainer
B	Piston	F	Spring
C	Shim	G	Sleeve
D	Seal	H	Screw

17   Using the new seals from the repair kit, assemble the pistons, making sure that the seal lips are the correct way round.

18   Dip the piston assemblies in clean hydraulic fluid and enter them into the cylinder bore.

19   Fit the pushrod complete with new dust excluder and secure with a new circlip.

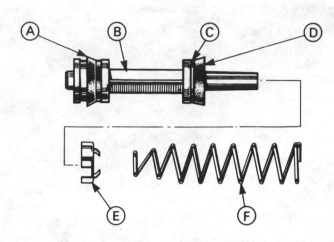

Fig. 8.13 Secondary piston dismantled (Sec 13)

A	Seal	D	Seal
B	Piston	E	Retainer
C	Shim	F	Spring

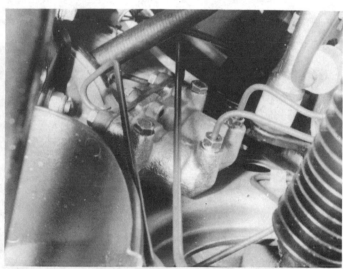

14.1 Location of pressure regulating valve

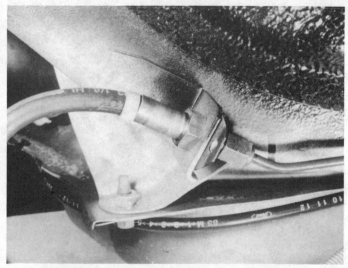

15.2 Typical flexible to rigid hydraulic pipe connection

20 Engage the dust excluder with the master cylinder.
21 Depress the pushrod and screw in the stop bolt.
22 Locate the two rubber seals and push the fluid reservoir into position.
23 It is recommended that a small quantity of fluid is now poured into the reservoir and the pushrod operated several times to prime the unit.
24 Refit the master cylinder by reversing the removal operations.
25 Bleed the complete hydraulic system on completion of the work (see Section 12).

14 Pressure regulating valve – removal and refitting

1 The brake pressure regulating valve is located within the engine compartment, just above the aperture in the wing inner panel through which the steering tie-rod passes (photo).
2 Unscrew the unions and disconnect the pipelines from the valve. Cap the ends of the pipes with bleed nipple dust caps to prevent loss of fluid.
3 Unscrew the valve mounting bolts and remove the valve.
4 Refitting is a reversal of removal, but bleed the complete hydraulic system when the work is finished (see Section 12).

15 Flexible and rigid hydraulic pipes – removal and fitting

1 Inspection has already been covered in Section 2 of this Chapter.
2 Always disconnect a flexible hose by prising out the spring anchor clip from the support bracket (photo) and then using two close-fitting spanners, disconnect the rigid line from the flexible hose.
3 Once disconnected from the rigid pipe, the flexible hose may be unscrewed from the caliper or wheel cylinder.
4 When reconnecting pipeline or hose fittings, remember that all union threads are to metric sizes. No copper washers are used at unions and the seal is made at the swaged end of the pipe, so do not try to wind a union in if it is tight yet still stands proud of the surface into which it is screwed.
5 A flexible hose must never be installed twisted, but a slight 'set' is permissible to give it clearance from an adjacent component. Do this by turning the hose slightly before inserting the bracket spring clip.
6 Rigid pipelines can be made to pattern by factors supplying brake components.
7 If you are making up a brake pipe yourself, observe the following essential requirements.
8 Before flaring the ends of the pipe, trim back the protective plastic coating by a distance of 5.0 mm (0.2 in).
9 Flare the end of the pipe as shown (Fig. 8.14).
10 The minimum pipe bend radius is 12.0 mm (0.5 in), but bends of less than 20.0 mm (0.8 in) should be avoided if possible.

16 Vacuum servo unit and connecting linkage – removal and refitting

1 Refer to Section 13 and complete the instructions given in paragraphs 1 to 3 and fit blanking plugs to the master cylinder fluid pipe connections to prevent the ingress of dirt.

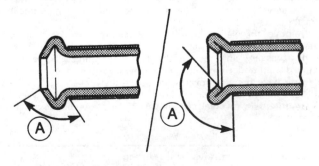

Fig. 8.14 Brake pipe flare (Sec 15)

A   Protective coating removed before flaring

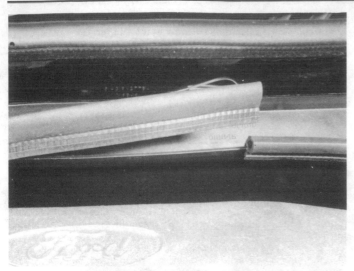

16.2A Prise free and lift away the heater plenum chamber surround trim ...

16.2B ... then lift out the chamber front section (for improved access on fuel injection models)

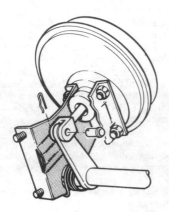

Fig. 8.15 Servo unit and connecting rod attachment – right-hand drive (Sec 16)

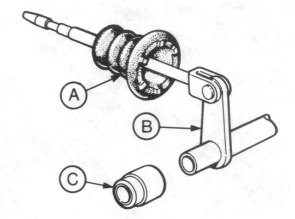

Fig. 8.16 Brake pedal pushrod to servo operating link – right-hand drive (Sec 16)

A   Grommet   C   Bush
B   Link

2   On fuel injection models unclip and lift out the front section of the heater plenum chamber to provide access to the connecting linkage across the lower bulkhead (photos).

3   Working inside the vehicle, remove the spring clip which attaches the pushrod to the arm of the brake pedal (photo 17.2).

4   Unscrew the nuts which hold the servo to its mounting bracket, also the servo support brace to the body.

5   Disconnect the vacuum hose from the servo.

6   Detach the linkage arm spring at the rear of the servo and then pull the servo forward until the servo operating rod can be unclipped from the linkage.

7   Remove the servo from the vehicle. It must be renewed if defective, no repair is possible.

8   If necessary, the rest of the servo operating linkage can be removed from under the instrument panel once the covering and cowl side trim have been removed from above the brake pedal inside the vehicle. Unbolt the connecting link bracket from the driver's side.

9   Refitting is a reversal of removal. Bleed the hydraulic system on completion.

17 Brake pedal – removal and refitting

1   Working within the vehicle, remove the under-dash cover panel.

2   Extract the spring clip which connects the pushrod to the arm of the brake pedal (photo).

17.2 Brake pedal and pushrod with securing clip (arrowed)

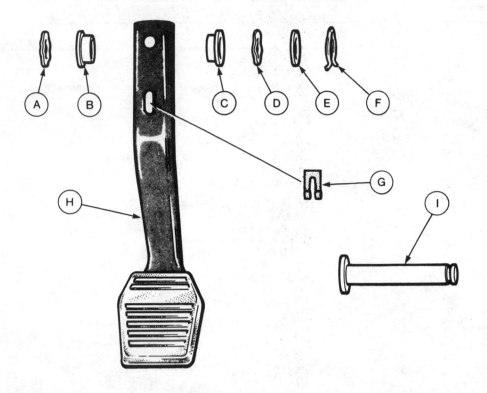

Fig. 8.17 Brake pedal components (Sec 17)

A   Washer
B   Bush
C   Bush
D   Washer
E   Washer
F   Spring clip
G   Pushrod clip
H   Pedal
I   Pedal pivot shaft

3   Extract the circlip from the end of the pedal pivot shaft and withdraw the shaft with clutch pedal and the flat and wave washers.
4   Renew the bushes as necessary.
5   Reassembly and refitting are reversals of removal and dismantling. Apply a little grease to the bushes when installing.

18 Brake warning lamps – description and renewal

1   As already mentioned, all models are fitted with a low fluid level warning switch in the master cylinder reservoir cap and a brake pedal stop-lamp switch.
2   Also fitted are front disc pad wear sensors and a handbrake ON warning switch.
3   Warning indicator lamps are mounted on the instrument panel. Their renewal is covered in Chapter 11.
4   Access to the handbrake switch is obtained after removal of the centre console, the switch cover is below it. Prise free the switch cover using a screwdriver, then unscrew and remove the switch lower retaining screw. Loosen the upper screw and slide the switch free.
5   Detach the wiring connector for complete removal of the switch.
6   Refitting is a reversal of the removal procedure, but on completion check the operation of the switch and warning light with the ignition on.

7   The stop-lamp switch can be removed by disconnecting the leads and unscrewing the locknut which holds the switch to its bracket.
8   When fitting the switch, adjust its position by screwing it in or out so that it does not actuate during the first 5.0 mm (0.2 in) of pedal travel.

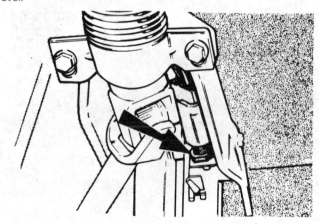

Fig. 8.18 Brake stop-lamp switch showing locknut – arrowed (Sec 18)

Fault diagnosis appears overleaf

19 Fault diagnosis – braking system

Symptom	Reason(s)
Pedal travels to floorboards before brakes operate	Brake fluid level too low Caliper leaking Master cylinder leaking (bubbles in master cylinder fluid) Brake flexible hose leaking Brake line fractured Brake system unions loose Rear automatic adjusters seized
Brake pedal feels springy	New linings not yet bedded-in Brake discs or drums badly worn or cracked Master cylinder securing nuts loose
Brake pedal feels spongy and soggy	Caliper or wheel cylinder leaking Master cylinder leaking (bubbles in master cylinder reservoir) Brake pipeline or flexible hose leaking Unions in brake system loose Air in hydraulic system
Excessive effort required to brake car	Pad or shoe linings badly worn New pads or shoes recently fitted – not yet bedded in Vacuum servo unit defective

Chapter 9 Steering

For modifications, and information applicable to later models, see Supplement at end of manual

Contents

Specifications

Steering gear

Type	Rack and pinion with universally-jointed shaft and deformable column
Turning circle (between kerbs)	10.08 m (33.1 ft)
Tie-rod diameter	11.8 mm (0.46 in) or 13.3 mm (0.52 in) depending on manufacturer
Pinion turning torque	0.3 to 1.3 Nm (0.22 to 0.96 lbf ft)
Pinion dust cover grease	To Ford specification SM1C-1021-A
Pinion plug sealant	To Ford specification EM-4G-14 or SPM-4G-9112F
Gear lubricant:	
Semi-fluid grease (70 cc)	To Ford specification SAM-1C-9106-A
Oil (120 cc)	To Ford specification SQM-2C-9003-AA

Front wheel alignment

Checking tolerance	0.5 mm (0.02 in) toe-in to 5.5 mm (0.22 in) toe-out
Setting tolerance	1.5 mm (0.06 in) to 3.5 mm (0.14 in) toe-out

Torque wrench settings

	Nm	lbf ft
Steering gear to bulkhead	45 to 50	33 to 37
Tie-rod to rack	68 to 90	50 to 66
Tie-rod locknut (to balljoint)	57 to 68	42 to 50
Coupling to pinion spline	45 to 56	33 to 41
Tie-rod end to steering arm	25 to 30	18 to 22
Steering wheel-to-shaft nut	27 to 34	20 to 25
Pinion slipper plug	4 to 5	3 to 4

1 General description

The steering is of rack-and-pinion type, with a safety steering column which incorporates a universally-jointed lower shaft and a convoluted column tube.

The pinion of the steering gear is supported in a needle roller bearing at its lower end and in a ball-bearing at its upper end. Pinion bearing preload adjustment has been eliminated.

The steering tie-rods are attached to the steering rack by means of balljoints working in nylon seats. The balljoints are precisely preloaded, set and locked in position during production.

The tie-rod outer balljoints are of screw-on type with a locking nut.

Rack-to-pinion contact is maintained by a spring-loaded slipper working against a threaded plug.

The tie-rods are adjustable for length in order to vary the front wheel alignment. Other steering angles are set in production and cannot be adjusted.

Integral lock stops are built into the steering gear and these are also non-adjustable.

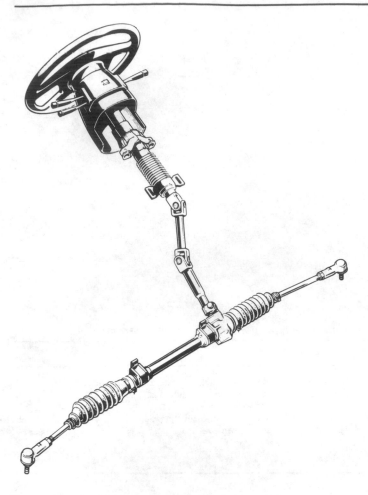

Fig. 9.1 Steering wheel, column and rack assembly (Sec 1)

The steering gear is lubricated with a semi-fluid grease but in case of difficulty in supply, use Hypoy 90 oil.

The steering wheel is located on a hexagon section shaft instead of the more conventional splined type. This arrangement makes the wheel easier to remove once the nut has been undone.

The steering column lock provides greater security through the large number of lock engagement slots in the column. It is impossible to remove the lock from the column unless the cylinder has first been unlocked.

2   Maintenance and precautions

1   Regularly check the condition of the steering gear bellows and the tie-rod balljoint dust excluders. If split, they must be renewed immediately and the steering gear lubricant cleared out and a fresh amount injected (see Section 3).
2   With an assistant turning the steering wheel from side-to-side, check for lost motion at the tie-rod end balljoints. If evident, renew the balljoints (see Section 4) as no repair or lubrication is possible.
3   When the front wheels are raised, avoid turning the steering wheel rapidly from lock-to-lock. This could cause hydraulic pressure build-up, with consequent damage to the bellows.

3   Steering gear bellows – renewal

1   At the first indication of a split or grease leakage from the bellows, renew them.
2   Loosen off the roadwheel bolts, raise the front of the vehicle and support on safety stands. Remove the roadwheels.
3   Measure and take note of the amount of thread on the tie-rod which is exposed (photo). This will ensure correct track alignment on reassembly.
4   Loosen off the tie-rod end ball-joint locknut.
5   Extract the split pin and remove the nut from the balljoint taper pin.
6   Using a suitable balljoint extractor, separate the balljoint taper pin from the eye of the steering arm (photo).
7   Unscrew the balljoint from the end of the tie-rod, also the locknut. As a double check for correct repositioning of the tie-rod end balljoint when reassembling, note the number of turns required to remove it.
8   Release the clip from the end of the damaged bellow and slide it from the rack and the tie-rod (photo).
9   When ordering the new bellows and retaining clips also specify the diameter of the tie-rod which will vary according to manufacture (see Specifications). This is important since if the wrong size bellows are fitted they will not seal or possibly be damaged on fitting.
10 If a damaged bellow has caused steering lubricant loss it will be necessary to drain any remaining lubricant and renew it. To do this turn the steering wheel gently to expel as much lubricant as possible from the rack housing. If the opposing bellow is not being renewed it is recommended that it is released from the rack housing to allow the old lubricant to be removed from that end, too.
11 Smear the narrow neck of the new bellows with grease and slide into position over the tie-rod, ensuring that the bellows are correctly located in the tie-rod groove on the outer bellow end.
12 If new bellows are being fitted to the pinion end of the rack, leave the bellows unclamped at this stage.
13 If the bellows are being fitted to the rack support bush end of the rack housing, clamp the inner end of the bellows.
14 Always use new screw-type clamps, never reuse the old factory-fitted wire type when securing the bellows.
15 Screw the locknut into position on the tie-rod, followed by the

3.3 Tie-rod balljoint assembly
Measure exposed thread on rod (A) before loosening locknut

3.6 Tie-rod to steering arm balljoint separator in position

3.8 Bellows to rack/pinion housing retaining clip – wire type as fitted during manufacture (discard on removal)

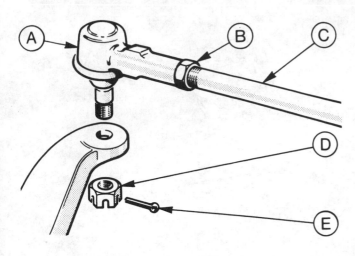

Fig. 9.2 Tie-rod outer balljoint (Sec 3)

A   Balljoint   D   Castellated nut
B   Locknut   E   Split pin
C   Tie-rod

outer tie-rod balljoint. Screw the joint the exact number of turns noted during removal.
16 Connect the tie-rod end balljoint to the steering arm, tighten the nut to the specified torque and insert a new split pin to secure.
17 If applicable, renew the steering gear lubricant, as described in Section 9, paragraph 26.
18 Tighten the bellow retaining clamp(s).
19 Refit the roadwheels and lower the vehicle to the ground. Settle the suspension by bouncing the front end.
20 Tighten the balljoint end locknut and check the amount of tie-rod thread exposed. It should be as noted when dismantling and therefore provide the correct tracking, but in any case the alignment should really be checked at the earliest opportunity, as described in Section 10, or by your Ford dealer.

4   Tie-rod end balljoint – renewal

1   If as the result of inspection the tie-rod end balljoints are found to be worn, remove them as described in the preceding Section.
2   When the balljoint nuts are unscrewed, it is sometimes found that the balljoint taper pin turns in the eye of the steering arm to prevent the nut from unscrewing. Should this happen, apply pressure to the top of the balljoint using a length of wood as a lever to seat the taper pin while the nut is unscrewed. When this condition is met with, a balljoint extractor is unlikely to be required to free the taper pin from the steering arm.
3   With the tie-rod removed, wire brush the threads of the tie-rod and apply grease to them.
4   Screw on the new tie-rod end to take up a position similar to the original. Due to manufacturing differences, the fitting of a new component will almost certainly mean that the front wheel alignment will require some adjustment. Check this as described in Section 10.
5   Connect the balljoint to the steering arm, as described in Section 3.

5   Steering wheel – removal and refitting

1   According to model, either pull off the steering wheel trim or prise out the insert which carries the Ford motif at the centre of the steering wheel. Insert the ignition key and turn it to position I.
2   Hold the steering wheel from turning and have the front road-wheels in the straight-ahead attitude, while the steering wheel retaining nut is unscrewed using a socket with extension.
3   Remove the steering wheel from the shaft. No effort should be

required to remove the steering wheel as it is located on a hexagonal section shaft which does not cause the binding associated with splined shafts.
4   Note the steering shaft direction indicator cam which has its peg uppermost.
5   Refitting is a reversal of removal. Check that the roadwheels are still in the straight-ahead position and locate the steering wheel so that the larger segment between the spokes is uppermost.

6   Steering column lock – removal and refitting

1   To remove the ignition switch/column lock, the shear-head bolt must be drilled out.
2   Access for drilling can only be obtained if the steering column is lowered. To do this, remove the shrouds from the upper end of the column by extracting the fixing screws. Disconnect the battery earth lead.
3   Unscrew the bonnet release lever mounting screw and position the lever to one side.
4   Disconnect the steering column clamps. The lower one is of bolt and nut type, while the upper one is of stud and nut design.
5   Lower the shaft/column carefully until the steering wheel rests on the seat cushion.
6   Centre-punch the end of the shear-bolt which secures the steering

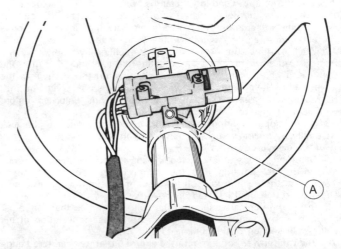

Fig. 9.3 Steering column lock unit showing position of shear-bolt (A) (Sec 6)

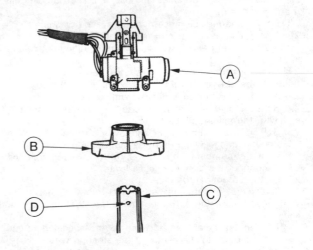

Fig. 9.4 Steering lock unit (A), upper clamp (B), column tube (C) and shear-bolt hole position (D) (Sec 6)

column lock and then drill it out. Remove the ignition switch/column lock.
7   When fitting the new lock, check for correct operation and then tighten the securing bolt until its head breaks off.
8   Raise the steering column and reconnect the clamps.
9   Refit the bonnet release lever and the column shrouds.

7   Steering column – removal, overhaul and refitting

1   Disconnect the battery.
2   Turn the ignition key and rotate the steering wheel to bring the front roadwheels to the straight-ahead position.
3   Working within the engine compartment, unscrew and remove the pinch-bolt which holds the steering shaft to the splined pinion shaft of the rack-and-pinion gear.
4   Remove the steering wheel, as described in Section 5.
5   Remove the direction indicator cam from the top end of the steering shaft.
6   Extract the fixing screws and remove the upper and lower shrouds from the upper end of the steering column.
7   Remove the insulation panel from the lower part of the dash panel.
8   Extract the screw, remove the bottom release lever mounting and place it to one side.
9   Take out the fixing screws and remove the switches from the steering column.
10   Disconnect the wiring harness multi-plug at the side of the column.
11   Unbolt the upper and lower clamps from the steering column and then withdraw the column/shaft into the vehicle. If any difficulty is experienced in separating the lower shaft from the pinion gear, prise the coupling open very slightly with a screwdriver.
12   Wear in the column bearings can be rectified by renewing them. Access to them is obtained by extracting the tolerance ring from the upper end of the column and then withdrawing the shaft from the lower end of the column. The lower bearing and spring will come with it. Make sure that the steering column lock is unlocked before withdrawing the shaft.
13   If the upper bearing is to be renewed, first remove the lock assembly by drilling out the shear-head bolt. The upper bearing may now be levered out of its seat.
14   Commence reassembly by tapping the new upper bearing into its seat in the lock housing. Refit the column upper clamp and bush.
15   Locate the column lock on the column tube and screw in a new shear-head bolt until its head breaks off.
16   Insert the conical spring into the column tube so that the larger diameter end of the spring is against the lowest convolution of the collapsible section of the column tube.
17   Slide the lower bearing onto the shaft so that its chamfered edge will mate with the corresponding one in the column lower bearing seat when the shaft is installed.
18   Insert the shaft into the lower end of the steering column. Make sure that the lock is unbolted and pass the shaft up carefully through the upper bearing.
19   Fit the bearing tolerance ring and waved washer.
20   Fit the direction indicator cancelling cam to the top of the shaft, making sure that the peg will be uppermost when the column is in the in-car attitude.
21   Fit the steering wheel to the shaft, screwing on the nut sufficiently tightly to be able to pull the lower bearing into the column tube with the bearing slots correctly aligned with the pegs on the tube.
22   Refit the column, making sure to engage the coupling at its lower end with the splined pinion shaft.
23   Bolt up the column upper and lower clamps.
24   Reconnect the wiring harness multi-plug.
25   Refit the combination switches to the steering column.
26   Reconnect the bonnet release lever.
27   Fit the column shrouds.
28   Check that the steering wheel is correctly aligned (wheels in the straight-ahead position). If not, remove the steering wheel and realign it.
29   Tighten the steering wheel nut to the specified torque and the insert the motif into the centre of the steering wheel.
30   Refit the insulation panel to the lower dash.
31   Tighten the coupling pinch-bolt at the base of the steering shaft.
32   Reconnect the battery.

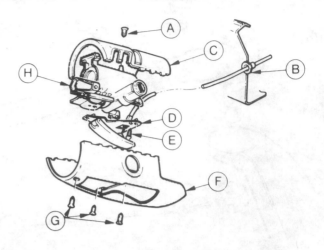

Fig. 9.5 Steering upper column attachments (Sec 7)

A   Screw   E   Screw
B   Bonnet release cable   F   Lower shroud
C   Upper shroud   G   Screws
D   Bonnet release lever   H   Lock housing

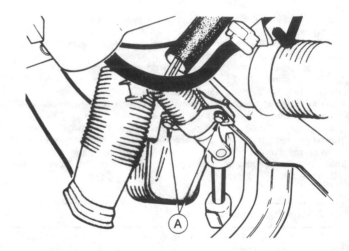

Fig. 9.6 Steering column lower clamp bolts (A) (Sec 7)

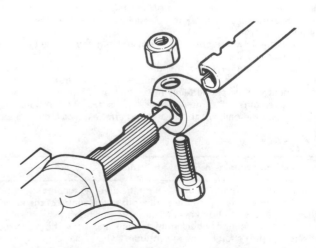

Fig. 9.7 Steering shaft coupling and pinch-bolt (Secs 7 and 8)

8 Steering gear – removal and refitting

1 Set the front roadwheels in the straight-ahead position.
2 Raise the front of the vehicle and fit safety stands.
3 Working under the bonnet, remove the pinch-bolt from the coupling at the base of the steering column shaft (Fig. 9.7).
4 Extract the split pins from the tie-rod balljoint taper pin nuts, unscrew the nuts and remove them.
5 Separate the balljoints from the steering arms using a suitable separator tool.
6 Flatten the locktabs on the steering gear securing bolts and unscrew and remove the bolts (photo). Withdraw the steering gear downwards to separate the coupling from the steering shaft and then take it out from under the front wing.

8.6 Steering gear-to-bulkhead mounting showing securing bolt and locktab

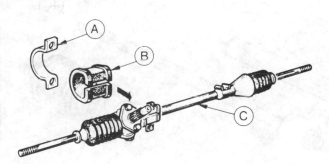

Fig. 9.8 Steering rack mounting components (Sec 8)

A Clamping saddle C Rack housing
B Rubber insulator

7 Refitting is a reversal of removal. If a new rack-and-pinion assembly is being installed, the tie-rods ends will have to be removed from the original unit and screwed onto the new tie-rods to approximately the same setting. If a note was not made of the position of the original tie-rod ends on their rods, inspection of the threads will probably indicate their original location. In any event it is important that the new tie-rod ends are screwed on an equal amount at this stage.
8 Make sure that the steering gear is centred. Do this by turning the pinion shaft to full lock in one direction and then count the number of turns required to rotate it to the opposite lock. Now turn the splined pinion shaft through half the number of turns just counted.
9 Check that the roadwheels and the steering wheel are in the straight-ahead attitude, offer up the steering gear and connect the shaft coupling without inserting the pinch-bolt.
10 Bolt up the gear housing and lock the bolts with their lockplate tabs.
11 Reconnect the tie-rod ends to the steering arms. Tighten the securing nuts to the specified torque setting and fit new split pins to secure.
12 Tighten the coupling pinch-bolt to the specified torque. Lower the vehicle to the floor.
13 If the tie-rods ends were disturbed or if a new assembly was installed, check and adjust the wheel alignment, as described in Section 10.

9 Steering gear – overhaul

1 The following operations should only be carried out by home mechanics having a reasonable level of engineering skill and the necessary tools, some of which are Ford special tools and their reference numbers are given, where necessary.
2 If the steering gear has given good service over a high mileage then it is strongly recommended that a new or factory reconditioned unit is installed, rather than overhaul the original assembly.
3 Remove the steering gear from the vehicle, as described in Section 8.
4 Remove the tie-rod ends and the bellows, as described in Section 3.
5 Drain the lubricant by turning the splined pinion shaft from lock-to-lock.
6 The steering rack must now be fully traversed in one direction (left or right) so that the rack teeth are fully exposed. Fit the rack into position in a vice fitted with protector jaws. Locate as shown in Fig. 9.9 and then unscrew the tie-rod ends from the steering rack.
7 Having removed the first tie-rod end mark it left or right, as applicable, to ensure that it is correctly refitted on reassembly.
8 Remove the opposite tie-rod in a similar manner.
9 Unscrew and remove the rack slipper plug using Ford special tool 13-009A, if available. Extract the spring and slipper.
10 Unscrew and remove the pinion retaining nut. The reverse end of Ford special tool 13-009A is designed for this purpose since it fits into the slots in the head of the nut. If this tool is not available, carefully drift the nut loose. Remove the nut seal.
11 The pinion and bearing assembly can now be withdrawn from the housing.
12 Withdraw the rack from the housing using a twisting action, then remove the rack support bush.
13 With the steering gear dismantled, clean and inspect all components. Check for excessive wear or damage of the various components and renew as necessary. Renewal of the pinion nut seal and the rack support bush should be undertaken as a matter of course.
14 Commence reassembly by inserting the new rack support bush into position in the rack tube.
15 Smear the rack lightly with specified semi-fluid grease and then fit the rack tube over the rack and position it so that the rack is centralised.
16 Smear the pinion teeth with the semi-fluid grease and locate the pinion and bearing unit into position in the rack housing. When fitted the pinion flat must be at 90° to the slipper plug (facing the tube pinion end).
17 Before fitting the pinion nut smear its threads with the specified sealant and then tighten it to the specified torque setting. If Ford special tool 13-009A is not available you will need to fabricate a castellated socket to locate into the slots of the nut to achieve this. When tightened, peen the edges of the nut into position with the steering rack housing.
18 Check that the steering rack is still centralised, then fit rack slipper and spring into position. Before fitting the retaining plug, coat its thread with a suitable thread sealant.
19 Tighten the slipper plug to the specified torque setting and then unscrew it 60° to 70°.
20 The pinion turning torque must now be set and for this you will need Ford special tool 13-004 which is a pinion socket and also tool 15-041 which is a preload gauge. If these tools are not available, have the pinion turning torque checked and set by a Ford dealer.

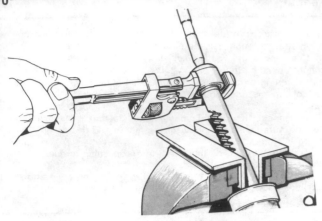

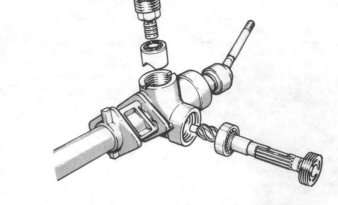

Fig. 9.9 Tie-rod removal/refitting method (Sec 9)

Failure to secure rack as shown can damage the pinion bearing

Fig. 9.10 The pinion, bearing and slipper assembly (Sec 9)

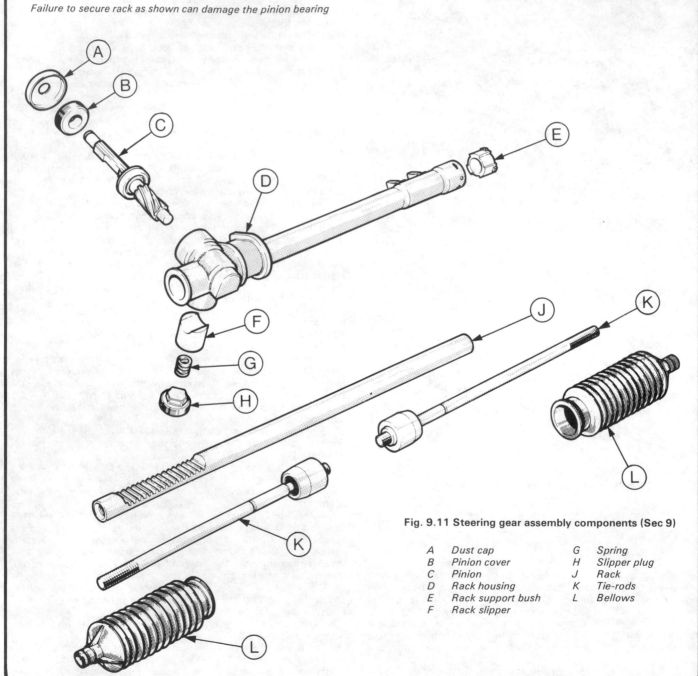

Fig. 9.11 Steering gear assembly components (Sec 9)

A	Dust cap	G	Spring
B	Pinion cover	H	Slipper plug
C	Pinion	J	Rack
D	Rack housing	K	Tie-rods
E	Rack support bush	L	Bellows
F	Rack slipper		

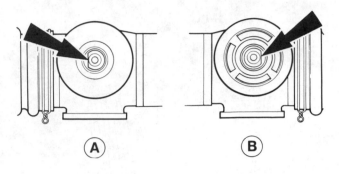

Fig. 9.12 Steering gear pinion alignment position for left-hand drive (A) and right-hand drive (B) models (Sec 9)

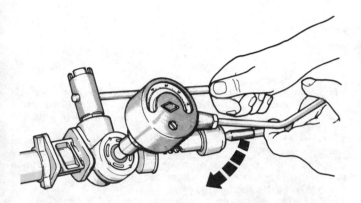

Fig. 9.13 Pinion turning torque check method using Ford special tools (Sec 9)

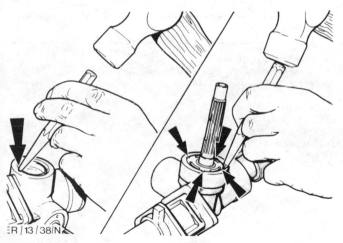

Fig. 9.14 Secure pinion cover and slipper plug in position by stake punching at points indicated (Sec 9)

21 Assuming the special tools are available, fit the socket and gauge into position on the pinion and turn the pinion through 180° anti-clockwise, then clockwise through 36° whilst noting the torque reading. Rotate the pinion back (anti-clockwise) 180°.
22 The pinion turning torque should be as given in the Specifications, but if adjustment is necessary, rotate the slipper plug in the direction required to increase or decrease the reading to that specified.
23 With the correct adjustment made, stake punch around the edge of the plug and housing surfaces to secure the plug in position.

24 Move the rack fully to the right or left and clamp the rack in a vice fitted with soft jaw protectors. Refit the appropriate tie-rod to the rack. If fitting the original tie-rods tighten them so that the stake marks align with the steering rack grooves when fully fitted. Service replacement tie-rods must be fitted and tightened to the specified torque setting using a suitable open-ended torque wrench adaptor. Service replacement tie-rods have flat sections on them for this purpose. When tightened, stake punch the tie-rod balljoints to the rack groove.
25 Smear the inner surface of the rack bellows where they contact the rack housing and tie-rod with grease and fit the bellows, ensuring correct location with the tie-rod groove.
26 Add 120 cc of the specified oil to the tube and 70 cc of semi-fluid grease to the gear housing end. If new bellows are being fitted ensure that the correct replacement types are fitted – refer to Section 3 for details.
27 Secure the bellows with new screw-type clamp clips, (do not reuse the original wire type clips).
28 The pinion cover must now be filled with grease and fitted to complete reassembly.
29 Refit the tie-rod ends, as described in Section 3.
30 Refit the steering gear to the vehicle, as given in Section 8.
31 When refitting is completed, check that the action of the steering is satisfactory before lowering the vehicle and road testing.
32 If the position of the tie-rod locknut was not altered from its original setting, the front wheel alignment (toe) will not have altered. but it is recommended that the alignment is checked at the earliest opportunity as described in Section 10.

10 Steering angles and wheel alignment

1 When reading this Section, reference should also be made to Chapter 10 in respect of front and rear suspension arrangement.
2 Accurate front wheel alignment is essential to good steering and for even tyre wear. Before considering the steering angles, check that the tyres are correctly inflated, that the roadwheels are not buckled, the hub bearings are not worn or incorrectly adjusted and that the steering linkage is in good order.
3 Wheel alignment consists of four factors:
Camber is the angle at which the road wheels are set from the vertical when viewed from the front or rear of the vehicle. Positive camber is the angle (in degrees) that the wheels are tilted outwards at the top from the vertical.
Castor is the angle between the steering axis and a vertical line when viewed from each side of the vehicle. Positive castor is indicated when the steering axis is inclined towards the rear of the vehicle at its upper end.
Steering axis iclination is the angle, when viewed from the front or rear of the vehicle, between the vertical and an imaginary line drawn between the upper and lower suspension swivel balljoints or upper and lower strut mountings.
Toe is the amount by which the distance between the front inside edges of the roadwheel runs differs from that between the rear inside edges. If the distance at the front is less than that at the rear, the wheels are said to toe-in. If the distance at the front inside edges is greater than that at the rear, the wheels toe-out.
4 Due to the need for precision gauges to measure the small angles of the steering and suspension settings, it is preferable to leave this work to your dealer. Camber and castor angles are set in production and are not adjustable. If these angles are ever checked and found to be outside specification then either the suspension components are damaged or distorted, or wear has occurred in the bushes at the attachment points.
5 If you wish to check front wheel alignment yourself, first make sure that the lengths of both tie-rods are equal when the steering is in the straight-ahead position. This can be measured reasonably accurately by counting the number of exposed threads on the tie-rod adjacent to the balljoint assembly.
6 Adjust, if necessary, by releasing the locknut from the balljoint assembly and the clamp at the small end of the bellows.
7 Obtain a tracking gauge. These are available in various forms from accessory stores, or one can be fabricated from a length of steel tubing, suitably cranked to clear the sump and bellhousing, and having a setscrew and locknut at one end.
8 With the gauge, measure the distance between the two inner rims

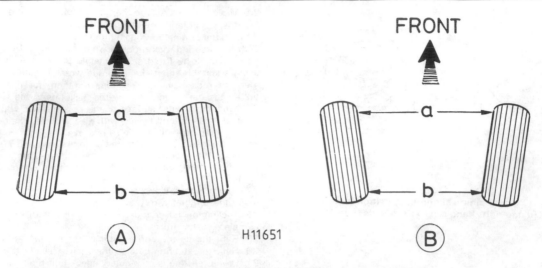

Fig. 9.15 Front wheel alignment (Sec 10)

A   Toe-in (a less than b)
B   Toe-out (a greater than b)

of the roadwheels (at hub height) at the rear of the wheel. Push the vehicle forward to rotate the wheel through 180° (half a turn) and measure the distance between the wheel inner rims, again at hub height, at the front of the wheel. This last measurement should differ from the first one by the specified toe-in/toe-out (see Specifications).

9 Where the toe setting is found to be incorrect, release the tie-rod balljoint locknuts and turn the tie-rods by an equal amount. Only turn them through a quarter turn at a time before re-checking the alignment. Do not grip the threaded part of the tie-rod during adjustment and make sure that the bellows outboard clip is released, otherwise the bellows will twist as the tie-rod is rotated. When each tie-rod is viewed from the rack housing, turning the rods clockwise will increase the toe-out. Always turn the tie-rods in the same direction when viewed from the centre of the vehicle, otherwise they will become unequal in length. This would cause the steering wheel spoke alignment to alter and also cause problems on turning with tyre scrubbing.

10 On completion of adjustment, tighten the tie-rod end locknuts without altering the setting of the tie-rods. Hold the balljoint assembly at the mid-point of its arc of travel (flats are provided on it for a spanner) while the locknuts are tightened.

11 Finally, tighten the bellows clamps.

12 Rear wheel alignment is set in production and is not adjustable, but when dismantling the tie-bar, it is essential that all washers are refitted in their original positions as they control the wheel setting for the life of the vehicle (see Chapter 10).

11 Fault diagnosis – steering

Symptom	Reason(s)
Steering feels vague, vehicle wanders	Uneven tyre pressures
	Worn tie-rod end balljoints
	Incorrect pinion adjustment
Stiff and heavy steering	Tyres under-inflated
	Dry suspension strut swivels
	Tie-rod end balljoints dry or corroded
	Incorrect toe setting
	Other steering angles incorrect
	Pinion adjusted too tightly
	Steering column misaligned

Chapter 10 Suspension

For modifications, and information applicable to later models, see Supplement at end of manual

Contents

Specifications

General

Front suspension	Independent, MacPherson strut with anti-roll bar. Double-acting shock absorbers incorporated in the struts
Rear suspension	Independent with coil spring and double-acting shock absorbers. Anti-roll bar on 1.6 fuel injection models

Track:
Front wheels .... 1399 mm (55.1 in)
Rear wheels .... 1422 mm (56.0 in)
Wheelbase .... 2400 mm (94.5 in)
Wheel bearing grease (to Ford specification) SAM-1C9111-A

Suspension angles (unladen)

	1.3	1.6
Castor (non-adjustable):		
Standard	2° 24′	2° 22′
Heavy duty	2° 19′	2° 19′
Maximum permissible variation (side to side)	1° 0′	1° 0′
Camber (non-adjustable):		
Standard	0° 10′	0° 03′
Heavy duty	0° 25′	0° 25′
Maximum permissible variation (side to side)	1° 15′	1° 15′

Roadwheels and tyres

Wheels:
Type .... Pressed-steel
Size .... $5\frac{1}{2}$J x 13
Tyres:
Type .... Steel radial
Tyre size:
1.6 Fuel injection models .... 175/70 HR 13
Other models .... 155 SR 13 or 175/70 SR 13

Tyre pressures (cold) bar (lbf/in^2):	Front	Rear
1.6 Fuel injection:		
Up to 3 people (normal use)	1.6 (23)	1.9 (28)
Fully laden (normal use)	1.9 (28)	2.3 (33)
Other models – 155 SR 13:		
Up to 3 people (normal use)	1.6 (23)	1.9 (28)
Fully laden (normal use)	1.9 (28)	2.3 (33)
Other models – 175/70 SR13:		
Up to 3 people (normal use)	1.6 (23)	1.9 (28)
Fully laden (normal use)	1.9 (28)	2.3 (33)

Increase the above pressures by 0.1 bar (1.5 lbf/in^2) for every 10 kph (6 mph) above 160 kph (100 mph) for sustained high speed use.

Torque wrench settings

	Nm	lbf ft
Front suspension		
Hub retaining nut	230	170
Arm inboard pivot bolt	60	44
Arm balljoint pinch-bolt	58	43
Balljoint-to-lower arm bolts	85	63
Suspension strut to stub axle carrier	85	63
Tie-bar to body bracket	50	37
Tie-bar bracket to body	50	37
Strut piston rod nut	50	37
Anti-roll bar clamp bolts	50	37
Anti-roll bar to suspension arm	110	81
Rear suspension		
Suspension arm inboard pivot bolt	85	63
Suspension arm outboard pivot bolt	65	48
Shock absorber top mounting nuts	50	37
Shock absorber bottom mounting bolts	85	63
Brake backplate bolts	50	37
Tie-bar-to-body pivot bolt	85	63
Tie-bar-to-stub axle carrier nut	85	63
Anti-roll bar clamp bolts	55	41
Roadwheel bolts	95	70

1 General description

The front suspension is of independent type with MacPherson struts. On both 1.3 and 1.6 versions the forged type suspension arm is located by an anti-roll bar.

The rear suspension is independent, incorporating a lower arm, a tie-bar and a coil spring with hydraulic shock absorber. 1.6 fuel injection models have a rear anti-roll bar.

2 Maintenance

This comprises a regular inspection of all suspension flexible bushes for wear, and periodically checking the torque wrench settings of all bolts and nuts with the weight of the vehicle on its roadwheels.

The roadwheels and tyres should be maintained as described in Section 16.

Fig. 10.1 Front suspension components (Sec 1)

A   Front strut assembly
C   Front strut upper
      mounting assembly
D   Hub carrier
E   Hub
J   Anti-roll bar
K   Lower suspension arm
      and balljoint assembly

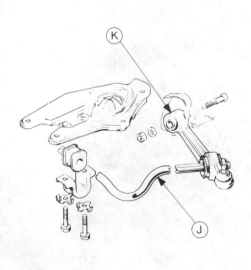
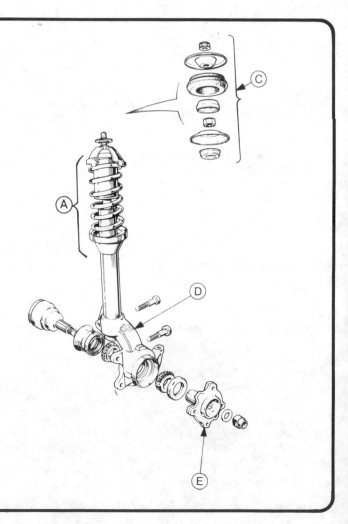

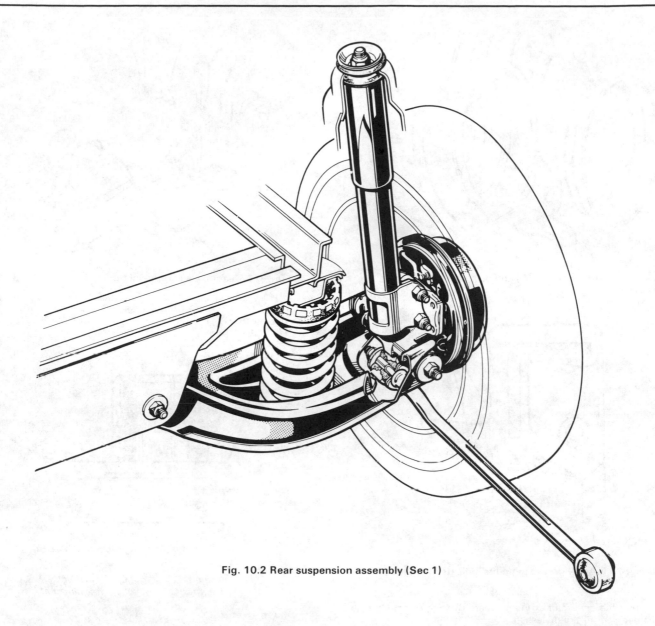

Fig. 10.2 Rear suspension assembly (Sec 1)

3 Front hub bearings – removal and refitting

1   Slacken the roadwheel bolts, raise and support the front of the vehicle with safety stands, and then remove the roadwheel.
2   Refit two of the roadwheel bolts as a means of anchorage for the disc when the hub nut is unscrewed.
3   Have an assistant apply the footbrake and then unscrew the staked hub nut and remove it, together with the plain washer. This nut should be renewed when refitting the hub.
4   Remove the temporary wheel bolts.
5   Unbolt the brake caliper and tie it up to the suspension strut to avoid strain on the flexible hose.
6   Withdraw the hub/disc. If it is tight, use a two-legged puller.
7   Extract the split pin and unscrew the castellated nut from the tie-rod end balljoint.
8   Using a suitable balljoint splitter, separate the balljoint from the steering arm.
9   Unscrew and remove the special Torx pinch-bolt which holds the lower arm balljoint to the stub axle carrier.
10 Support the driveshaft on a block of wood and remove the bolt which holds the stub axle carrier to the base of the suspension strut.
11 Using a suitable lever, separate the carrier from the strut by prising open the clamp jaws (Fig. 10.3).

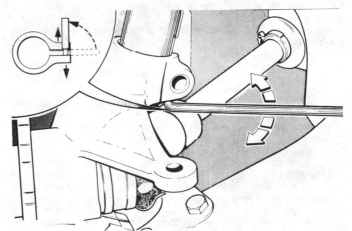

Fig. 10.3 Prise clamp jaws open to separate strut and carrier (Sec 3)

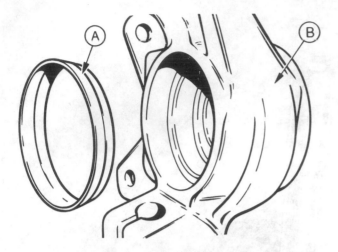

Fig. 10.4 Hub carrier (B) and dust shield (A) (Sec 3)

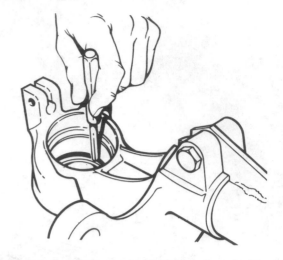

Fig. 10.5 Bearing track removal from hub carrier (Sec 3)

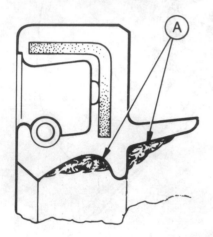

Fig. 10.6 Apply grease to points indicated (A) (Sec 3)

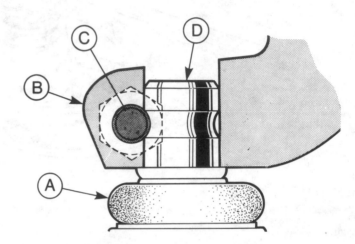

Fig. 10.7 Balljoint pinch-bolt location (Sec 3)

A   Balljoint   C   Pinch-bolt
B   Hub carrier   D   Balljoint stud

12 Support the driveshaft at the outboard CV joint and pull the stub axle carrier clear of the driveshaft.
13 Remove the stub axle carrier and grip it in a vice fitted with jaw protectors.
14 Using pliers, pull out the dust shield from the groove in the stub axle carrier.
15 Prise out the inner and outer oil seals.
16 Lift out the bearings.
17 With a suitable drift, drive out the bearing tracks. Take care not to damage the bearing track carrier surface during removal since any burrs on the surface could prevent the new tracks seating correctly during assembly.
18 Clean away all old grease from the stub axle carrier.
19 Drive the new bearing tracks squarely into their seats using a piece of suitable diameter tubing.
20 Liberally pack grease into the bearings, making sure to work plenty into the spaces between the rollers. Note that the cavity between the inner and outer bearings in the carrier **must not** be packed with grease since this could cause a pressure build-up and result in the seals leaking.
21 Install the bearing to one side of the carrier, then fill the lips of the new oil seal with grease and tap it squarely into position.
22 Fit the bearing and its seal to the opposite side in a similar way.
23 Fit the dust shield by tapping it into position using a block of wood.
24 Smear the driveshaft splines with grease, then install the carrier over the end of the driveshaft.

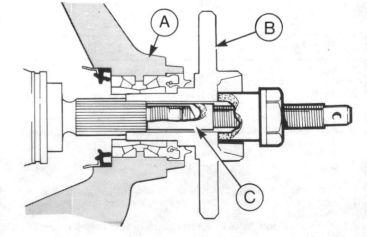

Fig. 10.8 Hub refitting method using Ford special tool 14-022 (Sec 3)

A   Hub carrier   C   Special tool
B   Hub

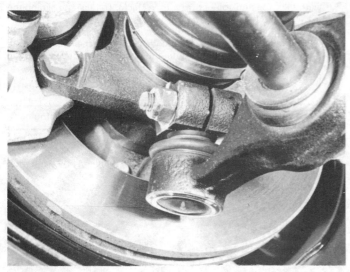

3.26 Lower arm balljoint to carrier
Note pinch-bolt orientation, nut to front of car

3.34 Tighten a new hub nut to the specified torque and stake punch it into the grooved section of driveshaft

25 Connect the carrier to the suspension strut and tighten the bolt to the specified torque.
26 Reconnect the suspension lower arm balljoint to the carrier and secure by passing the pinch-bolt through the groove in the balljoint stud. The head of the pinch-bolt should be to the rear (photo).
27 Reconnect the tie-rod to the steering arm, tighten the castellated nut to the specified torque (see Chapter 9) and secure with a new split pin.
28 Install the hub/disc and push it on to the driveshaft as far as it will go using hand pressure only.
29 In the absence of the special hub installer tool (14-022), draw the hub/disc onto the driveshaft by using a two or three-legged puller with legs engaged behind the carrier. On no account try to knock the hub/disc into position using hammer blows or the CV joint will be damaged.
30 Grease the threads at the end of the driveshaft, fit the plain washer and screw on a new nut, finger tight.
31 Fit the brake caliper, tightening the mounting bolts to the specified torque (see Chapter 8).
32 Screw in two wheel bolts and have an assistant apply the footbrake.
33 Tighten a new hub nut to the specified torque. This is a high torque and if a suitably calibrated torque wrench is not available, use a socket with a knuckle bar 457 mm (18 in) in length. Applying maximum hand leverage to the knuckle bar should tighten the nut to very close to its specified torque.
34 Stake the nut into the driveshaft groove (photo).
35 Remove the temporary roadwheel bolts.
36 Fit the roadwheel and lower the vehicle to the floor. Fully tighten the roadwheel bolts.

4 Front suspension lower arm – removal, overhaul and refitting

1 Raise the front of the vehicle and support it securely on safety stands.
2 Unbolt and remove the pivot bolt from the inboard end of the suspension arm.
3 At the outboard end of the suspension arm, disengage the arm from the hub carrier by unscrewing and removing the pinch-bolt.
4 Unscrew and remove the nut, washer and bush from the end of the anti-roll bar. Withdraw the suspension arm.
5 Renewal of the pivot bush at the inboard end of the suspension arm is possible using a nut and bolt, or a vice, and suitable distance pieces. Apply some brake hydraulic fluid to facilitate installation of the new bush. If the balljoint is worn or corroded, renew the suspension arm complete.

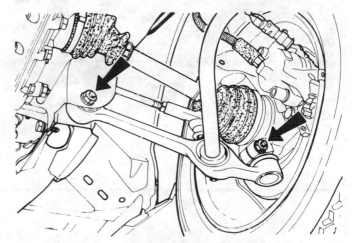

Fig. 10.9 Lower suspension arm-to-balljoint pinch-bolt and inboard pivot bolt (Sec 4)

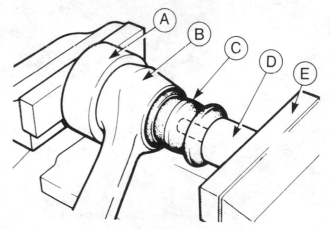

Fig. 10.10 Method of fitting suspension arm flexible bush (Sec 4)

A	Tubular spacer	D	Pilot
B	Lower arm	E	Vice jaws
C	Bush		

6 Refitting the arm is a reversal of removal. Tighten all nuts and bolts to the specified torque when the weight of the vehicle is again on the roadwheels.

5 Front anti-roll bar – removal and refitting

1 Jack up the front of the vehicle and support it securely on stands.
2 Flatten the lockplate tabs and unbolt the clamps which hold the anti-roll bar to the body (photo).
3 Disconnect the ends of the anti-roll bar by unscrewing the nuts, and removing the washers and the bushes (photo). Note that the nut on the right-hand side of the anti-roll bar has a left-hand thread and is unscrewed in a clockwise direction.
4 Unscrew a pivot bolt from the inboard end of one of the suspension arms.

5 Withdraw the anti-roll bar from the vehicle. To facilitate sliding the bushes from the bar, smear the bar with some brake fluid.
6 Refitting is a reversal of removal. When reassembling the bar to the lower arms ensure that the dished washers have their concave side away from the arm. Tighten all nuts and bolts to the specified torque after the weight of the vehicle is again on the roadwheels.
7 Lock the clamp bolts by bending up the lockplate tabs.

6 Front suspension strut – removal, overhaul and refitting

1 Slacken the roadwheel bolts, raise the front of the vehicle and support it securely on stands, then remove the roadwheel.
2 Support the underside of the driveshaft on blocks or by tying it up to the rack-and-pinion steering housing.
3 Detach the brake hose and location grommet from the strut

5.2 Front anti-roll bar-to-body clamp

5.3 Front anti-roll bar to suspension arm

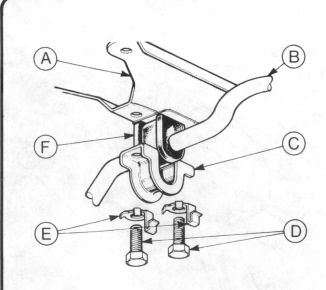

Fig. 10.11 Anti-roll bar mounting (Sec 5)

A Body   D Bolts
B Anti-roll bar E Lockplates
C Clamp   F Flexible bush

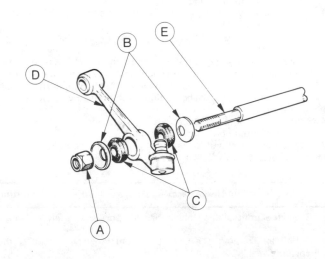

Fig. 10.12 Anti-roll bar-to-suspension arm assembly (Sec 5)

A Nut   D Lower arm
B Cupped washers E Anti-roll bar
C Bushes

6.3 Brake hose to strut bracket location

6.4A Remove the plastic cover ...

6.4B ... unscrew strut retaining nut
Note Allen key to prevent rod from turning

location bracket (photo), then unscrew and remove the pinch-bolt which holds the base of the suspension strut to the hub carrier. Using a suitable tool, lever the sides of the slot in the carrier apart until it is free from the strut.

4   Working at the top end of the strut, detach the cover and then unscrew the strut retaining nut (photos).

5   Withdraw the complete strut assembly from under the front wing.

6   Clean away external dirt and mud.

7   If the strut has been removed due to oil leakage or to lack of damping, then it should be renewed with a new or factory reconditioned unit. Dismantling of the original strut is not recommended and internal components are not generally available.

8   Before the strut is exchanged, the coil spring will have to be removed. To do this, a spring compressor or compressors will be needed. These are generally available from tool hire centres or they can be purchased at most motor accessory shops.

9   Engage the compressor over three coils of the spring and compress the spring sufficiently to release spring tension from the top mounting.

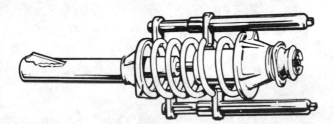

Fig. 10.13 Typical spring compressor in position (Sec 6)

10 Once the spring is compressed, unscrew and remove the nut from the end of the piston rod which retains the top mounting. As there will be a tendency for the piston rod to turn while the nut is unscrewed, provision is made at the end of the rod to insert a 6 mm Allen key to hold the rod still.

11 Remove the top mounting and lift off the spring and compressor.

12 The compressor need not be released if the spring is to be fitted immediately to a new strut. If the compressor is to be released from the spring, make sure that you do it slowly and progressively.

13 The top mounting can be dismantled by sliding off the thrust bearing and withdrawing the spring upper seat, gaiter spring and, where fitted, insulator. Also, if fitted, slide the bump stop from the piston rod.

14 Renew any worn or damaged components. If the front strut and/or coil spring is to be removed then it is advisable also to renew the equivalent assembly on the other side.

15 Fit the spring to the strut, making sure that the ends of the coils locate correctly in the shaped parts of the spring seats.

16 Fit the top mounting components, being very careful to maintain the correct order of assembly of the individual components.

17 Gently release and remove the spring compressor.

18 With the spring compressor removed, check that the ends of the spring are fully located in the shaped sections of the spring seatings, then refit the strut unit reversing the removal procedure. Lower the vehicle so that it is free standing before tightening the top mounting nut to its specified torque setting, then refit the plastic cover.

7   Rear hub bearings – adjustment

1   Raise and support the rear of the vehicle on safety stands. Release the handbrake.

2   This adjustment will normally only be required if, when the top and bottom of the roadwheel are gripped and 'rocked', excessive movement can be detected in the bearings. Slight movement is essential.

3   Remove the roadwheel. Using a hammer and cold chisel, tap off the dust cap from the end of the hub.

4   Extract the split pin and take off the nut retainer.

5   Tighten the hub nut to a torque of between 20 and 25 Nm (15 and 18 lbf ft), at the same time rotating the roadwheel in an anti-clockwise direction.

6   Unscrew the nut one half a turn and then tighten it only finger tight.

7   Fit the nut retainer so that two of its slots line up with the split pin hole. Insert a new split pin, bending the end **around** the nut, **not** over the end of the stub axle.

8   Tap the dust cap into position.

9   Recheck the play as described in paragraph 2. A fractional amount of wheel movement **must** be present.

10 Repeat the operations on the opposite hub, refit the roadwheels and lower the vehicle to the floor.

Fig. 10.14 Rear hub bearing adjustment (Sec 7)

8 Rear hub bearings – removal and refitting

1   Raise and support the rear of the vehicle with safety stands.
2   Remove the roadwheel then release the handbrake.
3   On fuel injected models remove the brake drum securing screw and withdraw the brake drum.
4   Tap off the dust cap from the end of the hub (photo).
5   Extract the split pin and remove the nut retainer.
6   Unscrew and remove the nut and take off the thrust washer.
7   Pull the hub towards you, then push it back slightly. This will now leave the outboard bearing ready to be taken off the stub axle.
8   Withdraw the hub.
9   Prise out the inner bearing oil seal using a screwdriver and then extract the inner bearing cone.
10 Using a suitable punch, drive out the bearing outer tracks, taking care not to burr the bearing seats.

11 If new bearings are being fitted to both hubs do not mix up the bearing components, but keep them in their individual packs until required.
12 Drive the new bearing tracks squarely into their hub recesses.
13 Pack both bearings with the specified grease, working plenty into the rollers. Be generous, but there is no need to fill the cavity between the inner and outer bearings.
14 Locate the inboard bearing and then grease the lips of a new oil seal and tap it into position.
15 Fit the hub onto the stub axle, taking care not to catch the oil seal lips.
16 Fit the outboard bearing and the thrust washer and screw on the nut.
17 Adjust the bearings, as described in Section 7.
18 On fuel injection models refit the brake drum and locate the securing screw.
19 Reft the roadwheel and lower the vehicle to the ground.

8.4 Remove the dust/grease cap from the rear hub

Fig. 10.15 Prise out the oil seal (Sec 8)

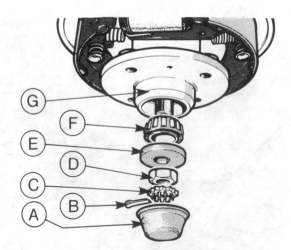

Fig. 10.16 Rear hub and outboard bearing assembly
(injection models) (Sec 8)

A	Dust cap	E	Washer
B	Split pin	F	Bearing cone
C	Nut retainer	G	Hub
D	Nut		

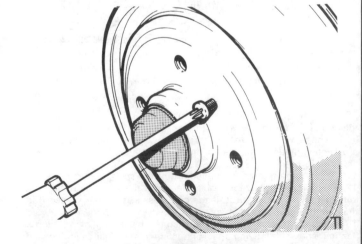

Fig. 10.17 Refit dust cap and secure drum with screw (injection
models) (Sec 8)

9 Rear stub axle – removal and refitting

1   Raise and support the rear of the vehicle and remove the roadwheel.
2   Remove the hub unit, as described in the previous Section.
3   Remove the rear brake shoe assembly, as described in Chapter 8. You will also need to disconnect the brake fluid pipe at its connection to the wheel cylinder. Plug the pipe and cylinder connections to prevent fluid loss and the ingress of dirt.
4   Extract the handbrake cable through the backplate, then unscrew the four backplate retaining bolts and withdraw the backplate.
5   Position a jack under the lower arm and support it.
6   Unscrew and remove the lower arm and shock absorber-to-stub axle retaining bolts.
7   Unscrew the tie-bar-to-stub axle retaining nut and withdraw the stub axle, noting the relative fitting positions of the spacers, washers and bushes of the tie bar (photo).
8   If the stub axle is damaged or worn excessively then it must be renewed.
9   Refitting is a reversal of the removal procedure, but note the following:
10 When reassembling the tie-bar to the stub axle ensure that the spacers, washers and bushes are correctly located (as noted during removal).
11 Do not fully tighten the suspension retaining nuts and bolts to their specified torque settings until the vehicle is lowered and free standing.
12 Refit and connect the brake assembly components, as given in Chapter 8. Leave bleeding the hydraulic circuit until after the hub and brake drum are refitted.
13 Adjust the hub axle bearings, as detailed in Section 7, before refitting the grease cap and roadwheel.

10 Rear shock absorber – removal, testing and refitting

1   Slacken the rear roadwheel bolts, raise and support the rear of the vehicle using safety stands. Remove the roadwheel.
2   Position a jack beneath the suspension arm and raise it to support the weight of the arm.
3   Open the tailgate and remove the rear parcels shelf.
4   Remove the cap from the top of the shock absorber. Hold the shock absorber strut against rotation by inserting an Allen key in its socket. Unscrew the nut and take off the mounting cushion.
5   Loosen the brake hose-to-shock absorber fixing and slide the hose free.

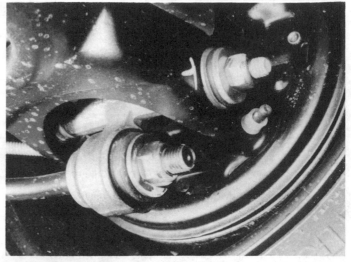

9.7 Tie-bar to rear stub axle location

6   Unscrew and remove the shock absorber lower mounting nuts and bolts then compress the shock absorber and remove it, together with the cup and bump rubber from underneath.
7   To test the shock absorber, grip its lower mounting in a vice so that the unit is vertical.
8   Fully extend and extract the shock absorber ten or twelve times. Any lack of resistance in either direction will indicate the need for renewal, as will evidence of leakage of fluid.
9   Refitting is a reversal of removal, but if a new unit is being installed, prime it first in a similar way to that described for testing.

11 Rear tie-bar – removal and refitting

1   Before attempting to remove a tie-bar, note the location of all washers and bushes. These control the rear wheel alignment and they must be returned to their original locations.
2   Raise the rear of the vehicle and support with stands.
3   Unscrew and remove the pivot bolt from the eye at the front end of the tie-bar.

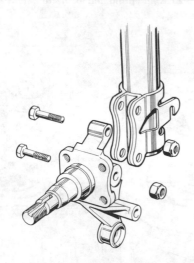

Fig. 10.18 Rear stub axle carrier (Sec 9)

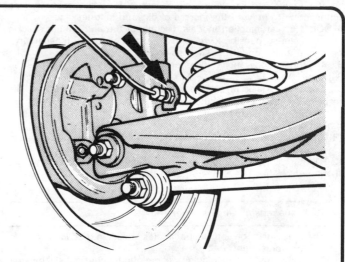

Fig. 10.19 Brake pipe connection at rear shock absorber (Sec 10)

4 Unscrew the nut from the rear end of the tie-bar, take off the washers and bushes as the tie-bar is withdrawn and keep them in strict sequence for refitting.
5 Renewal of the tie-bar flexible bush is quite easily carried out using sockets or distance pieces and applying pressure in the jaws of a vice.
6 Refit the tie-bar by reversing the removal operations. Tighten the retaining nuts to their specified torque settings.

12 Rear coil spring – removal and refitting

1 Slacken the roadwheel bolts, raise the rear of the vehicle and support it securely. Remove the roadwheel.
2 Support the suspension lower arm by placing a jack beneath the spring seating.
3 Unscrew and remove the suspension arm inboard pivot bolt. On 1.6 fuel injection models disconnect the anti-roll bar shackles.
4 Slowly lower the jack beneath the suspension arm and remove the spring and insulator pad.
5 Refitting is a reversal of removal. If applicable, the plastic sleeved end of the coil spring must be at the upper end when fitted.

13 Rear suspension lower arm – removal and refitting

1 Raise the rear of the vehicle and support it on safety stands.
2 On 1.6 fuel injection models disconnect the anti-roll bar shackles.
3 Position a jack under the lower arm spring seat to support it.
4 Unscrew and remove the pivot bolt from the inboard end of the suspension arm.
5 Unscrew and remove the pivot bolt from the outboard end of the suspension arm.
6 Lower the jack and withdraw the lower arm from the vehicle.
7 Refitting is a reversal of the removal procedure. When the pivot bolts are located, hand tighten the retaining nuts, then lower the vehicle before final tightening to the specified torque settings.

14 Rear suspension – removal and refitting

1 Raise the rear of the vehicle and support on stands.
2 Disconnect the handbrake cable at the connection to the primary cable and from the body guides (refer to Chapter 8).
3 Disconnect the tie-rod from its body bracket.
4 Unscrew and remove the pivot bolt from the inboard end of the suspension arm.
5 Disconnect the brake pipe line connection at the location bracket on the lower end of the shock absorber. Plug the exposed pipe connections to prevent the ingress of dirt and fluid leakage.
6 On 1.6 fuel injection models disconnect the anti-roll bar shackle link from the suspension lower arm (refer to Section 17 if necessary).
7 Place a jack under the suspension arm.
8 Disconnect the shock absorber upper mounting, as described in Section 10.
9 Lower the jack under the suspension arm and withdraw the suspension assembly from the vehicle.
10 Remove the suspension assembly from the opposite side in a similar way.
11 Refitting is a reversal of removal. Bleed the brake hydraulic system on completion and adjust the handbrake.
12 Tighten all nuts and bolts to the specified torque when the weight of the vehicle has been lowered onto the roadwheels.

15 Rear suspension angles – general

1 The rear wheel toe and camber angles are set in production and do not require adjustment.
2 The only time that the angles will need to be checked will be after an accident in which the rear end has suffered damage or where a rear end skid has caused a side impact on a rear roadwheel.
3 Severely worn components of the rear suspension can also cause the angles to be misaligned, in which case renewal of the defective components should rectify the suspension angles and alignment.

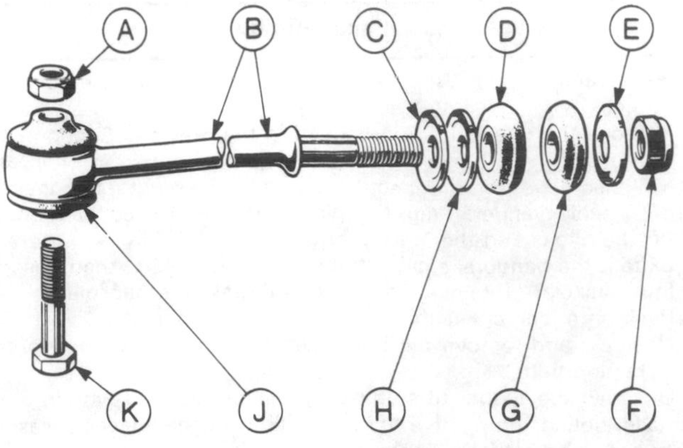

Fig. 10.20 Rear tie-bar components (Sec 11)

A *Nut*
B *Tie-bar*
C *Washer*
D *Flexible bush*
E *Washer*
F *Nut*
G *Flexible bush*
H *Washer*
J *Flexible bush*
K *Pivot bolt*

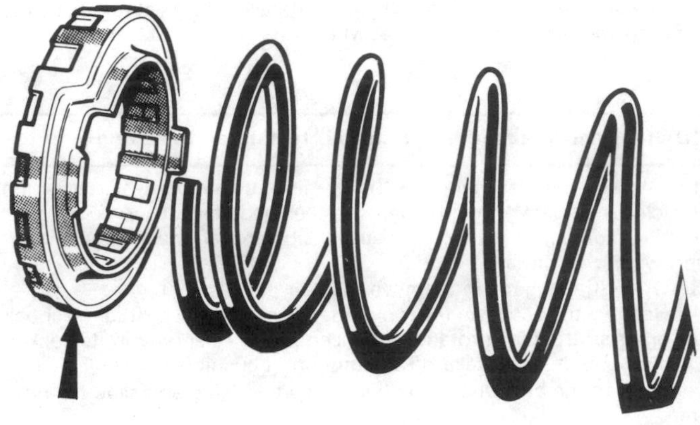

Fig. 10.21 Rear spring and insulator pad (Sec 12)

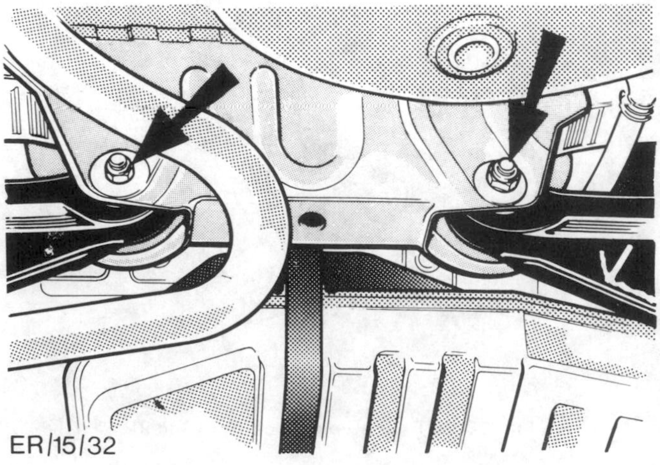

Fig. 10.22 Lower arm-to-body inboard mountings (Sec 13)

4   If the suspension angles need to be checked for any reason, entrust this task to your Ford dealer. The cost is relatively low and he will be able to advise you on any necessary action to be taken.

16 Roadwheels and tyres – general

1   All models are fitted with pressed-steel type wheels which are secured to the hubs by bolts.
2   The wheel trims differ according to model, but all trim types are of press-fit design and must be removed for access to the wheel bolts.
3   Periodically clean away the mud deposited on the inside rims of the roadwheels and touch up any rusty areas.
4   Avoid damaging the wheel rims through careless kerbing.
5   Whenever changing a roadwheel, always locate the jack as recommended in the introductory Section of this manual.
6   The tyres fitted during manufacture are steel radial type and this type should be used when replacements become necessary.
7   The tyre pressures should be checked weekly and at the same time the tread wear examined. Remove any flints or stones which may have become embedded in the tyres and also examine the tyres for damage and splits. Renew the tyres if the tread depth is approaching the legal minimum. The wheels should be rebalanced halfway through the life of the tyres to compensate for loss of rubber and also whenever the roadwheels have been repositioned.
8   Wheel balancing must be entrusted to your Ford dealer or a competent tyre specialist. If they have to fit balance weights to the wheels ensure that they fit the correct Ford type.

9   If it is desired to move the position of the roadwheels to minimise tyre wear, only move them front to rear or rear to front of the same side of the vehicle – never from side to side with radial tyres.
10 If snow chains are to be fitted at any time it is likely that you will need to reduce the size of the tyres fitted to allow for the additional clearance requirements. Check this with your Ford dealer before fitting.

17 Rear anti-roll bar – removal and refitting

1   Slacken the left-hand roadwheel bolts, raise and support the rear of the car on safety stands. Remove the roadwheel.
2   Lever the shackles from the right- and left-hand suspension lower arms.
3   Unbolt the anti-roll bar from the underbody, carefully noting the relative fixing locations.
4   Release the fuel lines from their securing clips. Support the fuel tank and remove the three tank mounting bolts. Carefully lower the tank on its support.
5   Withdraw the anti-roll bar from the left-hand side of the vehicle.
6   To remove the rubber bushes from the anti-roll bar simply prise open the bush retainers with a screwdriver. Press the retainers together so that the fixing holes are in line.
7   Refitting is a reversal of removal. The fuel tank must be bolted in position before securing the anti-roll bar. Ensure the underbody fixings are refitted in their original locations.
8   Lubricate the shackle bushes with soap solution before reconnecting them to the lower arms.

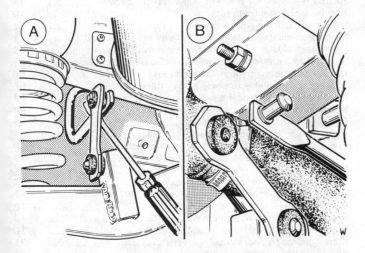

Fig. 10.23 Lever the rear anti-roll bar shackles from the suspension lower arm (Sec 17)

A   Left-hand side   B   Right-hand side

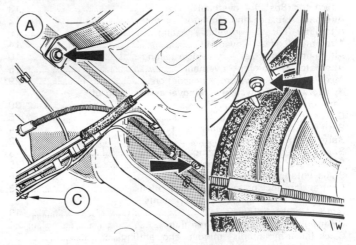

Fig. 10.24 Lower the fuel tank (Sec 17)

A   Mounting bolts (arrowed)   C   Fuel line securing clips
B   Mounting bolt (arrowed)

18 Fault diagnosis – suspension

Symptom	Reason(s)
Steering feels vague, car wanders and floats at speed	Tyre pressures uneven Shock absorbers worn Broken or weak coil springs Suspension geometry incorrect Suspension pick-up points out of alignment
Stiff and heavy steering	Suspension geometry incorrect Dry or corroded suspension balljoints Low tyre pressures
Wheel wobble and vibration	Roadwheel bolts loose Wheels/tyres out of balance Worn hub bearings Weak front coil springs Weak front struts

Chapter 11 Electrical system

For modifications, and information applicable to later models, see Supplement at end of manual

Contents

Specifications

System type

12V negative earth with belt-driven alternator and pre-engaged starter motor

Alternator

	Bosch	Lucas	Motorola
Rated output (13.5V at 6000 rpm engine speed)	28A (G1-28A)	28A (A115/28)	28A (9650D)
	35A (K1-35A)	35A (A115/36)	35A (2652F)
	45A (K1-45A)	45A (A133/45)	45A (2627G)
	55A (K1-55A)	55A (A133/55)	
Maximum continuous speed	15 000 rpm	15 000 rpm	15 000 rpm
Minimum brush length	5 mm (0.197 in)	5 mm (0.197 in)	4 mm (0.157 in)
Regulator voltage at 4000 rpm, 3 to 7A load	13.7 to 14.6 volts	13.7 to 14.6 volts	13.7 to 14.6 volts

Stator winding resistance (ohms/phase) ....

0.20 to 0.22 (G1-28A)	0.193 to 0.203 (A115/28)	0.333 to 0.368 (2650D)
0.130 to 0.143 (K1-35A)	0.128 to 0.138 (A115/36)	0.333 to 0.368 (2652F)
0.090 to 0.099 (K1-45A)	0.088 to 0.108 (A133/45)	0.266 to 0.294 (2627G)
0.070 to 0.077 (K1-55A)	0.193 to 0.213 (A133/55)	

Rotor winding resistance at 20°C (ohms) ....

3.40 to 3.74 (G1-28A)	3.088 to 3.413 (A115/28)	3.8 to 4.2 (all models)
3.40 to 3.74 (K1-35A)	3.04 to 3.36 (A115/36)	
4.00 to 4.34 (K1-45A)	3.04 to 3.36 (A133/45)	
4.00 to 4.34 (K1-55A)	3.04 to 3.36 (A133/55)	

Wiper blade .... Champion C-4501

Starter motor
Type .... Pre-engaged
Make:
    Lucas .... 8M90 or 9M90
    Bosch .... 0.8 kW, 0.85 kW or 0.9 kW
    Nippondenso .... 0.6 kW or 0.9 kW
Number of brushes .... 4, except Nippondenso 0.6 kW which has 2
Minimum brush length:
    Lucas .... 8.0 mm (0.32 in)
    Bosch .... 10.0 mm (0.39 in)
    Nippondenso 0.6 kW .... 10.0 mm (0.39 in)
    Nippondenso 0.9 kW .... 9.0 mm (0.35 in)
Minimum commutator dimension:
    Lucas .... 2.05 mm (0.08 in) thick
    Bosch .... 32.8 mm (1.29 in) diameter
    Nippondenso .... 0.6 mm (0.02 in) thick
Armature endfloat:
    Lucas .... 0.25 mm (0.010 in)
    Bosch .... 0.30 mm (0.012 in)
    Nippondenso .... 0.60 mm (0.024 in)
Number of pinion teeth (all models) 10
Number of flywheel teeth (all models) 135

Bulbs
Headlamp:
    Halogen 60/55W
    Tungsten 50/45W
Front parking lamp 4W
Front indicator lamp 21W
Stop/tail lamp 21/5W
Reversing lamp 21W
Rear foglamp 21W
Rear indicator lamp 21W
Rear number plate lamp 5W
Auxiliary lamp (Halogen) 55W
Foglamp (Halogen) 55W
Interior lights 10W
Glove compartment light 2W
Monitoring and warning lights .... 1.3 or 2.6W
Instrument lights .... 1.3 or 2.6W
Heater control unit light 1W
Automatic transmission selector quadrant light 1.2W
Cigar lighter illumination 1.4W
Luggage compartment light 10W

Battery
Type .... 12V lead-acid, 35 to 52Ah depending upon model
Charge condition:
    Poor .... 12.5 volts
    Normal .... 12.6 volts
    Good .... 12.7 volts

Torque wrench settings

	Nm	lbf ft
Electric window motor mounting bolts	5	4
Electric window regulator mounting bolts	5	4
Horn bracket bolt	35	26
Foglamp mounting bolt	9	7
Auxiliary lamp mounting bolt	45	33

1   General description

The electrical system is of 12V, negative earth type. The major components include an alternator, a pre-engaged starter and a lead/acid battery.

The electrical equipment varies according to the particular model. The system is fully fused, with circuit breakers and any necessary relays incorporated in the fusebox and under the facia panel.

2   Battery – maintenance

1   Every 12 000 miles (20 000 km) disconnect the leads from the battery and clean the terminals and lead ends. After refitting the leads smear the exposed metal with petroleum jelly.

2   The battery fitted as standard equipment is probably of the low maintenance type and only requires checking at 4 year (or 60 000 mile/100 000 km) intervals. However if a non-standard battery is fitted the following checks should be made on a monthly basis.

3   Check that the plate separators inside the battery are covered with electrolyte. To do this remove the battery covers and inspect through the top of the battery. On batteries with a translucent case it may be possible to carry out the check without removing the covers. If necessary top up the cells with distilled or de-ionized water as described in Section 3.

4   At the same time wipe clean the top of the battery with a dry cloth to prevent the accumulation of dust and dampness which may cause the battery to become partially discharged over a period.

5   Also check the battery clamp and platform for corrosion. If evident remove the battery and clean the deposits away. Then treat the affected metal with a proprietary anti-rust liquid and paint with the original colour.

6   Whenever the battery is removed it is worthwhile checking it for cracks and leakage. Cracks can be caused by topping up the cells with distilled water in winter *after* instead of *before* a run. This gives the water no chance to mix with the electrolyte, so the former freezes and splits the battery case. If the case is fractured, it may be possible to repair it with a proprietary compound, but this depends on the material used for the case. If electrolyte has been lost from a cell refer to Section 3 for details of adding a fresh solution.

7   If topping-up the battery becomes excessive and the case is not fractured, the battery is being over-charged and the voltage regulator may be faulty.

8   If the car covers a small annual mileage it is worthwhile checking the specific gravity of the electrolyte every three months to determine the state of charge of the battery. Use a hydrometer to make the check and compare the results with the following table:

	Ambient temperature above 25°C (77°F)	Ambient temperature below 25°C (77°F)
Fully charged	1.210 to 1.230	1.270 to 1.290
70% charged	1.170 to 1.190	1.230 to 1.250
Fully discharged	1.050 to 1.070	1.110 to 1.130

Note that the specific gravity readings assume an electrolyte temperature of 15°C (60°F); for every 10°C (18°F) below 15°C (60°F) subtract 0.007. For every 10°C (18°F) above 15°C (60°F) add 0.007.

9   If the battery condition is suspect first check the specific gravity of electrolyte in each cell. A variation of 0.040 or more between any cells indicates loss of electrolyte or deterioration of the internal plates.

10   In cases where a sealed-for-life maintenance-free battery is fitted, topping-up and testing of the electrolyte in each cell is not possible. The condition of the battery type can therefore only be tested using a battery condition indicator or a voltmeter, as with a standard or low maintenance type battery.

11   If testing the battery using a voltmeter, connect it across the battery and compare the result with those given in the Specifications under 'charge condition'. The test is only accurate if the battery has not been subject to any kind of charge for the previous six hours. If this is not the case switch on the headlights for 30 seconds then wait four to five minutes before testing the battery after switching off the headlights. All other electrical components must be switched off, so check that the doors and boot lid are fully shut when making the test.

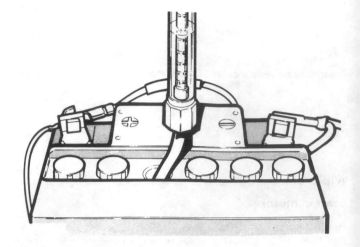

Fig. 11.1 Checking battery electrolyte specific gravity (Sec 2)

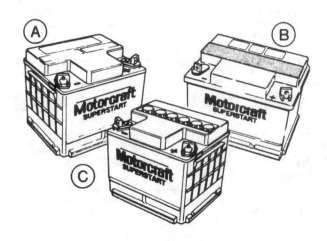

Fig. 11.2 Battery types (Sec 2)

A   Maintenance-free battery – sealed cell type
B   Maintenance-free battery – cell top removable
C   Low maintenance type

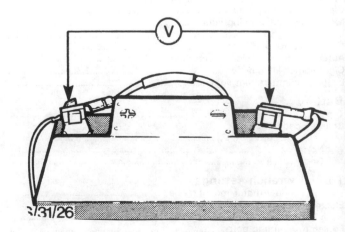

Fig. 11.3 Battery test method using voltmeter (Sec 2)

12 If the voltage reading is less than the 12.2 volts then the battery is discharged, whilst a reading of 12.2 to 12.5 volts indicates a partially discharged condition.

13 If the battery is to be charged, remove it from the vehicle and charge it as described in Section 4.

3 Battery – removal and refitting

1 Open the bonnet and support it on its stay.
2 The battery is mounted at the rear of the engine compartment.
3 Disconnect the negative (earth) lead, followed by the positive lead.
4 Unbolt and remove the clamps from the nibs at the base of the battery casing (photo).

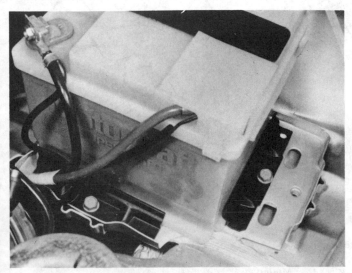

3.4 Battery showing lead connections and clamps

5 Lift the battery from its location, taking care not to spill electrolyte on the paintwork.
6 Refitting is a reversal of removal. Reconnect the positive and then the negative leads in that order.

4 Battery – electrolyte replenishment

1 If the battery is in a fully charged state and one or more of the cells maintains a specific gravity reading which is 0.040 or more lower than the others, then it is likely that electrolyte has been lost from the cell at some time.
2 Top up the cell with a solution of 1 part sulphuric acid to 2.5 parts of distilled water. If the cell is already topped up draw some electrolyte out of it with a pipette.
3 It is preferable to obtain ready mixed electrolyte, however if the solution is to be mixed note that **the water must never be added to the sulphuric acid otherwise it will explode**. Always pour the acid slowly onto the water in a glass or plastic container.

5 Battery – charging

1 In winter time when heavy demand is placed upon the battery, such as when starting from cold and much electrical equipment is continually in use, it is a good idea to occasionally have the battery fully charged from an external source.

Standard and low maintenance batteries

2 Charge the battery at a rate of 3.5 to 4 amps and continue to charge the battery at this rate until no further rise in specific gravity is noted over a four hour period.
3 Alternatively, a trickle charger charging at the rate of 1.5 amps can be safely used overnight.

4 Specially rapid 'boost' charges which are claimed to restore the power of the battery in 1 to 2 hours are not recommended as they can cause serious damage to the battery plates through overheating.
5 While charging the battery note that the temperature of the electrolyte should never exceed 100°F (37.8°C).

Maintenance-free batteries

6 This battery type takes considerably longer to fully recharge than the standard type, the time taken being dependent on the extent of discharge, but it can take anything up to three days.
7 A constant voltage type charger is required and this set, when connected, to 13.9 to 14.9 volts with a charger current below 25 amps. Using this method the battery should be useable within three hours, giving a voltage reading of 12.5 volts, but this is for a partially discharged battery and, as mentioned, full charging can take considerably longer.
8 If the battery is to be charged from a fully discharged state (condition reading less than 12.2 volts) have it recharged by your Ford dealer or local automotive electrician as the charge rate is higher and constant supervision during charging is necessary.

6 Drivebelt – removal, refitting and tensioning

1 A conventional vee drivebelt is used to drive the alternator, power being transmitted from a pulley on the front end of the crankshaft.
2 To remove a belt, slacken the alternator mounting bolts and the bolts on the adjuster link, push the alternator in towards the engine and slip the belt from the pulleys.
3 Fit the belt by slipping it over the pulley rims while the alternator is still loose on its mountings. Never be tempted to remove or fit a belt by prising it over a pulley without releasing the alternator. The pulley and possibly the alternator, will be distorted or damaged.
4 To retension the belt, pull the alternator away from the engine until the belt is fairly taut and nip up the adjuster strap bolt. Check that the total deflection of the belt is 4.0 mm (0.15 in) at the mid point of the longest run. A little trial and error may be required to obtain the correct tension. If the belt is too slack, it will slip and soon become glazed or burnt and the alternator will not perform correctly, with consequent low battery charge. If the belt is too tight, the bearings in the alternator will soon be damaged.
5 Do not lever against the body of the alternator to tension the belt, or damage may occur.

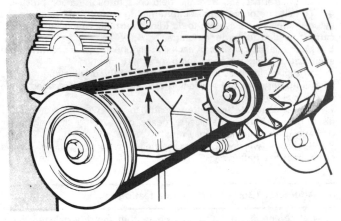

Fig. 11.4 Alternator drivebelt deflection (Sec 6)

X = 4.0 mm (0.15 in)

7 Alternator – description, maintenance and precautions

1 One of three different makes of alternator may be fitted, dependent upon model and engine capacity. The maximum output of the alternator varies similarly.
2 The alternator is belt-driven from the crankshaft pulley, it is fan cooled and incorporates a voltage regulator.
3 The alternator provides a charge to the battery at very low engine

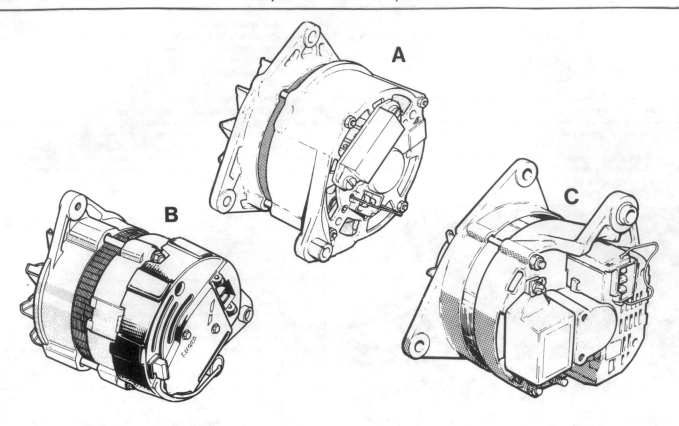

Fig. 11.5 Alternator types (Sec 7)

A   Bosch   B   Lucas   C   Motorola

revolutions and basically consists of a stator in which a rotor rotates. The rotor shaft is supported in ball-bearings, and slip rings are used to conduct current to and from the field coils through carbon brushes.

4   The alternator generates ac (alternating current) which is rectified by an internal diode system to dc (direct current) which is the type of current needed for battery storage.

5   Maintenance consists of occasionally checking the security of the electrical connections and wiping away external dirt.

6   At regular intervals check the tension of the drivebelt and also its condition. Renewal and tensioning of the drivebelt is described in the previous Section.

7   Never connect the battery leads to the wrong terminals, or disconnect a battery lead as a means of stopping the engine, as damage to the alternator may result.

8   If electric welding is being carried out on the vehicle, always disconnect the battery.

8   Alternator (Bosch) – in-vehicle testing

1   Before carrying out this test, check that the drivebelt tension is correct and that the battery is well charged.

2   A voltmeter and ammeter will be required, also a variable resistor and a tachometer.

3   Check the charging circuit wiring for continuity. To do this, pull out the alternator multi-plug, switch on the ignition and connect a 0 to 20V voltmeter between a good earthing point and each multi-plug terminal in turn.

4   The voltmeter should indicate battery voltage. If a zero reading is observed, this will mean an open-circuit which must be checked and repaired.

5   Rig the output test circuit using the voltmeter, ammeter and the variable resistor as shown in Fig. 11.7. The variable resistor must be capable of carrying a current of 30 amps.

6   Switch on the headlamps, the heater blower motor and the heated rear window. Start the engine and run it at 3000 rpm. Vary the resistance to increase the load current. The rated output (see Specifications) should be reached without the voltage dropping below 13V.

7   Switch off the engine and accessories and dismantle the test circuit.

8   Rig the 'positive side' volt-drop test circuit (Fig. 11.8) and reconnect the regulator multi-pin plug.

9   Switch on the headlamps, start the engine and check the voltage drop.

10   Run the engine at 3000 rpm. If the voltage drop is in excess of 0.5V, a high resistance is indicated on the positive side of the charging circuit. This must be located and remedied.

11   Switch off the headlamps and the engine.

12   Rig the 'negative side' voltage drop test circuit (Fig. 11.9).

13   Switch on the headlamps, start the engine and check the voltage drop. Run the engine at 3000 rpm and check the voltage reading. If the voltage drop is in excess of 0.25V then a high resistance is indicated on the negative (earth) side of the charging circuit which must be located and remedied. Check all earth terminals, earth straps etc for security.

14   Switch off the headlamps and the engine, and disconnect the test circuit.

15   Rig the control voltage test circuit (see Fig. 11.10). Start the engine and check the regulator voltage. Run the engine at 2000 rpm and observe the ammeter reading. When this falls between 3 and 5A, check the reading on the voltmeter which should be between 13.7 and 14.5V. If the reading is outside this range, then the integral regulator is faulty.

16   Switch off the ignition and dismantle the test circuit.

17   Refit the alternator multi-plug.

18   Where a fault is discovered as a result of the foregoing tests and its cause is not visually evident, the alternator must be overhauled as described in Section 13.

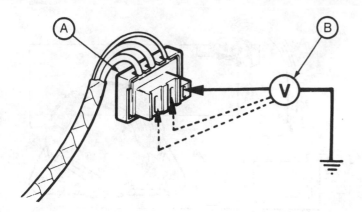

Fig. 11.6 Checking charging circuit continuity – Bosch (Sec 8)

A   Multi-plug   B   Voltmeter

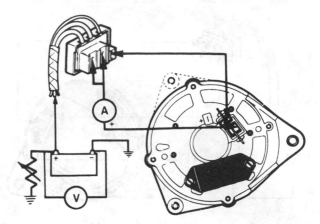

Fig. 11.7 Checking alternator output – Bosch (Sec 8)

A   Ammeter   V   Voltmeter

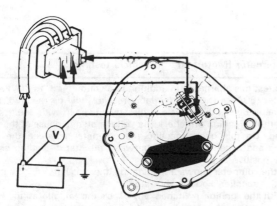

Fig. 11.8 Checking volt-drop (positive side) – Bosch (Sec 8)

V   Voltmeter

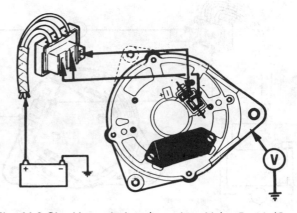

Fig. 11.9 Checking volt-drop (negative side) – Bosch (Sec 8)

V   Voltmeter

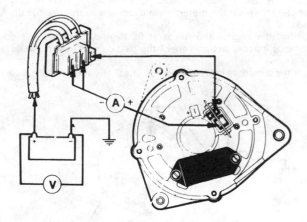

Fig. 11.10 Checking regulator control linkage – Bosch (Sec 8)

A   Ammeter   V   Voltmeter

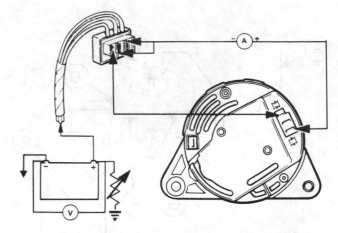

Fig. 11.11 Checking alternator output – Lucas (Sec 9)

A   Ammeter   V   Voltmeter

9   Alternator (Lucas) – in-vehicle testing

1   Remove the multi-plug and the alternator rear cover, then check the wiring circuit for continuity as described for the Bosch alternator in Section 8.

2   Check the alternator output as described in Section 8.
3   Check the 'positive side' voltage drop as described in Section 8.
4   Check the 'negative side' voltage drop as described in Section 8.
5   Check the control voltage as described in Section 8, but run the engine at 3000 rpm and check the voltage is between 13.7 and 14.5V when the current falls below 10A.

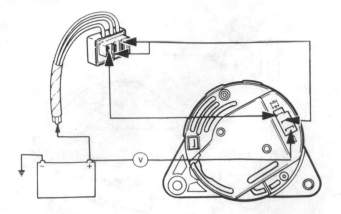

Fig. 11.12 Checking volt-drop (positive side) – Lucas (Sec 9)

V   Voltmeter

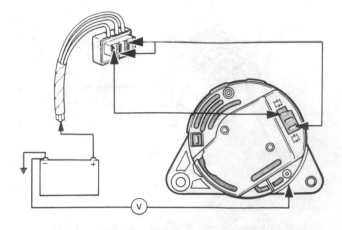

Fig. 11.13 Checking volt-drop (negative side) – Lucas (Sec 9)

V   Voltmeter

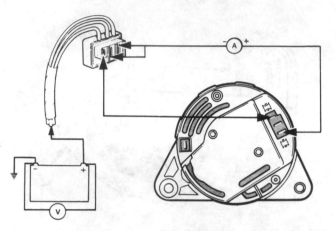

Fig. 11.14 Checking regulator control voltage – Lucas (Sec 9)

A   Ammeter   V   Voltmeter

10 Alternator (Motorola) – in-vehicle testing

1   To test this alternator, in addition to a voltmeter (0 to 20V) and an ammeter (50A), a rheostat (variable resistor) will be required, also a tachometer unless the vehicle is already equipped with one.
2   With the ignition off, check the voltage on one phase of the stator winding. Do this by connecting the voltmeter between the stator winding and a good earth and between the stator winding and the battery positive terminal.
3   If the voltmeter shows a reading in either case, it will indicate that a positive rectifier diode is shorting.
4   With the ignition switched off, check the voltage at the output terminal on the alternator and at the battery positive terminal.
5   The reading shown on the voltmeter should be the same at both test points. Otherwise, check for broken leads and for loose or corroded terminals.
6   Check the field current by rigging a test circuit as shown in Fig. 11.18, but use a rheostat (variable resistance) in series with the ammeter to protect the meter in the event of a short-circuit in the field windings.
7   Start the engine and run it at 3000 rpm. Reduce the rheostat resistance if necessary and check the field current, which should be 1 to 4 amps.
8   If the current is less than 1 amp, check the alternator brushes and

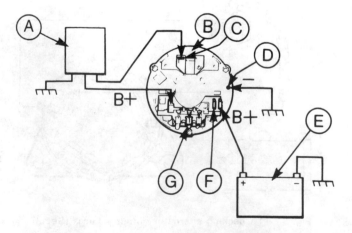

Fig. 11.15 Motorola alternator connections (Sec 10)

A   Regulator   E   Battery
B   Alternator   F   Multi-plug output
C   Field   G   Stator winding
D   Earth

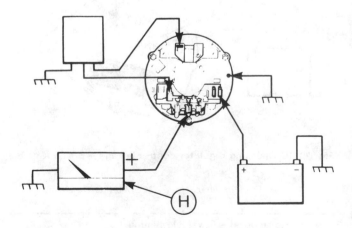

Fig. 11.16 Checking phase voltage – Motorola (Sec 10)

H   Voltmeter

slip rings. If the current is much more than 4 amps, a short-circuit is indicated.

9   To carry out a voltage comparison test, switch on the ignition, start the engine and run it at 3000 rpm. The voltage at the alternator output terminal and at the battery positive terminal should be indentical and between 13.7 and 14.7V at an ambient temperature of 25°C (77°F). Any difference in voltage will be due to corroded or loose terminals.

10   Switch off the ignition and dismantle the test rig.

11   Disconnect the regulator, short out the output terminal to the field terminal, switch on the ignition and run the engine at a fast idle. Check the voltage between the output terminal and a good earth. If the output voltage attains a level of between 14 and 16V, but failed to reach 14V when the test described in paragraph 9 was carried out,

then the regulator is at fault. If the output voltage does not rise and no fault was found in the field circuit during testing (paragraph 7), then the stator or the rectifier diodes are faulty.

12   Switch off the ignition and dismantle the test rig.

11 Alternator – removal and refitting

1   The operations are similar for all makes of alternator.

2   Disconnect the battery and disconnect the multi-plug or leads from the rear of the alternator. Remove the head shield (where fitted).

3   Release the mounting and adjuster link bolts, push the alternator in towards the engine and slip the drivebelt from the pulley.

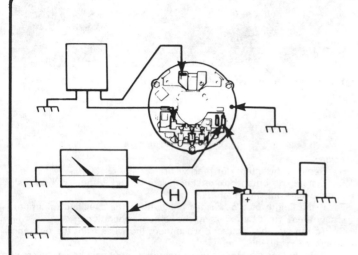

Fig. 11.17 Checking voltage at output terminals and position terminals – Motorola (Sec 10)

H   Voltmeters

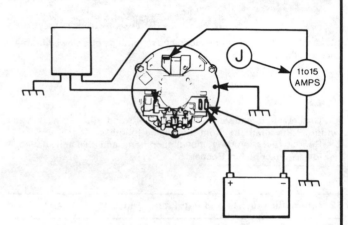

Fig. 11.18 Testing field circuits – Motorola (Sec 10)

J   Ammeter

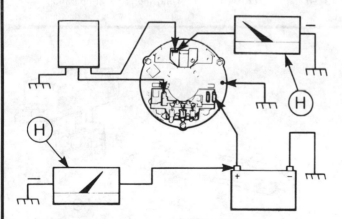

Fig. 11.19 Comparing output and battery voltage – Motorola (Sec 10)

H   Voltmeters

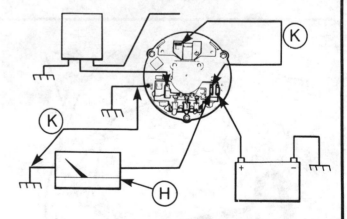

Fig. 11.20 Checking voltage between output terminal and earth – Motorola (Sec 10)

H   Voltmeter   K   Connecting leads

11.4A Alternator lead connections and mounting bolts viewed from underneath

11.4B Alternator adjuster link bolt (arrowed)

4   Unscrew and remove the mounting bolts and adjuster link bolt and withdraw the alternator from the engine (photos).
5   Refit by reversing the removal operations, and adjust the drivebelt tension as described in Section 6.

12 Alternator brushes and regulator – renewal

1   With the alternator removed from the engine, clean the external surfaces free from dirt.

Bosch
2   Remove the regulator screws from the rear cover and withdraw the regulator. Check the brush length, if less than the specified minimum, renew them.
3   Unsolder the brush wiring connectors and remove the brushes and the springs.
4   Refit by reversing the removal operations.

Lucas
5   Remove the alternator rear cover.
6   Extract the brush box retaining screws and withdraw the brush assemblies from the brush box.
7   If the length of the brushes is less than the specified minimum, renew them. Refit by reversing the removal operations.
8   To remove the regulator, disconnect the wires from the unit and unscrew the retaining screw.
9   Refit by reversing the removal operations, but check that the small plastic spacer and the connecting link are correctly located.

Motorola
10 Extract the two regulator securing screws, disconnect the two regulator leads and withdraw the unit.
11 Extract the brush box retaining screw and pull and tilt the brush box from its location, taking care not to damage the brushes during the process.
12 If necessary, unsolder the brush connections.
13 Fit the new brushes by reversing the removal operations.

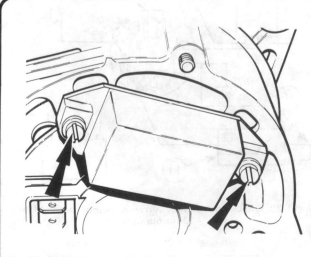

Fig. 11.21 Regulator screws – Bosch (Sec 12)

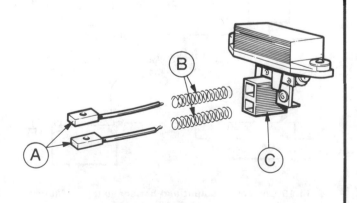

Fig. 11.22 Brush box – Bosch (Sec 12)

A   Brushes   C   Brush box
B   Springs

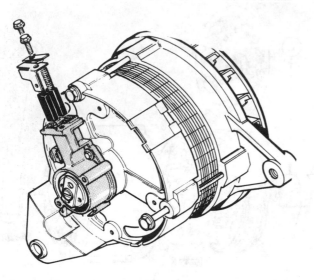

Fig. 11.23 Brush box – Lucas (Sec 12)

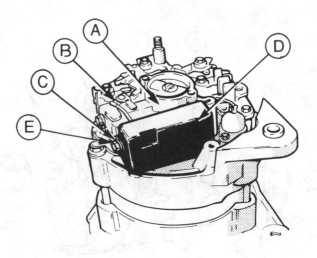

Fig. 11.24 Regulator – Lucas (Sec 12)

A   Brush box   D   Regulator
B   Field link   E   Retaining screw
C   Plastic spacer

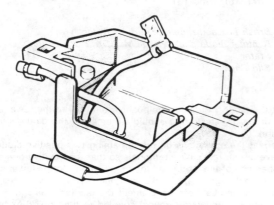

Fig. 11.25 Regulator – Motorola (Sec 12)

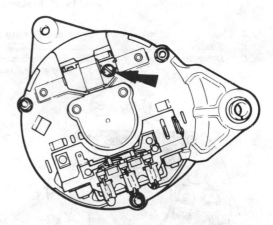

Fig. 11.26 Brush box retaining screw (arrowed) – Motorola
(Sec 12)

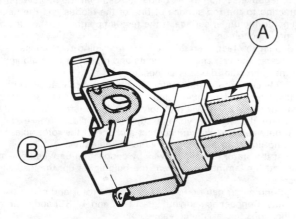

Fig. 11.27 Brush box – Motorola (Sec 12)

A   Brush   B   Brush box

13 Alternator (Bosch) – overhaul

1   With the alternator removed from the vehicle, unscrew the pulley retaining nut. To prevent the pulley rotating, place an old drivebelt in the pulley grooves and grip both runs of the belt in a vice as close to the pulley as possible.
2   Take off the washer, pulley, fan, spacer and the Woodruff key.
3   Remove the brush box.
4   Remove the tie-bolts and separate the drive end housing and rotor from the slip ring end housing.
5   Press out the rotor from the drive end housing.
6   Remove the drive end bearing and its retainer.
7   Remove the slip ring end bearing from the rotor shaft.
8   Extract the rectifier diode pack retaining screws and lift out the stator and the rectifier pack.
9   Unsolder the stator-to-diode pack connections, using a pair of pliers as a heat sink to prevent the heat spreading to the diodes.
10 With the alternator dismantled, check the positive diodes by connecting a 12V supply through a 5W test bulb wired to form a circuit through one of the diodes. Connect to the positive section of the diode pack with the negative terminal attached to the upper side of

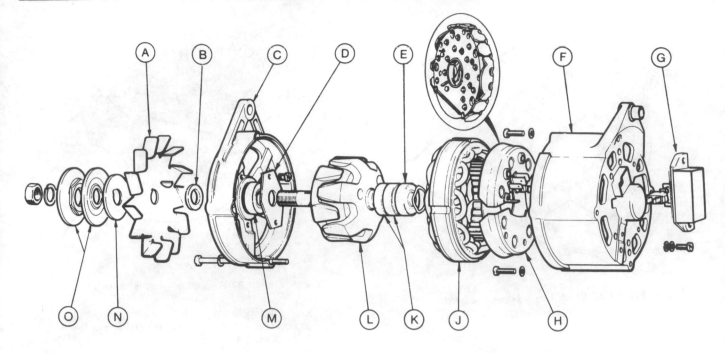

Fig. 11.28 Exploded view of Bosch alternator (Sec 13)

A	Fan	D	Drive end bearing retaining
B	Spacer		plate
C	Drive end housing	E	Slip ring end bearing
		F	Slip ring end housing

G	Brush box and regulator	L	Rotor
H	Rectifier diode pack	M	Drive end bearing
J	Stator	N	Spacer
K	Slip rings	O	Pulley

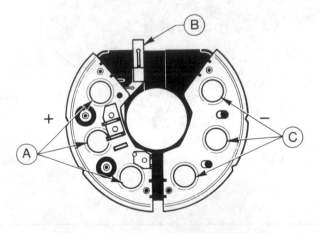

Fig. 11.29 Diode pack – Bosch (Sec 13)

A Positive diodes   C Negative diodes
B Brush box terminal

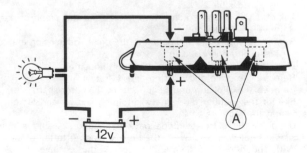

Fig. 11.30 Positive diodes (A) – Bosch (Sec 13)

one of the diodes. Connect the positive terminal to the lower surface of the diode. The test lamp should illuminate if the diode is in good condition.
11 Repeat the operations on the remaining two positive diodes.
12 Reverse the test circuit terminals so that the positive one goes to the upper side of the diode and the negative one to the lower surface. If the test bulb lights up, the diode is defective.
13 To check the field diodes, connect the test lamp as shown in Fig. 11.30 with the negative terminal coupled to the brush box terminal and the positive one to the diode. The bulb will light up if the diode is in good condition.
14 Repeat the test on the remaining two diodes.
15 Now reverse the terminals and repeat the test. If the bulb lights up then the diode is defective.
16 Now check the negative diodes by connecting the test lamp circuit to the negative section of the diode pack so that the positive terminal is attached to the top surface of one of the diodes and the negative terminal to the under surface. If the test lamp lights up then the diode is in good condition.
17 Repeat the test operations on the remaining two diodes.
18 Reverse the test circuit terminals and repeat. If the bulb lights up then that particular diode is defective.
19 To check the rotor and stator insulation, a 110V ac power supply and test lamp will be required and as this is unlikely to be available, the testing of these items will probably have to be left to your dealer.
20 Where the suitable voltage supply is available, make the test circuit between one slip ring contact and one of the rotor poles. If the test lamp lights up then the insulation is defective.
21 Test the stator in a similar way by connecting between one stator cable and the lamination pack. If the bulb lights up, the insulation is defective.
22 An ohmmeter can be used to determine rotor and stator winding continuity. Connect as shown (Figs. 11.34 and 11.35) and refer to the Specifications for resistance values.
23 Commence reassembly by resoldering the stator-to-diode pack connections, again using a pair of pliers as a heat sink to reduce heat spread.
24 Install the stator and diode pack into the slip ring end housing.

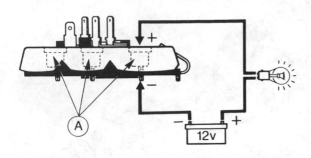

Fig. 11.31 Negative diodes (A) – Bosch (Sec 13)

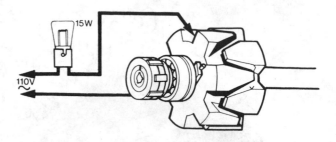

Fig. 11.32 Checking rotor winding insulation – Bosch (Sec 13)

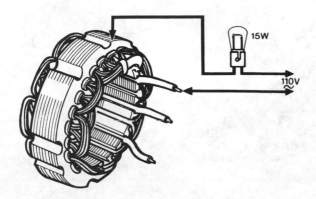

Fig. 11.33 Checking stator winding insulation – Bosch (Sec 13)

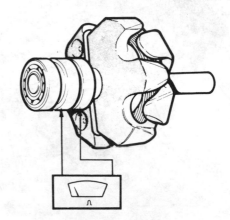

Fig. 11.34 Checking rotor winding continuity – Bosch (Sec 13)

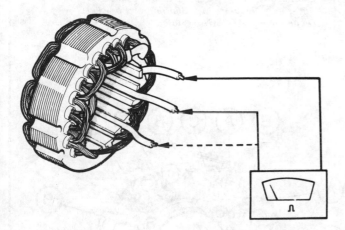

Fig. 11.35 Checking stator winding continuity – Bosch (Sec 13)

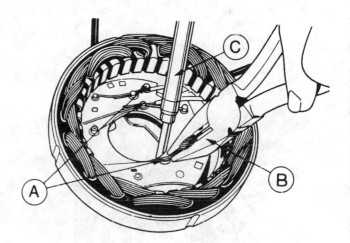

Fig. 11.36 Soldering stator-to-diode pack connections – Bosch (Sec 13)

A   Stator pack   C   Soldering iron
B   Pliers

25 Press the slip ring end housing onto the rotor shaft.
26 Refit the drive end bearing and secure with its retainer plate.
27 Fit the rotor into the drive end housing and assemble the rotor and drive end housing to the slip ring end housing.
28 Refit the brush box and the fan/pulley assembly. Make sure that the pulley spacer has its concave face against the fan as it acts as a vibration damper.

14 Alternator (Lucas) – overhaul

1   With the alternator removed from the vehicle and cleaned, remove the pulley and fan as described in the preceding Section, paragraph 1.
2   Remove the rear cover.
3   Remove the regulator.

4   Remove the surge protection diode and the brush box.
5   Unsolder the stator connections from the rectifier pack, using a pair of pliers as a heat sink as described in the preceding Section.
6   Extract the three bolts and remove the pack.
7   Checking the diodes should be carried out in a similar way to that described in the preceding Section, but note the different design of the diode pack.
8   Remove the tie-bolts, separate the drive end and slip ring end housing and withdraw the stator.
9   Unsolder the leads from the slip rings and remove the slip rings from the rotor shaft.

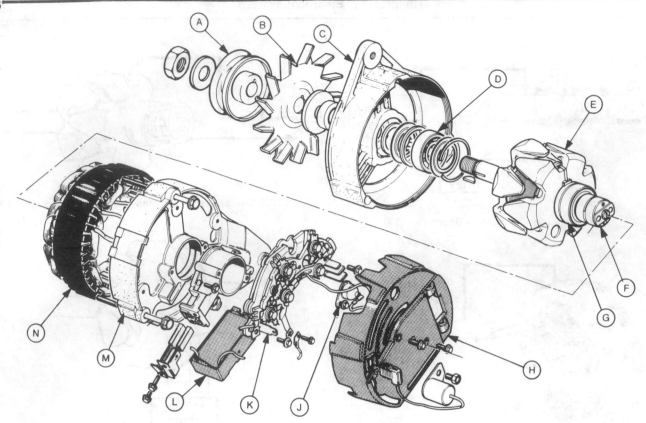

Fig. 11.37 Exploded view of Lucas alternator

A	Pulley	E	Rotor	H	End cover	L	Voltage regulator
B	Fan	F	Slip ring	J	Anti-surge diode	M	Slip ring end bracket
C	Drive end bracket	G	Slip ring end bearing	K	Diode plate	N	Stator
D	Drive end bearing						

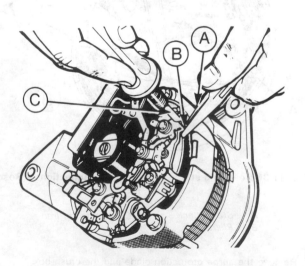

Fig. 11.38 Unsoldering stator/diode connections (Sec 14)

A Pliers C Soldering iron
B Rectifier pack

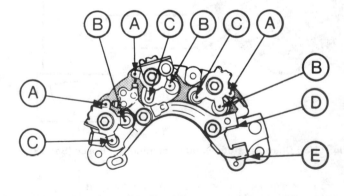

Fig. 11.39 Diode pack – Lucas (Sec 14)

A Field diodes D Field terminal
B Positive diodes E Positive terminal
C Negative diodes

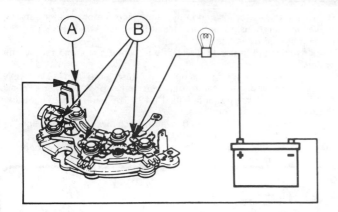

Fig. 11.40 Checking positive diodes – Lucas (Sec 14)

A   Positive terminals   B   Positive diodes

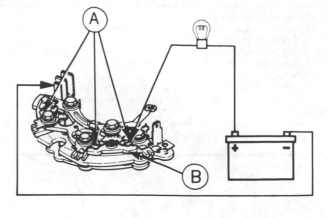

Fig. 11.41 Checking field diodes – Lucas (Sec 14)

A   Field diodes   B   Field plate

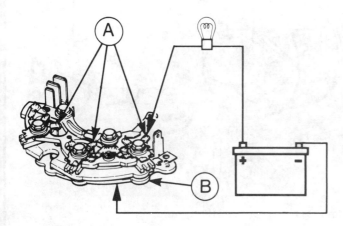

Fig. 11.42 Checking negative diodes – Lucas (Sec 14)

A   Negative diodes   B   Negative plate

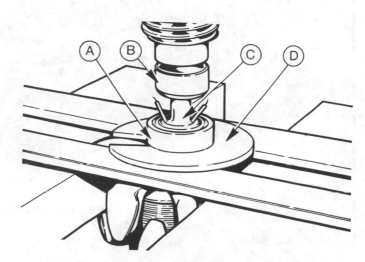

Fig. 11.43 Slip ring end bearing removal (Sec 14)

A   Bearing   D   Special slotted support
B   Press   washer
C   Rotor shaft

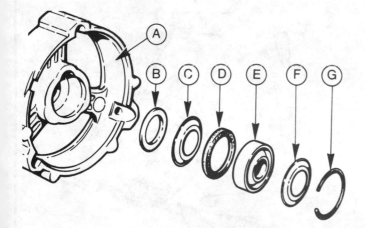

Fig. 11.44 Drive end bearing components – Lucas (Sec 14)

A   Drive end housing   E   Drive end bearing
B   Felt ring   F   Thrust washer
C   Thrust washer   G   Circlip
D   O-ring

10 Press out the slip ring end bearing and the rotor assembly from the slip ring end housing. Press off the slip ring end bearing.
11 To facilitate extraction of the drive end bearing circlip, apply light pressure to the rear face of the bearing.
12 Remove the circlip, thrust washer, the drive end bearing and shim pack.
13 Check the rotor and stator for winding continuity and insulation as described in the preceding Section, paragraphs 19 to 22.
14 Commence reassembly by fitting the drive end bearing shim pack, the bearing and the thrust washer. If the original bearing is being used again, work some high melting-point grease into it. Fit the retaining circlip (Fig. 11.44).
15 Make sure that the rotor wires are correctly located in their grooves in the rotor shaft and install the slip ring end bearing to the shaft. If the original bearing is being used, work some high melting-point grease into it. Refit the slip rings and resolder their leads.
16 Fit the rotor assembly to the slip ring end housing.
17 Locate the stator in the slip ring end housing and reconnect the slip ring and drive end housings. Pull the housings evenly together by tightening the tie-bolts.
18 Fit the rectifier diode pack and resolder the stator-to-rectifier diode pack wiring.
19 Fit the brush and the surge protection diode.
20 Fit the regulator, the rear cover and the pulley/fan assembly.

15 Alternator (Motorola) – overhaul

1 With the alternator removed from the engine and cleaned, remove the pulley/fan assembly as described in Section 13, paragraph 1.
2 Remove the rear cover and the regulator.
3 Remove the brush box.
4 Check the rotor by connecting test probes from an ohmmeter to each slip ring. The resistance must be within the limits given in the Specifications.
5 Connect an ohmmeter between a slip ring and the alternator housing. No reading should be indicated.

6 Check the stator insulation by connecting the ohmmeter between the alternator housing and each stator phrase winding in turn. No reading should be indicated.
7 Unsolder the stator-to-diode bridge connections and remove the bridge.
8 Test the diode bridge using a 5W test lamp and 12V supply. Connect the indicator lamp between each positive diode phase terminal and the B+ terminal (Fig. 11.49). The lamp should light up if the diode is in good condition.
9 Reverse the test lead probes and the lamp should not light up unless the diode is faulty.
10 To check the negative diodes, connect the test lamps between

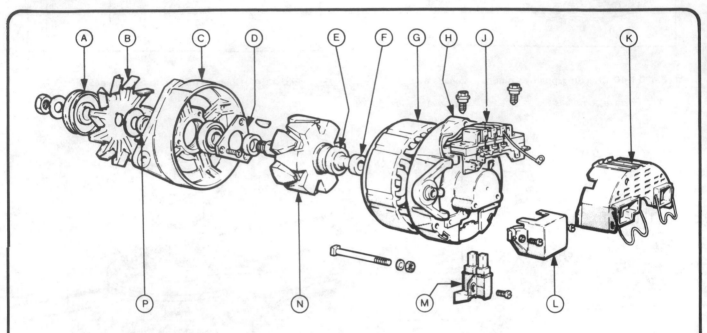

Fig. 11.45 Exploded view of Motorola alternator (Sec 15)

A Pulley
B Fan
C Drive end bearing
D Drive end bearing retaining plate
E Slip ring
F Slip ring end bearing
G Stator
H Slip ring end bearing
J Diode bridge
K End cover
L Regulator
M Brush box
N Rotor
P Spacer

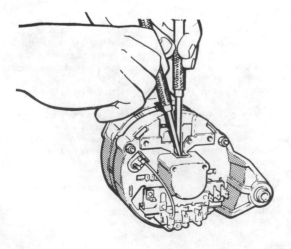

Fig. 11.46 Checking rotor resistance – Motorola (Sec 15)

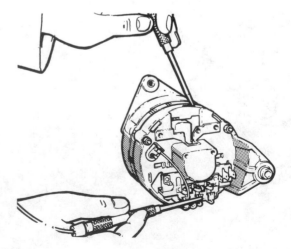

Fig. 11.47 Checking stator condition – Motorola (Sec 15)

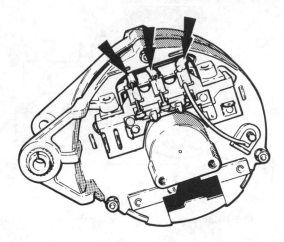

Fig. 11.48 Diode bridge and stator lead soldered connections –
Motorola (Sec 15)

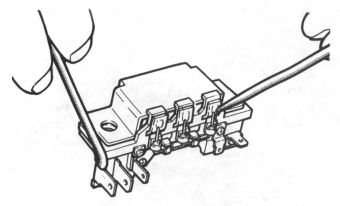

Fig. 11.49 Checking positive diodes – Motorola (Sec 15)

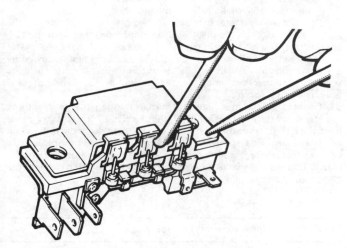

Fig. 11.50 Checking negative diodes – Motorola (Sec 15)

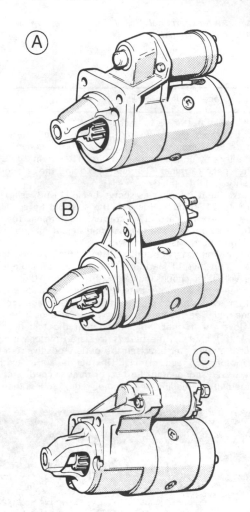

Fig. 11.51 Starter motor identification features (Sec 16)

A   Lucas   C   Nippondenso
B   Bosch

each phase terminal and earth. If the diode is in good condition, the
bulb should light up. Now reverse the test probes when the bulb
should not light up unless the diode is faulty.
11 Remove the tie-bolts, separate the drive end and slip ring end
housings and withdraw the stator.
12 Pull off the rear bearing using a two-legged extractor.
13 Unsolder the wires from the slip rings.
14 Extract the three screws which hold the bearing plate at the drive
end and press out the bearing assembly.
15 Commence reassembly by installing the drive end bearing and the
bearing plate and screws. If the original bearing is being used, work
some high melting-point grease into it.
16 Locate the inner slip ring on the rotor shaft, making sure that the
lead holes are correctly aligned. Press the slip ring into position and
solder the lead.
17 Install the outer slip ring in a similar way.
18 Fit the rotor and drive end bearing to the drive end housing. If the
original bearing is being used, work some high melting-point grease
into it.
19 Locate the stator in the slip ring end housing and connect it to the
drive end housing. Pull the assemblies evenly together using the tie-
bolts.
20 Fit the diode bridge and resolder the stator/diode wiring connections.
21 Fit the brush box, the regulator and the rear cover.
22 Fit the Woodruff key and the fan/pulley assembly.

16 Starter motor – description

The starter motor is of pre-engaged type and incorporates an
integral solenoid.
One of three different makes may be fitted. Lucas, Bosch or
Nippondenso. The power output of the starter motor varies according
to make and model.

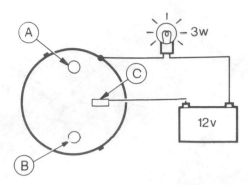

Fig. 11.52 Checking solenoid winding (Sec 17)

A   Battery terminal   C   Spade terminal
B   Feed terminal

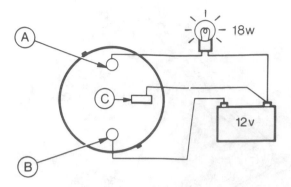

Fig. 11.53 Checking solenoid for continuity (Sec 17)

A   Battery terminal   C   Spade terminal
B   Feed terminal

17 Starter motor – in-vehicle testing

1   Check that the battery is fully charged.
2   First test the solenoid. To do this, disconnect the battery negative lead and both leads from the solenoid. Check the continuity of the solenoid windings by connecting a test lamp (12V with 2 to 3W bulb) between the spade terminal (C in Fig. 11.52) and the solenoid body. The lamp should light up.
3   Now make the test circuit as shown in Fig. 11.53, using a higher wattage (18 to 21W) bulb. Energise the solenoid by applying 12V between the spade terminal and the starter feed terminal. The solenoid should be heard to operate and the test bulb should light up, indicating that the solenoid contacts have closed.
4   Connect a voltmeter directly between the battery terminals. Disconnect the positive LT lead from the ignition coil and operate the starter. The voltmeter should indicate not less than 10.5V.
5   Now connect the voltmeter between the starter main terminal and the body of the starter motor. Operate the starter, with the coil LT lead still disconnected. The reading on the voltmeter should be no more than 0.5V lower than that indicated during the test described in paragraph 4. If it is, check the battery-to-starter motor wiring.
6   Connect the voltmeter between the battery positive terminal and the starter motor main feed terminal. Operate the starter (with the LT coil positive lead disconnected) for two or three seconds and observe the meter readings. A reading of 12V should drop to less than 1.0V. If

the reading is higher, a high resistance is indicated (refer to paragraph 7). If the reading is lower, refer to paragraph 8.
7   Connect the voltmeter between the two main stud terminals of the starter solenoid. With the positive LT lead disconnected from the coil, operate the starter for two or three seconds and note the meter readings. Battery voltage (12V) should be indicated first, followed by a voltage drop of less than 0.5V. If outside this tolerance, a faulty switch or connections may be the cause, or loose or corroded terminals in the circuit.
8   Connect a voltmeter between the battery negative terminal and the starter motor main casing. With the positive LT lead disconnected from the coil, operate the starter for two or three seconds. If the earth line is satisfactory, the reading should be less than 0.5V. If it is 0.6V or more then there is a high resistance in the earth return side of the circuit. This may be due to a loose or corroded connection either at the battery or at the engine block.

18 Starter motor – removal and refitting

1   Disconnect the battery.
2   Working from under the vehicle, disconnect the main starter motor cable and the two wires from the starter solenoid (photo).
3   Unbolt the starter motor and withdraw it from its location (photo).
4   Refit by reversing the removal operations.

18.2 Detach solenoid wires (Bosch starter motor shown)

18.3 Starter motor retaining bolts

19 Starter motor (Bosch) – overhaul

1   With the starter motor removed from the vehicle and cleaned, grip the starter motor in the jaws of a vice which have been fitted with soft metal protectors.
2   Disconnect the field winding connector link from the solenoid stud.
3   Extract the solenoid fixing screws and withdraw the solenoid yoke from the drive end housing and the solenoid armature. Unhook the solenoid armature from the actuating lever.
4   Extract the two screws and remove the commutator end cap and rubber seal.
5   Wipe away any grease and withdraw the C-clip and shims.
6   Remove the tie-nuts and remove the commutator end housing.
7   Remove the brushes by prising the brush springs clear and sliding the brushes from their holders. Remove the brushplate.
8   Separate the drive end housing and armature from the yoke by tapping apart with a plastic-faced hammer.

9   Remove the tie-studs to release the drive pinion clutch stop bracket.
10 Withdraw the armature assembly and unhook the actuating arm from the drive pinion flange.
11 To remove the drive pinion from the armature shaft, drive the stop collar down the shaft with a piece of tubing to expose the clip. Remove the clip from its groove and slide the stop collar and drive pinion off the shaft.
12 Examine the components and renew as necessary.
13 If the brushes have worn to less than the specified minimum, renew them as a set. To renew the brushes, cut their leads at their midpoint and make a good soldered joint when connecting the new brushes.
14 The commutator face should be clean and free from burnt spots. Where necessary burnish with fine glass paper (not emery) and wipe with a fuel-moistened cloth. If the commutator is in really bad shape it can be skimmed on a lathe provided its diameter is not reduced below the specified minimum. If recutting the insulation slots, take care not to cut into the commutator metal.

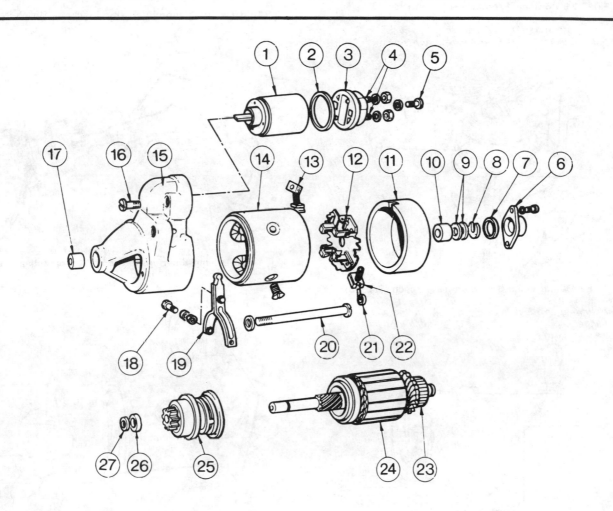

Fig. 11.54 Exploded view of Bosch starter motor (Sec 19)

1 Solenoid body	8 C-clip	15 Drive end housing	22 Brush
2 Gasket	9 Shim	16 Solenoid fixing screw	23 Commutator
3 Contact switch assembly	10 Bearing	17 Bearing	24 Armature
4 Main terminals	11 Commutator end housing	18 Pivot screw	25 Drive pinion/roller clutch
5 Retaining screws	12 Brush box	19 Actuating lever	26 Bearing
6 End cover	13 Link connector	20 Tie-bolt	27 Thrust washer
7 Seal	14 Main casing (yoke)	21 Brush spring	

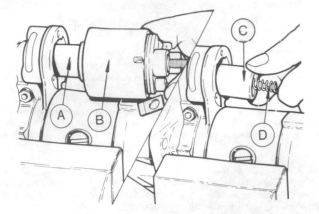

Fig. 11.55 Solenoid removal – Bosch (Sec 19)

A   Armature   C   Armature
B   Yoke   D   Armature return spring

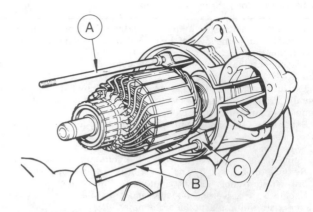

Fig. 11.56 Tie-studs and clutch stop bracket – Bosch (Sec 19)

A   Stud   C   Clutch stop bracket
B   Stud

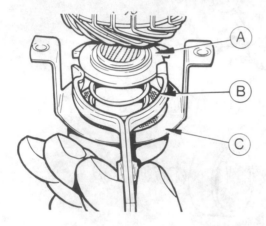

Fig. 11.57 Withdrawing the armature – Bosch (Sec 19)

A   Actuating arm locating   B   Actuating arm
    flange   C   Clutch stop bracket

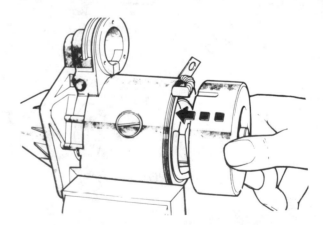

Fig. 11.58 Driving down armature shaft stop collar – Bosch
(Sec 19)

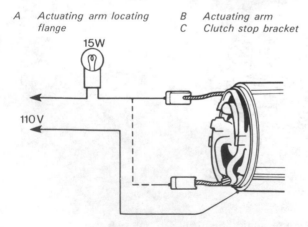

Fig. 11.59 Testing field winding for continuity – Bosch (Sec 19)

Fig. 11.60 Fitting commutator end housing and rubber insulator –
Bosch (Sec 19)

15 The field winding can be checked for continuity only if a 110V ac power source is available, probably a job for your dealer. Where facilities are to hand, connect the test lamp between each field winding brush in turn and a clean, unpainted area of the yoke. The test lamp should not light up.

16 Renew the end housing bushes which are of self-lubricating type and should have been soaked in clean engine oil for at least 20 minutes before installation. Drive out the old bushes, whilst supporting the endplate/housing, using a suitable mandrel or drlft.

17 Commence reassembly by sliding the drive pinion and stop collar onto the armature shaft. Fit the C-clip into the shaft groove and then use a two-legged puller to draw the stop collar over the clip.

18 Align the clutch retaining bracket and secure it with the two tie-studs.

19 Fit the rubber insert into the drive end housing.

20 Guide the yoke over the armature and tap home onto the drive end housing.

21 Fit the brush plate, the brushes and their springs.

22 Guide the commutator end housing into position, at the same time sliding the rubber insulator into the cut-out in the commutator

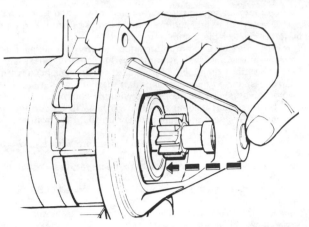

Fig. 11.61 Checking the endfloat of the armature – Bosch (Sec 19)

housing. Secure the commutator end housing with the stud nuts and washers.

23 Slide the armature into position in its bearings so that the shaft has the maximum projection at the commutator bearing end.

24 Fit sufficient shims onto the armature shaft to eliminate endfloat when the C-clip is installed, which should now be done.

25 Fit the armature shaft bearing cap seal, apply a little lithium-based grease to the end of the shaft and refit the bearing cap with its two screws.

26 Apply some grease to the solenoid armature hook and engage the hook with the actuating arm in the drive end housing. Check that the solenoid armature return spring is correctly located and then guide the solenoid yoke over the armature. Align the yoke with the drive end housing and fit the three securing screws.

27 Connect the field wire link to the solenoid terminal stud.

20 Starter motor (Lucas) – overhaul

1 With the starter removed from the vehicle and cleaned, grip it in a vice fitted with soft metal jaw protectors.

2 Remove the plastic cap from the commutator endplate.

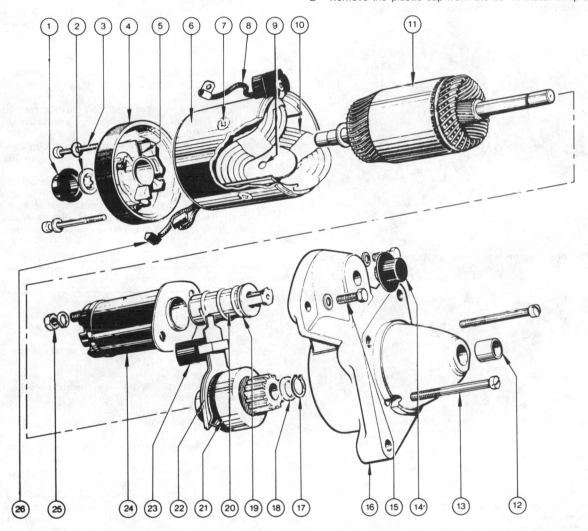

Fig. 11.62 Exploded view of Lucas starter motor (Sec 20)

1 Dust cap	8 Link connector	15 Solenoid fixing screw	21 Drive assembly
2 Star-clip	9 Pole screw	16 Drive end housing	22 Engagement lever
3 Endplate bolt	10 Field coils	17 C-clip	23 Pivot
4 Endplate	11 Armature	18 Spacer	24 Solenoid body
5 Brush housing	12 Bearing	19 Return spring	25 Terminal nut and washer
6 Main casing (yoke)	13 Housing screws	20 Solenoid armature	26 Brushes
7 Pole screw	14 Dust cover		

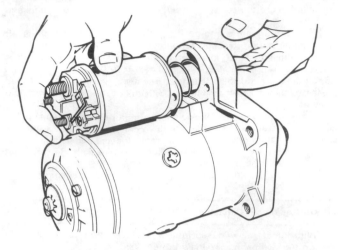

Fig. 11.63 Removing the solenoid – Lucas (Sec 20)

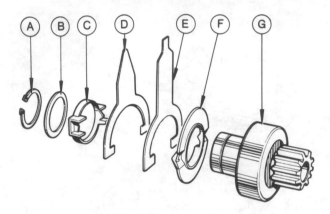

Fig. 11.64 The drive pinion and clutch unit components – Lucas
(Sec 20)

A	C-clip	E	Actuating lever
B	Spacer	F	Drive collar
C	Drive collar	G	Drive pinion
D	Actuating lever		

3   Using a very small cold chisel, remove the star clip from the end of the armature shaft. Do this by distorting the prongs of the clip until it can be removed.
4   Disconnect the main feed link from the solenoid terminal.
5   Unscrew the two mounting nuts and withdraw the solenoid from the drive end housing, at the same time unhooking the solenoid armature from the actuating lever.
6   Extract the two drive end housing fixing screws. Guide the housing and the armature clear of the yoke.
7   Withdraw the armature from the drive end housing and the actuating lever assembly will come out with it, complete with plastic pivot block and rubber pad.
8   Use a piece of tubing to drive the stop collar down the armature shaft to expose the C-clip. Remove the C-clip and take off the stop collar and drive pinion.
9   To separate the actuating lever from the drive pinion, extract the C-clip and remove the spacer. Separate the two halves of the plastic drive collar and withdraw the actuating lever.
10 Remove the commutator endplate screws and tap the plate free of the yoke.

11 Lift the plate far enough to give access to the two field winding brushes. Disconnect two of the brushes from the brush box to permit complete removal of the commutator endplate.
12 The brush box and commutator endplate are only supplied as a complete assembly and should be renewed together, if necessary.
13 Examine all the components for wear. If the brushes have worn to less than the specified minimum length, renew them as a set.
14 Two of the brushes come complete with the commutator endplate terminal, but the field winding brushes will have to be cut and new ones soldered. Cut the original leads 6.0 mm (0.24 in) from the field winding conductor.
15 New brush springs are only supplied complete with a new brush box.
16 Recondition the commutator where necessary as described in Section 19, paragraph 14.
17 Check the field winding for continuity as described in Section 19, paragraph 15.
18 Renewal of the field winding is not usually within the scope of the home mechanic unless a pressure driver is available to release the pole piece retaining screws.
19 The endplate bearing bushes should be renewed as described in Section 19, paragraph 16.
20 Commence reassembly by locating two field winding brushes in their brush box channels. Align the commutator endplate and secure it with four screws.
21 Fit the actuating lever to the drive pinion, the two halves of the drive collar and the spacer. Secure with the C-clip.
22 Slide the drive pinion and thrust collar onto the armature shaft. Fit the C-clip and use a two-legged puller to draw the stop collar over the clip.
23 Hook the plastic pivot block over the actuating arm, position the rubber pad and insert into the solenoid mounting housing.
24 Guide the armature into the drive end housing.
25 Guide the armature and drive end housing through the yoke and align the armature shaft with the endplate bush. Secure the yoke and housing with two fixing screws.
26 Fit a new star clip to the end of the armature shaft, making sure that it is firmly fixed to eliminate shaft endfloat. Fit the plastic cap.
27 Locate the solenoid armature onto the actuating arm, guide the solenoid yoke over the armature and secure with studs and nuts.
28 Refit the connecting link between the solenoid and the main feed terminal.

21 Starter motor (Nippondenso) – overhaul

1   With the starter motor removed from the engine and cleaned, secure it in a vice with jaws protected with soft metal.
2   Disconnect the field winding connector from the solenoid terminal.
3   Remove the solenoid retaining nuts.
4   Withdraw the solenoid and unhook the armature hook from the actuating lever.
5   Remove the bearing cap (two screws).
6   Slide the C-washer from its groove in the armature shaft and take off the coil spring.
7   Unbolt and remove the rear housing cover.
8   Withdraw two field brushes and remove the brush gear mounting plate.
9   Withdraw the armature and drive end housing from the main housing.
10 Withdraw the armature and the actuating lever from the drive end housing. Remove the actuating lever.
11 Use a piece of tubing to tap the stop collar down the armature shaft to expose the C-clip. Remove the clip and pull off the stop collar and drive pinion. To avoid damaging the clutch, do not clamp it in a vice when driving the stop collar down the armature.
12 Inspect all components for wear. If the brushes have worn to less than the specified minimum, renew them as a set. To do this, the original brush leads will have to be cut at the midpoint of their length and the new ones joined by soldering.
13 Recondition the commutator as described in Section 19, paragraph 14.
14 Check the field winding for continuity as described in Section 19, paragraph 15.
15 Renew the commutator and drive end housing bushes where necessary, as described in Section 19, paragraph 16.

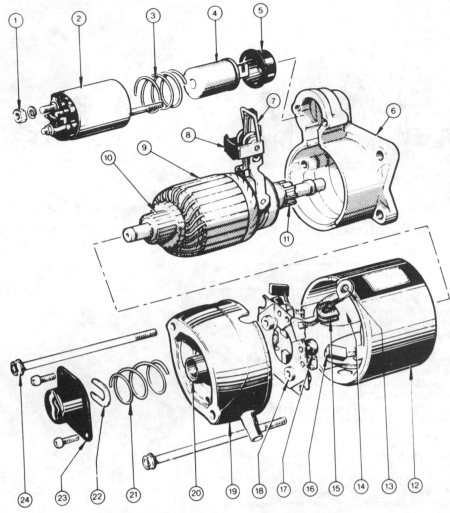

Fig. 11.65 Exploded view of Nippondenso starter motor (Sec 21)

1 Solenoid terminal nut	8 Pivot	13 Link connector	19 Commutator end housing
2 Solenoid body	9 Armature	14 Pole shoe	20 Bush
3 Return spring	10 Commutator	15 Seal	21 Spring
4 Solenoid armature	11 Drive pinion/roller	16 Brush	22 C-clip
5 Seal	clutch	17 Brush spring	23 End cover
6 Drive end housing	12 Main casing	18 Brush plate	24 Tie-bolt
7 Actuating lever			

16 Commence reassembly by sliding the drive pinion and stop collar onto the armature shaft. Fit the C-clip and using a two-legged puller, draw the stop collar over the clip.

17 Align the actuating lever in the drive end housing. Guide the armature into position, at the same time locating the actuating lever onto the drive pinion flange.

18 Tap the yoke into engagement with the drive end housing.

19 Locate the brush plate, aligning the cut-outs in the plate with the loops in the field winding. The brush assembly will be positively located when the fixing screws are screwed in.

20 Position the brushes in their brush box locations and retain with their springs.

21 Guide the commutator end housing into position and secure with the fixing nuts.

22 To the commutator end of the armature shaft, fit the coil spring and the C-clip.

23 Smear the end of the shaft with lithium based grease and then fit the cap (two screws).

24 Connect the solenoid armature hook onto the actuating lever in the drive end housing. Align the solenoid yoke and fit the two fixing bolts.

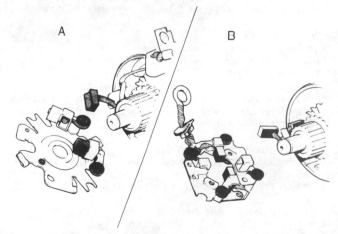

Fig. 11.66 Locate brushes in their boxes in the mounting plate (Sec 21)

A   0.6 kW brushes   B   0.9 kW brushes

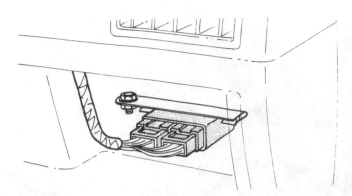

Fig. 11.67 Fuse and relay box showing plastic cover removal (2), fuse removal (3) and relays (4). Check if fuse has blown at point indicated in inset (Sec 22)

Fig. 11.68 Auxiliary relay – central door locking (Sec 22)

22 Fuses, relays and circuit breakers

1   The fuses and most of the relays are contained in a plastic box attached to the bulkhead on the driver's side under the bonnet.

2   The fuses are numbered to identify the circuit which they protect and the circuits are represented by symbols on the plastic cover of the box (photo).

3   When an accessory or other electrical component or system fails, always check the fuse first. The fuses are coloured red (10A), blue (15A), yellow (20A) clear (25A) and green (30A). Never replace a fuse with one of higher rating or bypass it with tinfoil, and if the new fuse blows immediately, check the reason before renewing again. The most common cause of a fuse blowing is faulty insulation creating a short-circuit.

4   Spare fuses are carried in the fusebox lid.

5   The radio and, where fitted, heated seats have their own in-line circuit fuses or are fused in the rear of the radio casing.

6   Relays are of the plug-in type and will be found within the main fuse/relay box, below the facia panel on the driver's side or, in the case of the central locking system, under the instrument panel (next to the glove compartment).

7   Circuit breakers are only fitted to vehicles equipped with electrically operated windows or a central door lock system.

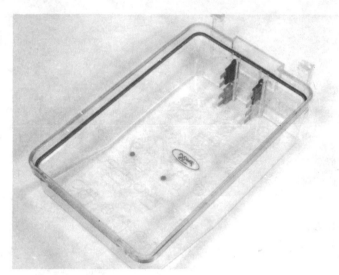

22.2 Fusebox cover gives circuit information
Note spare fuses

23 Switches – removal and refitting

Disconnect the battery before removing any switches

1   Reference should also be made to Chapter 9 for details of steering column switches and to Chapter 8 for braking system switches.

Wiper delay switch

2   Remove the switch knob and the bezel nut.

3   Withdraw the switch through the parcels tray and disconnect it from the wiring harness.

Heated rear window and remote boot lid release switches

4   Using a screwdriver, gently prise the switch from the facia panel.

5   Disconnect the switch multi-plug.

Luggage compartment lamp switch

6   Open the boot lid, then using a suitable cross-head screwdriver, unscrew the switch retaining screw.

7   Withdraw the switch and disconnect the lead plug.

Instrument cluster light switch

8   Open the small tidy tray by pulling it downwards.

9   Extract the two screws from its top edge.

10 Pull the knob from the switch and unscrew the bezel nut.

11 Remove the switch through the tidy tray aperture and disconnect the electrical leads from it.

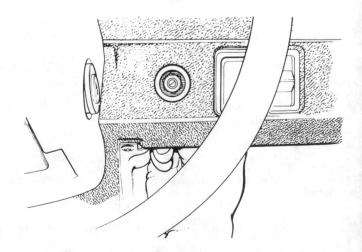

Fig. 11.69 Removing wiper delay switch (Sec 23)

207

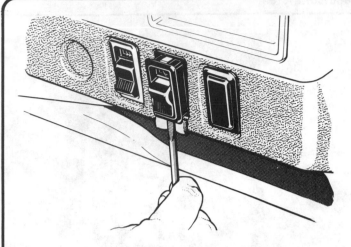

Fig. 11.70 Lever switch from facia – remote release for the boot lid (Sec 23)

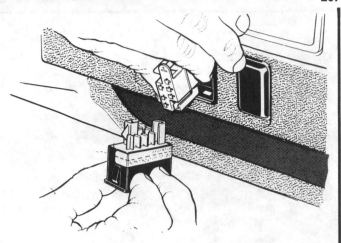

Fig. 11.71 Switch removal from multi-plug (Sec 23)

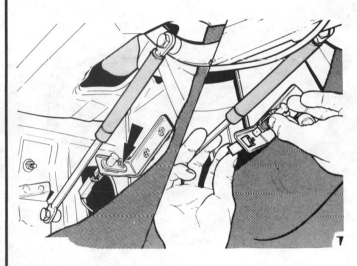

Fig. 11.72 Luggage compartment lamp switch removal (Sec 23)

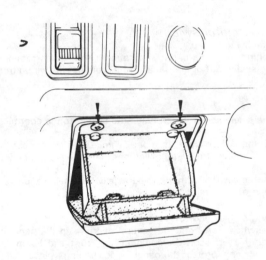

Fig. 11.73 Facia tidy tray securing screws (Sec 23)

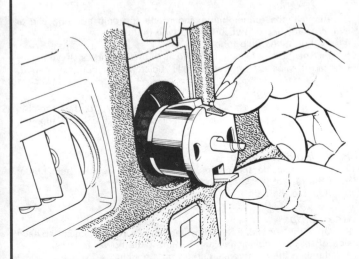

Fig. 11.74 Heater blower motor switch removal (Sec 23)

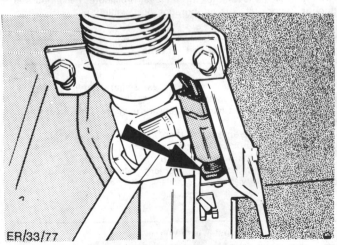

Fig. 11.75 Stop-light switch location and locknut – arrowed (Sec 23)

23.14 Door courtesy lamp switch

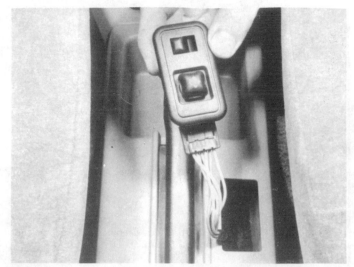

23.18 Door mirror control switch removal

Heater blower motor switch

12 Pull off the switch knob.
13 Reach behind the facia panel and squeeze the switch retaining tangs. Pull the switch out of the panel and disconnect the wiring from it.

Courtesy lamp switch

14 Extract the single screw which holds the switch to the door pillar (photo).
15 Withdraw the switch from its rubber shroud and disconnect the electrical lead. To prevent the lead falling back into the pillar, tape it to retain it.
16 Smearing the switch with petroleum jelly will help to prevent corrosion which often causes failure.

Door mirror control switch

17 Prise the switch free from its location aperture in the panel by inserting a thin-bladed screwdriver under the front end lip of the switch. When levering, protect the panel by positioning a piece of thin cardboard under the screwdriver blade.
18 Pull the switch from the panel and disconnect the wiring connector (photo).

All switches

19 Refitting is the reverse of the removal procedure. Reconnect the battery and check for correct operation on completion.

24 Cigar lighter – removal and refitting

1 Disconnect the battery.
2 Remove the ashtray, and, after extracting the fixing screws, withdraw the ashtray housing.
3 Disconnect the electrical leads and remove the bulb holder from the lighter.
4 Pull out the light element and then, from the rear, press the lighter body and the illumination ring from the ashtray.
5 Remove the illumination ring from the lighter body.
6 To remove the coil from the element, release the locknut while gripping the spindle with a pair of pliers.
7 Refitting is a reversal of removal.

25 Bulbs (exterior lamps) – renewal

Headlamp

1 Open the bonnet.
2 Working inside the engine compartment, pull the multi-plug from the rear of the headlamp (photo).

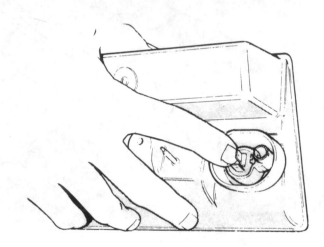

Fig. 11.76 Cigar lighter removal (Sec 24)

3 Remove the rubber gaiter and rotate the bulb securing clip or extract the spring clip according to type (photo).
4 Withdraw the bulb (photo).
5 Fit the bulb, avoiding handling it with the fingers. If you have touched it, wipe the bulb with a pad moistened in methylated spirit.

Front parking lamp

6 The operations are similar to those just described for the headlamp bulb. Twist the parking lamp bulb holder from the headlamp unit (photo).

Front indicator lamp

7 Working inside the engine compartment, twist the bulb holder from the rear of the lamp (photo).
8 Remove the bulb from the holder.

Rear lamps

9 Open the boot lid. Reach down and depress the retaining tab each side of the bulb holder unit and withdraw the holder (photos).
10 Remove the bulb concerned from its holder.

Rear number plate lamp

11 Prise the light unit from the bumper using a screwdriver (photo).

25.2 Detach headlamp multi-plug ...

25.3 ... remove rubber cover, squeeze together clip arms and pivot back retaining clip

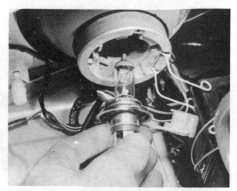

25.4 Withdraw headlight bulb

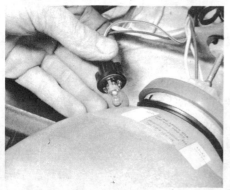

25.6 Extract parking lamp

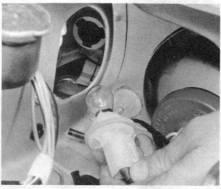

25.7 Front indicator lamp bulb removal

25.9A Depress tab each side of rear light unit to withdraw it

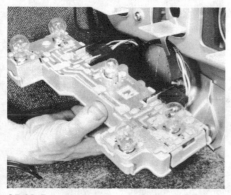

25.9B Rear lamp unit removed for bulb inspection/renewal

25.11 Prising free the number plate lamp

25.12 Extracting number plate lamp bulb and holder

12 Rotate the holder socket anti-clockwise and withdraw it for access to the bulb (photo).

All lamps
13 Replacement of the bulb and holder is a reversal of removal in all cases. Check operation of the lights on completion.

26 Bulbs (interior lamps) – renewal

Glove compartment lamp
1 This is simply a matter of gently pulling the bulb from its holder.

Heater control illumination lamp
2 Slide the heater control levers to the top of their travel.

3 Pull off the heater motor switch knob and then unclip the control trim panel from the facia.
4 Pull the bulb from the lamp socket.

Hazard warning switch
5 Grip the switch cover and pull it off.
6 Gently pull the bulb from its socket.

Interior front lamp and centre console-mounted lamp
7 Carefully prise the lamp from its location and remove the bulb from its spring contact on the lamp body (photo).

Luggage compartment lamp
8 Using a thin screwdriver, prise the lamp from its location.
9 Remove the bulb from its spring contact clip.
10 Refitting the bulb is a reversal of removal.

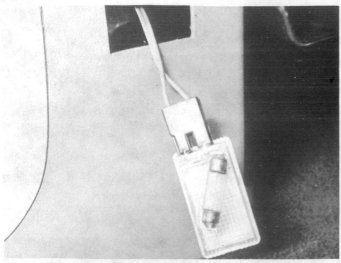

26.7 Console-mounted lamp removed

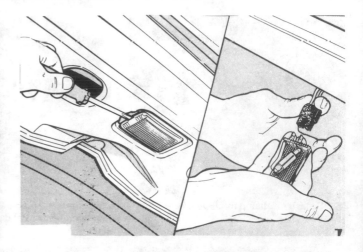

Fig. 11.77 Luggage compartment lamp removal (Sec 26)

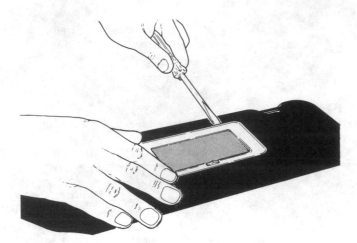

Fig. 11.78 Vanity mirror removal (Sec 26)

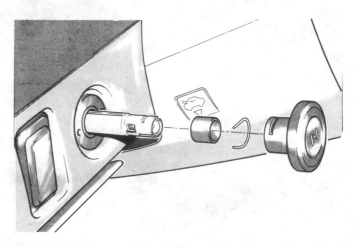

Fig. 11.79 Choke knob, retaining clip and sleeve (Sec 26)

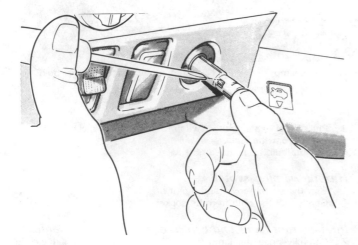

Fig. 11.80 Choke warning lamp bulb removal (Sec 26)

Vanity mirror lamp

11 With the sun visor lowered, carefully prise free the mirrors and diffuser unit from the visor using a thin-bladed screwdriver.
12 Remove the festoon bulb from its location contacts for renewal.

Manual choke knob warning lamp

13 Prise free the knob retaining clip, withdraw the knob and the sleeve.
14 To extract the bulb, push it against the spring pressure then push down the bulb retainer using a thin-bladed screwdriver as shown to release the bulb (Fig. 11.80).

All lamps

15 Refitting is a reversal of the removal for all lamp assemblies, but note that when inserting the choke knob bulb the retainer must be pushed upwards to secure the bulb in position.
16 Check the operation of the lights on completion.

27 Exterior lamps – removal and refitting

Headlamp

1 Remove the radiator grille, as described in Chapter 12.

2   Working inside the engine compartment, disconnect the headlamp multi-plug and pull out the parking lamp bulb holder.

3   Twist the top and side clip plastic heads through 90° to release them from their retainers (photos).

4   With the headlamp unit released, pull it sharply forward off its ballstud (photo).

Front direction lamp

5   Working inside the engine compartment, disconnect the indicator bulb holder from the lamp.

6   Remove the headlamp, as described in earlier paragraphs of this Section.

7   Remove the spring clip from the ball-headed bolt and remove the bolt (photo).

8   Remove the lower adjuster by turning the knurled collar (photo).

9   Release the lamp from its retaining clips and tangs, the latter by prising up with a screwdriver (photo).

Rear lamp

10 Remove the bulb holder, as described in Section 25.

11 Remove the lamp retaining nuts and bolts and remove the lamp assembly from the body (photo). One nut is located under the black trim.

27.3A Headlamp unit top mounting and plastic retainer

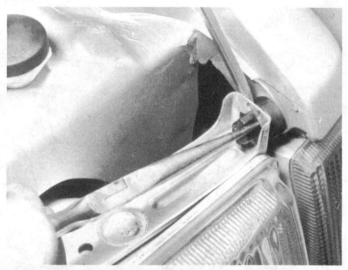

27.3B Headlamp unit side mounting detachment method

27.4 Headlamp ball-stud

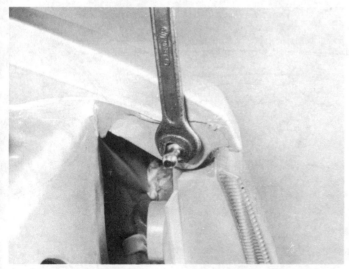

27.7 Remove ball-head bolt

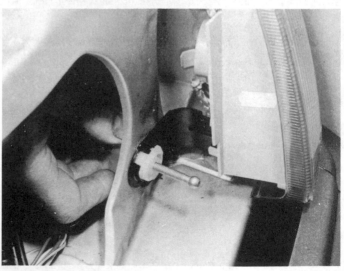

27.8 Removing lower adjuster

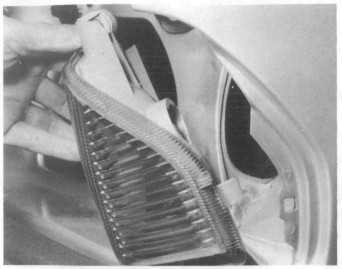

27.9 Indicator lamp removal

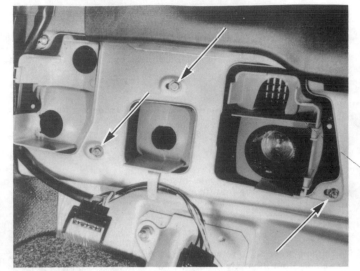

27.11 Rear lamp lens unit retaining nuts (arrowed)

All lamps
12   Refitting is a reversal of removal for all lamp assemblies. Check headlight alignment, if necessary.

28   Headlamps – alignment

1   The headlights are adjustable individually for both horizontal and vertical alignment from within the engine compartment.
2   Adjustments should not normally be necessary and, if their beam alignment is suspect, they should be checked by a Ford garage with optical alignment equipment.
3   A temporary adjustment can be made by turning the vertical and/or horizontal adjuster screws at the rear of each headlight unit. When making an alignment check, the car tyre pressures must be correct and the car standing unladen on level ground.

29   Auxiliary warning system – description

1   This system monitors the fluid levels and front brake pads for excessive wear. In the event of a fluid level dropping below the specified level, or the brake pads wearing down to the minimum allowable thickness, the driver is warned of the particular malfunction by means of a warning lamp.
2   When the ignition is first switched on, all warning lamps will illuminate as a means of verifying that all bulbs are working. This illumination period is of five seconds duration.
3   The system embraces the following components:

   Fuel low level warning lamp. Activated by a sensor in the fuel level transmitter when the quantity of fuel in the tank falls below 7.0 litres (1.5 gallons).

   Coolant low level warning lamp. Activated by a float-operated reed switch mounted in the expansion vessel.

   Washer fluid low level warning lamp. A similar device to the coolant switch, it activates when the fluid is down to about 25% of capacity.

   Engine oil low level warning lamp. Activated by a dipstick whose resistance increases when its marked lower section is not immersed in oil.

   Brake pad wear indicator. The sensing of worn disc pads is carried out by electrodes built into the pad. When the friction material has worn down to about 2 mm (0.079 in) thick, the electrodes cause the warning lamp to illuminate. In this instance the brake pads must be renewed at the earliest opportunity, as described in Chapter 8.

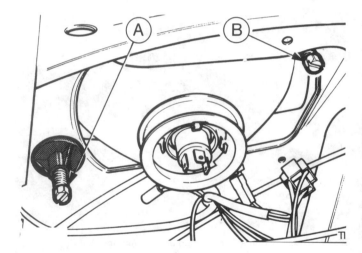

Fig. 11.81 Headlight adjuster screws (Sec 28)

A   *Vertical adjustment*   B   *Horizontal adjustment*

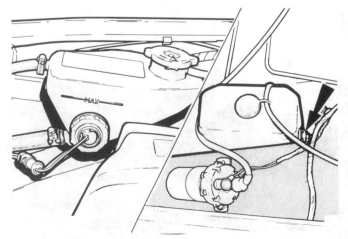

Fig. 11.82 Coolant and washer low level warning sensor switch positions (Sec 29)

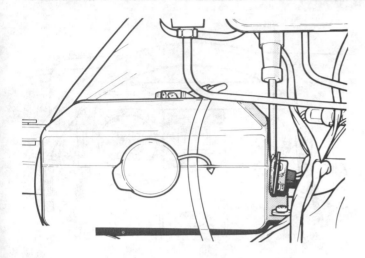

Fig. 11.83 Low washer fluid warning switch removal – prise free at point shown with screwdriver (Sec 30)

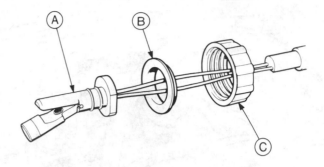

Fig. 11.84 Low coolant warning switch (Sec 30)

A   Switch   C   Retainer
B   Spacer

30 Auxiliary warning system – removal and refitting of components

Low washer fluid warning switch
1   Drain or syphon out the reservoir fluid then disconnect the switch multi-plug. Lever the switch away from the seal grommet using the flat blade of a suitable screwdriver. Do not allow fluid to enter the connectors.
2   Refit in reverse order of removal, checking that the grommet is correctly seated. On completion, check that the switch is operational and that there are no leaks around the grommet.

Low coolant warning switch
3   Drain the coolant from the expansion tank (see Chapter 2), having first depressurised the system if necessary.
4   Detach the switch multi-plug and then unscrew the threaded retainer. The switch can then be levered from the seal grommet using a flat-bladed screwdriver. Do not allow coolant to enter the connectors.
5   Refit in reverse and, on completion, check switch operation and, when reservoir is refilled to the specified level, that there are no signs of leaks from the grommet/retainer.

Warning indicator control unit
6   Remove the radio speaker grille and speaker from the facia.
7   Disconnect the multi-plug from the warning indicator/control assembly and then remove the two nylon fixing nuts which hold the assembly in position on the facia panel. Take care when withdrawing and handling the unit not to knock it, as the integral micro-electronics could be damaged.
8   Refit in the reverse order of removal. On completion check that the warning lights function for the initial period of five seconds after the ignition is switched on.

Low fuel sensor unit
9   This is integral with the fuel tank sender unit and is removed from the tank as described in Section 7, Chapter 3.

Brake pad wear indicators
10   The removal and refitting of the brake pad sensors is described in Chapter 8.

Auxiliary system warning light bulbs
11   The auxiliary warning light bulbs are integral with the instrument panel and are welded in position. They cannot be individually renewed. To remove the instrument panel cluster refer to Section 32.

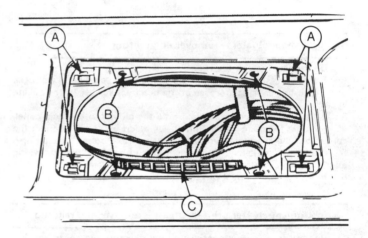

Fig. 11.85 Loudspeaker fixings (A,B) and auxiliary warning system control assembly (C) (Sec 30)

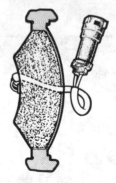

Fig. 11.86 Brake pad and wear sensor (Sec 30)

31 Instrument cluster glass – removal and refitting

1   Remove the instrument cluster bezel by extracting the two retaining screws and pulling the bezel from its lower clips.
2   Extract the six glass securing screws.
3   Refitting is a reversal of removal.

Fig. 11.87 Removing the instrument cluster glass (Sec 31)

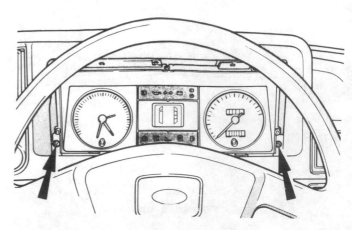

Fig. 11.88 Instrument cluster retaining screws (Sec 32)

4   Very carefully prise the printed circuit from its fixing pegs and remove it.
5   Refitting is a reversal of removal.

32 Instrument cluster – removal and refitting

1   Disconnect the battery.
2   Extract the screws and pull the instrument panel bezel from the panel. The two clips at the base of the bezel will release by the pulling action.
3   Extract the two screws which hold the cluster to the facia panel.
4   Remove the dash under-trim panel, reach up and disconnect the cable from the speedometer by depressing the serrated plastic ring.
5   Gently pull the cluster forwards and to one side so that the wiring multi-plug can be disconnected. Withdraw the cluster.
6   Refitting is a reversal of removal.

33 Instrument cluster printed circuit – removal and refitting

1   Remove the instrument cluster, as described in the preceding Section.
2   Place the cluster face downwards on a clean bench and remove all the bulb holders and multi-plug retainers.
3   Remove the terminal nuts and washers.

34 Speedometer cable – removal and refitting

1   Disconnect the battery and remove the instrument cluster, as described in Section 32.
2   Disconnect the cable from the transmission and release it from its clips and grommet.
3   Withdraw the cable through the bulkhead.
4   Refitting is a reversal of removal. The inner and outer cables are supplied as a complete assembly.

35 Speedometer – removal and refitting

1   Remove the instrument cluster as described in Section 32.
2   Split the cluster by extracting the securing screws.
3   Remove the speedometer fixing screws and remove the unit.
4   Refit by reversing the removal operations.

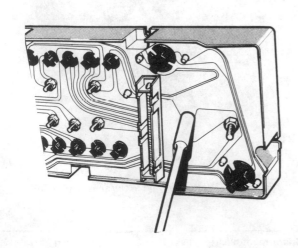

Fig. 11.89 Remove cluster terminal nuts and washers (Sec 33)

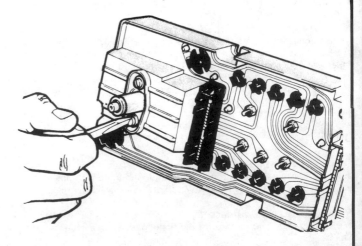

Fig. 11.90 Speedometer head retaining screws (Sec 35)

36 Tachometer – removal and refitting

The operations are very similar to those described for the speedometer in the preceding Section.

37 Fuel and temperature gauges – removal and refitting

1 Access to these instruments is obtained in a similar way to that described for the speedometer (Section 35).
2 Remove the five fixing nuts and withdraw the fuel gauge, temperature gauge and voltage stabiliser as an assembly. The individual components cannot be obtained separately. Refit by reversing the removal operations.

38 Clock (facia-mounted) – removal and refitting

1 Disconnect the battery.
2 Remove the instrument cluster (Section 32).
3 Separate the cluster as previously described in Section 33.

4 Unscrew the two fixing nuts and remove the clock.
5 Refit by reversing the removal operations.
6 The clock can be adjusted by depressing the button and turning the hands.

39 Clock (roof-mounted, digital) – removal and refitting

1 Disconnect the battery.
2 Extract the two screws which hold the clock to the header panel (photo).
3 Disconnect the clock and courtesy lamp wiring plug.
4 Detach the lamp from the clock.
5 Refit by reversing the removal operations. Once the battery is reconnected, the time must be set in the following way.
6 Turn the ignition key to position II. The clock will indicate a random time and the colon will be flashing at one second intervals to prove that the clock is running.
7 Using a balljoint pen or similar, gently depress the upper recessed button. For each depression of the button, the clock will advance one hour.
8 If the clock indicates am instead of pm advance the clock through a full twelve hours.

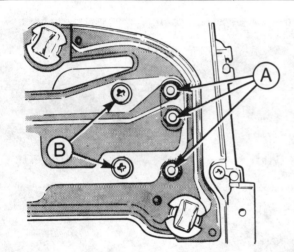

Fig. 11.91 Tachometer retaining screws (B) and terminal nuts (A) (Sec 36)

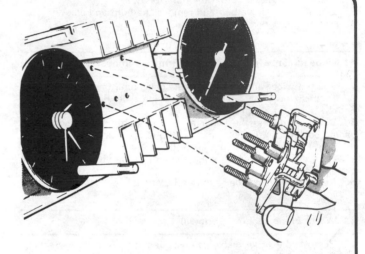

Fig. 11.92 Fuel and temperature gauge removal (Sec 37)

39.2 Roof-mounted clock showing two retaining screws (arrowed)

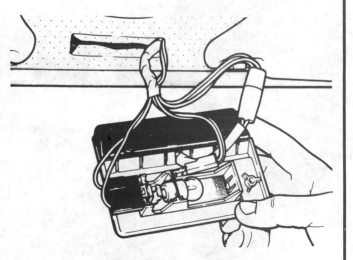

Fig. 11.93 Roof-mounted clock removal (Sec 39)

9   To regulate the minutes, depress the lower recessed button. For each depression, the clock will advance one minute.

10 The colon will now be static and the set time will not advance until the stop/start button is depressed. This is a feature of great advantage when setting the clock accurately to a radio time check. Once the clock has started, the colon will flash.

11 To set the calendar function, again turn the ignition key to position II. Depress the function control once. The clock will now indicate a random date. Continue adjustment within four seconds of having depressed the function button.

12 Using a ballpoint pen or similar, depress the upper recessed button.

13 For each successive depression of the button the clock calendar will advance one day.

14 Once the correct day is obtained move the ballpoint pen to the lower recessed button and depress to obtain the correct month.

15 The clock automatically compensates for months of varying numbers of days.

40 Horn(s) – removal and refitting

1   The horn(s) are located in the left-hand front corner of the engine compartment. Before removing, disconnect the battery.

2   Disconnect the lead from the horn (photo).

3   Unscrew the single bolt and remove the horn and bracket.

4   Refitting is a reversal of removal.

41 Windscreen wiper blades and arms – removal and refitting

1   Pull the wiper arm away from the glass until the arm locks.

2   Depress the small clip on the blade and slide the blade out of the hooked part of the arm (photo).

3   Before removing the wiper arms it is worthwhile marking their parked position on the glass with a strip of masking tape as an aid to refitting. Raise the plastic nut cover (photo).

4   Unscrew the nut which holds the arm to the pivot shaft and pull the arm from the shaft splines.

5   Refit by reversing the removal operations.

42 Wiper blade rubber – renewal

1   Remove the wiper blade, as described in the preceding Section.

2   Using the thumb, draw back the rubber insert until the spring clip can be removed.

3   Slide the rubber insert from the blade.

4   Refit by reversing the removal operations.

43 Windscreen wiper motor and linkage – removal and refitting

1   Remove the wiper arms and blades, as previously described.

2   Disconnect the battery.

3   Remove the nut covers, the fixing nuts, washers and spacers from the pivot shafts.

4   Withdraw the cover from the motor (photo) and disconnect the motor wiring at the multi-pin socket connection.

5   Unscrew the two fixing bolts and withdraw the motor, complete with linkage, from the engine compartment.

6   Remove the spacers from the pivot shafts.

7   The motor can be separated from the linkage by removing the nut from the crankarm and then unbolting the motor from the mounting.

8   Refitting is a reversal of removal, but connect the motor crankarm when the link is aligned with it as shown in Fig. 11.95.

44 Windscreen washer pump (engine compartment reservoir) – removal and refitting

1   Drain the washer fluid container (photo).

2   Disconnect the lead and washer pipe.

40.2 Horn location showing lead connection

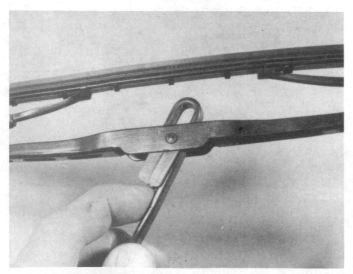

41.2 Disconnecting wiper blade from arm

41.3 Unscrewing wiper arm nut

43.4 Wiper motor cover removal

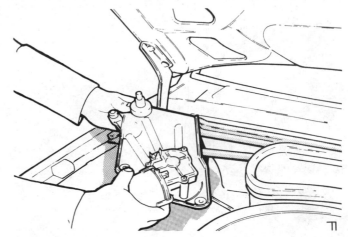

Fig. 11.94 Withdrawing the wiper motor unit (Sec 43)

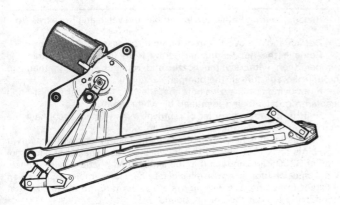

Fig. 11.95 Wiper motor crankarm alignment for refitting (Sec 43)

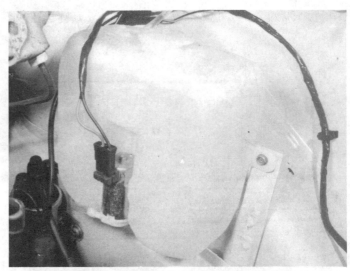

44.1 Windscreen washer fluid reservoir and pump — engine compartment type

3   Ease the top of the washer pump away from the fluid container and remove it.
4   Refitting is a reversal of removal; check that the pump sealing grommet is a good fit.

---

45 Windscreen washer pump (wing-mounted reservoir) – removal and refitting

1   On some models the windscreen washer pump and fluid reservoir are mounted on the forward end of the underside of the left-hand front wing panel. It also incorporates the headlamp washer pump which draws its fluid from this reservoir also.
2   To remove the reservoir and pump units withdraw the level dipstick and syphon the fluid out of the reservoir through the filler neck.
3   Unscrew and remove the reservoir retaining bolts at its top end from inside the engine compartment.
4   Working under the wheel arch, unscrew and remove the two lower retaining bolts.
5   Withdraw the reservoir, carefully pulling its filler neck through the grommet on the inner wing panel. Disconnect the pump hoses.
6   The pump and fluid level sensor unit can be eased away from their location apertures in the reservoir.
7   Refitting is a reversal of the removal; check that the pump and fluid level sensor grommets are in good condition when reassembling, and check for leaks on completion.

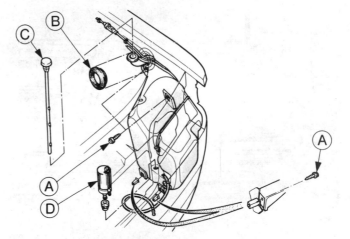

Fig. 11.96 Wing-mounted washer reservoir (Sec 45)

A   Retaining screws   C   Cap/dipstick
B   Grommet   D   Headlamp washer pump

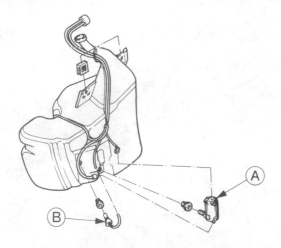

Fig. 11.97 Wing-mounted reservoir (Sec 45)

A   Windscreen washer pump   B   Fluid level sensor

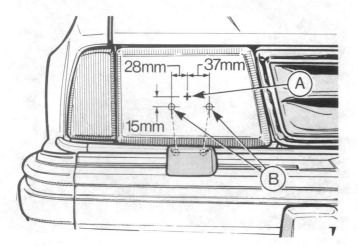

Fig. 11.99 Headlamp washer jet alignment (Sec 46)

A   Headlamp centre   B   Jet direction points

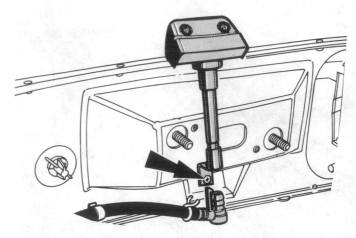

Fig. 11.98 Headlamp washer nozzle and retaining screw (Sec 46)

46 Headlamp washer nozzles – removing and refitting

1   Reach underneath the nozzle and pull the valve and hose free from it.
2   Detach and remove the front bumper, as described in Chapter 12.
3   Remove the nozzle retainer screw from its location within the bumper, then withdraw the nozzle and retainer – pulling them up through the aperture in the bumper.
4   If removing both nozzles note that they are handed, the right-hand headlamp nozzles being identified by white stems.
5   Refit in the reverse order of removal. When fitted, reconnect the fluid hose and check the jet application.
6   If adjustment is necessary, mark the headlamp lens with crayon at the points shown in Fig. 11.99. If available, use special service tool number 32004 and engage it in the slots of the nozzle circumference. If the special tool is not available fabricate a suitable tool, get an assistant to operate the washer system and rotate the nozzles so that they hit the lens at the correct points.
7   The interconnecting nozzle supply hoses are a push-fit on the nozzles and connectors and are secured by spring clips (photo). To renew a hose simply compress the clips with pliers to expand the clip and pull the hose from its connector. When hoses are reconnected operate the washer system and check for any signs of leaks from the connections.

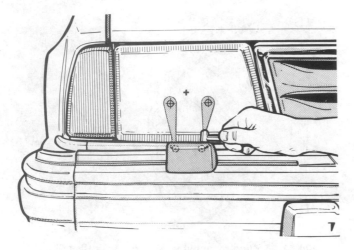

Fig. 11.100 Headlamp washer jet adjustment using special tool
(Sec 46)

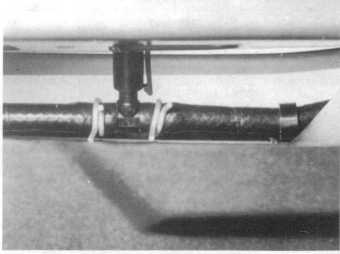

46.7 Nozzle supply hoses and connecting clips

47 Windscreen washer jet nozzles – removal and refitting

1   Open the bonnet and disconnect the washer pipe from the jet.
2   If the pipe stub on the jet assembly is now pushed to one side, the jet retaining tang will be released and the jet can be removed from the bonnet grille slots.
3   Refit by reversing the removal operations. The end of the plastic washer pipe should be warmed in very hot water to make it easier to push onto the jet pipe stub and so avoid breaking it.
4   Adjustment of the jet spray pattern can be done using a pin in the jet nozzle.

48 Central door locking system – description

1   This system is an optional fitting on the GL model, but a standard fitting on the Ghia and Ghia fuel injection variants.
2   The system allows all door locks and the boot lock to be operated by the driver by turning the key or using the door lock plunger inside the vehicle.

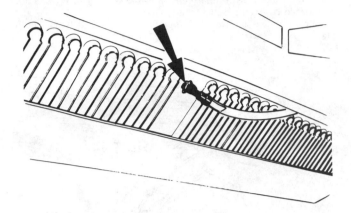

Fig. 11.101 Windscreen washer jet (arrowed) at bonnet grille (Sec 47)

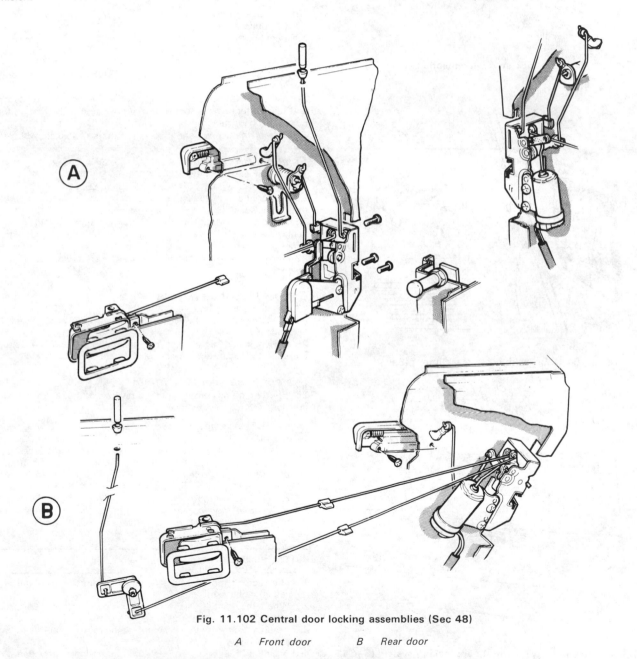

Fig. 11.102 Central door locking assemblies (Sec 48)

A   Front door   B   Rear door

3   The door locks, with the exception of the one on the driver's door are actuated by solenoids.
4   An overload circuit breaker is located in the fusebox to protect the system.

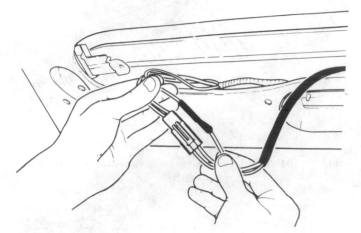

Fig. 11.103 Door lock switch connections (Sec 49)

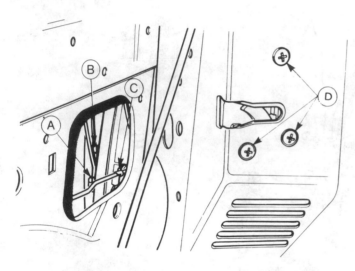

Fig. 11.104 Door locking rod attachment (Sec 49)

A   Clip   C   Clip
B   Clip   D   Lock retaining screws

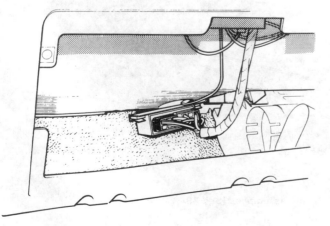

Fig. 11.105 Solenoid relay – central door locking system (Sec 49)

49 Central door locking system components – removal and refitting

Switch (driver's door lock)
1   Raise the driver's door lock fully.
2   Disconnect the battery.
3   Remove the door trim panel (Chapter 12).
4   Disconnect the wiring plugs inside the door cavity and release the wires from their clips.
5   Release the lock control rods and remove the lock fixing screws.
6   Remove the lock from the door interior by guiding it round the glass guide channel.
7   Extract the two screws and remove the switch from the lock.

Solenoid control relay
8   Disconnect the battery.
9   Remove the under-facia trim panel from the passenger side.
10 Pull the relay from its securing clips.
11 Disconnect the multi-plug and remove the relay.

Solenoid (rear door)
12 Disconnect the battery.
13 Remove the door trim panel (Chapter 12).
14 Remove the bellcrank and operating lever by extracting the securing screws.
15 Release the operating rod rubber insulators from the door and disconnect the wiring.
16 Extract the lock securing screws, push the lock into the door cavity and then withdraw the lock with the operating rods through the cut-out in the door panel.
17 Extract the screws and disconnect the solenoid from the lock.

Solenoid (front door)
18 Disconnect the battery.
19 Remove the door trim panel (Chapter 12).
20 Disconnect the lock operating rods and extract the three lock fixing screws.
21 Release the wiring from the clips, manoeuvre the lock round the door glass guide channel and remove it through the cut-out in the door panel.
22 Separate the solenoid from the lock after extracting the fixing screws.

Solenoid (boot lid release)
23 Disconnect the battery.
24 Remove the boot lid lock unit, as described in Chapter 12, and disconnect the solenoid wiring.
25 Unscrew and remove the two solenoid retaining screws, unhook the operating shaft and withdraw the solenoid.

System components refitting
26 Refitting off all components is a reversal of the removal procedure, but note the following special points:

   a)   When fitting the door lock solenoids, locate the guide lock assembly into position, but do not fully tighten the retaining screws until after the bellcrank and rubber operating rod guides, and the internal lock operating lever are fitted
   b)   Check that, when the solenoid is in the unlocked position, the gaiter has an uncompressed length of 20mm (0.78 in)
   c)   Before refitting the door trim panel check that the wires within the door cavity are out of the way of the window regulating mechanism and secured by strap clips

50 Electrically operated windows – description

1   The electric motor drivegear engages directly with the window regulator mechanism.
2   When the ignition is switched on, power is supplied through a relay mounted in the fusebox.
3   When a control switch is actuated, the motor operates to lower or raise the window.
4   A circuit breaker type of overload protection is provided.

221

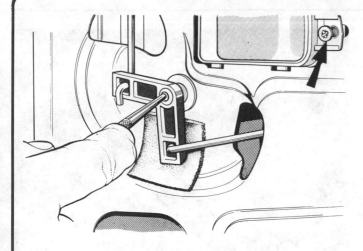

Fig. 11.106 Bellcrank removal – note remote lock handle screw (arrowed) – rear door (Sec 49)

Fig. 11.107 Withdraw the door lock and rods – rear door (Sec 49)

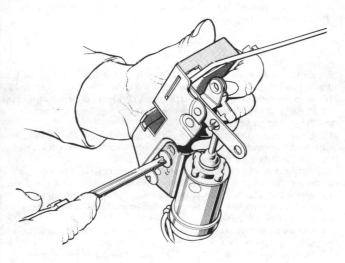

Fig. 11.108 Solenoid removal from lock – rear door (Sec 49)

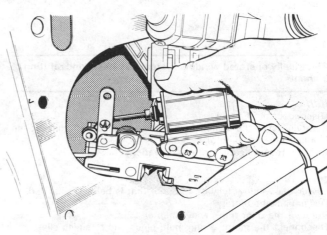

Fig. 11.109 Front door lock and solenoid removal (Sec 49)

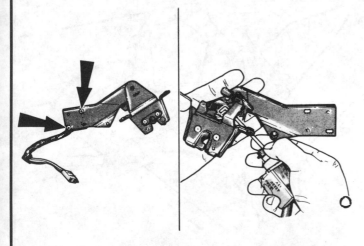

Fig. 11.110 Luggage compartment solenoid showing retaining screws (arrowed) and unhooking of operating shaft (Sec 49)

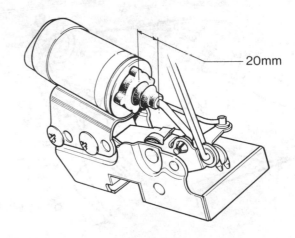

Fig. 11.111 Solenoid gaiter uncompressed length when fitted (Sec 49)

51.2 Window regulating switch removal from armrest

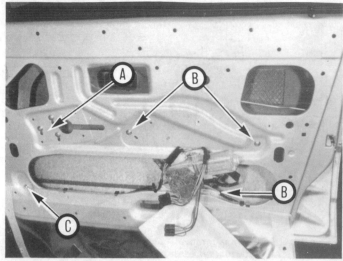

51.8 Electric window winding mechanism
A   Regulator mounting screws   C   Glass channel fixing screw
B   Motor mounting screws

51 Electrically operated window system – removal and refitting of components

Switch
1   Disconnect the battery.
2   Carefully lever the switch from the armrest and disconnect the multi-plug connector (photo).
3   Refit by reversing the removal operations.

Motor
4   Lower the window fully on the door that is being dismantled.
5   Disconnect the battery.
6   Remove the door trim panel (Chapter 12).
7   Disconnect the motor wiring multi-plugs and retaining clips.
8   Remove the mounting screws from the motor and the regulator – three screws each (photo).

9   Extract the retaining screw from the door glass channel. Detach the channel from the door and remove the door glass (see Chapter 12).
10   Grip the motor mounting plate in one hand and the regulator in the other. Raise the regulator and at the same time pull the motor towards the hinge end of the door.
11   Slowly twist the motor in a clockwise direction and at the same time fold the regulator over the top of the motor so that it comes to rest on the lock side of the door.
12   Rotate the motor mounting in an anti-clockwise direction until a corner of the mounting comes into view in the cut-out of the door.
13   Move the assembly so that this corner projects through the cut-out and then turn the whole assembly in a clockwise direction and guide it out of the cut-out.
14   Remove the two Allen screws from the regulator travel stop, and the single screw from the regulator gear guide.
15   Extract the circlip from the motor driveshaft and remove the drivegear.

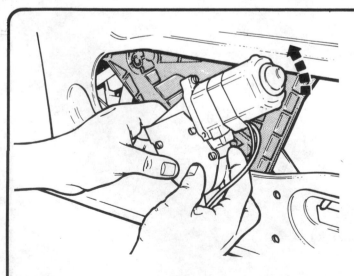

Fig. 11.112 Window motor removal – pull towards hinge end of door (Sec 51)

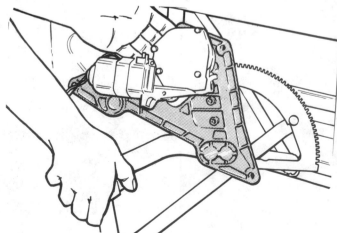

Fig. 11.113 Window motor and fixing removed (Sec 51)

16 Move the regulator to expose the motor mounting bolts. Extract the bolts and separate the motor from the regulator.
17 Reassembly and refitting is a reversal of the dismantling and removal procedure. Before refitting the door trim check that the wiring is secured out of the way of the window regulating system.

52 In-car entertainment equipment

1 The following Sections (53 to 60) cover radio/cassette player equipment fitted during production which is of Ford manufacture.
2 Where equipment is to be installed at a later date and is not necessarily of Ford make, refer to Section 61.

53 Radio – removal and refitting

1 Disconnect the battery.
2 Remove the radio control knobs and withdraw the tuning knob spacer and the tone control lever.
3 Unscrew and remove the facia plate retaining nuts and washers, then withdraw the facia plate.
4 The radio retaining tangs can now be pulled inwards (towards the centre of the radio) and the radio withdrawn from its aperture. You may need to make a suitable hook-ended rod (welding rod is ideal) to pull the tangs inwards to release the radio.
5 With the radio withdrawn, disconnect the power lead, the speaker plug, earth lead, the aerial cable and feed.
6 From the rear of the radio remove the plastic support bracket and locating plate, then remove the radio from the front bracket.
7 Refitting is the reversal of the removal procedure.

54 Radio/cassette player – removal and refitting

1 Disconnect the battery earth lead.
2 To withdraw the radio/cassette unit from its aperture you will need to fabricate the U-shaped extractor tools from wire rod of suitable gauge to insert into the withdrawal slots on each side of the unit (in the front face).
3 Insert the withdrawal tools as shown (see Figs. 11.16 and 11.17) then, pushing each outwards simultaneously, pull them evenly to withdraw the radio/cassette unit. It is important that an equal pressure is applied to each tool as the unit is withdrawn.
4 Once withdrawn from its aperture disconnect the aerial cable, the power lead, the aerial feed, the speaker plugs, the earth lead and the light and memory feed (where applicable).
5 Push the retaining clips inwards to remove the removal tool from each side (Fig. 11.19).
6 Refit in the reverse order of removal. The withdrawal tools do not have to be used, simply push the unit into its aperture until the securing clips engage in their slots.

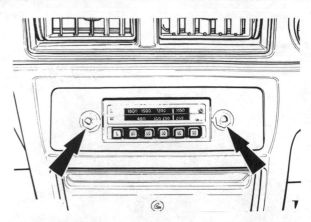

Fig. 11.114 Remove radio facia plate nuts (Sec 53)

Fig. 11.115 Press the securing tangs inwards to remove radio (Sec 53)

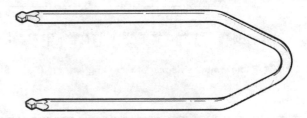

Fig. 11.116 Radio/cassette extractor tool (Sec 54)

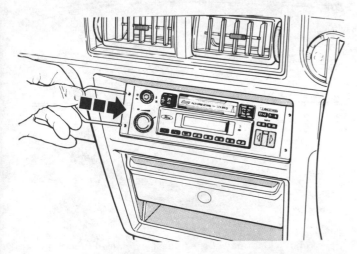

Fig. 11.117 Insert extractor tools into location on each side of the radio/cassette unit front face (Sec 54)

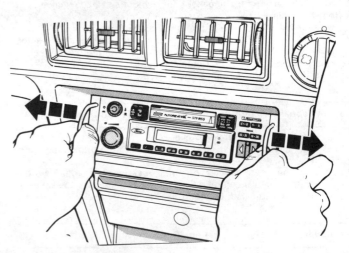

Fig. 11.118 Radio/cassette withdrawal (Sec 54)

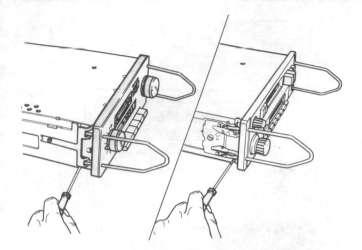

Fig. 11.119 Releasing the removal tool (Sec 54)

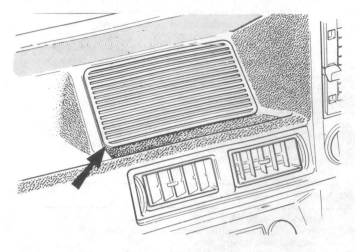

Fig. 11.120 Facia-mounted speaker grille (Sec 55)

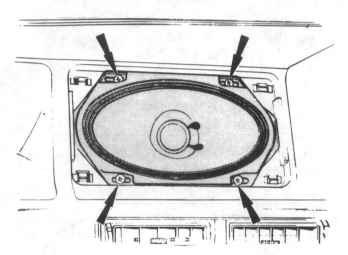

Fig. 11.121 Facia-mounted speaker retaining screws (Sec 55)

Fig. 11.122 Cowl-mounted speaker removal (Sec 56)

55 Loudspeaker (facia) – removal and refitting

1   Carefully prise up the speaker grille using a small screwdriver. Lift it from the facia.
2   Extract the speaker mounting screws which are now exposed.
3   Lift the speaker up until the connecting wires can be disconnected by pulling on their terminals. The wires have different connecting terminals to prevent incorrect connections.
4   Refitting is a reversal of removal.

56 Loudspeaker (cowl panel) – removal and refitting

1   Prise out the grille retaining clip.
2   Extract screws as necessary to be able to remove the cowl panel/grille.
3   Extract the four speaker mounting screws and withdraw the speaker until the leads can be disconnected at the rear of the speaker.
4   Refitting is a reversal of removal.

57 Loudspeaker (rear parcel shelf) – removal and refitting

1   Lever up the speaker cover using a screwdriver with a flat blade

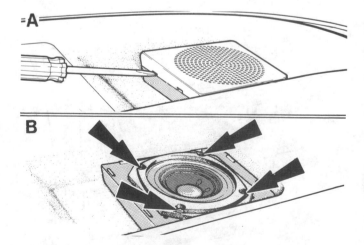

Fig. 11.123 Rear parcel shelf speaker removal (Sec 57)

A   *Prise speaker cover free*   B   *Remove retaining screws*

which will fit into the lever slot in the side of the cover. Remove the speaker cover.

2   Remove the four speaker retaining screws, lift up the speaker and detach the wires.

3   Refit in the reverse order to removal.

58 Heated rear window aerial amplifier – removal and refitting

1   On the Orion the radio aerial is incorporated in the heated rear window element and to assist reception an amplifier is fitted. This is located under the trim panel of the C-pillar on the left-hand side.

2   To remove the C-pillar trim panel, disconnect the rear seat belt upper mounting and remove the rear seat backrest as described in Chapter 12, Section 33. Extract the two screws and pull the panel from its clips.

3   With the amplifier now accessible, remove the two retaining screws, detach the wiring connections and withdraw the amplifier unit.

4   Refitting is a reversal of the removal procedure.

59 Heated rear window element – general

1   The rear window heater element/aerial is fixed to the interior surface of the glass.

2   When cleaning the window use only water and a leather or soft cloth, and avoid scratching with rings on the fingers.

3   Avoid sticking labels over the element and packing luggage so that it can rub against the glass.

4   In the event of the element being damaged, it can be repaired using one of the special conductive paints now available.

60 Speaker fader joystick – removal and refitting

1   Disconnect the battery.

2   Use a screwdriver and carefully prise free the fader unit bezel.

3   Pull free the cassette stowage box from its aperture.

4   Rotate the securing clip anti-clockwise to remove it and the fader from the box. Detach the wiring multi-plug.

5   Refit in the reverse order of removal.

61 Radio equipment (non-standard) – installation

1   This Section covers briefly the installation of in-car entertainment equipment purchased from non-Ford sources.

Radio/cassette player

2   It is recommended that a standard sized receiver is purchased and fitted into the location provided in the facia panel or centre console.

3   A fitting kit is normally supplied with the radio or cassette player.

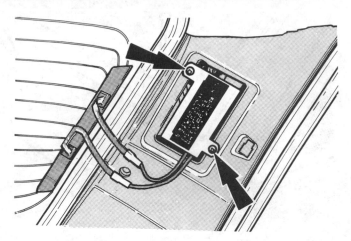

Fig. 11.124 Aerial amplifier retaining screws (Sec 58)

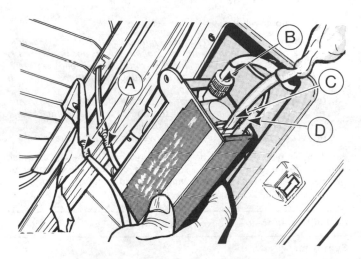

Fig. 11.125 Wiring connections of aerial amplifier (Sec 58)

A   Heated rear window   C   Heated rear window feed
B   To radio   D   Aerial feed

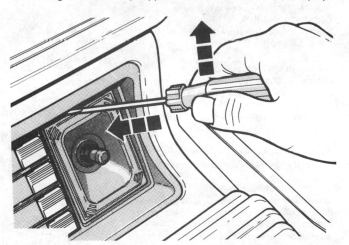

Fig. 11.126 Fader bezel removal (Sec 60)

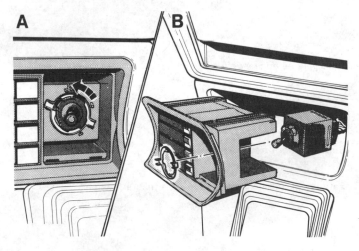

Fig. 11.127 Speaker fader assembly (Sec 60)

A   Release retaining clip   B   Remove assembly

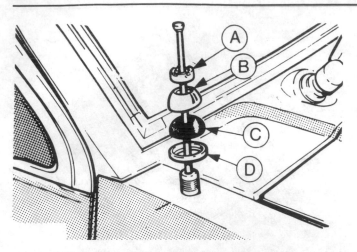

Fig. 11.128 Typical mast aerial mounting components (Sec 61)

A	Collar nut	C	Spacer
B	Bezel	D	Seal

4   Connections will be required as follows:

(a) *Power supply, taken from the ignition switch so that the radio is only operational with the ignition key in position I or II. Always insert a 2A in-line fuse in the power lead*

(b) *Earth. The receiver must have a good clean earth connection to a metal part of the body*

(c) *Aerial lead. From an aerial which itself must be earthed. Avoid routing the cable through the engine compartment or near the ignition, wiper motor or flasher relay*

(d) *Loudspeaker connections, between speaker and receiver*

5   A mast type aerial can be fitted if preferred to the existing rear window heater element/aerial. Location of the aerial is a matter of choice. A roof-mounted or rear wing-mounted aerial usually provides

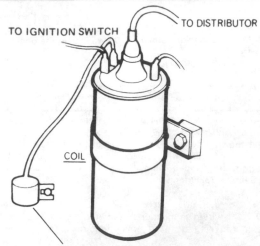

1µf CAPACITOR WITH A PIGGYBACK CONNECTOR

Fig. 11.129 Radio interference suppressor capacitor fitted to coil + terminal (Sec 61)

the most interference-free reception. Cut the hole by drilling and filing or by means of a tank hole cutter. Paint the edges of the hole to prevent rusting.

6   If the radio is being installed for the first time, interference will almost certainly present a problem when the engine is running.

7   The ignition HT leads will have been suppressed during production, but a 1µF capacitor should be connected between the + terminal of the coil and the coil mounting bracket bolt.

8   Sometimes an in-line choke can be fitted into the power supply lead as close as possible to the radio to reduce interference.

9   The alternator often gives rise to a whine through the radio which can be eliminated by connecting a 1.0 to 3.0µF capacitor between the large terminal (B+) on the alternator and earth.

10   Further interference suppression will be on a trial and error basis.

62 Fault diagnosis – electrical system

Symptom	Reason(s)
Starter fails to turn engine	Battery discharged Battery defective internally Leads loose, or terminals corroded Loose connections at starter motor Engine earth strap loose, broken or missing Starter motor faulty or solenoid not functioning Starter motor brushes worn Commutator dirty or worn Starter motor armature faulty Field coils earthed
Starter turns engine very slowly	Battery in discharged condition Starter brushed badly worn, sticking or brush wires loose Loose wires in starter motor circuit
Starter spins but does not turn engine	Pinion or flywheel gear teeth broken or worn Battery discharged
Starter motor noisy or excessively rough engagement	Pinion or flywheel gear teeth broken or worn Starter motor retaining bolts loose
Battery will not hold charge for more than a few days	Battery defective, internally Electrolyte level too low or electrolyte too weak due to leakage Plate separators no longer fully effective Battery plates severely sulphated Alternator drivebelt slipping Battery terminal connections loose or corroded Alternator not charging Short-circuit causing continual battery drain Integral regulator unit not working correctly

Symptom	Reason(s)
Ignition light fails to go out, battery runs flat in a few days	Alternator drivebelt loose and slipping or broken Alternator brushes worn, sticking, broken or dirty Alternator brush springs weak or broken Internal fault in alternator

Failure of individual electrical equipment to function correctly is dealt with under the headings listed below

Horn

Horn operates all the time	Horn push either earthed or stuck down Horn cable to horn push earthed
Horn fails to operate	Blown fuse Cable or cable connection loose, broken or disconnected Horn has an internal fault
Horn emits intermittent or unsatisfactory noise	Cable connections loose Horn incorrectly adjusted

Lights

Lights do not come on	If engine not running, battery discharged Wire connections loose, disconnected or broken Light switch shorting or otherwise faulty Light bulb filament burnt out or bulbs broken
Lights give very poor illumination	Lamp glasses dirty Lamps badly out of adjustment
Lights work erratically — flashing on and off, especially over bumps	Battery terminals or earth connection loose Lights not earthing properly Contacts in light switch faulty

Wipers

Wiper motor fails to work	Blown fuse Wire connections loose, disconnected or broken Brushes badly worn Armature worn or faulty Field coils faulty
Wiper motor works very slowly and takes excessive current	Commutator dirty, greasy or burnt Armature bearings dirty or unaligned Armature badly worn or faulty
Wiper motor works slowly and takes little current	Brushes badly worn Commutator dirty, greasy or burnt Armature badly worn or faulty
Wiper motor works but wiper blades remain static	Wiper motor gearbox parts badly worn

Electrically operated windows

Glass will only move in one direction	Defective switch
Door glass slow to move	Stiff regulator or glass guide channels
Door glass will not move: With motor running	Binding glass guide channels Faulty regulator
Motor not running	Faulty relay Blown fuse Fault in motor Broken or disconnected wire

Central door locking system

Complete failure	Blown fuse Faulty master switch Faulty relay Broken or disconnected wire
Latch locks but will not unlock, or unlocks but will not lock	Faulty master switch Poor contact in pulse relay multi-plugs Faulty relay
One solenoid will not operate	Poor circuit connections Broken wire Faulty solenoid Binding bellcrank rod Binding driver's remote control lock button Fault in latch

1983-86 Model

COMMON POINT	DIAGRAM/GRID REF.
S103	1/H1
	2/H2
S104	1/J1
	2/K2
S105	1/H1
	3/G1
	4/H1
S106	1/K5
	2/F6
	3/F6
	4/K5
S107	1/L1
	2/K1
	3/K2
S108	1/A8
	2/B8
	4/A8
S109	1/A1
	2/B1
S110	1/J6
	2/J5
	3/J5
S113	1/H1
	2/G1
S120	1/A4
	4/A4
S123	1/H5
	2/J5
	3/J5

COMMON EARTH POINT	DIAGRAM/GRID REF.
G102	1/L5
	2/F7
	3/F7
	4/L5
G103	1/A8
	2/B8
	4/A8
G104	1/A2
	2/B1
G107	1/D3
	3/B4

1986-90 Model

COMMON POINT	DIAGRAM/GRID REF.	COMMON POINT	DIAGRAM/GRID REF.
S116	3a/F6	S1024	1a/D3
	4/E6		3a/C4
S1002	1a/G8		4a/D2
	2a/H1		4b/D2
	4/H1	S1025	1a/G3
	4a/G1		2a/G3
	4b/G1		3a/G3
S1012	1a/F2		4/K5
	2a/C3	S1032	1a/B2
	3a/C3		4/A4
	4a/F2	S1043	2a/F5
	4b/F2		3a/F5
	5/H6	S1044	1a/J5
S1014	2a/E3		2a/C5
	4/K1		4/K5
	4b/K1		4b/J5
	5/B5	S1052	2a/E5
	5/C6		3a/E5
	5/J1		4/K8
	5/K4		4b/H8
S1021	1a/A8		5/B4
	2a/B8		5/C6
	4/A8		5/D1
			5/H1
			5/J4

COMMON EARTH POINT	DIAGRAM/GRID REF.	COMMON EARTH POINT	DIAGRAM/GRID REF.
G1002	1a/F8	G1006	1a/D3
G1003	1a/A8		3a/B5
	2a/B8		4a/D2
	4/A8		4b/D2
G1005	1a/G4	G1009	1a/K8
	2a/G4		4/M7
	3a/G3		4a/M7
	4/L5		4b/M7

Wire Colours

B	Blue	Rs	Pink
Bk	Black	S	Grey
Bn	Brown	V	Violet
Gn	Green	W	White
R	Red	Y	Yellow

NOTES:

1. Feed wires are coloured red (black when switched) and originate from diagrams 1 and 1a.
2. Earth wires on all diagrams are coloured brown.
3. The above tables show where common connecting points and earths interconnect between diagrams.
4. Not all items are fitted to all models.
5. Brackets show how the circuit may be connected in more than one way.

Table of common points/earths, wire colours and notes

ITEM	DESCRIPTION	DIAGRAM/ GRID REF.	ITEM	DESCRIPTION	DIAGRAM/ GRID REF.
1	ABS Warning Relay	1a/C1	34	Door Lock Actuator LH Rear	3/L8
2	ABS Warning Switch	1a/B2	35	Door Lock Actuator RH Rear	3/L1
		1a/B8	36	Door Lock Motor LH Front	3a/K8
3	Air Temp. Sensor	1a/B6	37	Door Lock Motor LH Rear	3a/M8
		4a/C3	38	Door Lock Motor RH Front	3a/K1
		4b/C3	39	Door Lock Motor RH Rear	3a/M1
4	Alternator	1/B3	40	Door Lock Relay	3/K6
		1a/A3	41	Door Switch	2/G1
5	Antenna Module	3/M7			2/G8
		3a/M2			2/K1
		5/F2			2/K8
		5/F4			2a/H1
		5/F7			2a/H8
		5/M2			2a/K1
		5/M5			2a/K8
6	Auto. Trans. Inhibitor Switch	1/D7	42	Econolight Switch (amber)	1/F3
		1a/D7	43	Econolight Switch (red)	1/F3
		2/B7	44	E-DIS Module	4b/F4
		2a/B7	45	EEC IV Module	4a/K3
7	Auto. Trans. Relay 1983-86	1/E1			4b/K3
8	Auto. Trans. Relay 1986 On	1a/E1	46	Electric Choke	1/F5
9	Auto. Trans. Selector Illumination	2/K5	47	Electric Door Mirror 1983-86	3/F1
		2a/J5			3/F8
10	Auxiliary Air Device	4/F4	48	Electric Door Mirror 1986 On	3a/F1
11	Auxiliary Warning System Module	1/K3			3a/F8
12	Battery	1/F8	49	Electric Mirror Cont. Switch 1983-86	3/G6
		1a/F8	50	Electric Mirror Cont. Switch 1986 On	3a/H2
13	Brake Pad Sender LH	1/C8	51	Electric Window Motor LH	3/G8
14	Brake Pad Sender RH	1/C1			3a/G8
15	Canister Purge Valve	4a/F7	52	Electric Window Motor RH	3/G1
16	Choke Switch	1/K5			3a/G1
		1a/K5	53	Electric Window Relay	3/D1
17	Cigar Lighter	2/K6	54	Electric Window Switch LH 1983-86	3/H8
		2a/K6	55	Electric Window Switch LH 1986 On	3a/H8
18	Clock	2/G5	56	Electric Window Switch RH 1983-86	3/H1
		2a/G5	57	Electric Window Switch RH 1983-86	3/K1
19	C.O. Adjuster Pot.	4b/K6		(LH window driver controlled)	
20	Cold Running Valve	1a/C8	58	Electric Window Switch RH 1986 On	3a/H1
21	Cold Starting Valve	4/F3	59	Engine Management Relay	4b/H1
22	Coolant Temp. Sensor	1/B7	60	Engine Temp. Sensor	1a/D6
		1a/B7			4a/C4
23	Cooling Fan	1/A6			4b/C4
		1a/A6	61	ESC II Ignition Module	1a/B5
24	Cooling Fan Switch	1/A7	62	Fader Control (4 way)	5/B6
		1a/A7	63	Flasher/Hazard Switch	2a/K3
25	Crank. Position Sensor	1a/C6	64	Flasher Lamp LH	2/A8
		4b/C7			2a/A8
26	Dim/Dip Relay V	2a/D1	65	Flasher Lamp RH	2/A1
27	Dim/Dip Relay D	2a/E1			2a/A1
28	Dim/Dip Relay L4/L5	2a/F1	66	Flasher Lamp LH Side Mark	2/C8
29	Diode Block	4/J6			2a/C8
30	Dip Beam Relay	2a/A5	67	Flasher Lamp RH Side Mark	2/C1
		3a/A2			2a/C1
31	Distributor	1/D4	68	Flasher Relay 1983-86	2/D1
		1a/C4	69	Flasher Relay 1986 On	2a/J3
		4/C3	70	Fog Lamp Switch 1983-86	2/K6
		4/C6	71	Fog Lamp Switch 1986 On	2a/K6
		4a/B6	72	Footwell Illumination	2/E3
32	Door Lock RH Front	3/J1			2/E6
33	Door Lock Actuator LH Front	3/J8	73	Fuel Computer	4/L2
					4b/K2

Key to wiring diagrams

ITEM	DESCRIPTION	DIAGRAM/ GRID REF.	ITEM	DESCRIPTION	DIAGRAM/ GRID REF.
74	Fuel Flow Sensor	4/D7	107	Ignition Coil (Double Ended)	1a/D4
75	Fuel Injection Relay	4/J2			4b/B6
76	Fuel Pump	4/L7	108	Ignition Relay	1/D1
		4a/L7			1a/D1
		4b/L7			2a/C1
77	Fuel Pump Relay	4a/E1	109	Ignition Switch	1/K1
		4b/E1			1a/K1
78	Fuel Sender	1/L7			3/K2
		1a/L7			5/D1
		4/L7			5/D4
		4b/L8			5/D6
79	Fuel Shut Off Valve	1/C7			5/K1
		1a/B8			5/L5
80	Glove Box Lamp/Switch	2/H7	110	Inertia Switch	4a/L5
		2a/G7			4b/L5
81	Graphic Equalizer	5/H5	111	Injector Ballast Resistor	4a/F6
82	Handbrake Warning Switch	1/K7	112	Injector Valve	4a/B3
		1a/K7			4b/C3
83	Headlamp Unit LH	2/A7			4b/C4
		2a/A7	113	Instrument Cluster 1983-86	1/K3
84	Headlamp Unit RH	2/A2			2/F3
		2a/A2			4/K3
85	Headlamp Washer Pump	3/A7	114	Instrument Cluster 1986 On	1a/K3
		3a/A7			2a/F4
86	Headlamp Washer Relay	3/C6			4/L3
		3a/B4			4a/L2
87	Heated Door Mirror Relay	3/E5			4b/L3
88	Heated Rear Window	3/M5	115	Interior Lamp Delay Relay	2/G4
		3a/M3	116	Interior Lamp/Switch	2/G4
89	Heated Rear Window Relay 1983-86	3/C3			2/L4
90	Heated Rear Window Relay 1986 On	1a/B1			2a/G4
		3a/C1			2a/K4
		4/B1	117	Licence Plate Lamp	2/M4
91	Heated Rear Window Switch 1983-86	3/H3			2/M5
92	Heated Rear Window Switch 1986 On	3a/K6			2a/M5
93	Heated Windscreen	3a/F6	118	Light Cluster LH Rear	2/M8
94	Heated Windscreen Relay	1a/H1			2a/M8
		3a/E1	119	Light Cluster RH Rear	2/M1
95	Heated Windscreen Switch	3a/K6			2a/M1
96	Heater Blower Illumination	2/G6	120	Light/Dimmer Switch	2a/K4
		2a/G6	121	Light/Wiper Switch	2/K3
97	Heater Blower Motor	3/G5			3/J3
		3a/G6	122	Low Brake Fluid Sender	1/E7
98	Heater Blower Switch	3/G3			1a/E7
		3a/G4	123	Low Coolant Sender	1/B1
99	H.E.G.O. Sender	4a/A4	124	Low Oil Sender	1/F4
100	High Beam Relay	2a/A6	125	Low Washer Fluid Sender	1/B8
101	Horn	3/A6	126	Luggage Comp. Lamp	2/L3
		3a/A6			2a/L2
102	Horn Relay	3a/B1	127	Luggage Comp. Lamp Switch	2/M3
103	Horn Switch	3a/K5			2a/M3
104	Idle Speed Relay	1a/D1	128	Luggage Comp. Release Relay	1/H3
105	Idle Speed Valve	1/F6			3/E5
		1a/F7	129	Luggage Comp. Release Switch	3/H4
		4/E3	130	Map Sensor	4a/F5
		4b/C6			4b/F5
106	Ignition Coil (Conventional)	1/C4	131	Multifunction Switch	2/K4
		1a/C3			3/J4
		4/B3	132	Oil Pressure Switch	1/F5
		4/B5			1a/F5
		4a/A6			

Key to wiring diagrams (continued)

ITEM	DESCRIPTION	DIAGRAM/ GRID REF.	ITEM	DESCRIPTION	DIAGRAM/ GRID REF.
133	Overrun Shut Off Valve	4/C7	155	Throttle Sensor	4a/B4
134	Power Timer Delay Relay	4a/J1			4b/C4
135	Radio Unit	3/H6	156	Throttle Switch	4/E6
		5/C8	157	Vanity Mirror Illumination	2/G6
		5/D2	158	Warm-Up Regulator	4/F5
		5/D5	159	Windscreen Washer Pump	3/C7
		5/J3			3a/C7
		5/K6	160	Wiper Intermittent Relay	3/C1
136	Reversing Lamp Switch	2/C7			3a/D1
		2a/C7	161	Wiper Intermittent Speed Control	3/F3
137	Spark Plugs	1/E4	162	Wiper Motor	1/E2
		1a/C4			1a/E2
		1a/E4			3/C4
		4/D3			3a/C4
		4/D6	163	Wiper Switch	3a/K4
		4a/C6			
		4b/B6			
138	Speaker LH Front	5/A2			
		5/A5			
		5/A8			
		5/G3			
		5/G6			
139	Speaker LH Rear	5/F8			
		5/M3			
		5/M6			
140	Speaker RH Front	5/A1			
		5/A4			
		5/A6			
		5/G1			
		5/G4			
141	Speaker RH Rear	5/F6			
		5/M1			
		5/M4			
142	Speed Sender Unit	4a/C7			
		4b/D7			
143	Speed Sensor	4/D8			
		4b/D8			
144	Speed Sensor Relay	4/J3			
145	Spot Lamp	2/A3			
		2/A6			
		2a/A3			
		2a/A6			
146	Spot Lamp Relay	2/E1			
147	Starter Motor	1/B5			
		1a/A5			
148	Stop Lamp Switch	2/C5			
		2a/C4			
149	Suppressor	1a/E4			
		1a/E6			
		3a/B2			
		4/D2			
		4a/B8			
		4b/A7			
		4b/B8			
150	Tailgate Lock Motor	3a/M5			
151	Tailgate Release Actuator	3/M4			
152	TFI Module	4a/F4			
153	Thermal Time Switch	1a/C7			
		4/D5			
154	Throttle Control Motor	4a/C4			

Key to wiring diagrams (continued)

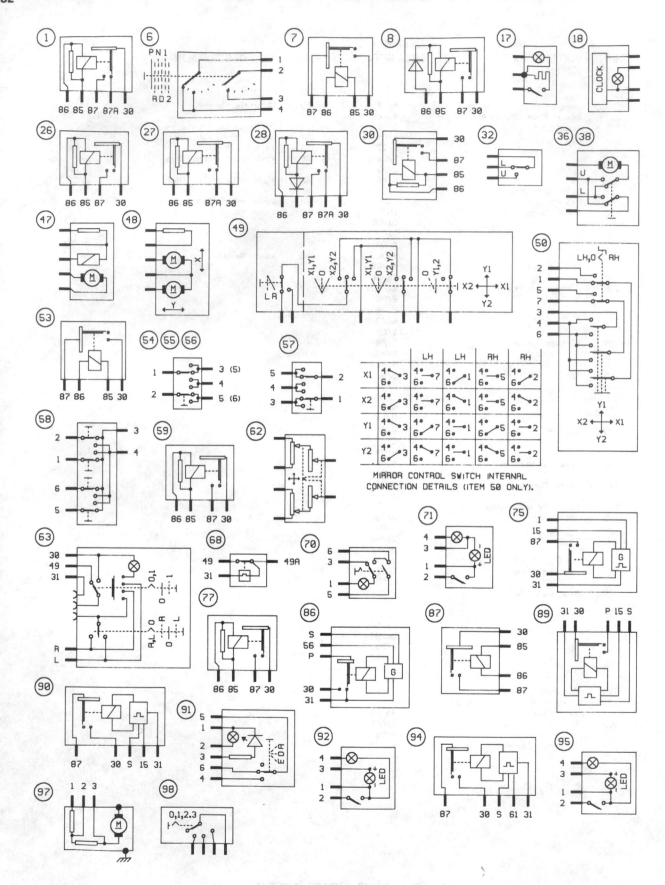

MIRROR CONTROL SWITCH INTERNAL
CONNECTION DETAILS (ITEM 50 ONLY).

Internal connection details all models

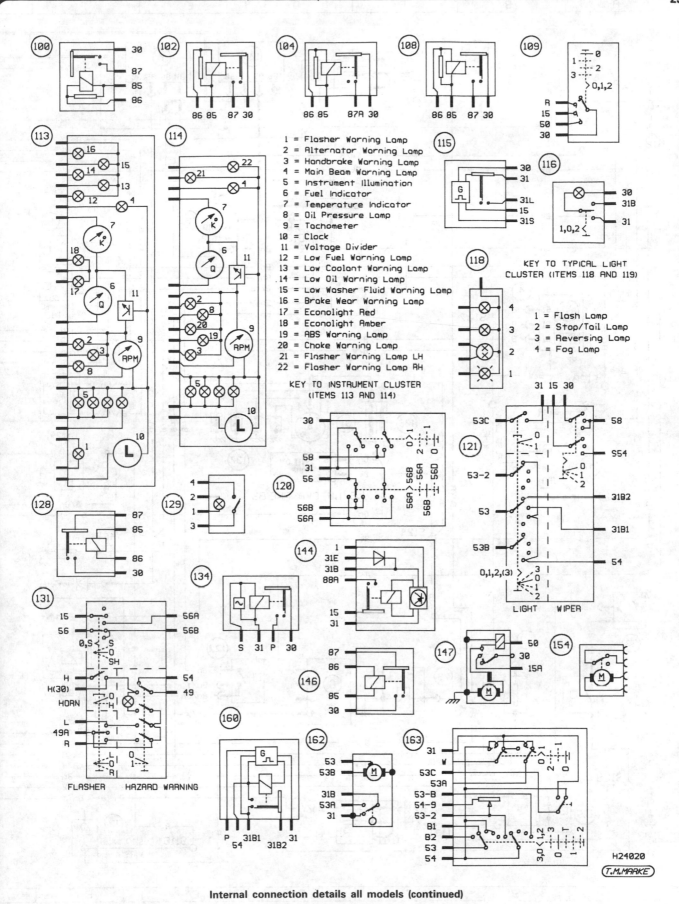

KEY TO INSTRUMENT CLUSTER
(ITEMS 113 AND 114)

1 = Flasher Warning Lamp
2 = Alternator Warning Lamp
3 = Handbrake Warning Lamp
4 = Main Beam Warning Lamp
5 = Instrument Illumination
6 = Fuel Indicator
7 = Temperature Indicator
8 = Oil Pressure Lamp
9 = Tachometer
10 = Clock
11 = Voltage Divider
12 = Low Fuel Warning Lamp
13 = Low Coolant Warning Lamp
14 = Low Oil Warning Lamp
15 = Low Washer Fluid Warning Lamp
16 = Brake Wear Warning Lamp
17 = Econolight Red
18 = Econolight Amber
19 = ABS Warning Lamp
20 = Choke Warning Lamp
21 = Flasher Warning Lamp LH
22 = Flasher Warning Lamp RH

KEY TO TYPICAL LIGHT
CLUSTER (ITEMS 118 AND 119)

1 = Flash Lamp
2 = Stop/Tail Lamp
3 = Reversing Lamp
4 = Fog Lamp

H24020

T.M.MARKE

Internal connection details all models (continued)

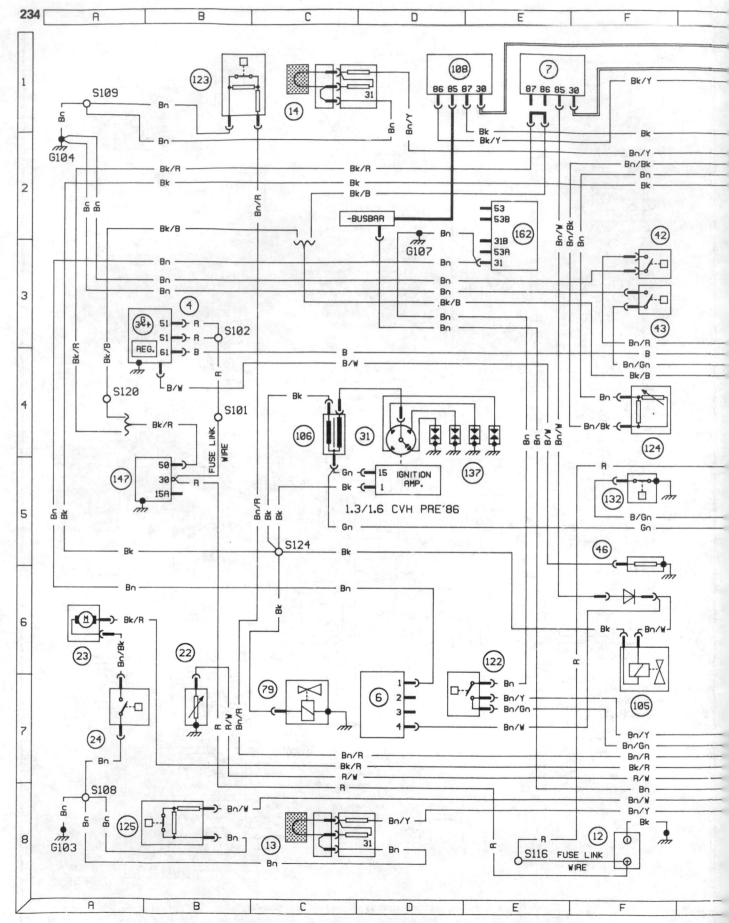

Diagram 1: 1983-86 Starting, charging and ignition (except fuel injection) all models

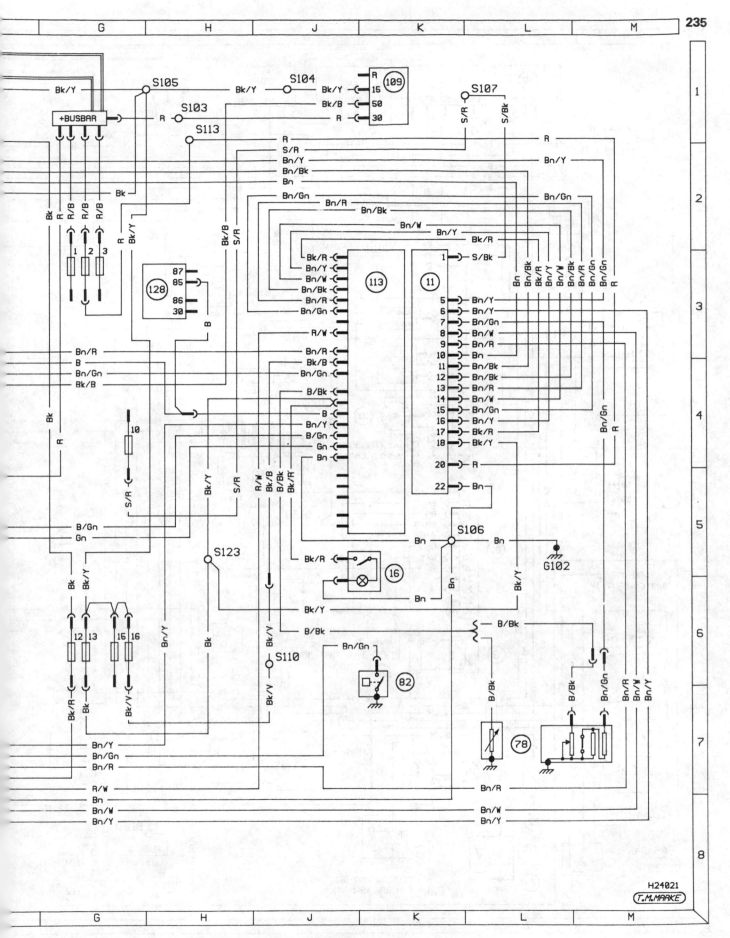

Diagram 1 (continued)

H24021

T.M.MARKE

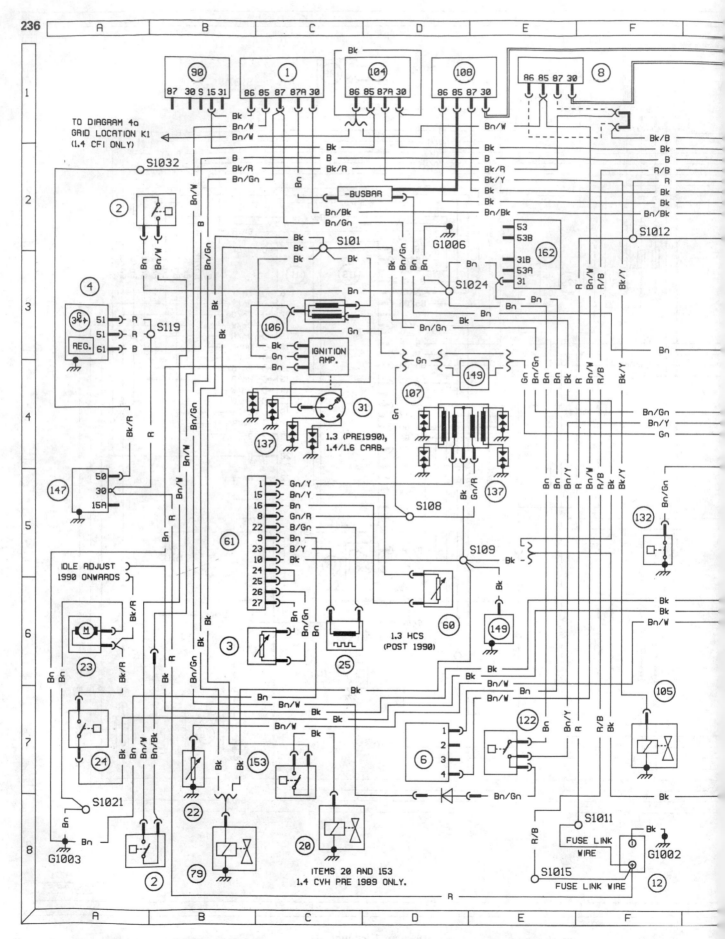

Diagram 1a: 1986 onward – starting, charging and ignition (except fuel injection) all models

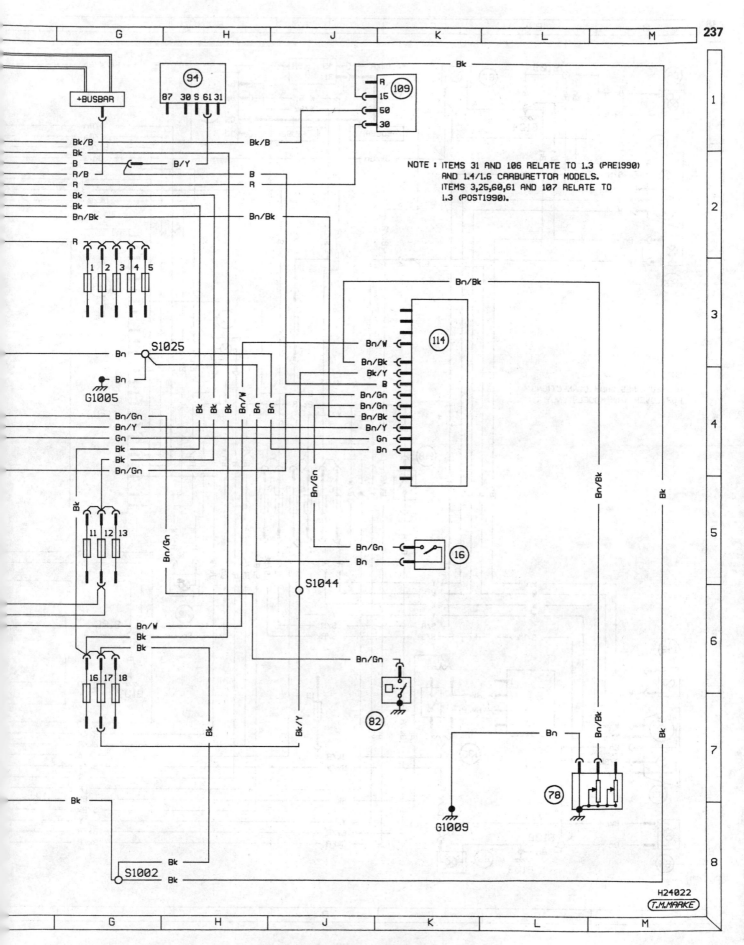

NOTE : ITEMS 31 AND 106 RELATE TO 1.3 (PRE1990)
AND 1.4/1.6 CARBURETTOR MODELS.
ITEMS 3,25,60,61 AND 107 RELATE TO
1.3 (POST1990).

H24022
T.M.MARKE

Diagram 1a (continued)

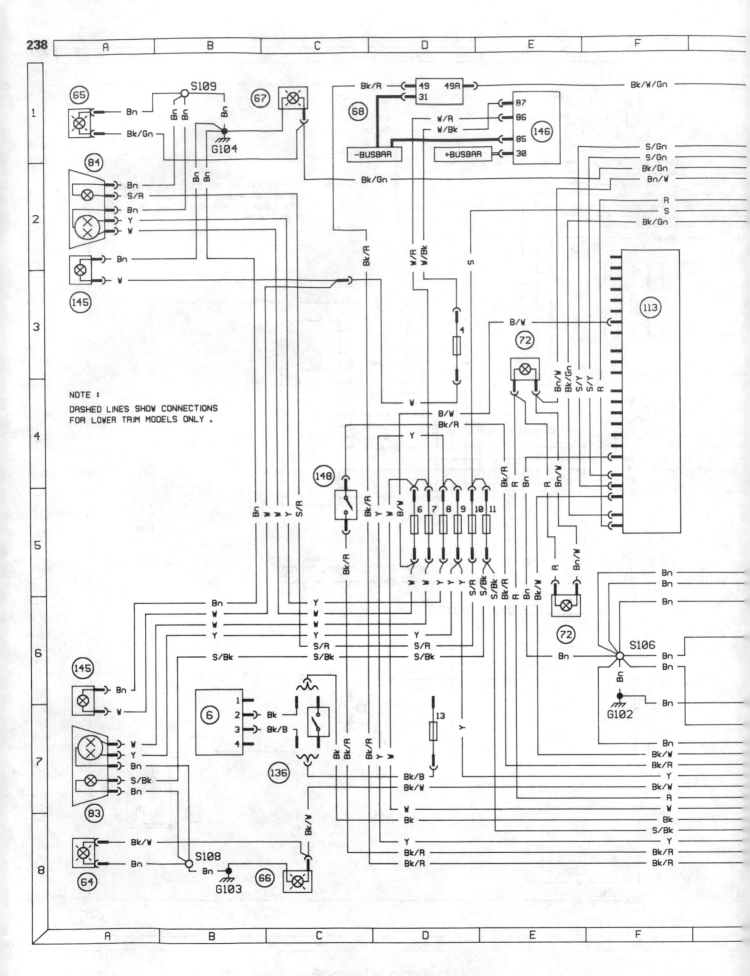

Diagram 2: 1983-86 – lighting all models

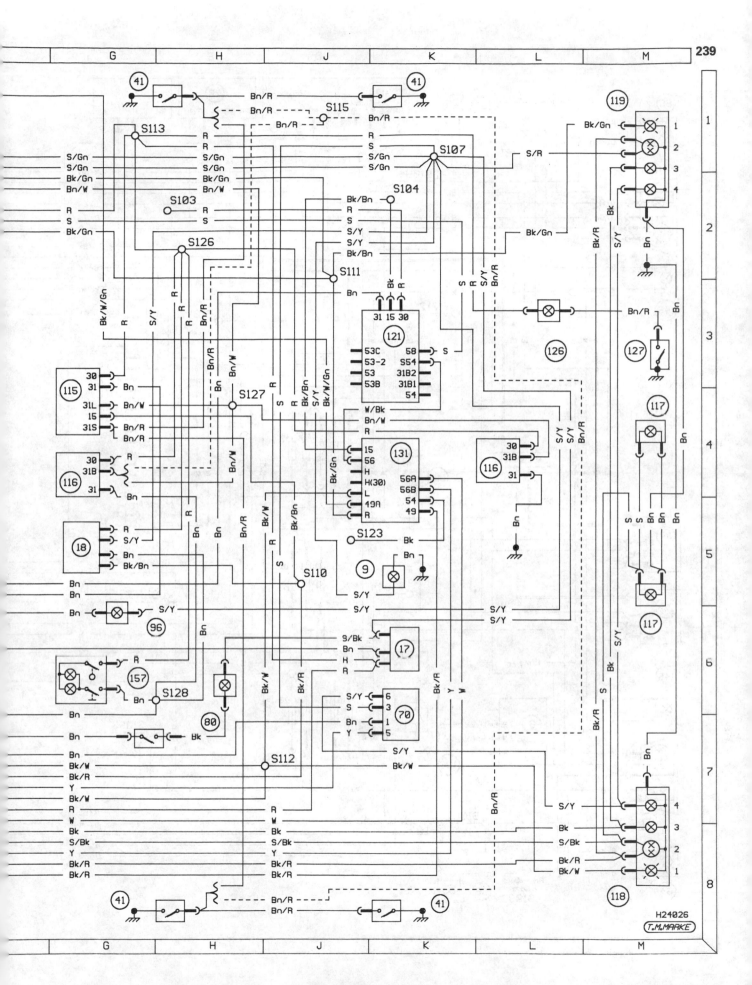

Diagram 2 (continued)

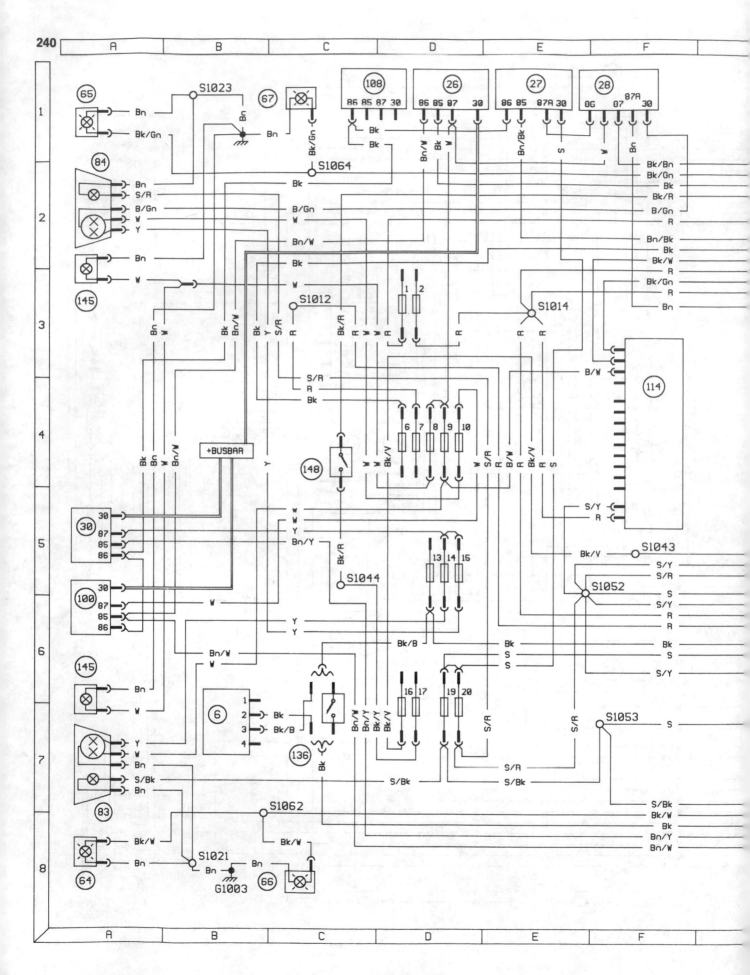

Diagram 2a: 1986 onward – lighting all models

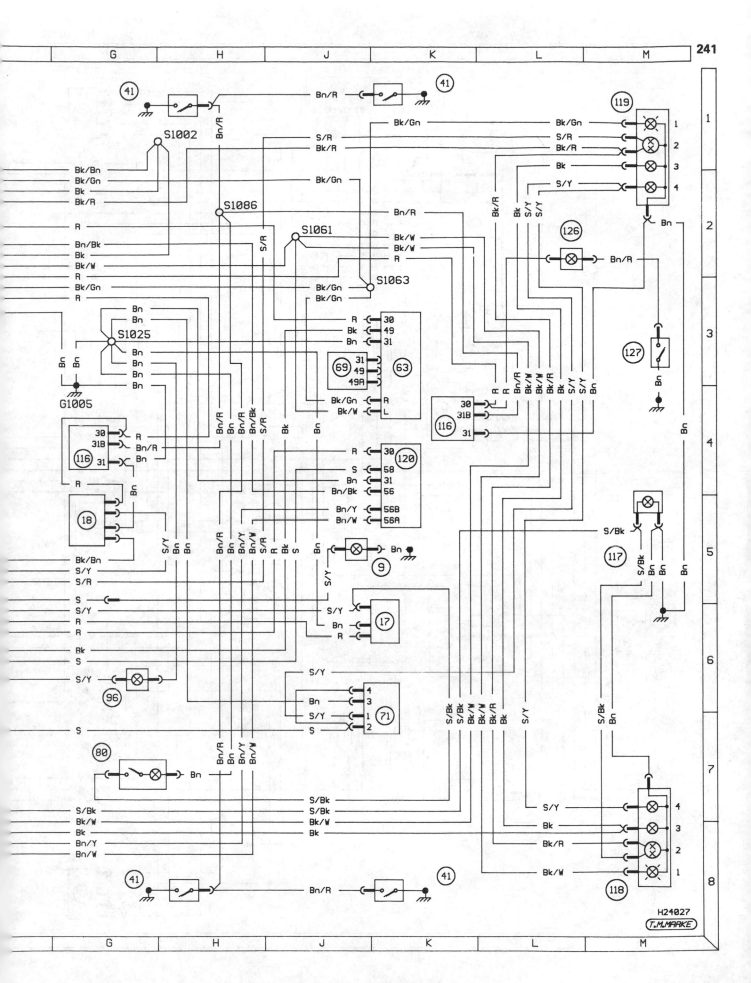

Diagram 2a (continued)

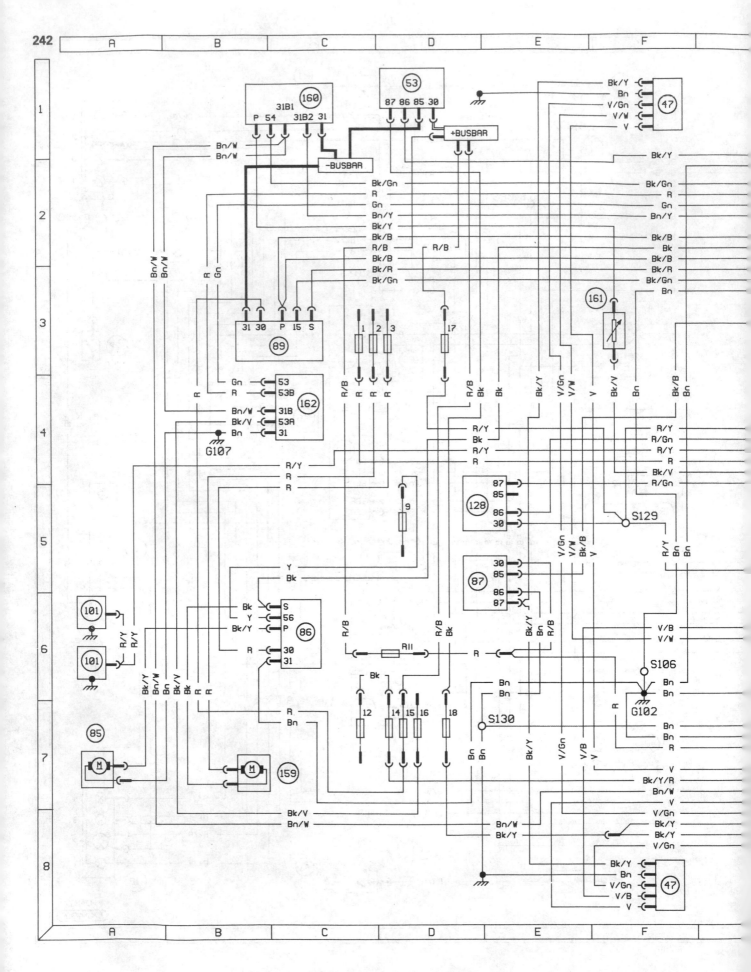

Diagram 3: 1983-86 – ancillary circuits all models

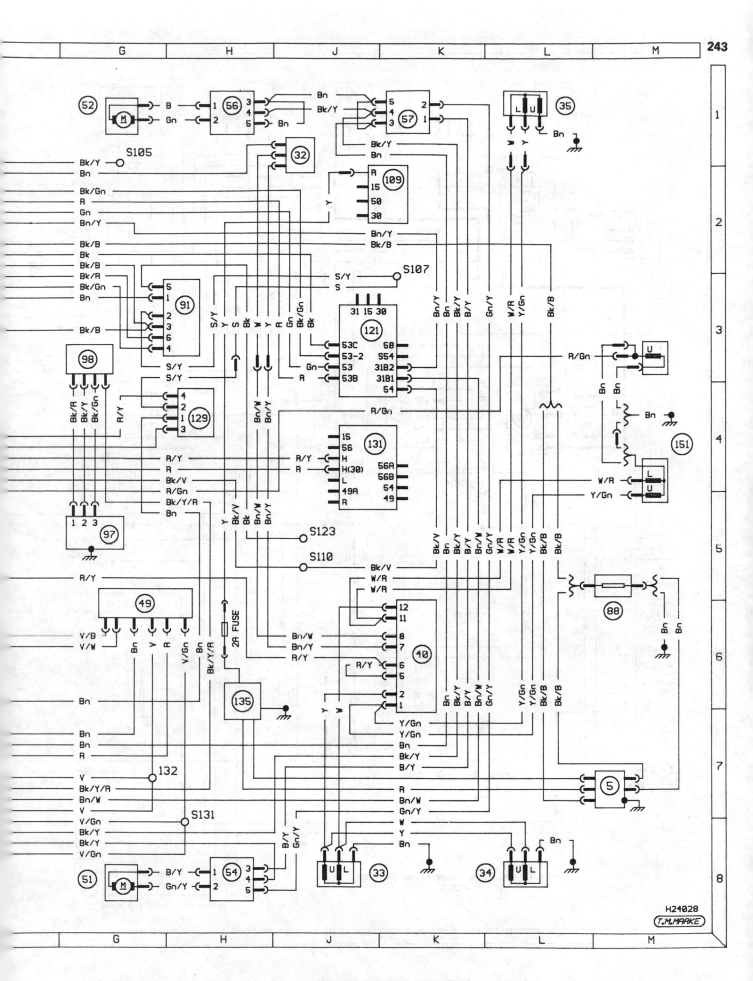

Diagram 3 (continued)

H24028
T.M.MARKE

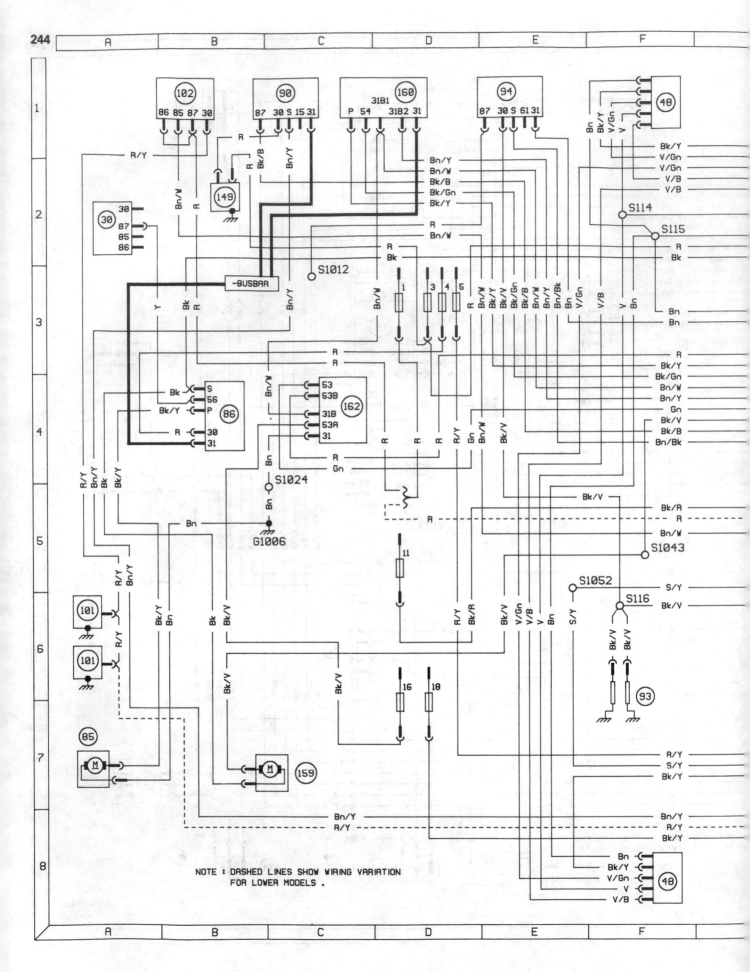

NOTE : DASHED LINES SHOW WIRING VARIATION
FOR LOWER MODELS .

Diagram 3a: 1986 onward - ancillary circuits all models

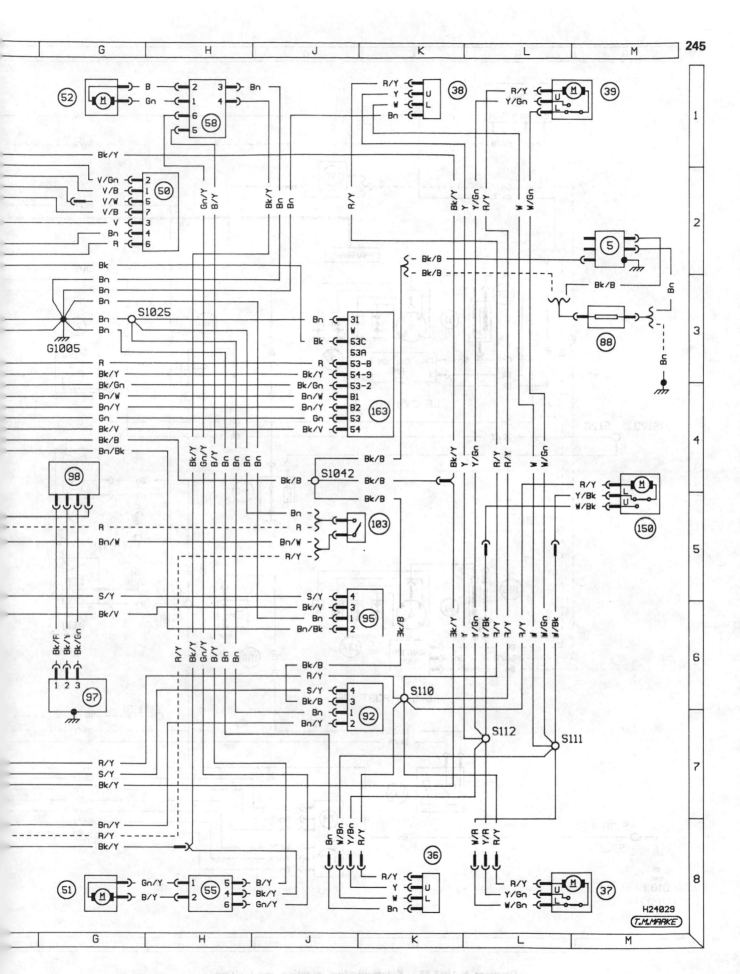

Diagram 3a (continued)

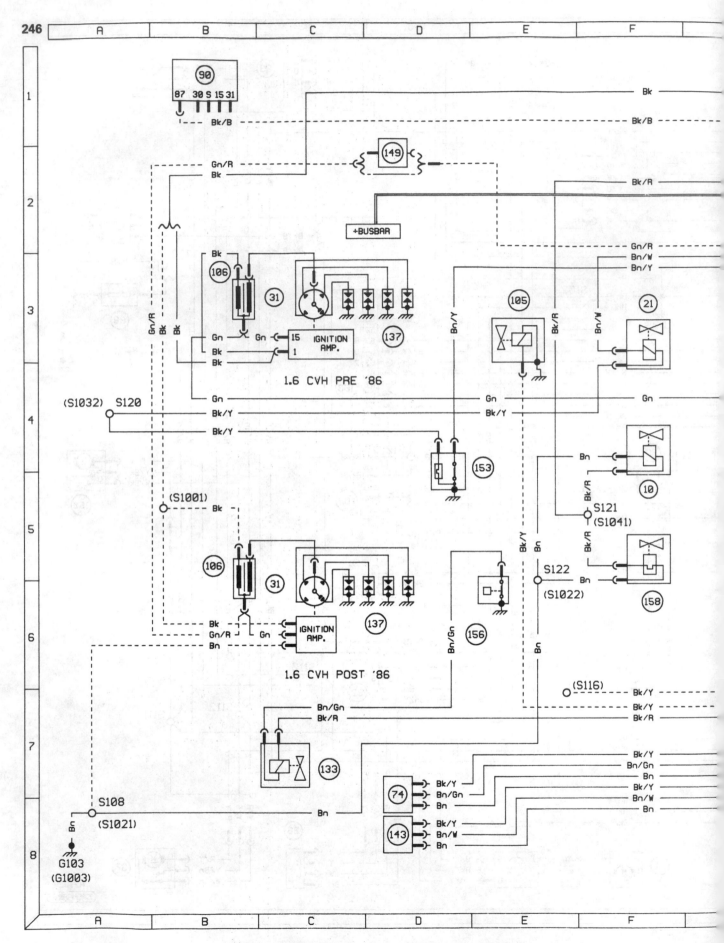

Diagram 4: 1983-89 - K-Jetronic fuel injection and ignition

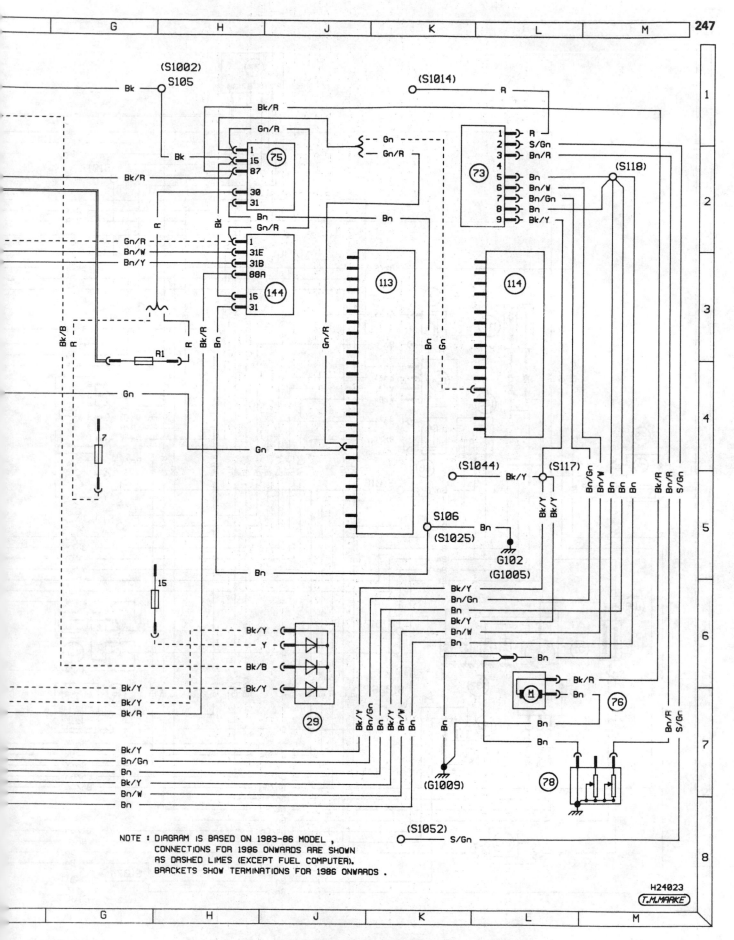

Diagram 4 (continued)

NOTE : DIAGRAM IS BASED ON 1983-86 MODEL ,
CONNECTIONS FOR 1986 ONWARDS ARE SHOWN
AS DASHED LINES (EXCEPT FUEL COMPUTER).
BRACKETS SHOW TERMINATIONS FOR 1986 ONWARDS .

H24023
T.M.MARKE

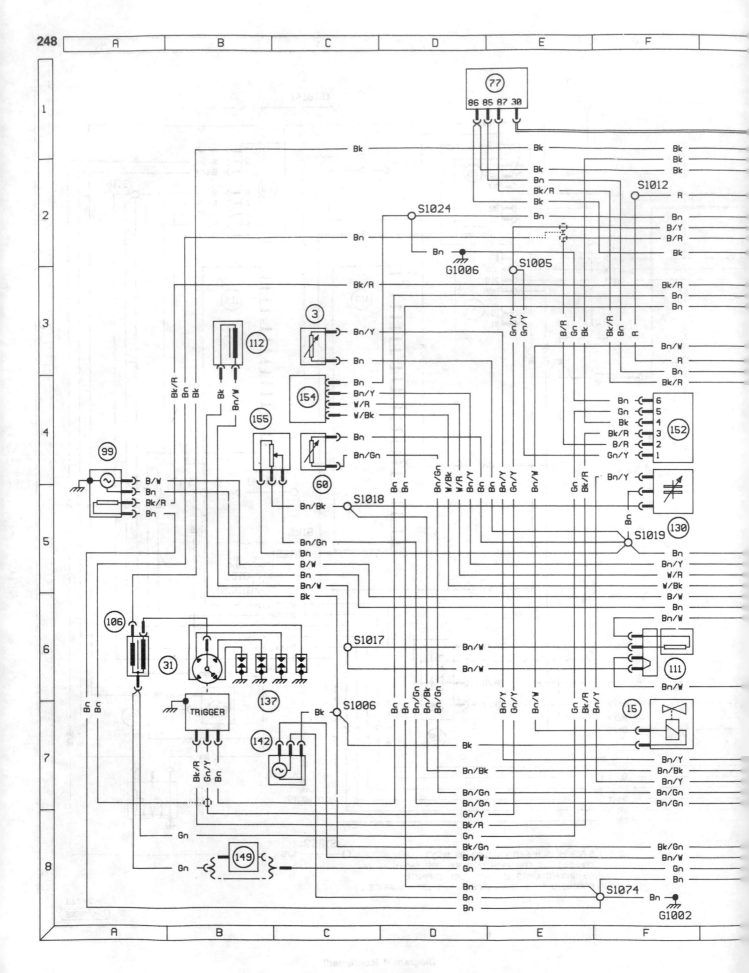

Diagram 4a: 1990 - 1.4 CFi fuel injection and ignition

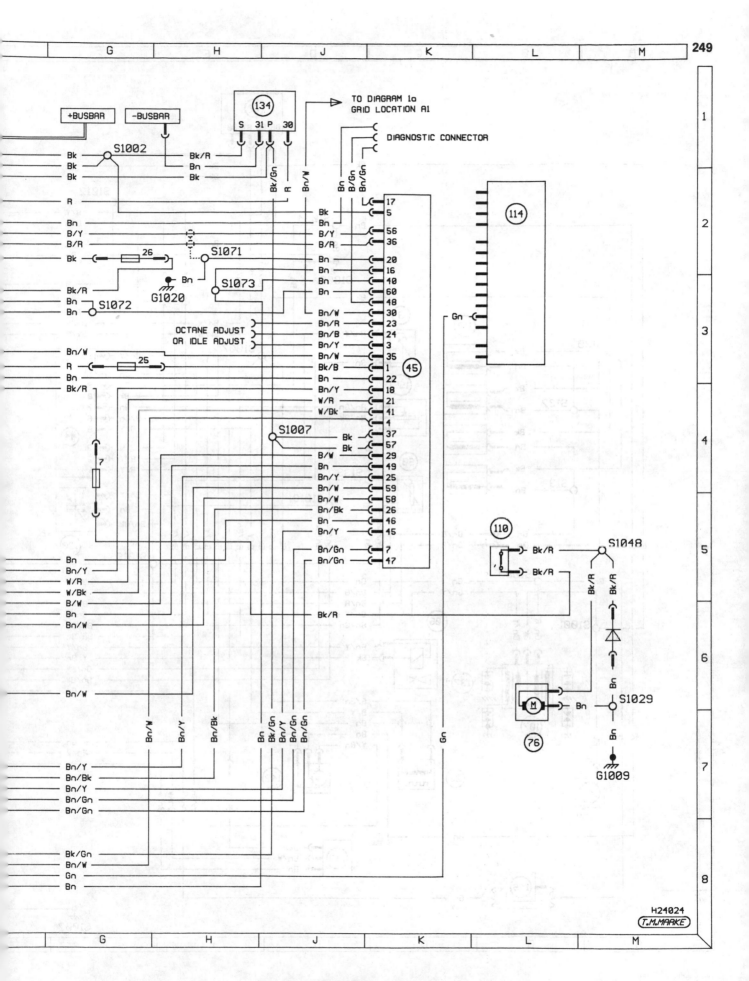

Diagram 4a (continued)

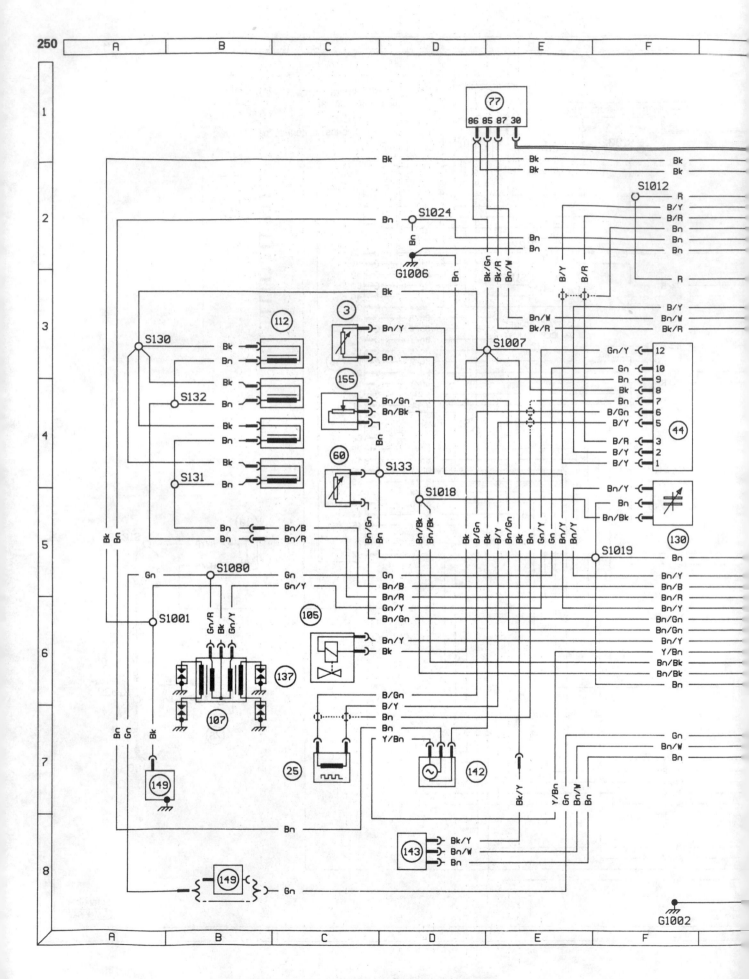

Diagram 4b: 1990 – 1.6 EFi fuel injection and ignition

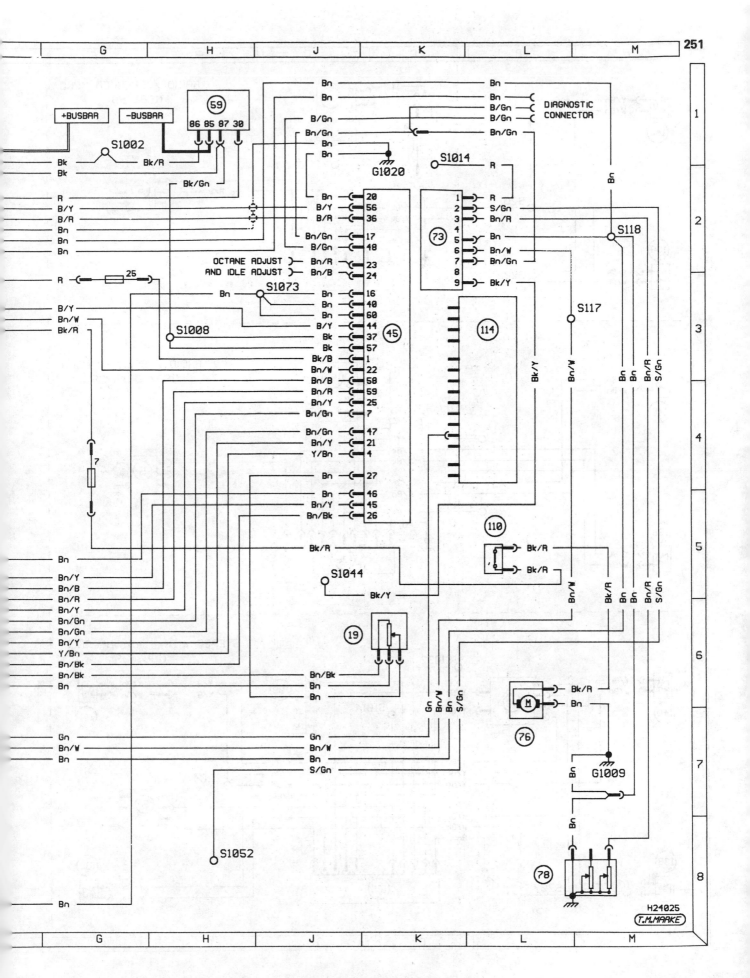

Diagram 4b (continued)

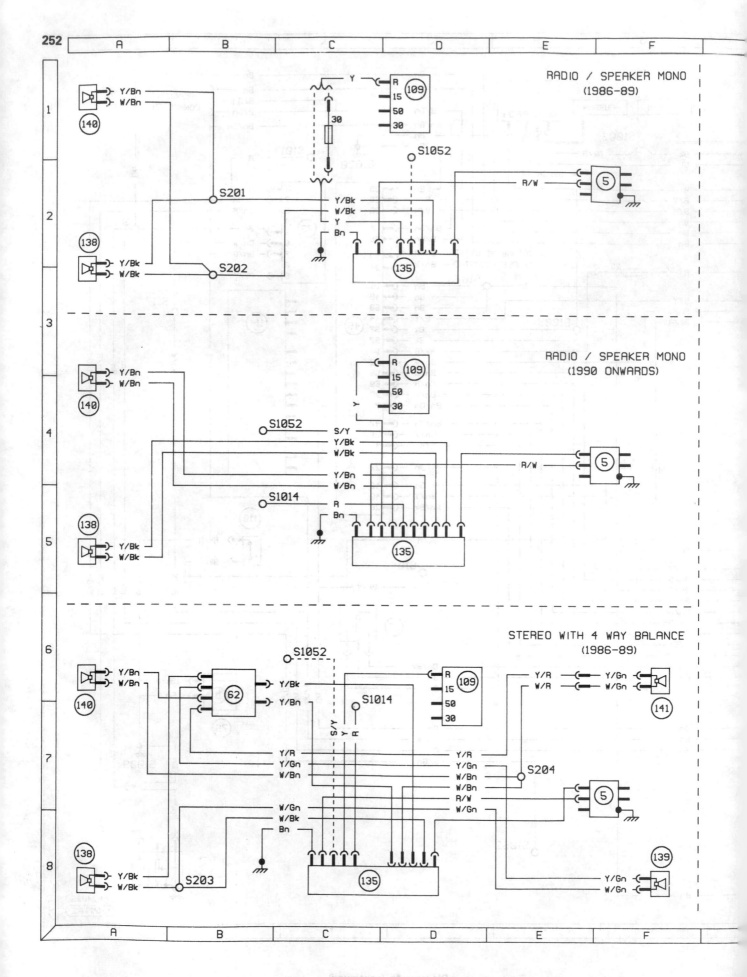

RADIO / SPEAKER MONO
(1986-89)

RADIO / SPEAKER MONO
(1990 ONWARDS)

STEREO WITH 4 WAY BALANCE
(1986-89)

Diagram 5: 1986 onward – in-car entertainment, all models

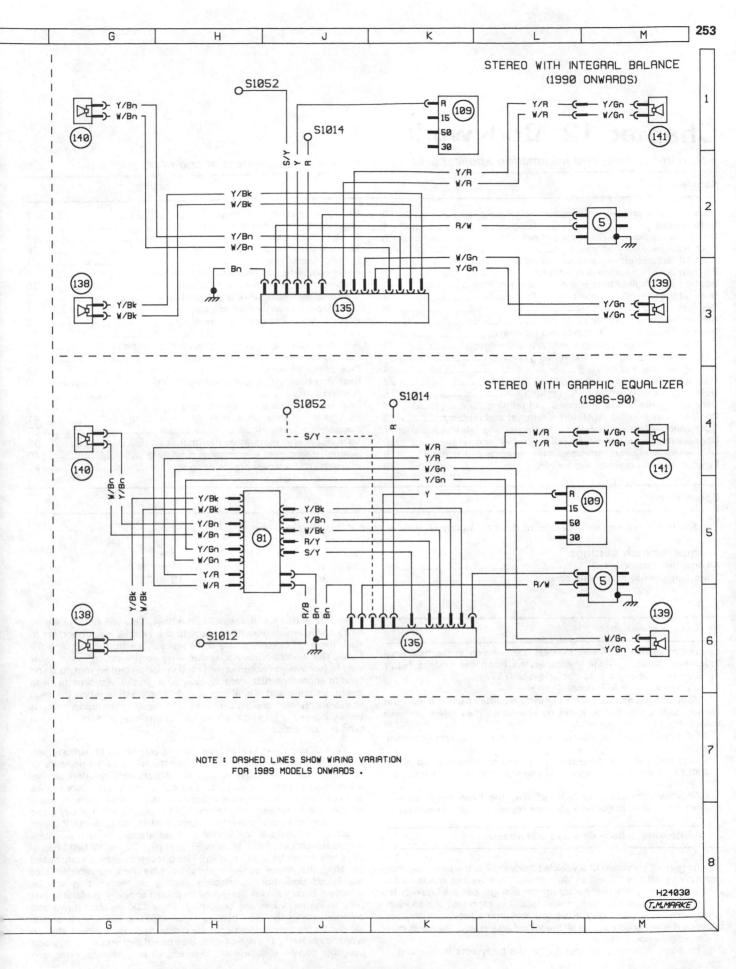

STEREO WITH INTEGRAL BALANCE (1990 ONWARDS)

STEREO WITH GRAPHIC EQUALIZER (1986-90)

NOTE : DASHED LINES SHOW WIRING VARIATION FOR 1989 MODELS ONWARDS .

H24030
T.M.MAAKE

Diagram 5 (continued)

Chapter 12 Bodywork

For modifications, and information applicable to later models, see Supplement at end of manual

Contents

Specifications

For details of sizes and weights refer to the introductory sections at start of this manual

Torque wrench settings

	Nm	lbf ft
All seat belt anchor bolts	29 to 41	21 to 30
Front belt stalk-to-seat frame screws	25 to 30	18 to 22

1 General description

The bodyshell is of welded steel construction in the traditional 'three-box' styling. Wedge-shaped at the front, the body is highly aerodynamic, having a drag coefficient of 0.37.

All models have four doors.

Wrap around polycarbonate bumpers are fitted front and rear, and further body protection is given by side mouldings which are also manufactured in this material.

The body is of monocoque construction and is of energy-absorbing design.

Rust and corrosion protection is applied to all new vehicles and includes zinc phosphate dipping and wax injection of box sections and door interiors.

All body panels are welded, including the front wings, so it is recommended that major body damage repairs are left to your dealer.

2 Maintenance – bodywork and underframe

1 The general condition of a vehicle's bodywork is the one thing that significantly affects its value. Maintenance is easy but needs to be regular. Neglect, particularly after minor damage, can lead quickly to further deterioration and costly repair bills. It is important also to keep watch on those parts of the vehicle not immediately visible, for instance the underside, inside all the wheel arches and the lower part of the engine compartment.

2 The basic maintenance routine for the bodywork is washing – preferably with a lot of water, from a hose. This will remove all the loose solids which may have stuck to the vehicle. It is important to flush these off in such a way as to prevent grit from scratching the finish. The wheel arches and underframe need washing in the same way to remove any accumulated mud which will retain moisture and tend to encourage rust. Paradoxically enough, the best time to clean the underframe and wheel arches is in wet weather when the mud is thoroughly wet and soft. In very wet weather the underframe is usually cleaned of large accumulations automatically and this is a good time for inspection.

3 Periodically, except on vehicles with a wax-based underbody protective coating, it is a good idea to have the whole of the underframe of the vehicle steam cleaned, engine compartment included, so that a thorough inspection can be carried out to see what minor repairs and renovations are necessary. Steam cleaning is available at many garages and is necessary for removal of the accumulation of oily grime which sometimes is allowed to become thick in certain areas. If steam cleaning facilities are not available, there are one or two excellent grease solvents available, such as Holts Engine Cleaner or Holts Foambrite, which can be brush applied. The dirt can then be simply hosed off. Note that these methods should not be used on vehicles with wax-based underbody protective coating or the coating will be removed. Such vehicles should be inspected annually, preferably just prior to winter, when the underbody should be washed down and any damage to the wax coating repaired using Holts Undershield. Ideally, a completely fresh coat should be applied. It would also be worth considering the use of such wax-based protection for injection into door panels, sills, box sections, etc, as an additional safeguard

2.4A Keep drain tubes clear

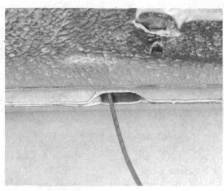

2.4B Probe body drain slots with wire to keep clear ...

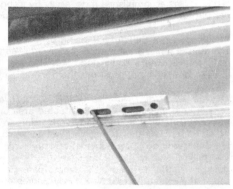

2.4C ... and the same applies to the door drain slots

against rust damage where such protection is not provided by the vehicle manufacturer.

4   After washing paintwork, wipe off with a chamois leather to give an unspotted clear finish. A coat of clear protective wax polish, like the many excellent Turtle Wax polishes, will give added protection against chemical pollutants in the air. If the paintwork sheen has dulled or oxidised, use a cleaner/polisher combination such as Turtle Extra to restore the brilliance of the shine. This requires a little effort, but such dulling is usually caused because regular washing has been neglected. Care needs to be taken with metallic paintwork, as special non-abrasive cleaner/polisher is required to avoid damage to the finish. Always check that the door and ventilator opening drain holes and pipes are completely clear so that water can be drained out (photos). Bright work should be treated in the same way as paint work. Windscreens and windows can be kept clear of the smeary film which often appears by the use of a proprietary glass cleaner like Holts Mixra. Never use any form of wax or other body or chromium polish on glass.

3   Maintenance – upholstery and carpets

Mats and carpets should be brushed or vacuum cleaned regularly to keep them free of grit. If they are badly stained remove them from the vehicle for scrubbing or sponging and make quite sure they are dry before refitting. Seats and interior trim panels can be kept clean by wiping with a damp cloth and Turtle Wax Carisma. If they do become stained (which can be more apparent on light coloured upholstery) use a little liquid detergent and a soft nail brush to scour the grime out of the grain of the material. Do not forget to keep the headlining clean in the same way as the upholstery. When using liquid cleaners inside the vehicle do not over-wet the surfaces being cleaned. Excessive damp could get into the seams and padded interior causing stains, offensive odours or even rot. If the inside of the vehicle gets wet accidentally it is worthwhile taking some trouble to dry it out properly, particularly where carpets are involved. *Do not leave oil or electric heaters inside the vehicle for this purpose.*

4   Body damage – repair

The photographic sequences on pages 262 and 263 illustrate the operations detailed in the following sub-sections.
Note: *For more detailed information about bodywork repair, the Haynes Publishing Group publish a book by Lindsay Porter called The Car Bodywork Repair Manual. This incorporates information on such aspects as rust treatment, painting and glass fibre repairs, as well as details on more ambitious repairs involving welding and panel beating.*

Repair of minor scratches in bodywork

If the scratch is very superficial, and does not penetrate to the metal of the bodywork, repair is very simple. Lightly rub the area of

the scratch with a paintwork renovator like Turtle Wax New Color Back, or a very fine cutting paste like Holts Body + Plus Rubbing Compound to remove loose paint from the scratch and to clear the surrounding bodywork of wax polish. Rinse the area with clean water.

Apply touch-up paint, such as Holts Dupli-Color Color Touch or a paint film like Holts Autofilm, to the scratch using a fine paint brush; continue to apply fine layers of paint until the surface of the paint in the scratch is level with the surrounding paintwork. Allow the new paint at least two weeks to harden: then blend it into the surrounding paintwork by rubbing the scratch area with a paintwork renovator or a very fine cutting paste, such as Holts Body + Plus Rubbing Compound or Turtle Wax New Color Back. Finally, apply wax polish from one of the Turtle Wax range of wax polishes.

Where the scratch has penetrated right through to the metal of the bodywork, causing the metal to rust, a different repair technique is required. Remove any loose rust from the bottom of the scratch with a penknife, then apply rust inhibiting paint, such as Turtle Wax Rust Master, to prevent the formation of rust in the future. Using a rubber or nylon applicator fill the scratch with bodystopper paste like Holts Body + Plus Knifing Putty. If required, this paste can be mixed with cellulose thinners, such as Holts Body + Plus Cellulose Thinners, to provide a very thin paste which is ideal for filling narrow scratches. Before the stopper-paste in the scratch hardens, wrap a piece of smooth cotton rag around the top of a finger. Dip the finger in cellulose thinners, such as Holts Body + Plus Cellulose Thinners, and then quickly sweep it across the surface of the stopper-paste in the scratch; this will ensure that the surface of the stopper-paste is slightly hollowed. The scratch can now be painted over as described earlier in this Section.

Repair of dents in bodywork

When deep denting of the vehicle's bodywork has taken place, the first task is to pull the dent out, until the affected bodywork almost attains its original shape. There is little point in trying to restore the original shape completely, as the metal in the damaged area will have stretched on impact and cannot be reshaped fully to its original contour. It is better to bring the level of the dent up to a point which is about $\frac{1}{8}$ in (3 mm) below the level of the surrounding bodywork. In cases where the dent is very shallow anyway, it is not worth trying to pull it out at all. If the underside of the dent is accessible, it can be hammered out gently from behind, using a mallet with a wooden or plastic head. Whilst doing this, hold a suitable block of wood firmly against the outside of the panel to absorb the impact from the hammer blows and thus prevent a large area of the bodywork from being 'belled-out'.

Should the dent be in a section of the bodywork which has a double skin or some other factor making it inaccessible from behind, a different technique is called for. Drill several small holes through the metal inside the area – particulary in the deeper section. Then screw long self-tapping screws into the holes just sufficiently for them to gain a good purchase in the metal. Now the dent can be pulled out by pulling on the protruding heads of the screws with a pair of pliers.

The next stage of the repair is the removal of the paint from the damaged area, and from an inch or so of the surrounding 'sound' bodywork. This is accomplished most easily by using a wire brush or abrasive pad on a power drill, although it can be done just as effectively by hand using sheets of abrasive paper. To complete the preparation for filling, score the surface of the bare metal with a screwdriver or the tang of a file, or alternatively, drill small holes in the affected area. This will provide a really good 'key' for the filler paste.

To complete the repair see the Section on filling and re-spraying.

Repair of rust holes or gashes in bodywork

Remove all paint from the affected area and from an inch or so of the surrounding 'sound' bodywork, using an abrasive pad or a wire brush on a power drill. If these are not available a few sheets of abrasive paper will do the job just as effectively. With the paint removed you will be able to gauge the severity of the corrosion and therefore decide whether to renew the whole panel (if this is possible) or to repair the affected area. New body panels are not as expensive as most people think and it is often quicker and more satisfactory to fit a new panel than to attempt to repair large areas of corrosion.

Remove all fittings from the affected area except those which will act as a guide to the original shape of the damaged bodywork (eg headlamp shells etc). Then, using tin snips or a hacksaw blade, remove all loose metal and any other metal badly affected by corrosion. Hammer the edges of the hole inwards in order to create a slight depression for the filler paste.

Wire brush the affected area to remove the powdery rust from the surface of the remaining metal. Paint the affected area with rust inhibiting paint like Turtle Wax Rust Master; if the back of the rusted area is accessible treat this also.

Before filling can take place it will be necessary to block the hole in some way. This can be achieved by the use of aluminium or plastic mesh, or aluminium tape.

Aluminium or plastic mesh or glass fibre matting, such as the Holts Body + Plus Glass Fibre Matting, is probably the best material to use for a large hole. Cut a piece to the approximate size and shape of the hole to be filled, then position it in the hole so that its edges are below the level of the surrounding bodywork. It can be retained in position by several blobs of filler paste around its periphery.

Aluminium tape should be used for small or very narrow holes. Pull a piece off the roll and trim it to the approximate size and shape required, then pull off the backing paper (if used) and stick the tape over the hole; it can be overlapped if the thickness of one piece is insufficient. Burnish down the edges of the tape with the handle of a screwdriver or similar, to ensure that the tape is securely attached to the metal underneath.

Bodywork repairs – filling and re-spraying

Before using this Section, see the Sections on dent, deep scratch, rust holes and gash repairs.

Many types of bodyfiller are available, but generally speaking those proprietary kits which contain a tin of filler paste and a tube of resin hardener are best for this type of repair, like Holts Body + Plus or Holts No Mix which can be used directly from the tube. A wide, flexible plastic or nylon applicator will be found invaluable for imparting a smooth and well contoured finish to the surface of the filler.

Mix up a little filler on a clean piece of card or board – measure the hardener carefully (follow the maker's instructions on the pack) otherwise the filler will set too rapidly or too slowly. Alternatively, Holts No Mix can be used straight from the tube without mixing, but daylight is required to cure it. Using the applicator apply the filler paste to the prepared area; draw the applicator across the surface of the filler to achieve the correct contour and to level the filler surface. As soon as a contour that approximates to the correct one is achieved, stop working the paste – if you carry on too long the paste will become sticky and begin to 'pick up' on the applicator. Continue to add thin layers of filler paste at twenty-minute intervals until the level of the filler is just proud of the surrounding bodywork.

Once the filler has hardened, excess can be removed using a metal plane or file. From then on, progressively finer grades of abrasive paper should be used, starting with a 40 grade production paper and finishing with 400 grade wet-and-dry paper. Always wrap the abrasive paper around a flat rubber, cork, or wooden block – otherwise the surface of the filler will not be completely flat. During the smoothing of the filler surface the wet-and-dry paper should be periodically rinsed in water. This will ensure that a very smooth finish is imparted to the filler at the final stage.

At this stage the 'dent' should be surrounded by a ring of bare

metal, which in turn should be encircled by the finely 'feathered' edge of the good paintwork. Rinse the repair area with clean water, until all of the dust produced by the rubbing-down operation has gone.

Spray the whole repair area with a light coat of primer, either Holts Body + Plus Grey or Red Oxide Primer – this will show up any imperfections in the surface of the filler. Repair these imperfections with fresh filler paste or bodystopper, and once more smooth the surface with abrasive paper. If bodystopper is used, it can be mixed with cellulose thinners to form a really thin paste which is ideal for filling small holes. Repeat this spray and repair procedure until you are satisfied that the surface of the filler, and the feathered edge of the paintwork are perfect. Clean the repair area with clean water and allow to dry fully.

The repair area is now ready for final spraying. Paint spraying must be carried out in a warm, dry, windless and dust free atmosphere. This condition can be created artificially if you have access to a large indoor working area, but if you are forced to work in the open, you will have to pick your day very carefully. If you are working indoors, dousing the floor in the work area with water will help to settle the dust which would otherwise be in the atmosphere. If the repair area is confined to one body panel, mask off the surrounding panels; this will help to minimise the effects of a slight mis-match in paint colours. Bodywork fittings (eg chrome strips, door handles etc) will also need to be masked off. Use genuine masking tape and several thicknesses of newspaper for the masking operations.

Before commencing to spray, agitate the aerosol can thoroughly, then spray a test area (an old tin, or similar) until the technique is mastered. Cover the repair area with a thick coat of primer; the thickness should be built up using several thin layers of paint rather than one thick one. Using 400 grade wet-and-dry paper, rub down the surface of the primer until it is really smooth. While doing this, the work area should be thoroughly doused with water, and the wet-and-dry paper periodically rinsed in water. Allow to dry before spraying on more paint.

Spray on the top coat using Holts Dupli-Color Autospray, again building up the thickness by using several thin layers of paint. Start spraying in the centre of the repair area and then, with a single side-to-side motion, work outwards until the whole repair area and about 2 inches of the surrounding original paintwork is covered. Remove all masking material 10 to 15 minutes after spraying on the final coat of paint.

Allow the new paint at least two weeks to harden, then, using a paintwork renovator or a very fine cutting paste such as Turtle Wax New Color Back or Holts Body + Plus Rubbing Compound, blend the edges of the paint into the existing paintwork. Finally, apply wax polish.

---

5   Bonnet – removal and refitting

1   Open the bonnet and support it on its stay.
2   Detach the anti-static strap at the bonnet hinge.
3   Mark round the hinge plates on the underside of the bonnet lid as an aid to refitting.

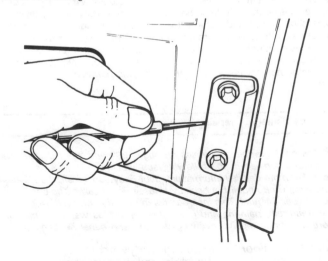

Fig. 12.1 Marking bonnet hinge position (Sec 5)

5.8 Bonnet striker and safety catch

6.3 Cable to latch release

4   With an assistant supporting the bonnet lid, unbolt the hinges and lift the lid from the vehicle.
5   Refit by reversing the removal operations. If a new bonnet is being installed, position it so that an equal gap is provided at each side when it is being closed.
6   The bonnet should close smoothly and positively without excessive pressure. If it does not, carry out the following adjustment.
7   Screw in the bump stops which are located on the front upper cross rail. Close the bonnet and then readjust the bump stops until the bonnet is flush with the wing upper surfaces.
8   Adjust the striker centrally in relation to the latch (photo). Release it by unscrewing its pressed steel locknut.
9   Screw the striker in or out until the bonnet fully closes under its own weight when allowed to drop from a point 300 mm (12 in) above its released position.

6   Bonnet release cable – removal and refitting

1   Working inside the vehicle, extract the three screws and remove the steering column shroud. Open the bonnet.
2   Extract the single screw and remove the cable bracket from the steering column.
3   Working within the engine compartment, pull the cable grommet from the bonnet latch bracket and then disengage the cable end fitting from the latch (photo).
4   Unclip the cable from the side of the engine compartment.
5   Withdraw the cable through the engine compartment rear bulkhead into the vehicle interior.
6   Refitting is a reversal of removal.

7   Bonnet lock – removal and refitting

1   Extract the three securing screws from the lock and lower it until the cable can be disconnected.
2   Withdraw the lock from below the top rail.
3   Refit by reversing the removal operations.

8   Radiator grille – removal and refitting

1   The grille is held in position by four spring clips (photo).
2   Once these clips are released, the grille can be removed from the body panel.
3   Refit by reattaching the spring clips.

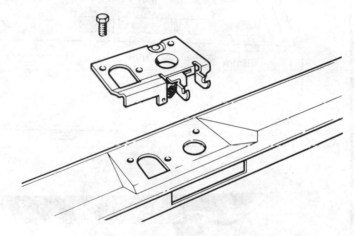

Fig. 12.2 Bonnet lock components (Sec 7)

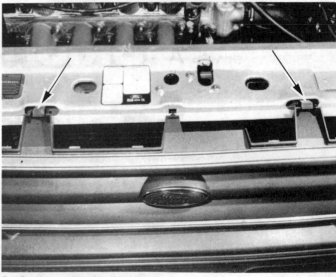

8.1 Radiator grille clips (arrowed)

9 Body adhesive emblems – removal and refitting

1   The radiator grille emblem, the front wing motif, the boot lid emblems and the body side mouldings are all of the self-adhesive type.

2   To remove them, it is recommended that a length of nylon cord is used to separate them from their mounting surfaces.

3   New emblems have adhesive already applied and a protective backing. Before sticking them into position, clean off all the old adhesive from the mounting surface of the vehicle with a suitable solvent.

10 Boot lid – removal and refitting

1   Disconnect the battery.

2   Raise and support the boot lid.

3   Disconnect the multi-plug of the boot release wiring. Prise free the rubber grommet protecting the wiring at its entry into the boot lid cavity near the left-hand hinge.

4   Detach the wiring loom from the retaining clips and then tie a piece of cord to the plug and pull the loom and cord from the lid panel. The cord must now be untied from the wiring loom, but left in position

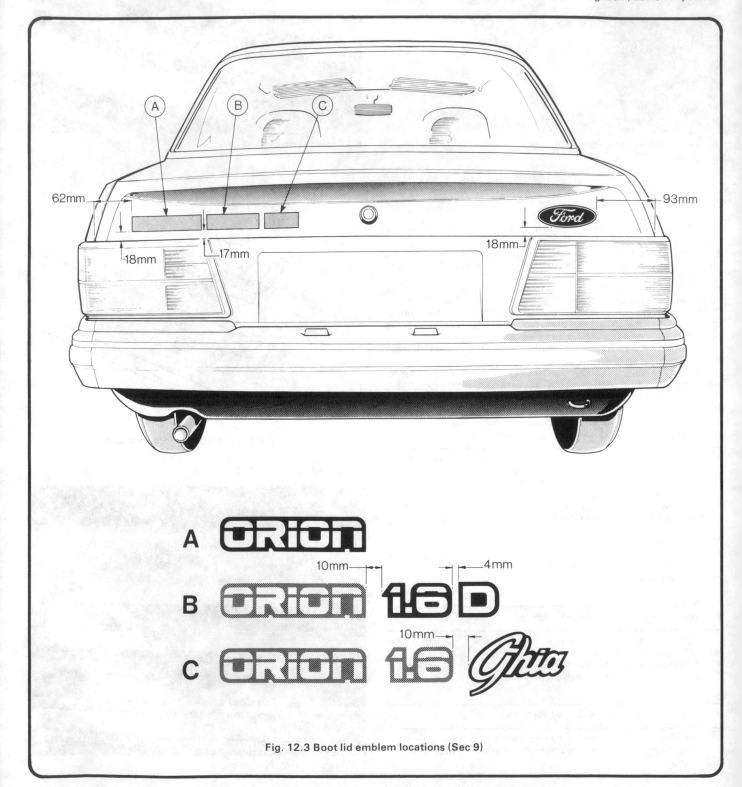

Fig. 12.3 Boot lid emblem locations (Sec 9)

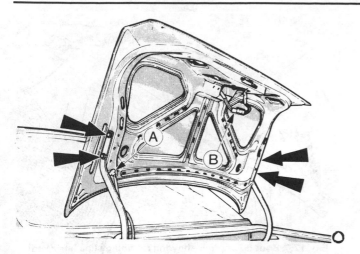

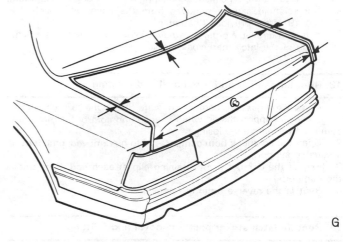

Fig. 12.4 Boot lid showing positions of retaining bolts (arrowed), rubber grommet (A) and multi-plug (B) (Sec 10)

Fig. 12.5 Check boot lid alignment at points indicated (Sec 10)

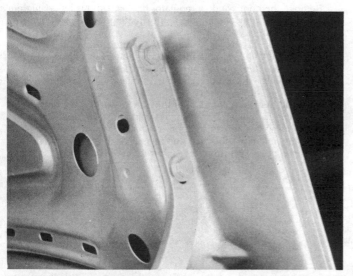

10.6 Boot lid hinge bolts

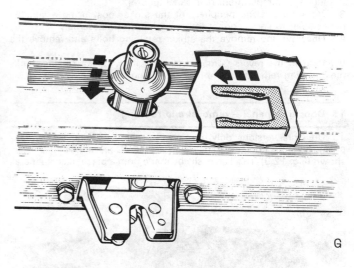

Fig. 12.6 Boot lid lock barrel and retaining clip (Sec 11)

in the panel, so that the wiring loom can be re-routed during assembly.
5   Mark around the boot lid hinge plates to indicate their fitting positions during reassembly.
6   Get an assistant to support the lid, unscrew and remove the hinge bolts (photo) and lift the lid clear.
7   Refit in the reverse order to removal, but do not fully tighten the hinge bolts until the lid is aligned and adjusted correctly.

11 Boot lid lock barrel – removal and refitting

1   Open and support the boot lid.
2   Prise free and remove the barrel retaining clip from the underside of the panel.
3   Where fitted, detach the central door locking rod – the lock barrel can then be withdrawn from the lid.
4   Refitting is a reversal of removal. Check latch operation is satisfactory prior to closing the lid.

12 Boot lid latch – removal and refitting

1   Open and support the boot lid.
2   Disconnect the multi-plug from the wiring loom within the lid cavity.
3   Unscrew and remove the three latch retaining screws (photo) and

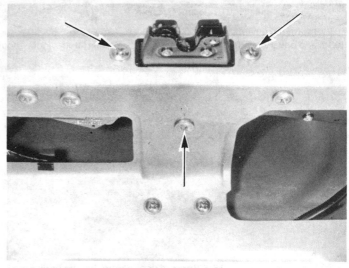

12.3 Boot lid latch securing screws (arrowed)

extract the latch from the lid, manoeuvring it free through the aperture.

4   The solenoid can be removed from the latch, as described in Section 49 of the previous Chapter.

5   Refit in the reverse order of removal. When reconnected check the operation of the latch then close the lid.

13 Boot lid damper unit – removal and refitting

1   Pressurised gas ram damper units are fitted, one to each boot lid hinge, which support the lid when opened and control the movement during lid opening and closing.

2   Open the lid and, if both dampers are to be removed, prop it using a suitable support.

3   Extract the damper pivot retaining clip at each end then remove the damper(s).

4   Refit in the reverse order of removal.

14 Boot lid latch striker post – removal and refitting

1   Raise and support the boot lid.

2   Grip one end of the covering panel and carefully pull it free from the luggage compartment rear panel (photo).

3   Mark around the periphery of the striker post using a suitable marker pen to show correct fitting position for reassembly.

4   Unscrew and remove the striker retaining bolts and remove the striker.

5   Refit in the reverse order, realigning the striker with the marks made during removal before fully tightening the retaining bolts.

15 Door trim panel – removal and refitting

1   On Ghia versions only, remove the panel capping by carefully prising out the retaining clips using a forked tool similar to the one shown (Fig. 12.9). This can easily be made from a piece of scrap metal.

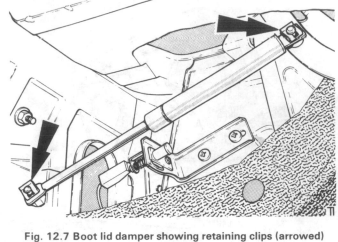

Fig. 12.7 Boot lid damper showing retaining clips (arrowed) (Sec 13)

2   Remove the door window regulator handle. Do this by prising out the plastic insert from the handle and extracting the screw which will now be exposed.

3   On vehicles fitted with electrically operated front windows, pull out the switches and remove the door pocket finisher (photo).

4   Remove the door pull/armrest. This is held by two screws (photo). On Base models with a door pull only, the end caps will have to be prised up to reveal the screws.

5   Push the door lock remote control handle bezel towards the rear of the vehicle to release it from its retaining lugs (photo).

6   Again using the forked tool, pass it round the edge of the panel between the panel and the door and release each of the panel clips in turn. Lift the panel from the door (photo).

14.2 Boot lid latch striker post, securing bolts and covering panel

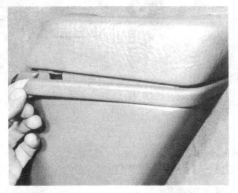

15.3 Remove finisher strip (electrically operated window door trim) ...

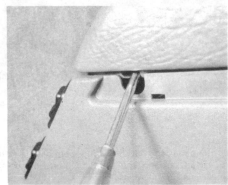

15.4 ... then remove the armrest/door pull screws

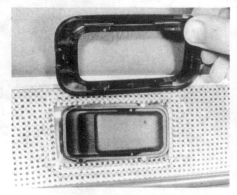

15.5 Remove door control handle bezel

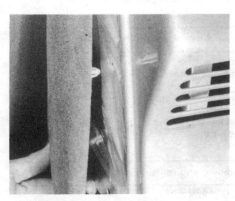

15.6 Prising free the trim panel from the door

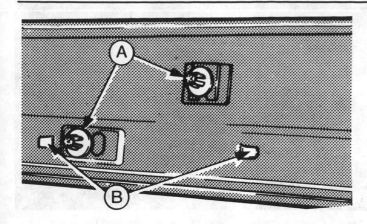

Fig. 12.8 Door trim panel capping – Ghia (Sec 15)

A   Panel fixing clip   *B   Moulding tray*

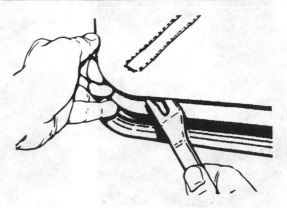

Fig. 12.9 Tool for releasing trim panel clips (Sec 15)

7   The door tidy is attached directly to the trim panel without any anchor screws being used; for this reason the tidy should not be used as a means of closing the door.
8   Refitting the panel is a reversal of removal.

16 Door trim panel pocket – removal and refitting

1   Remove the door trim panel, as given in the previous Section.
2   On models fitted with the electric window operating mechanism, remove the three U-shaped retainer plates and single push-on clip.
3   Unhook the pocket from the lower edge of the trim panel.
4   Refit in reverse order of removal.
5   On models fitted with the manual window operating mechanism, remove the central securing screw, withdraw the two U-shaped retainer plates and then unhook the pocket from the lower edge of the trim panel.
6   Refit in the reverse order of removal.

17 Door window (manual regulator) – removal and refitting

1   Remove the door trim panel, as described in Section 15.
2   Carefully peel back the waterproof sheet from the door.
3   Prise off the inner and outer glass weatherstrips.
4   Lower the window so that the regulator connector is level with the door lower aperture.
5   On the front door, remove the single screw which retains the glass run extension (accessible through the small aperture at the lower corner of the door).
6   On the rear door, remove the upper and lower screws which secure the divisional channel and quarter window in position. Remove the door quarter window.
7   On front and rear doors, detach the window channel from the regulator ball and socket joints then raise and remove the window from the exterior side of the door (front) or interior side of the door (rear).
8   Refitting of the door glass is the reversal of the removal procedure. On completion check that the window operates freely before refitting the waterproof sheet and trim to the door.

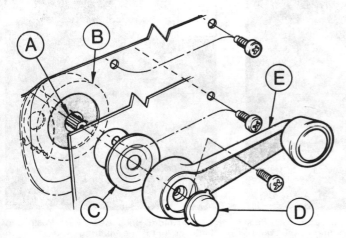

Fig. 12.10 Door window regulator handle components (Sec 15)

A   Shaft   *D   Insert*
B   Anti-rattle pad   *E   Handle*
C   Bezel

18 Door window (electric regulator) – removal and refitting

Refer to Section 51 in Chapter 11, paragraphs 4 to 9 inclusive. Remove the glass, as given in paragraph 7, Section 17 of this Chapter.

19 Door window regulator (mechanical) – removal and refitting

1   Remove the door trim panel, as described in Section 15.
2   Carefully peel back the waterproof sheet from the door.
3   Lower the glass so that the channel and regulator attachments are accessible through the door aperture. Detach the ball and socket joints (two for the front door, one for the rear door).

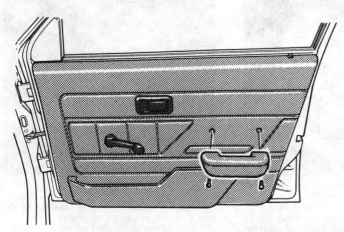

Fig. 12.11 Door pull/armrest – Base model (Sec 15)

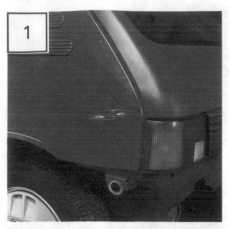

This photographic sequence shows the steps taken to repair the dent and paintwork damage shown above. In general, the procedure for repairing a hole will be similar; where there are substantial differences, the procedure is clearly described and shown in a separate photograph.

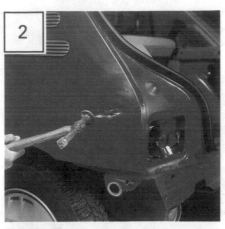

First remove any trim around the dent, then hammer out the dent where access is possible. This will minimise filling. Here, after the large dent has been hammered out, the damaged area is being made slightly concave.

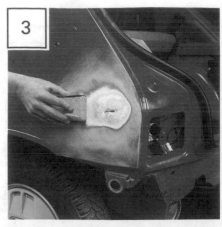

Next, remove all paint from the damaged area by rubbing with coarse abrasive paper or using a power drill fitted with a wire brush or abrasive pad. 'Feather' the edge of the boundary with good paintwork using a finer grade of abrasive paper.

Where there are holes or other damage, the sheet metal should be cut away before proceeding further. The damaged area and any signs of rust should be treated with Turtle Wax Hi-Tech Rust Eater, which will also inhibit further rust formation.

For a large dent or hole mix Holts Body Plus Resin and Hardener according to the manufacturer's instructions and apply around the edge of the repair. Press Glass Fibre Matting over the repair area and leave for 20-30 minutes to harden. Then ...

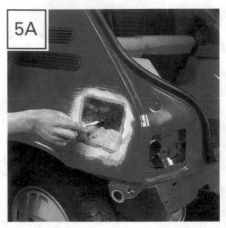

... brush more Holts Body Plus Resin and Hardener onto the matting and leave to harden. Repeat the sequence with two or three layers of matting, checking that the final layer is lower than the surrounding area. Apply Holts Body Plus Filler Paste as shown in Step 5B.

For a medium dent, mix Holts Body Plus Filler Paste and Hardener according to the manufacturer's instructions and apply it with a flexible applicator. Apply thin layers of filler at 20-minute intervals, until the filler surface is slightly proud of the surrounding bodywork.

For small dents and scratches use Holts No Mix Filler Paste straight from the tube. Apply it according to the instructions in thin layers, using the spatula provided. It will harden in minutes if applied outdoors and may then be used as its own knifing putty.

Use a plane or file for initial shaping. Then, using progressively finer grades of wet-and-dry paper, wrapped round a sanding block, and copious amounts of clean water, rub down the filler until glass smooth. 'Feather' the edges of adjoining paintwork.

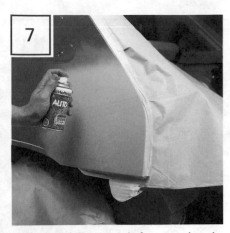

Protect adjoining areas before spraying the whole repair area and at least one inch of the surrounding sound paintwork with Holts Dupli-Color primer.

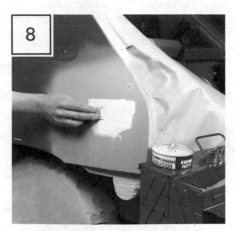

Fill any imperfections in the filler surface with a small amount of Holts Body Plus Knifing Putty. Using plenty of clean water, rub down the surface with a fine grade wet-and-dry paper – 400 grade is recommended – until it is really smooth.

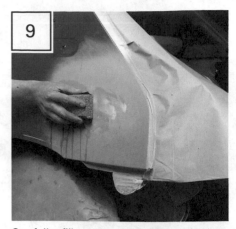

Carefully fill any remaining imperfections with knifing putty before applying the last coat of primer. Then rub down the surface with Holts Body Plus Rubbing Compound to ensure a really smooth surface.

Protect surrounding areas from overspray before applying the topcoat in several thin layers. Agitate Holts Dupli-Color aerosol thoroughly. Start at the repair centre, spraying outwards with a side-to-side motion.

If the exact colour is not available off the shelf, local Holts Professional Spraymatch Centres will custom fill an aerosol to match perfectly.

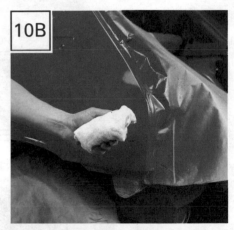

To identify whether a lacquer finish is required, rub a painted unrepaired part of the body with wax and a clean cloth.

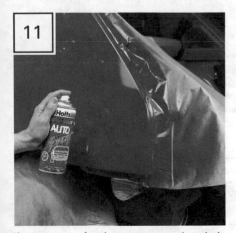

If *no* traces of paint appear on the cloth, spray Holts Dupli-Color clear lacquer over the repaired area to achieve the correct gloss level.

The paint will take about two weeks to harden fully. After this time it can be 'cut' with a mild cutting compound such as Turtle Wax Minute Cut prior to polishing with a final coating of Turtle Wax Extra.

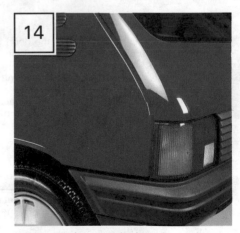

When carrying out bodywork repairs, remember that the quality of the finished job is proportional to the time and effort expended.

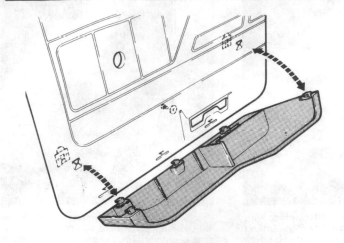

Fig. 12.12 Door trim panel pocket (Sec 16)

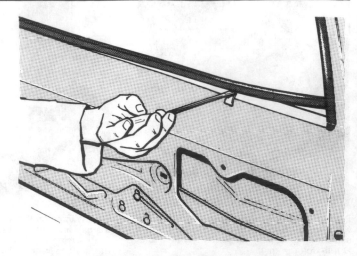

Fig. 12.13 Door weatherstrip removal (Sec 17)

Fig. 12.14 Door window channel and regulator connections (A) and glass run extension retaining screw (B) (Sec 17)

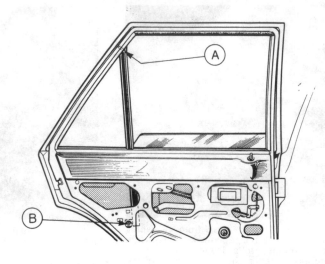

Fig. 12.15 Rear door divisional channel securing screw positions, upper (A) and lower (B) (Sec 17)

4   Lower the glass to the base of the door, then drill out the seven rivets which secure the regulator in position. The rivet positions are shown in Fig. 12.16.
5   With the rivets removed, the regulator unit can be withdrawn from the aperture in the door.
6   Refitting is a reversal of the removal procedure. Align the regulator with the respective rivet holes before pop riveting it to secure. The ball and socket joints are a push-fit to the glass channel, but support the channel when pushing on the joint.

20 Door window regulator (electrical) – removal and refitting

Refer to Chapter 11 Section 51 for details of the removal and refitting of the electrically operated door window winder mechanism.

21 Rear door quarter window – removal and refitting

1   Proceed as given in Section 17, paragraphs 1 to 6 inclusive.
2   Refit in reverse order of removal. On completion check that the adjustable window can be freely regulated before refitting the water-proof sheet and door trim.

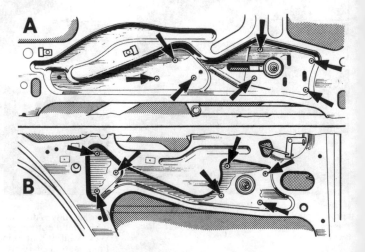

Fig. 12.16 Regulator retaining rivet positions for the front (A) and rear (B) doors (Sec 19)

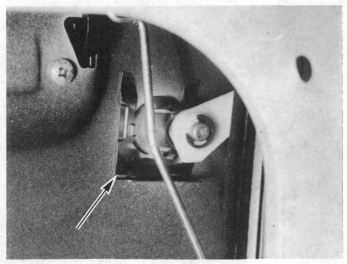

22.4 Door lock cylinder securing clip (arrowed)

22.5 Door lock securing screws

22 Door lock and cylinder – removal and refitting

1   Remove the door trim panel, as described in Section 15.
2   Pull away the waterproof sheet as necessary to gain access to the lock.
3   Disconnect the control rods from the lock.
4   To remove the lock cylinder, pull out the retaining clip (photo) and seal and withdraw the cylinder.
5   Remove the lock by extracting the three securing screws (photo) and lowering the lock sufficiently to permit the cylinder lock rod to clear the lock housing. Turn the latch around the door frame and withdraw the assembly through the rear cut-out in the door.
6   The remote control handle can be removed once its connecting rod has been disconnected and the single securing screw extracted.
7   Refitting is a reversal of removal.

23 Central door locking system – removal and refitting

Refer to Section 49 in Chapter 11 for details of system components removal and refitting.

24 Door – removal and refitting

Front door
1   Open the door fully and support its lower edge on a jack or blocks covered with a pad of rag.
2   Unscrew the two bolts which hold the check arm bracket to the body and disconnect the arm.
3   Remove the scuff plate from the sill at the bottom of the door aperture.
4   Unclip the lower cowl side trim panel.
5   Remove the heater duct.
6   Unbolt the door lower hinge from the body pillar.
7   Unbolt the upper hinge from the body pillar, then lift the door from the vehicle.

Rear door
8   The operations are similar to those described for removal of the front door, except that the centre pillar trim panels must be removed for access to the hinge bolts.

All doors
9   When refitting the doors, do not fully tighten the hinge bolts until the alignment of the door within the body aperture has been checked.

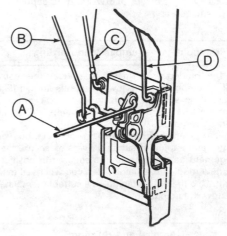

Fig. 12.17 Door lock connections (Sec 22)

A   Interior handle   C   Lock barrel
B   Exterior handle   D   Sill button

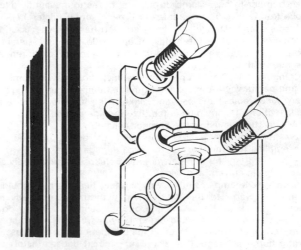

Fig. 12.18 Door check arm brackets (Sec 24)

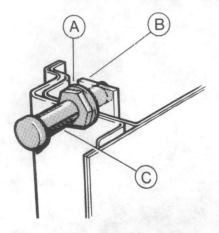

Fig. 12.19 Door striker components (Sec 24)

A   Body pillar   C   Striker pin
B   Reinforcement plate

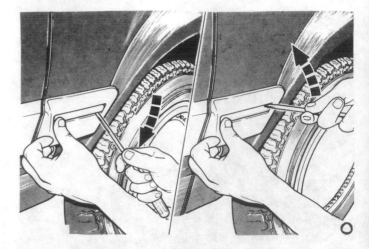

Fig. 12.20 Moulding insert removal and refitting method (Sec 25)

10 The door striker can be adjusted to provide smooth positive closure by unscrewing it a turn or two from its captive retaining nut and sliding it as necessary.

25 Body side mouldings – removal and refitting

1   Using a thin-bladed screwdriver, prise away the moulding insert strip, carefully levering from the lower edge as shown (Fig. 12.20).
2   The moulding is secured by rivets and these can be drilled out using a 3 mm (0.12 in) drill. With the rivets drilled through the moulding can be removed.
3   Refitting is a reversal of the removal procedure, but you will need a pop rivet gun and supply of suitable rivets to secure the moulding. Check its alignment as the moulding is secured in position.
4   Where a new moulding is being fitted you will need to first drill the rivet holes in it. Use the old moulding as a suitable template to drill the holes in the new moulding.

26 Front bumper – removal and refitting

1   Open and support the bonnet. Remove the radiator grille, as described in Section 8.
2   Working under each wheel arch in turn unscrew and remove the bumper bracket nut each side (photo).
3   Where applicable, disconnect the headlamp washer supply hoses to their bumper fixings. Clamp or plug the hoses to prevent fluid loss. Remove the nozzles from the bumper if necessary (Chapter 11).
4   Unscrew and remove the right- and left-hand bumper securing nuts located just below the headlight each side. Get an assistant to support the bumper whilst these nuts are being removed. On removal of the nuts withdraw the bumper.
5   If required the front bumper quarter panel(s) can now be removed. Prise and peel away the moulding from the bumper then, laying it on its front face, release the securing clips at the joint to separate the bumper sections. It should be noted that damage around the joint area will necessitate renewal of the bumper assembly.
6   To refit the bumper quarter panels align the dowel pegs and push the assemblies together so that the clips engage.
7   Before refitting the bumper moulding clean off the old adhesive using a suitable solvent and wipe dry.
8   Using a blow lamp or similar, very carefully heat the new moulding so that it is warm to the touch then, with the bumper securely positioned rear face down with the quarter sections hanging down each side, peel a portion of backing strip away from the moulding. Fit 12 mm (0.5 in) of moulding through the bumper cut-out and press the moulding home to locate it, making sure that it doesn't distort and wrinkle.

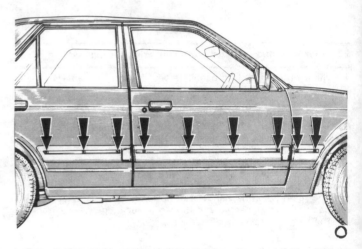

Fig. 12.21 Side moulding rivet positions (arrowed) (Sec 25)

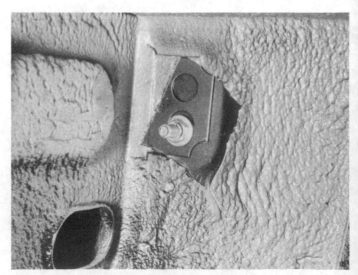

26.2 Bumper bracket nut inside front wheel arch

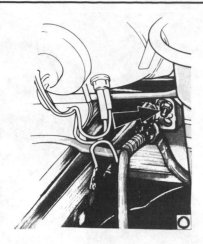

Fig. 12.22 Front bumper securing nut location in engine compartment (Sec 26)

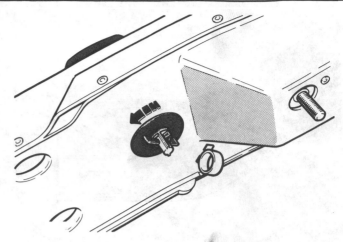

Fig. 12.23 Turn clip to detach overridder from front bumper (where fitted) (Sec 26)

Fig. 12.24 Release clips to detach quarter bumper (front) (Sec 26)

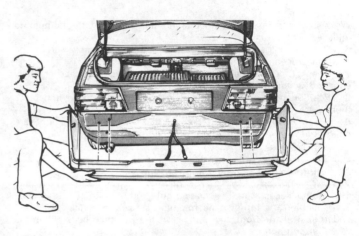

Fig. 12.25 Removing the rear bumper (Sec 27)

9   Continue applying the moulding, working progressively towards the opposing end of the bumper. Just before the other end is reached, peel off the rest of the backing paper and then press and manipulate that end into its location in the bumper.

10   Refitting of the bumper to the car is a reversal of the removal procedure.

27 Rear bumper – removal and refitting

1   Remove the number plate lamps from the bumper, detach the wiring and bulbholders from each unit and extract them through their apertures in the bumper (see Section 25 in Chapter 11).

2   Open the boot lid then, reaching down in the luggage compartment, unscrew and remove the bumper support securing nuts from each side. Get an assistant to support the bumpers when removing these nuts, then withdraw the bumper, detaching the location pegs at each end from the retaining clip on the body.

3   The quarter bumpers can be removed by tapping them free from the main bumper using a soft drift or piece of wood. Remove the quarter bumper retaining tangs by pulling them free with pliers.

4   To remove the side retaining clip from the body panel each side rotate them through 90° and withdraw them.

5   To remove the moulding from the main bumper compress the retainer clip jaws together and simultaneously pull the moulding free.

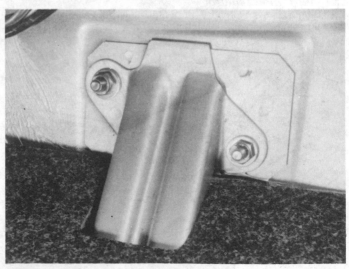

27.2 Rear bumper retaining nuts within luggage compartment

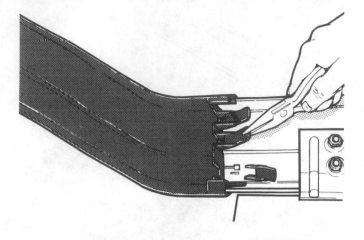

Fig. 12.26 Quarter bumper retaining tangs removal (Sec 27)

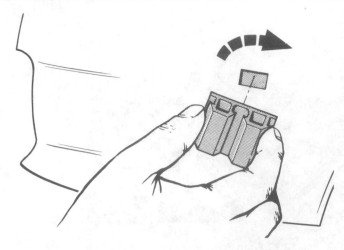

Fig. 12.27 Side retaining clip removal from wing panel (Sec 27)

Work in a progressive manner along the length of the bumper to release all of the clips.
6   Reassembly and refitting of the bumper is a reversal of the removal procedure.
7   Check that the main bumper moulding securing clips are fully engaged when fitted.
8   Position the quarter bumpers onto the main bumper and press them fully home so that the tangs engage.
9   When the bumper is refitted check that the number plate lights are operational when the lights are switched on.

28 Front spoiler – removal and refitting

1   The spoiler is in two sections, right- and left-hand.
2   Unscrew and remove the retaining screws from the wings and underpanel at the front edge, and also the retaining bolts within the wheel arch (photo).
3   Remove the spoiler, disengaging it from the location pegs.
4   Refit in the reverse order of removal.

29 Exterior mirror – removal and refitting

Without remote control
1   Using a screwdriver, prise off the triangular trim panel from inside the mirror mounting position (photo).

28.2 Spoiler securing bolt within front wheel arch (arrowed)

29.1 Remove trim panel for access to exterior mirror

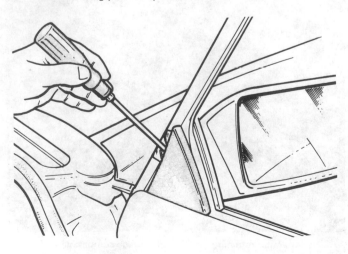

Fig. 12.28 Exterior mirror trim panel removal method (Sec 29)

2   Unscrew and remove the three mirror fixing screws and withdraw the mirror.

With remote control
3   Unscrew and remove the mirror actuator bezel nut from the triangular trim panel. A special wrench will be needed to release the nut but a C-spanner may serve as a suitable substitute.

All mirrors
4   Refitting both types of mirror is a reversal of removal.

---

30 Interior mirror – removal and refitting

---

1   The interior mirror is bonded to the windscreen glass. If it must be removed, use a length of thin nylon cord as shown (Fig. 12.29) to break the adhesive bond between the stem of the mirror and the windscreen patch.
2   When refitting the mirror, the following preliminary work must first be carried out.
3   Remove existing adhesive from the windscreen glass using a suitable solvent. Allow the solvent to evaporate. The location of the mirror base is marked on the glass with a black patch, so that there

should not be any chance of an error when fitting.
4   If the original mirror is being refitted, clean away all the old adhesive from the mirror mounting base, and apply a new adhesive patch to it.
5   If a new windscreen is being installed, peel off the protective layer from the black patch, which is pre-coated with adhesive.
6   Peel off the protective layer from the mirror adhesive patch and locate the mirror precisely onto the black patch on the screen. Hold it in position for at least two minutes.
7   For best results, the fitting of a bonded type mirror should be carried out in an ambient temperature of 70°C (158°F). The careful use of·a blower heater on both the glass and mirror should achieve this temperature level.

---

31 Centre console – removal and refitting

---

1   Unclip and pull off the console end cover or, where fitted, the console extension.
2   Remove the gear lever knob.
3   Pull the flexible gaiter up the control lever and remove it.
4   Extract the four securing screws and remove the console.
5   Refitting is a reversal of removal.

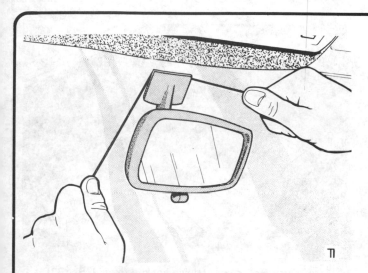

Fig. 12.29 Break adhesive bond of mirror to windscreen using cord (Sec 30)

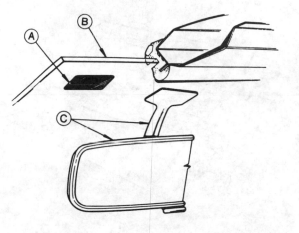

Fig. 12.30 Interior mirror mounting (Sec 30)

A   Adhesive black patch   C   Mirror and mounting stem
B   Windscreen

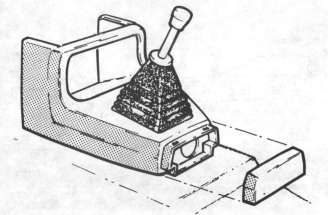

Fig. 12.31 Centre console end cover (Sec 31)

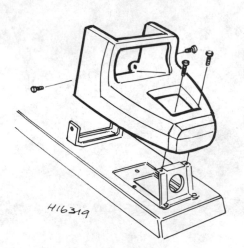

Fig. 12.32 Centre console retaining screws (Sec 31)

32 Front seat and slide – removal and refitting

1   Slide the seat as far forward as it will go.
2   Unscrew and remove the bolts which retain the rear of the seat slides to the floor pan.
3   Slide the seat as far to the rear as it will go and remove the bolts which secure the front ends of the slides to the floor.
4   Remove the seat from the vehicle interior.
5   If the seat slides must be detached from the seat, invert the seat and remove the two bolts from each side. Detach the cross-rod and clips.
6   Refitting is a reversal of removal. Tighten the front bolts before the rear ones to ensure that the seat is located evenly on the floor pan.

33 Rear seat – removal and refitting

Cushion

1   Unscrew and remove the Torx (socket-headed) screws from the seat cushion hinges which are located on each side.

2   Push the cushion rearwards and simultaneously lift it to disengage it from the retaining hook. Lift the cushion clear.

Backrest

3   Remove the rear seat cushion, as previously described.
4   Remove the seat back retaining screws (from the cushion side).
5   Unscrew and remove the upper retaining nuts, working from the luggage compartment side. Remove the backrest from within the vehicle.

Both parts

6   Refitting is a reversal of removal. Do not fully tighten the backrest securing screws until they are all in position.

34 Rear seat backrest release mechanism and cable – removal and refitting

1   Hinge the backrest forward, but should this not be possible, due to a broken catch or cable, remove the catch cover and manually release

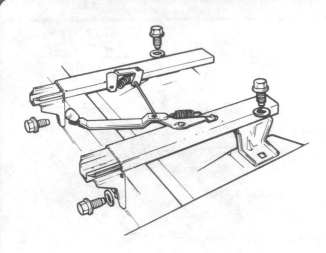

Fig. 12.33 Front seat mounting bolts (Sec 32)

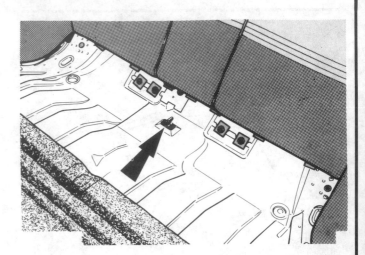

Fig. 12.34 Rear seat retaining hook (arrowed) (Sec 33)

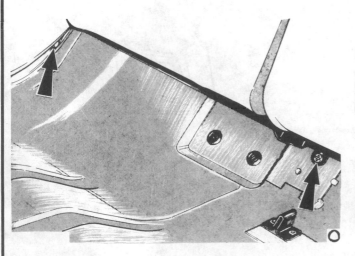

Fig. 12.35 Seat backrest retaining screws (arrowed) (Sec 33)

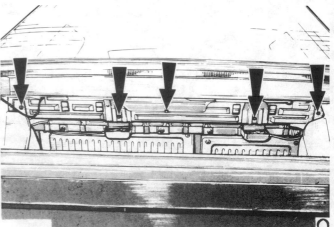

Fig. 12.36 Seat backrest retaining nuts on luggage compartment side (arrowed) (Sec 33)

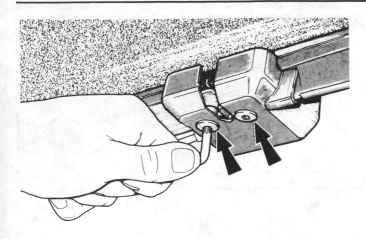

Fig. 12.37 Seat catch securing screws (Sec 34)

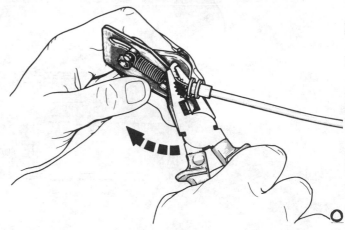

Fig. 12.38 Cable disconnection from catch (Sec 34)

the mechanism by reaching through from the luggage compartment side.
2   Remove the two securing screws from the catch and cover then detach the operating cable using suitable pliers as shown (Fig. 12.38).
3   Pull the operating handle and cable from the seat bracket by pushing down the cushion around the catch (to grip the operating handle for its removal).
4   Refit in reverse and, on completion, check operation.

35 Rear parcel shelf – removal and refitting

1   Remove the rear seat cushion and seat backrest, as described in Section 33.
2   Disconnect the leads to the parcel shelf mounted loudspeakers.
3   Disconnect the rear seat belts at their upper anchor points on the C-pillar, then remove the C-pillar trim panel securing screws and remove the trim.
4   Remove the parcel shelf retaining screws. Lift the shelf at its front edge and pull it free.
5   Refitting is a reversal of removal.

36 Glove compartment – removal and refitting

1   Open the glovebox lid and extract the screws which hold the glovebox to the crash pad.
2   Remove the latch (two screws).
3   Remove the single screw inside the top of the glove compartment which holds it to the moulded bracket. Withdraw the glove compartment.
4   Refitting is a reversal of removal.

37 Facia – removal and refitting

1   Disconnect the battery.
2   Refer to Chapter 9 and remove the steering wheel and the column shroud.
3   Remove the steering column switches and detach the electrical wiring harness.
4   Remove the underdash cover panels.
5   Unbolt the steering column mountings and carefully lower the assembly to rest on the front seat.
6   Remove the screw and detach the bonnet release lever.
7   Refer to Chapter 11 and remove the instrument cluster.
8   Detach the heater controls, switches and wiring multi-plugs, referring to Chapter 11 where necessary.
9   Remove the ashtray and cigar lighter mounting panel.
10 Remove the radio and its mounting bracket (Chapter 11)
11 Remove the glovebox (Section 36).
12 Remove the instrument warning module (Chapter 11).

13 Detach the vent ducts and demister hoses from the heater.
14 Extract the three securing screws and remove the facia panel complete with crash pad.
15 The crash padding can be detached by removing the glove compartment mounting bracket and lock bracket, withdrawing the side and centre face level vents and extracting all the securing clips.
16 Refitting is a reversal of removal. Check operation of all instruments and controls on completion.

38 Sunroof – adjustment

1   When correctly fitted the sunroof peripheral clearance to the car roof should be 8.23 ± 0.5 mm (0.32 ± 0.02 in). The front edge of the sunroof panel should be within 1 mm (0.04 in) below the roof line whilst the rear edge must be equally flush, but above the roof line.
2   The sunroof panel can be adjusted within its aperture and for flush fitting with the roof panel in the following way.
3   To correct the panel-to-aperture gap, bend the weatherstrip flange as necessary.
4   To adjust the panel height at its front edge, release the corner screws, raise or lower the panel as necessary and then tighten the screws.
5   To adjust the panel height at its rear edge, release the two screws at each side on the link assemblies and push the links up or down within the limits of the elongated screw holes. Retighten the screws when alignment is correct.

39 Sunroof panel – removal and refitting

1   To remove this type of glass panel, pull the sun blind into the open position and have the sliding roof closed.
2   Wind the sliding roof handle in an anti-clockwise direction for one complete turn.
3   Remove the three screws and clips which connect the lower frame and glass.
4   Turn the handle to close the sliding roof and remove the three screws from each side which hold the glass to the sliding gear.
5   Remove the glass panel by lifting it from the outside of the vehicle.
6   To refit the panel, have the roof closed, locate the glass and secure with the three screws on each side. Once the screws are secure give the handle one complete turn in a clockwise direction.
7   Set the glass to align with the roof panel and locate the lower frame to glass brackets. Insert the clips through the brackets.
8   Insert the retaining screws in the sequence shown in Fig. 12.41.

40 Sunroof sliding gear – removal and refitting

1   Remove the glass panel, as described in the preceding Section.
2   Turn the sliding roof regulator handle clockwise to the fully closed

272

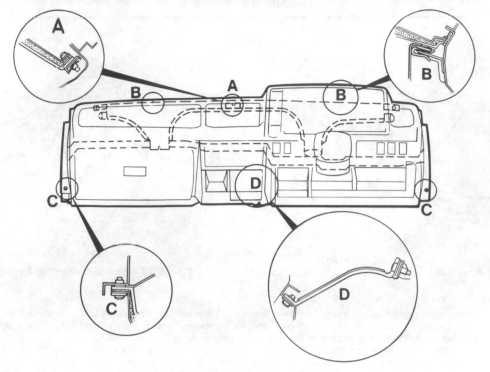

Fig. 12.39 Crash pad retainers (Sec 37)

A Screw   B Clip   C Screw   D Screw

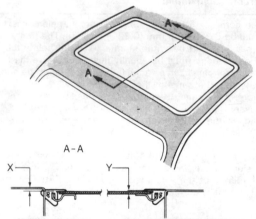

Fig. 12.40 Sunroof panel alignment diagram (Sec 38)

X Flush to within 1.0 mm below roof line
Y Flush to within 1.0 mm above roof line

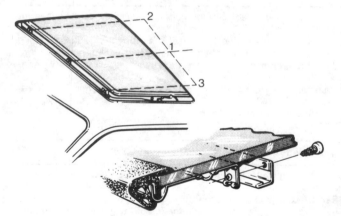

Fig. 12.41 Sunroof glass-to-frame screws. Numbers indicate insertion order (Sec 39)

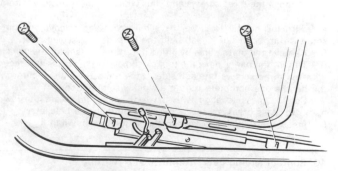

Fig. 12.42 Sunroof glass-to-gear screws (Sec 40)

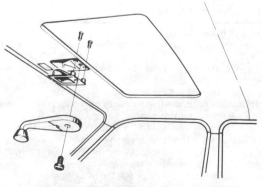

Fig. 12.43 Sliding roof handle and cup (Sec 40)

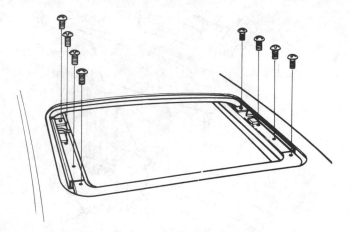

Fig. 12.44 Sliding roof gear-to-roof screws (Sec 40)

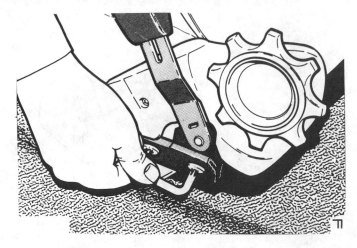

Fig. 12.45 Seat belt stalk removal (Sec 41)

position. Extract the three screws and remove the regulator handle and the handle cup.

3   Extract the four screws from each side which hold the sliding gear to the roof. Lift up the front of the gear and withdraw it from the front of the sliding roof aperture.

4   Refitting is a reversal of removal.

5   Adjust if necessary as described in Section 38.

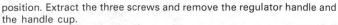

41 Seat belts – maintenance, removal and refitting

1   Periodically check the belts for fraying or other damage. If evident, renew the belt.

2   If the belts become dirty, wipe them with a damp cloth using a little liquid detergent only.

3   Check the tightness of the anchor bolts and if they are ever disconnected, make quite sure that the original sequence of fitting of washers, bushes and anchor plate is retained.

4   Never modify the belt or alter its attachment point to the body.

Front seat belt

5   On the side being worked on, push the seat back as far as its travel allows. Push the other front seat fully forward.

6   Detach the seat belt stalk from the seat frame.

7   Push free the upper seat belt anchor cover, then unscrew and remove the retaining bolt and spacers.

8   Unscrew the four pillar trim screws, pull the trim free then slide the belt webbing through the panel slot.

9   Unscrew the lower retaining bolt and remove the seat belt.

10   To refit, extend the belt, attach the upper mounting checking that the locator pin on the spacer engages in the location hole in the pillar. Tighten the bolt to the specified torque setting and refit the anchor cover.

11   Refit the reel assembly into the aperture in the pillar and check that the mounting plate tang locates in the inner door sill panel.

12   Locate the inertia reel retaining bolt and tighten it to the specified torque setting. The pillar trim can then be refitted.

13   Refit the belt stalk to the seat frame and tighten the retaining screws to the specified torque setting.

14   Check the seat belt for satisfactory operation when the seats are readjusted to their normal positions.

Rear seat belt

15   Remove the rear seat cushion and backrest, as described in Section 33.

16   Unscrew and remove the inertia reel webbing lower attachment bolts.

17   Prise free the belt upper attachment cover, then unscrew and remove the retaining bolt and fixings.

18   Manipulate the webbing free from the C-pillar trim then let the webbing rewind onto its reel.

19   Unscrew the retaining bolt and remove the inertia reel unit from

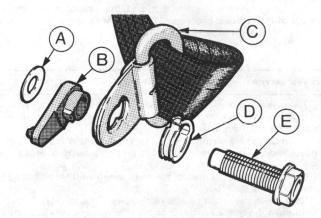

Fig. 12.46 Seat belt upper anchorage components (Sec 41)

A   Paper washer   D   Bush
B   Spacer and pin   E   Bolt
C   Anchor

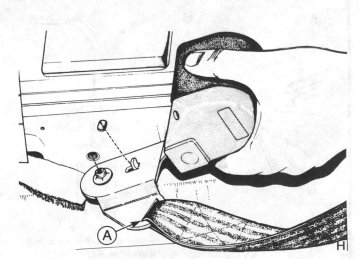

Fig. 12.47 Front seat belt inertia reel mounting showing lower webbing anchorage (A) and pillar aperture location tang and slot (Sec 41)

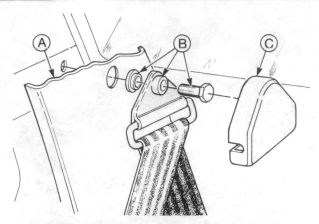

Fig. 12.48 Rear seat belt anchorage to C-pillar (Sec 41)

> A   Trim
> B   Anchor and fixings   C   Cover

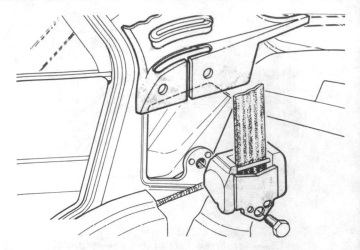

Fig. 12.49 Rear seat belt inertia reel retaining bolt (Sec 41)

the side panel. The remaining belt and buckle assemblies can be removed as necessary.
20 Refitting of the rear seat belts and the associate fittings is a reversal of the removal procedure. Tighten the retaining bolts to their specified torque settings.

42 Windscreen – removal and refitting

The average DIY mechanic is advised to leave windscreen removal and refitting to an expert. For the owner who insists on doing it himself, the following paragraphs are given.

1   All models are fitted with a laminated glass screen and in consequence, even if cracked, it will probably be removed as one piece.
2   Cover the bonnet in front of the windscreen with an old blanket to protect against scratching.
3   Remove the wiper arms and blades (see Chapter 11).
4   Remove the rear view mirror from the windscreen, as described in Section 30.
5   Working inside the vehicle, push the lip of the screen weatherseal under the top and the sides of the body aperture flange.
6   With an assistant standing outside the car to restrain the screen, push the glass complete with weatherseal out of the bodyframe.

7   Where fitted, extract the bright moulding from the groove in the weatherstrip and then pull the weatherstrip off the glass.
8   Unless the weatherstrip is in good condition, it should be renewed. If using the old weatherstrip, check that its glass groove is free from old sealant and glass chippings.
9   Check with a Ford dealer regarding the application of sealant to the weatherstrip before fitting. Various weatherstrip types are used, depending on model.
10 Commence refitting by fitting the weatherstrip to the glass. Locate a length of nylon or terylene cord in the body flange groove of the weatherstrip so that the ends of the cord emerge at the bottom centre and cross over by a length of about 150 mm (6.0 in).
11 Offer the screen to the body and engage the lower lip of the weatherstrip on its flange. With an assistant applying gentle, even pressure on the glass from the outside, pull the ends of the cord simultaneously at right-angles to the glass. This will pull the lip of the weatherstrip over the body flange. Continue until the cord is released from the centre top and the screen is fully fitted.
12 If a bright moulding was removed, refit it now. This can be one of the most difficult jobs to do without a special tool. The moulding should be pressed into its groove just after the groove lips have been prised open to receive it. Take care not to cut the weatherstrip if improvising with a made-up tool.
13 On completion, refit the rear view mirror, as described in Section 30.

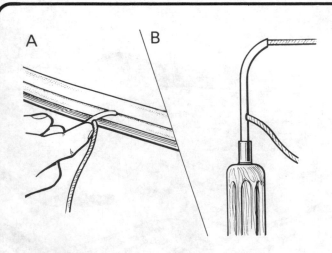

Fig. 12.50 Insert cord into weatherstrip as shown (A), using special tool (B) if available (Sec 42)

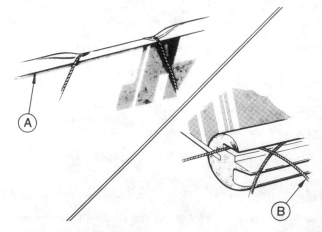

Fig. 12.51 Lip weatherstrip (A) over aperture flange with draw-cord ends crossed over (B) (Sec 42)

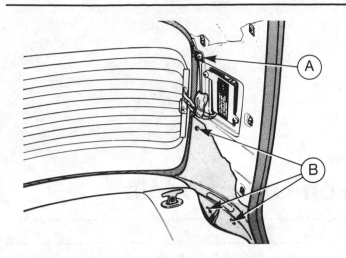

Fig. 12.52 Rear window showing C pillar trim, retaining clamp (A) and trim securing screws (B) (Sec 43)

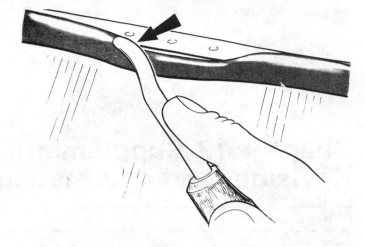

Fig. 12.53 Prise weatherstrip underneath the rear window surround aperture flange (Sec 43)

43 Rear window – removal and refitting

1 The advisory notes given in the previous Section are also applicable for the rear window.
2 Cover the boot lid and rear wings with a suitable cloth to avoid damaging or scratching them.
3 From inside the car, remove the C panel trims by disconnecting the rear seat belt upper mountings and folding down the rear seat backrest. Unscrew the securing screws (five a side) and withdraw the trim panel.

4 Disconnect the wiring to the rear window element and remove the weatherstrip clamps.
5 Using a suitable lipped tool and working from the inside, prise the weatherstrip lip under the side and top aperture surround flanges.
6 With an assistant outside the car to restrain the window, push the glass and weatherseal out of the aperture.
7 Refitting is a reversal of the removal procedure and similar to the instructions given in the previous Section for windscreen refitment, see paragraphs 8 to 12 inclusive.
8 With the window in position reconnect the element wires and refit the C-panel trim on each side.

Chapter 13 Supplement:
Revisions and information on later models

Contents

1 Introduction

Since its inception in 1983 the Ford Orion has been modified in several areas to keep pace with current technological innovations.

At the beginning of 1986 a 1.3 litre OHV engine was introduced to replace the 1.3 CVH engine. At the same time a 1.4 litre CVH engine became available.

In 1989 the 1.3 litre OHV engine was modified to take account of Ford's lean burn technology, resulting in the 1.3 OHV HCS (High Compression Swirl) engine, incorporating an electronic distributorless ignition system (DIS).

In 1990, the 1.4 litre CVH CFi (Central Fuel Injection) engine with an exhaust catalyst, and the 1.6 litre CVH EFI EEC-IV (Electronic Fuel Injection with Electronic Engine Control) were introduced, incorporating the latest in engine management systems.

Other changes include modifications to the bodywork, electrical and interior components, and a new optional anti-lock braking system. Other minor changes to the transmission, suspension and steering systems have also been carried out.

The Supplement contains information which is additional to, or a revision of, the material in the first twelve Chapters.

The Sections in this Supplement follow the same order as the Chapters to which they relate. The Specifications are all grouped together at the beginning for convenience, and also follow Chapter order.

It is recommended that before any work is started, reference is made to the appropriate Section(s) of the Supplement in order to establish any changes to procedures or specifications before reading the main Chapter(s).

The models used in the preparation of this Supplement and in many of the photographic sequences were a 1989 Orion L fitted with a 1.3 litre OHV HCS engine and a 1990 model Orion GLS with a 1.6 litre EFI EEC-IV engine.

2   Specifications

The specifications listed below are revisions of, or supplementary to, the main Specifications listed at the beginning of each Chapter

Engine (1.3 litre OHV)
General
Engine type	Four-cylinder, in-line overhead valve
Engine code	JLA
Power output (DIN)	60 PS (44 kW) at 5000 rpm
Maximum torque (DIN)	74 lbf ft (100 Nm) at 3000 rpm
Bore	73.96 mm (2.91 in)
Stroke	75.48 mm (2.97 in)
Cubic capacity	1297 cc
Compression ratio	9.3:1

Cylinder block
Material	Cast iron
Number of main bearings	5
Cylinder bore (diameter):	
Standard (1)	73.940 to 73.950 mm (2.9110 to 2.9114 in)
Standard (2)	73.950 to 73.960 mm (2.9114 to 2.9118 in)
Standard (3)	73.960 to 73.970 mm (2.9118 to 2.9122 in)
Standard (4)	73.970 to 73.980 mm (2.9122 to 2.9126 in)
Oversize 0.5 mm	74.500 to 74.510 mm (2.9331 to 2.9335 in)
Oversize 1.0 mm	75.000 to 75.010 mm (2.9528 to 2.9531 in)
Main bearing shell inner diameter:	
Standard	57.009 to 57.036 mm (2.2444 to 2.2455 in)
0.254 mm undersize	56.755 to 56.782 mm (2.2344 to 2.2355 in)
0.508 mm undersize	56.501 to 56.528 mm (2.2244 to 2.2255 in)
0.762 mm undersize	56.247 to 56.274 mm (2.2144 to 2.2155 in)
Camshaft bearing inner diameter	39.662 to 39.682 mm (1.5615 to 1.5623 in)

Crankshaft
Main bearing journal diameter:	
Standard	56.990 to 57.000 mm (2.2437 to 2.2441 in)
0.254 mm undersize	56.726 to 56.746 mm (2.3330 to 2.2341 in)
0.508 mm undersize	56.472 to 56.492 mm (2.2233 to 2.2241 in)
0.762 mm undersize	56.218 to 56.238 mm (2.2133 to 2.2141 in)
Main bearing running clearance	0.009 to 0.046 mm (0.0004 to 0.0018 in)
Main bearing running clearance wear limit	5.056 mm (0.0022 in)
Crankpin (big-end) diameter:	
Standard	42.99 to 43.01 mm (1.6925 to 1.6933 in)
0.254 mm undersize	42.74 to 42.76 mm (1.6827 to 1.6835 in)
0.508 mm undersize	42.49 to 42.51 mm (1.6728 to 1.6736 in)
0.762 mm undersize	42.24 to 42.26 mm (1.6630 to 1.6638 in)
Thrust washer thickness:	
Standard	2.80 to 2.85 mm (0.1102 to 0.1122 in)
Oversize	2.99 to 3.04 mm (0.1177 to 0.1197 in)
Crankshaft endfloat	0.079 to 0.279 mm (0.0031 to 0.0110 in)
Maximum permissible journal and crankpin ovality and taper	0.0254 mm (0.001 in)

Camshaft
Number of bearings	3
Drive	Single chain
Thrust plate thickness	4.457 to 4.508 mm (0.175 to 0.177 in)
Inlet cam lift	5.300 mm (0.209 in)
Exhaust cam lift	5.300 mm (0.209 in)
Inlet cam length	32.288 to 32.516 mm (1.272 to 1.281 in)
Exhaust cam length	32.618 to 32.846 mm (1.285 to 1.294 in)
Camshaft bearing diameter	39.615 to 39.636 mm (1.561 to 1.562 in)
Camshaft bearing bush internal diameter	39.662 to 39.682 mm (1.563 to 1.564 in)
Camshaft endfloat	0.02 to 0.19 mm (0.0008 to 0.0075 in)

Piston and piston rings

Diameter:

Standard (1)	73.910 to 73.920 mm (2.9098 to 2.9012 in)
Standard (2)	73.920 to 73.930 mm (2.9102 to 2.9106 in)
Standard (3)	73.930 to 73.940 mm (2.9106 to 2.9110 in)
Standard (4)	73.940 to 73.950 mm (2.9110 to 2.9114 in)
0.5 mm oversize	74.460 to 74.485 mm (2.9315 to 2.9325 in)
1.0 mm oversize	74.960 to 74.985 mm (2.9152 to 2.9522 in)
Piston-to-bore clearance	0.015 to 0.050 mm (0.006 to 0.0020 in)

Piston ring end gap:

Compression	0.25 to 0.45 mm (0.010 to 0.018 in)
Oil control	0.20 to 0.40 mm (0.008 to 0.016 in)

Gudgeon pin

Pin length	63.0 to 63.8 mm (2.48 to 2.51 in)

Pin diameter:

White	20.622 to 20.625 mm (0.8118 to 0.8120 in)
Red	20.625 to 20.628 mm (0.8120 to 0.8121 in)
Blue	20.628 to 20.631 mm (0.8121 to 0.8122 in)
Yellow	20.631 to 20.634 mm (0.8122 to 0.8124 in)
Interference fit in connecting rod at 21°C (70°F)	0.013 to 0.045 mm (0.0005 to 0.0017 in)
Clearance in piston at 21°C (70°F)	0.005 to 0.011 mm (0.0002 to 0.0004 in)

Cylinder head

Material	Cast iron
Maximum permissible cylinder head distortion measured over entire length	0.15 mm (0.006 in)
Minimum combustion chamber depth after skimming	9.07 mm (0.357 in)
Valve seat angle	45°

Valve seat width:

Inlet	1.20 to 1.75 mm (0.047 to 0.068 in)
Exhaust	1.20 to 1.70 mm (0.047 to 0.067 in)

Seat cutter correction angle:

Upper	30°
Lower	75°
Valve guide bore (standard)	7.907 to 7.938 mm (0.311 to 0.312 in)

Valves – general

Operation	Cam followers and pushrods

Valve timing:

Inlet valve opens	14° BTDC
Inlet valve closes	46° ABDC
Exhaust valve opens	65° BBDC
Exhaust valve closes	11° ATDC

Valve clearances (cold):

Inlet	0.22 mm (0.009 in)
Exhaust	0.59 mm (0.023 in)
Cam follower diameter	13.081 to 13.094 mm (0.515 to 0.516 in)
Cam follower clearance in bore	0.016 to 0.062 mm (0.0006 to 0.0024 in)
Valve spring free length	42.4 mm (1.67 in)

Inlet valve

Length	105.45 to 106.45 mm (4.155 to 4.194 in)
Head diameter	38.02 to 38.28 mm (1.498 to 1.508 in)

Stem diameter:

Standard	7.866 to 7.868 mm (0.309 to 0.3010 in)
0.076 mm oversize	7.944 to 7.962 mm (0.3130 to 0.3137 in)
0.38 mm oversize	8.249 to 8.267 mm (0.3250 to 0.3257 in)
Valve stem clearance in guide	0.021 to 0.070 mm (0.0008 to 0.0028 in)
Valve lift	8.367 mm (0.330 in)

Exhaust valve

Length	106.04 to 107.04 mm (4.178 to 4.217 in)
Head diameter	29.01 to 29.27 mm (1.142 to 1.153 in)

Stem diameter:

Standard	7.846 to 7.864 mm (0.3089 to 0.3096 in)
0.076 mm oversize	7.922 to 7.940 mm (0.3119 to 0.3126 in)
0.38 mm oversize	8.227 to 8.245 mm (0.3239 to 0.3246 in)
Valve stem clearance in guide	0.043 to 0.092 mm (0.0017 to 0.0036 in)
Valve lift	8.367 mm (0.330 in)

Lubrication

Oil pump type	Rotor, external drive by gear on camshaft
Minimum oil pressure at 80°C (175°F):	
Engine speed 750 rpm	0.6 bar (8.5 lbf/in²)
Engine speed 2000 rpm	1.5 bar (21.3 lbf/in²)
Oil pressure warning lamp operates	0.32 to 0.53 bar (4.5 to 7.5 lbf/in²)
Relief valve opens	2.41 to 2.75 bar (34.3 to 39.1 lbf/in²)
Oil pump clearances:	
Outer rotor-to-body	0.14 to 0.26 mm (0.0055 to 0.0102 in)
Inner rotor-to-body	0.051 to 0.127 mm (0.0020 to 0.0050 in)
Rotor endfloat	0.25 to 0.06 mm (0.0010 to 0.0024 in)
Oil filter	Champion C104
Engine oil capacity:	
Without filter change	2.75 litre (4.8 pints)
With filter change	3.25 litre (5.7 pints)
Engine oil type/specification	Multigrade engine oil, viscosity SAE 10W/30 to API SF/CD (Duckhams QXR, Hypergrade or 10W/40 Motor oil)

Torque wrench settings

	Nm	lbf ft
Main bearing cap bolts	88 to 102	65 to 75
Connecting rod (big end) bolts	29 to 36	21 to 27
Rear oil seal retainer bolts	16 to 20	12 to 15
Flywheel bolts	64 to 70	47 to 52
Timing chain tensioner	7 to 9	5 to 7
Camshaft thrust plate	4 to 5	3 to 4
Camshaft sprocket bolt	16 to 20	12 to 15
Timing cover bolts	7 to 10	5 to 8
Crankshaft pulley bolt	54 to 59	40 to 44
Oil pump to crankcase	16 to 20	12 to 15
Oil pump cover bolts	8 to 12	6 to 9
Sump bolts:		
Stage 1	6 to 8	4 to 6
Stage 2	8 to 11	6 to 8
Stage 3 (after 15 minute warm-up)	8 to 11	6 to 8
Sump drain plug	21 to 28	15 to 21
Oil pressure switch	13 to 15	10 to 11
Rocker shaft pedestal bolts	40 to 46	30 to 34
Cylinder head bolts:		
Stage 1	10 to 15	8 to 11
Stage 2	40 to 50	30 to 37
Stage 3	80 to 90	59 to 66
Stage 4 (after 10 to 20 minutes)	100 to 110	74 to 81
Rocker cover	4 to 5	3 to 4
Engine to transmission	35 to 45	26 to 33
Right-hand engine mounting to body	41 to 58	30 to 43
Right-hand engine mounting bracket to engine	54 to 72	40 to 53
Right-hand engine mounting rubber insulator to brackets	70 to 95	52 to 70
Left-hand engine mounting to transmission	28 to 40	21 to 30
Left-hand engine mounting rubber insulator nuts	41 to 58	30 to 43
Transmission mountings to transmission	80 to 100	59 to 74
Transmission support crossmember to body	52	38
Exhaust manifold bolts	21 to 25	15 to 18
Inlet manifold bolts	16 to 20	12 to 15

Engine (1.3 litre HCS)

Specifications as for 1.3 litre OHV engine except for the following

General

Engine code	JBA
Compression ratio	9.5 to 1
Power output (DIN)	63 PS (46 kW) at 5000 rpm

Cylinder block

Cylinder bore diameter	As for 1.3 litre OHV engine but there is no 4th standard oversize

Crankshaft

Crankpin (big-end) diameter:	
Standard	40.99 to 41.01 mm (1.6150 to 1.6157 in)
0.254 mm undersize	40.74 to 40.76 mm (1.6051 to 1.6059 in)
0.508 mm undersize	40.49 to 40.51 mm (1.5933 to 1.5960 in)
0.762 mm undersize	40.24 to 40.26 mm (1.5854 to 1.5862 in)
Main bearing running clearance	0.009 to 0.056 mm (0.0003 to 0.002 in)
Big-end bearing running clearance	0.006 to 0.060 mm (0.0002 to 0.002 in)
Crankshaft endfloat	0.075 to 0.285 mm (0.0029 to 0.012 in)

Camshaft
Inlet cam lift .... 5.70 mm (0.224 in)
Exhaust cam lift .... 5.76 mm (0.226 in)
Inlet cam length .... 32.586 to 32.814 mm (1.283 to 1.292 in)
Exhaust cam length .... 32.646 to 33.874 mm (1.286 to 1.334 in)

Connecting rod
Bore diameter:
  Big-end .... 43.99 to 44.01 mm (1.733 to 1.734 in)
  Small-end .... 17.99 to 18.01 mm (0.708 to 0.795 in)
Connecting rod endfloat .... 0.10 to 0.25 mm (0.0039 to 0.0098 in)
Note: *the HCS engine has four connecting rod weight classes, A, B, C and D stamped on the rod opposite the oil drilling*

Gudgeon pin
Pin length .... 63.6 to 64.4 mm (2.505 to 2.537 in)
Pin diameter:
  White .... 18.026 to 18.029 mm (0.7102 to 0.7103 in)
  Red .... 18.029 to 19.032 mm (0.7103 to 0.7498 in)
  Blue .... 18.032 to 18.035 mm (0.7104 to 0.7105 in)
  Yellow .... 18.035 to 18.038 mm (0.7105 to 0.716 in)
Interference fit in connecting rod at 21°C (70°F) .... 0.013 to 0.048 mm (0.0005 to 0.0018 in)
Clearance in piston at 21°C (70°F) .... 0.008 to 0.014 mm (0.0003 to 0.0005 in)

Cylinder head
Minimum combustion chamber depth after skimming .... 14.4 ± 0.15 mm (0.567 ± 0.005 in)
Valve seat width .... 1.18 to 1.75 mm (0.046 to 0.068 in)
(Note: *No repair to valve seats using conventional tools is possible)*

Valves – general
Valve timing:
  Inlet opens .... 16° BTDC
  Inlet closes .... 44° ABDC
  Exhaust opens .... 51° BBDC
  Exhaust closes .... 9° ATDC
Valve clearances (cold):
  Inlet .... 0.22 mm (0.008 in)
  Exhaust .... 0.32 mm (0.012 in)
Valve spring free length .... 41.0 mm (1.615 in)

Inlet valve
Length .... 103.70 to 104.40 mm (4.085 to 4.113 in)
Head diameter .... 34.40 to 34.60 mm (1.355 to 1.363 in)
Stem diameter:
  Standard .... 7.025 to 7.043 mm (0.276 to 0.277 in)
  0.76 mm oversize .... 7.225 to 7.243 mm (0.284 to 0.235 in)
  0.381 mm oversize .... 7.425 to 7.443 mm (0.292 to 0.293 in)
Valve stem clearance in guide .... 0.021 to 0.690 mm (0.0008 to 0.027 in)
Valve lift .... 9.350 mm (0.368 in)

Exhaust valve
Length .... 104.02 to 104.72 mm (4.098 to 4.125 in)
Head diameter .... 28.90 to 29.10 mm (1.138 to 1.146 in)
Stem diameter:
  Standard .... 6.999 to 7.017 mm (0.275 to 0.276 in)
  0.076 mm oversize .... 7.199 to 7.217 mm (0.283 to 0.284 in)
  0.381 mm oversize .... 7.399 to 7.417 mm (0.291 to 0.292 in)
Valve stem clearance in guide .... 0.043 to 0.091 mm (0.001 to 0.003 in)
Valve lift .... 9.450 mm (0.372 in)

Torque wrench settings
As for OHV engine except for the following

	Nm	lbf ft
Big-end bearing cap bolts:		
Stage 1	4	3
Stage 2	Tighten by a further 90°	Tighten by a further 90°
Crankshaft pulley bolt	100 to 120	74 to 89
Cylinder head bolts (M11 – necked):		
Stage 1	30	22
Stage 2	Tighten by a further 90°	Tighten by a further 90°
Stage 3	Tighten by a further 90°	Tighten by a further 90°

Engine (1.3 and 1.6 litre CVH, up to 1990)

Oil pump
Clearances – gear type pump – mm (in):

Outer rotor-to-housing	0.069 to 0.140 (0.0027 to 0.0055)
Inner rotor-to-housing	0.070 to 0.165 (0.0028 to 0.0065)
Rotor-to-cover endfloat	0.028 to 0.078 (0.0011 to 0.0031)

Clearances – rotor type pump – mm (in):

Outer rotor-to-housing	0.060 to 0.190 (0.0024 to 0.0075)
Inner-to-outer rotor	0.050 to 0.180 (0.0020 to 0.0071)
Rotor-to-cover endfloat	0.014 to 0.100 (0.0006 to 0.0039)
Oil filter	Champion C104

Engine (1.4 litre CVH carburettor)
The Specifications are the same as for the 1.3 litre CVH engine given at the beginning of Chapter 1, except for the following

General
Data:

Engine code	FUA
Power output (DIN)	75 PS (55 kW) at 5600 rpm
Maximum torque	80.4 lbf ft (109 Nm) at 4000 rpm
Bore	77.24 mm (3.04 in)
Stroke	74.30 mm (2.93 in)
Cubic capacity	1392 cc

Cylinder block
Cylinder bore diameter – mm (in):

Standard (1)	77.220 to 77.230 (3.0402 to 3.0406)
Standard (2)	77.230 to 77.240 (3.0406 to 3.0409)
Standard (3)	77.240 to 77.250 (3.0409 to 3.0413)
Standard (4)	77.250 to 77.260 (3.0413 to 3.0417)
Oversize (A)	77.510 to 77.520 (3.0516 to 3.0520)
Oversize (B)	77.520 to 77.530 (3.0520 to 3.0524)
Oversize (C)	77.530 to 77.540 (3.0524 to 3.0528)
Oversize 0.29	77.525 to 77.535 (3.0522 to 3.0526)
Oversize 0.50	77.745 to 77.755 (3.0608 to 3.0612)

Pistons and piston rings
Diameter – mm (in):

Standard (1)	77.190 to 77.200 (3.0390 to 3.0394)
Standard (2)	77.200 to 77.210 (3.0394 to 3.0398)
Standard (3)	77.210 to 77.220 (3.0398 to 3.0402)
Standard (4)	77.220 to 77.230 (3.0402 to 3.0406)
Standard service	77.210 to 77.235 (3.0398 to 3.0407)
Oversize (A)	77.480 to 77.490 (3.0504 to 3.0508)
Oversize (B)	77.490 to 77.500 (3.0508 to 3.0512)
Oversize (C)	77.500 to 77.510 (3.0512 to 3.0516)
Oversize 0.29	77.490 to 77.515 (3.0508 to 3.0518)
Oversize 0.50	77.710 to 77.735 (3.0594 to 3.0604)

Gudgeon pin length (1990 – on)
63.000 to 63.800 mm (2.4822 to 2.5137 in)

Cylinder head
Minimum combustion chamber depth (after refacing) – mm (in)   17.40 (0.685)

Valve timing

Inlet valve opens	15° ATDC
Inlet valve closes	30° ABDC
Exhaust valve opens	28° BBDC
Exhaust valve closes	13° BTDC

Inlet valve

Length – mm (in)	136.29 to 136.75 (5.368 to 5.384)
Head diameter – mm (in)	39.90 to 40.10 (1.571 to 1.579)

Stem diameter – mm (in):

Standard	8.025 to 8.043 (0.316 to 0.317)
Oversize 0.2	8.225 to 8.243 (0.324 to 0.325)
Oversize 0.4	8.425 to 8.443 (0.331 to 0.332)

Exhaust valve

Length – mm (in)	132.97 to 133.43 (5.235 to 5.253)
Head diameter – mm (in)	33.90 to 34.10 (1.335 to 1.343)

Stem diameter – mm (in):

Standard	7.999 to 8.017 (0.315 to 0.316)
Oversize 0.2	8.199 to 8.217 (0.323 to 0.324)
Oversize 0.4	8.399 to 8.417 (0.330 to 0.331)

Lubrication

Oil pump type	Rotor, driven by crankshaft
Oil pump clearances – mm (in):	
Outer rotor-to-housing	0.060 to 0.190 (0.0024 to 0.0075)
Inner-to-outer rotor	0.050 to 0.180 (0.0020 to 0.0071)
Rotor-to-cover endfloat	0.014 to 0.100 (0.0006 to 0.0039)
Oil filter	Champion C104

Engine (1.4 litre CVH CFi)
As carburettor 1.4 litre CVH except for the following

General

Engine code	F6D
Compression ratio	8.5 to 1
Power output (DIN)	73 PS (54 kW) at 5600 rpm
Maximum torque (DIN)	76 lbf/ft (103 Nm) at 4000 rpm

Engine (1.6 litre CVH carburettor, 1986-on)
As earlier 1.6 litre CVH carburettor engine except for the following

General

Engine code	LUC
Power output (DIN)	90 PS (66 kW) at 5800 rpm
Maximum torque (DIN)	98 lbf ft (103 Nm) at 4000 rpm

Camshaft

Camlift (inlet and exhaust)	6.09 mm (0.2399 in)
Cam length (heel-to-toe):	
Inlet	38.606 mm (1.5199 in)
Exhaust	37.590 mm (1.4799 in)

Valves

Valve timing:	
Inlet valve opens	4° ATDC
Inlet valve closes	32° ABDC
Exhaust valve opens	38° BBDC
Exhaust valve closes	10° BTDC
Valve lift:	
Inlet	10.09 mm (0.3975 in)
Exhaust	10.06 mm (0.3963 in)

Engine (1.6 CVH EFI)
As for earlier 1.6 engines except for the following:

General

Engine code	LJA
Power output (DIN)	108 PS (79 kW) at 6000 rpm
Maximum torque (DIN)	102 lbf ft (138 Nm) at 4800 rpm
Compression ratio	9.75 to 1

Pistons and piston rings

Piston diameter:	
Standard 1	79.915 to 79.925 mm (3.1486 to 3.1490 in)
Standard 2	79.925 to 79.935 mm (3.1490 to 3.1494 in)
Standard 3	79.935 to 79.945 mm (3.1494 to 3.1498 in)
Standard 4	79.945 to 79.955 mm (3.1498 to 3.1502 in)
Standard service	79.935 to 79.955 mm (3.1494 to 3.1498 in)
Oversize 0.29 mm	79.215 to 79.235 mm (3.1289 to 3.1218 in)
Oversize 0.50 mm	80.435 to 80.455 mm (3.1691 to 3.1699 in)
Piston-to-bore clearance (service)	0.010 to 0.040 mm (0.0003 to 0.0015 in)

Piston ring gap

Compression	0.30 to 0.50 mm (0.011 to 0.019 in)
Oil control	0.25 to 0.40 mm (0.009 to 0.015 in)

Gudgeon pin

Pin length	63.00 mm (2.482 in)

Valve (general)

Valve lift:	
Inlet	10.80 mm (0.425 in)
Exhaust	10.80 mm (0.425 in)
Valve timing:	
Inlet valve opens	4° BTDC
Inlet valve closes	30° ABDC
Exhaust valve opens	44° BBDC
Exhaust valve closes	10° ATDC

Torque wrench settings
(applicable to all CVH engines)

	Nm	lbf ft
Oil pump cover	10	7
Sump (with one piece gasket)	7	5
Left-hand engine mounting to transmission (1986 models onwards)	36	26
Left-hand engine mounting rubber insulator nuts (1986 models onwards)	50	40
Right-hand engine mounting to body (1986 models onwards)	50	40
Right-hand engine mounting rubber insulator to bracket (1986 models onwards)	50	40
Right-hand engine mounting bracket to engine (1986 models onward)	90	66
Transmission mountings to transmission (1986 models onward)	90	66
Transmission to crossmember to body (1986 models onward)	52	38
Cylinder head bolts:		
Stage 1	30	22
Stage 2	50	40
Stage 3	Tighten through further 90°	Tighten through further 90°
Stage 4	Tighten through further 90° from Stage 3	Tighten through further 90° from Stage 3

Note: *Cylinder head bolts must not be retorqued*

	Nm	lbf ft
Timing belt cover	10	7

Cooling system CVH engine (1990-on)

Coolant capacity:
- 1.4 litre .... 7.6 litres (13.4 pints)
- 1.6 litre .... 7.8 litres (13.7 pints)

Thermostat (all models):
- Temperature when fully open .... 102°C (223°F) allow tolerance of ± 3°C (5°F) for used thermostat

Torque wrench settings

	Nm	lbf ft
Thermostat housing (OHV engines)	17 to 21	13 to 15
Water pump (OHV engines)	7 to 10	5 to 7
Water pump pulley	9 to 11	6 to 8

Fuel and exhaust systems

Ford VV carburettor specification

Application	1.3 litre OHV engines
Part number	86 BF 9510 KAA
Idle speed (cooling fan on)	750 to 850 rpm
Idle CO content	1.0 to 2.0%
Air cleaner	Champion W153

Weber carburettor specification

Weber 2V DFTM:

Application	1.4 litre engines
Idle speed (cooling fan on)	750 to 850 rpm
Idle CO content	1.25 to 1.75%
Throttle kicker speed	1250 to 1350 rpm
Fast idle speed	2600 to 2800 rpm
Choke pull-down	2.7 to 3.2 mm (0.10 to 0.12 in)
Float height	7.5 to 8.5 mm (0.30 to 0.33 in)

	Primary	Secondary
Venturi diameter	21 mm	23 mm
Air correction jet	200	165
Emulsion tube	F22	F60
Idle jet	42	60
Main jet	102	125
Air cleaner	Champion W179	

Weber 2V TLD:

Application	1.6 litre engines (1986-on)
Idle speed (cooling fan on):	
Manual transmission	750 to 850 rpm
Automatic transmission	850 to 950 rpm
Idle mixture CO content:	
Up to 1990	1.0 to 2.0%
1990-on	1.25 to 1.75%
Throttle kicker speed	1050 to 1150 rpm
Fast idle speed:	
Manual transmission	1850 to 1950 rpm
Automatic transmission	1950 to 2050 rpm
Choke pull-down:	
Manual transmission	4.0 to 5.0 mm (0.15 to 0.19 in)
Automatic transmission	3.5 to 4.5 mm (0.13 to 0.17 in)
Float height	28.5 to 29.5 mm (1.12 to 1.16 in)

	Primary	Secondary
Venturi diameter	21 mm	23 mm
Air correction jet	185	125
Emulsion tube	F105	F71
Main jet:		
Manual transmission	117	127
Automatic transmission	115	130
Air cleaner	Champion W201	

Weber 2V TLDM:
Application	1.3 HCS engine	
Idle speed (fan on)	700 to 800 rpm	
Idle mixture (CO content)	0.5 to 1.5%	
Fast idle speed	2500 rpm	
Float height	28.0 to 30.0 mm (1.10 to 1.18 in)	

	Primary	Secondary
Venturi diameter	26	28
Main jet	90	122
Emulsion tube	F113	F75
Air correction jet	185	130
Air cleaner	Champion W153	

Fuel requirement
Fuel octane rating (HCS engines)	97 RON (leaded) or 95 RON (unleaded)

Electronic Fuel Injection EEC-IV
Application	1.6 litre fuel injection models, 1990-on
Idle speed	850 to 950 rpm
Mixture (CO content) at idle	0.55 to 1.05%
Fuel pump:	
Make	Ford
Type	In-tank, electric, roller cell
Output	Greater than 3.0 bar (43.5 lbf/in^2)
Pressure regulator:	
Type	Weber
Control pressure:	
Engine running	2.3 to 2.7 bar (33.3 to 39.1 lbf/in^2)
Engine off	3.0 bar (43.5 lbf/in^2)
Lubricant for pressure regulator seals	Clean engine oil
Injectors:	
Make	Weber
Type	Electronic
Lubricant for injector seals	Clean engine oil

Air cleaner element
	Champion U502

Fuel filter
	Champion L204

Torque wrench settings
	Nm	lbf ft
Idle speed control valve bolts	4	3
Fuel pressure regulator bolts	10	7
Fuel rail retaining bolts	23	17
Air charge temperature sensor	15	11
Engine coolant temperature sender	15	11
Fuel filter unions	17	12.5

Central Fuel Injection (Catalyst)
Application	1.4 litre fuel injection models, 1990-on
Idle speed	850 to 950 rpm (only adjustable in service set mode)
Engine speed in service set mode 60	1150 to 1250 rpm (when adjusted and self test disengaged normal idle speed should be obtained)
Fuel pump:	
Make	Bosch
Type	Electric, roller cell
Output pressure	Greater than 3.0 bar (43.5 lbf/in^2) at 12 volts, engine off
CFi unit:	
Make	Weber
Fuel delivery	Electronic injector
Pressure regulator	Diaphragm operated
Regulated pressure	0.5 to 1.5 bar (7.2 to 21.7 lbf/in^2)
Silicone grease for injector seals	ESEM-1C171A

Torque wrench settings
	Nm	lbf ft
CFi unit to intake manifold	14	10
Fuel filter unions	18	13

Torque wrench settings (continued)

	Nm	lbf ft
Engine coolant temperature sensor	23	17
Air charge temperature sensor	23	17
HEGO sensor	60	44
Knock sensor	18	13

Ignition system (1.3 litre OHV engines)

General
System type	Breakerless electronic
Ignition timing:	
For leaded fuel	6° BTDC
For unleaded fuel	2° BTDC
Advance at 2000 rpm, no load, crankshaft degrees (initial advance not included):	
Mechanical	5° to 12.5°
Vacuum	14° to 22°
Total	19° to 34.5°

Distributor
Make	Bosch 86BF-FA
Automatic advance method	Mechanical and vacuum
Drive	Skew gear on camshaft
Rotation	Anti-clockwise
Dwell angle	Non-adjustable (governed by ignition amplifier module)
Firing order	1-2-4-3 (No 1 cylinder at crankshaft pulley end)

Coil
Output (open circuit condition)	25 kV (minimum)
Primary resistance	0.72 to 0.88 ohms
Secondary resistance	4500 to 7000 ohms

Spark plugs
Type	Champion RS9YCC or RS9YC
Electrode gap:	
Champion RS9YCC	0.8 mm (0.032 in)
Champion RS9YC	0.7 mm (0.028 in)

HT leads
	Champion CLS 8 boxed set

Torque wrench settings
	Nm	lbf ft
Spark plugs	13 to 20	10 to 15
Distributor clamp pinch-bolt	4	3
Distributor clamp plate bolt	10	7

Ignition system – (HCS engine)

3-D Electronic ignition system 1989-on
Application	1.3 litre HCS engine
Type	Fully electronic, distributorless ignition
Ignition timing:	
For leaded fuel	15° BTDC
For unleaded fuel	15° BTDC
Firing order	1-2-4-3

Coil
Type	High output
Output	37kV (minimum) open circuit
Primary resistance (measured at coil)	0.50 to 1.00 ohms

Spark plugs
Type	Champion RS9YCC or RS9YC
Electrode gap:	
Champion RS9YCC	0.8 mm (0.032 in)
Champion RS9YC	0.7 mm (0.028 in)

HT leads
Resistance	30 000 ohms maximum per lead
Type	Champion CLS 8 boxed set

Ignition system (1.3, 1.4 and 1.6 litre CVH engines)

Ignition timing
1.4 litre engines:	
For leaded fuel	12° BTDC
For unleaded fuel	8° BTDC

Ignition timing (continued)

	Mechanical	Vacuum	Total
Advance at 2000 rpm, no load, crankshaft degrees (initial advance not included)	3° to 11°	15° to 23°	18° to 34°

1.6 litre engines (pre-1986 models with automatic transmission and VV carburettor):

Advance at 2000 rpm, no load, crankshaft degrees (initial advance not included):

	Mechanical	Vacuum	Total
Bosch distributor 81SF-12100-ANA.......................	0.6° to 6.2°	6.5° to 14°	7.1° to 20.2°
Lucas distributor 82SF-12100-LA	–2.4° to 3°	3° to 10.4°	0.6° to 13.4°

1.6 litre carburettor engines (1986-on):

For leaded fuel	12° BTDC
For unleaded fuel	8° BTDC

1.6 litre fuel injection engines (1986-on):

For leaded fuel	12° BTDC
For unleaded fuel	6° BTDC

Advance at 2000 rpm, no load, crankshaft degrees (initial advance not included):

	Mechanical	Vacuum	Total
Bosch distributor 84SF-12100-TA and Lucas distributor 84SF-12100-SA	6° to 14°	9° to 17°	15° to 31°
Bosch distributor 86SF-12100-ARA and Lucas distributor 86SF-12100-AMA	5.5° to 13.4°	9° to 17°	14.5° to 30.4°
Bosch distributor 84SF-12100-FA (fuel injection engines)....................	7.5° to 16.2°	8.5° to 17°	16° to 33.2°
Bosch distributor 84SF-12100-LA (fuel injection engines)....................	8.2° to 16°	9° to 17°	17.2° to 33°

Spark plugs
Application:

1.3 HCS, 1.4 CVH carburettor models...	Champion RC7YCC or RC7YC

Ignition system (1.6 EFI engines)

General

System type	EEC-IV engine management system with fully electronic distributorless ignition system (E-DIS 4) controlled by EEC-IV module
Firing order...	1-3-4-2

Coil

Type..	High output distributorless ignition coil
Output..	37.0 Kvolt (minimum) – open circuit condition on vehicle
Primary resistance..	4.5 to 5.0 ohms

Spark plugs

Type..	Champion RC7YCC or RC7YC
Electrode gap...	1.0 mm (0.040 in)

HT leads

Resistance	30 000 ohms (maximum) per lead

Ignition system (1.4 CFi Catalyst engine)

General

Type..	TFi IV

Distributor

Type..	Breakerless, 'Hall effect'
Drive	Offset dog from camshaft
Direction of rotation	Anti-clockwise (when viewed end on)

Ignition timing

Auto advance	Totally controlled by engine management system
Static advance..	10° BTDC (must be set in service code 60)
Dwell angle	Controlled by TFi IV module

Coil

Type..	High output breakerless ignition coil
Output..	30.0 Kvolt (minimum) – open circuit condition on vehicle
Primary resistance..	0.72 to 0.88 ohms
Secondary resistance	4500 to 7000 ohms

Spark plugs

Type..	Champion RC7YCC or RC7YC
Electrode gap...	1.0 mm (0.040 in)

HT leads
Resistance... 30 000 ohms maximum per lead

Torque wrench settings
	Nm	lbf ft
Distributor to cylinder head..	6	4

Clutch
Diameter – 1.6 litre engines 1986-on........................... 220.0 mm (8.7 in)

Torque wrench settings
	Nm	lbf ft
Pressure plate-to-flywheel bolts, all models, 1987- on...............................	30	22

Manual transmission

Gear ratios
Four-speed transmission
1.3 litre OHV engines:

1st................................	3.15:1
2nd...............................	1.91:1
3rd................................	1.28:1
4th................................	0.95:1
Reverse..........................	3.62:1

1.4 litre CVH engines:

1st................................	3.58:1
2nd...............................	2.04:1
3rd................................	1.32:1
4th................................	0.95:1
Reverse..........................	3.77:1

Five-speed transmission:
1.3 litre OHV engines:

1st................................	3.15:1
2nd...............................	1.91:1
3rd................................	1.28:1
4th................................	0.95:1
5th................................	0.76:1
Reverse..........................	3.62:1

1.4 litre CVH engines:

1st................................	3.58:1
2nd...............................	2.04:1
3rd................................	1.32:1
4th................................	0.95:1
5th................................	0.76:1
Reverse..........................	3.77:1
Final drive ratio (1.3 and 1.4 litre engines).........................	3.84:1

Torque wrench settings
	Nm	lbf ft
Transmission mountings to transmission (1986 models onwards)..........	80 to 100	59 to 74
Transmission crossmember to body (1986 models onwards)..................	52	38
Gearchange mechanism bolts (1987-on)..	22	16

Automatic transmission

Automatic transmission fluid
Type (see text):

Early type transmission with identification number prefix E3RP........ Automatic transmission fluid to Ford specification SQM-2C 9010- A or ESP-M2C 138-CJ (Duckhams Uni-Matic or D-Matic)

Later type transmission with identification number prefix E6RP....... Automatic transmission fluid to Ford specification ESP-M2C 166H (Duckhams Uni-Matic or Q-Matic)

Driveshafts

CV joint lubricant type/specification........................... Lithium-based grease to Ford specification A77SX 1C 9004 AA (Duckhams LB 10)

Braking system

Torque wrench settings
	Nm	lbf ft
Modulator pivot bolt (ABS)...	22 to 28	16 to 21
Modulator adjuster bolt (ABS).......................................	22 to 28	16 to 21
Modulator drivebelt cover (ABS)....................................	8 to 11	6 to 8
Load apportioning valve adjusting bracket nuts (ABS).............................	21 to 29	15 to 21
Load apportioning valve to mounting bracket (ABS)...............................	21 to 29	15 to 21

Steering

Torque wrench settings
	Nm	lbf ft
Steering gear tie-rod to rack (using Loctite 270).........................	72 to 88	53 to 65

Suspension

Suspension angles (unladen) – 1986 models onwards
Castor:
   Standard.. 2° 32′ ± 1° 0′
   Heavy duty .... 2° 18′ ± 1° 0′
   Maximum permissible variation (side to side).............. 1° 0′
Camber:
   Standard.. 0° ± 1° 0′
   Heavy duty .... 0° 21′ ± 1° 0′
   Maximum permissible variation (side to side).............. 1° 15′

Roadwheels and Tyres
Wheel size .... 6.0 J x 14
Tyres:

	Front	Rear
Size ... 185/60 R 14		
Pressures (cold) bar (lbf/in²):		
Up to 3 people (normal use)	1.6 (23)	2.0 (29)
Fully laden/speed	2.0 (29)	2.3 (33)

Electrical system

Alternator

	Lucas	Mitsubishi
Rated output (13.5 V at 6000 rpm engine speed)	55A (A127/55)	55A (A500T)
	70A (A127/70)	
Maximum continuous speed	15 000 rpm	15 000 rpm
Minimum brush length	5 mm (0.197 in)	5 mm (0.197 in)
Regulated voltage at 4000 rpm, 3 to 7A load	13.7 to 14.6 volts	13.7 to 14.6 volts
Stator winding resistance (ohms/phase)	0.195 – 10%	0.8 ± 5%
Rotor winding resistance at 20°C (ohms)	3.2 ± 5%	2.7 to 3.1

Starter motor
Make .... Lucas M79
Number of brushes 4
Minimum brush length .... 8.0 mm (0.32 in)
Armature endfloat... 0.25 mm (0.010 in)

Torque wrench settings

	Nm	lbf ft
Alternator mounting bolts	25	18
Starter motor retaining bolts	35 to 45	26 to 33

General dimensions, weights and capacities

Dimensions (1986 models onwards)
Overall length .... 4230 mm (166.5 in)
Overall height .... 1391 mm (54.8 in)
Overall width (including driver's and passenger's door mirrors).............. 1834 mm (72.2 in)

Weights (1986 models onwards)
Gross vehicle weight:
   1.3 and 1.4 litre.. 1325 kg (2921 lb)
   1.6 litre manual (carburettor models)................... 1350 kg (2976 lb)
   1.6 litre manual (fuel injection models) and 1.6 litre automatic .... 1375 kg (3032 lb)
Basic kerb weight:
   1.3 litre .... 875 kg (1929 lb)
   1.4 litre .... 880 kg (1940 lb)
   1.6 litre manual (carburettor model).................... 890 kg (1962 lb)
   1.6 litre manual (fuel injection model) .... 935 kg (2062 lb)
   1.6 litre automatic .... 920 kg (2029 lb)

Capacities (1986 models onwards)
Engine oil with filter change (OHV engine)..................... 3.25 litres (5.7 Imp pints)
Engine oil without filter change (OHV engine) .... 2.75 litres (4.8 Imp pints)
Cooling system capacity:
   1.3 litre .... 7.1 litres (12.5 pints)
   1.4 litre .... 7.6 litres (13.4 pints)
   1.6 litre .... 7.8 litres (13.7 pints)

3 Routine maintenance

1   Various changes have been made to the maintenance and servicing schedules for the Orion range since its introduction. The following list is applicable to all models since the start of production. The 1990 models have the 6000 mile service carried out at 12 000 mile intervals (including those items under the existing 12 000 mile service) after the initial first 6000 mile service, effectively giving a 12 000 mile service interval.

2   The Chapter numbers shown in brackets refer to the main Chapters of the manual, but reference must be made to applicable Sections of this Supplement for any modifications or changes to procedures which may be relevant.

Every 250 miles (400 km) or weekly

Engine, cooling system and brakes
Check the oil level and top up if necessary
Check the coolant level and top up if necessary
Check the brake fluid level in the master cylinder and top up if necessary

Lights and wipers
Check the operation of all interior and exterior lights, wipers and washers
Check, and if necessary top up, the washer reservoir(s)

Tyres
Check the tyre pressures and adjust if necessary
Visually examine the tyres for wear or damage

Every 6000 miles (10 000 km) or 6 months – whichever comes first

Engine (Chapter 1)
Renew the engine oil and filter
On OHV engines remove and clean the oil filler cap

Cooling system (Chapter 2)
Check the hoses, hose clips and visible joint gaskets for leaks and any signs of corrosion or deterioration

Fuel, exhaust and emission control systems (Chapter 3)
Visually check the fuel pipes and hoses for security, chafing, leaks and corrosion
Check the fuel tank for leaks and any sign of damage or corrosion
Check, and if necessary adjust, the idle speed and mixture settings (engines without idle speed control only)

Ignition system (Chapter 4)
Clean the distributor cap, coil tower and HT leads and check for tracking

Braking system (Chapter 8)
Check the front disc pad and rear brake shoe lining thickness
Check the condition and security of all brake pipes, hoses and unions including the servo vacuum hose (where fitted)

Suspension and steering (Chapters 9 and 10)
Check the steering components for any signs of damage
Check tightness of wheel nuts/bolts (wheels on ground)

Electrical system (Chapter 11)
Check the condition and adjustment of the alternator drivebelt

Bodywork (Chapter 12)
Check the seat belt webbing for cuts or damage and check the seat belt operation
Carefully inspect the paintwork for damage and the bodywork for corrosion

Every 12 000 miles (20 000 km) or 12 months – whichever comes first

In addition to all the items in the 6000 mile (10 000 km) service, carry out the following:

Engine (Chapter 1)
On OHV engines check and if necessary adjust the valve clearances (pre-1989 only)

Fuel, exhaust and emission control systems (Chapter 3)
Check the underbody for signs of fuel or exhaust leaks and check the exhaust system condition and security

Ignition system (Chapter 4)
Renew the spark plugs

Manual transmission (Chapter 6)
Visually check for oil leaks around the transmission joint faces and oil seals
Check, and if necessary top up, the transmission oil

Automatic transmission (Chapter 6)
Visually check for fluid leaks around the transmission joint faces and seals
Check, and if necessary top up, the automatic transmission fluid
Check the operation of the selector mechanism
Check and adjust as necessary the throttle/downshift linkage

Driveshafts (Chapter 7)
Check the driveshafts for damage or distortion and check the condition of the constant velocity joint bellows

Suspension and steering (Chapters 9 and 10)
Check the condition and security of all steering gear components, front and rear suspension joints and linkages, and steering gear bellows condition
Check the front and rear shock absorbers for fluid leaks
Inspect the roadwheels for damage
Check the tightness of the roadwheel bolts
Check the wheel bearings for wear

Bodywork (Chapter 12)
Lubricate all hinges, door locks, check straps and the bonnet release mechanism
Check the operation of all doors, tailgate, bonnet release and window regulator components

Road test
Check the operation of all instruments and electrical equipment
Check for any abnormalities in the steering, suspension, handling or road feel
Check the performance of the engine, clutch and transmission
Check the operation and performance of the braking system

Every 24 000 miles (40 000 km) or two years – whichever comes first

In addition to all the items in the 12 000 mile (20 000 km) and 6000 mile (10 000 km) services, carry out the following:

Engine (Chapter 1)
On OHV and HCS engines 1989-on, check and adjust the valve clearances

Cooling system (Chapter 2)
Renew the antifreeze in the cooling system

Fuel, exhaust and emission control systems (Chapter 3)
Renew the air cleaner filter element
On HCS and CVH carburettor engines, renew the adaptor on the underside of the air cleaner housing
On CVH engines, renew the crankcase emission control filter
On fuel injected engines, renew the fuel filter
On OHV engines, clean the oil filler cap and wire mesh filter
Where fitted, check the operation of the temperature controlled air cleaner inlet valve

Every 36 000 miles (60 000 km) or 3 years – whichever comes first

In addition to all the items listed in the previous services, carry out the following:

Engine (Chapter 1)
On CVH engines renew the timing belt

Braking system (Chapter 8)
Make a thorough inspection of all brake components and rubber seals for signs of leaks, general deterioration and wear
Drain and refill the hydraulic system with fresh fluid

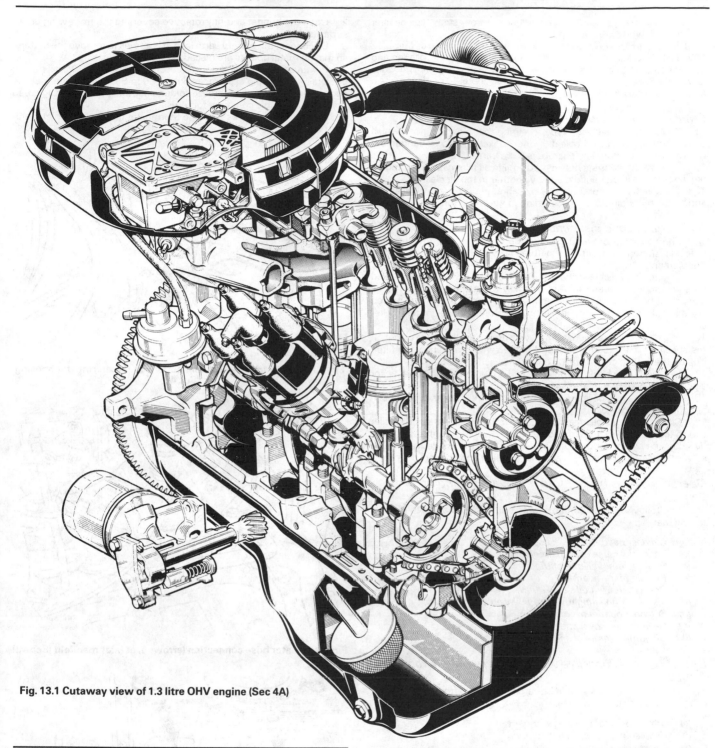

Fig. 13.1 Cutaway view of 1.3 litre OHV engine (Sec 4A)

---

4   Engine (1.3 litre OHV)

PART A: GENERAL

General description

1   At the beginning of 1986, the 1296 cc CVH engine was deleted from the Orion range and replaced by an OHV (overhead valve) unit of 1297 cc capacity. The new engine is based upon the 'Kent' design used in many earlier Ford models, including the Fiesta and Escort.

2   As with previous installations, the engine is mounted transversely at the front of the car together with the transmission to form a combined power train. The engine is of water-cooled, four-cylinder in-line type, having overhead valves operated by tappets, pushrods and rocker arms.

3   The camshaft is located within the cylinder block and chain-driven from the crankshaft. A gear on the camshaft drives the oil pump and the distributor, while an eccentric operates the fuel pump lever.

4   The cylinder head is of crossflow type, having the exhaust manifold mounted on the opposite side of the inlet manifold.

5   The crankshaft runs in five main bearings, with endfloat controlled by semi-circular thrust washers located on either side of the centre main bearing.

6   The oil pump is mounted externally on the cylinder block just below the distributor, and the full-flow type oil filter is screwed directly into the oil pump.

Lubrication system – description

7   Engine oil contained in the sump is drawn through a strainer and pick-up tube by an externally-mounted oil pump of twin rotor design.

8   The oil is then forced through a full-flow, throw-away type oil filter which is screwed onto the oil pump.
9   Oil pressure is regulated by a relief valve integral in the oil pump.
10   The pressurised oil is directed through the various galleries and passages to all bearing surfaces. A drilling in the big-end provides lubrication for the gudgeon pins and cylinder bores. The timing chain and sprockets are lubricated by an oil ejection nozzle.

Crankcase ventilation system – description
11   The system is a closed type, ensuring that blow-by gases which pass the piston rings and collect in the crankcase, also oil vapour, are drawn into the combustion chambers to be burnt.
12   The system consists of a vented engine oil filler cap connected by one hose to the inlet manifold and by another to the air cleaner.
13   The gas flow is controlled by a calibrated port in the oil filler cap and by the manifold vacuum according to throttle setting.

Maintenance and inspection
14   The following procedures must be carried out at the specified intervals shown in 'Routine maintenance' at the beginning of this Supplement.
15   Engine oil level check: check the engine oil level with the car parked on level ground, preferably after allowing the engine to cool. The oil level must be kept between the minimum and maximum markings on the dipstick. Top up the oil level through the filler neck in the rocker cover.
16   Engine oil change and filter renewal: drain the old engine oil hot, at the specified mileage intervals, and at the same time renew the filter. Top up the engine oil level using oil of the specified grade.
17   Occasionally check the engine and associated components for signs of oil, coolant or fuel leakage.
18   Check and, if necessary, adjust the valve clearances at the specified mileage intervals.
19   Clean the crankcase emission control orifice: detach the filler cap-to-intake manifold hose and remove the control orifice from the filler cap unit by pulling and rotating it free. Clean the orifice in a suitable solvent. Renew the orifice if it is damaged. Refit and connect the hose.

Operations possible without removing engine from vehicle
20   The following work can be carried out without having to remove the engine:

(a) Cylinder head – removal and refitting
(b) Valve clearances – adjustment
(c) Sump – removal and refitting
(d) Rocker gear – overhaul
(e) Crankshaft front oil seal – renewal
(f) Pistons/connecting rods – removal and refitting
(g) Engine mountings – renewal
(h) Oil filter – removal and refitting
(i) Oil pump – removal and refitting

Operations only possible with engine removed from vehicle
21   The following work should be carried out only after the engine has been removed from the vehicle:

(a) Crankshaft main bearings – renewal
(b) Crankshaft – removal and refitting
(c) Flywheel – removal and refitting
(d) Crankshaft rear oil seal – renewal
(e) Camshaft – removal and refitting
(f) Timing gears and chain – removal and refitting

Fault diagnosis – OHV engine
22   Refer to Chapter 1, Section 27 but ignore all references to fuel injection systems or components.

PART B: OPERATIONS POSSIBLE WITH ENGINE IN CAR

Cylinder head – removal and refitting
1   If the engine is in the vehicle, carry out the preliminary operations described in paragraphs 2 to 15.

2   Open the bonnet and fit protective covers to the front wing upper surfaces.
3   Disconnect the battery earth lead. It is as well to remove the battery, so that no metal objects are placed across its terminals.
4   Remove the air cleaner unit, as described in Section 10.
5   Drain the cooling system, as described in Section 9. Note that the coolant should have an antifreeze solution mix and can be used again, so drain into a suitable container for re-use.
6   Disconnect the hoses from the thermostat housing and inlet manifold.

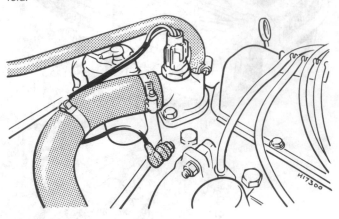

Fig. 13.2 Hose and electrical connections at the thermostat housing (Sec 4B)

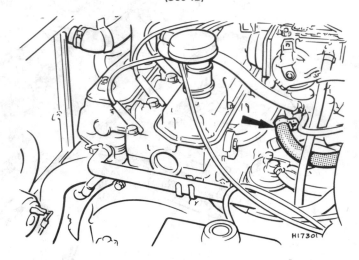

Fig. 13.3 Heater hose connection (arrowed) at inlet manifold (Sec 4B)

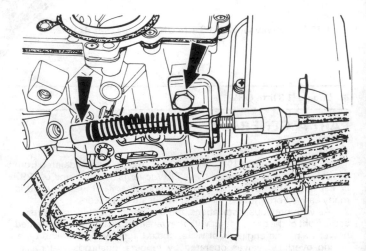

Fig. 13.4 Throttle cable attachment at carburettor (Sec 4B)

Fig. 13.5 Remove the rocker shaft assembly (Sec 4B)

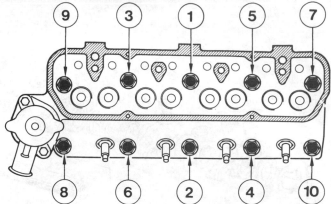

Fig. 13.6 Cylinder head bolt tightening sequence (Sec 4B)

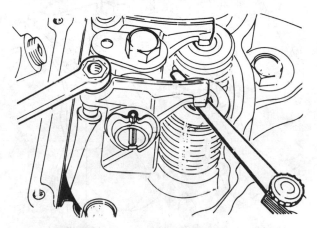

Fig. 13.7 Valve clearance adjustment (Sec 4B)

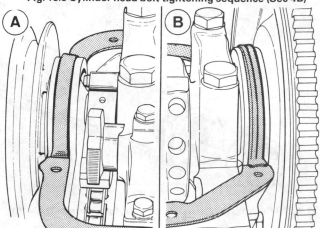

Fig. 13.8 Sump gasket fitting details at timing cover end (A) and flywheel end (B) (Sec 4B)

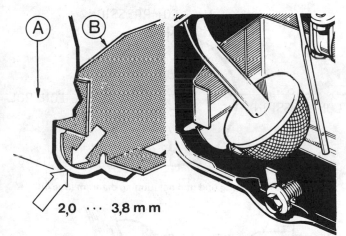

Fig. 13.9 Sump and oil baffle clearance (Sec 4B)

A   Sump   *B   Baffle*

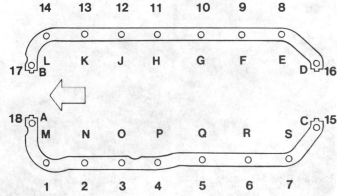

Fig. 13.10 Sump bolt tightening sequence – arrow points to timing cover end (Sec 4B)

7   Detach the choke cable.

8   Release the throttle cable from the carburettor operating lever by moving the spring clip and removing the bracket fixing bolt.

9   Disconnect the fuel and vacuum pipes from the carburettor.

10   Disconnect the breather hose from the inlet manifold.

11   Disconnect the brake servo vacuum hose from the inlet manifold.

12   Disconnect the HT leads from the spark plugs.

13   Disconnect the electrical leads from the temperature sender unit, inlet manifold, carburettor, and radiator fan thermal switch.

14   Unbolt and remove the heated air box from the exhaust manifold (where fitted).

15   Disconnect the exhaust downpipe from the manifold by unbolting

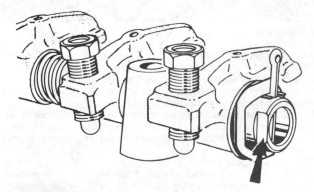

Fig. 13.11 Flat on rocker shaft (arrowed) and retaining split pin (Sec 4B)

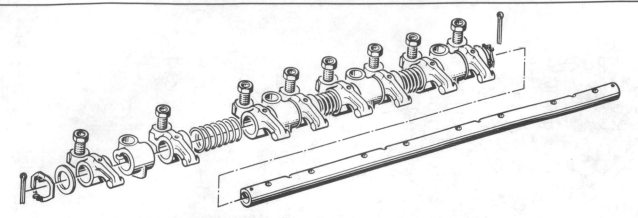

Fig. 13.12 Rocker shaft assembly components (Sec 4B)

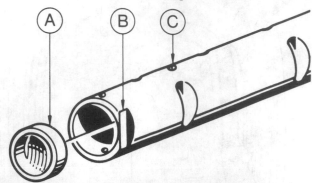

Fig. 13.13 Rocker shaft front end plug (A), flat (B) and oil hole (C) (Sec 4B)

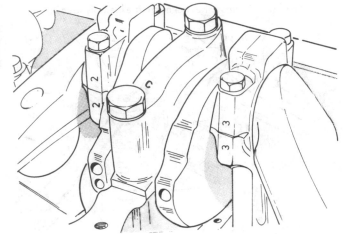

Fig. 13.14 Connecting rod and big-end cap identification numbers (Sec 4B)

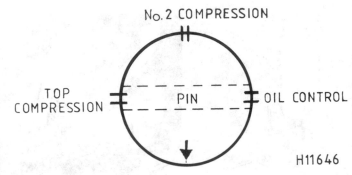

Fig. 13.15 Piston ring end gap positioning diagram (Sec 4B)

4B.19 Remove the pushrods

the connecting flanges. Support the exhaust system at the front end.
16   Pull free and remove the oil filler cap with breather hoses.
17   Extract the four screws and remove the rocker cover.
18   Unscrew and remove the four fixing bolts and lift away the rocker shaft assembly from the cylinder head.
19   Withdraw the pushrods, keeping them in their originally fitted sequence. A simple way to do this is to punch holes in a piece of card and number them 1 to 8 from the thermostat housing end of the cylinder head (photo).
20   Remove the spark plugs.
21   Unscrew the cylinder head bolts progressively in the reverse order to that given for tightening (see Fig. 13.6). Remove the cylinder head.
22   Dismantling of the cylinder head is described in Part D.
23   Before refitting the cylinder head, remove every particle of carbon,

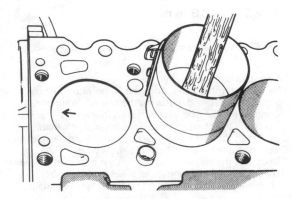

Fig. 13.16 Installing a piston/connecting rod assembly (Sec 4B)

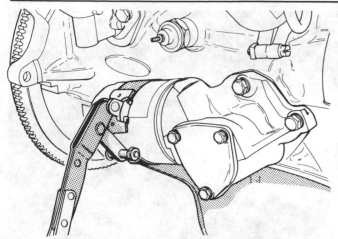

Fig. 13.17 Using a strap wrench to unscrew the oil filter cartridge (Sec 4B)

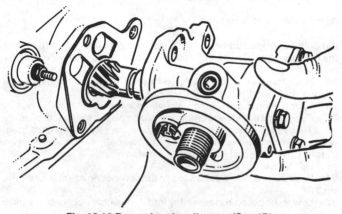

Fig. 13.18 Removing the oil pump (Sec 4B)

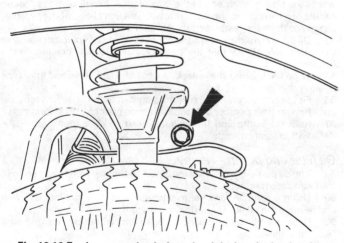

Fig. 13.19 Engine mounting bolt under right-hand wheel arch (Sec 4B)

old gasket and dirt from the mating surfaces of the cylinder head and block. Do not let the removed material drop into the cylinder bores or waterways; if it does, remove it. Normally, when a cylinder head is removed, the head is decarbonised and the valves ground in, as described in Part D, to remove all traces of carbon. Clean the threads of the cylinder head bolts and mop out oil from the bolt holes in the cylinder block. In extreme cases, screwing a bolt into an oil-filled hole can cause the block to fracture due to hydraulic pressure.

24   If there is any doubt about the condition of the inlet or exhaust gaskets, unbolt the manifolds and fit new ones to perfectly clean mating surfaces.

25   Locate a new cylinder head gasket on the cylinder block, making

quite sure that the bolt holes, coolant passages and lubrication holes are correctly aligned.

26   Lower the cylinder head carefully into position on the block.

27   Screw in all the bolts finger tight and then tighten them in four stages, in the sequence shown in Fig. 13.6 to the specified torque.

28   Refit the pushrods in their original order.

29   Lower the rocker shaft assembly into position, making sure that the rocker adjusting screws engage in the sockets at the ends of the pushrods.

30   Screw in the rocker pedestal bolts finger tight. At this stage, some or the rocker arms will be applying pressure to the ends of the valve stems and some of the rocker pedestals will not be in contact with the cylinder head. The pedestals will be pulled down, however, when the bolts are tightened to the specified torque, which should now be done.

31   Adjust the valve clearances, as described in the next sub-Section.

32   Refit the rocker cover. If the gasket is in anything but perfect condition, renew it.

33   Fit the oil filler cap and breather hose and the spark plugs. Tighten these to the specified torque. They are of tapered seat type, no sealing washers being used.

34   Connect the exhaust downpipe and fit the heated air box.

35   Reconnect all electrical leads, vacuum and coolant hoses.

36   Reconnect the cables. Refit the battery (if removed) and reconnect the battery terminals.

37   Fit the air cleaner.

38   Refill the cooling system, as described in Chapter 2.

Valve clearances – adjustment

39   This operation should be carried out with the engine cold and the air cleaner and rocker cover removed.

40   Using a ring spanner or socket on the crankshaft pulley bolt, turn the crankshaft in a clockwise direction until No 1 piston is at tdc on its compression stroke. This can be verified by checking that the pulley and timing cover marks are in alignment and that the valves of No 4 cylinder are rocking. When the valves are rocking, this means that the slightest rotation of the crankshaft pulley in either direction will cause one rocker arm to move up and the other to move down.

41   Numbering from the thermostat housing end of the cylinder head, the valves are identified as follows:

Valve No	Cylinder No
1 – Exhaust	1
2 – Inlet	1
3 – Exhaust	2
4 – Inlet	2
5 – Exhaust	3
6 – Inlet	3
7 – Exhaust	4
8 – Inlet	4

42   Adjust the valve clearances by following the sequence given in the following table. Turn the crankshaft pulley 180° (half a turn) after adjusting each pair:

Valves rocking	Valves to adjust
7 and 8	1 (Exhaust), 2 (Inlet)
5 and 6	3 (Exhaust), 4 (Inlet)
1 and 2	7 (Exhaust), 8 (Inlet)
3 and 4	5 (Exhaust), 6 (Inlet)

43   The clearances for the inlet and exhaust valves are different (see Specifications). Use a feeler gauge of the appropriate thickness to check each clearance between the end of the valve stem and the rocker arm. The gauge should be a stiff sliding fit. If it is not, turn the adjuster bolt with a ring spanner. These bolts are of stiff thread type and require no locking nut. Turn the bolt clockwise to reduce the clearance and anti-clockwise to increase it.

44   Refit the air cleaner and rocker cover on completion of adjustment.

Sump – removal and refitting

45   Disconnect the battery earth lead and drain the engine oil.

46   Unbolt and withdraw the starter motor. Support the motor to avoid straining the electrical wiring.

47   Unbolt and remove the clutch cover plate.
48   Extract the sump securing bolts and remove the sump. If it is stuck, prise it gently with a screwdriver, but do not use excessive leverage. If it is very tight, cut round the gasket joint using a sharp knife.
49   Before refitting the sump, remove the front and rear sealing strips and gaskets. Clean the mating surfaces of the sump and cylinder block.
50   Stick new gaskets into position on the block using thick grease to retain them, then install new sealing strips into their grooves so that they overlap the gaskets.
51   Before offering up the sump, check that the gap between the sump and oil baffle is between 2.0 and 3.8 mm (0.08 and 0.15 in) – Fig. 13.9.
52   Screw in the sump bolts and tighten in three stages to the specified torque, in accordance with Fig. 13.10.

Stage 1 – in alphabetical order
Stage 2 – in numerical order
Stage 3 – in alphabetical order

53   It is important to follow this procedure in order to provide positive sealing against oil leakage.
54   Refit the clutch cover plate and the starter motor and reconnect the battery.
55   Refill the engine with the correct grade and quantity of oil.

Rocker gear – dismantling and reassembly
56   With the rocker gear removed as described previously, extract the split pin from one end of the rocker shaft.
57   Take off the spring and plain washers from the end of the shaft.
58   Slide off the rocker arms, support pedestals and coil springs, keeping them in their originally fitted order. Clean out the oil holes in the shaft.
59   Apply engine oil to the rocker shaft before reassembling and make sure that the flat on the end of the shaft is to the same side as the rocker arm adjuster screws. This is essential for proper lubrication of the components.
60   If a new rocker shaft is being fitted, check that the end plug is correctly located (Fig. 13.13).

Crankshaft front oil seal – renewal
61   Disconnect the battery earth lead.
62   Slacken the alternator mounting and adjuster bolts, and after pushing the alternator in towards the engine, slip off the drivebelt.
63   Unscrew and remove the crankshaft pulley bolt. To prevent the crankshaft turning while the bolt is being released, jam the teeth of the starter ring gear on the flywheel, after removing the clutch cover plate or starter motor for access.
64   Remove the crankshaft pulley. This should come out by hand, but, if it is tight, prise it carefully with two levers placed at opposite sides under the pulley flange.
65   Using a suitable claw tool, prise out the defective seal and wipe out the seat.
66   Install the new seal using a suitable distance piece, the pulley and its bolt to draw it into position. If it is tapped into position, the seal may be distorted or the timing cover fractured.
67   When the seal is fully seated, remove the pulley and bolt, apply grease to the seal rubbing surface of the pulley, install it and tighten the securing bolt to the specified torque.
68   Refit the clutch cover or starter motor.
69   Fit and tension the drivebelt (Chapter 11) and reconnect the battery.

Pistons/connecting rods – removal and refitting
70   Remove the cylinder head and the sump, as described previously. Do not remove the oil pick-up filter or pipe, which is an interference fit.
71   Note the location numbers stamped on the connecting rod big-ends and caps, and to which side they face. No 1 assembly is nearest the timing cover, and the assembly numbers are towards the camshaft side of the engine.
72   Turn the crankshaft by means of the pulley bolt until the big-end cap bolts for No 1 connecting rods are in their most accessible position. Unscrew and remove the bolts and the big-end cap complete with bearing shell. If the cap is difficult to remove, tap it off with a plastic-faced hammer.
73   If the bearing shells are to be used again keep the shell taped to its cap.
74   Feel the top of the cylinder bore for a wear ridge. If one is detected,

4B.88 Oil filter and pump unit

it should be scraped off before the piston/rod is pushed out of the top of the cylinder block. Take care when doing this not to score the cylinder bore surfaces.
75   Push the piston/connecting rod out of the block, retaining the bearing shell with the rod if it is to be used again.
76   Dismantling the piston/rod is covered in Part C.
77   Repeat the operations on the remaining piston/rod assemblies.
78   To install a piston/rod assembly, have the piston ring gaps staggered, as shown in the diagram (Fig. 13.15), oil the rings and apply a piston ring compressor. Compress the piston rings.
79   Oil the cylinder bores.
80   Wipe out the bearing shell seat in the connecting rod and insert the shell.
81   Lower the piston/rod assembly into the cylinder bore until the base of the piston ring compressor stands squarely on the top of the block.
82   Check that the directional arrow on the piston crown faces towards the timing cover end of the engine, and then apply the wooden handle of a hammer to the piston crown. Strike the head of the hammer sharply to drive the piston into the cylinder bore.
83   Oil the crankpin and draw the connecting rod down to engage with the crankshaft. Check that the bearing shell is still in position in the connecting rod.
84   Wipe the bearing shell seat in the big-end cap clean and insert the bearing shell.
85   Fit the cap, screw in the bolts and tighten to the specified torque.
86   Repeat the operations on the remaining pistons/connecting rods.
87   Refit the sump and the cylinder head as described previously. Refill with oil and coolant.

Oil filter and pump – removal and refitting
88   The oil pump is externally mounted on the rearward facing side of the crankcase (photo).
89   Using a suitable removal tool (strap wrench or similar), unscrew and remove the oil filter cartridge and discard it.
90   Unscrew the three mounting bolts and withdraw the oil pump from the engine.
91   Clean away the old gasket.
92   If a new pump is being fitted, it should be primed with engine oil before installation. Do this by turning its shaft while filling it with clean engine oil.
93   Locate a new gasket on the pump mounting flange, insert the pump shaft and bolt the pump into position.
94   Grease the rubber sealing ring of a new filter and screw it into position on the pump, using hand pressure only, **not** the removal tool.
95   Top up the engine oil to replenish any lost during the operations.

Engine mountings – removal and refitting
96   The engine mountings can be removed if the weight of the engine/transmission is first taken by one of the three following methods.
97   Either support the engine under the sump using a jack and a block of wood, or attach a hoist to the engine lifting lugs. A third method is to

make up a bar with end pieces which will engage in the water channels at the sides of the bonnet lid aperture. Using an adjustable hook and chain connected to the engine lifting lugs, the weight of the engine can be taken off the mountings.

Right-hand mounting

98 Unscrew and remove the mounting side bolt from under the right-hand wheel arch, just to the rear and above the brake hose bracket.

99 Unscrew and remove the mounting retaining nut and washer from the body bracket in the engine compartment.

100 Undo the three bolts securing the mounting to the cylinder block (working from underneath). The mounting unit and bracket can then be lowered from the engine.

101 Unbolt and remove the mounting from its support bracket.

Left-hand mountings

102 Undo the nuts securing both mountings to the longitudinal crossmember beneath the transmission.

103 Unbolt the crossmember at the front and at the rear and remove it from under the car.

104 Unbolt the front or rear rubber mounting, as applicable, from the transmission brackets, and remove the relevant mounting.

All mountings

105 Refitting of all mountings is a reversal of removal. Make sure that the original sequence of assembling the washers and plates is maintained.

PART C: REMOVAL AND DISMANTLING

Engine/transmission – removal and separation

1 The engine is removed from the vehicle complete with transmission (gearbox and final drive) in a downward direction.

2 Disconnect the battery negative lead.

3 Place the transmission in fourth gear on four-speed versions, or reverse gear on the five-speed unit, to aid adjustment of the gearchange linkage when refitting. On models produced from February 1987 onwards, place the transmission in second gear on four-speed versions, or fourth gear on five-speed versions.

4 Refer to Chapter 12 and remove the bonnet.

5 Refer to Section 10 and remove the air cleaner.

6 Refer to Section 9 and drain the cooling system.

7 Disconnect the radiator top and bottom hoses and the expansion tank hose at the thermostat housing.

8 Disconnect the heater hoses from the stub on the lateral coolant pipe and inlet manifold.

9 Disconnect the choke cable and the throttle cable from the carburettor throttle lever. Unbolt the cable support bracket and tie the cable assembly to one side of the engine compartment.

10 Disconnect the fuel pipe from the fuel pump and plug the pipe.

11 Disconnect the brake servo vacuum hose from the inlet manifold.

12 Disconnect the leads from the following electrical components:

(a) Alternator and electric fan temperature switch
(b) Oil pressure sender
(c) Coolant temperature sender
(d) Reversing lamp switch
(e) Anti-run-on solenoid valve

13 Disconnect the HT and LT (distributor) wires from the coil terminals.

14 Unscrew the speedometer drive cable from the transmission and release the breather hose.

15 Disconnect the clutch cable from the release lever and from its transmission support.

16 Unbolt and remove the hot air box from the exhaust manifold.

17 Disconnect the exhaust downpipe from the manifold by extracting the two flange bolts. Support the exhaust pipe to avoid straining it.

18 The vehicle should now be jacked up and safety stands fitted to

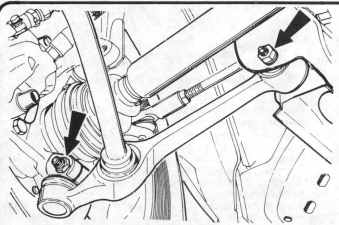

Fig. 13.20 Front suspension arm pivot bolt and balljoint clamp bolt (Sec 4C)

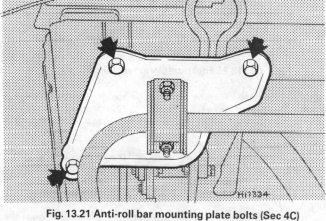

Fig. 13.21 Anti-roll bar mounting plate bolts (Sec 4C)

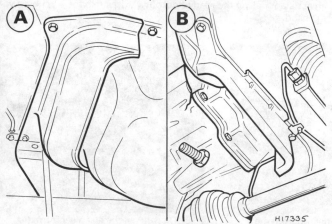

Fig. 13.22 Plastic splash shield locations under engine (A) and transmission (B) (Sec 4C)

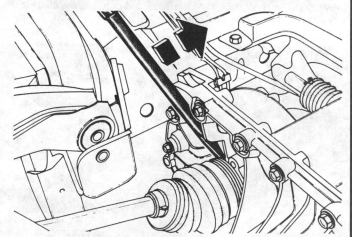

Fig. 13.23 Driveshaft removal from transmission (Sec 4C)

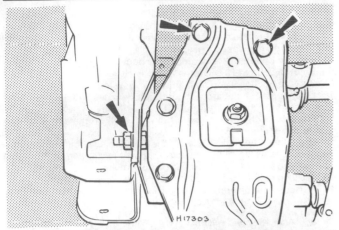

Fig. 13.24 Transmission support crossmember rear attachments to body (Sec 4C)

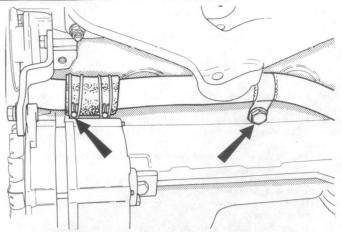

Fig. 13.25 Engine lateral coolant pipe attachments (Sec 4C)

Fig. 13.26 Fuel pump removal (Sec 4C)

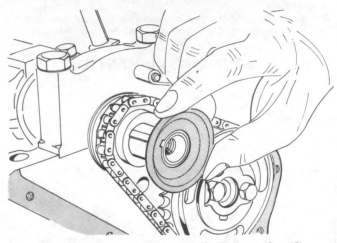

Fig. 13.27 Removing the crankshaft oil slinger (Sec 4C)

provide sufficient clearance beneath it to be able to remove the engine/transmission from below. A distance of 686 mm (27.0 in) is recommended between the floor and the bottom edge of the front panel.

19   Disconnect the exhaust system from its flexible mountings and remove the system complete.

20   Disconnect the starter motor leads and the engine earth strap.

21   Disconnect the gearchange rod from the transmission selector shaft by releasing the clamp bolt and withdrawing the rod (photos). Tie the rod to the stabiliser and then where fitted, unhook the tension spring.

22   Unscrew the single bolt and disconnect the stabiliser from the transmission housing, noting the washer fitted between the stabiliser trunnion and the transmission (photo).

23   Unscrew and remove the pivot bolt and nut from the inboard end of both front suspension lower arms.

24   Unscrew and remove the nut and bolt which secures the balljoint at the outboard end of the suspension lower arms. Use a Torx type socket bit to hold the bolt as the nut is unscrewed.

25   Undo the three bolts each side securing the anti-roll bar mounting plates to the body, then remove the anti-roll bar complete with both suspension lower arms.

26   Remove the engine and transmission plastic splash shields from under the inner wheel arches.

27   Release both driveshafts from the transmission by inserting a lever between the inboard constant velocity joint and the transmission. With an assistant pulling the roadwheel outwards, strike the lever hard with the hand.

4C.21A Release the gearchange rod clamp bolt ...

4C.21B ... and withdraw the rod from the selector shaft

4C.22 Disconnect the stabiliser from the transmission housing

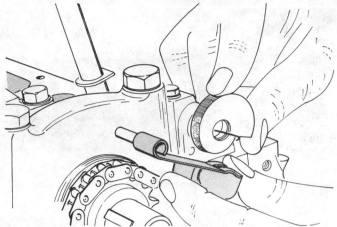

Fig. 13.28 Sliding off the chain tensioner arm (Sec 4C)

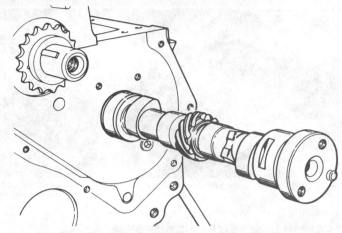

Fig. 13.29 Camshaft removal (Sec 4C)

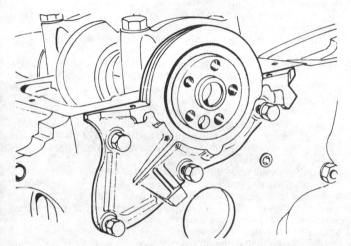

Fig. 13.30 Crankshaft rear oil seal retainer (Sec 4C)

28   With the driveshafts released, tie them up, or support them in such a way that they do not hang down at an angle of more than 45° from the horizontal.

29   Support the engine/transmission assembly securely on a jack, or preferably attach a suitable hoist using chains and brackets.

30   Just take the weight of the engine/transmission assembly so that the tension is relieved from the mountings.

31   Unbolt the right-hand engine mounting from the support bracket in the engine compartment (one nut) and from the inner wing panel, accessible from under the wheel arch (one bolt).

32   Undo the nuts and bolts securing the transmission support crossmember to the body. The crossmember is removed with the engine/transmission assembly.

33   Carefully lower the engine/transmission and withdraw it from under the car. To ease the withdrawal operation, lower the engine/transmission onto a crawler board or a sheet of substantial chipboard placed on rollers or lengths of pipe.

Separation

34   Unscrew and remove the starter motor bolts and remove the starter.

35   Unbolt and remove the clutch cover plate from the lower part of the clutch bellhousing.

36   Unscrew and remove the bolts from the clutch bellhousing-to-engine mating flange.

37   Withdraw the transmission from the engine. Support its weight, so that the clutch assembly is not distorted while the input shaft is still in engagement with the splined hub of the clutch driven plate.

Engine – complete dismantling

38   Position the engine so that it is upright on a bench or other convenient working surface. If the exterior is very dirty it should be cleaned before dismantling using paraffin and a stiff brush or a water-soluble solvent.

39   Remove the coolant pipe from the side of the engine by disconnecting the hose clips and the securing bolt.

40   If not already done, drain the engine oil.

41   Remove the dipstick and unscrew and discard the oil filter.

42   Disconnect the HT leads from the spark plugs, release the distributor cap and lift it away complete with leads.

43   Unscrew and remove the spark plugs.

44   Disconnect the breather hose from the inlet manifold and remove it complete with the oil filler cap.

45   Disconnect the fuel and vacuum pipes from the carburettor and unbolt and remove the carburettor.

46   Unbolt the thermostat housing cover and remove it, together with the thermostat.

47   Remove the rocker cover.

48   Remove the rocker shaft assembly (four bolts).

49   Withdraw the pushrods, keeping them in their originally fitted order.

50   Remove the cylinder head, complete with manifolds, as described in Part B.

51   Remove the bolt that holds the distributor clamp plate to the cylinder block and withdraw the distributor.

52   Unbolt and remove the fuel pump.

53   Remove the oil pump.

54   Pinch the two runs of the water pump drivebelt together at the pump pulley to prevent the pulley rotating, and release the pulley bolts.

55   Release the alternator mounting and adjuster link bolts, push the alternator in towards the engine and remove the drivebelt.

56   Unbolt the alternator bracket and remove the alternator.

57   Unbolt and remove the water pump.

58   Unscrew the crankshaft pulley bolt. To do this, the flywheel starter ring gear will have to be jammed to prevent the crankshaft from turning.

59   Remove the crankshaft pulley. If this does not pull off by hand, carefully use two levers behind it placed at opposite points.

60   Place the engine on its side and remove the sump. Do not invert the engine at this stage, or sludge and swarf may enter the oilways.

61   Unbolt and remove the timing chain cover (photo).

62   Take off the oil slinger from the front face of the crankshaft sprocket.

63   Slide the chain tensioner arm from its pivot pin on the front main bearing cap.

64   Unbolt and remove the chain tensioner.

65   Bend back the lockplate tabs from the camshaft sprocket bolts and unscrew and remove the bolts.

66   Withdraw the sprocket complete with timing chain.

67   Unbolt and remove the camshaft thrust plate.

68   Rotate the camshaft until each cam follower (tappet) has been pushed fully into its hole by its cam lobe.

69   Withdraw the camshaft, taking care not to damage the camshaft bearings.

70   Withdraw each of the cam followers, keeping them in their originally fitted sequence by marking them with a piece of numbered tape or using a box with divisions (photo).

71   From the front end of the crankshaft, draw off the sprocket using a two-legged extractor.

72   Check that the main bearing caps are marked F (Front), C (Centre)

4C.61 Remove the timing chain cover

4C.70 Lift out the cam followers (tappets) using a valve grinding tool

4C.73 Connecting rod and big-end cap markings

4C.74 Removing the big-end cap

and R (Rear). The caps are also marked with an arrow which indicates the timing cover end of the engine, a point to remember when refitting the caps.

73   Check that the big-end caps and connecting rods have adjacent matching numbers facing towards the camshaft side of the engine. Number 1 assembly is nearest the timing chain end of the engine. If any markings are missing or indistinct, make some of your own with quick-drying paint (photo).

74   Unbolt and remove the big-end bearing caps. If the bearing shell is to be used again, tape the shell to the cap (photo).

75   Now check the top of the cylinder bore for a wear ridge. If one can be felt, it should be removed with a scraper before the piston/rod is pushed out of the cylinder.

76   Remove the piston/rod by pushing it out of the top of the block. Tape the bearing shell to the connecting rod.

77   Remove the remaining three piston/rod assemblies in a similar way.

78   Unbolt the clutch pressure plate cover from the flywheel. Unscrew the bolts evenly and progressively until spring pressure is relieved, before removing the bolts. Be prepared to catch the clutch driven plate as the cover is withdrawn.

79   Unbolt and remove the flywheel. It is heavy, do not drop it. If necessary, the starter ring gear can be jammed to prevent the flywheel rotating. There is no need to mark the fitted position of the flywheel to its mounting flange as it can only be fitted one way. Take off the adaptor plate (engine backplate).

80   Unbolt and remove the crankshaft rear oil seal retainer.

81   Unbolt the main bearing caps. Remove the caps, tapping them off if necessary with a plastic-faced hammer. Retain the bearing shells with their respective caps if the shells are to be used again, although unless the engine is of low mileage this is not recommended.

82   Lift the crankshaft from the crankcase and lift out the upper bearing shells, noting the thrust washers either side of the centre bearing. Keep these shells with their respective caps, identifying them for refitting to the crankcase if they are to be used again.

83   With the engine now completely dismantled, each component should be examined, as described in Part D before reassembling.

PART D: ENGINE OVERHAUL AND REASSEMBLY

Engine – examination and renovation

1   Clean all components using paraffin and a stiff brush, except the crankshaft, which should be wiped clean and the oil passages cleaned out with a length of wire.

2   Never assume that a component is unworn simply because it looks

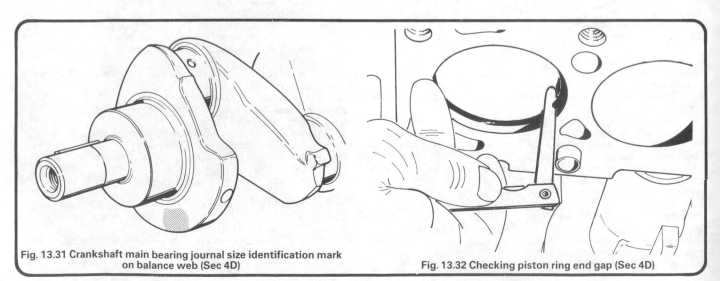

Fig. 13.31 Crankshaft main bearing journal size identification mark on balance web (Sec 4D)

Fig. 13.32 Checking piston ring end gap (Sec 4D)

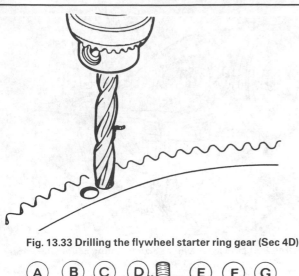

Fig. 13.33 Drilling the flywheel starter ring gear (Sec 4D)

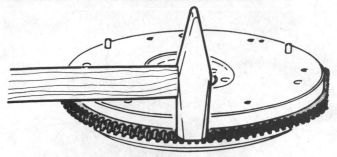

Fig. 13.34 Removing the ring gear from the flywheel (Sec 4D)

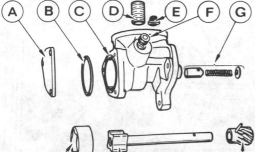

Fig. 13.35 Oil pump components (Sec 4D)

A Cover	F Plug
B O-ring	G Relief valve
C Pump body	H Outer rotor
D Threaded insert	J Inner rotor
E Filter (relief valve)	K Drive pinion

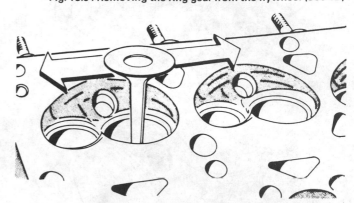

Fig. 13.36 Checking valve guide wear (Sec 4D)

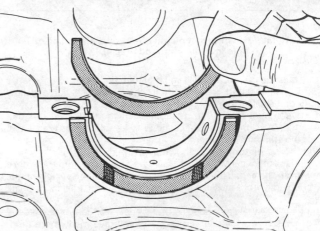

Fig. 13.38 Crankshaft endfloat thrust washers (Sec 4D)

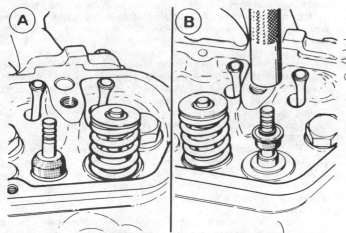

Fig. 13.37 Valve stem oil seals (Sec 4D)

A Exhaust valve type   B Inlet valve type

all right. After all the effort which has gone into dismantling the engine, refitting worn components will make the overhaul a waste of time and money. Depending on the degree of wear, the overhauler's budget and the anticipated life of the vehicle, components which are only slightly worn may be refitted, but if in doubt it is always best to renew.

Crankshaft, main and big-end bearings

3   The need to renew the main bearing shells or to have the crankshaft reground will usually have been determined during the last few miles of operation when perhaps a heavy knocking has developed from within the crankcase or the oil pressure warning lamp has stayed on, denoting a low oil pressure probably caused by excessive wear in the bearings.

4   Even without these symptoms, the journals and crankpins on a high mileage engine should be checked for out-of-round (ovality) and taper. For this a micrometer will be needed to check the diameter of the journals and crankpins at several different points around them. A motor factor or engineer can do this for you. If the readings show that either out-of-round or taper is present, then the crankshaft should be reground by your dealer or engine reconditioning company, to accept the undersize main and big-end shell bearings which are available. Normally, the company doing the regrinding will supply the necessary undersize shells.

5   If the crankshaft is in good condition, it is wise to renew the bearing shells, as it is almost certain that the original ones will have worn. This is often indicated by scoring of the bearing surface, or by the top layer of the bearing metal having worn through to expose the metal underneath.

6   Each shell is marked on its back with the part number. Undersize shells will have the undersize stamped additionally on their backs.

7   Standard size crankshafts having main bearing journal diameters at the lower end of the tolerance range are marked with a yellow spot on

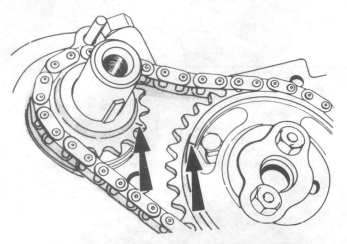

Fig. 13.39 Crankshaft and camshaft sprocket timing marks (arrowed) (Sec 4D)

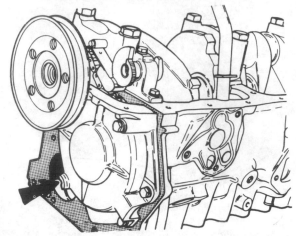

Fig. 13.40 Bolt (arrowed) which secures timing cover and water pump (Sec 4D)

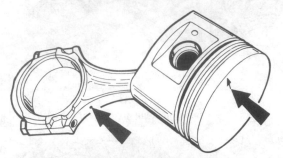

Fig. 13.41 Relative positions of piston directional arrow and oil feed hole in connecting rod (Sec 4D)

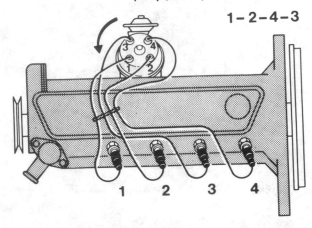

Fig. 13.42 Distributor cap to spark plug HT lead connections (Sec 4D)

the front balance weight. You will find that with this type of crankshaft, a standard shell is fitted to the seat in the crankcase but a yellow colour-coded shell is fitted to the main bearing cap.

8   If a green spot is seen on the crankshaft then this indicates that 0.254 mm (0.01 in) undersize main and/or big-end bearings are used in place of the standard diameter.

Cylinder bores, pistons, rings and connecting rods

9   Cylinder bore wear will usually have been evident from the smoke emitted from the exhaust during recent operation of the vehicle on the road, coupled with excessive oil consumption and fouling of spark plugs.

10   Engine life can be extended by fitting special oil control rings to the pistons. These are widely advertised, and will give many more thousands of miles without the need for a rebore, although this will be inevitable eventually. If this remedy is decided upon, remove the piston/connecting rods, as described in Part B, and fit the proprietary rings in accordance with the manufacturer's instructions.

11   Where a more permanent solution is decided upon, the cylinder block can be rebored by your dealer or engineering works, or by one of the mobile workshops which now undertake such work. The cylinder bore will be measured both for out-of-round and for taper to decide how much the bores should be bored out. A set of matching pistons will be supplied in a suitable oversize to suit the new bores.

12   Due to the need for special heating and installing equipment for removal and refitting of the interference type gudgeon pin, the removal and refitting of pistons to the connecting rods is definitely a specialist job, preferably for your Ford dealer.

13   The removal and refitting of piston rings is however well within the scope of the home mechanic. Do this by sliding two or three old feeler blades round behind the top compression ring so that they are at equidistant points. The ring can now be slid up the blades and removed. Repeat the removal operations on the second compression ring and then the oil control ring. This method will not only prevent the ring from dropping onto empty grooves as they are withdrawn, but it will also avoid ring breakage.

14   Even when new piston rings have been supplied to match the pistons, always check that they are not tight in their grooves and also

check their end gaps by pushing them squarely down their particular cylinder bore and measuring with a feeler blade. Adjustment of the end gap can be made by careful grinding to bring it within the specified tolerance.

15   If new rings are being fitted to an old piston, always remove any carbon from the grooves beforehand. The best tool for this job is the end of a broken piston ring. Take care not to cut your fingers, piston rings are sharp. The cylinder bores should be roughened with fine glass paper to assist the bedding-in of the new rings.

Timing sprockets and chain

16   The teeth on the timing sprockets rarely wear, but check for broken or hooked teeth even so.

17   The timing chain should always be renewed during a major engine overhaul. A worn chain is evident if, when supported horizontally at both ends, it takes on a deeply bowed appearance.

18   Finally check the rubber cushion on the tensioner spring leaf. If grooved or chewed up it should be renewed.

Flywheel

19   Inspect the starter ring gear on the flywheel for wear or broken teeth. If evident, the ring gear should be renewed in the following way. Drill the ring gear with two holes, approximately 7 or 8 mm (0.3 in) diameter and offset as shown (Fig. 13.33). Make sure that you do not drill too deeply or you will damage the flywheel.

20   Tap the ring gear downwards off its register and remove it.

21   Place the flywheel in the household refrigerator for about an hour and then heat the new ring gear to between 260 and 280°C (500 and 536°F) in an electric oven. Do not heat it above 290° (554°F) or its hardness will be lost.

22   Slip the ring onto the flywheel and gently tap it into position against its register. Allow it to cool without quenching.

23   The clutch friction surface on the flywheel should be checked for grooving or tiny hair cracks, the latter being caused by overheating. If

these conditions are evident, it may be possible to surface grind the flywheel provided its balance is not upset. Otherwise, a new flywheel will have to be fitted – consult your dealer about this.

Oil pump

24 The oil pump should be checked for wear by unbolting and removing the cover plate and checking the following tolerances (photo).

(a) *Outer rotor-to-pump body gap*
(b) *Inner rotor-to-outer rotor gap*
(c) *Rotor endfloat (use a feeler blade and straight-edge across pump body)*

Use feeler blade to check the tolerances, and if they are outside the specified values, renew the pump.

25 If the pump is serviceable, renew the O-ring and refit the cover (photo).

Oil seals and gaskets

26 Renew the oil seals on the timing cover and the crankshaft rear retainer as a matter of routine at time of major overhaul. Oil seals are cheap, oil is not! Use a piece of tubing as a removal and installing tool. Apply some grease to the oil seal lips and check that the small tensioner spring in the oil seal has not been displaced by the vibration caused during fitting of the seal.

27 Renew all the gaskets by purchasing the appropriate 'de-coke', short, or full engine set. Oil seals may be included in the gasket sets.

Crankcase

28 Clean out the oilways with a length of wire or by using compressed air. Similarly clean the coolant passages. This is best done by flushing through with a cold water hose. Examine the crankcase and block for stripped threads in bolt holes; if evident, thread inserts can be fitted.

29 Renew any core plugs which appear to be leaking, or which are excessively rusty.

30 Cracks in the casting may be rectified by specialist welding, or by one of the cold metal key interlocking processes available.

Camshaft and bearings

31 Examine the camshaft gear and lobes for damage or wear. If evident a new camshaft must be purchased, or one which has been 'built-up' such as are advertised by firms specialising in exchange components.

32 The bearing internal diameters should be checked against the Specifications if a suitable gauge is available; otherwise, check for movement between the camshaft journal and the bearing. Worn bearings should be renewed by your dealer.

33 Check the camshaft endfloat by temporarily refitting the camshaft and the thrust plate.

Cam followers

34 It is seldom that the cam followers wear in their bores, but it is likely that after a high mileage, the cam lobe contact surfaces will show signs of depression or grooving.

35 Where this condition is evident, renew the cam followers. Grinding out the wear marks will only reduce the thickness of the hardened metal of the cam follower, and further accelerate wear.

Cylinder head and rocker gear

36 The usual reason for dismantling the cylinder head is to decarbonise and to grind in the valves. Reference should therefore be made to the next sub-Section in addition to the dismantling operations described here. First remove the manifolds.

37 Using a standard valve spring compressor, compress the spring on

No 1 valve (valve nearest the timing cover). Do not overcompress the spring or the valve stem may bend. If it is found that, when screwing down the compressor tool, the spring retainer does not release from the collets, remove the compressor and place a piece of tubing on the retainer so that it does not impinge on the collets, and strike the end of the tubing a sharp blow with a hammer. Refit the compressor and compress the spring.

38 Extract the split collets and then gently release the compressor and remove it.

39 Remove the valve spring retainer, the spring and the oil seal.

40 Withdraw the valve.

41 Repeat the removal operations on the remaining seven valves. Keep the valves in their originally fitted sequence by placing them in a piece of card which has holes punched in it and numbered 1 to 8 (from the timing cover end).

42 Place each valve in turn in its guide so that approximately one third of its length enters the guide. Rock the valve from side to side. If there is any more than a barely perceptible movement, the guides will have to be reamed (working from the valve seat end) and oversize stemmed valves fitted. If you do not have the necessary reamer (tool 21-042 or 21-043), leave this work to your Ford dealer.

43 Examine the valve seats. Normally, the seats do not deteriorate but the valve heads are more likely to burn away in which case, new valves can be ground in as described in the next sub-Section. If the seats require re-cutting, use a standard cutter available from most accessory or tool stores, or consult your motor engineering works, but note that *hardened valve seats need special tools*.

44 Renewal of any valve seat which is cracked or beyond recutting is definitely a job for your dealer or motor engineering works.

45 If the cylinder head mating surface is suspected of being distorted due to persistent leakage of coolant at the gasket joint, then it can be checked and surface ground by your dealer or motor engineering works. Distortion is unlikely under normal circumstances with a cast iron head.

46 Check the rocker shaft and rocker arms pads which bear on the valve stem and faces for wear or scoring, also for any broken coil springs. Renew components as necessary after dismantling, as described in Part B. If the valve springs have been in use for 50 000 miles (80 000 km) or more, they should be renewed.

47 Reassemble the cylinder head by fitting new valve stem oil seals. Install No 1 valve (lubricated) into its guide and fit the valve spring with the closer coils to the cylinder head, followed by the spring retainer. Compress the spring and engage the split collets in the cut-out in the valve stem. Hold them in position while the compressor is gently released and removed.

48 Repeat the operations on the remaining valves, making sure that each valve is returned to its original guide, or if new valves have been fitted, into the seat into which it was ground.

49 On completion, support the ends of the cylinder head on two wooden blocks and strike the end of each valve stem with a plastic or copper-faced hammer, just a light blow to settle the components.

Cylinder head and pistons – decarbonising

50 With the cylinder head removed, as described in Part B, the carbon deposits should be removed from the combustion spaces using a scraper and a wire brush fitted into an electric drill. Take care not to damage the valve heads, otherwise no special precautions need be taken as the cylinder head is of cast iron construction.

4D.24 Check the oil pump rotor-to-body clearance at (A) and the inner-to-outer rotor clearance at (B)

4D.25 Oil pump O-ring seal (arrowed) must be renewed

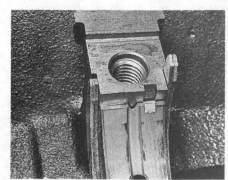

4D.66 Fit the centre main bearing upper shell and thrust washers

4D.74 Secure the camshaft sprocket retaining bolts with the lockplate tabs

4D.78 Refit the crankshaft rear oil seal retainer

4D.79 Locate the engine backplate over the two dowels

51   Where a more thorough job is to be carried out, the cylinder head should be dismantled as described previously, so that the valves may be ground in and the ports and combustion spaces cleaned, brushed and blown out, after the manifolds have been removed.

52   Before grinding-in a valve, remove the carbon and deposits completely from its head and stem. With an inlet valve, this is usually quite easy, simply scraping off the soft carbon with a blunt knife and finishing with a wire brush. With an exhaust valve the deposits are very much harder, and those on the head may need a rub on coarse emery cloth to remove them. An old woodworking chisel is a useful tool to remove the worst of the head deposits.

53   Make sure that the valve heads are really clean, otherwise the rubber suction cup of the grinding tool will not stick during the grinding-in operations.

54   Before starting to grind-in a valve, support the cylinder head so that there is sufficient clearance underneath for the valve stem to project fully without being obstructed.

55   Take the first valve and apply a little coarse grinding paste to the bevelled edge of the valve head. Insert the valve into its guide and apply the suction grinding tool to its head. Rotate the tool between the palms of the hands in a back-and-forth rotary movement until the gritty action of the grinding-in process disappears. Repeat the operation with the fine paste, and then wipe away all traces of grinding paste and examine the seat and bevelled edge of the valve. A matt silver mating band should be observed on both components, without any sign of black spots. If some spots do remain, repeat the grinding-in process until they have disappeared. A drop or two of paraffin applied to the contact surfaces will increase the speed of grinding-in, but do not allow any paste to run down into the valve guide. On completion, wipe away every trace of grinding paste using a paraffin-moistened cloth.

56   Repeat the operations on the remaining valves, taking care not to mix up their originally fitted sequence.

57   The valves are refitted as described previously.

58   An important part of the decarbonising operation is to remove the carbon deposits from the piston crowns. To do this, turn the crankshaft so that two pistons are at the top of their stroke and press some grease between these pistons and the cylinder walls. This will prevent carbon particles falling down into the piston ring grooves. Stuff rags into the other two bores.

59   Cover the oilways and coolant passages with masking tape and then, using a blunt scraper, remove all the carbon from the piston crowns. Take care not to score the soft alloy of the crown or the surface of the cylinder bore.

60   Rotate the crankshaft to bring the other two pistons to tdc and repeat the operations.

61   Wipe away the circle of grease and carbon from the cylinder bores.

62   Clean the top surface of the cylinder block by careful scraping.

Engine – reassembly

63   With everything clean, commence reassembly by oiling the bores for the cam followers and inserting them fully in their original sequence.

64   Lubricate the camshaft bearings and insert the camshaft from the timing cover end of the engine.

65   Fit the thrust plate and tighten the fixing bolts to the specified torque. The endfloat will already have been checked, as described previously.

66   Wipe clean the main bearing shell seats in the crankcase and fit the shells, noting that the lower shells do not have the lubrication groove. Using a little grease, stick the semi-circular thrust washers on either side of the centre bearing so that the oil grooves are visible when the washers are installed (photo).

67   Check that the Woodruff key is in position on the front end of the crankshaft and tap the crankshaft sprocket into place using a piece of tubing.

68   Oil the bearing shells and lower the crankshaft into the crankcase.

69   Wipe the seats in the main bearing caps and fit the bearing shells into them. Install the caps so that their markings are correctly positioned, as explained at dismantling.

70   Screw in the cap bolts and tighten evenly to the specified torque.

71   Now check the crankshaft endfloat. Ideally a dial gauge should be used, but feeler blades are an alternative if inserted between the face of the thrust washer and the machined surface of the crankshaft balance weight, after having prised the crankshaft first in one direction and then the other. Provided the thrust washers at the centre bearing have been renewed, the endfloat should be within the specified tolerance. If it is not, oversize thrust washers are available (see Specifications).

72   Rotate the crankshaft so that the timing mark on its sprocket is directly in line with the centre of the crankshaft sprocket mounting flange.

73   Engage the camshaft sprocket within the timing chain and then engage the chain around the teeth of the crankshaft sprocket. Push the camshaft sprocket onto its mounting flange. The camshaft sprocket bolt holes should now be in alignment with the tapped holes in the camshaft flange and both sprocket timing marks in alignment (Fig. 13.39). Turn the camshaft as necessary to achieve this, also withdraw the camshaft sprocket and reposition it within the loop of the chain. This is a 'trial and error' operation which must be continued until exact alignment of bolt holes and timing marks is achieved.

74   Screw in the sprocket bolts to the specified torque and bend up the tabs of a new lockplate (photo).

75   Bolt the timing chain tensioner into position, retract the tensioner cam spring and then slide the tensioner arm onto its pivot pin. Release the cam tensioner so that it bears upon the arm.

76   Fit the oil slinger to the front of the crankshaft sprocket so that its convex side is against the sprocket.

77   Using a new gasket, fit the timing cover, which will already have been fitted with a new oil seal. One fixing bolt should be left out at this stage as it also holds the water pump. Grease the oil seal lips and fit the crankshaft pulley. Tighten the pulley bolt to the specified torque (lock the crankshaft as described in paragraph 80).

78   Using a new gasket, bolt the crankshaft rear oil seal retainer into position. Tighten the bolts to the specified torque (photo).

79   Locate the engine adaptor (back) plate on its dowels and then fit the flywheel (photo).

80   Screw in and tighten the flywheel bolts to the specified torque. To prevent the flywheel turning, the starter ring gear can be jammed or a piece of wood placed between a crankshaft balance weight and the inside of the crankcase.

81   Install and centralise the clutch, as described in Chapter 5.

82   The pistons/connecting rods should now be installed. Although new pistons will have been fitted to the rods by your dealer or supplier, it is worth checking to ensure that with the piston crown arrow pointing

to the timing cover end of the engine, the oil hole in the connecting rod is on the left as shown (Fig. 13.41). Oil the cylinder bores.

83   Install the pistons/connecting rods.

84   Fit the sump.

85   Fit the oil pressure sender unit, if removed.

86   Turn the crankshaft until No 1 piston is at tdc (crankshaft pulley and timing cover marks aligned) and fit the oil pump complete with new gasket and a new oil filter.

87   Using a new gasket, fit the fuel pump. If the insulating block became detached from the crankcase during removal, make sure that a new gasket is fitted to each side of the block.

88   Fit the water pump using a new gasket.

89   Fit the cylinder head.

90   Refit the pushrods in their original sequence, and the rocker shaft.

91   Adjust the valve clearances and refit the rocker cover using a new gasket.

92   Fit the inlet and exhaust manifolds using new gaskets, and tighten the nuts and bolts to the specified torque.

93   Refit the carburettor using a new flange gasket and connect the fuel pipe from the pump.

94   Screw in the spark plugs and the coolant temperature switch (if removed).

95   Refit the thermostat and the thermostat housing cover.

96   Fit the pulley to the water pump pulley flange.

97   Fit the alternator and the drivebelt and tension the belt, as described in Chapter 11.

98   Refit the distributor, as described in Section 11.

99   Refit the distributor cap and reconnect the spark plug HT leads.

100   Bolt on and connect the water pipe to the side of the cylinder block.

101   Fit the breather pipe from the oil filler cap to the inlet manifold and fit the cap.

102   Check the sump drain plug for tightness. A new seal should be fitted at each oil change to prevent leakage. Refit the dipstick.

103   Refilling with oil should be left until the engine is installed in the vehicle.

Engine/transmission – reconnection and refitting

104   This is a direct reversal of the removal and separation from the transmission. Take care not to damage the engine ancillary components and body panels when raising the unit into position.

Reconnection

105   Reconnection of the engine and transmission is a reversal of separation, but if the clutch has been dismantled, check that the driven plate has been centralised as described in Chapter 5.

Refitting

106   Manoeuvre the engine/transmission under the vehicle and position it on the jack, or attach the lifting hoist. Raise the unit carefully until the right-hand mounting can be fitted, but leave the mounting nut and bolt slack at this stage.

107   Refit the transmission support crossmember and mountings to the body and transmission.

108   Lower the jack or hoist and let the power unit rest on its mountings. Ensure that none of the mountings are under strain, then tighten all the mounting nuts and bolts. Remove the jack or hoist.

109   Insert a finger into the driveshaft hole in the differential and align the gears ready to receive the driveshafts.

110   Using a new snap-ring on the inboard joint splines, reconnect the right-hand driveshaft to the transmission by having an assistant apply pressure on the roadwheel. Check that the snap-ring has locked in position.

111   Reconnect the left-hand driveshaft using the same procedure.

112   Refit the anti-roll bar and both suspension lower arms using the reverse of the removal procedure. When connecting the suspension arms to the hub carrier, ensure that the head of the Torx type bolt faces the rear of the car.

113   Refit the engine/transmission splash shields to the inner wheel arches.

114   Reconnect the gearchange rod to the transmission selector shaft, and the stabiliser to the transmission housing. Adjust the gearchange linkage as described in Section 13.

115   Fit the starter motor leads to their terminals.

116   Connect the engine earth leads.

117   Refit the exhaust system and bolt the downpipe to the manifold.

118   Refit the hot air box which connects with the air cleaner.

119   Reconnect the clutch operating cable.

120   Reconnect the electrical leads, the fuel pipe, the brake vacuum hose and speedometer cable.

121   Reconnect the throttle cable and the choke cable.

122   Reconnect the radiator coolant hoses, and heater hoses.

123   Fill up with engine oil, transmission oil and coolant, then reconnect the battery.

124   Refit the bonnet, bolting the hinges to their originally marked positions. Reconnect the screen washer pipe.

125   Fit the air cleaner and reconnect the hoses and the air cleaner intake spout.

126   Once the engine is running, check the ignition timing, idle speed and mixture adjustment.

127   If a number of new internal components have been installed, run the vehicle at restricted speed for the first few hundred miles to allow time for the new components to bed in. It is also recommended that with a new or rebuilt engine, the engine oil and filter are changed at the end of the running-in period.

5 Engine (1.3 litre HCS)

General description

The 1.3 litre OHV HCS engine was introduced at the beginning of 1989 and is the only 1.3 litre engine now fitted to the Orion range.

This engine was a development of the old 1.3 OHV unit and comprised Ford's latest lean burn technology. Virtually every aspect of the HCS engine was of new design but there was still a similarity to the old engine.

The major differences began in the cylinder head, where the inlet valve ports and combustion chambers were designed to impart a high degree of swirl to the incoming fuel/air mixture. The valve arrangement was also different, using a 'mirror' design where the inlet valves of the centre cylinders were opposing one another.

Combined with the new 3-D fully electronic ignition system which lacked any moving parts, the result was an economical engine with cleaner exhaust emissions, able to run on leaded or unleaded fuel without adjustment to the ignition timing.

Servicing the new HCS engine could follow similar lines to the old OHV engine as described in Section 4, the only differences being those mentioned in this Section.

Cylinder head – removal and refitting

1   The procedure is covered in Section 4, Part D, but reference should be made to the relevant Sections in this Supplement for disconnection of differing individual components.

2   Note, the new cylinder head bolt tightening procedure is completed in the three stages as shown in the Specifications. This procedure is applicable to M11 sized bolts with a necked shank (a reduced diameter section between the bolt head and the threaded portion).

3   At each stage, all the bolts must be tightened in the order shown in Fig.1.8, Chapter 1. Cylinder head bolts may be used a total of three times (including initial fit) and must be suitably marked to indicate each removal operation. If doubt exists as to how many times the bolts have been used, obtain and fit new bolts.

Valve clearances – adjustment

4   The procedure is as described in Section 4, Part B, but note that valve arrangement has been altered and is now as follows.

Valve No	Cylinder No
1 – Exhaust	1
2 – Inlet	1
3 – Exhaust	2
4 – Inlet	2
5 – Inlet	3
6 – Exhaust	3
7 – Inlet	4
8 – Exhaust	4

Engine – method of removal

5   The engine can be lifted from the engine bay provided the radiator and certain other ancillary components are removed first to give room for manoeuvring. These are detailed in the removal procedure.

5.6 A locally made up lifting eye

5.7 Lifting off the bonnet

5.12A Radiator lower mounting bolt ...

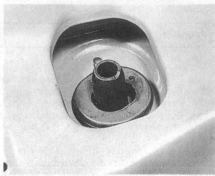

5.12B ... and upper locating peg

5.12C Lifting out the radiator

6   Before commencing work it will be necessary to make up two lifting eyes from $\frac{1}{4}$ in mild steel bar, approximately 3 in long and $1\frac{1}{2}$ in wide, with two $\frac{1}{2}$ in holes drilled in them (photo).

Engine – removal

7   Remove the bonnet as described in Chapter 12, Section 5, but additionally disconnect the earth lead between the bonnet and body-work (photo).
8   Disconnect the battery negative lead.
9   Remove the air cleaner as described in Section 10 of this Supplement.
10   Drain the engine oil.
11   Drain the coolant (Chapter 2, Section 3).
12   Remove the radiator (Chapter 2, Section 9) (photos).
13   Disconnect the heater hoses from the inlet manifold and the water pump.
14   Disconnect the lead at the anti-run-on valve solenoid on the carburettor.
15   Disconnect the throttle cable (see Section 10).
16   Disconnect the choke cable (see Section 10).
17   Disconnect the fuel inlet (blue clip) and outlet (green clip) pipes from the fuel pump (see Section 10).
18   Disconnect the brake servo vacuum hose from the inlet manifold by depressing the outer ring and pulling the hose out (photo).
19   Disconnect the earth lead from the inlet manifold.
20   Disconnect the following electrical connections:

(a)   *Cooling fan thermal switch on thermostat housing (photo)*
(b)   *Coolant temperature sender (photo)*
(c)   *Alternator*
(d)   *Ignition coil (see Section 11)*
(e)   *Oil pressure switch*
(f)   *Ignition thermal switch in inlet manifold (see Section 11)*
(g)   *Ignition TDC sender*
(h)   *Reversing light switch*
(i)   *Transmission housing earth lead*

21   Disconnect the speedometer cable (photo).
22   Disconnect the exhaust downpipe from the exhaust manifold flange (photo). The nuts are easier to reach from underneath the vehicle and once undone support the exhaust on wire.
23   Disconnect the starter motor and engine earth lead which is under one of the starter motor bolts (Chapter 11, Section 19).
24   Remove the starter lead support bracket from the transmission housing.
25   Disconnect the gearchange mechanism (Chapter 6, Section 4).
26   Remove the driveshafts (Chapter 8, Section 5). **Note:** *On removal of the driveshafts push a length of wooden dowel into the hole vacated by the driveshaft in the transmission housing to prevent the sun gears of the differential becoming misaligned. A piece of broom handle is ideal, but will have to be turned down somewhat.*
27   Support the right-hand side of the engine on a trolley jack and just take the weight of the engine.
28   Remove the right-hand engine mounting by undoing the top nut on the wing panel, removing the bolt accessible from inside the wheel arch, and the three bolts securing the mounting bracket to the engine (photos).
29   Once removed, undo the Torx headed bolt securing the mounting to the bracket (photo).
30   Refit the bracket to the cylinder block and bolt one of the made-up lifting eyes to the bracket using one of the spare bolts (photo).
31   Fit the other lifting eye to the transmission housing (photo).
32   Secure suitable lifting gear to the engine and just begin to take the weight. **Note:** *If because of the angle of the lifting sling/chain the carburettor is likely to be damaged, remove the carburettor as described in Section 10.*
33   Remove the alternator (Chapter 11, Section 11) to give more room for manoeuvring the engine out.
34   Pull the transmission breather hoses from inside the wing panel.
35   Remove the nut from the left-hand front engine mounting.
36   Remove the nut from the left-hand rear mounting and also remove the nuts securing the mounting bracket to the transmission housing and remove the bracket (photos).
37   Commence lifting the engine slowly, checking all round that every-

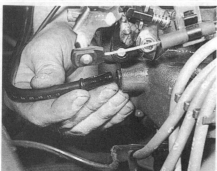
5.18 Disconnecting the brake vacuum servo hose

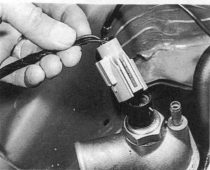
5.20A Disconnecting the cooling fan thermal switch ...

5.20B ... and coolant temperature sender

5.21 Disconnecting the speedometer cable

5.22 View of the exhaust downpipe from below

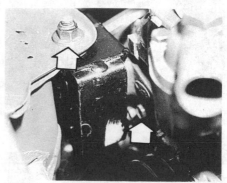
5.28A Right-hand engine mounting nuts/bolts (arrowed)

5.28B One bolt (arrowed) is accessible from within the wheel arch

5.29 Torx headed bolt (arrowed) securing the mounting to the bracket

thing has been disconnected and that the engine does not foul other components as it is lifted. Swing the engine and tilt it as necessary to clear obstacles (photos).

38   Once out of the engine bay, swing the engine clear and lower it onto a suitable work surface.

39   Remove the starter motor (Chapter 11, Section 18) and then separate the transmission from the engine (Chapter 1, Section 16).

Engine – dismantling

40   Follow the procedure given in Chapter 1, Section 18, noting the following differences:

41   There is no coolant transfer pipe along the front of the engine.

42   Disconnect and remove the HT leads as described in Section 11.

43   There is no distributor to remove. The procedure for removal of the coil is given in Section 11.

44   The big-end cap bolts are Torx type bolts (photo).

45   Remove the ignition system TDC sender as described in Section 11, before removing the flywheel to prevent damage to the sender.

46   There are five main bearings, numbered 1 to 5 from the timing chain end. The caps have an arrow on them which points to the timing chain end (photo).

47   The crankshaft thrust bearings are still fitted either side of the centre main bearing.

48   The rear oil seal carrier is secured in place by Torx type bolts.

Engine – examination and renovation

49   The procedure is as described in Chapter 1, Section 19.

Cylinder head and pistons – decarbonising

50   The procedure is as described in Chapter 1, Section 21, noting the following.

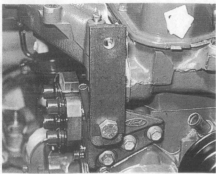

5.30 Lifting eye bolted to right-hand mounting position ...

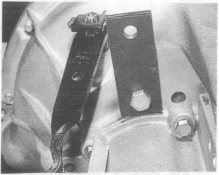

5.31 ... and on transmission housing

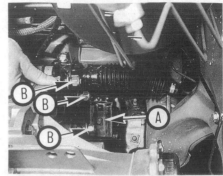

5.36A Mounting nut location A and bracket-to-transmission housing nuts B

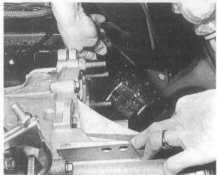

5.36B Removing the mounting bracket

5.37A Lifting the engine and transmission upwards ...

5.37B ... and out of the engine compartment

5.44 Big-end cap bolts are Torx type bolts

5.46 Crankshaft laid in position

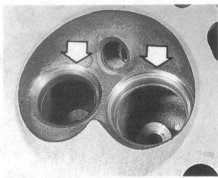

5.51 View of the swirl chamber in the cylinder head showing the valve seals (arrowed)

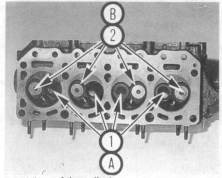

5.52 View of the cylinder head with valves fitted

5.53A Tape the end of the valve stem before fitting the valve stem seal

5.53B Use a double-depth socket to push the seal fully home

A Inlet side   1 Inlet valves
B Exhaust side 2 Exhaust valves

5.57 Line up the flange using a spanner

51   When cleaning out the swirl ports, great care must be exercised not to damage the valve seats, especially if using power tools (photo).
52   The valve arrangement is different, being of mirror effect, where the inlet valves for number 2 and 3 cylinders are next to each other (photo).
53   When refitting the valve stem oil seals, tape the end of the stem to prevent damage to the seal as it is fitted, and use a double-depth socket or length of tube to push the seals fully down (photos). Remove the tape on completion.
54   Hardened valve seats cannot be re-worked using conventional tools.

Engine – reassembly

55   Follow the procedure in Chapter 1, Section 23, noting the following.
56   Tighten the main bearing cap bolts to the specified torque (see Chapter 1) before fitting the oil pick-up tube.
57   When fitting the oil pick-up tube, use a spanner on the flats of the flange to line it up (photo).
58   The flywheel is dowelled to the crankshaft and cannot be fitted off-centre (photo).
59   The big-end bearing cap bolts are angle tightened after an initial torque load (see Specifications). Use the correct tool if it is available or make up a card template with the specified angle marked on it (photos).
60   Apart from lining up the camshaft and crankshaft sprocket timing marks (for valve timing), there is no ignition timing mark to worry about.

Engine – refitting

61   The engine refitting procedure is a reversal of the removal procedure given earlier.

6   Engine (1.3, 1.4 and 1.6 litre CVH)

Sump and gasket – modifications

1   In April 1985 a modified sump and one-piece sump gasket were introduced on CVH engines to improve sealing in the region of the oil pump and rear oil seal carrier-to-cylinder block joints.
2   Removal and refitting procedures are essentially the same as for the earlier four-piece gasket arrangement but note the following when refitting:

  (a)   The gasket should be fitted dry but jointing compound should be applied to the oil pump and rear oil seal carrier-to-cylinder block joints as shown in Fig. 13.43.
  (b)   To aid installation it is helpful if a few studs can be screwed into the retaining bolt holes on each side to locate the gasket as the sump is fitted. As the sump is placed in position make sure that the spacing pips in the sump face locate in the holes in the gasket, then fit the retaining bolts finger tight. Remove the studs and fit the rest of the bolts
  (c)   Tighten the bolts evenly in two stages to the specified torque

3   The one-piece gasket can be fitted to earlier engines provided that it is used in conjunction with the modified sump. The four-piece gasket is still available for use with earlier sumps.

Timing belt – general

4   Should damage occur to the teeth of the timing belt or teeth shear off, when the belt tension is known to be correct, check that the coolant pump and tensioner pulley turn freely and are not partially seized.
5   If these components are in good order then remove the sump pan and check that the oil pump pick-up mounting flange is tight and not distorted. Air entering at this point can cause the oil supply to the hydraulic tappets to foam. This in turn will prevent the tappets from operating correctly and apply excessive strain on the belt.
6   Renew of the timing belt has now been included in the service schedule, and this must be carried out at 36 000 mile (60 000 km) intervals. This applies retrospectively to all CVH engines covered by this manual. **Note:** *From April 1988 (build code JG) a modified timing belt tensioner incorporating a larger diameter tensioner roller was introduced, and from October 1988 an improved timing belt is used. When renewal of the timing belt becomes necessary, only the latest, improved timing belt must be used (the older type will no longer be available). On models produced before April 1988 this will entail renewal of the tensioner roller.*

Timing belt cover – modifications

7   A two-piece timing belt cover has been progressively introduced on all later CVH engines covered by this manual. The upper half of the cover is visually similar to the earlier one-piece type and can be removed after undoing the two retaining bolts. To withdraw the lower half it will first be necessary to remove the crankshaft pulley, and this procedure is described in Chapter 1. The two retaining bolts can then be undone and the cover removed.
8   When carrying out any repairs which entail removal of the crankshaft pulley (ie timing belt renewal, crankshaft front oil seal renewal, etc) remember to place the cover lower half in position before refitting the pulley.

5.58 Fitting the flywheel to the crankshaft

5.59A Using the correct tool ...

5.59B ... and utilising a card template to angle tighten the big-end cap bolts

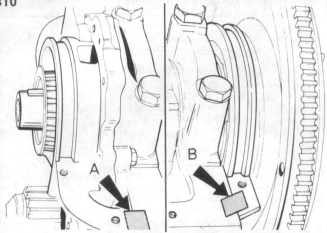

Fig. 13.43 Sealing compound application with one-piece sump gasket (Sec 6)

A   Oil pump joint
B   Rear oil seal carrier joint
Apply sealer to shaded areas arrowed

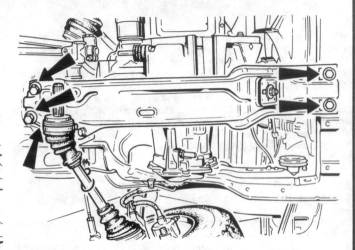

Fig. 13.44 Ensure spacing pips and gasket holes (inset) engage when fitting modified sump and one-piece gasket (Sec 6)

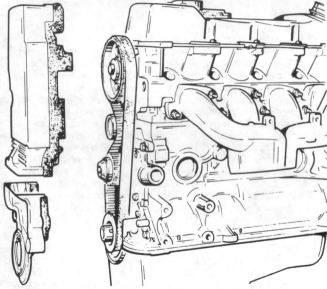

Fig. 13.45 Two-piece timing belt cover arrangement (Sec 6)

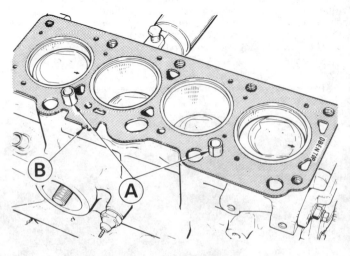

Fig. 13.46 Transmission support crossmember front and rear attachments (Sec 6)

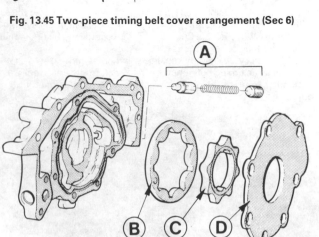

Fig. 13.47 Exploded view of the rotor type oil pump (Sec 6)

A   Pressure relief valve   C   Inner rotor
B   Outer rotor   D   Oil pump cover

Fig. 13.48 Cylinder head gasket details (Sec 6)

A   Locating dowels   B   Gasket identification teeth
                                   (1.4 litre version shown)

6.12A Where a two-piece timing belt cover is fitted, undo the bolts ...

6.12B ... and remove the upper half

6.18A Crankshaft sprocket projection aligned with mark on pump housing (arrowed)

6.18B Timing mark on camshaft sprocket aligned with TDC mark on cylinder head

Timing belt – removal, refitting and adjustment (engine in car)

Note: *The following procedure supersedes that given in Chapter 1, Section 4 but it must be pointed out that accurate adjustment of the belt entails the use of Ford special tools. An approximate setting can be achieved using the method described in this Section, but the tension should be checked on completion.*

9   Disconnect the battery negative lead.

10   Release the alternator mounting and adjuster link bolts, push the alternator in towards the engine and slip the drivebelt off the pulleys.

11   Using a spanner on the crankshaft pulley bolt, turn the crankshaft until the notch on the pulley is aligned with the TDC (O) mark on the timing belt cover scale. Now remove the distributor cap and check that the rotor arm is pointing towards the No 1 cylinder HT lead segment in the cap. If the rotor arm is pointing towards the No 4 cylinder segment, turn the crankshaft through another complete turn and realign the pulley notch with the TDC mark.

12   On early models unscrew the four bolts and remove the one-piece timing belt cover. On later models fitted with a two-piece cover, unscrew the two upper bolts and remove the top half, then unscrew the two lower bolts. The lower half cannot be removed at this stage (photos).

13   Undo the bolts and remove the right-hand engine splash shield.

14   Using a ring spanner unscrew the crankshaft pulley retaining bolt by removing the starter motor as described in Chapter 11 and by locking

the flywheel ring gear with a cold chisel or similar tool to prevent the crankshaft rotating. Remove the pulley followed by the lower half of the timing belt cover.

15   Slacken the two bolts which secure the timing belt tensioner and, using a large screwdriver, prise the tensioner to one side to relieve the tension of the belt. If the tensioner is spring-loaded, tighten one of the bolts to retain it in the slackened position.

16   If the original belt is to be refitted, mark it for direction of travel and also the exact tooth positions on all three sprockets.

17   Slip the timing belt off the camshaft, water pump and crankshaft sprockets.

18   Before refitting the belt, check that the crankshaft is still at TDC (the small projection on the belt sprocket front flange in line with the TDC mark on the oil pump housing – photo) and that the timing mark on the camshaft sprocket is opposite the TDC mark on the cylinder head (photo). Adjust the position of the sprockets slightly, but avoid any excessive movement of the sprockets while the belt is off, as the piston crowns and valve heads may make contact.

19   Engage the timing belt with the teeth of the crankshaft sprocket and then pull the belt vertically upright on its right-hand run. Keep it taut and engage it with the teeth of the camshaft sprocket. Check that the positions of the sprockets have not altered.

20   Wind the belt round the camshaft sprocket, around and under the tensioner and over the water pump sprocket.

21   Refit the crankshaft pulley and tighten the bolt to the specified

torque, using the same procedure as used previously to stop the crankshaft turning. On later models make sure that the timing belt cover lower half is placed in position before refitting the pulley.

22   To adjust the belt tension, slacken the tensioner and move it towards the front of the car to apply an initial tension to the belt. Secure the tensioner in this position.

23   Rotate the crankshaft through two complete revolutions, then return to the TDC position. Check that the camshaft sprocket is also at TDC as previously described.

24   Grasp the belt between thumb and forefinger at a point midway between the crankshaft and camshaft sprocket on the straight side of the belt. When the tension is correct it should just be possible to twist the belt through 90° at this point. Slacken the tensioner and using a large screwdriver as a lever, move it as necessary until the tension is correct. Tighten the tensioner bolts, rotate the camshaft to settle the belt, then recheck the tension. It will probably take two or three attempts to achieve success.

25   It must be emphasised that this is an approximate setting only and should be rechecked by a Ford dealer at the earliest opportunity.

26   Refit the starter motor, engine splash shield, distributor cap and timing belt cover/s.

27   Refit the alternator driveshaft and adjust its tension as described in Chapter 11.

28   Reconnect the battery (earth lead last).

Engine mountings – removal and refitting

29   At the beginning of 1986 the method of supporting the engine/transmission assembly was changed. A longitudinal support crossmember, attached to the body at the front and rear, is now used and the two left-hand mountings beneath the transmission are attached to the crossmember.

30   The removal and refitting procedure is the same as for the OHV engine, and reference should be made to Section 4, Part B of this Supplement.

Engine/transmission – removal and refitting (general)

31   When removing the engine/transmission assembly on models produced from 1986 onwards, the procedures described in Chapter 1 are still applicable, but note the following points:

(a)   Some difficulty may be experienced in removing the selector shaft cap nut and locking assembly to drain the transmission oil. This is due to the close proximity of the transmission mounting bracket, making access to the cap nut awkward. This is of no great consequence, as it is not absolutely necessary to drain the transmission oil for the removal operation. Note, however, that a quantity of oil will be released when the driveshafts are removed, so have a container at the ready

(b)   On models produced from February 1987 onwards, select 2nd gear for four-speed transmissions, or 4th gear for five-speed transmissions, before disconnecting the gearchange linkage

(c)   When disconnecting the engine mountings, the two mountings on the left-hand side under the transmission should not be removed, but instead undo the bolts at the front and rear securing the crossmember to the body. The crossmember and mountings can then be detached if necessary, after the engine/transmission assembly has been removed

(d)   On models equipped with the Anti-lock Braking System, refer to Section 16 of this Supplement and remove the modulator drivebelts before releasing the driveshafts. Refit and adjust the drivebelts as described in Section 16 after installation

Oil pump – modifications

32   From 1986 onwards the previously used gear type oil pump has been superseded by a new low friction rotor type pump.

33   The removal and refitting procedures remain the same for the new unit, as does the examination and renovation information contained in Chapter 1, Section 19. Note however that wear limit tolerances are now supplied for both pump types, and the clearances can be checked with a feeler blade as follows:

34   Measure the outer rotor-to-housing clearance by inserting the feeler blade between the outer rotor and the pump body wall.

35   Measure the inner-to-outer rotor clearance by inserting the feeler blade between the peak of one of the inner rotor gear teeth or lobes, and the outer rotor.

36   Measure the rotor-to-cover endfloat by placing a straight edge across the pump body face and inserting a feeler blade between the straight edge and the rotors.

37   If any of the measured clearances are outside the tolerances given in the Specifications at the beginning of this Supplement, renew the pump. Note that the rotor type pump can only be fitted to post-1986 engines, due to the modified drive slot on the front of the crankshaft.

Cylinder head gasket – modifications

38   From 1986 onwards the configuration of the holes on the cylinder head gasket have been changed, and a different gasket is used for each size of engine. Identification is by teeth on the rear facing edge of the gasket, as shown in Fig. 13.48 according to engine as follows:

    1.6 litre: 4 teeth
    1.4 litre: 2 teeth

39   Earlier engines are unaffected by this change.

1.4 litre engine – description

40   At the beginning of 1986 a new 1.4 litre version of the CVH engine was introduced, to replace the 1.3 litre engine which was deleted from the range.

41   The change in capacity is achieved by using the 1.6 litre cylinder block with a reduced bore size, and the 1.3 litre crankshaft with increased stroke. Other changes include revisions to the cylinder head shape, the exhaust ports and the valves, modifications to the pistons and flywheel, and the inclusion of all the modifications described previously in this Section for all CVH engines.

42   The servicing, repair and overhaul procedures are the same as for the other CVH engines, and reference should be made to the earlier parts of this Section and to Chapter 1.

Cylinder head bolts – revised tightening torque

43   Note the revised cylinder head tightening torque given in the Specifications. The four stage procedure remains the same.

44   Note also that cylinder heads tightened in this manner **should not be re-torqued** as this is **unnecessary**.

7   Engine (1.6 CVH EFI EEC-IV)

General description

The 1.6 CVH EFI engine introduced in 1990 replaces the previous 1.6 FI unit. It is basically the same CVH engine, modified in certain areas to take account of the new Electronic Engine Management system.

Only those differences affecting the servicing procedures given in Chapter 1 and Section 6 of this Supplement are dealt with in this Section, all other procedures remaining as before.

A crankshaft position sensor (CPS) is fitted axially on the cylinder block rear flange, similar to that on the 1.3 HCS engine. The CPS transmits engine speed and crankshaft position signals. The indexing for the CPS is cast into the rear of the flywheel.

New pistons with modified crown patterns which match the hemispherical combustion chambers and increase compression ratio are fitted. The piston oil control rings have been improved and the piston pin is shorter and lighter.

As the distributor has been replaced by the solid-state E-DIS 4 ignition system and drive from the camshaft no longer required, a plastic blanking plate covers the housing where the distributor was originally fitted.

The camshaft differs in having increased overlap at high speed improving engine operating characteristics.

The valve shape has been modified to improve the gas flow through the inlet and exhaust ports. Improved material is also used on the exhaust valve seats.

A redesigned air intake system for use with the EEC is fitted, the valve cover being changed to accommodate the intake ducting.

The exhaust manifold is new and incorporates an exhaust heatshield.

Pistons – removal and refitting

1   The pistons are made of light alloy, are not slotted, and have two oil return holes on each side.

2   The piston crown pattern is governed by the position of the valves.

3   New piston ring profiles are shown in Fig. 13.51.

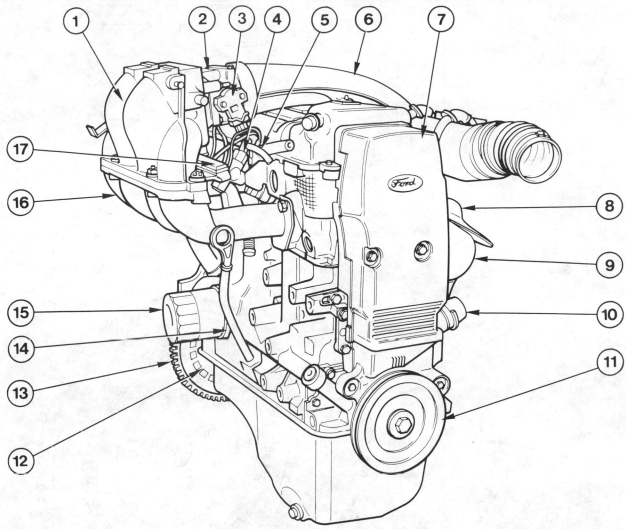

Fig. 13.49 View of 1.6 litre CVH EFI engine (Sec 7)

1　Intake manifold (upper)
2　Throttle housing
3　Throttle position sensor
4　Fuel rail
5　Fuel hose
6　Air intake duct
7　Timing belt cover
8　Heat shield
9　Exhaust manifold
10　Coolant inlet pipe
11　Crankshaft pulley
12　Flywheel indexing
13　Flywheel
14　Oil cooler (special-to-type)
15　Oil filter
16　Intake manifold (lower)
17　Cable duct

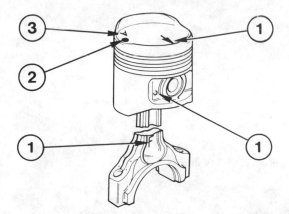

Fig. 13.50 Piston and connecting rod markings on 1.6 litre EFI EEC-IV engine (Sec 7)

1　Arrow, pimple and F mark
2　Piston pin bore grade
3　Piston diameter grade

4　When fitting piston/connecting rod assemblies, the arrow on the piston crown or the cast pimple on the piston side by the piston pin bore must be in relation to the F for front mark on the connecting rod, and all three marks must face the timing belt end of the engine.

Flywheel – removal and refitting
5　The flywheel has been modified to incorporate the indexing for the CPS.
6　A larger cut-out in the indexing denotes 90° BTDC on number one cylinder.
7　The six bolt holes are asymmetric so the flywheel can only be fitted to the crankshaft in one position.

Engine – removal and refitting
Note: *the procedure is basically as described in Chapter 1 except for those components associated with the EFI and EEC systems. Where necessary, reference should be made to the relevant Sections of this Supplement for details of these components.*
8　Disconnect the battery negative terminal.
9　Pull the HT leads from the spark plugs and remove the leads from the air intake duct and guide clip on the rocker cover.

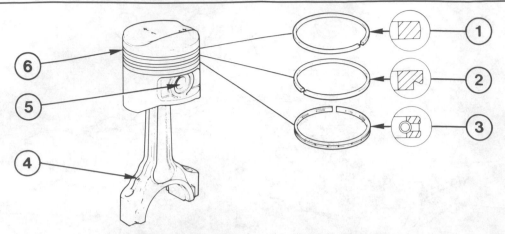

Fig. 13.51 Piston ring profile on 1.6 litre EFI EEC-IV engine (Sec 7)

1   Top compression ring   3   Oil control rings   5   Piston pin
2   Second compression ring   4   Oil squirt hole   6   Piston ring grooves

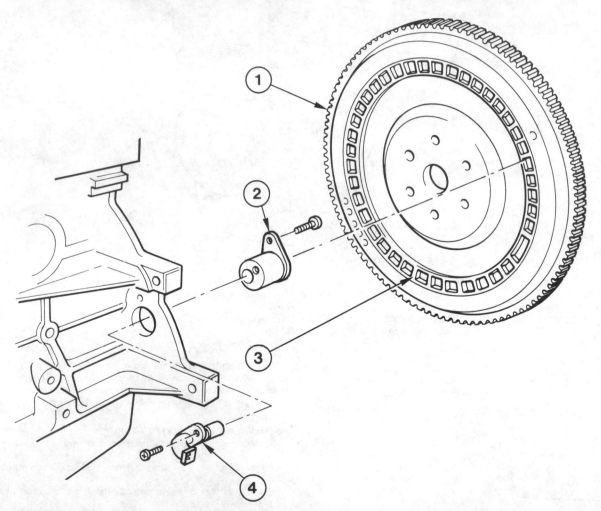

Fig. 13.52 Flywheel and CPS sensor assembly on 1.6 litre EFI EEC-IV engine (Sec 7)

1   Flywheel   2   CPS holder   3   Index cut-outs   4   CPS sensor

10   Remove the bolts from the intake duct and disconnect the duct from the throttle housing.

11   Disconnect the idle speed control valve multiplug and its vacuum hose at the inlet manifold.

12   Unclip the air cleaner housing cover and withdraw the cover, idle speed control valve and its vacuum hose, and the air intake duct as one unit.

13   Remove the air cleaner element.

14   Drain the cooling system as described in Chapter 2.

15   Disconnect the radiator lower hose from the water pump and the

7.19 Oil trap hose connections

A   Vent hose   B   Rocker cover   C   Oil trap

7.25 Ignition coil suppressor connection

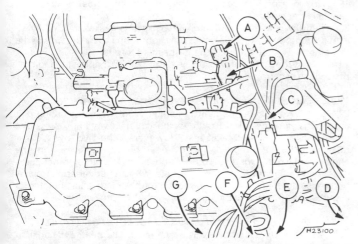

Fig. 13.53 Multi-plug location on 1.6 litre CVH EFI engine (Sec 7)

A Engine wiring loom	E Cooling fan temperature
B Speed sensor	sensor
C Ignition coil	F Temperature gauge
D Reversing lamp switch	sender unit
	G CPS sensor

coolant hoses from the thermostat housing.
16   Disconnect the accelerator cable.
17   Disconnect the MAP sensor vacuum hose from the inlet manifold.
18   Disconnect the crankcase breather hose from the rocker cover.
19   Disconnect the vent pipe from the oil trap-to-T-piece and the oil trap hose to the rocker cover (photo).
20   Disconnect the brake servo vacuum hose from the inlet manifold.
21   Depressurise the fuel system, then disconnect the fuel inlet pipe from the fuel rail and the outlet pipe from the pressure regulator.
22   Disconnect the engine earth lead from the transmission housing.
23   Disconnect the speedometer drive.
24   Disconnect the following multiplugs.

    (a)   engine wiring loom
    (b)   speed sensor
    (c)   ignition coil
    (d)   reversing lamp switch
    (e)   cooling fan temperature sensor
    (f)   temperature gauge sender unit
    (g)   CPS sensor

25   Disconnect the ignition coil suppressor where fitted (photo).
26   The remaining procedure is as described in Chapter 1, Section 16,

paragraph 15 onwards, with the additional operations as appropriate.
27   Remove the under-engine splash panels.
28   Disconnect the heater hose from the inlet manifold.
29   Unbolt the brake pipe bracket from the transmission bearer.
30   Refitting is a reversal of the removal procedure.

Engine – overhaul
31   Overhaul of the EFI engine is basically as described in Chapter 1, but note that the valve seats in the cylinder head cannot be reworked using conventional cutting tools.

8   Engine (1.4 litre CVH CFi engine)

General description
    The 1.4 litre CVH CFi engine is basically similar to earlier 1.4 litre CVH engines but is modified as follows.
    A knock sensor is screwed into the cylinder block near to the oil filter.
    The inlet manifold is similar to earlier CVH engines, but modified to house the injection unit.
    The pistons have a modified crown pattern adapted to the low compression of the engine.
    An electric fuel pump is used, so there is no mechanical pump mounted on the cylinder block.
    Servicing and overhaul procedures are as described for 1.4 litre CVH engines, taking account of the changes to the fuel and ignition systems given in later Sections.

9   Cooling system

Cooling system draining – general
1   On later models a drain plug is fitted to the radiator, located at the bottom left-hand corner. When draining the system on models so equipped, refer to the procedure given in Chapter 2, Section 3 but instead of removing the bottom hose, unscrew the drain plug using a large screwdriver. Refit the drain plug securely before filling.

Radiator fan unit (1986-on) – removal and refitting
2   When removing the radiator fan and cowling on 1986 models onwards, note that the cowling is secured by two bolts at the top and two clips at the bottom. Bearing this in mind, the remainder of the procedure is as given in Chapter 2, Section 8.

Radiator (1986-on) – removal and refitting
3   At the beginning of 1986 a new lightweight aluminium crossflow

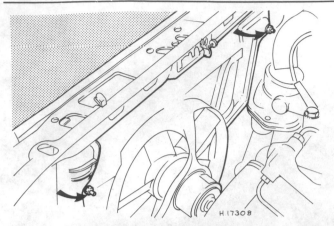

Fig. 13.54 Radiator fan cowling upper securing bolts (arrowed) –
1986 models onward (Sec 9)

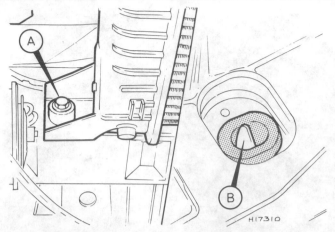

Fig. 13.55 Radiator attachments – 1986 models onwards (Sec 9)

A   Lower retaining bolts   B   Upper retaining lugs

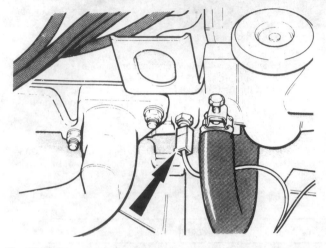

Fig. 13.56 Temperature gauge sender unit location in cylinder head
(Sec 9)

radiator with plastic side tanks was fitted to all models. Removal and refitting procedures for the new unit are as follows.

4   Drain the cooling system as described previously.

5   Disconnect the battery negative lead.

6   Release the retaining clips and disconnect all the hoses from the radiator.

7   Remove the radiator fan unit as described previously.

8   To provide greater clearance for radiator removal, slacken the alternator mounting and adjustment arm bolts and push the alternator in towards the engine as far as it will go.

9   Unscrew the two radiator retaining bolts.

10   Move the bottom of the radiator in towards the engine, then lower it to disengage the two upper retaining lugs. Carefully lift the radiator from the engine compartment.

11   Inspection and cleaning recommendations remain unchanged, and are described in Chapter 2, Section 9.

12   Refitting is the reversal of removal. Refill the system as described in Chapter 2, and adjust the alternator drivebelt as described in Chapter 11.

Water pump (OHV engine) – removal and refitting

13   Drain the cooling system as described previously.

14   Release the water pump pulley bolts now while the drivebelt is still in position. Any tendency for the pulley to turn as the bolts are unscrewed can be restrained by depressing the top run of the belt.

15   Release the alternator mounting and adjuster link bolts, push the alternator in towards the engine and slip the drivebelt from the pump pulley.

16   Disconnect the coolant hose from the pump. Remove the previously slackened pulley bolts and take off the pulley.

17   Unbolt the water pump and remove it.

18   Peel away the old gasket from the engine block and clean the surface.

19   No provision is made for repair and if the pump is leaking or noisy it should be renewed.

20   Refitting is a reversal of removal. Use a new gasket, smeared with jointing compound, and apply the same compound to the threads of the fixing bolts. Tighten the bolts to the specified torque.

21   Adjust the drivebelt tension, as described in Chapter 11, and refill the cooling system.

Water pump (CVH engines) – removal and refitting

22   On CVH engines fitted with the later type two-piece timing belt cover it is not possible to remove the cover lower half unless the crankshaft pulley is removed first. However, if the two lower cover retaining bolts are removed, the cover can be moved away from the engine sufficiently for the pump removal and refitting procedures described in Chapter 2 to be carried out with the cover still in place. Refer also to the timing belt removal, refitting and adjustment procedures described in the previous Section before proceeding.

Water pump (1.6 litre EFI engine – removal and refitting)

23   The procedure is basically as described in Chapter 2 and earlier in this Section.

24   However, in order to gain access the air cleaner housing must first be removed.

25   To do this, first remove the air cleaner element as described in Section 10.

26   Remove the right-hand wheel arch liner.

27   Undo the bolts securing the air cleaner housing to the inner wing panel and withdraw the housing.

28   Refitting is a reversal of removal.

Thermostat (OHV engine) – removal, testing and refitting

29   On the OHV engine, the thermostat housing is located at the crankshaft pulley end of the cylinder head.

30   Drain the cooling system as described previously.

31   Disconnect the electrical lead from the thermal switch and the coolant hoses from the thermostat housing outlets.

32   Undo the two bolts and lift off the thermostat housing, then withdraw the thermostat.

33   Testing of the thermostat is described in Chapter 2, Section 7.

34   Refitting is the reversal of removal, but use a new housing gasket lightly smeared with jointing compound. Refill the cooling system as described in Chapter 2.

Heating and ventilation system (1986-on) description

35   Certain changes have been made to the heating and ventilation system for 1986 models onwards. The most significant of these being the modification to the heater controls, which are now of a rotary type instead of the lever type used previously.

36   Apart from the following information, the procedures given in Chapter 2 are still applicable to later models.

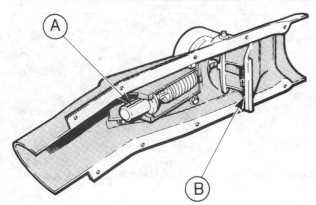

Fig. 13.57 Waxstat type air cleaner components in air cleaner spout (Sec 10A)

A   Wax capsule   B   Flap valve

Heater controls (1986-on) – adjustment

37   Set the air temperature control just off the cold position, and the air distribution control just off the closed position.

38   Release the securing bolts on the cable clamps, and pull the temperature control and air direction flap valve arms to the COLD and CLOSED positions respectively. Check to see that the setting of the knobs on the control panel has not changed and retighten the cable clamps.

Heater controls (1986-on) – removal and refitting

39   Pull the air ducts off the heater on the right-hand side and move them clear.

40   Detach the right-hand cable from the heater casing and temperature control flap lever.

41   Pull the cover off the left-hand actuating lever and detach the cable from the heater casing and air distribution flap lever.

42   Pull off the heater control knobs and undo the two screws, one located under each outer control knob, then remove the control panel bezel. Remove the centre vents.

43   Undo the two control panel screws and withdraw the panel with cables, through the aperture.

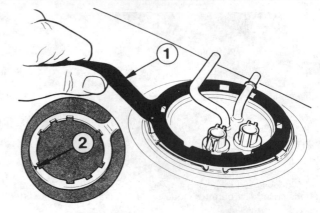

Fig. 13.58 Using special tool 23-026 (1) to remove the lock ring. Alignment mark (2) also shown (1.6 EFI models) (Sec 10A)

44   Refitting is a reversal of removal. On completion adjust as described previously.

Temperature gauge sender unit – removal and refitting

45   With the engine cold remove the expansion tank cap to release any pressure in the system. This will minimise coolant loss when the sender unit is removed. Refit the expansion tank cap.

46   Disconnect the lead from the sender and unscrew the sender from the cylinder head (adjacent to the thermostat housing).

47   Refit in reverse order using a sealing compound on the threads of the sender unit.

48   On completion, top up the cooling system as described in Chapter 2.

10   Fuel and exhaust systems

PART A: GENERAL

Waxstat controlled air cleaner – description

1   From 1986 onwards a waxstat type air cleaner was progressively

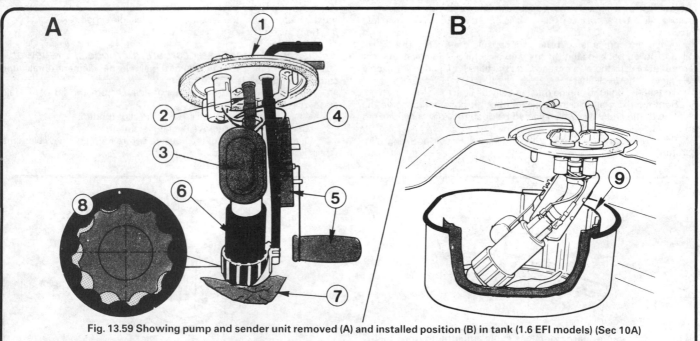

Fig. 13.59 Showing pump and sender unit removed (A) and installed position (B) in tank (1.6 EFI models) (Sec 10A)

1 Fuel pump/sender unit cover	3 Pulsation damper	6 Fuel pump and pressure relief valve	8 Section through roller cell pump
2 Fuel feed pipe	4 Fuel return pipe	7 Fuel filter	9 Plastic reservoir chamber
	5 Sender unit		

10A.11 Air cleaner lid retaining screw locations on later carburettor models

10A.12 Release the air cleaner lid retaining caps (where fitted)

10A.16 Disconnecting the crankcase ventilation hose at the air cleaner body

10A.17 Cold air intake hose removal from air cleaner spout

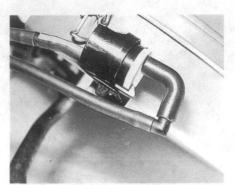

10A.18 Fuel trap on side of air cleaner housing on 1.3 litre HCS engine

10A.20 Adaptor on underside of air cleaner housing

A   Hose from oil   B   Hose from
    filler cap   crankcase

introduced on certain engines to replace the thermostatically controlled type used previously.
2   The waxstat air cleaner performs the same hot and cold air blending operation using a flap valve as described in Chapter 3, but the flap valve is controlled by a wax capsule and is not dependent on manifold vacuum.
3   When the engine is cold the wax capsule contracts and the flap valve is pulled back to shut off the cold air intake. As engine ambient temperature rises the wax expands and the flap is opened to admit only cold air into the air cleaner.
4   To test the unit the engine must initially be cold.
5   Remove the manifold-to-air cleaner hot air hose and observe the position of the flap valve which should be open to allow only hot air to enter.
6   Refit the hose and warm up the engine to normal operating temperature.

7   Remove the hot air hose again and check the position of the flap valve. With the engine at normal operating temperature the flap should be closed to admit only cold air into the air cleaner.
8   If this is not the case the waxstat is defective and the air cleaner must be renewed as the waxstat is not available separately.
9   Refit the hot air hose on completion of the checks.

Air cleaner element (later carburettor models) – renewal

10   The procedure for renewal of the air cleaner element on all later carburettor models is as follows.
11   Undo and remove the securing screws from the lid of the air cleaner housing (photo).
12   Where fitted, release the lid securing clips (photo).
13   Lift off the lid and remove the filter element.
14   Clean out the inside of the housing before fitting the new element which is a reversal of removal.

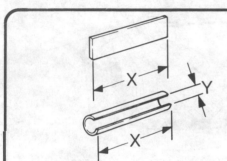

Fig. 13.60 Suitable spacer for choke cable adjustment – pre-1986 models (Sec 10A)

X = 37.0 to 37.5 mm   Y = 12.0 mm (0.47 in)
(1.45 to 1.47 in)   minimum

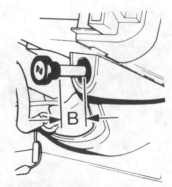

Fig. 13.61 Insert previously made spacer in position (B) for choke cable adjustment – pre-1986 models (Sec 10A)

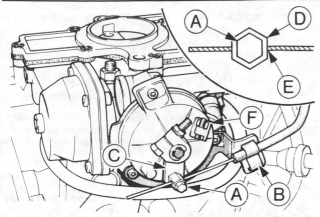

Fig. 13.62 Choke cable attachments at carburettor (Sec 10A)

A   Lower cable clamp bolt
B   Outer cable clip
C   Operating lever
D   Cable clamp
E   Point 22.0 mm from cable
    end
F   Full choke stop

Note: *the crankcase ventilation system adaptor on the underside of the air cleaner housing must be renewed at the same routine maintenance intervals as the air cleaner element. Refer to part G for details.*

Air cleaner housing (later carburettor models) – removal and refitting

15   Disconnect the battery negative terminal.
16   Where they are accessible from above, disconnect the crankcase ventilation hoses (photo).
17   Disconnect the cold air intake hose from the housing (photo).
18   On HCS engines, unclip the fuel trap (part of the ignition system) from the side of the housing (photo).
19   Undo the retaining screws or bolts on the air cleaner lid and lift the housing from the carburettor.
20   On HCS and CVH engines, either disconnect the crankcase ventilation hoses from the adaptor on the underside of the housing, or alternatively, unclip the adaptor from the housing, leaving the hoses connected (photo).
21   Remove the air cleaner housing from the engine.
22   Refitting is a reversal of removal.

Air cleaner element (1.6 EFI EEC-IV engines) – renewal

23   The air cleaner element is located in a plastic housing on the front right-hand inner wing.
24   To renew the element, unclip the cleaner housing top cover and lift it back, then withdraw the element.
25   Clean the inside of the housing before fitting the new element which is a reversal of removal.

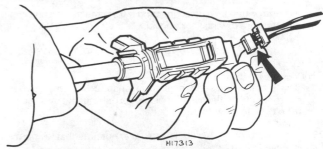

Fig. 13.63 Choke warning light wire connection at choke cable assembly – 1986 models onwards (Sec 10A)

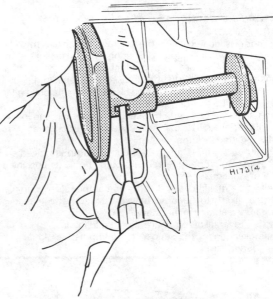

Fig. 13.64 Using a small probe to release the choke knob locking pin – 1986 models onward (Sec 10A)

Air inlet duct (1.6 EFI EEC-IV engines) – removal and refitting

26   A plastic air inlet duct is fitted between the air cleaner housing and the throttle housing. The duct also provides a channelling route for the spark plug HT leads.
27   To remove the duct, first disconnect the HT leads from the spark plugs and lay them to one side.
28   Disconnect the duct from the air cleaner housing.
29   Remove the two bolts securing the duct to the valve cover (photo).

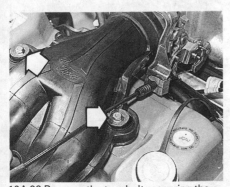

10A.29 Remove the two bolts securing the duct to the valve cover (arrowed)

10A.32 Fuel pump location on OHV engines

10A.33 Fuel pump connections on HCS engine

A   Inlet from tank
B   Outlet to carburettor
C   Return to tank

30   Withdraw the duct, disconnecting it from the throttle housing.
31   Refitting is a reversal of removal.

Fuel pump (carburettor engines) – testing, removal and refitting
OHV engine
32   The procedure is as described in Chapter 3, Section 6, but the pump is mounted on the cylinder block, and is actuated by an eccentric cam from the camshaft (photo).
HCS engine
33   The same comments apply as above, but note that the pump has three connections (photo).
34   The additional hose is the fuel return to the tank which is fitted to the carburettor on OHV engines.

Fuel pump and sender unit (1.6 EFI EEC-IV engines) – removal and refitting
35   The fuel pump is located inside the fuel tank, so the tank must first be removed as described in Chapter 3, Section 7 noting the following.
36   The sender unit/pump are located under a plate on the top of the tank. The tank must be lowered sufficiently for the sender unit/pump, fuel outlet and return and vent hoses to be disconnected before the tank can be removed, leaving the fuel filler pipe in position.
37   Once the tank is removed, the sender unit/pump can be un-screwed using special tool 23-026 or a suitable lever engaged in the cut-outs of the screwed lockring.
38   No overhaul procedures for the sender or pump are given so if either is defective it must be renewed, although it may be possible to renew each item individually.
39   There may be a fuel filter fitted at the end of the fuel pick up pipe, and this is quite likely to become blocked on some high mileage vehicles, ultimately resulting in fuel starvation.
40   Refitting is a reversal of removal noting the following.
41   Use a new seal under the sender unit/pump as the old seal will have distorted during removal.

42   When fitting the sender unit/pump to the tank ensure the locating lug fits into the cut-out in the tank.
43   Use a light smear of grease on the fuel filler neck seal to assist in fitting.

Accelerator cable (1989-on) – removal and refitting
44   Disconnect the accelerator cable from the accelerator pedal and remove it, as described in Chapter 3.
45   To disconnect the cable from the carburettor or throttle housing, release the cable end fitting from the throttle valve lever, pull the clip from the rubber grommet and release the grommet and cable from the bracket (photo).
46   Refit in reverse order and adjust as described later.
47   If the accelerator cable is being disconnected for reasons other than cable renewal, then disconnect the cable from the throttle lever as described above. Unbolt and release the cable bracket from the carburettor or throttle housing, leaving the rubber grommet and clip secured in the bracket. This will eliminate the need for adjustment when refitting.

Accelerator cable (1989-on) – adjustment
48   On carburettor models, remove the air cleaner housing.
49   On all models, pull out the clip securing the rubber grommet to the bracket (photo).
50   Have an assistant fully depress the accelerator pedal and keep it depressed.
51   Refit the clip to the grommet.
52   Release the accelerator pedal, then fully depress it once more and check that full throttle opening is achieved.
53   On carburettor models, refit the air cleaner housing.

Choke control cable – removal, refitting and adjustment
Pre-1986 models
54   Removal and refitting of the cable is as described in Chapter 3,

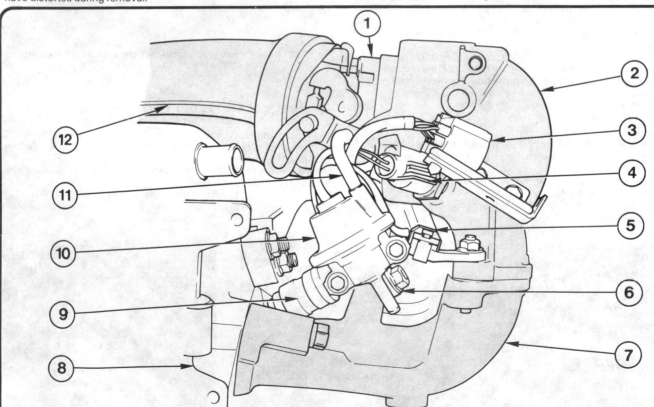

Fig. 13.65 Upper and lower sections of inlet manifold and components attached (1.6 EFI EEC-IV models) (Sec 10A)

1	Throttle housing	4	Air charge temperature sensor	7	Lower section of inlet manifold	10	Fuel pressure regulator
2	Upper section of manifold	5	Cable duct	8	Cylinder head	11	Vacuum line
3	EEC IV control line with holder	6	Fuel rail	9	Injector	12	Air inlet duct

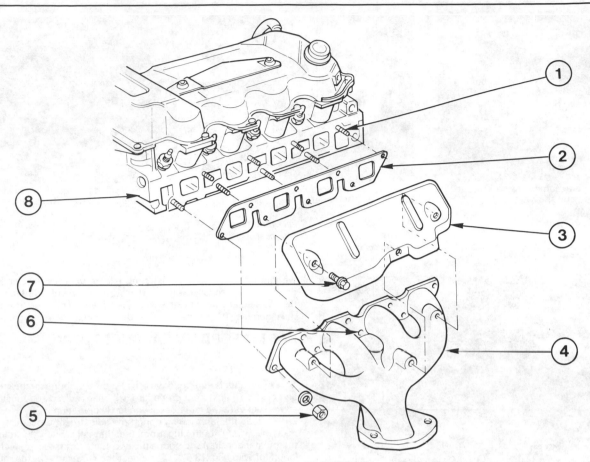

Fig. 13.66 Exhaust manifold on 1.6 EFI EEC-IV models (Sec 10A)

1 Stud	3 Heat shield	5 Nut	7 Bolt (for heat shield)
2 Gasket	4 Exhaust manifold	6 Centring hole	8 Cylinder head

Section 10, but the adjustment procedure has been revised and is now as follows.

55 From either a flat strip of metal or preferably metal tubing make up a spacer as shown in Fig. 13.60.

56 Pull out the choke and locate the spacer behind the choke knob. Ensure that the spacer remains in position throughout the procedure.

57 At the carburettor end, mark the inner cable at a point 22 mm (0.86 in) from the end using pencil or tape. On some cables the cable may be kinked for reference at this point, or a ferrule may be fitted.

58 Insert the cable in the cable clamp until the mark or ferrule is against the edge of the clamp. Tighten the clamp bolt.

59 Pull the outer cable so that the operating lever on the choke is against the 'full choke' stop on the housing. Secure the outer cable to its bracket, in this position, using the retaining clip.

60 Remove the spacer and check that the operating lever contacts the 'choke off' stop and 'full choke' stop on the housing when the choke knob is pushed in and pulled out respectively. On completion of the adjustment ensure that there is a small clearance between the lever and the 'off stop' when the choke knob is pushed in.

1986 models onwards

61 Disconnect the battery negative lead.

62 Remove the air cleaner as described previously.

63 At the carburettor end of the cable, loosen the cable clamp bolt, detach the outer cable securing clip at the choke control bracket and disconnect the cable (photo).

64 Working inside the car remove the steering column shrouds for access to the cable.

65 From behind the facia disconnect the warning light wire from the choke control assembly.

66 Using a small probe, depress the locking pin on the underside of the choke knob collar and remove the knob.

67 Unscrew the choke control retaining collar and withdraw the cable from under the facia. Pull the cable through the bulkhead and remove it from inside the car.

68 Refitting is the reversal of removal, but in conjunction with the following adjustment procedure.

69 With the cable in position in the facia and routed through the bulkhead, push the choke knob fully in and engage the inner cable end with the clamp at the carburettor.

70 Pull the cable through the clamp up to the cable ferrule, then tighten the clamp bolt.

71 Pull out the choke knob to the full choke position and also hold the choke lever on the carburettor in the full choke position. Secure the cable to the bracket with the clip.

72 Check that with the choke knob pulled fully out the choke lever contacts the full choke stop on the carburettor and returns fully to the choke off position when the knob is pushed in. On models fitted with the Ford VV carburettor, ensure that there is a small clearance between the choke lever and the choke off stop when the choke knob is pushed fully in.

HCS engines

73 The procedure is as described above, but additionally disconnect the cable from the carburettor by releasing the outer cable securing clip and unhooking the cable end fitting from the choke lever (photo).

Inlet manifold (1.6 EFI EEC-IV engines) – description, removal and refitting

74 A cast aluminium, two section inlet manifold is used on these models.

75 The lower section is bolted to the cylinder head in much the same way as on earlier models, the upper section being bolted to the lower section to form an attachment for the throttle housing.

10A.45 Accelerator cable support bracket
(1.3 litre HCS engine shown)

A   Securing bolt
B   Securing clip

10A.49 Accelerator cable assembly on 1.6
litre EFI EEC-IV model

A   Throttle lever   C   Grommet
B   Grommet   D   Bracket
    securing clip

10A.63 Releasing the choke cable clamp bolt
(OHV models, 1986-on) (arrowed)

10A.73 Choke cable outer cable clamp (A) and end fitting (B) on 1.3
HCS engine

76   The complete inlet manifold can be removed after disconnec-
tion/removal of the components mounted on the manifold (refer to
Fig. 13.65) and the relevant paragraphs of Section E.
77   When refitting the manifold, or bolting the two halves together,
ensure that all traces of old gasket are removed from the manifold and
cylinder head and use new gaskets throughout.

Exhaust manifold (1.6 EFI EEC-IV engines) – description, removal and refitting
78   The exhaust manifold on these models has been redesigned and is
slightly different to earlier models, although removal and refitting
procedures are basically the same.
79   Note that the centre lower hole is smaller than the others and is
used as a centering point.
80   A steel heat shield is bolted to the upper half of the manifold.

Operation on unleaded fuel
81   To operate continuously on unleaded fuel an engine must be fitted
with hardened valve seat inserts. Most engines built from 1986-on have
hardened valve seats and can operate on unleaded fuel.
82   However, some may require ignition timing adjustment to prevent
detonation or pinking.
83   Engines built before 1986, which do not have hardened valve seats
can run on unleaded fuel, however leaded fuel must be used on every
fourth refill of the fuel tank. The ignition timing must also be adjusted by
the recommended amount.
84   From 1990, all engines can run on either leaded or unleaded fuel

without ignition timing adjustment, except vehicles with an **exhaust
catalyst** which **must be** operated exclusively on **unleaded fuel**.
85   Where any doubt exists as to the suitability of an engine to run on
unleaded fuel, the advice of a Ford dealer should be sought.

PART B: FORD VV CARBURETTOR

Adjustments
1   On all models equipped with the Ford VV carburettor the idle speed
and mixture adjustment procedure has been revised and must now be
carried out with the radiator cooling fan in operation.
2   To keep the fan running during the adjustment procedure, disconnect the wiring multi-plug from the thermal switch (located in the
thermostat housing) and bridge the two contacts in the plug with a short
length of wire (Fig. 13.67). Disconnect the wire and refit the multi-plug
on completion of the adjustments. Make sure that the engine and
ignition are switched off when connecting and disconnecting the bridging wire.
3   On 1984 models onwards equipped with automatic transmission,
the following additional information should be noted.
4   Slacken the downshift adjusting screw (refer to Chapter 6, Fig. 6.74)
to provide a clearance of between 2.0 and 3.0 mm (0.08 to 0.12 in).
5   Adjust the idle speed and mixture as described in Chapter 3 in
conjunction with the previous information.
6   On completion adjust the downshift screw to give a clearance of
between 0.1 and 0.3 mm (0.004 and 0.012 in).
7   Increase the engine speed, allow it to return to idle and recheck the
downshift clearance.
8   On all VV carburettors produced from November 1985, the mixture
adjustment screw has been changed from a slotted screw head type to
an internal 4 mm hexagonal socket-head type. A suitable Allen key
should now be used for adjustment.

Fig. 13.67 Temporary bridging wire in cooling fan thermal switch
multi-plug (Sec 10B)

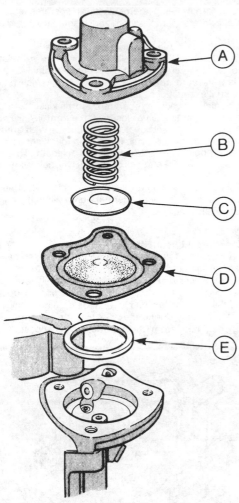

Fig. 13.68 Exploded view of the modified pump – Ford VV carburettor (Sec 10B)

A   Pump cover   D   Diaphragm
B   Spring   E   Spacer
C   Metal plate   F   Vacuum passage

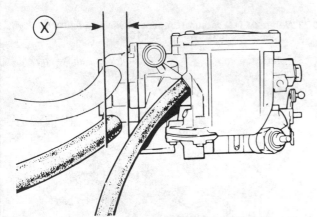

Fig. 13.71 Fuel and choke hose clearance – Ford VV carburettor (Sec 10B)

X = 11.0 mm (0.40 in)

Accelerator pump and air control diaphragm – modifications

9   If, during carburettor overhaul, it is found that the accelerator pump or air control diaphragms are perished and in need of removal, then the

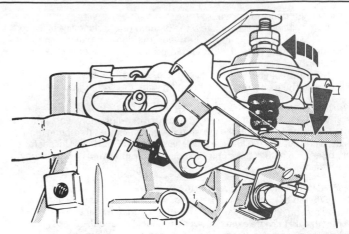

Fig. 13.69 Setting throttle damper clearance using a feeler blade (arrowed) – Ford VV carburettor (Sec 10B)

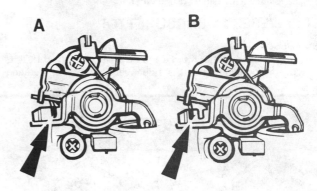

Fig. 13.70 Choke spring leg position – Ford VV carburettor (Sec 10B)

A   Correctly located   B   Incorrectly located

latest type modified components should be fitted.
10   The accelerator pump diaphragm is supplied as a repair kit and comprises the diaphragm, coloured spacer, metal plate, and spring, as shown in Fig. 13.68.
11   With the accelerator pump cover, spring and original diaphragm removed from the carburettor, clean away all traces of old gasket from the cover, if one was fitted.
12   Fit the coloured spacer into the pump body recess, followed by the diaphragm, gasket side towards the cover.
13   Place the metal plate on the diaphragm, followed by the spring, then fit the new cover and secure with the three screws.
14   The latest type air control diaphragm is manufactured from a material having a high resistance to deterioration due to fuel and fuel additives, and can be identified from the earlier type by being held in colour. The previous type was black.
15   Renew of the diaphragm is covered in Chapter 3, Section 18.

Throttle damper – removal, refitting and adjustment

16   Certain later models are fitted with a throttle damper mounted on a bracket on the side of the carburettor to allow progressive closure of the throttle linkage.
17   To remove the damper, remove the air cleaner as described in Part A, slacken the locknut and remove the damper from its bracket.
18   Refit the damper by screwing it into place in the bracket, then adjust the unit as follows.
19   Warm up the engine to normal operating temperature, then switch off. Connect a tachometer in accordance with the manufacturer's instructions and bridge the radiator cooling fan multi-plug as described previously.
20   Start the engine and increase its speed to 3200 ± 50 rpm by means of the idle speed adjustment screw. When the speed has stabilised, switch off the engine.
21   Rotate the secondary throttle lever clockwise to remove any play between the primary and secondary throttle levers, but ensure that the

primary lever does not move.
22   Using a feeler blade, unscrew the damper until a clearance of 0.1 to 0.3 mm (0.004 to 0.01 in) exists between the damper plunger and the secondary throttle lever. Hold the damper in this position and tighten the locknut.
23   Start the engine and return the idle speed to the specified rpm. Disconnect the tachometer and bridging wire, then refit the air cleaner.

Manual choke – general

24   When carrying out any repair, overhaul or adjustment work which entails removal of the choke housing cover, check that the spring leg is located correctly in the linkage lever, as shown in Fig. 13.70. Unsatisfactory operation of the choke unit can occur if the spring leg is not properly positioned.

Fuel and choke hose clearances

25   Whenever the fuel or choke hoses to this carburettor are detached for any reason it is essential when refitting to ensure that a clearance of 11 mm (0.4 in) or more exists between the fuel line and the choke hoses. If the clearance between them is less than this the heat transference from the choke hoses may cause fuel vaporization which will in turn give poor engine idling and possibly stalling when the engine is hot.

PART C: WEBER 2V CARBURETTOR

General description

1   The Weber 2V carburettor fitted to 1.3 HCS, and the 1.4 and 1.6 litre CVH engines from 1986 onwards is a dual venturi type incorporating bypass idling, fixed main jet system, vacuum operated secondary venturi, manual accelerator pump system and vacuum operated power valve.
2   The choke operates on the primary venturi only and is manually controlled on the 1.3 HCS and 1.4 CVH engine, and automatically controlled by coolant temperature on 1.6 CVH engines. Included in the choke system is a vacuum operated pull-down unit which pulls the choke off during cruise conditions.
3   On 1.4 CVH engines, a vacuum operated throttle kicker, acting as a damper, is used to allow progressive closure of the throttle linkage. This same throttle kicker is also used on 1.6 CVH models with automatic transmission, but it performs a reverse function in that it serves to hold the throttle linkage open slightly when drive is selected. There is no throttle kicker fitted to 1.3 HCS engines or 1.6 CVH models with manual transmission.
4   A back-bleed solenoid is used on 1.4 CVH versions which reduces the amount of fuel supplied to the accelerator pump when the engine is at normal operating temperature.

Adjustments

Idle speed and mixture adjustment

5   Before carrying out the following adjustments ensure that all other engine variables, ie, ignition timing, spark plug gap etc have been checked, and where necessary adjusted to their specified settings. The air cleaner must be fitted, the engine must be at normal operating temperature and the radiator cooling fan must be running.
6   To keep the fan running during the adjustment procedure, disconnect the wiring multi-plug from the thermal switch (located in the

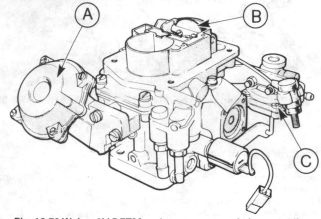

Fig. 13.72 Weber 2V DFTM carburettor general view – 1.4 litre models (Sec 10C)

A   Secondary venturi vacuum unit
B   Choke plate operating on primary venturi
C   Throttle kicker

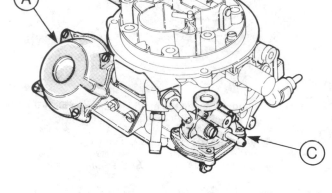

Fig. 13.73 Weber 2V TLD carburettor general view – 1.6 litre models, 1986 onwards (Sec 10C)

A   Secondary venturi vacuum unit
B   Automatic choke unit
C   Throttle kicker

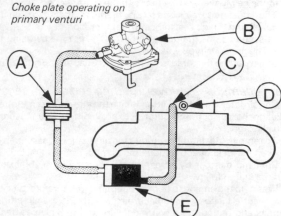

Fig. 13.74 Weber carburettor throttle kicker system – 1.4 litre models (Sec 10C)

A   Vacuum sustain valve
B   Throttle kicker
C   Vacuum port
D   Mixture adjustment screw
E   Fuel trap

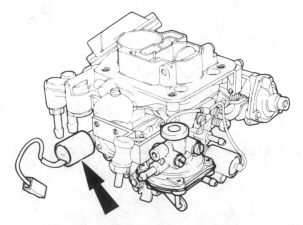

Fig. 13.75 Weber carburettor back bleed solenoid – 1.4 litre models (Sec 10C)

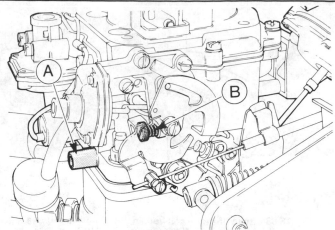

Fig. 13.76 Idle mixture adjustment screw (A) and idle speed adjustment screw (B) – 1.4 litre models (Sec 10C)

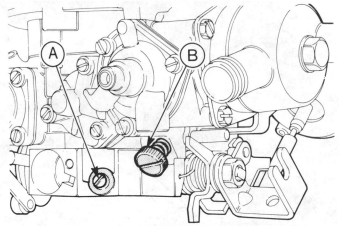

Fig. 13.77 Idle mixture adjustment screw (A) and idle speed adjustment screw (B) – 1.6 litre models, 1986 onwards (Sec 10C)

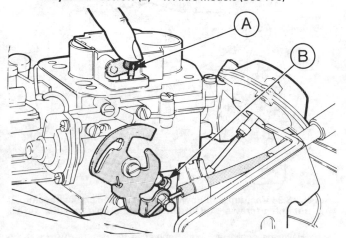

Fig. 13.78 Fast idle speed adjustment – 1.3 and 1.4 litre models (Sec 10C)

A Choke plate held open   B Fast idle adjusting screw

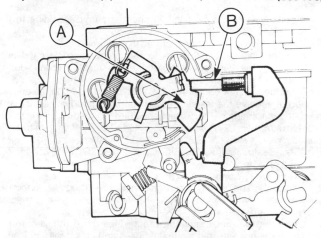

Fig. 13.79 Fast idle speed adjustment – 1.6 litre models, 1986 onwards (Sec 10C)

A Fast idle cam   B Fast idle adjusting screw on third step of cam

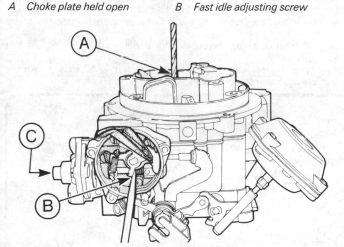

Fig. 13.80 Choke vacuum pull-down adjustment – 1.6 litre models, 1986 onwards (Sec 10C)

A Twist drill   C Adjusting screw
B Diaphragm held fully open

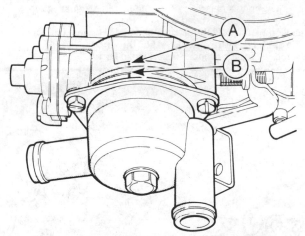

Fig. 13.81 Bi-metal coil housing and choke body alignment marks – 1.6 litre models, 1986 onwards (Sec 10C)

A Dot punch mark   B Choke alignment mark on housing

thermostat housing) and bridge the two contacts in the plug with a short length of wire (Fig. 13.67).

7 Start the engine and turn the idle speed adjustment screw (Figs. 13.76 and 13.77) (photos) as necessary to obtain the specified idle speed. If available use a tachometer for this operation to ensure accuracy.

8 Adjustment of the idle mixture setting should not be attempted in territories where this may cause a violation of exhaust emission regulations. Where these regulations are less stringent the following procedure may be used.

9 Using a small screwdriver, prise out the tamperproof plug (if fitted)

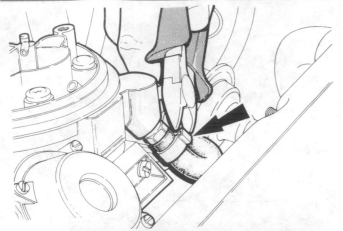

Fig. 13.82 Cutting off crimped type fuel hose clip (Sec 10C)

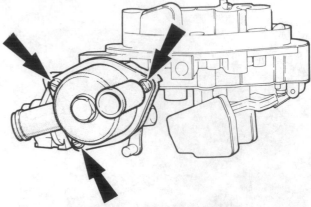

Fig. 13.83 Choke bi-metal coil housing retaining screws – 1.6 litre models, 1986 onwards (Sec 10C)

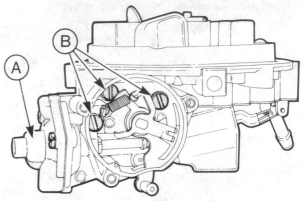

Fig. 13.84 Vacuum pull-down housing (A) and choke housing (B) retaining screws – 1.6 litre models, 1986 onwards (Sec 10C)

over the idle mixture screw (photo).

10   If a CO meter is to be used, connect the unit according to the manufacturer's instructions.

11   Adjust the idle speed, as described in paragraph 7.

12   Run the engine at 3000 rpm for 30 seconds to clear the inlet manifold of excess fuel. Repeat this operation every 30 seconds during the adjustment procedure.

13   Turn the idle mixture screw (Figs. 13.76 and 13.77) in the desired direction to achieve the fastest possible engine speed consistent with smooth even running or the correct specified CO reading on the meter scale. **Note** that on 1.3 HCS engines, an Allen key is required to turn the mixture screw.

14   If necessary, readjust the idle speed setting. Refit the cooling fan multi-plug on completion.

Fast idle speed (1.3 and 1.4 litre models)

15   Adjust the engine idle speed and mixture settings as previously described, then switch off the engine. Leave the tachometer connected from the previous operation.

16   Undo the four bolts securing the air cleaner to the carburettor, disconnect the hot and cold air intake hoses and lift off the air cleaner. Position the air cleaner clear of the carburettor, but leave the crankcase breather hoses and the vacuum supply hose connected.

17   Pull the choke knob fully out and start the engine.

18   Using a finger on the linkage lever as shown in Fig. 13.78 hold the choke plate open and note the fast idle speed.

19   If adjustment is necessary turn the fast idle adjusting screw (Fig. 13.78) until the specified speed is obtained (photo).

20   On completion refit the air cleaner and disconnect the tachometer.

Fast idle speed (1.6 litre models – 1986 onwards)

21   Remove the air cleaner as described in Part A.

22   Have the engine at normal operating temperature with a tachometer connected in accordance with the manufacturer's instructions.

23   With the engine stopped, open the throttle linkage slightly by hand and close the choke plate until the fast idle adjusting screw lines up with the third (middle) step of the fast idle cam (Fig. 13.79). Release the throttle so that the fast idle screw rests on the cam. Release the choke plate.

24   Without touching the accelerator pedal, start the engine by just turning the key.

25   Note the fast idle speed and if adjustment is necessary, turn the fast idle adjusting screw until the specified speed is obtained.

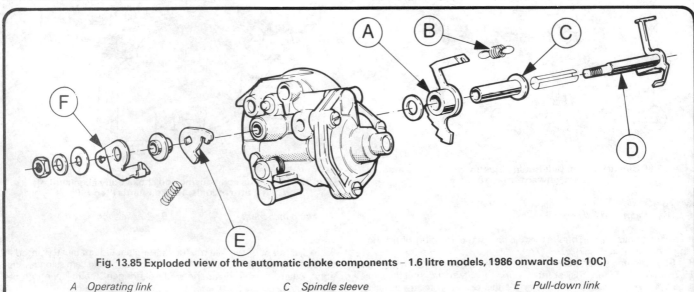

Fig. 13.85 Exploded view of the automatic choke components – 1.6 litre models, 1986 onwards (Sec 10C)

A   Operating link
B   Fast idle cam return spring
C   Spindle sleeve
D   Connecting rod and lever
E   Pull-down link
F   Actuating lever

10C.7A Idle speed screw (A) and mixture adjustment screw (B) on Weber 2V TLDM carburettor (1.3 litre models)

10C.7B Idle speed screw (arrowed) on Weber 2V DFTM carburettor (1.4 litre CVH models)

10C.9 Mixture (CO content) adjustment screw tamperproof plug on Weber 2V DFTM carburettor (1.4 litre models)

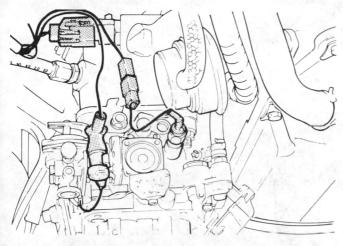
Fig. 13.86 Wiring disconnection points for carburettor removal – 1.4 litre models (Sec 10C)

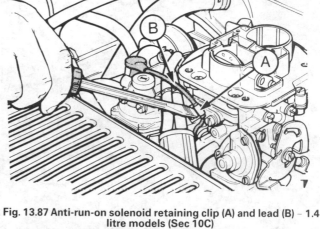
Fig. 13.87 Anti-run-on solenoid retaining clip (A) and lead (B) – 1.4 litre models (Sec 10C)

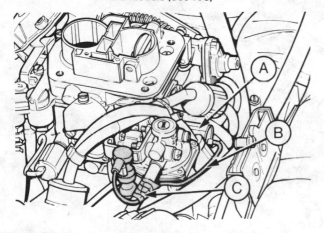
Fig. 13.88 Anti-run on solenoid (A), lead (B) and insulating tape (C) securing lead to vacuum hose – 1.4 litre models (Sec 10C)

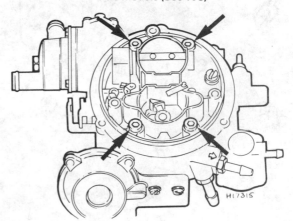
Fig. 13.89 Carburettor-to-manifold retaining screws – 1.6 litre models, 1986 onwards (Sec 10C)

26   On completion refit the air cleaner and disconnect the tachometer.
Throttle kicker (1.4 litre models)
27   Remove the air cleaner as described in Part A. Plug the vacuum supply from the manifold.
28   Have the engine at normal operating temperature with a tachometer connected in accordance with the manufacturer's instructions.
29   With the engine running and the idle speed and mixture correctly adjusted, manually operate the throttle kicker by lifting the operating lever upwards. Note the increase in engine speed.
30   If the increased speed is outside the figure given in the Specifications, remove the tamperproof plug from the top of the kicker body and adjust the unit to give the specified speed.
31   Remove the tachometer and refit the air cleaner on completion.

Automatic choke unit (1.6 litre models) – 1986 onwards – adjustment
32   Remove the air cleaner as described in Part A.
33   Release any pressure in the cooling system by loosening the pressure cap on the expansion tank (protect the hands using a cloth if the engine is hot), then disconnect the water inlet and outlet hoses at the automatic choke unit. Clamp the hoses or position them with their ends facing upwards to minimise the coolant leakage.
34   Undo the three screws and detach the choke bi-metal coil housing, followed by the internal heat shield.
35   Fit a rubber band to the choke plate lever, open the throttle to allow the choke plate to close, and then secure the band to keep the plate closed (Fig. 13.80).
36   Using a screwdriver, push the diaphragm open to its stop and measure the clearance between the lower edge of the choke plate and

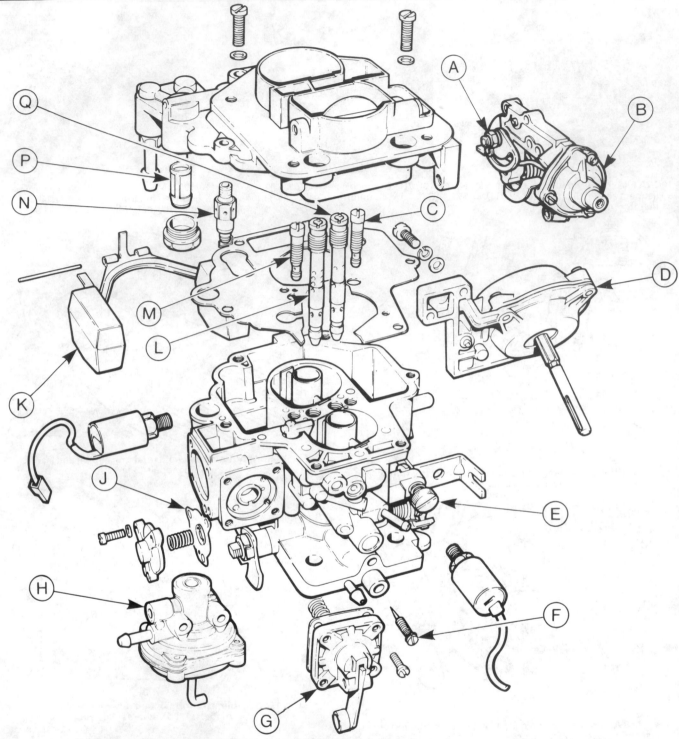

Fig. 13.90 Exploded view of the Weber 2VDFTM carburettor as fitted to 1.4 litre models (Sec 10C)

A   Manual choke unit
B   Choke vacuum pull-down
C   Secondary idle jet
D   Secondary venturi vacuum
     unit

E   Idle speed adjustment
     screw
F   Idle mixture adjustment
     screw
G   Accelerator pump assembly

H   Throttle kicker
J   Power valve diaphragm
K   Float
L   Primary emulsion tube

M   Primary idle jet
N   Needle valve
P   Fuel inlet filter
Q   Secondary emulsion tube

the air horn, using a twist drill or other gauge rod. Where the clearance is outside that specified, remove the tamperproof plug from the diaphragm housing and turn the screw, now exposed, in or out as necessary.

37   Fit a new diaphragm housing tamperproof plug, and remove the rubber band.

38   Refit the heat shield, making sure that the locating peg is correctly engaged in the notch in the housing.

39   Place the bi-metal coil housing in position, with the coil engaged with the slot in the choke lever which projects through the cut-out in the heat shield.

40   Screw in the retaining screws finger tight, and then rotate the housing to set the housing mark opposite the dot punch mark on the choke body. Secure the housing.

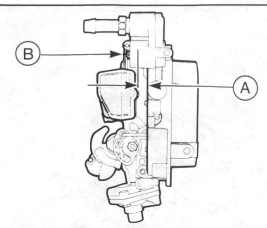

Fig. 13.91 Float setting adjustment – 1.4 litre models (Sec 10C)

A *Checking dimension*   B *Float arm tag*

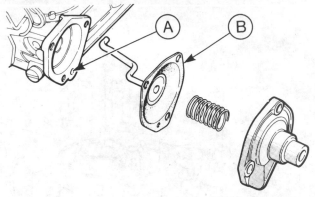

Fig. 13.92 Choke vacuum pull-down assembly installation – 1.4 litre models (Sec 10C)

A *Upper body vacuum gallery*   B *Diaphragm*

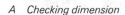

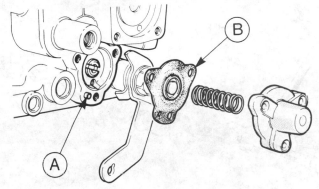

Fig. 13.93 Power valve installation – 1.4 litre models (Sec 10C)

A *Upper gallery*   B *Diaphragm*

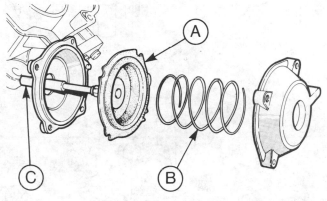

Fig. 13.94 Secondary venturi vacuum unit installation – 1.4 litre models (Sec 10C)

A *Diaphragm*   C *Operating rod*
B *Return spring*

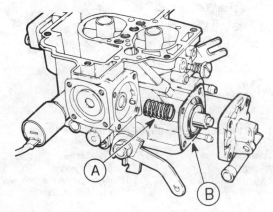

Fig. 13.95 Accelerator pump installation – 1.4 litre models (Sec 10C)

A *Return spring*   B *Diaphragm*

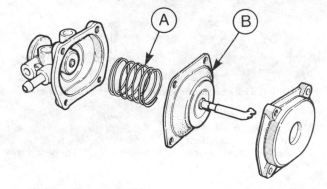

Fig. 13.96 Throttle kicker installation – 1.4 litre models (Sec 10C)

A *Return spring*   B *Diaphragm*

41   Reconnect the hoses and refit the air cleaner.
42   Check, and if necessary top up, the cooling system as described in Chapter 2.

Automatic choke unit (1.6 litre models – 1986-on) – removal and refitting

43   Remove the air cleaner as described in Part A.
44   Release any pressure in the cooling system by loosening the pressure cap, then detach the water inlet and outlet hoses at the automatic choke unit. Clamp the hoses or position them with their ends facing upwards to minimise coolant leakage.
45   Disconnect the lead at the anti-run on valve solenoid.
46   Disconnect the fuel supply and return hoses at the carburettor. If crimped type hose clips are used, cut them off and use screw type clips at reassembly.
47   Undo the six carburettor upper body retaining screws and remove the upper body. Note that four of the screws are of the Torx type and a suitable key or socket bit will be needed for their removal.
48   With the upper body removed, undo the three screws and remove the choke bi-metal coil housing followed by the internal heat shield.
49   Undo the three screws securing the choke housing to the upper body, disconnect the link rod and remove the choke housing.
50   Undo the three screws and remove the vacuum pull-down housing cover, then withdraw the spring, diaphragm and operating rod assembly.

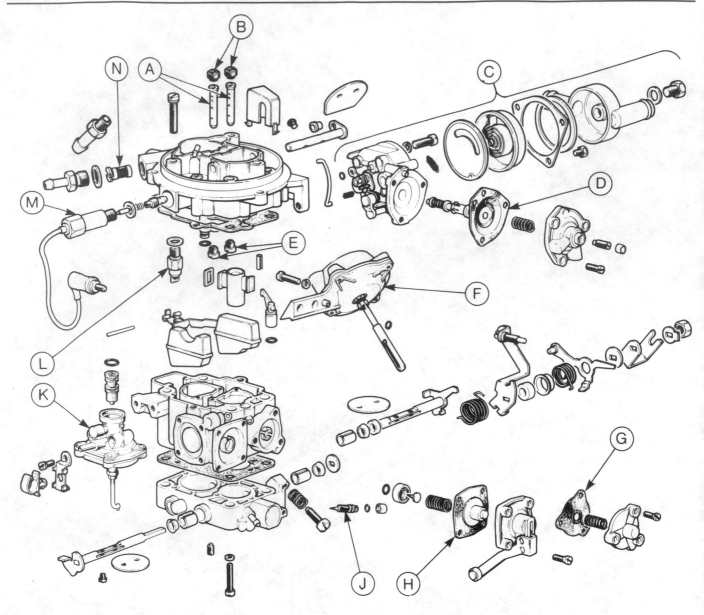

Fig. 13.97 Exploded view of the Weber 2V TLD carburettor as fitted to 1.6 litre models from 1986 onwards (Sec 10C)

A	Emulsion tube	E	Main jets	H	Accelerator pump	K	Throttle kicker
B	Air correction jets	F	Secondary venturi vacuum		diaphragm	L	Needle valve
C	Automatic choke assembly		unit	J	Idle mixture adjustment	M	Anti-run-on solenoid valve
D	Choke vacuum pull-down	G	Power valve diaphragm#		screw	N	Fuel inlet filter
	diaphragm						

51   Make a note of the exact position of the choke mechanism return and tension springs, then undo the nut and remove the connecting rod, levers and link from the choke housing (Fig. 13.85).

52   Clean and inspect all the parts for wear, damage, cracking or distortion. Pay particular attention to the condition of the pull-down diaphragm and the choke housing O-ring seal. Renew any parts as necessary.

53   Reassemble the choke mechanism connecting rod, levers, link and springs with reference to Fig. 13.85 and the notes made during removal. Secure the assembly with the retaining nut.

54   Locate the vacuum pull-down diaphragm and operating rod in the choke housing and with the diaphragm laying flat on the housing face, refit the cover and secure with the three screws.

55   Locate the O-ring seal on the choke housing, then connect the housing to the link rod.

56   Position the housing on the carburettor upper body and secure with the three screws.

57   Refit the upper body to the carburettor.

58   Before refitting the bi-metal coil housing, refer to paragraphs 35 and 36 and adjust the vacuum pull-down, then fit the coil housing as described in paragraph 37 onwards.

Removal and refitting

1.4 litre models

59   Disconnect the battery negative lead.

60   Remove the air cleaner as described in Part A.

61   Disconnect the electrical leads at the solenoids.

62   Disconnect the vacuum pipe at the carburettor outlet (photo).

63   Disconnect the accelerator cable by releasing the spring clip securing the end fitted to the ball-stud on the linkage, and then unscrewing the cable bracket fixing bolts (photo).

64   Release the choke cable from the linkage lever and move the

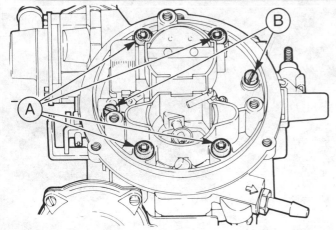

Fig. 13.98 Carburettor mounting screws (A) and upper body retaining screws (B) – 1.6 litre models, 1986 onwards (Sec 10C)

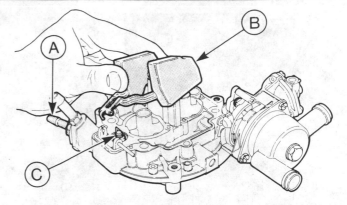

Fig. 13.99 Float and needle valve removal – 1.6 litre models, 1986 onwards (Sec 10C)

A Fuel outlet connection   C Needle valve
B Float

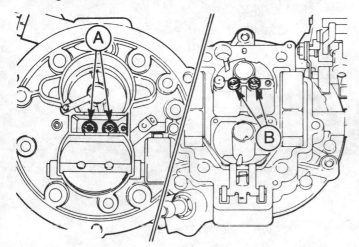

Fig. 13.100 Upper body jet locations – 1.6 litre models, 1986 onwards (Sec 10C)

A Air correction jets   B Main jets

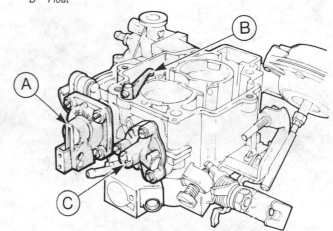

Fig. 13.101 Carburettor main body external components – 1.6 litre models, 1986 onwards (Sec 10C)

A Accelerator pump   C Power valve
B Accelerator pump
   discharge nozzle

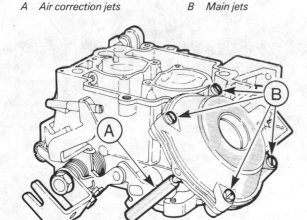

Fig. 13.102 Secondary venturi vacuum unit operating rod (A) and cover screws (B) – 1.6 litre models, 1986 onwards (Sec 10C)

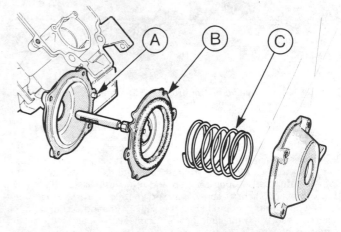

Fig. 13.103 Secondary venturi vacuum unit installation – 1.6 litre models, 1986 onwards (Sec 10C)

A Vacuum gallery   C Return spring
B Diaphragm

bracket with both cables attached, to one side (photo).
65 Disconnect the fuel inlet and return hoses, noting their respective positions, and plug them after removal (photo). If crimped type clips are used, cut them off and use new screw type clips when refitting.
66 Undo the four mounting flange nuts and washers and withdraw the carburettor from the manifold.
67 Refitting is the reversal of removal, but use a new flange gasket and ensure that the mating surfaces are perfectly clean. Reconnect the choke and accelerator cables and refit the air cleaner using the proce-

dures described in Part A, then adjust the idle speed and mixture settings as described previously in this Section.

10C.19 Fast idle speed screw on Weber 2V TLDM carburettor (1.3 litre models)

10C.62 Disconnect the vacuum pipes at the outlet (Weber 2V DFTM carburettor)

10C.63 Accelerator cable end fitting spring clip (Weber 2V DFTM carburettor)

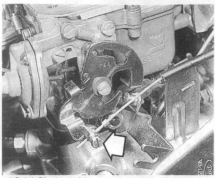

10C.64 Choke cable attachment at linkage lever (arrowed) (Weber 2V DFTM carburettor)

10C.65 Disconnect the fuel inlet and return hoses (arrowed) (Weber 2V DFTM carburettor)

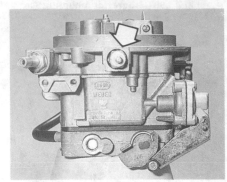

10C.83 Anti-run-on valve (arrowed) on Weber 2V TLDM carburettor

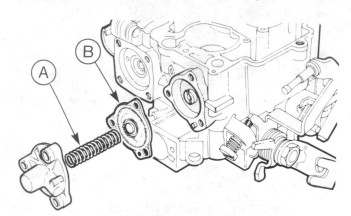

Fig. 13.104 Power valve installation – 1.6 litre models, 1986 onwards (Sec 10C)

A   Return spring   B   Diaphragm

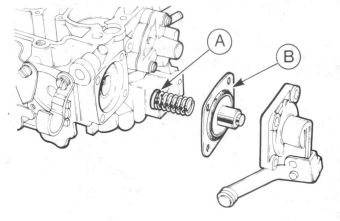

Fig. 13.105 Accelerator pump installation – 1.6 litre models, 1986 onwards (Sec 10C)

A   Return spring and valve   B   Diaphragm

68   If the carburettor has been renewed, and the new unit utilises a metal clip to secure the anti-run-on solenoid lead to the carburettor body, carefully prise open the clip and remove the lead (Fig. 13.87). Undo the clip retaining screw, discard the clip and refit the screw securely. Route the lead as shown in Fig. 13.88, and secure it to the vacuum hose using insulating tape. Connect the lead to the wiring harness connector.

1.6 litre models (1986 onwards)

69   Disconnect the battery negative lead.
70   Remove the air cleaner as described in Part A.
71   If the engine is still hot, depressurise the cooling system by carefully releasing the pressure cap (see Chapter 2).
72   Disconnect the coolant inlet and outlet hose at the automatic choke and clamp or plug their ends to prevent coolant loss.
73   Disconnect the throttle cable by releasing the spring clip securing the end fitting to the ball-stud, and unscrew the cable bracket fixing bolts.
74   Disconnect the fuel inlet and return hoses, noting their respective positions, and plug them after removal. If crimped type clips are used, cut them off and use screw type clips when refitting.
75   Disconnect the distributor vacuum pipe.
76   Disconnect the electrical lead at the anti-run-on valve solenoid.
77   Using a suitable Torx type key or socket bit, unscrew the four mounting through-bolts from the top of the carburettor and remove the unit from the manifold.
78   Refitting is the reverse sequence to removal, but use a new flange gasket and ensure that the mating faces are perfectly clean. On completion top up the cooling system as described in Chapter 2, and check the idle speed and mixture settings as described previously in this Section.

10C.84A Removing the four Torx bolts on the Weber 2V TLDM carburettor

10C.84B Lifting off the carburettor (Weber 2V TLDM)

10C.85 Fitting a new flange gasket

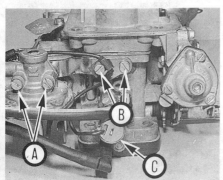
10C.88 Throttle kicker retaining screws (A), kicker bracket screws (B) and anti-run-on solenoid valve (C) on Weber 2V DFTM

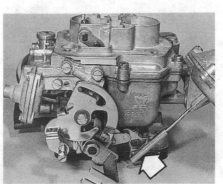
10C.92 Secondary venturi vacuum unit operating rod ball and socket end fitting (arrowed) on Weber 2V DFTM carburettor

10C.93 Secondary venturi vacuum unit cover retaining screws (arrowed) on Weber DFTM carburettor

1.3 litre models (HCS engine)

79   Disconnect the battery negative terminal.
80   Remove the air cleaner housing as described in Part A.
81   Disconnect the accelerator cable and choke cable as described in Part A.
82   Disconnect the fuel inlet hose. If the existing connection is of the crimped type, cut through it and use a worm drive clip (jubilee) when refitting the hose.
83   Disconnect the lead from the anti-run-on valve (photo).
84   Unscrew and remove the four Torx bolts securing the carburettor to the inlet manifold and lift off the carburettor (photos).
85   Refitting is a reversal of removal using a new gasket (photo).
86   On completion adjust the accelerator and choke cables as described in Part A.

Overhaul

1.4 litre models

87   Remove the carburettor from the engine as described previously in this Section.
88   Undo the two screws and nuts securing the throttle kicker to its mounting bracket and remove the kicker (photo).
89   Undo the screws and detach the throttle kicker bracket from the carburettor body. Note the anti-run-on valve solenoid lead located by one of the retaining screws.
90   Undo the four screws and lift off the throttle kicker cover, then take out the diaphragm and spring.
91   Undo the four screws and lift off the accelerator pump cover, then take out the diaphragm and spring.
92   Disconnect the secondary venturi vacuum unit operating rod by pushing the end of the rod downwards and twisting to release the ball and socket end fitting (photo).
93   Undo the four screws and lift off the secondary venturi vacuum unit cover (photo). Withdraw the spring and lift out the diaphragm.
94   Undo the three screws and lift off the power valve cover (photo), then take out the spring and diaphragm.

95   Using a sharp pointed instrument, carefully prise out the idle mixture adjusting screw tamperproof plug (where fitted) and unscrew the mixture screw.
96   Undo the six screws and lift off the carburettor upper body (photos).
97   Undo the three screws (photo) and lift off the vacuum pull-down cover, then take out the spring and diaphragm (photo).
98   Undo the brass nut in the upper body, remove the washer and take out the fuel inlet filter (photos).
99   Extract the float retaining pin, unhook the float arm from the needle valve and remove the float assembly (photos).
100   Withdraw the needle valve and unscrew the needle valve housing (photo).
101   Mop out the fuel from the float chamber and extract the jets from the carburettor main body (photos). Identify the jet locations before removal with reference to Fig. 13.90.
102   If required, separate the idle jets from their holders (photo) and the main jets from the emulsion tubes (photo).
103   Withdraw the accelerator pump discharge tube and remove the carburettor gasket.
104   Carry out a careful inspection of the carburettor components. Blow out all jets and passages, and renew the gaskets and diaphragms. Do not use wire to clean the jets, as this may cause damage.
105   Commence reassembly by fitting the accelerator pump discharge tube and the jets to their main body locations.
106   Refit the float needle valve assembly, hook the float arm under the needle valve and secure the float with the retaining pin. Refit the fuel inlet filter and brass nut.
107   Check the float setting by holding the carburettor vertically so that the float is hanging down and closing the needle valve. Measure the distance between the upper body mating face and the upper surface of the float. If adjustment is necessary to achieve the correct setting (see Specifications) bend the float arm tag as necessary (Fig. 13.91).
108   Refit the vacuum pull-down assembly ensuring that the diaphragm lies flat, and that the hole in the diaphragm and notch in the cover are aligned with the gallery in the upper body.

10C.94 Power valve location (arrowed) on Weber 2V DFTM carburettor

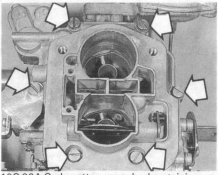
10C.96A Carburettor upper body retaining screws (arrowed) on Weber 2V DFTM carburettor

10C.96B Removing the upper body on Weber 2V DFTM carburettor

10C.97A Undo the three screws (arrowed) ...

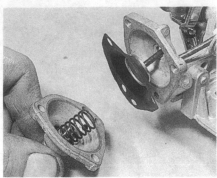
10C.97B ... and remove the vacuum pull-down cover and spring, followed by the diaphragm (Weber 2V DFTM carburettor)

10C.98A Remove the brass nut and washer ...

10C.98B ... followed by the fuel inlet filter (Weber 2V DFTM carburettor)

10C.99A Extract the float retaining pin ...

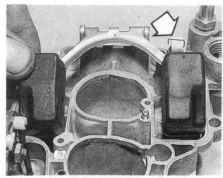
10C.99B ... unhook the float arm from the needle valve (arrowed) ...

10C.100 ... then remove the needle valve (Weber 2V DFTM carburettor)

10C.101A Removing the secondary idle jet and holder ...

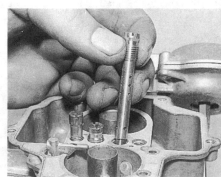
10C.101B ... and secondary main jet and emulsion tube (Weber 2V DFTM carburettor)

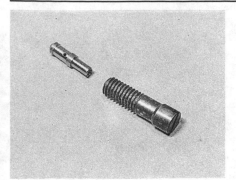

10C.102A Idle jet and holder ...

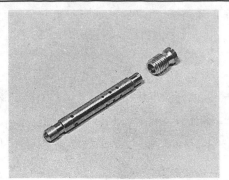

10C.102B ... and main jet and emulsion tube (Weber 2V DFTM carburettor)

10C.142 Choke assembly mounting screws (arrowed) on Weber 2V TLDM carburettor

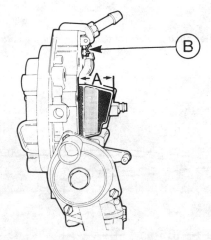

Fig. 13.106 Float setting adjustment – 1.6 litre models, 1986 onwards (Sec 10C)

A   *Checking dimension*   B   *Float tag*

109   Move the choke mechanism to the fully closed position, then manually push the vacuum pull-down diaphragm operating rod up to its stop.
110   Using a twist drill shank or other gauge rod, measure the clearance between the lower edge of the choke plate and the air horn. Where the clearance is outside that specified, remove the tamperproof plug in the diaphragm cover and turn the adjustment screw as necessary. Fit a new plug on completion.
111   Position a new gasket on the carburettor body, refit the upper body and secure with the six screws.
112   Refit the power valve, secondary venturi vacuum unit, accelerator pump and throttle kicker assemblies, using the reverse of the removal procedure, and with reference to the accompanying photos and illustrations.
113   Screw in the mixture adjusting screw until it lightly contacts its seat, then unscrew it three times. This will provide an initial adjustment and allow the engine to be started.
114   Once the carburettor has been refitted to the car, check and adjust the idle speed and mixture settings, the fast idle speed and the throttle kicker adjustment as described previously in this Section.
1.6 litre models (1986 onwards)
115   Remove the carburettor from the engine as described previously in this Section.
116   Undo the two screws, hold the throttle open and separate the carburettor upper body from the main body.
117   Tap out the float retaining pin, remove the float and lift out the needle valve. Remove the carburettor gasket.
118   Unscrew the needle valve housing and remove the washer.
119   Unscrew the fuel inlet in the upper body and remove the filter.
120   Unscrew the two air correction jets from the upper body. Identify the jet locations before removal with reference to Fig. 13.100. Now turn the upper body over and withdraw the emulsion tubes which are located beneath the air correction jets.

121   Unscrew the two main jets from the underside of the upper body, again noting their respective positions.
122   Mop out the fuel from the float chamber in the main body, then carefully prise out the accelerator pump discharge tube and O-ring seal.
123   Undo the four screws, lift off the accelerator pump cover and remove the diaphragm and spring. Ensure that the inlet valve, valve seat and O-ring have been withdrawn with the spring. If not, remove them from their locations in the main body.
124   Disconnect the secondary venturi unit operating rod by pushing the end of the rod downwards and twisting to release the ball and socket end fitting.
125   Undo the four screws and lift off the secondary venturi vacuum unit cover. Withdraw the spring and lift out the diaphragm.
126   Using a sharp pointed instrument, prise out the idle mixture adjusting screw tamperproof plug (if fitted) and unscrew the mixture screw.
127   Undo the three screws and lift off the power valve cover, then remove the spring and diaphragm.
128   Carry out a careful inspection of the carburettor components. Blow out all jets and passages, and renew the gaskets and diaphragms. Do not use wire to clean the jets, as this may cause damage.
129   Commence reassembly by screwing in the mixture adjusting screw until it lightly contacts its seat, then unscrew it three turns. This will provide an initial adjustment and allow the engine to be started.
130   Position the secondary venturi vacuum unit diaphragm on the housing. Ensure that the diaphragm lies flat and that the hole in the diaphragm and the notch in the cover are aligned with the vacuum gallery in the main body. Refit the spring and cover, then connect the operating rod.
131   Refit the power valve diaphragm and spring, then fit the cover

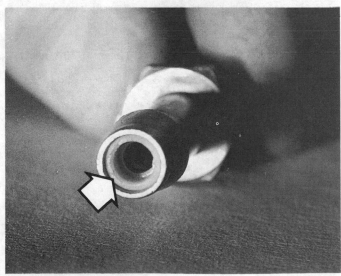

10C.143 Fuel inlet filter gauze (arrowed) inside the fuel inlet union (Weber 2V TLDM carburettor)

ensuring that the vacuum galleries are aligned and the diaphragm lies flat.

132 Refit the accelerator pump O-ring, valve seat, inlet valve, spring and diaphragm, then fit the cover with the diaphragm lying flat.

133 Refit the accelerator pump discharge tube and O-ring.

134 Locate the emulsion tubes in their original positions, then refit the air correction jets.

135 Refit the two main jets to their original locations.

136 Refit the filter and fuel inlet.

137 With a new gasket in position, refit the needle valve assembly and the float.

138 Check the float setting by holding the carburettor body vertically so that the float is hanging down and closing the needle valve. Measure the distance between the surface of the gasket and the base of the float. If adjustment is necessary to achieve the correct setting, bend the float tag (Fig. 13.106).

139 Hold the throttle partially open and refit the carburettor upper body. Secure with the two screws.

140 Once the carburettor has been refitted to the car, check and adjust the idle speed and mixture settings, and the fast idle speed and throttle kicker adjustment as described previously in this Section.

1.3 litre models (HCS engine)

141 The procedure is basically as described for 1.6 litre models (1986 onwards), but using the specifications (at the front of this Supplement) for the Weber 2V TLDM carburettor and noting the following differences.

142 The secondary venturi vacuum unit is mounted on the choke assembly bracket and is removed with the choke assembly after disconnection of the vacuum hose (photo).

143 The fuel inlet union filter is a different arrangement, being located inside the union (photo).

Unstable idle speed (1.3 HCS engines) – rectification

144 Unstable idle speed can be attributable to a defective O-ring seal or collet at the brake vacuum hose connection in the inlet manifold. It can also cause a fluctuating CO reading.

145 If this symptom is diagnosed a new seal and collet available from Ford dealers should be fitted.

146 Apply light even pressure to hold the flange of the collet against the manifold and pull gently on the vacuum hose to release it from the connection. Do not pull at an angle or use excessive force which can cause the collet to jam the hose.

147 Withdraw and discard the collet, being careful not to damage the brass insert in the manifold.

148 Carefully prise the O-ring seal from the connector in the manifold, then insert the new seal. There is no need to push the seal fully into the connector as the fitting of the collet will position the seal correctly.

149 Fit the new collet, taking care not to damage its spring legs.

150 Ensure the end of the vacuum hose is not damaged or distorted which can cause a bad seal. Renew it as necessary.

151 Push the hose into the collet until its swaged end contacts the flange of the collet. Pull gently on the hose to ensure it is locked in the connector.

152 Check and adjust idle speed and mixture (CO).

PART D: FUEL INJECTION SYSTEM (K-Jetronic)

Modifications (1986 models onwards)

1 The fuel injection system on later models has been modified with respect to the throttle housing and the location of the fuel accumulator.

2 On the latest type throttle housing the idle speed adjustment screw is located on the top of the housing beneath a tamperproof cap (Fig. 13.107). The procedures in Chapter 3 are unchanged, but it will be necessary to prise out the tamperproof cap before adjusting the idle speed.

3 The fuel accumulator on later models is located on the left-hand side of the engine compartment. The removal and refitting procedures given in Chapter 3 are unchanged, but it is not necessary to raise the rear of the car.

Fuel filter – electrostatic charge

4 To overcome electrostatic charge which may be generated in either the fuel filter or fuel mixture control unit on fuel injection systems, a wiring harness, as shown in Fig. 13.108, can be made up and fitted as follows.

5 Remove the fuel filter as described in Chapter 3, Section 30, then

Fig. 13.107 Idle speed adjustment screw location on later type throttle housing (K-Jetronic fuel injection) (Sec 10D)

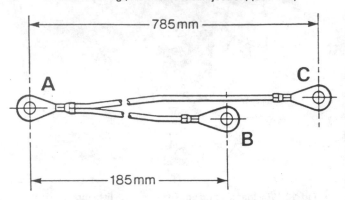

Fig. 13.108 Wiring harness dimensions for K-Jetronic fuel injection models (Sec 10D)

Eyelet – 6.0 mm inside diameter
Cable – 0.75 or 1.0 mm^2 (brown)

remove the filter label from the filter canister, being careful not to score or scratch the filter surface.

6 Refit the filter, fitting connection 'A' of the harness under the clamp screw.

7 Fit connection 'B' to one of the fuel mixture control unit upper-to-lower half securing screws.

8 Route cable A – C underneath the air cleaner and across to the ignition coil, using existing cable ties to secure the cable in place. Fit connection 'C' to one of the ignition coil clamp screws.

Note: *that on vehicles with this modification, when subsequently renewing the fuel filter, the filter label must be removed.*

Fault diagnosis – fuel injection system

9 Where an engine will not start, first check that there is sufficient fuel in the tank.

10 Next, switch on the ignition and listen to see if the fuel pump is running.

11 If not, check the fuel pump fuse is intact, then that the fuel injection relay (safety module) is serviceable.

12 If these components are working correctly or the pump is running, then the fault lies elsewhere in the system.

PART E: ELECTRONIC FUEL INJECTION SYSTEM (EFI EEC-IV)

General description

From 1990 model year, an Electronic Fuel Injection system (EFI) controlled by an Electronic Engine Management System (EEC-IV) and incorporating an Electronic Distributorless Ignition system (E-DIS 4) is

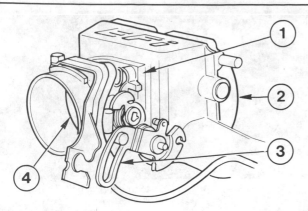

Fig. 13.109 View of throttle housing on 1.6 litre EFI models (Sec 10E)

1 Throttle housing	3 Control gate
2 Inlet manifold	4 Throttle butterfly

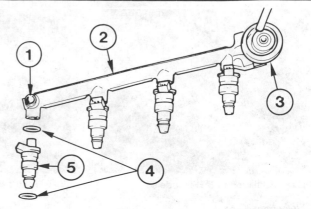

Fig. 13.110 Fuel rail and injector assembly on 1.6 litre EFI models (Sec 10E)

1 Fuel inlet	4 O-ring seals
2 Fuel rail	5 Injector
3 Pressure regulator	

used on all 1.6 fuel injection models. The system is designed to meet the requirements of the European 15.04 exhaust emission control laws. Those components more easily related to the ignition system are described in Section 11 (EEC-IV module, E-DIS 4 module, DIS coil and engine coolant temperature sensor). Those relating to the fuel system are described here and more fully dealt with in the ensuing paragraphs.

Air intake system
The volume of air drawn into the system depends on both fixed and variable factors. Fixed factors are governed by the design of the intake system. Variable factors are air pressure and density, throttle valve position, engine speed and the cleanliness of the air cleaner element. The EEC-IV module evaluates these factors through the Air Charge Temperature sensor (ACT), Manifold Absolute Pressure sensor (MAP), Throttle Position Sensor (TPS) and controls engine idle speed via the Idle Speed Control Valve (ISCV).

The air cleaner is similar to earlier assemblies. A flexible hose connected to the valve cover acts as a cylinder head and crankcase breather. A further connection leads to the idle speed control valve. The ISCV, controlled by the EEC-IV module operates by varying the amount of time this auxiliary air passage, which by-passes the throttle valve, is open, and also varies the valve opening time to stabilise engine idle speed under all conditions. A throttle housing bolted to the upper section of the intake manifold houses the throttle valve, limit stops, accelerator cable connection and TPS. The TPS measures throttle opening.

The MAP sensor, mounted on the engine bulkhead and connected to the inlet manifold by vacuum tube and electrically to the EEC-IV module measures the vacuum in the inlet manifold. If the MAP fails in service, the EEC-IV module uses the TPS to provide one of three values:

(a)   Idle.
(b)   Part load.
(c)   Full load.

Inlet air temperature is measured by an electrical resistive element screwed into the upper half of the inlet manifold (ACT) and is connected to the EEC- IV module.

The fuel system
The fuel pump, fuel tank level sender and fuel return flow are all contained within one unit installed in the fuel tank. The fuel pump is electric, its supply being via a fuel pump relay which is controlled by the EEC-IV module. When the ignition is switched on the fuel pump is given a lead time of approximately one second in order to build up pressure in the system. The pump also incorporates a non-return valve which prevents system pressure dropping after the ignition is switched off, to improve the warm start.

An inertia switch, installed between the fuel pump relay and fuel pump will break the supply to the pump in the event of sudden impact thus switching off the pump. If the switch has been activated, the re-set button will be in the raised position.

The fuel rail is made of forged aluminium and is bolted to the lower section of the inlet manifold. The fuel rail holds the four injectors in the inlet manifold. A fuel filter is installed between the fuel pump and fuel rail.

A pressure regulator, mounted on the outlet end of the fuel rail and connected by tube to the inlet manifold to sense manifold pressure, controls fuel pressure in the fuel rail. Excess fuel is returned to the fuel tank.

The electro-magnetic fuel injectors have only two positions, on or off. The volume of fuel injected is regulated by varying the time the injectors remain open, which is controlled by the EEC-IV module.

A plastic cable duct mounted alongside the fuel rail contains the wiring looms for the engine coolant temperature sensor, main loom, injectors, ACT sensor and TPS.

Idle speed and mixture – adjustment
1   Idle speed is totally controlled by the EEC-IV module and cannot be adjusted.
2   To adjust mixture (CO content), first run the engine until it reaches normal operating temperature.
3   Connect a CO meter and tachometer to the engine in accordance with the manufacturer's instructions.
4   Stabilise the engine by running it at 3000 rev/min for approximately 15 seconds, then allow it to idle.
5   Record the CO content and idle speed.
6   If adjustment of the mixture (CO content) is necessary, remove the cap from the CO adjustment potentiometer (on inner wing behind the left-hand suspension tower) and adjust the CO content to the specified level.

Note: *Any adjustment must be made within thirty seconds from the initial stabilisation (paragraph 4). If more than thirty seconds elapse, the stabilisation process must be repeated.*

7   On completion, stop the engine and remove all test equipment. Fit a new tamperproof cap to the CO adjustment potentiometer.

Fuel system – depressurising

Caution: *Before disconnecting any fuel pipe the system must be depressurised as follows. Take all necessary fire precautions before commencing and read the Safety First Section at the beginning of this manual.*

8   Disconnect the battery negative terminal.
9   Place a drain tray under the fuel filter.
10   Cover the outlet union on the fuel filter with absorbent cloth to prevent fuel being sprayed around the engine bay, then slowly undo the outlet union and allow all pressure to dissipate.
11   Tighten the union on completion unless the filter is being renewed.

Note: *The system will remain depressurised until the engine or fuel pump is started.*

EFI EEC-IV – component renewal
Fuel filter
12   The fuel filter must be renewed at the intervals given in the

10E.13 Fuel filter on 1.6 EFI models

A   Inlet from pump
B   Outlet to fuel rail
C   Clamp

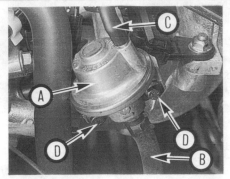

10E.20 Fuel pressure regulator on 1.6 litre EFI models

A   Regulator
B   Fuel return hose (to tank)
C   Vacuum hose
D   Mounting bolts

10E.34 Injector multi-plug on 1.6 litre EFI models (arrowed)

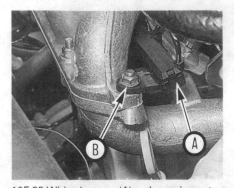

10E.35 Wiring harness (A) and securing nut (B) on 1.6 litre EFI models

10E.36 Fuel supply pipe union on fuel rail on 1.6 litre EFI models (arrowed)

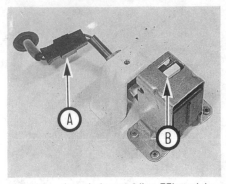

10E.42 Inertia switch on 1.6 litre EFI models

A   Multi-plug
B   Reset button

Routine maintenance Section at the beginning of this Supplement.
13   The filter is located in the engine bay on the left-hand inner wing (photo).
14   First, depressurise the system as described earlier.
15   Unscrew the filter outlet and inlet unions.
16   Remove the filter clamp screw and withdraw the filter, remembering there will still be fuel in the filter, so take precautions against spillage.
17   Refit in reverse order, ensuring the flow direction arrows on the filter face toward the fuel rail and renewing the washers on the inlet and outlet unions.

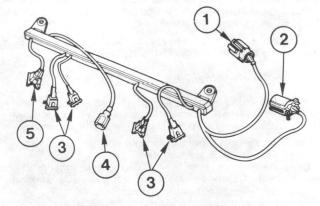

Fig. 13.111 Wiring harness connections on 1,6 litre EFI models (Sec 10E)

1   Engine coolant temperature sensor
2   Connection to main loom
3   Injector plugs
4   Air charge temperature sensor
5   Throttle position sensor

Fuel pressure regulator
18   Disconnect battery negative terminal.
19   Depressurise the fuel system as described earlier.
20   Being prepared for spillage, disconnect the fuel return hose and the vacuum hose from the regulator (photo).
21   Unscrew the regulator retaining bolts and withdraw the unit from the fuel rail.
22   Refitting is a reversal of removal, noting that new sealing rings lubricated with clean engine oil must be fitted every time the regulator is removed.
23   On completion, switch the ignition on and off five times without cranking the engine and check for fuel leaks from the regulator.
Throttle housing
24   Disconnect the battery negative terminal.
25   Depressurise the system as described earlier.
26   Remove the air intake duct.
27   Unbolt the accelerator cable bracket and disconnect the cable at the throttle housing.
28   Disconnect the throttle position sensor.
29   Remove the four bolts and withdraw the throttle housing from the inlet manifold.
30   Refit in reverse order using a new gasket between the throttle housing and the manifold.
Fuel rail and injectors
31   Disconnect the battery negative terminal.
32   Depressurise the fuel system.
33   Remove the throttle housing.
34   Disconnect the injector multiplug (photo), air charge temperature sensor, and engine coolant temperature sensor.
35   Unbolt the wiring harness and lay it clear of the fuel rail (photo).
36   Disconnect the fuel supply pipe to the fuel rail (photo) and the fuel return pipe and vacuum hose from the pressure regulator.
37   Unbolt and remove the fuel rail and injectors.
38   Remove the injectors from the fuel rail.
39   Refit in reverse order, noting that new seals must be fitted to all

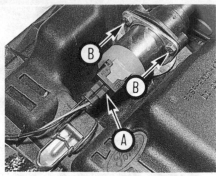

10E.46 Throttle position sensor on 1.6 litre EFI models

A Multi-plug
B Retaining screws

10E.50 Idle speed control valve on 1.6 litre EFI models

A Multi-plug
B Retaining bolts

10E.66 Manifold absolute pressure sensor on 1.6 litre EFI models

A Sensor
B Vacuum connection
C Multi-plug

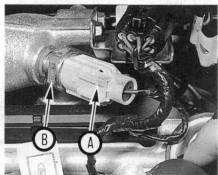

10E.68 Fuel trap is fitted with white end toward sensor (1.6 litre EFI models)

10E.70 Air charge temperature sensor on 1.6 litre litre EFI models

A Multi-plug
B Sensor

10E.72 Vehicle speed sensor on 1.6 litre EFI models (arrowed)

injectors even if only one has been renewed, and the seals must be lubricated with clean engine oil before fitting to the injectors.

Inertia switch (fuel shut off)

40   Disconnect the battery negative terminal.
41   Open the boot and remove the spare wheel.
42   Disconnect the inertia switch multiplug (photo).
43   Remove the screws securing the switch to the bracket and with-draw the switch.
44   Refit in reverse order, checking that the reset button has remained down after the spare wheel has been fitted.

Throttle position sensor

45   Disconnect the battery negative terminal.
46   Disconnect the sensor multi-plug (photo).
47   Remove the retaining screws and withdraw the sensor from the throttle plate shaft.
Warning: *while removed, do not rotate the sensor beyond its normal operating range.*
48   Refit in reverse order ensuring the moulded side of the sensor faces the inlet manifold.

Idle speed control valve

49   Disconnect the battery negative terminal.
50   Disconnect the control valve multi-plug (photo).
51   Unscrew the retaining bolts and remove the valve.
52   Clean the mating surfaces of the valve and air cleaner housing then refit the valve, ensuring that the locating lug on the valve locates in the slot in the housing.
53   Fit and tighten the retaining bolts to the specified torque.
54   Connect the multi-plug.
55   Connect the battery.
56   Start the engine and check that idle speed is stable and there are no induction air leaks at the valve.
57   Connect a tachometer to the engine in accordance with the

manufacturer's instructions. Allow the engine to reach normal operating temperature.
58   Check that the idle speed is as specified, then turn on all available electrical loads (heater, rear screen heater, lights etc.) and check that the system compensates for the increased load and the idle speed remains as specified.
59   Switch off the engine and remove the test equipment.

Idle speed control valve – cleaning

60   Remove the valve as described earlier.
61   Immerse the valve in a container of clean petrol and allow it to soak for approximately three minutes.
62   Use a clean paint brush to clean the bore, slots and piston of the valve.
63   Carefully, using a small screwdriver, move the valve piston up and down in the bore (do not use the slots to do this), then rinse and dry the valve preferably using compressed air.
64   Refit the valve as described earlier.

Manifold absolute pressure sensor

65   Disconnect the battery negative terminal.
66   Disconnect the vacuum hose and multi-plug from the sensor (photo).
67   Remove the screws and withdraw the sensor from the engine bulkhead.
68   Refit in reverse order. Note that the fuel trap between the inlet manifold and the sensor is fitted with the white end toward the sensor (photo).

Air charge temperature sensor

69   Disconnect the battery negative terminal.
70   Disconnect the multi-plug and unscrew the sensor from the inlet manifold (photo).
71   Refit in reverse order, applying a suitable sealant to the threads of the sensor.

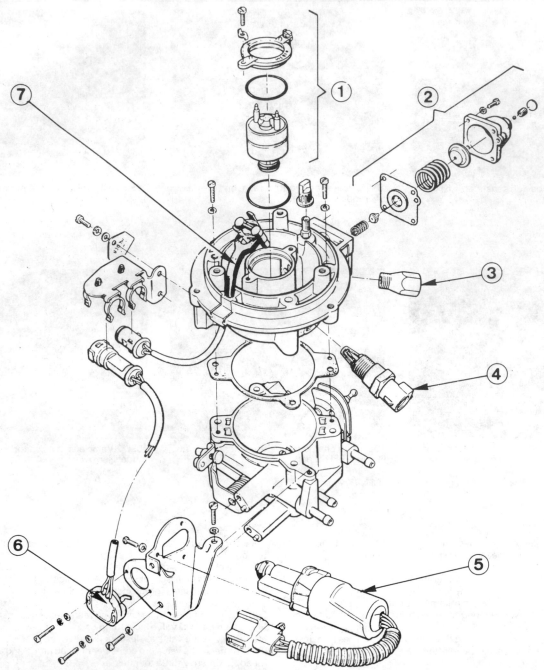

Fig. 13.112 Exploded view of the CFi unit (1.4 litre CFi engine) (Sec 10F)

1 Fuel injector assembly	4 ACT sensor	6 Throttle position sensor
2 Fuel pressure regulator components	5 Throttle plate control motor	7 Fuel injector wiring
3 Fuel inlet connection		

Vehicle speed sensor unit
72   Refer to Section 19. The sensor is the same as fitted to models with a fuel computer (photo).

Mixture (CO) adjustment potentiometer
73   Disconnect the battery negative terminal.
74   Disconnect the multi-plug from the potentiometer.
75   Remove its securing screw and withdraw the potentiometer from the suspension tower (photo).
76   Refit in reverse order, then check and adjust the CO (mixture) content.

Engine temperature sensor
77   The engine temperature sensor is similar to that fitted to the 3-D ignition system on the HCS engine, but is screwed into the cylinder block below the inlet manifold.

Fault diagnosis (EFI EEC-IV)
78   Complete and accurate fault diagnosis is only possible using special test equipment available through authorised Ford dealers. For this reason the home mechanic has no recourse but to enlist the help of a Ford dealer, except for the general checks given here and minor overhaul procedures in the previous paragraphs.
79   Where a component is obviously defective, it can be removed and a new component fitted in its place.
80   Although certain electrical checks can be done to establish continuity or resistance this is not recommended as the incorrect use of test probes between component connector pins can cause damage to the internal circuitry of some components.
81   The home mechanic should therefore confine his activities to the following general checks and the limited overhaul procedures men-

10E.75 Mixture (CO) adjustment potentiometer on 1.6 litre EFI models

General checks

82 Following disconnection of the battery, all Keep Alive Memory (KAM) values will be erased, which can result in engine surge, hesitation, erratic idle or a deterioration of drive.

83 After reconnecting the battery, start the engine and allow it to idle for at least three minutes. After normal operating temperature is reached, increase engine speed to 1200 rpm and maintain this speed for at least two minutes.

84 This procedure will allow the module to 're-learn' idle values. However, it may be necessary to drive the vehicle for five miles of varied driving to complete the re-learning process.

85 If the idle speed is still erratic after the re-learning process has been completed, check that the air intake system is in good condition with no leaks. Also check the air cleaner element is not blocked, although the idle speed system will compensate for the filter becoming partially clogged under normal operating conditions.

86 Remove and clean the idle speed valve as described earlier if idle speed is still erratic.

87 To check if the system is running in Limited Operation Strategy (LOS), switch on the ignition and listen for the fuel pump running. The pump should switch off after one second.

88 If the pump runs continuously, the system is in LOS. Switch off the ignition and investigate the cause.

89 Check that all electrical connections are made and free from dirt, moisture and corrosion.

90 Check all vacuum lines and fuel hoses/pipes are in good condition and free from leaks.

Fuel pump – testing

91 Remove the fuel tank filler cap and switch on the ignition. The fuel pump should be heard running for approximately one second before stopping. If the pump continues to run then the system is operating in Limited Operation Strategy.

92 If the pump fails to run, first check that the inertia switch in the boot is in the fully depressed position.

93 Secondly check the fuel pump fuse and relay in the main fusebox.

Relays

94 The EFI EEC-IV power relay is located up under the dash on the driver's side. Access is by removal of the lower sound insulation panel.

95 The fuel pump relay is located in the central fusebox panel in the engine compartment.

PART F: CENTRAL FUEL INJECTION SYSTEM (1.4 CFi CATALYST ENGINES)

General description

The system is best described by dividing it into four separate sub-systems – air, fuel, engine management (EEC-IV module) and ignition.

Air system

The air system consists of an air cleaner, connecting inlet duct, Central Fuel Injection (CFi) unit, Manifold Absolute Pressure (MAP) sensor and inlet manifold.

Air is drawn in through the air cleaner and inlet duct to the CFi unit. The CFi unit contains an Air Charge Temperature (ACT) sensor and a throttle plate. The ACT passes information to the EEC-IV module, which uses the information to determine engine fuel requirement. The inlet air then passes the throttle plate and on to the inlet manifold. Below the throttle plate is a take-off point for the Manifold Absolute Pressure (MAP) sensor which measures pressure in the manifold, passing this information to the EEC-IV module. The EEC-IV module uses this information as another factor in determining fuel and ignition timing at full throttle or during ignition key 'on' engine 'off' conditions. Using the information from the ACT and MAP sensors, the EEC-IV module can calculate the mass of air entering the engine and adjust fuelling and ignition timing accordingly.

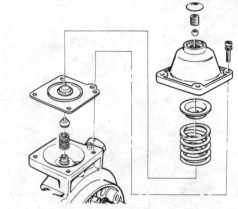

Fig. 13.113 Exploded view of the fuel pressure regulator (Sec 10F)

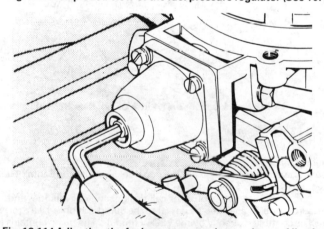

Fig. 13.114 Adjusting the fuel pressure regulator using an Allen key (Sec 10F)

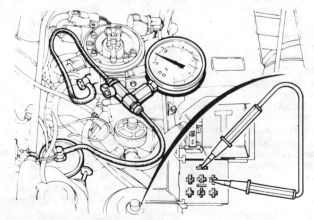

Fig. 13.115 Pressure gauge connected between the CFi unit and fuel filter (Sec 10F)

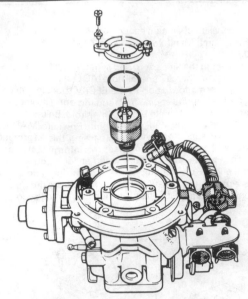

Fig. 13.116 Components of the fuel injector (Sec 10F)

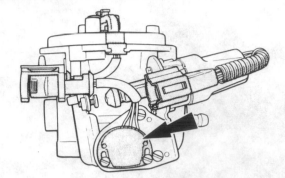

Fig. 13.117 Throttle position sensor (TPS) on side of CFi unit (Sec 10F)

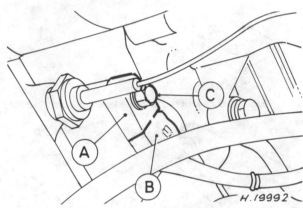

Fig. 13.118 Knock sensor on 1.4 litre CFi engine (Sec 10F)

A   *Knock sensor*   C   *Securing bolt*
B   *Multi-plug*

Fuel system

The fuel system consists of a fuel pump, fuel filter and the Central Fuel Injection (CFi) unit.

The fuel pump is electric, of roller cell design, and delivers fuel under pressure to the engine. Electric power to the pump is supplied via a relay which is controlled directly by the EEC-IV module. The pump contains a non-return valve which maintains pressure in the system after the ignition is switched off, to assist in starting.

From the pump the fuel passes through an in-line filter to the CFi unit. A fuel pressure regulator, mounted on the CFi unit maintains fuel pressure to the injector at 1 bar. Excess fuel is returned from the regulator to the fuel tank.

The CFi unit, resembling a carburettor, hoses the throttle plate, throttle plate control motor, Throttle Position Sensor (TPS), ACT, electronic injector unit and pressure regulator. These components work in conjunction with the EEC-IV module and are explained later except for the fuel pressure regulator which is a simple mechanical device, adjustable by means of an external Allen screw.

Engine management and emission system

The Engine Electronic Control (EEC) IV module is a microprocessor based system containing within its memory the necessary strategy and calibration data. It provides control signals to the output actuators according to the input signals received from the various engine condition sensors. The EEC-IV module will calculate the necessary requirements against data stored or programmed in its memory. Accurate control of the engine is thus maintained.

Ignition system

The ignition system consists of a distributor, TFI IV module, ignition coil

and HT cables. These components are more fully described in Section 11.

Catalytic converter

The function of the catalytic converter (or catalyst) is to control and reduce exhaust gas emissions, keeping oxides of nitrogen (NOx), hydrocarbons (HC) and carbon monoxide (CO) to an acceptable level.

The catalyst consists of a ceramic honeycomb coated with platinum and rhodium, housed in a metal exhaust box. The honeycomb design presents a large surface area to the exhaust gas promoting maximum conversion.

A heated exhaust gas sensor (HEGO) screwed into the exhaust down-pipe allows the engine management system to control the air/fuel ratio

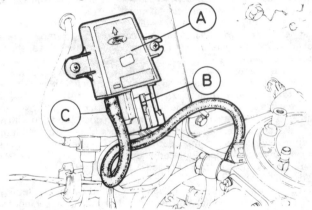

Fig. 13.119 Manifold absolute pressure sensor (MAP) (Sec 10F)

A   *Sensor*   C   *Vacuum hose*
B   *Multi-plug*

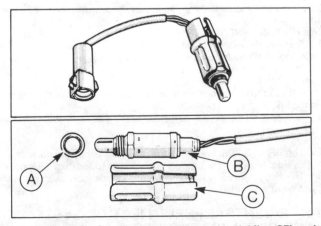

Fig. 13.120 Heated exhaust gas oxygen sensor on 1.4 litre CFi engine (Sec 10F)

A   *Sealing ring*   C   *Sensor shield*
B   *HEGO sensor*

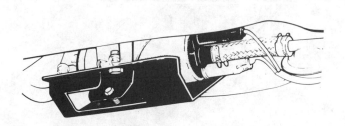

Fig. 13.121 Electric fuel pump on underside of vehicle on 1.4 litre CFi model (Sec 10F)

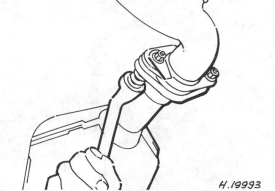

H.19993

Fig. 13.122 Removing the bolts from the catalyst front flange (Sec 10F)

at the ideal of 14.7 to 1, which is needed for the catalyst to function most effectively.

NOTE: *where a vehicle fitted with a catalytic converter is being used to tow a trailer, a heat shield (obtainable from Ford dealers) must be fitted to the alternator and starter motor to prevent them being damaged by the increased heat from the exhaust caused by the towing.*

CFi system sensors – description

Air Charge Temperature (ACT) sensor
The ACT sensor is a resistive device measuring the temperature of the air passing through the CFi unit. The temperature of the incoming air changes the resistance of the sensor which is monitored by the EEC IV module, which determines the air temperature from the resistive value.

Engine Coolant Temperature (ECT) sensor
Functions in a similar manner to the ACT measuring engine coolant temperature.

Heated Exhaust Gas Oxygen (HEGO) sensor
A HEGO sensor is fitted to enable very accurate control of engine fuel requirement ensuring effective operation of the catalyst in the exhaust system. The HEGO enables the mixture (CO) content to be controlled around the ideal air/fuel ratio for complete combustion.
Located in the exhaust downpipe, the HEGO consists of a two-part chemical cell that has air, with a high oxygen content, on one side, and exhaust gas, with a low oxygen content, on the other. The conduction of ions through the sensor cells, from high to low content produces a voltage across the cell. This voltage is proportional to the oxygen content of the exhaust gas. For the HEGO to function, an operating temperature in excess of 400°C and the engine being run on lead free fuel is required. To enable this temperature to be quickly achieved the HEGO sensor is electrically heated. This heating of the sensor also gives improved temperature stability under varying climatic or drive conditions, as well as enabling 'closed loop' operation to be quickly established. Under cold start conditions or when engine operating conditions dictate, information from the HEGO is ignored by the EEC-IV module, allowing the system to operate under an 'open loop' mode, enabling enrichment for cold engine running.
WARNING: HEGO *sensors will be permanently damaged if leaded fuel is used.*

Knock sensor
Detects engine detonation which may occur when using low octane fuel. Screwed into the cylinder block in such a position as to detect detonation in any of the four cylinders, it passes a signal based on vibration to the EEC-IV module. The module analyses the signal and adjusts ignition timing accordingly.

Manifold Absolute Pressure (MAP) sensor
A solid state electronic device containing a pressure sensing element and signal conditioning electronics. The MAP sensor is connected to the inlet manifold by vacuum hose and is powered by a 5 volt reference supply from the EEC-IV module. As pressure varies within the inlet manifold the frequency of the output signal changes. The output signal is in square wave form and frequency can vary from 162.4 Hz at full throttle (low vacuum) to 80.9 Hz at idle (high vacuum), and even lower during deceleration. The information from the MAP is used by the EEC-IV module to modify fuelling and spark advance. When the engine is switched off the EEC-IV module is kept supplied with power (through the power relay) for a few seconds, the MAP supplying it with atmospheric pressure, which is used by the memory to provide high altitude fuelling requirements.

Speed sender unit
Mounted on the speedometer take off point on the gearbox the speed sender unit produces an alternating output voltage proportional to vehicle speed.

Throttle Position Sensor (TPS)
Mounted on the CFi unit and connected to the 'D' shaped drive end of the throttle plate shaft the TPS, being a rotary potentiometer (variable resistor) provides throttle position information to the EEC-IV module. Supplied with a 5 volt reference supply from the module, a wiper contact inside the potentiometer moves with the throttle plate, providing an output voltage proportional to throttle plate opening. This information is used by the EEC-IV to determine the following:

(a) Closed throttle for idle speed control
(b) Part throttle for normal engine operation
(c) Wide open throttle for fuel enrichment
(d) Wide open throttle for clearing a flooded engine
(e) Rate of change of throttle plate position for acceleration enrichment

CFi system actuators – description

Fuel pump
Refer to previous paragraphs.

Fuel pump relay
The relay is controlled by the EEC-IV module and is mounted on the central fuse box.

Power relay
The relay is mounted under the facia, and fitted to protect the system against sudden voltage fluctuations. The relay has a built-in timer which allows the throttle plate motor to continue to operate after the engine is switched off, allowing an anti-dieselling function to be performed by the motor. This will prevent the engine from running on.

Throttle plate control motor
The throttle plate control motor is mounted on the side of the CFi unit. The motor controls the throttle stop position and thus idle speed. The throttle stop also acts as a switch to determine when the throttle is

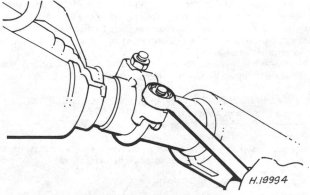

H.19994

Fig. 13.123 Removing a nut from the catalyst rear flange 'A' clamp (Sec 10F)

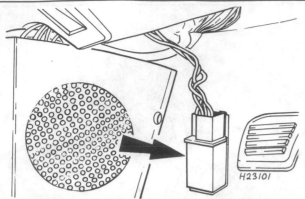

Fig. 13.124 CFi system power relay location (Sec 10F)

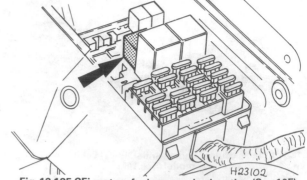

Fig. 13.125 CFi system fuel pump relay location (Sec 10F)

closed. Under the control of the EEC-IV module, the motor controls the position of the throttle plate during the following conditions:

(a) Idle speed control
(b) Deceleration/part throttle
(c) Engine shut off
(d) Engine start up

Fuel injector
The fuel injector is a solenoid valve used to meter and atomise the fuel entering the engine. The injector is fitted in the CFi unit in such a position so as to direct the fuel downwards into the inlet manifold.
Consisting of a solenoid operated pintle and needle valve assembly, an electrical signal from the EEC-IV module energises the solenoid, lifting the pintle valve off its seat allowing the fuel (which is under pressure) to be sprayed into the manifold. The EEC-IV module gives two signals to the injector, one high current to open the injector, the other low current to hold the injector open. This latter signal is sent via a ballast resistor. At idle the injector is pulsed every other inlet stroke, and at every inlet stroke during drive conditions.

Idle speed and mixture (CO) – adjustment
1   Both the idle speed and mixture (CO) content are controlled by the engine management system. Their adjustment requires the use of specialist equipment at present only likely to be held by authorised Ford dealers. If the idle speed is suspected of being incorrect the vehicle must be taken to a Ford dealer for diagnostic checks and, if necessary, adjustment.

Fuel system – depressurising

Warning: *the fuel system will remain pressurised after the engine is switched off. Comply with all relevant safety precautions during this operation*

2   Disconnect the battery negative terminal.
3   Remove the air cleaner assembly.
4   Position a suitable tray or sufficient absorbent cloth beneath the fuel inlet connection on the fuel injection unit.
5   Use an open ended spanner on the flats of the inlet union screwed into the injection unit to prevent it turning while the inlet pipe union is disconnected. Allow all pressure/fuel seepage to dissipate, before fully undoing the union if it is to be disconnected, or tightened if another part of the system is to be worked on.
6   The system will remain depressurised until the fuel pump is primed, prior to starting the engine. Remove the tray or cloths on completion.

Central Fuel Injection system – component renewal
Central fuel injection (CFI) unit
7   Disconnect the battery negative terminal.
8   Remove the air cleaner assembly.
9   Depressurise the fuel system as described earlier, undoing the fuel inlet pipe completely once all pressure has been relieved.
10   Disconnect the fuel return pipe.
11   Disconnect the accelerator cable.
12   Clamp the coolant hoses as close as possible to the CFI unit then disconnect the hoses. Alternatively, drain the coolant system before

disconnecting the pipes.
13   Disconnect the multi-plugs from the Air Charge Temperature sensor, Throttle Plate sensor and throttle plate control motor.
14   Disconnect the vacuum pipe from the CFI unit.
15   Unscrew the four retaining bolts and lift the CFI unit from the inlet manifold.
16   Refit in reverse order, on completion topping up the cooling system as necessary.
Fuel pressure regulator
17   Remove the CFI unit as described earlier.
18   With the regulator side of the CFI unit held uppermost, remove the core plug and Allen screw from the centre of the regulator and recover the ball from under the screw.
19   With the regulator still uppermost, remove the regulator housing retaining screws and lift off the housing, recovering the cup and large spring, diaphragm, valve and small spring.
20   Inspect these components for signs of wear or splitting of the diaphragm, renewing as necessary.
21   Commence reassembly by again holding the regulator side of the CFI unit uppermost and fitting the small spring and valve, then the diaphragm.
22   Fit the large spring and cup, then position the regulator housing over the assembly and fit and tighten the retaining screws evenly to prevent distortion of the housing.
23   Drop the ball into the housing ensuring it locates correctly in the spring cup.
24   Fit the Allen screw and screw it in until it bottoms, then screw it out by three complete turns.
25   Refit the CFI unit as described earlier and make all connections, but do not connect the fuel inlet pipe.
26   Disconnect the other end of the fuel inlet pipe from the fuel filter and connect a 0 to 10 bar (0 to 145 psi) pressure gauge between the filter and CFI unit.
27   Bridge the contacts on the fuel pump relay and switch on the ignition, when the fuel pump should run continuously.
28   The reading on the pressure gauge should be as given in the Specifications.
29   If the reading is incorrect, adjust the regulator Allen screw to achieve a pressure of 0.5 bar (7.0 psi), then bring the pressure back up to that specified.
30   On completion, switch off the engine, depressurise the system as described earlier and remove the pressure gauge and pipes.
31   Refit the fuel inlet pipe between the filter and the CFI unit.
32   Start the engine and check for leaks.
33   Using a suitable sealant, fit a new core plug over the regulator adjustment screw.
34   Refit the air cleaner assembly.
Fuel injector
35   Disconnect the battery negative terminal.
36   Remove the air cleaner assembly.
37   Depressurise the fuel system as described earlier then undo the fuel inlet pipe.
38   Disconnect the multi-plug from the fuel injector.
39   Bend back the injector retaining screw locking tabs then undo the retaining screws.
40   Remove the injector retaining collar then withdraw the injector from the CFI unit.
41   Carefully remove the seals from the injector unit. These seals must

be renewed whenever the injector is removed.

42   Lubricate the new seals with silicone grease (see Specifications) and fit them into the injection unit. Also fit a new seal to the injector retaining collar.

43   Fit the injector into the injection unit, ensuring the lug on the injector locates correctly into the cut-out in the injection unit.

44   Fit the injector retaining collar and secure it with the screws, then lock the screws by bending up the locking tabs.

45   Connect the injector multi-plug, refit the air cleaner assembly and connect the battery negative terminal.

Throttle Position Sensor (TPS)

46   Disconnect the battery negative terminal.

47   Unclip and disconnect the sensor multi-plug.

48   Remove the two retaining screws and withdraw the sensor from the throttle plate shaft.

49   Refit in reverse, ensuring that the sensor actuating arm is correctly located.

Throttle plate control motor

50   Disconnect the battery negative terminal.

51   Remove the air cleaner assembly.

52   Disconnect the multi-plugs from the control motor and the throttle position sensor (TPS).

53   Unscrew the motor bracket screws and remove the bracket from the injection unit.

54   Unscrew the motor retaining screws and withdraw the motor from the bracket.

55   To refit, fit the motor to the bracket and secure it with the two screws.

56   Fit the bracket to the injection unit, ensuring the throttle position sensor is located on the accelerator linkage and the bracket aligns with the locating pegs.

57   Secure the bracket to the injection unit with the two screws.

58   Connect the throttle position sensor and motor multi-plugs.

59   Reconnect the battery.

60   Refit the air cleaner assembly.

Note: *the checking of the motor and adjustment of the idle speed requires the use of special test equipment.*

Air charge temperature sensor

61   The ACT is screwed into the central fuel injection unit housing.

62   Disconnect the battery negative terminal.

63   Remove the air cleaner housing from the CFi unit.

64   Disconnect the multi-plug from the ACT.

65   Unscrew the ACT from the central fuel injection unit.

66   Refit in reverse order, using suitable sealant on the sensor threads.

Engine temperature sensor (ECT)

67   The ECT is screwed into the inlet manifold.

68   Disconnect the battery negative terminal.

69   Drain the coolant system to below the level of the sensor.

70   Disconnect the multi-plug from the sensor.

71   Unscrew the sensor from the manifold.

72   Refit in reverse order, tightening the sensor to the specified torque.

Knock sensor

73   The knock sensor is screwed into the cylinder block near the oil filter.

74   Disconnect the battery negative terminal.

75   Disconnect the knock sensor multi-plug by depressing the plug locking lugs and pulling the plug from the sensor.

76   Unscrew the sensor securing bolt and withdraw the sensor from the cylinder block.

77   Refit in reverse order.

Manifold absolute pressure sensor

78   Disconnect the battery negative terminal.

79   Disconnect the vacuum hose from the MAP sensor.

80   Disconnect the multi-plug from the MAP sensor.

81   Unscrew and remove the sensor from the engine bulkhead.

82   Refit in reverse order.

Heated Exhaust Gas Oxygen sensor (HEGO)

83   Raise the front of the vehicle onto ramps or axle stands.

84   Disconnect the battery negative terminal.

85   Disconnect the sensor multi-plug, unclipping the lead from adjacent components as necessary.

86   Remove the HEGO sensor heat shield.

87   Unscrew the sensor from the exhaust downpipe and retrieve the sealing ring.

Warning: *do not touch the tip of the HEGO sensor.*

88   Refitting is a reversal of removal using a new sealing ring and suitable sealant on the sensor threads.

89   On completion, start the engine and check for exhaust gas leaks from the sensor.

Fuel pump

90   Raise the rear of the vehicle onto ramps or axle stands.

91   Disconnect the battery negative terminal.

92   Depressurise the system as described earlier.

93   Clamp the fuel inlet hose from the fuel tank as close as possible to the fuel pump.

94   Disconnect the fuel inlet hose from the pump.

95   Disconnect the fuel outlet pipe and drain any fuel in the pipe into a suitable container.

96   Disconnect the electrical connections on the pump.

97   Loosen the pump securing bracket bolt and slide the pump from the bracket.

98   Refit in reverse order.

Fuel filter

99   The fuel filter is similar to that fitted on 1.6 litre EFI models. Refer to Part E.

Fuel cut-off (inertia) switch

100   The fuel cut-off switch is similar to that used on the 1.6 litre EFI models. Refer to Part E.

Vehicle speed sender unit

101   The vehicle speed sender unit is similar to vehicles with a fuel computer. Refer to Section 19 of this Supplement.

Catalyst (1.4 CFi models) – removal and refitting

Caution: *handle the catalyst with care. Any sudden knocks or dropping of the catalyst can cause damage to the internal substrates.*

102   Disconnect the battery negative terminal.

103   Raise the front of the vehicle onto axle stands.

104   Remove the bolts from the exhaust downpipe-to-catalyst front flange.

105   Remove the nut from the catalyst-to-rear exhaust pipe clamp.

106   Unhook the catalyst from the front and rear exhaust insulator support mountings and carefully withdraw the catalyst from underneath the vehicle.

107   Ensure that all exhaust pipe and catalyst mating faces and joints are clean.

108   Check that the exhaust insulator mountings are in good condition. If they are not, renew them. Note that the insulators used on versions with a catalyst are of a special high temperature type.

109   Locate the catalyst into the rear exhaust pipe, but do not tighten the clamp.

110   Reconnect the exhaust insulator supports.

111   Fit a new gasket and bolts to the front flange, but do not tighten the bolts at this stage.

112   Align the catalyst and exhaust pipes so that no strain is imposed upon them, then tighten the front flange bolts and rear clamp.

113   Remove the vehicle from axle stands, reconnect the battery, start the engine and check for exhaust gas leaks. No leakage is permitted.

Relays (CFi Cat) – location

114   The CFi power relay is located up under the dash on the driver's side. Access is by removal of the lower sound insulation panel.

115   The fuel pump relay is located on the central fusebox panel in the engine compartment as shown in Fig. 13.124.

Fault diagnosis – Central Fuel injection system

116   The comments given in Part E for the Electronic fuel injection system on Fault diagnosis apply equally to the Central Fuel injection system, ignoring paragraphs 83 onward.

PART G: EMISSION CONTROL, CRANKCASE VENTILATION AND EXHAUST SYSTEM

Emission control system – general

1   On 1984 and later automatic transmission models, the emission control system is as shown in Fig. 13.126 or 13.127 according to operating territory.

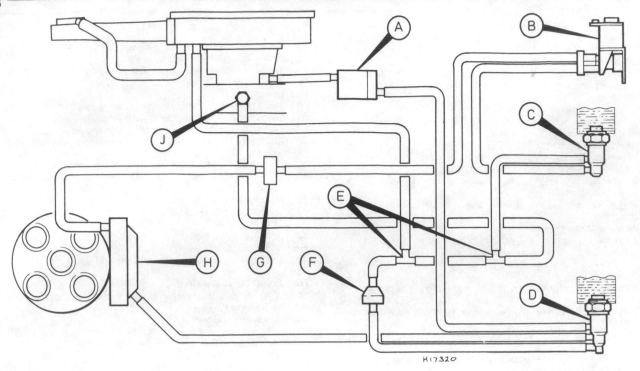

H17320

Fig. 13.126 Emission control system layout for UK automatic transmission models with Ford VV carburettor (Sec 10G)

A	Fuel trap	D	Ported vacuum switch (green)	G	Restrictor
B	Two-way solenoid	E	T-connectors	H	Dual diaphragm distributor
C	Ported vacuum switch (blue)	F	Check valve	J	Inlet manifold connection

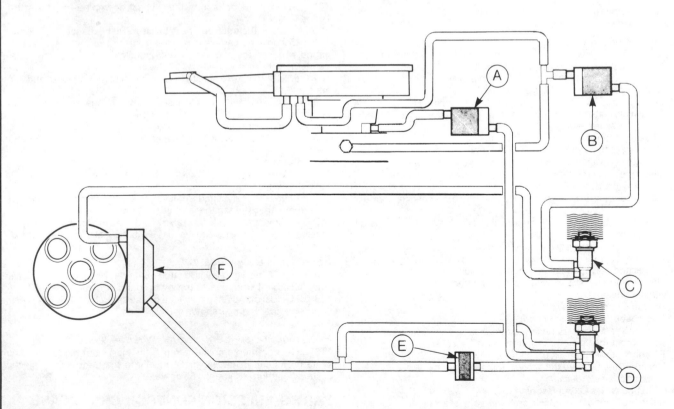

Fig. 13.127 Emission control system for later Swedish automatic transmission models (Sec 10G)

A	Fuel trap	C	Ported vacuum switch (PVS) – blue	E	Spark sustain valve (SSV)
B	Fuel trap	D	Ported vacuum switch (PVS) – brown	F	Dual diaphragm vacuum capsule

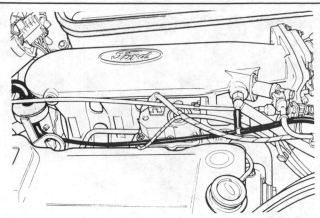

Fig. 13.128 Early (Mk1) crankcase ventilation system on K-Jetronic fuel injection models (Sec 10G)

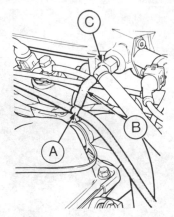

Fig. 13.129 Components of Mk1 crankcase ventilation system (Sec 10G)

A T-connector   C Plenum chamber
B Short vacuum pipe   connector

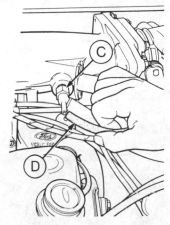

Fig. 13.130 Overrun fuel shut-off valve hose (D) and plenum chamber connector (C) on Mk1 type crankcase ventilation system (Sec 10G)

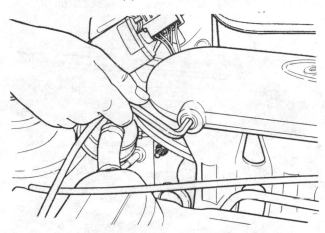

Fig. 13.131 Unscrewing the plenum chamber plug (Sec 10G)

Crankcase ventilation system (K-Jetronic fuel injection models) – modifications

2 During the course of production modifications have been made to the crankcase ventilation system on fuel injected engines to eliminate stalling and rough idling caused by oil from the crankcase venting system contaminating the throttle housing.

3 Currently three versions of the system may be fitted on fuel injected models. If the stalling and rough idling problems are encountered on cars equipped with the Mk 1 or Mk 2 system, then they should be uprated to Mk 3 specification as described in the following paragraphs. It should be noted that even the latest (Mk 3) level system failed to cure the problem completely, and at the beginning of 1986 a revised throttle housing was introduced. These can be identified by having their idle speed adjustment screw located on the top of the housing under a tamperproof cap, rather than underneath the housing as on early versions. The latest version of throttle housing can be fitted to early cars but the work should be carried out by a dealer, as numerous modifications are involved. The latest version of crankcase ventilation system should always be fitted first however, as follows.

4 As a preliminary operation, remove the idle speed adjustment screw and blow out the idle passage in the throttle housing.

5 Refit the screw.

Cars with earliest type (Mk 1) crankcase ventilation system

6 Remove and discard the crankcase ventilation filter vacuum hose.

7 Remove and discard the T-connector (A – Fig. 13.129) and also the short hose (B).

8 Fit the overrun fuel shut off valve hose (D – Fig. 13.130) to the plenum chamber connector (C).

9 Remove and discard the crankcase ventilation filter bracket.

10 Remove and discard the hose which runs between the ventilation filter and the rocker cover.

11 Turn the filter and its hose, which is connected to the air cleaner, so that the small spigot on the filter is uppermost,.

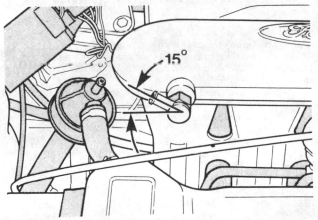

Fig. 13.132 Correct setting of plenum chamber angled connector (Sec 10G)

12 Fit a new hose between the filter and rocker cover, secure it with the original hose clips.

13 Remove and discard the plug from the plenum chamber (Fig. 13.131) and in its place, screw in the angled connectors. Set the connector as shown in Fig. 13.132.

14 Connect the ventilation filter to the angled connector using a new hose.

15 Seat the idle speed screw gently and then unscrew it two complete turns.

16 Bring the engine to normal working temperature and adjust the

10G.26A Engine oil filler cap and ventilation hose on 1.3 litre HCS engine

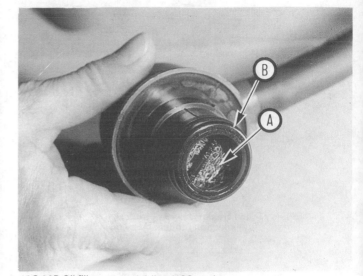

10G.26B Oil filler cap on 1.3 litre HCS engine

A   Filter mesh   B   O-ring seal

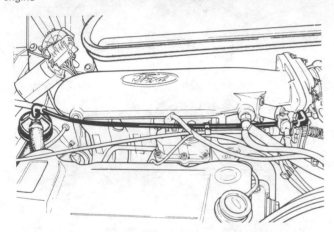

Fig. 13.133 Mk2 crankcase ventilation system (Sec 10G)

idle speed and mixture as described in Chapter 3.

Cars with Mk 2 crankcase ventilation system

17   Remove and discard the crankcase ventilation filter vacuum hose and fit a blanking cap to the hose connector on the throttle housing end of the plenum chamber.

18   Remove and discard the plug from the plenum chamber and substitute the new angled connector as described in paragraph 13.

19   Fit the new hose between the ventilation filter and the angled connector.

20   Repeat the operations described in paragraphs 15 and 16.

21   Later model cars have the crankcase ventilation filter hose connections as shown in Fig. 13.134.

Crankcase ventilation system (1.3 HCS and CVH engines) – description

22   Under all conditions blowby gases flow from the crankcase to the valve cover, through the oil filler cap to the adaptor in the bottom of the air cleaner housing.

23   At idle and part load these gases are directed into the combustion chamber via a restricted outlet on the underside of the adaptor which is linked to the inlet manifold (the 'mushroom' valve being held closed by manifold vacuum) and an air bleed.

24   Under full load conditions the mushroom valve is allowed to open and blowby gases are allowed up into the air cleaner where they are then passed to the combustion chamber for burning.

Crankcase ventilation system (1.3 HCS and CVH VV carburettor engines) – servicing

25   The crankcase ventilation system must be inspected and serviced

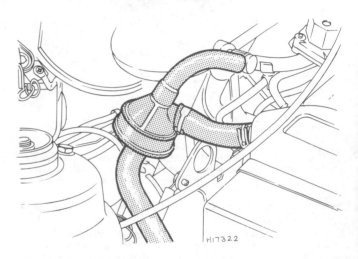

Fig. 13.134 Latest (Mk3) crankcase ventilation system (Sec 10G)

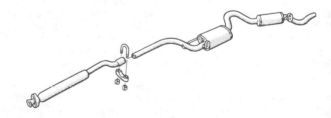

Fig. 13.135 Exhaust pipe resonator and connector (Sec 10G)

at the intervals given in the Routine maintenance Section at the beginning of this Supplement.

26   Visually inspect the filter mesh in the oil filler cap for blockage. Renew or clean the cap as necessary (photos).

27   The adaptor on the underside of the air cleaner housing must be renewed at the same intervals as for the air cleaner element. If at any time the adaptor is found blocked, it must be renewed (independently of the air cleaner element).

28   To renew the adaptor, remove the air cleaner housing as described in Part A.

29   Disconnect the two hoses from the adaptor, then swivel the

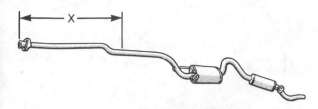

Fig. 13.136 Exhaust pipe cutting diagram (Sec 10G)
X = 895.0 mm (35.2 in)

adaptor out of its retaining clips and pull it from the air cleaner housing.

30   Refit in reverse order.

Exhaust pipe – modification

31   The following modification may be carried out to the exhaust pipe if there is a tendency to backfire or a popping noise occurs during overrun conditions.

32   Disconnect the exhaust system from the downpipe and then cut the exhaust pipe at a point 895.0 mm (35.2 in) from the flared end.

33   Replace the removed section with a purpose made Ford resonator assembly available from your dealer.

---

11   Ignition system

Electronic ignition system (OHV engine) – description

1   1.3 litre Orion models from 1986 onwards are fitted with an electronic ignition system, incorporating a breakerless distributor with integral electronic module. The distributor is of Bosch manufacture and is located on the rear facing side of the engine. Drive is by a skew gear from the camshaft.

2   The operation of the electronic ignition system is the same as on CVH engines, and a description is contained in Chapter 4, Section 1.

Distributor (OHV engine) – removal and refitting

3   Disconnect the leads from the spark plugs, spring back the retaining clips and lift off the distributor cap.

4   Disconnect the distributor LT wiring multi-plug and the vacuum hose at the distributor vacuum unit.

5   Remove No 1 spark plug (nearest the crankshaft pulley).

6   Place a finger over the plug hole and turn the crankshaft in the normal direction of rotation (clockwise viewed from the crankshaft pulley end) until pressure is felt in No 1 cylinder. This indicates that the piston is commencing its compression stroke. The crankshaft can be turned with a spanner on the pulley bolt.

7   Refer to the Specifications and look up the ignition timing setting for the engine being worked on.

8   Continue turning the crankshaft until the notch in the pulley is aligned with the correct setting on the scale located just above and to the right of the pulley. The 'O' mark on the scale represents top dead centre (TDC) and the raised projections to the left of TDC are in increments of 4° BTDC (Fig. 13.138).

9   Check that the rotor arm is pointing to the notch on the rim of the distributor body.

10   Make a mark on the distributor body and a corresponding mark on the cylinder block to aid refitting.

11   Undo the bolt securing the distributor clamp plate to the cylinder block, then withdraw the distributor from its location. As the distributor is removed, the rotor arm will move a few degrees clockwise. Note the new position of the rotor arm and make an alignment mark on the distributor body rim.

12   Before installing the distributor, make sure that the crankshaft is still positioned at TDC as previously described. If a new distributor is being fitted, transfer the markings made during removal to the new unit.

13   Hold the distributor over its hole in the cylinder block, with the mark made on the distributor body aligned with the mark made on the cylinder block.

14   Position the rotor arm so that it points to the mark made on the distributor rim after removal, and push the distributor fully home. As the skew gears mesh, the rotor arm will move anti-clockwise and should align with the manufacturer's mark on the distributor rim.

15   With the distributor in place, turn the body slightly, if necessary so that the arms of the trigger wheel and stator are aligned, then refit and tighten the clamp plate bolt.

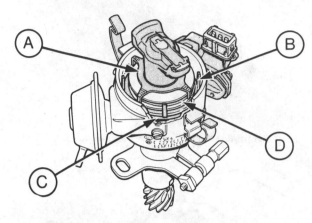

Fig. 13.137 Electronic ignition distributor – 1.3 litre OHV engine (Sec 11)

A   *Trigger wheel*   C   *Magnet*
B   *Stator*   D   *Trigger coil*

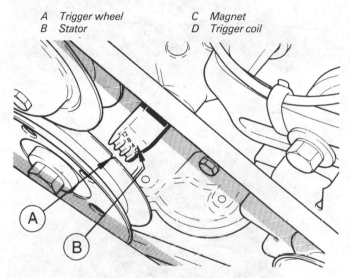

Fig. 13.138 Timing mark details – 1.3 litre OHV engine (Sec 11)

A   *Notch on crankshaft pulley*   B   *Timing cover scale*

Fig. 13.139 Rotor arm must point toward notch in distributor body rim before removal – 1.3 litre OHV engine (Sec 11)

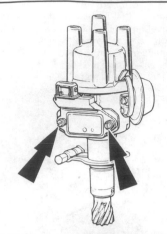

Fig. 13.140 Electronic amplifier module retaining screws – 1.3 litre OHV engine (Sec 11)

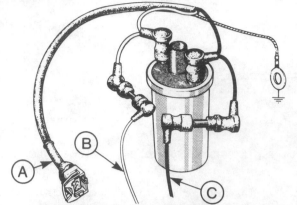

Fig. 13.141 LT wiring adaptor kit to suit modified distributor – CVH engines (Sec 11)

A   Wiring multi-plug to   B   Green wire
     amplifier module   C   Black wire

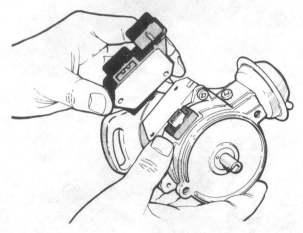

Fig. 13.142 Removing the electronic amplifier module – later type Lucas distributor, CVH engines (Sec 11)

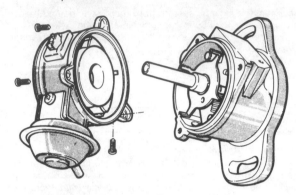

Fig. 13.143 Separating distributor body halves – later type Lucas distributor, CVH engines (Sec 11)

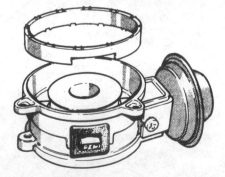

Fig. 13.144 Removing the plastic spacer ring – later type Lucas distributor, CVH engines (Sec 11)

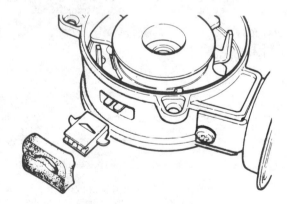

Fig. 13.145 Trigger coil terminal connector and rubber seal – later type Lucas distributor, CVH engines (Sec 11)

16   Reconnect the LT wiring multi-plug and vacuum hose, then refit the distributor cap, spark plug and plug leads.
17   Adjust the ignition timing as described in this Section.

Distributor (OHV engine) – overhaul

Note: *Ensure that replacement parts are readily available before carrying out any overhaul or repair work on the distributor.*

18   Remove the distributor from the engine as described previously.
19   Remove the rotor arm.
20   Extract the circlip securing the vacuum unit rod to the baseplate pivot post.
21   Undo the two vacuum unit retaining screws, tip the unit to release the rod from the baseplate pivot post and withdraw it from the distributor body.

22   Undo the two screws securing the electronic amplifier module to the distributor body and detach the module from the distributor.
23   To remove the drive gear at the base of the distributor, support the gear in a vice or on a block and drive out the retaining pin using a hammer and punch. It may be necessary to resort to the use of a press if the pin is excessively tight. Withdraw the drive gear from the distributor shaft.
24   This is the limit of dismantling that can be undertaken on these distributors. Should the distributor be worn or unserviceable in any other respect, renewal of the complete unit will be necessary.
25   Reassembly and refitting is the reverse of the dismantling and removal procedures. Lubricate the baseplate pivot post with a high melting point grease and apply heat sink compound, available from Ford parts dealers, to the back of the amplifier module before fitting.

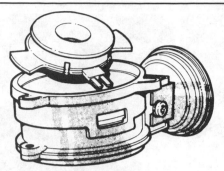

Fig. 13.146 Removing the trigger coil – later type Lucas distributor, CVH engines (Sec 11)

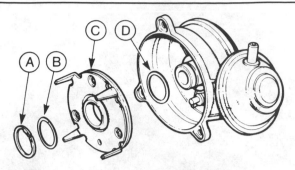

Fig. 13.147 Stator and shim details – later type Lucas distributor, CVH engines (Sec 11)

A Circlip   C Stator
B Upper shim   D Lower shim

Also check the condition of the amplifier module rubber grommet, where fitted, and renew if necessary.

Distributor (CVH engines) – modifications

26   From approximately January 1985 a new type of distributor was introduced on CVH engine models. The new distributor may be of either Bosch or Lucas manufacture, and is most easily identifiable from the earlier type by only having two retaining bolt flanges instead of the three used originally.

27   Although of different design and construction the new distributors operate on the same principles as the earlier type, and reference should be made to Chapter 4.

Distributor (CVH engines) – removal and refitting

28   Removal and refitting of the later type distributor is the same as for earlier versions, as described in Chapter 4, Section 4.

29   Should it be necessary to obtain a new distributor for a vehicle produced prior to January 1985, only the later type distributor will be supplied by Ford parts dealers. It will also therefore be necessary to obtain an LT wiring adaptor kit, as the later type distributors are not directly compatible with the wiring loom used on early cars. The wiring adaptor kit is also supplied by Ford parts dealers, and should be connected as shown in Fig. 13.141.

Distributor (CVH engines) – overhaul

Note: *Ensure that replacement parts are readily available before carrying out any overhaul or repair work on the distributor.*

Bosch distributor (later type)

30   Remove the distributor from the engine as described previously.

31   Remove the rotor arm and the plastic shield (photos).

32   Undo the two screws securing the vacuum unit to the side of the distributor body (photos). Tip the unit to release the rod from the baseplate pivot post and withdraw it from the distributor.

33   Undo the two screws securing the electronic amplifier module and remove the module (photos).

34   Extract the circlip securing the trigger wheel to the distributor shaft (photo).

35   Withdraw the trigger wheel from the shaft by carefully levering it up with two screwdrivers (photo). Recover the locating pin as the trigger wheel is removed.

36   Extract the second circlip from the distributor shaft (photo), undo the retaining screw on the side of the distributor body, and lift out the baseplate with stator and trigger coil assembly (photo).

11.31A Removing the rotor arm ...

11.31B ... and plastic shield

11.32A Vacuum unit ...

11.32B ... securing screws (arrowed)

11.33A Electronic amplifier retaining screw (arrowed)

11.33B Removing the amplifier

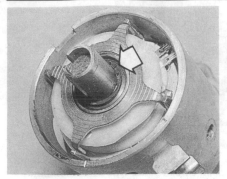

11.34 Trigger wheel retaining circlip (arrowed)

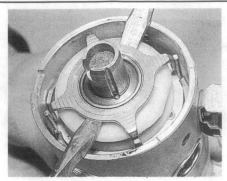

11.35 Trigger wheel removal

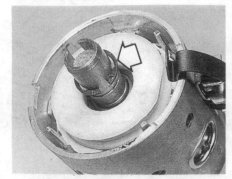

11.36A Distributor shaft second circlip (arrowed)

11.36B Removing the baseplate

11.65 3-D Electronic ignition system ESC module (1.3 litre HCS models)

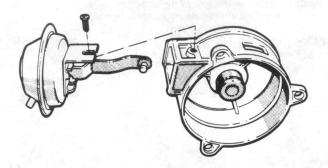

Fig. 13.148 Vacuum unit removal – later type Lucas distributor, CVH engines (Sec 11)

37   To remove the drive dog, turn the distributor shaft to align the retaining pin with the slots in the distributor body flange.

38   Scribe a mark on each side of the body flange in line with the dog teeth, and also suitably mark the distributor shaft to ensure correct orientation of both components when refitting.

39   Remove the drive dog retaining spring clip.

40   Support the drive dog in a vice or on a block, and drive out the retaining pin using a hammer and punch. **Do not** support the body flange during this operation – only the drive dog. It may be necessary to resort to the use of a press if the pin is excessively tight.

41   With the pin removed, withdraw the drive dog from the shaft.

42   This is the limit of dismantling that can be undertaken on these distributors. Should the distributor be worn or unserviceable in any other respect, renewal of the complete unit will be necessary.

43   Reassembly is the reverse of the dismantling procedure. Lubricate the baseplate pivot post with a high melting point grease and apply heat sink compound, available from Ford parts dealers, to the back of the

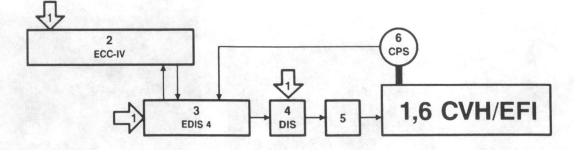

Fig. 13.149 Schematic diagram of E-DIS 4 ignition system, 1.6 litre EFI models (Sec 11)

1 Power supply (ignition switch, battery and power relay)	3 E-DIS 4 module	5 Spark plugs
2 EEC-IV module	4 DIS coil	6 CPS

11.66A Engine speed sensor mounted on cylinder block (1.3 litre HCS models)

11.66B The cut-outs in the flywheel – larger cut-out arrowed

11.68A Vacuum connection on inlet manifold ...

amplifier module before fitting. When refitting the drive dog, align the marks made during removal and secure the drive dog using a new retaining pin.

Lucas distributor (later type)

44 Remove the distributor from the engine as described previously.
45 Remove the rotor arm.
46 Undo the two screws securing the electronic amplifier module and remove the module.
47 Undo the three screws and separate the two halves of the distributor body.
48 Withdraw the plastic spacer ring from the body upper half.
49 Withdraw the rubber seal, then pull the connector off the trigger coil terminals. Note the fitted direction of the connector to aid refitting.
50 Tip the trigger coil up and remove it from the body upper half.
51 Extract the stator retaining circlip and the upper shim.
52 Lift out the stator and the lower shim.
53 Slacken the vacuum unit retaining screw and remove the vacuum unit.
54 This is the limit of dismantling that can be undertaken on these distributors. Should the distributor be worn or unserviceable in any other respect, renewal of the complete unit will be necessary.
55 Reassembly is the reverse of the dismantling procedures. Lubricate the vacuum unit peg with a high melting point grease and apply heat sink compound, available from Ford parts dealers, to the back of the amplifier module before refitting.

Ignition timing (OHV engine) – adjustment

56 Refer to the Specifications for the appropriate ignition timing setting, then highlight the crankshaft pulley notch and the applicable mark on the timing scale with a dab of quick-drying white paint (see Fig. 13.138).
57 Connect a stroboscopic timing light in accordance with the manufacturer's instructions.
58 Disconnect the vacuum pipe from the distributor and plug the pipe with a piece of rod.
59 Start the engine and allow it to idle.

60 If the timing light is now directed at the engine timing marks, the pulley notch will appear to be stationary and opposite the specified mark on the scale. If the marks are not in alignment, release the distributor clamp pinch-bolt and turn the distributor in whichever direction is necessary to align the marks.
61 Retighten the pinch-bolt, switch off the engine, remove the timing light and reconnect the vacuum pipe.
62 It may now be necessary to check and adjust the engine idle speed if the distributor setting has to be varied to any extent.

3-D Electronic ignition system (HCS engine) – general description

63 A fully electronic ignition system is fitted to all HCS engines.
64 The '3-D' system is so called because it computes a three-dimensional map of 256 calibration points drawing information from three sources – engine vacuum (load), engine speed, and spark advance. These form the X, Y and Z axis of the 3-D map.
65 The ESC module (control unit), mounted on the left-hand inner wing panel, monitors engine load, speed and operating temperature and computes the correct degree of spark advance under all engine operating conditions (photo).
66 Engine speed is monitored through the speed sensor mounted on the cylinder block, facing the flywheel. The sensor is 'triggered' by cut-outs in the flywheel. A larger cut-out in the flywheel denotes 90° BTDC for No 1 cylinder (photos).
67 As speed increases, so does the frequency and amplitude of the signal sent to the ESC module.
68 Engine load is monitored by a vacuum hose between the inlet manifold and the ESC module (photos).
69 Engine temperature is monitored through a thermal sender screwed into the bottom of the inlet manifold and connected electrically to the ESC module.
70 A DIS coil assembly is mounted on the cylinder block by number one cylinder. The coil has two primary and two secondary windings. It is connected to the battery and ESC module via a three pin plug.
71 The HT leads connect to the coil by 'quick-fit' type plugs and to the spark plugs by conventional connectors.

11.68B ... and ESC module (1.3 litre HCS models)

11.76A Undo the central retaining bolt on ESC module multi-connector ...

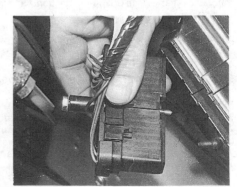

11.76B ... and withdraw the connector

11.77 ESC module securing screws (arrowed)

11.79 Showing wire clip on coil multi-plug

11.80 Compress the clips (arrowed) and pull off the HT lead connections (coil removed for clarity)

11.81 Removing the coil (engine removed for clarity)

11.82 Push the HT leads firmly back in place

11.83 Disconnecting the plug from the sensor

72   One coil supplies current to numbers 1 and 4 cylinders simultaneously, the other to 2 and 3 cylinders. Whenever either of the coils is energised, two sparks are released. One is routed (for instance) to number 1 cylinder on compression stroke, the other to number 4 cylinder on exhaust stroke. This spark is 'redundant' and has no detrimental effect on combustion.

3-D Electronic ignition system (HCS engine) – servicing and overhaul

Warning: *Electronic ignition systems carry very much higher voltages when working on such systems. Refer to the Safety First Section at the beginning of this manual and always disconnect the battery negative terminal before working on any part of the system.*

73   No routine maintenance is required on the 3-D ignition system, there being no moving parts, apart from spark plug inspection adjustment and renewal (see Chapter 4, Section 7 and later paragraphs of this Section).
74   Because of the need for specialist equipment to test the system and diagnose faults, the help of a Ford dealer will have to be sought should a fault occur.

3-D Electronic ignition system (HCS engine) – component renewal

ESC module (control unit)
75   Disconnect the vacuum hose from the module.
76   Undo the central retaining bolt and pull out the multi-connector (photos).
77   Remove the screws securing the module to the left-hand inner wing panel and withdraw the module (photo).
78   Refit in reverse order.
DIS coil
79   Pull back the wire clip and pull off the multi-plug (photo).
80   Compress the clips on the side of each HT lead connection and remove the HT leads (photo).

81   Unscrew the three Torx screws securing the coil to the cylinder block and withdraw the unit (photo).
82   Refit in reverse order, pushing the HT lead connections firmly back into place (photo).
Engine speed (TDC) sensor
83   Disconnect the electrical connection from the sensor (photo).
84   Remove the securing screw and withdraw the sensor (photo).
85   Refit in reverse order.
Engine temperature sensor
86   Drain the cooling system as described in Chapter 2, Section 3.
87   Disconnect the plug from the sensor.
88   Unscrew the sensor from the bottom of the inlet manifold (photo).
89   Refit in reverse order, being careful not to overtighten the sensor in the aluminium manifold. Refill the cooling system as described in Chapter 2 on completion.
Fuel trap
90   A fuel trap is fitted in the vacuum hose between the inlet manifold and the ESC module (see also Section 10).
91   When refitting a fuel trap, the side marked DIST faces the ESC module and the side marked CARB faces the inlet manifold.
Spark plugs
92   The spark plugs themselves are conventional and should be inspected and adjusted, the gap being set to that shown in the Specifications at the beginning of this Supplement, and renewed, at the intervals given in the Routine maintenance Section.
93   Disconnect the HT leads by pulling on the rubber cover and not on the lead (photo).
94   Brush out the spark plug recesses in the cylinder head.
95   Use a double depth socket and ratchet to remove each plug in turn.
96   Refit in reverse, starting each plug off in its thread by hand to avoid cross threading them.

Ignition system (1.6 EFI EEC-IV) – general description
The components of the EEC-IV) ignition system are shown in Fig. 13.149.

11.84 Sensor and securing screw

11.88 Engine temperature sensor screwed into bottom of inlet manifold

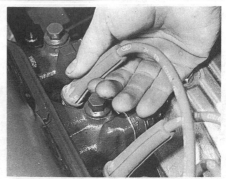

11.93 Disconnecting an HT lead from a spark plug

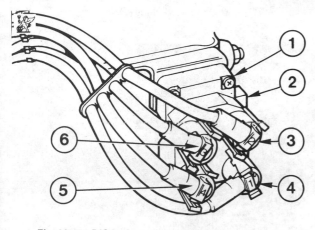

Fig. 13.150 DIS ignition coil, 1.6 litre EFI models (Sec 11)

1 Coil windings	4 To number 1 cylinder
2 Connection to E-DIS 4	spark plug
module	5 To number 4 cylinder
3 To number 2 cylinder	spark plug
spark plug	6 To number 3 cylinder
	spark plug

The EEC-IV module is the heart of the electronic engine control system and is based on a microprocessor-controlled electronic circuit. It compares signals from its various sensors with stored engine operating parameters, varying the engines operating settings directly according to engine load and environment.

Ignition is electronic via a DIS coil and E-DIS 4 module. From signals generated by the Crankshaft Position Sensor (CPS), the E-DIS 4 module generates a Profile Ignition Pulse (PIP). From this PIP, the EEC-IV module calculates a Spark Advance Word (SAW) as a means of defining ignition timing (or firing point). The E-DIS 4 module uses the SAW signal to control the DIS coil. If the EEC-IV module develops a fault, a Limited Operation Strategy (LOS) comes into effect allowing the driver to continue the journey but with restricted power and economy. Under LOS conditions the SAW and PIP signals are not used.

The EEC-IV module is provided with a memory which is used for control matching, diagnosis and self testing.

With the engine running the E-DIS IV module receives the SAW signal in a 'window' extending from 10° ATDC to 170° BTDC. The signal is therefore outside the ignition advance and retard range (10° ATDC to 57° BTDC) and cannot be influenced by HT disturbances.

When the engine is started or running at low speed, or operating in LOS, ignition is triggered by the E-DIS 4 module at 10° BTDC and not controlled by the SAW.

The DIS ignition coil (DIS refers to distributorless) consists of two coil windings converting the voltage signal from the E-DIS 4 module into HT and supplying this HT to the spark plugs in the correct firing order.

The crankshaft position sensor (CPS) is an inductive proximity switch reacting to the thirtysix webs cast into the rear of the flywheel. One web is missing causing a gap and is used to denote 90° BTDC on

number one cylinder in the firing order. The signal generated by the CPS is used by the E-DIS 4 module to determine actual ignition timing. On engines with an open-loop operating principle (as opposed to those with a closed-loop system incorporating a catalyst and HEGO sensor), the CO adjustment pot, a 5 kohm potentiometer supplies a substitute CO value to the EEC-IV module in place of the HEGO sensor (Heated Exhaust Gas Oxygen sensor)

Ignition system (1.6 EFI EEC-IV) – testing and fault diagnosis

97   At the time of writing the testing and fault diagnosis of EEC-IV ignition system can only be undertaken using special test equipment not yet available to the DIY market and only likely to be held by authorised Ford dealers.

98   For this reason there is no recourse but to leave testing and fault diagnosis to a Ford dealer, except where a component is obviously defective and can be removed and a replacement fitted.

99   It is expected that in the future reasonably priced diagnostic equipment will become available for the DIY market.

Ignition system (1.6 EFI EEC-IV) – component renewal
EEC-IV module
100   The EEC-IV module is located behind the centre console underneath a stiff carpeting cover. To remove the module proceed as follows.
101   Disconnect the battery negative terminal.
102   Working from the passenger side of the vehicle, lift off the cover from the module and pull the module from its bracket behind the centre console (photo).
103   Undo the bolt securing the multiplug in place, disconnect the multiplug, and withdraw the module (photo).
104   Refitting is a reversal of removal.

Note: *Different versions of the EEC-IV module are available and are not interchangeable. The modules can only be identified by a code in the hollow for the module multi-plug, by an adhesive label on the module itself and on the inside of the driver's door. If the wrong module is fitted, engine performance may be seriously affected. Always ensure a replacement module has the same part number as the one removed.*

E-DIS 4 module
105   Disconnect the battery negative terminal.
106   The E-DIS 4 module is located on the left-hand inner wing in the engine compartment just above the fuel filter (photo).
107   Pull the multi-plug from the module by pulling on the plug and not the wiring.
108   Unscrew and withdraw the module.
109   Refitting is a reversal of removal.

Note: *The E-DIS 4 module is similar to other modules used in other systems but is externally marked to prevent confusion. The multi-plug cut-outs are also different to prevent wrong connection. 1990 model year modules have a blue identity plate.*

DIS coil
110   Disconnect the battery negative terminal.
111   The DIS coil is mounted on the left-hand end of the engine under a plastic cover (photo).

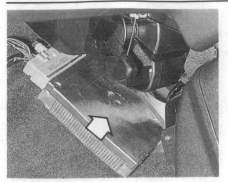

11.102 EEC-IV module and bracket (arrowed) – 1.6 litre EFI models

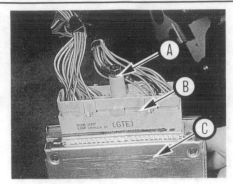

11.103 EEC-IV module showing (A) multi-plug bolt, (B) multi-plug, and (C) module

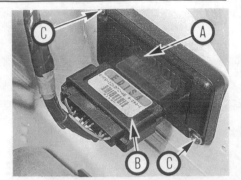

11.106 E-DIS 4 module on 1.6 litre EFI models

A   module
B   multi-plug
C   module securing screws

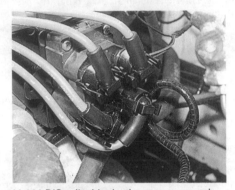

11.111 DIS coil with plastic cover removed – 1.6 litre EFI models

11.118 Showing the spark plugs with HT leads correctly routed – 1.6 litre EFI models

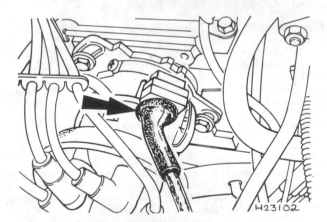

Fig. 13.151 Distributor multi-plug (arrowed) on 1.4 CFi catalyst models (Sec 11)

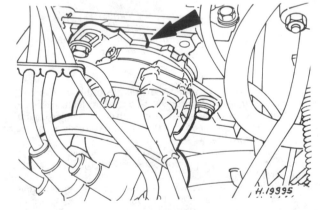

Fig. 13.152 Distributor alignment marks on 1.4 CFi catalyst models (Sec 11)

112   Unscrew and remove the cover.
113   Disconnect the coil multi-plug.
114   Disconnect each HT lead in turn by depressing both locking lugs and pulling the lead from the coil.
115   Unscrew the four Torx type screws and withdraw the coil.
116   Refit in reverse order ensuring the HT leads are connected correctly in the right firing order (see Fig. 13.150).

Spark plugs
117   The spark plugs are conventional and are removed and refitted in a similar fashion to the 3-D ignition system.
118   Ensure that during refitting, each lead is pushed back into its routing in the air intake duct and into the clips on the valve cover (photo).

Crankshaft position sender (CPS)
119   The CPS is similar to the engine speed sensor on the 3-D system and is removed and refitted in the same way.

120   The gap between the sensor tip and the flywheel must be between 0.5 and 1.0 mm (0.02 and 0.04 in). If this gap is incorrect, the sensor will malfunction.

Ignition system (1.4 CFi catalyst) – general description
The ignition system on 1.4 CFi catalyst models consists of a distributor, TFI IV module, coil and EEC-IV module.
The distributor is similar to that used on earlier CVH engines being mounted on the cylinder head and driven by the camshaft, but has no centrifugal or vacuum advance mechanisms, these functions being carried out by the EEC-IV module. Working on the 'Hall' effect principle, the distributor provides a square wave pulse signal to the EEC-IV module.
HT distribution is achieved using a conventional resistive rotor arm

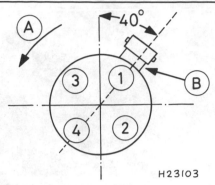

Fig. 13.153 Correct orientation of distributor on 1.4 CFi catalyst models (Sec 11)

A   Direction of rotation

B   Centre line through distributor (multi-plug at 40° to vertical).

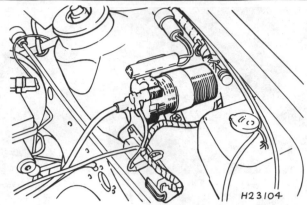

Fig. 13.154 Ignition coil on 1.4 CFi catalyst models (Sec 11)

and distributor cap. The distributor performs the following functions:

   (a)   *Sends signals to the EEC-IV module to trigger the ignition firing process*
   (b)   *From the pulses, the EEC-IV module calculates engine speed*
   (c)   *Distributes HT voltage to the appropriate cylinder*

   The TFI IV (Thick Film Integration) module functions as a high current switch by controlling the ignition coil primary LT circuit. The module is controlled by one of two input signals, either from the Hall effect sensor – Profile Ignition Pickup (PIP), or from the EEC-IV module – Spark Out (SPOUT). Both of these signals are in square wave form.

   The PIP signal from the distributor passes through the TFI module to the EEC-IV. The EEC-IV module modifies the wave form to provide ignition timing advancement relative to engine speed, load and temperature, before returning it to the TFI module, as the SPOUT signal.

   The operation of the TFI module can be simplified by assuming that it is accepting two series of on/off signals, one PIP the other SPOUT. The module will accept an 'on' or 'off' command depending on what condition it is currently in. If, for example the module is in the off state, it will accept the next on command from either source, switching on the LT current. The next off command will then cut the LT current, generating the HT voltage in the coil.

   When the engine is operating in the Limited Operation Strategy (LOS) mode, or being cranked, the TFI module is controlled solely by the PIP signal.

   The Electronic Engine Control (EEC) IV module is a powerful microprocessor programmed to provide total engine management. From signals received from the various system sensors the module controls the following functions:

   (a)   *Ignition timing*
   (b)   *Fuel delivery*
   (c)   *Deceleration fuelling*
   (d)   *Idle speed*
   (e)   *Engine overspeed protection*

   If the module should fail, the ignition timing will be switched by the TFI module (there will be no ignition advance) and fuel will be delivered at a constant rate. This is known as the Limited Operation Strategy (LOS) and allows the vehicle to be driven, but with greatly reduced engine performance and fuel economy.

   Should any of the system sensors fail or send signals without their normal operating range, the EEC-IV module will sense this and substitute a single predetermined value for the failed input. Again, this will allow continued engine operation but with reduced driveability, performance, starting and economy. Under these conditions a self test code will be stored in the module memory to aid in subsequent fault diagnosis.

   The module contains a Keep Alive Memory (KAM) which continuously adjusts the module calibration, compensating for wear and ageing of the calibrated components. This 'adaptive strategy' is retained in the memory and is not lost when the ignition is switched off. A further function of the KAM is to store intermittent fault codes. The codes are kept for a cycle of forty engine starts.

Important: *Whenever the battery is disconnected all the values stored in the KAM will be erased. Upon reconnection, the engine must be allowed to idle at normal operating temperature for three minutes. Engine speed must then be increased to 1200 rpm for approximately two minutes. This will allow the module to re-learn idle values. It may also be necessary to drive the vehicle for five miles of varied driving to complete the relearning process.*

Ignition system (1.4 CFi catalyst) – testing and fault diagnosis

121   The same comments as given for the 1.6 EFI EEC-IV ignition system apply equally to the 1.4 CFi catalyst ignition system.

Ignition timing (1.4 CFi catalyst) – adjustment

122   The ignition timing can only be set accurately using the special test equipment available at a Ford main dealer.

123   If the fitting and alignment procedures given in the following paragraphs under 'component renewal' have been adhered to, the timing should be sufficiently adjusted to allow the vehicle to be started, and driven to the nearest Ford dealer where accurate adjustments may be made.

Ignition system (1.4 CFi catalyst) – component renewal

Distributor

Note: *during production, engines are timed to within half a degree using a microwave timing system. Subsequent timing requires the use of special test equipment. Unless absolutely necessary* **do not** *remove the distributor.*

124   Disconnect the battery negative terminal.

125   Disconnect the HT lead from the coil, remove the distributor cap and position it to one side.

126   Disconnect the distributor multi-plug.

127   Ensure there are alignment marks across the distributor base and cylinder head. If there are not, make them now using a scribe or centre punch.

128   Remove the distributor retaining bolts and withdraw the distributor from the end of the cylinder head.

129   Before refitting, check that the seal on the distributor is in good condition, renewing it if necessary. Lubricate the seal (old or new) with clean engine oil.

130   Align the distributor drive dog with the slot in the camshaft. The dog will only fit one way as the slot is offset.

131   Loosely secure the distributor to the cylinder head with the two bolts, then turn the distributor body until either the alignment marks line up or if a new distributor/cylinder head has been fitted, orientate the multiplug as shown in Fig. 13.153. Tighten the bolts.

132   Reconnect the multi-plug, fit the distributor cap and connect the HT lead from the coil.

133   Connect the battery negative terminal.

134   Refer to earlier paragraphs on ignition timing.

Coil

135   Disconnect the battery negative terminal.

12.3 One-piece clutch fork in-situ

12.7 Clutch release lever pinch bolt

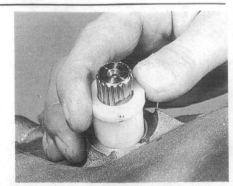
12.9 Remove the nylon bush

12.10 Remove the release bearing

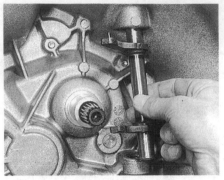
12.11 Lift out the fork assembly

136   Disconnect the HT and LT terminals from the coil.
137   Remove the coil clamp screws and withdraw the coil.
138   Refitting is a reversal of removal, noting that the LT positive terminal is the larger of the two LT terminals.

TFI IV module
139   The TFI IV module is located on the left-hand inner wing.
140   Disconnect the battery negative terminal.
141   Depress the multi-plug locking tabs and disconnect the plug by pulling it from the module.
142   Unscrew and remove the module.
143   Refitting is a reversal of removal.

EEC-IV module
144   The procedure is as described for the EEC-IV module fitted to EFI models.
Note: *all EEC-IV modules look identical from the outside but must not be interchanged. The module is programmed for specific engine control systems and incorrect replacement could seriously affect performance and economy. Identification of modules is by part number only.*

Spark plugs and HT cables
145   The spark plugs and HT leads are conventional and removed and refitted as described for earlier ignition systems.

12   Clutch

Clutch (1.6 models, 1988-on) – Low-lift
1   From May 1988, 1.6 models are fitted with a 'Low-lift' clutch assembly. This simply means that the internal components have been modified resulting in reduced pressure plate lift.
2   The components of the 'Low-lift' clutch are not interchangeable with 'High-lift' clutches and the clutch driven plate and pressure plate are stamped, 'Low-lift' for identification.

Clutch fork (June 1988-on) – removal and refitting
3   From June 1988 (build code JC), all models are fitted with a one piece clutch fork assembly (photo).
4   These components are not interchangeable with earlier versions.
5   To remove a one piece fork assembly proceed as follows.
6   Remove the transmission as described in Chapter 6.
7   Undo and remove the pinch bolt and then lift off the release lever (photo).
8   Remove the rubber cover from the end of the shaft.
9   Remove the nylon bush (photo).
10   Remove the release bearing (photo).
11   Lift the fork assembly from the lower bearing then lower it out of the bellhousing (photo).
12   Refit in reverse order, using a little lithium based grease on all pivot points, but note that only the special Ford grease must be used on the release bearing guide sleeve (refer to Section 13).

13   Manual transmission

Transmission oil levels – revisions
1   The following procedure should be adopted when checking the oil level on all transmission types.
2   Ensure that the car is standing on level ground and has been stationary for some time.
3   Unscrew the combined filler/level plug from the front face of the transmission. The plug is of socket-headed type and a suitable key will be required for removal.
4   With the plug removed, check the oil level. To do this accurately, make up an oil level check dipstick from a short length of welding rod or similar material. Make a 90° bend in the rod, then mark the downward leg in 5 mm increments. The dipstick is then inserted through the filler plug orifice so that the unmarked leg rests flat on the plug orifice threads, with the marked leg dipped in the oil. Withdraw the dipstick and read off the level of oil.

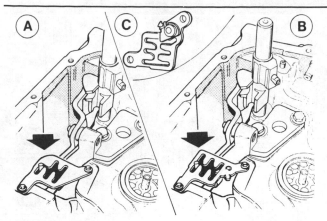

Fig. 13.155 Modified gearshift gates – February 1987-on (Sec 13)

A Four-speed transmission   C Reverse gear lock on
B Five-speed transmission   underside of gate

Note: *The selector block boss must engage in the gate. On five-speed transmissions, the reverse gear should point downwards towards the selector shaft*

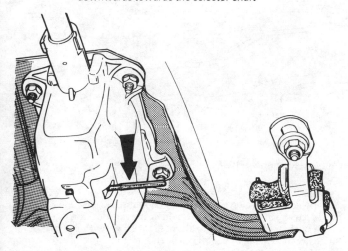

Fig. 13.157 Using a drift to lock the gear lever prior to adjustment (Sec 13)

5   On transmissions manufactured up to August 1985, the oil level must be maintained between 5 and 10 mm below the lower edge of the filler plug hole.
6   On transmissions manufactured from September 1985 onwards, the oil level must be maintained between 0 and 5 mm below the lower edge of the filler plug hole.
7   To determine the date of transmission manufacture, locate the aluminium build code tag, which will be attached to one of the transmission housing retaining bolts. The transmission part number is stamped on the tag, and if the last letter of the part number suffix is a 'D', then the transmission is of the early type. If the last letter of the suffix is an 'E', then the transmission is of the later type.
8   Top up the transmission with the specified type of oil if necessary until the level is correct for the transmission type. Take care not to overfill the unit as this can lead to excessive heat build-up, increased leakage and impaired gear changing.

Gearchange mechanism – modifications
9   At the beginning of 1987 the remote control gearchange mechanism was modified on all four- and five-speed transmissions.
10   Removal and refitting procedures are basically the same as described in Chapter 6, Section 4 or 15, except that the gearchange housing is bolted directly to the floor and the four retaining nuts are accessible from inside the car, beneath the centre console.
11   Note also that from February 1987, the gearshift gate must be detached before removing the main selector shaft (Fig. 13.155). On reassembly, the gate should be fitted after the main selector shaft, and

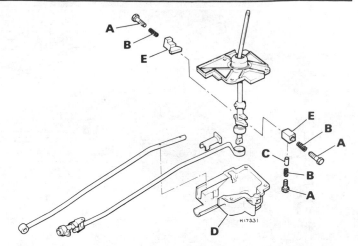

Fig. 13.156 Later type gearchange housing component locations – five-speed transmission shown (Sec 13)

A Locking screws   D Housing body
B Tension springs   E Locking bar
C Locking pin

before the relay levers. Tighten the bolts to the specified torque.
12   Overhaul follows the procedures given in Chapter 6, but refer to Fig. 13.156.

Gearchange mechanism (February 1987-on) – adjustment
13   Place the transmission in 2nd gear for four-speed transmissions, or 4th gear for five-speed transmissions.
14   Jack up the front of the car and support it on stands.
15   Slacken the gearchange rod clamp bolt, and ensure that the clamp is free to slide on the transmission selector shaft.
16   Lock the gear lever in its 2nd or 4th gear position, as applicable, by inserting a 3.0 mm (0.12 in) diameter rod through the alignment hole at the base of the gearchange housing (Fig. 13.157).
17   Now turn the selector shaft clockwise, as viewed from the rear of the car, to take up any free play, then tighten the clamp bolt. Remove the alignment rod and lower the car.

Transmission – removal and refitting (general)
18   When removing either the four- or five-speed transmission on 1986 models onwards using the procedures described in Chapter 6., some difficulty may be experienced in removing the selector shaft cap nut and locking assembly to drain the transmission oil. This is due to the close proximity of the transmission mounting bracket making access to the cap nut awkward. This is of no great consequence, as it is not strictly necessary to drain the oil for transmission removal. Note however that a quantity of oil will be released when the driveshafts are removed, so have a container at the ready.
19   If working on the later type transmission with modified gearchange mechanism (see previous sub-Section) place the transmission in 2nd gear on four-speed models, or 4th gear for five-speed models, before disconnecting the gearchange linkage. Adjust after refitting, as previously described.
20   On cars equipped with the Anti-lock Braking System, remove the modulator drivebelts as described in Section 16, before releasing the driveshafts. Refit and adjust the drivebelts as described in Section 16 after installation.
21   On 1986 models onwards the engine/transmission mountings on the left-hand side have been modified, and the transmission is now supported on a longitudinal crossmember. When removing the transmission, unbolt the crossmember at the front and rear and remove the transmission with mountings and crossmember still attached.

Input shaft and 5th gear – renewal
22   As from March 1984, the input shaft and 5th gear are supplied in matched pairs. If either component must be renewed, always renew both.

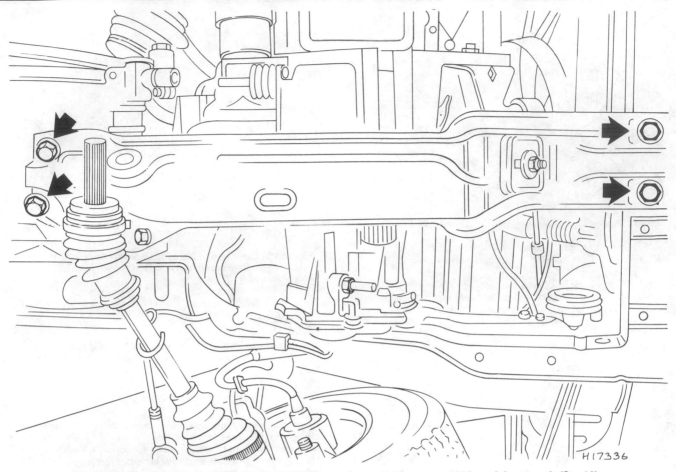

Fig. 13.158 Transmission support crossmember front and rear attachments – 1986 models onwards (Sec 13)

Gearchange stabiliser bar bush – renewal

23   If the stabiliser bush is in poor condition, it can cause engine and transmission noises to be transmitted to the vehicle interior. To renew the bush, raise and support the vehicle on safety stands.

24   Disconnect the stabiliser bar at the transmission end, then press out the bush using a suitable bolt, nut and two washers, used together with a pair of suitable diameter sockets as shown (Fig. 13.159). During bush removal and refitting do not pull down excessively on the stabiliser bar. Use sockets of different diameters so that one is the same as that of the bush housing, and one the same diameter as the fitted bush.

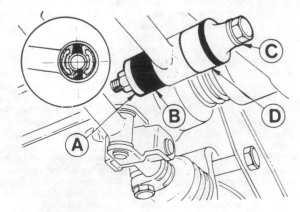

Fig. 13.159 Method of fitting gearchange stabiliser bar bush. Note location of bush channels (Sec 13)

A   Washer   C   Washer
B   Bush   D   Socket

25   Having withdrawn the old bush, insert the new one drawing it into position using the sockets, bolt, washers and nut. Position the channels in the bush as shown in the inset in Fig. 13.159 and take care during fitting not to damage or distort the bush.

26   Reconnect the stabiliser bar to the transmission, and tighten the retaining bolt to the specified torque wrench setting.

Input shaft and clutch release bearing guide sleeve – lubrication

27   Whenever the transmission unit is separated from the engine the splines on the input shaft, internal splines on the clutch disc and the clutch release bearing guide sleeve must be thoroughly cleaned to remove all traces of old grease. The splines must then be re-greased using only the special grease obtainable from Ford dealers.

28   The use of other greases may cause gearchange problems.

---

14   Automatic transmission

Automatic transmission fluid type – revisions

1   An improved type of transmission fluid is used in later models, and before topping-up or refilling it is necessary to identify the transmission being worked on, so that the correct fluid may be obtained.

2   Locate the transmission identification number, which is stamped on a metal tag attached to the top of the valve body cover. If, at the end of the second line on the metal tag, the prefix E3RP appears, then the transmission is of the early type. If the prefix is E6RP then the unit is of the later type. Later transmissions can also be identified by having a black dipstick stating the fluid specification and type. Having determined whether the transmission is of the early or later type, refer to the Specifications for the fluid requirement. Under no circumstances may

the later type fluid be used in the early type transmission, and *vice versa*.
3   The fluid level checking procedures are contained in Chapter 6, Section 19.

Automatic transmission starter inhibitor – renewal
4   All models with automatic transmission have a starter inhibitor relay mounted in the fuse/relay box.
5   When renewing the relay, only the correct relay obtainable from Ford dealers must be fitted.
6   An incorrect relay can allow the engine to be started in any gear selector position and also allow the starter motor to continue turning after the engine has started.

15   Driveshafts

Driveshaft inboard constant velocity joint – modifications
1   Since April 1986, Orion 1.4 and 1.6 litre models with manual transmission, but without the Anti-lock Braking system, have been fitted with a modified inboard constant velocity joint of the tripode type (Fig. 13.161).
2   The driveshaft repair and overhaul procedures described in Chapter 7 are still applicable, but bear in mind the following:

   (a)   When removing the driveshaft from the car, ensure that the joint member is released from the transmission before pulling outwards on the driveshaft. If this is not done the bellows may be strained, and the joint may come apart internally
   (b)   To dismantle the joint for bellows renewal, release the bellows retaining clips and slide back the bellows. With the suspension disconnected slide the driveshaft and spider out of the outer member, extract the circlip and remove the spider. Slide off the bellows. Refitting is a reversal of removal, but pack the joint with the specified Ford lubricant (see Chapter 7 Specifications)

Driveshaft joint bellows – setting dimension
3   The driveshaft joint bellows dimension (Chapter 7, Fig. 7.8) for both inboard and outboard joints on models from 1986 onwards is now 95 mm (3.74 in).

Driveshaft and driveshaft joint – removal (general)
4   When removing the driveshafts or driveshaft joints on 1986 models onwards from the transmission using the procedures described in Chapter 7, some difficulty may be experienced in removing the selector shaft cap nut and locking assembly to drain the transmission oil. This is due to the close proximity of the transmission mounting bracket, making access to the cap nut awkward. This is of no great consequence as it is not absolutely necessary to drain the oil for these operations. Note however that a quantity of oil will be released when the driveshaft or driveshaft joint is released, so have a container at the ready.

Driveshafts (anti-lock brakes) – removal and refitting
5   The procedure for removing and refitting the driveshafts on vehicles with anti-lock brakes is as described in Chapter 7, Section 5, but the modulator drivebelts must first be released as described in Section 16 of this Supplement.
6   When refitting a driveshaft, use a new locating circlip on the inner joint (item 'G' in Fig. 7.2 of Chapter 7), and ensure that the circlip engages correctly in the differential.
7   Failure to observe correct engagement of the circlip can lead to 'wandering' of the driveshaft in the differential with subsequent loss of fluid and/or drive.

16   Braking system

Handbrake adjuster – modification
1   As from September 1985, a lockpin is used to secure the handbrake cable adjuster nut in position (photo).
2   Before adjusting the handbrake cable, the pin must be withdrawn using a pair of pliers.
3   Tap the lockpin into position on completion of adjustment.

Brake pedal travel – general
4   Although the braking system may be in a satisfactory condition generally, it is possible that some drivers may feel that the brake pedal

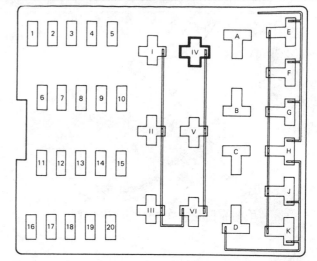

Fig. 13.160 Starter inhibitor relay location in fusebox (Sec 14)

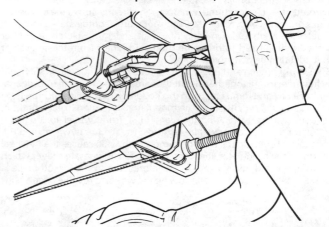

Fig. 13.161 Tripode type inboard constant velocity joint components (Sec 15)

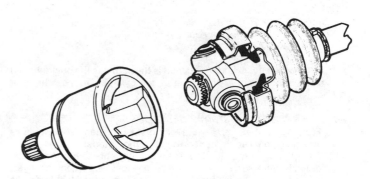

Fig. 13.162 Removing handbrake adjuster lockpin (Sec 16)

travel is excessive. The travel can be reduced in the following way if the upper surface of the pedal pad is less than 200.0 mm above the metal surface of the floor.
5   Remove the brake pedal as described in Chapter 8, Section 17.
6   Remove the white plastic bush (A) Fig. 13.164.
7   Fit a new bush which is red in colour and will increase the pedal height. Once this type of bush has been fitted it will not be possible to refit the anti-rattle retainer (B). This does not matter.
8   Adjust the stop-lamp switch as described in Chapter 8, Section 18.

Rear wheel cylinder – identification
9   Should it be necessary to renew a rear wheel cylinder, note that any

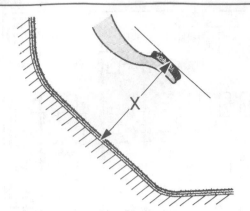

Fig. 13.163 Brake pedal height (Sec 16)

$X = 200.0\ mm\ (7.9\ in)$

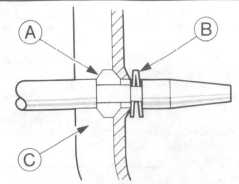

Fig. 13.164 Sectional view of brake pedal arm and pushrod (Sec 16)

A   Bush   C   Pedal arm
B   Retainer

of three different sizes may be fitted, according to model and year. The wheel cylinders are identified by a letter stamped on the rear face (Fig. 13.165) which corresponds to the following:

Letter 'T' = 22.20 mm diameter cylinder
Letter 'L' = 19.05 mm diameter cylinder
Letter 'H' = 17.78 mm diameter cylinder

Ensure that the new cylinder obtained is the same as the one removed and more importantly, is the same as the cylinder on the other rear brake.

Anti-lock braking system – description

10   From 1986 onwards, an anti-lock braking system is available as standard or optional equipment on certain Orion models.
11   The system comprises four main components: two modulators, one for each brake circuit, and two rear axle load apportioning valves, again, one for each brake circuit. Apart from the additional hydraulic piping the remainder of the braking system is the same as for conventional models.
12   The modulators are located in the engine compartment with one mounted on each side of the transmission, directly above the driveshaft inner constant velocity joints. Each modulator contains a shaft which actuates a flywheel by means of a ball and ramp clutch. A rubber toothed belt is used to drive the modulator shaft from the driveshaft inner constant velocity joint.
13   During driving and under normal braking the modulator shaft and the flywheel rotate together and at the same speed through the engagement of a ball and ramp clutch. In this condition hydraulic pressure from the master cylinder passes to the modulators and then to each brake in the conventional way. In the event of a front wheel locking, the modulator shaft rotation will be less than that of the flywheel, and the flywheel will overrun the ball and ramp clutch. This causes the flywheel to slide on the modulator shaft, move inward and operate a lever which in turn opens a dump valve. Hydraulic pressure to the locked brake is released via a de-boost piston allowing the wheel to revolve once again .

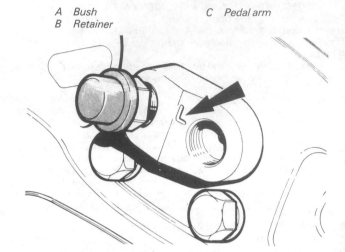

Fig. 13.165 Wheel cylinder identification letter location – arrowed (Sec 16)

Fluid passes through the dump valve is returned to the master cylinder reservoir via the modulator return pipes. At the same time hydraulic pressure from the master cylinder causes a pump piston to contact an eccentric cam on the modulator shaft. The flywheel is then decelerated at a controlled rate by the flywheel friction clutch. When the speed of the modulator shaft and flywheel are once again equal the dump valve closes and the cycle repeats. This complete operation takes place many time a second until the vehicle stops or the brakes are released.
14   The load apportioning valves are mounted on the rear crossmember and connected to each rear suspension arm via a linkage. The valves regulate hydraulic pressure to the rear brakes in accordance with vehicle load and attitude, in such a way that brake force at the front brakes will always be greater than that at the rear.
15   A belt break warning switch is fitted to the cover which surrounds each modulator drivebelt. The switch contains an arm which is in contact with the drivebelt at all times. If the belt should break, or if the

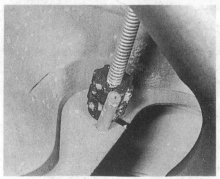

16.1 Handbrake cable adjuster lockpin

16.17 Removing the belt break switch from the modulator drivebelt cover

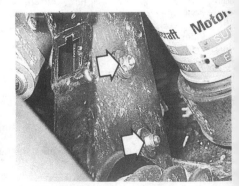

16.18 Drivebelt cover retaining nuts (arrowed)

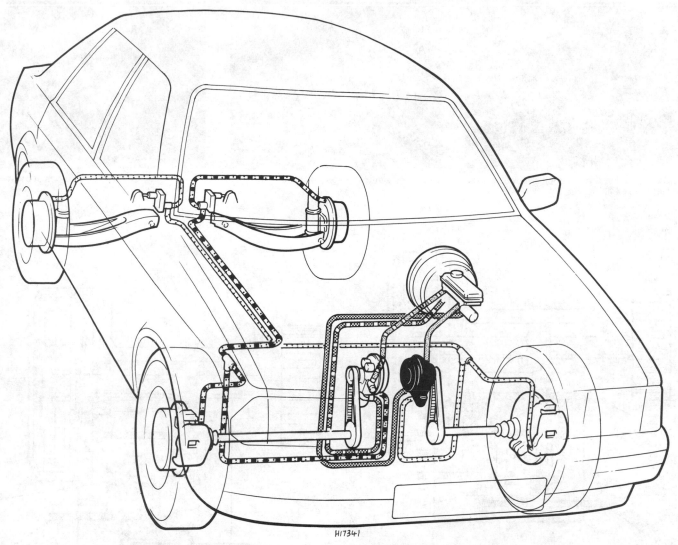

Fig. 13.166 Anti-lock braking system hydraulic pipe arrangement and component layout (Sec 16)

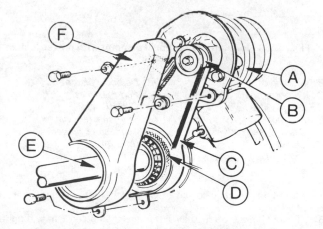

Fig. 13.167 Modulator and drivebelt details (Sec 16)

A Modulator
B Sprocket
C Drivebelt
D Constant velocity joint
E Driveshaft
F Drivebelt cover

adjustment of the belt is too slack, the arm will move out closing the switch contacts and informing the driver via an instrument panel warning light.

Modulator drivebelt (anti-lock braking system) – removal and refitting
Right-hand side
16   Jack up the front of the car, support it on stands and remove the roadwheel.
17   Remove the belt break switch from the drivebelt cover by pushing it in the direction of the arrow moulded on the switch body (Fig. 13.171). With the switch flexible leg compressed by approximately 1.5 mm (0.06 in), withdraw the switch from the drivebelt cover (photo).
18   Undo the two drivebelt cover retaining nuts and washers (photo), and on later models, the bolt from the additional support leg on the modified right-hand drivebelt cover.
19   Withdraw the cover from the studs and remove it by moving it upwards to clear the oil filter (photo).
20   Slacken the modulator adjuster bolt (photo), move the modulator to relieve the tension on the drivebelt then slip the belt off the modulator sprocket.
21   Extract the split pin, undo the retaining nut and separate the tie-rod balljoint from the steering arm using a suitable balljoint separator tool.
22   Disconnect the front suspension lower arm balljoint from the hub carrier by removing the nut and pinch-bolt. Note that the pinch-bolt is of the socket-headed (Torx) type and a special key or socket bit will be required for this purpose. These are readily available from most accessory shops.
23   Place a suitable container beneath the driveshaft inner constant velocity joint.
24   Insert a lever between the inner constant velocity joint and the

16.19 Removing the drivebelt cover upwards to clear the oil filter

16.20 Modulator adjuster bolt (arrowed)

16.45 Modulator fluid return pipes at master cylinder reservoir

A   To right-hand modulator
B   To left-hand modulator

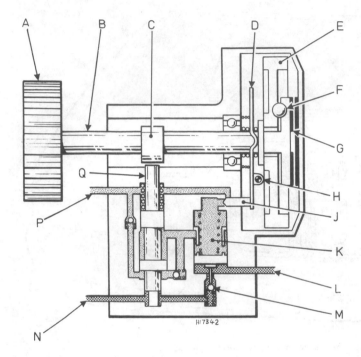

Fig. 13.168 Modulator operational diagram for normal braking (Sec 16)

A   Sprocket
B   Modulator shaft
C   Eccentric cam
D   Dump valve lever
E   Flywheel
F   Ball and ramp drive
G   Clutch
H   Pivot

J   Dump valve
K   De-boost piston
L   Port to brakes
M   Cut-off valve
N   From master cylinder
P   To master cylinder
     reservoir
Q   Pump piston

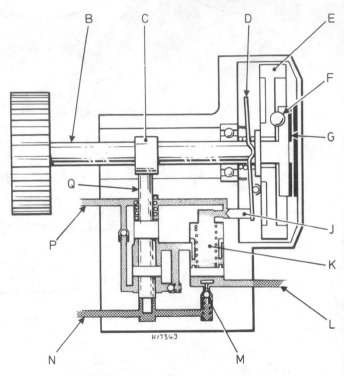

Fig. 13.169 Modulator operational diagram with brakes locked (Sec 16)

B   Modulator shaft
C   Eccentric cam
D   Dump valve lever
E   Flywheel
F   Ball and ramp drive
G   Clutch
J   Dump valve

K   De-boost piston
L   Port to brakes
M   Cut-off valve
N   From master cylinder
P   To master cylinder
     reservoir
Q   Pump piston

transmission housing. Firmly strike the lever to release the constant velocity joint from the differential.
25   Pull the driveshaft out of the transmission and slip the modulator drivebelt off the joint. Allow the transmission oil to drain into the container.
26   With the driveshaft disconnected, suspend it in such a way so as not to adopt an angle of more than 45° from the outer constant velocity joint.
27   Before refitting the drivebelt, renew the snap-ring fitted to the splines of the inner constant velocity joint.
28   Ensure that the modulator sprocket and constant velocity joint splines are clean and dry then slip the drivebelt over the joint.
29   Engage the joint splines with the differential and firmly push the hub carrier inwards to force the joint home.
30   Reconnect the lower arm balljoint to the hub carrier and insert the

Torx bolt with its head to the rear. Refit the nut and tighten to the specified torque.
31   Reconnect the tie-rod balljoint to the steering arm, fit and tighten the nut to the specified torque and secure with a new split pin.
32   Slip the drivebelt over the modulator sprocket ensuring that it sits squarely in the sprocket teeth.
33   Move the modulator as necessary to tension the belt so that the belts deflection, under light finger pressure, is 5.0 mm (0.2 in). Check this using a ruler at a point midway between the two sprockets.
34   With the belt tensioned correctly, tighten the modulator adjuster bolt.
35   Refit the drivebelt cover and secure with the two nuts and washers.

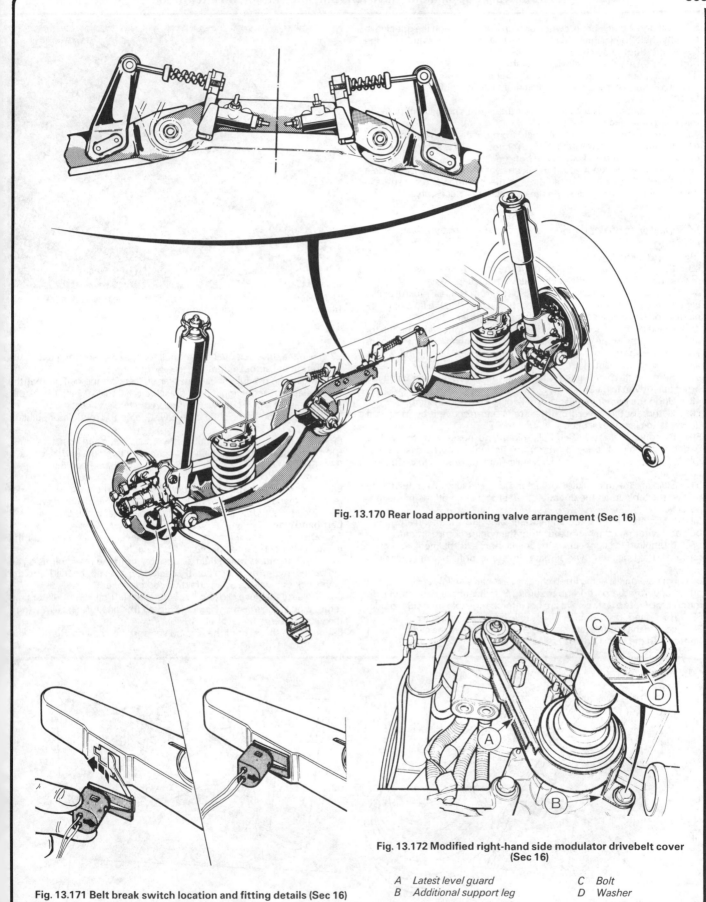

Fig. 13.170 Rear load apportioning valve arrangement (Sec 16)

Fig. 13.172 Modified right-hand side modulator drivebelt cover
(Sec 16)

Fig. 13.171 Belt break switch location and fitting details (Sec 16)

A   Latest level guard   C   Bolt
B   Additional support leg   D   Washer

36   Engage the belt break switch arm upwards through the opening in the drivebelt cover, then locate the flexible leg of the switch into the cover aperture. Push the switch in the direction of the arrow on the body, and locate the non-flexible leg into position.
37   Refit the roadwheel and lower the car to the ground.
38   Top the transmission oil as described in Chapter 6.
Left-hand side
39   The procedure is the same as for the right-hand side but note the following differences.
40   Remove the engine splash shield from the inner wheel arch.
41   When removing the drivebelt cover note that it is secured by three bolts, two at the top and one at the bottom.
42   To move the modulator for adjustment of the belt tension, use a suitable length of wood inserted through the steering tie-rod aperture in the inner wheel arch, to push on the modulator as necessary.

Modulator (anti-lock braking system) – removal and refitting

Right-hand side
43   Disconnect the wiring plug from the level warning switch in the master cylinder reservoir filler cap. Remove the cap.
44   Syphon out as much fluid as possible from the reservoir using an old battery hydrometer or a poultry baster. Do not drip the fluid onto the paintwork as it will act as an effective paint stripper.
45   Release the hose clip and disconnect the right-hand modulator fluid return pipe at the master cylinder reservoir (nearest to the vacuum servo unit – photo).
46   Jack up the front of the car and support it on stands.
47   Remove the belt break switch from the drivebelt cover using the procedure given in paragraph 17.
48   Undo the two drivebelt cover retaining nuts and washers.
49   Withdraw the cover from the studs and remove it by moving it upwards to clear the oil filter.
50   Disconnect the two hydraulic pipes and hoses with the yellow bands at the pipe bracket on the transmission support crossmember (photo). Allow the remaining hydraulic fluid to drain into a suitable container.
51   Slacken the modulator adjuster bolt, move the modulator to relieve the tension on the drivebelt then slip the belt off the modulator sprocket.
52   Undo and remove the adjustment bolt and the modulator pivot bolt and withdraw the modulator from the engine compartment.
53   If required, disconnect the hydraulic hoses at the modulator after removal. Plug or tape over all pipe ends and orifices to prevent dirt ingress.
54   If a new unit is being fitted check that it has a yellow arrow marked on its cover and a part number suffix 'A' indicating a right-hand side modulator. Note that the units are not interchangeable from side to side.
55   Reconnect the modulator hydraulic hoses if applicable.
56   Locate the modulator on its mounting bracket, fit the pivot bolt and tighten it to the specified torque.

16.50 Hydraulic pipe and hose unions at the pipe bracket on the transmission support crossmember.

57   Slip the drivebelt over the modulator sprocket ensuring that it sits squarely in the sprocket teeth.
58   Move the modulator as necessary to tension the belt so that the belt deflection, under light finger pressure is 5.0 mm (0.2 in). Check this using a ruler at a point midway between the two sprockets.
59   With the belt tensioned correctly, tighten the modulator adjuster bolt.
60   Reconnect the two modulator hydraulic pipes and hoses.
61   Refit the drivebelt cover and secure with two nuts and washers.
62   Refit the belt break switch, as described in paragraph 36.
63   Lower the car to the ground.
64   Reconnect the modulator fluid return pipe to the master cylinder reservoir then fill the reservoir with fresh fluid of the specified type.
65   Bleed the hydraulic system as described later in this Section.
Left-hand side
66   Disconnect the wiring plug from the level warning switch in the master cylinder reservoir filler cap. Remove the cap.
67   Syphon out as much fluid as possible from the reservoir using an old battery hydrometer or a poultry baster. Do not drip the fluid onto the paintwork as it will act as an effective paint stripper.
68   Release the hose clip and disconnect the left-hand modulator fluid return pipe at the master cylinder reservoir (the one furthest away from the vacuum servo unit – photo 16.45).
69   Jack up the front of the car and support it on stands. Remove the left-hand roadwheel.

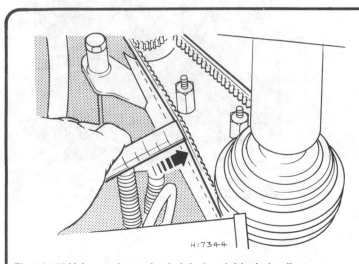

Fig. 13.173 Using a ruler to check right-hand drivebelt adjustment (Sec 16)

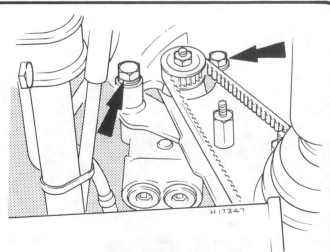

Fig. 13.174 Right-hand modulator adjuster and pivot bolts – arrowed (Sec 16)

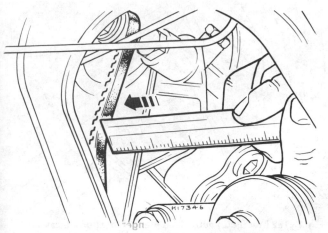

Fig. 13.175 Using a ruler to check left-hand drivebelt adjustment (Sec 16)

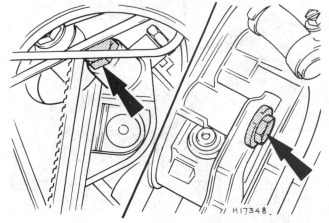

Fig. 13.176 Left-hand modulator adjusted and pivot bolts – arrowed (Sec 16)

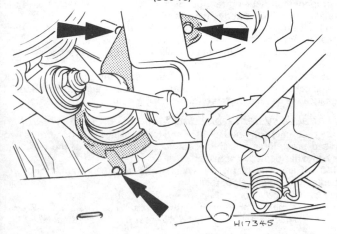

Fig. 13.177 Left-hand drivebelt cover retaining bolt locations (Sec 16)

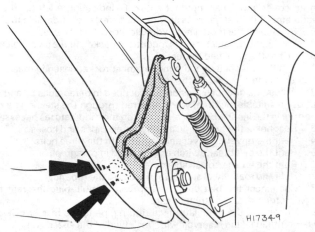

Fig. 13.178 Load apportioning valve adjusting bracket retaining bolt locations – arrowed (Sec 16)

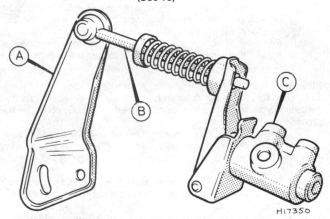

Fig. 13.179 Load apportioning valve assembly (Sec 16)

A Adjusting bracket   C   Apportioning valve
B Valve pushrod

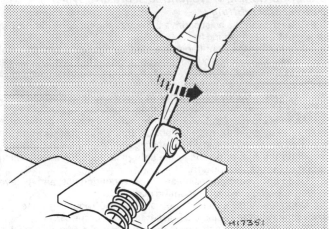

Fig. 13.180 Separating apportioning valve pushrod from adjusting bracket (Sec 16)

70   Remove the engine splash shield from the inner wheel arch.
71   Remove the belt break switch from the drivebelt cover using the procedure given in paragraph 17.
72   Undo the three bolts, two at the top and one at the bottom, securing the drivebelt cover to the modulator bracket. Remove the cover.
73   Disconnect the two hydraulic pipes and hoses with the white bands at the pipe bracket on the transmission support crossmember (photo 16.45). Allow the remaining hydraulic fluid to drain into a suitable container.

74   Slacken the modulator adjuster bolt, move the modulator to relieve the tension on the drivebelt then slip the belt off the modulator sprocket.
75   Remove the distributor cap, rotor arm and shield. Disconnect the left-hand belt break switch wiring at the multi-plug.
76   Undo and remove the adjuster bolt and the modulator pivot bolt and withdraw the modulator upwards out of the engine compartment.
77   If required, disconnect the hydraulic hoses at the modulator after removal. Plug or tape over all pipe ends and orifices to prevent dirt ingress.
78   If a new unit is being fitted, check that it has a white arrow marked

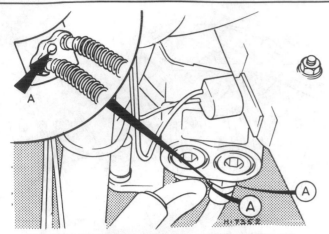

Fig. 13.181 Modulator bypass valve location (A) (Sec 16)

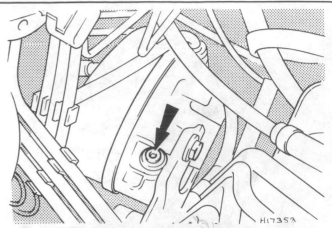

Fig. 13.182 Modulator auto bleed plunger location – arrowed (Sec 16)

on its cover and a part number suffix 'C' indicating a left-hand side modulator. Note that the units are not interchangeable from side to side.
79   Reconnect the modulator hydraulic pipes if applicable.
80   Locate the modulator on its mounting bracket, fit the pivot bolt and tighten it to the specified torque.
81   Slip the drivebelt over the modulator sprocket ensuring that it sits squarely in the sprocket teeth.
82   Adjust the drivebelt tension as described in paragraphs 58 and 59, but use a suitable length of wood inserted through the steering tie-rod aperture in the inner wheel arch, to push on the modulator as necessary.
83   Reconnect the two modulator hydraulic pipes and hoses.
84   Refit the drivebelt cover and secure with the three bolts.
85   Refit the belt break switch as described in paragraph 36.
86   Refit the engine splash shield.
87   Refit the roadwheel and lower the car to the ground.
88   Reconnect the belt break switch wiring multi-plug the refit the shield, rotor arm and distributor cap.
89   Reconnect the modulator fluid return pipe to the master cylinder reservoir then fill the reservoir with fresh fluid of the specified type.
90   Bleed the hydraulic system as described later in this Section.

Load apportioning valve (anti-lock braking system) – removal and refitting

91   Raise the car on a hoist or drive the rear of the car up on ramps. The rear wheels must not hang free.
92   If removing the right-hand side load apportioning valve on fuel injected models, undo the nut and bolt securing the fuel pump mounting bracket to the underbody. Move the fuel pump aside to gain access to the valve.
93   Disconnect the hydraulic pipes at the valve, then plug the pipes and orifices to prevent loss of fluid and dirt ingress.
94   As an aid to reassembly accurately mark the position of the valve adjusting bracket on the rear suspension arm. This will ensure that the valve adjustment is not lost when refitting.
95   Undo the nuts and remove the stud plate securing the adjusting bracket to the suspension arm.
96   Undo both rear suspension arm inner mounting nuts and remove the load apportioning valve mounting plate.
97   Undo the bolts securing the valve to the mounting plate and remove the valve and adjusting bracket from under the car.
98   If required separate the valve pushrod from the adjusting bracket by levering off the pushrod trunnion with a screwdriver. Lubricate the trunnion rubber bush to aid removal.
99   If a new valve is being fitted it will be supplied with nylon setting spacers and ties attached, to ensure correct adjustment of the valve. Leave these in position until the valve is installed.
100   Refit the pushrod trunnion to the adjusting bracket using a suitable socket and a vice.
101   Locate the valve on its mounting plate and secure with the retaining bolts.
102   Position the mounting plate over the suspension arm mounting bolts and secure with the nuts tightened to the specified torque.
103   Reconnect the hydraulic pipes to the valve.
104   Refit the stud plate and adjusting bracket to the suspension arm ensuring that the previously made marks are aligned if the original

components are being refitted. Secure the adjusting bracket with the retaining nuts tightened to the specified torque.
105   If a new valve assembly is being fitted, remove the nylon setting spacers and ties.
106   Where applicable refit the fuel pump mounting bracket.
107   Lower the car to the ground.
108   It is recommended that the load apportioning valve adjustment be checked by a dealer if the original unit has been refitted. Special gauges are needed for this operation and it is not a DIY proposition.

Hydraulic system – bleeding (anti-lock braking system)

109   On cars equipped with the anti-lock braking system there are two bleed procedures possible according to which part of the hydraulic system has been disconnected.
110   If any one of the following conditions are present, bleed procedure A should be adopted:

    (a)   A modulator has been removed
    (b)   A modulator-to-master cylinder return hose has been drained
    (c)   The two modulator hydraulic hoses have been removed

111   If any one of the following conditions are present, bleed procedure B should be adopted:

    (a)   Any condition where the master cylinder has been drained providing that the modulator fluid return pipe has not lost its head of fluid
    (b)   Removal of any of the basic braking system components ie brake caliper, flexible hose or pipe, wheel cylinder, load apportioning valve

Bleed procedure A
112   Top up the master cylinder reservoir to the MAX mark using the specified type of fluid and keep it topped up throughout the bleed procedure.
113   Using a Torx type key or socket bit, slacken the bypass valve on the relevant modulator by one to one and a half turns. The bypass valve is located between the two flexible hoses on the side of the modulator (Fig. 13.181).
114   Fully depress and hold depressed the auto bleed plunger on the modulator so that the plunger circlip contacts the modulator body (Fig. 13.182).
115   Have an assistant speedily pump the brake pedal at least twenty times while you observe the fluid returning to the master cylinder reservoir. Continue this operation until the returning fluid is free from air bubbles.
116   Release the auto bleed plunger ensuring that it has fully returned. Pull it out by hand if necessary.
117   Tighten the bypass valve on the modulator.
118   Now carry out bleed procedure B.
Bleed procedure B
119   This procedure is the same as for conventional braking systems and reference should be made to Chapter 8. Note, however, that all the weight of the car must be on the roadwheels, not suspended wheel free, otherwise the load apportioning valves will not bleed.
120   The bleeding sequence is slightly different for the anti-lock braking system – start with right-hand front, then left-hand front, right-hand rear and left-hand rear, in that order.

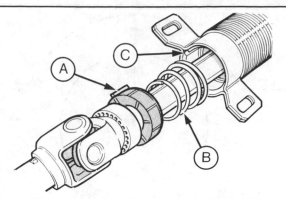

Fig. 13.183 Steering column later type cover bearing (Sec 17)

A Locating key   C Slot
B Spring

121   As with conventional systems, the master cylinder should never be allowed to run dry during bleeding. Top up to the 'MAX' mark on completion.

17 Steering

Steering wheel alignment – general

1   Owing to the fact that the steering wheel is located on a hexagon shaped steering shaft, it may be difficult to obtain perfect steering wheel alignment due to lack of fine adjustment.
2   It is therefore acceptable to adjust the tie-rods to give unequal lengths.
3   Check that the front roadwheels are in the straight-ahead position and that the toe setting is as specified.
4   If the steering wheel is more than 30° out of alignment, remove it and centralise it as much as possible on its shaft.
5   To adjust the steering wheel through a small angle, carry out the following operations.
6   Release the tie-rod and locknuts.
7   Turn one tie-one clockwise and the opposite one anti-clockwise by the identical amount. For every 1° of steering wheel angular error, turn each tie-rod through 30°.
8   Once the steering wheel has been centralised (front wheels in straight-ahead position), retighten the tie-rod end locknuts.
9   Although the toe setting should not have altered, check the front wheel alignment as described in Chapter 9.

Steering gear – overhaul (general)

10   The method of securing the steering gear tie-rods to the rack has been revised on all models, eliminating the need to stake the tie-rod balljoints to the rack.
11   Whenever a tie-rod is removed or renewed using the procedures described in Chapter 9, Section 9, the threads of the tie-rod balljoint should be coated with Loctite 270 prior to refitting. The balljoint should then be tightened to the revised torque setting given in the Specifications, using an open-ended torque wrench adaptor.
12   Follow the manufacturer's instructions when using Loctite 270, which can be obtained from Ford parts suppliers.

Steering rack (1988-on) – description

13   From September 1988 all Orion models are fitted with a new 'variable-ratio' steering rack.
14   The system gives greater response at high speeds and makes for easier parking.
15   The procedures covering the steering rack given in Chapter 9 remain unchanged.

Steering column lower bearing – later models

16   When renewing the steering column lower bearing as described in Chapter 9, Section 7, note that on later models the lower bearing has a locating key which fits into the keyway on the column tube. This prevents the bearing from rotating in the tube, causing a squealing noise.
17   The spring is fitted with its larger diameter end in the column tube and smaller diameter end located in the bearing. This is the opposite of the spring fitting direction in Chapter 9, Section 7.

18 Suspension

Rear wheel alignment – checking and adjustment

1   Should the rear tyres show evidence of excessive wear, or the car

Ride height measured	Toe-in measured												
	0 to 2.5	2.6 to 3.5	3.6 to 4.5	4.6 to 5.5	5.6 to 6.5	6.6 to 7.5	7.6 to 8.5	8.6 to 9.5	9.6 to 10.5	10.6 to 11.5	11.6 to 12.5	12.6 to 13.5	13.6 to 14.5
	Number of washers to be added to/or deleted from each tie bar												
290 – 299	−1	−1	−1	0	0	0	0	+1	+1	+1	+1	+2	+2
300 – 309	−1	−1	0	0	0	0	+1	+1	+1	+1	+2	+2	+2
310 – 319	−1	0	0	0	0	+1	+1	+1	+1	+2	+2	+2	+2
320 – 329	0	0	0	0	+1	+1	+1	+1	+2	+2	+2	+2	+3
330 – 394	0	0	0	+1	+1	+1	+1	+2	+2	+2	+2	+3	+3
395 – 407	0	0	0	0	+1	+1	+1	+1	+2	+2	+2	+2	+3
408 – 417	−1	0	0	0	0	+1	+1	+1	+1	+2	+2	+2	+2
418 – 427	−1	−1	0	0	0	0	+1	+1	+1	+1	+2	+2	+2
428 – 440	−1	−1	−1	0	0	0	0	+1	+1	+1	+1	+2	+2

All dimensions in mm

− = delete
+ = add

Fig. 13.184 Ride height/toe-in data (Sec 18)

become partially unstable on icy or snowy surfaces, check the rear wheel toe setting in a similar way to that described for the front wheels in Chapter 9, Section 10. Record the toe setting.

2   Now measure and record the ride heights at the rear left and right-hand sides. The measurements should be taken between the centre of each roadwheel and the highest point of the wheel arch rim.

3   Take the average of the two measurements, and then compare the toe and ride height dimensions with the following chart to determine the washer variation required to alter the rear wheel alignment.

4   The number of washers to be removed or added just forward of the tie-bar compliance bush is indicated in the chart.

5   The same number of washers must always be fitted to each side of the car, and always have at least one washer remaining at each side.

6   Failure to bring rear wheel alignment within specified tolerance will be due to worn suspension components or accident damage.

Wheels and tyres – general care and maintenance

7   Wheels and tyres should give no real problems in use provided that a close eye is kept on them with regard to excessive wear or damage. To this end, the following points should be noted.

8   Ensure that tyre pressures are checked regularly and maintained correctly. Checking should be carried out with the tyres cold and not immediately after the vehicle has been in use. If the pressures are checked with the tyres hot, an apparently high reading will be obtained owing to heat expansion. Under no circumstances should an attempt be made to reduce the pressures to the quoted cold reading in this instance, or effective underinflation will result.

9   Underinflation will cause overheating of the tyre owing to excessive flexing of the casing, and the tread will not sit correctly on the road surface. This will cause a consequent loss of adhesion and excessive wear, not to mention the danger of sudden tyre failure due to heat built-up.

10   Overinflation will cause rapid wear of the centre part of the tyre tread coupled with reduced adhesion, harsher ride, and the danger of shock damage occurring in the tyre casing.

11   Regularly check the tyres for damage in the form of cuts or bulges, especially in the sidewalls. Remove any nails or stones embedded in the tread before they penetrate the tyre to cause deflation. If removal of a nail *does* reveal that the tyre has been punctured, refit the nail so that its point of penetration is marked. Then immediately change the wheel and have the tyre repaired by a tyre dealer. Do *not* drive on a tyre in such a condition. In many cases a puncture can be simply repaired by the use of an inner tube of the correct size and type. If in any doubt as to the possible consequences of any damage found, consult your local tyre dealer for advice.

12   Periodically remove the wheels and clean any dirt or mud from the inside and outside surfaces. Examine the wheel rims for signs of rusting, corrosion or other damage. Light alloy wheels are easily damaged by 'kerbing' whilst parking, and similarly steel wheels may become dented or buckled. Renew of the wheel is very often the only course of remedial action possible.

13   The balance of each wheel and tyre assembly should be maintained to avoid excessive wear, not only to the tyres but also to the steering and suspension components. Wheel imbalance is normally signified by vibration through the vehicle's bodyshell, although in many cases it is particularly noticeable through the steering wheel. Conversely, it should be noted that wear or damage in suspension or steering components may cause excessive tyre wear. Out-of-round or out-of-true tyres, damaged wheels and wheel bearing wear/maladjustment also fall into this category. Balancing will not usually cure vibration caused by such wear.

14   Wheel balancing may be carried out with the wheel either on or off the vehicle. If balanced on the vehicle, ensure that the wheel-to-hub relationship is marked in some way prior to subsequent wheel removal so that it may be refitted in its original position.

15   General tyre wear is influenced to a large degree by driving style – harsh braking and acceleration or fast cornering will all produce more rapid tyre wear. Interchanging of tyres may result in more even wear, but this should only be carried out where there is no mix of tyre types on the vehicle. However, it is worth bearing in mind that if this is completely effective, the added expense of replacing a complete set of tyres simultaneously is incurred, which may prove financially restrictive for many owners.

16   Front tyres may wear unevenly as a result of wheel misalignment. The front wheels should always be correctly aligned according to the settings specified by the vehicle manufacturer.

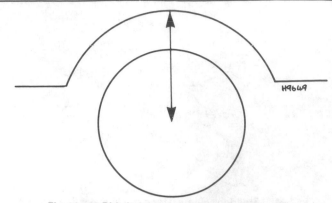

Fig. 13.185 Ride height measuring points (Sec 18)

17   Legal restrictions apply to the mixing of tyre types on a vehicle. Basically this means that a vehicle must not have tyres of differing construction on the same axle. Although it is not recommended to mix tyre types between front axle and rear axle, the only legally permissible combination is crossply at the front and radial at the rear. When mixing radial ply tyres, textile braced radials must always go on the front axle, with steel braced radials at the rear. An obvious disadvantage of such mixing is the necessity to carry two spare tyres to avoid contravening the law in the event of a puncture.

18   In the UK, the Motor Vehicles Construction and Use Regulations apply to many aspects of tyre fitting and usage. It is suggested that a copy of these regulations is obtained from your local police if in doubt as to the current legal requirements with regard to tyre condition, minimum tread depth, etc.

---

19   Electrical system

Alternator – removal and refitting

1   In order to prevent strain on the alternator mounting lugs, it is important to make sure that the mounting washers are located exactly as shown in Fig. 13.186.

2   Tighten the mounting bolts to the specified torque as shown in the Specifications Section of this Supplement.

Alternator brushes and regulator – renewal
Lucas A127/55 and A127/70

3   Remove the alternator from the engine as described in Chapter 11.

4   Remove the alternator rear cover.

5   Extract the brush box retaining screws and withdraw the regulator and brush box assembly from the alternator.

6   If the brushes are worn beyond the minimum length specified, disconnect the field connector and renew the regulator/brush box complete. The brushes are not supplied separately.

7   Refitting is a reversal of removal.

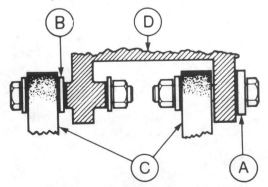

Fig. 13.186 Alternator mounting (Sec 19)

A   Large washer
B   Small washer (pre-1985 only)
C   Mounting bracket
D   Mounting lugs

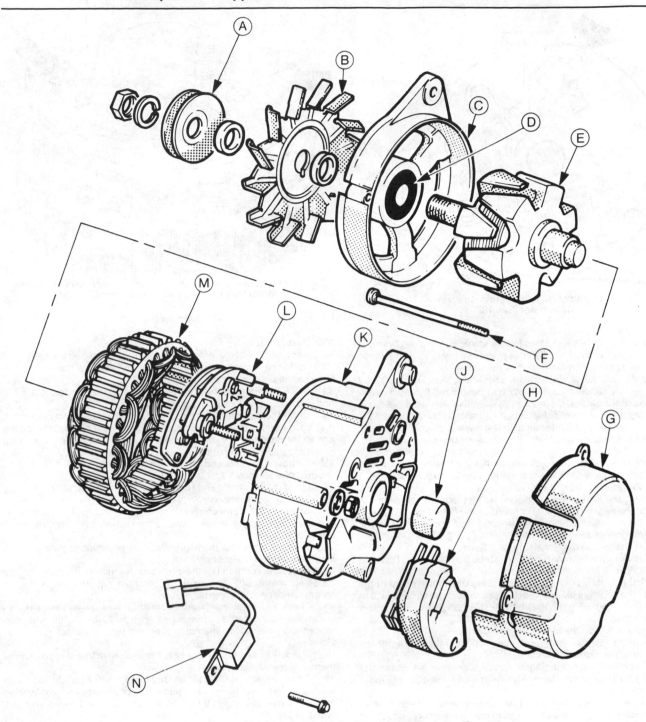

Fig. 13.187 Exploded view of the Lucas A127 alternator (Sec 19)

A Pulley
B Fan
C Drive end housing
D Drive end bearing

E Rotor
F Through-bolt
G End cover

H Brush box and regulator
J Slip ring end bearing
K Slip ring end housing

L Rectifier pack
M Stator
N Suppressor

Mitsubishi A500T

8   Renewal of the brushes on these alternators entails considerable dismantling, and reference should be made to the next sub-Section.

Alternator – overhaul
Lucas A127/55 and A127/70

9   Remove the alternator from the engine as described in Chapter 11.
10   Remove the alternator rear cover.

11   Undo the retaining nut and washer and remove the pulley, fan and spacers.
12   Extract the brush box retaining screws, remove the field connector and withdraw the brush box and regulator assembly.
13   Unscrew the terminal nuts and, remove the washers and insulators, then unscrew the rectified retaining screws and through-bolts.
14   Separate the drive end housing and rotor from the stator, rectifier pack and slip ring end housing.

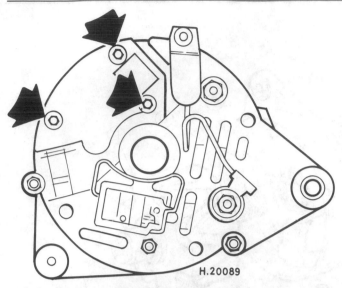

Fig. 13.188 Regulator and brush box retaining screws – Lucas A127 alternator (Sec 19)

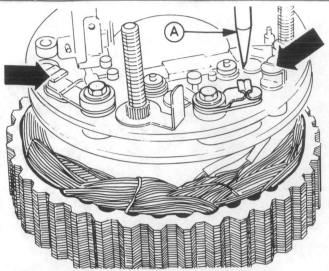

Fig. 13.189 Unsoldering the stator connections from the rectifier (diode) pack – Lucas A127 alternator (Sec 19)

A   Soldering iron

15   Refer to Fig. 13.189 and unsolder the stator connections from the rectifier pack. Use a pair of needle-nose pliers as a heat sink on the diode terminal pins, to prevent overheating of the diodes.
16   With the alternator dismantled, check the positive diodes by connecting a 12V supply through a 5W test bulb wired to form a circuit through one of the diodes. Connect to the positive section of the diode pack with the negative terminal attached to the upper side of one of the diodes. Connect the positive terminal to the lower surface of the diode. The test lamp should illuminate if the diode is in good condition.
17   Repeat the operations on the remaining two positive diodes.
18   Reverse the test circuit terminals so that the positive one goes to the upper side of the diode and the negative one to the lower surface. If the test bulb lights up, the diode is defective.
19   To check the field diodes, connect the test lamp as shown in Fig. 13.191 with the negative terminal coupled to the field diode module or single small terminal, and the positive one to a diode stem. The bulb will light if the diode is in good condition.
20   Repeat the test on the remaining two diodes.
21   Now reverse the terminals and repeat the test. If the bulb lights up then the diode is defective.
22   Check the negative diodes by connecting the negative lead of the test lamp to the negative plate of the diode pack, and the positive lead to one of the diode stems (Fig. 13.192). If the test lamp lights up the diode is in good condition.
23   Repeat the test on the remaining two diodes.
24   Reverse the test circuit terminals and repeat. If the bulb lights up, then that particular diode is defective.
25   To check the rotor winding continuity, connect an ohmmeter between the two slip ring contacts. The resistance should be as given in the Specifications.
26   Check the rotor insulation by connecting one lead of the ohmmeter to one of the slip rings, and the other lead to one of the rotor poles. There should be no reading on the ohmmeter.
27   Check the stator winding insulation by connecting the ohmmeter between one of the stator wires and the lamination pack. Again there should be no reading.
28   Examine the bearings in the drive end and slip ring end housings, and check for roughness or excessive free play. If the bearing in the drive end housing is worn, a new housing complete with bearing must be obtained. If the bearing in the slip ring end housing is worn it can be renewed separately. Drive the old bearing out and the new bearing in using suitable mandrels.
29   Finally inspect the brushes for length, and renew the regulator/brush box assembly if the brushes are below the minimum specified length.
30   Reassembly is a reversal of the dismantling procedure. If the slip ring end bearing has not been renewed, pack it with a high melting-point grease prior to reassembly. Use the needle nose pliers to insulate the diodes when resoldering, as was done during dismantling.

Mitsubishi A500T
31   Remove the alternator from the engine as described in Chapter 11.
32   Undo the retaining nut and washer, and remove the pulley, fan, large spacer and dust seal.
33   Make an alignment mark on the drive end housing, stator and slip ring end housing to facilitate reassembly.
34   Undo the through-bolts and remove the slip ring end housing. It may be necessary to apply heat from a high power (200 watt) soldering iron to the centre of the end housing for a few minutes if the housing refuses to free from the rotor.
35   Remove the drive end housing from the rotor shaft, followed by the dust seal and small spacer.
36   Undo the four bolts and remove the stator and rectifier assembly from the slip ring end housing.
37   Unsolder the stator connections from the rectifier pack terminals, and the connecting terminal between the rectifier pack and the brush box assembly.
38   With the alternator dismantled, clean the components and check for visible signs of wear or damage.
39   Check the condition of the diodes as described previously for the Lucas alternator, but refer to the accompanying illustrations for the ohmmeter connection points.
40   Check the rotor and stator continuity and insulation using an ohmmeter connected as shown in Figs. 13.197 to 13.199 and with reference to the Lucas alternator checking procedure described previously.
41   Check the bearings for roughness or excessive free play and renew them if necessary as follows.
42   To renew the bearing in the drive end housing, undo the three screws and remove the retaining plate. Drift or press out the old bearing and fit the new bearing in the same way. Secure the bearing with the retaining plate.
43   To renew the slip ring end bearing, remove the clip and pull off the bearing using a suitable puller. Press on the new bearing, ensuring that the groove is towards the slip rings. Fit the clip into the bearing eccentric groove, ensuring that the thickest part of the clip fits into the deepest part of the groove, marked by a chamfered edge.
44   Renew the brush box and brushes if they are worn down to the specified minimum.
45   Reassembly is a reversal of the dismantling procedure. Insert a suitable piece of wire through the housing access hole to keep the brushes retracted as the housing is fitted. Release the brushes by withdrawing the wire after reassembly.

Starter motor (Lucas M78) – overhaul
46   With the starter motor removed from the car and cleaned, grip it in a vice fitted with soft jaw protectors.
47   Disconnect the connecting link from the solenoid terminal.
48   Undo the two endplate cap screws and remove the cap.

Fig. 13.190 Diode pack arrangement – Lucas A127 alternator (Sec 19)

A   *Field diodes*   C   *Negative diodes*   D   *Field terminal*   E   *Positive terminal*
B   *Positive diodes*

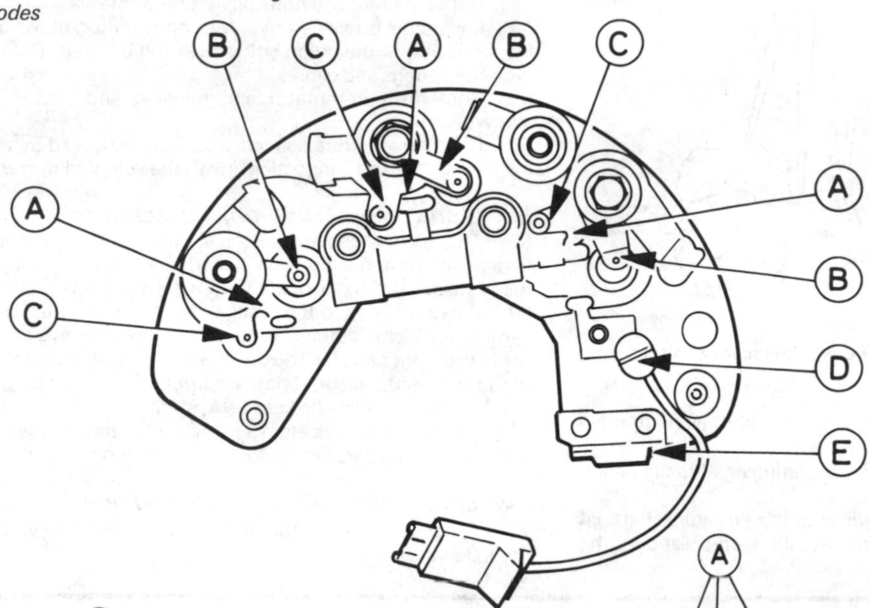

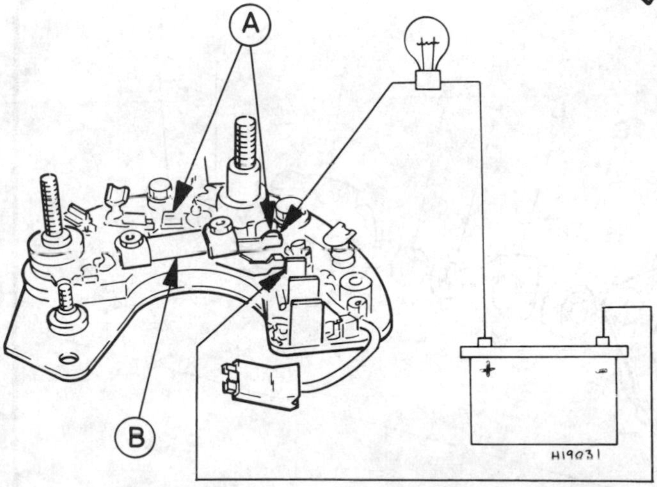

**Fig. 13.191 Test circuit for checking field diodes – Lucas A127
alternator (Sec 19)**

A   *Field diodes*   B   *Field diode module*

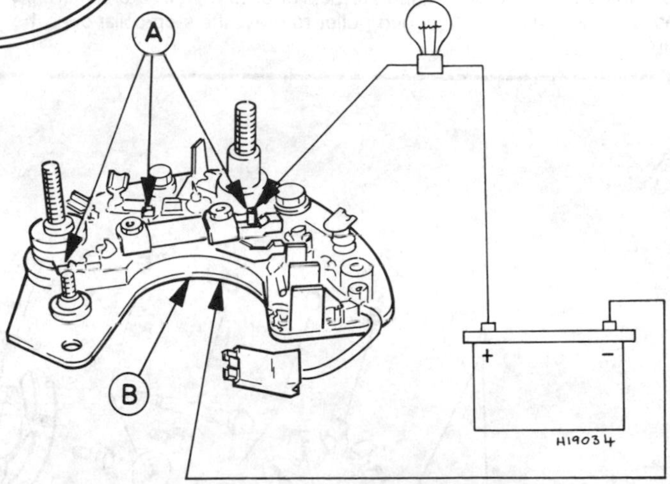

**Fig. 13.192 Test circuit for checking negative diodes – Lucas A127
alternator (Sec 19)**

A   *Negative diodes*   B   *Negative plate*

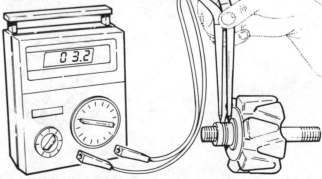

**Fig. 13.193 Rotor winding continuity check – Lucas A127 alternator
(Sec 19)**

49   Extract the C-clip and remove the spacers from end of the armature shaft.
50   Undo the two commutator end housing screws and withdraw the end housing.
51   Undo the solenoid yoke screws and slide the yoke off the drive and housing armature.
52   Disconnect the solenoid armature from the actuating lever and remove the armature.
53   Undo the two drive end housing screws and withdraw the housing from the yoke and armature.
54   Slide the armature out of the yoke, taking care not to damage the brushes. The actuating lever, plastic support block and rubber pad will be removed with the armature.
55   Use a piece of tubing to drive the stop collar down the armature shaft to expose the C-clip. Remove the C-clip and take off the stop collar and drive pinion.
56   To remove the actuating lever, remove the circlip and slide the lever and pivot assembly off the pinion.
57   Remove the retaining springs and remove the brushes from the

brush box. Examine all the components for wear and renew as necessary.
58   Two of the brushes come complete with the brush link wire, but

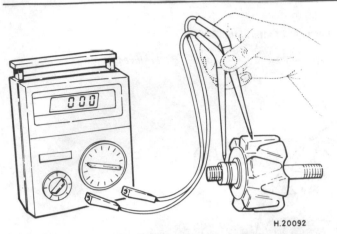

Fig. 13.194 Rotor winding insulation check – Lucas A127 alternator (Sec 19)

the field winding brushes will have to be cut and new ones soldered in place.

59   Commence reassembly by fitting the actuating lever to the pinion and securing with the circlip.

60   Slide the drive pinion and stop collar onto the armature shaft. Fit the C-clip and use a two-legged puller to draw the stop collar over the clip.

61   Fit the armature to the yoke and locate the actuating lever plastic support and rubber block in the drive end housing.

62   Engage the solenoid armature with the actuating lever, then refit and secure the solenoid yoke.

63   Refit the drive end housing retaining screws.

64   Locate the brush box over the commutator, fit the brushes in their locations and fit the nylon cover over the brushes. Retain the brushes with the springs and clips.

65   Refit the commutator end housing and secure with the two screws.

66   Refit the armature spacers and C-clip followed by the end cap.

67   Re-attach the connecting link to the solenoid terminal.

Fuses and relays (1986-on) – description

68   The fusebox and its location are the same on later models, but the fuse positions and circuits protected have been rearranged. Additional fuses are still used and located as for early models.

69   Relays located in the fusebox have their circuits designated by a symbol for identification. Up to six additional relays are located under the instrument panel on the driver's side. These are used in conjunction with the speed sensor, diode assembly, fuel injection system, heated windscreen, and dim-dip lighting system.

70   The direction indicator/hazard flasher relay is located at the rear of the direction indicator multi-function switch on the steering column.

Switches (1986-on) – removal and refitting

71   The procedures are the same as described in Chapter 11 except for the following.

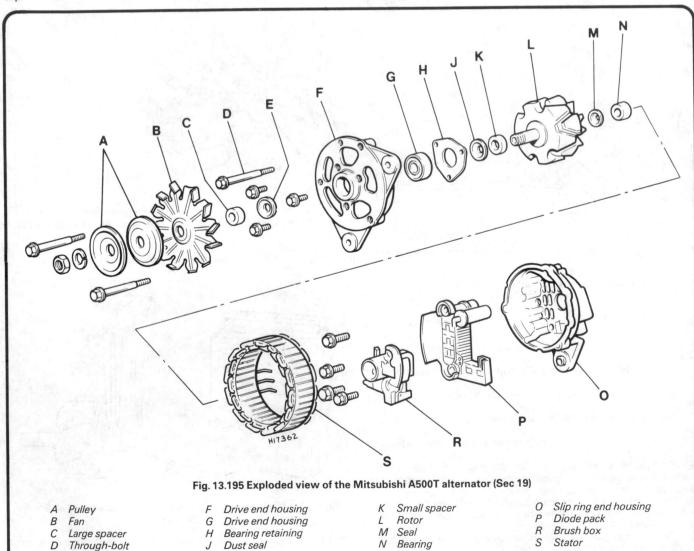

Fig. 13.195 Exploded view of the Mitsubishi A500T alternator (Sec 19)

A Pulley	F Drive end housing	K Small spacer	O Slip ring end housing
B Fan	G Drive end housing	L Rotor	P Diode pack
C Large spacer	H Bearing retaining	M Seal	R Brush box
D Through-bolt	J Dust seal	N Bearing	S Stator
E Dust cap			

19.73 Rear foglamps switch removal

19.76A Unscrewing the steering column shroud upper ...

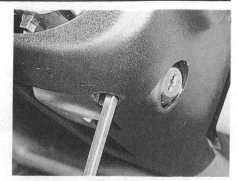

19.76B ... and lower retaining screws

19.76C Removing the two shrouds

19.77 Steering column switch retaining screws (arrowed)

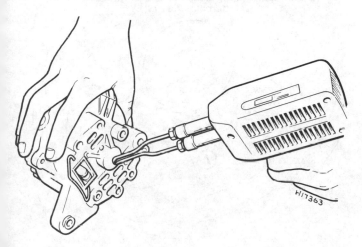

Fig. 13.196 Using a soldering iron to heat the slip ring end housing – Mitsubishi alternator (Sec 19)

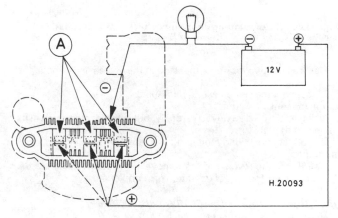

Fig. 13.197 Test circuit for checking positive diodes – Mitsubishi A500T alternator (Sec 19)

A   Positive diodes

72   Always disconnect the battery negative lead before removing any switches.

Heated windscreen/rear window, rear foglamp switches
73   Undo the two screws, carefully remove the instrument panel bezel then prise out the switch with a screwdriver taking care not to damage the surrounding facia (photo).
74   Disconnect the wiring multi-plug and remove the switch.

Steering column multi-function switches
75   Remove the steering wheel as described in Chapter 9.
76   Undo the screws and remove the upper and lower steering column shroud (photos).
77   Undo the retaining screws and remove the switch from the steering column (photo).
78   Disconnect the switch wiring multi-plug.
79   If removing the direction indicator multi-function switch, remove the hazard flasher switch and relay if required.

Ignition switch
80   Undo the screws and remove the steering column lower shroud.
81   Insert the ignition key into the switch and turn it to position 1.
82   Using a thin pointed tool, depress the lock spring through the access hole in the lock housing. Pull on the key while holding the lock spring depressed, and remove the switch. It may be necessary to move the key slightly to the left and right to align the key barrel and lock housing cam, so permitting removal.

Heater blower motor switch
83   Carefully pull off the three heater control knobs.
84   Undo the two retaining screws and remove the heater control panel.
85   Undo the two switch panel-to-facia securing screws and withdraw the panel.

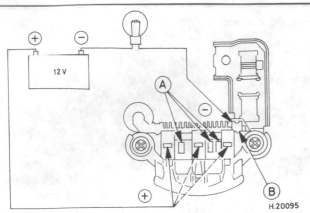

Fig. 13.198 Test circuit for checking field diodes – Mitsubishi A500T alternator (Sec 19)

A   Positive diodes   B   Brush box terminal

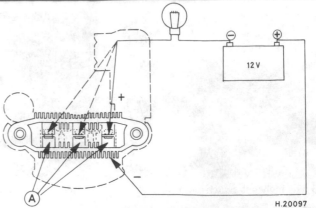

Fig. 13.199 Test circuit for checking negative diodes – Mitsubishi A500T alternator (Sec 19)

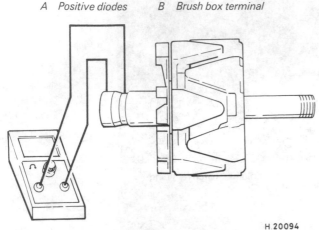

Fig. 13.200 Rotor winding continuity check – Mitsubishi A500T alternator (Sec 19)

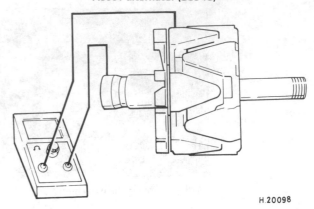

Fig. 13.201 Rotor winding insulation check – Mitsubishi A500T alternator (Sec 19)

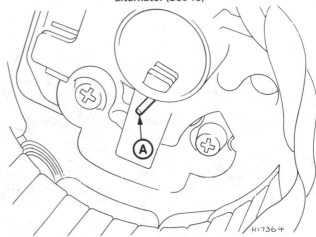

Fig. 13.202 Using a length of wire (A) to hold brushes retracted – Mitsubishi A500T alternator (Sec 19)

86   Depress the two tabs on either side of the switch and remove the switch.
87   Disconnect the switch wiring multi-plug.

Door mirror control switch
88   Using a thin screwdriver carefully prise the switch out of its location in the facia.
89   Disconnect the wiring multi-plug and remove the switch.

All switches
90   Refitting is the reverse of the removal procedure. Reconnect the battery and check for correct operation on completion.

Cigar lighter (1986-on) – removal and refitting
91   Disconnect the battery negative lead.
92   Remove the radio/cassette player as described later in this Section.
93   Disconnect the wiring from the cigar lighter body.
94   Pull out the cigar lighter element.
95   Push the cigar lighter body and illuminating ring out of their locations, then separate the ring from the body.
96   Refitting is a reversal of removal.

Interior lamp bulbs (1986-on) – renewal
97   The procedures are the same as described in Chapter 11 except for the following.

Glove compartment lamp
98   From inside the glove compartment, undo the two switch assembly retaining screws and withdraw the assembly.
99   Using a thin screwdriver, carefully prise out the switch and remove the bulb by pushing and turning ant-clockwise.

Heater control illumination lamp
100   Carefully pull off the three heater control knobs.
101   Undo the two retaining screws and withdraw the heater control panel.

102   From the rear of the panel, push and turn the bulb anti-clockwise to remove.

Manual choke knob warning lamp
103   Remove the choke knob by depressing the pin located on the underside of the knob.
104   Withdraw the sleeve, then remove the bulb by pushing it down, then pushing down the bulb retainer using a thin screwdriver.

All lamps
105   Refitting is the reversal of removal.

Front direction indicator side repeater lamp bulb (1986-on) – renewal
106   From under the front wing, compress the lamp body retaining clips and withdraw the lamp assembly.
107   Turn the bulbholder anti-clockwise and withdraw it from the

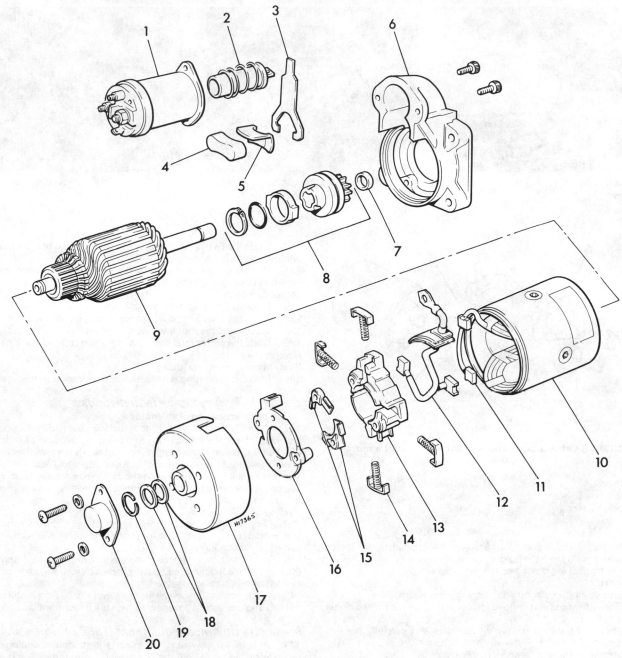

Fig. 12.203 Exploded view of the Lucas M79 starter motor (Sec 19)

1 Solenoid yoke	6 Drive end housing	11 Field bushes	16 Brush box insulator
2 Solenoid armature	7 Stop collar	12 Brush link	17 Commutator end housing
3 Actuating lever	8 Pinion assembly	13 Brush box	18 Spacers
4 Rubber block	9 Armature	14 Retaining spring	19 C-clip
5 Plastic support block	10 Main casing (yoke)	15 Insulator	20 End plate cap

lamp assembly. Pull out the push-fit bulb from the holder.
108   Refitting is the reversal of removal.

Instrument cluster (1986-on) – removal and refitting
109   Refer to Chapter 9 and remove the steering wheel.
110   Extract the two screws and pull the instrument cluster bezel from the cluster. The two clips at the base will release by the pulling action (photo).
111   Undo the four screws securing the cluster to the facia (photos).
112   Pull the cluster away from the facia and disconnect the wiring multi-plug and speedometer cable from the rear of the instrument

cluster. It may be necessary to feed the speedometer cable slack through the bulkhead from the engine compartment to facilitate removal. Withdraw the cluster.
113   Refitting is a reversal of removal.

Instrument cluster (1986-on) – dismantling and reassembly
114   Remove the instrument cluster as described previously.
Panel illumination and warning lamp bulbs
115   Turn the bulbholders anti-clockwise and remove them from the rear of the instrument cluster.

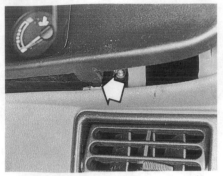
19.110 Bezel lower retaining clip (arrowed)

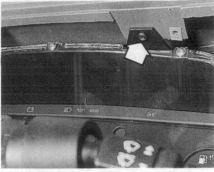
19.111A Instrument cluster upper retaining screw (arrowed) ...

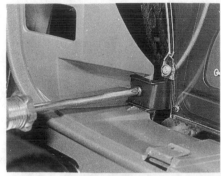
19.111B ... and lower screw removal

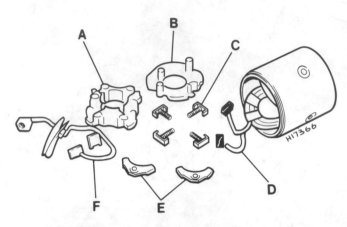

Fig. 13.204 Brush box components – Lucas M79 starter motor (Sec 19)

A Brush box
B Brush box insulator
C Retaining springs

D Field brushes
E Insulators
F Brush link

116   The bulbs and bulbholders are renewed complete, the bulbs cannot be removed from the holders separately.
117   Refit by pushing down and turning clockwise.
Printed circuit
118   Remove all illumination and warning lamp bulbholders.
119   Undo all the nuts and remove the washers from the printed circuit terminals.
120   Remove the wiring multi-plug retainers and carefully pull the printed circuit off the pins on the rear of the cluster.
121   Refitting is the reverse sequence to removal.
Speedometer
122   Undo the retaining screws and around the edge of the panel at the rear and separate the two panel halves.
123   Undo the two screws and remove the speedometer.
124   Refitting is the reverse sequence to removal.
Tachometer
125   The procedure is the same as for the speedometer except that the unit is secured by three nuts.
Fuel and temperature gauges
126   Proceed as for the speedometer but remove the combined gauge assembly after undoing the four nuts.

Central door locking system components (1986-on) – removal and refitting

127   From 1986 models onwards the central door locking system is operated by electric motors instead of the solenoids used previously. Removal and refitting of the system components is as follows.
Motor (front and rear doors)
128   Disconnect the battery negative lead.
129   Remove the door trim panel as described in Section 20.

130   Undo the two retaining screws, or drill out the bracket rivets and withdraw the motor.
131   Disconnect the motor from the operating rod, disconnect the wiring multi-plug and remove the motor.
Motor (boot lid)
132   Disconnect the battery negative lead.
133   Open the boot lid and where applicable, remove the trim panel.
134   Disconnect the motor wiring multi-plug.
135   Undo the motor retaining bolts, disconnect the operating rod and remove the motor.
System components refitting
136   In all cases refitting is a reversal of the removal procedure.

Central locking system – fault diagnosis
Jamming/overheating of solenoids
137   On early models with central locking solenoids (as opposed to locking motors), if a solenoid is to be renewed because of jamming or overheating, the central locking relay must also be renewed, as jamming or overheating of the solenoid can be a direct result of relay malfunction. The relay must be renewed even though it may appear to be working correctly. Make sure that the part number of the new relay is identical to the one removed.
Cycling of lock motors
138   If cycling (repeated locking and unlocking) of the lock motors on later models occurs, first check for short circuits and/or defective wiring, and rectify accordingly.
139   Also check that the lock motors are all of the same manufacture (Klaxon – made in France and casing halves riveted together, or SWF – casing halves screwed together).
140   If the lock motors are all identical and the cycling is still present, the lock motors should be renewed with the latest standard motors.

In-car entertainment equipment (1986-on – general)
141   Although a new range of in-car entertainment equipment became available from 1986 models onwards, the removal and refitting procedures described in Chapter 11 are still applicable, apart from the following exceptions.
142   On care equipped with a graphic equaliser, the removal and refitting procedures are the same as for the radio/cassette player.
143   When renewing the cowl panel mounted loudspeaker proceed as follows.
144   Extract sufficient screws from the scuff plate to facilitate cowl panel removal.
145   Insert a screwdriver into the captive plastic retainers and turn 90° anti-clockwise to remove them. Withdraw the cowl panel.
146   Undo the three speaker retaining screws, disconnect the leads and remove the speaker.
147   Refitting is a reversal of removal.
148   When removing the speaker fader joystick, proceed as follows.
149   Disconnect the battery negative lead, then remove the instrument cluster as previously described.
150   Carefully prise off the trim bezel using a screwdriver.
151   Turn the retaining clip anti-clockwise and remove the clip.
152   From within the instrument panel aperture disconnect the wiring multi-plug and remove the unit.
153   Refit in the reverse order of removal.

Fig. 13.205 Main fuse/relay box on 1986 models onwards (Sec 19)

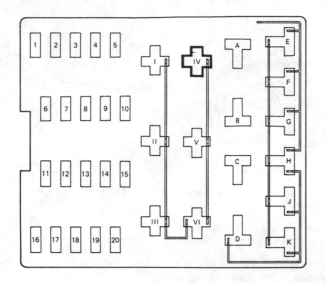

Relays in fusebox

I	Headlamp wash
II	Heated rear window time delay
III	Intermittent wiper (front)
IV	Automatic transmission starter inhibitor
V	Fuel pump, voltage protection, dim-dip
VI	Ignition switch
A	Idle speed, driving lamps
B	Free
C	Dual horn
D	Rear foglamp, dim-dip (sidelamps)
E	Free
F	Heated seats
G	Daytime running lamps (I)
H	Daytime running lamps (II)
J	Main beam
K	Dipped beam

Relays in relay box below instrument panel

L1	Speed sensor
L2	Diode assembly
L3	Fuel injection
L4	Heated windshield
L5	Daytime running lamps, dim-dip
L6	Anti-lock braking

Additional relays

M1	EGR system (engine compartment, RH side)

Fuse No	Rating	Circuit
1	15	Horn, hazard warning
2	15	Cigar lighter, interior lamps
3	30	Heated rear window, power mirror
4	30	Headlamp wash/wipe
5	15	Central door locking
6	15	Heated seats
7	20	Fuel pump
8	15	Driving lamps
9	10	LH main beam
10	10	RH main beam
11	20	Heater blower motor
12	25	Cooling fan
13	10	Flasher, reversing lamps
14	10	LH dipped beam
15	10	RH dipped beam
16	20	Wiper motors, washer pumps
17	10	Stop lamps, gauges
18	30	Electric windows
19	10	LH side lamps
20	10	RH side lamps

Additional fuses (located below instrument panel)

25	3	EEC IV Module
26	10	HEGO sensor, voltage protection.

In-car entertainment equipment – anti-theft

154   Certain later models are fitted with radio/cassettes with an electronic anti-theft device.

155   Whenever the power supply to the radio/cassette is interrupted (ie unit is removed or battery disconnected), then the radio/cassette unit must be reprogrammed with the correct security code – the 'Keycode' known only to the owner.

156   The unit will accept only three attempts at Keycode entry, after which a period of thirty minutes must elapse between each of up to ten subsequent attempts. Any further attempts will render the unit inoperative until reprogrammed by a Ford dealer.

Dim-dip lighting system – general

157   Later Orion models covered by this manual are equipped with a dim-dip lighting system which became a legal requirement in the UK for all cars registered from April 1st, 1987 onwards.

158   The system provides the headlamps with a brightness level

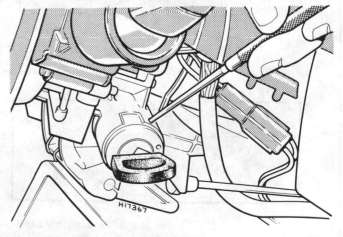

Fig. 13.206 Ignition switch removal using a pointed tool to depress the lock spring – 1986 models onwards (Sec 19)

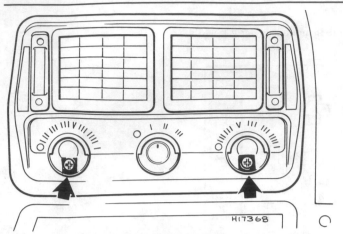

Fig. 13.207 Heater control panel retaining screw locations – 1986 models onwards (Sec 19)

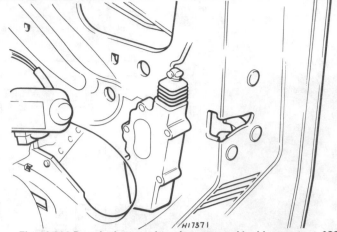

Fig. 13.208 Door lock motor location – central locking system, 1986 models onwards (Sec 19)

between that of the sidelamps and the normal dipped headlamp beam. The purpose of this legislation is to prevent cars being driven on sidelamps only.

159   The electrical control of the system is by additional relays located in the fuse unit. Circuit changes are shown in the applicable wiring diagrams at the end of this Supplement.

Fuel computer – removal and refitting

160   Disconnect the battery negative terminal.
161   Undo the two instrument panel bezel retaining screws and ease the bezel out to release the lower clips.

162   Withdraw the computer module from the facia to the right of the instrument panel.
163   Disconnect the wiring multi-plug and remove the computer.
164   Refitting is the reverse sequence to removal.

Fuel computer speed sender unit – removal and refitting

165   Undo the retaining nut and detach the speedometer cable from the speed sender unit.
166   Unclip and disconnect the wiring multi-plug.
167   Undo the retaining nut and withdraw the speed sender unit from the transmission.
168   Refitting is the reverse sequence to removal.

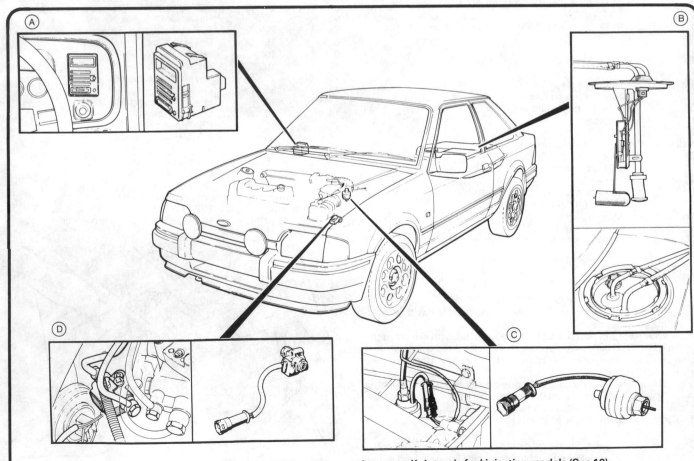

Fig. 13.209 Fuel computer component layout on K-Jetronic fuel injection models (Sec 19)

A   Fuel computer   B   Fuel tank sender unit   C   Speed sender unit   E   Fuel flow sensor

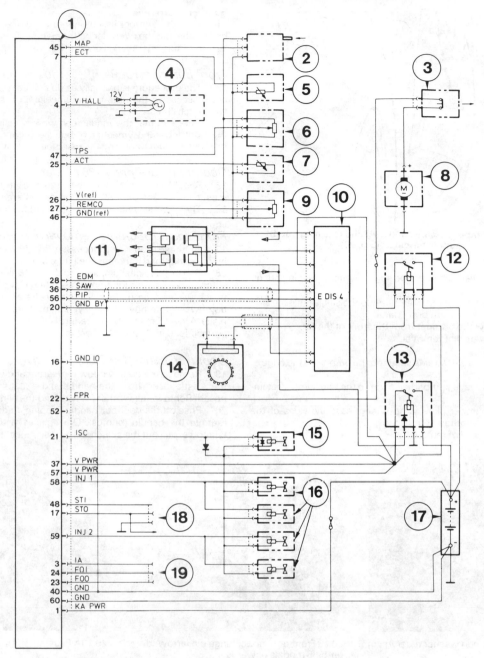

Fig. 13.210 Schematic diagram of engine management system on 1.6 litre EFI models (Sec 19)

1 EEC-IV module
2 Manifold absolute pressure sensor (MAP)
3 Inertia switch
4 Vehicle speed sensor
5 Engine coolant temperature sensor (ECT)
6 Throttle position sensor (TPS)
7 Air charge temperature sensor (ACT)
8 Fuel pump
9 CO adjustment pot
10 E-DIS 4 module
11 Ignition coil (DIS)
12 Fuel pump relay
13 Power relay
14 Crankshaft position sensor (CPS)
15 Idle speed control valve (ISCV)
16 Fuel injectors
17 Battery
18 Self test connector
19 Service connector

Fuel computer fuel flow sensor – removal and refitting

169   The fuel flow sensor is used in conjunction with the fuel computer on fuel-injected models and is located on the fuel distributor at the front left-hand side of the engine compartment.
170   Disconnect the wiring multi-plug then undo the two banjo unions on the side of the unit. Note the position of the sealing washers.
171   Undo the two retaining screws and remove the fuel flow sensor.
172   Refitting is the reverse sequence to removal. Ensure that the sealing washers are correctly fitted.

20 Bodywork

Radiator grille (1988-on) – removal and refitting
1   The radiator grille is integral with the front bumper moulding and is removed with the bumper (see later paragraphs).

Bumper assembly (1986-on) – removal and refitting
Front bumper
2   Undo the single screw each side securing the bumper to the edge of the wheel arch.

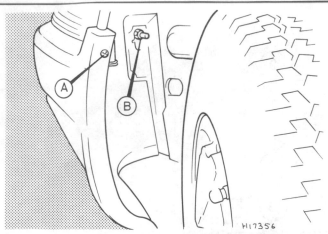

Fig. 13.211 Front bumper-to-arch screw (A) and retaining nut (B) – 1986 models onwards (Sec 20)

3   From under the wheel arch undo the single bumper retaining nut on each side.

4   From within the engine compartment undo the single nut each side securing the bumper to the front body panel.

5   Carefully withdraw the bumper from the front of the car.

6   Refitting is the reversal of removal.

Rear bumper

7   Undo the three screws each side securing the bumper to the edge of the wheel arch.

8   From inside the luggage compartment undo the two bumper retaining nuts each side.

9   Disconnect the number plate lamp wiring, ease the sides of the bumper outward and withdraw it from the car.

10   Refitting is a reversal of removal.

Bumper overriders

11   With the bumper assembly removed, the two retaining nuts can be undone and the overrider withdrawn.

12   Refitting is a reversal of removal.

Front bumper (1988-on) – removal and refitting

13   The procedure is basically as described for 1986-on models but if more access to the nuts in the wheelarches is required, remove the wheelarch liners.

14   Note also that the windscreen washer reservoir is now located in the front left-hand wheel arch, but the bumper retaining nut can be reached without removing the reservoir (photo).

Door renewal – pre-1986 models

15   Should a new door need to be fitted to a pre-1986 model, the door must be reworked as 1986-on doors are different to early doors.

16   The necessary parts can be obtained from Ford dealers.

Front door (1986-on) – removal and refitting

17   On these models it is necessary to extract the pin from the upper hinge, rather than unbolting the hinge from the pillar.

18   To do this, ideally special tool 41-018 is needed, but a suitable alternative can be made from a piece of metal with a U-shaped cut-out which will engage under the head of the pin (photo). Strike the tool downward to remove the pin. When refitting, tap the pin upwards into place. Apart from this the procedure is the same as for pre-1986 models, as described in Chapter 12, Section 24.

Door trim panel (1986-on) – removal and refitting

19   Remove the door window regulator handle. Do this by prising out the plastic insert from the handle and extracting the screw now exposed. Remove the washer from behind the handle (photos).

20   Prise off the door pull handle capping, undo the three screws and remove the handle (photos). On vehicles with electrically operated windows, pull out the switches and disconnect the wiring.

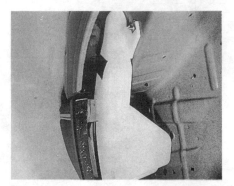

20.14 View of windscreen washer reservoir in wheel arch (liner removed)

20.18 Front door upper hinge pin (arrowed) on 1986 models onwards

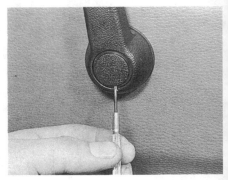

20.19A Prise out the insert ...

20.19B ... unscrew and remove the regulator handle ...

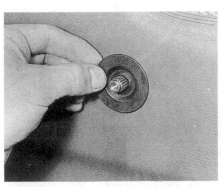

20.19C ... and washer

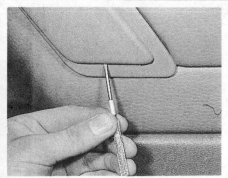

20.20A Prise out the door pull handle capping ...

20.20B ... undo the screws ...

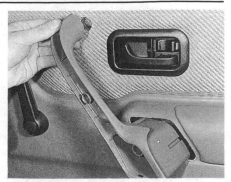

20.20C ... and remove the handle

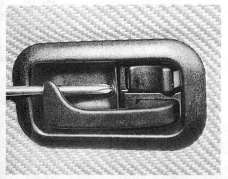

20.21A Undo the remote control handle bezel retaining screw ...

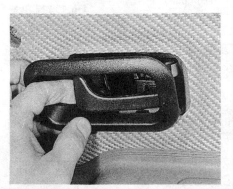

20.21B ... and remove the bezel

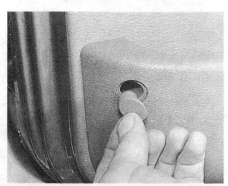

20.22A Release the trim cap and undo the screw ...

20.22B ... followed by the side screws

20.23 Lift the trim panel upwards to disengage the lower brackets

21   Undo the door lock remote control handle bezel retaining screw and remove the bezel (photos).
22   Prise out the plastic trim cap and unscrew the lower front panel retaining screw. Unscrew the three remaining screws, one at the upper front and two at the rear of the panel (photos).
23   Carefully release the retaining clips at the top of the panel and lift upwards to disengage the lower brackets (photo).
24   Refitting is a reversal of removal.

Door trim panel (1988-on) – removal and refitting
25   From 1989, a new foam watershield is fitted under the door trim panel, secured in position by a strip of butyl.
26   To remove the watershield, the butyl strip must not be touched with the hands or subsequent adhesion will be impaired.
27   If the foam watershield is damaged beyond re-use on removal, all traces of it, and the butyl must be removed from the door inner skin. The butyl can be removed by 'rolling' it up on itself to form a ball.

28   New butyl strips can then be applied and a new watershield fitted. Use a roller to press the shield into contact with the butyl strip.
29   Alternatively, an alkathene sheet can be used, which is secured in place with double sided tape.
30   Vehicles which are fitted with an alkathene sheet in production must not subsequently be fitted with a foam shield as certain other components (eg remote handle seal) are different to allow for the thickness of the foam.

Door lock plunger – general
31   Although the door lock rod is threaded, the plastic pushbutton is not.
32   To fit a button, have the latch unlocked and push the button onto the rod, making sure that the flat inside the button aligns with the flat on the rod.
33   Push the button down until the top of the button is flush with the panel grommet.

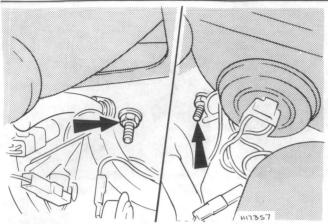

Fig. 13.212 Front bumper retaining nuts in engine compartment –
1986 models onwards (Sec 20)

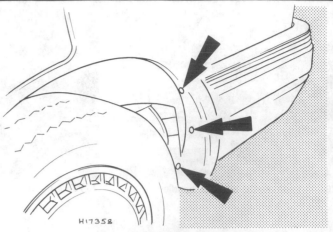

Fig. 13.213 Rear bumper-to-wheel arch screws – 1986 models
onwards (Sec 20)

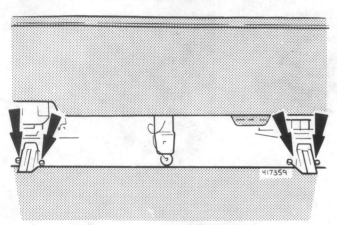

Fig. 13.214 Rear bumper attachments in luggage compartment –
1986 models onwards (Sec 20)

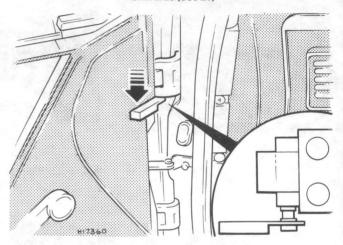

Fig. 13.215 Front door upper hinge pin removal using special tool –
1986 models onwards (Sec 20)

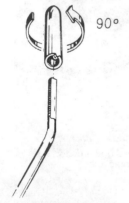

Fig. 13.216 Door lock pushbutton fixing diagram (Sec 20)

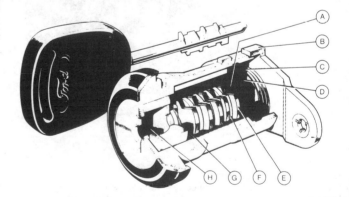

Fig. 13.217 'Tibbe' high security lock (Sec 20)

A   Housing   E   Tumbler
B   Lever   F   Spacer
C   Bush   G   Retaining ring
D   Barrel   H   Shutter assembly

34   Operate the door interior lock lever to raise the button, and then fix
the button to the rod by turning it through 90°. This will cause the
threads on the rod to cut into the inside of the button. Do not turn button
round and round.

Door locks (1987-on) – removal and refitting

35   From August 1987 all models are fitted with 'Tibbe' high security
locks to all doors, the ignition switch and fuel filler lid.
36   Repair/overhaul kits are available for these locks from Ford dealers,
and locks can be re-built to any key combination code.
37   The removal and refitting procedure for the high security locks is
as described in Chapter 12, Section 22.

Glove compartment (1986-on) – removal and refitting

38   Undo the two screws and remove the glove compartment lid.

39   Remove the latch (two screws) and disconnect the lamp wiring
(where fitted).
40   Undo the three screws and remove the glove compartment.
41   Refitting is a reversal of removal.

Facia (1986-on) – removal and refitting

42   Disconnect the battery negative lead.
43   Refer to Chapter 9 and remove the steering column assembly.

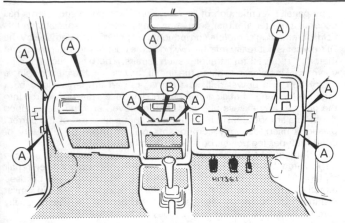

Fig. 13.218 Crash pad and facia attachments – 1986 models onwards (Sec 20)

A Retaining screws B Retaining nut

Fig. 13.219 Electrically operated door mirror switches (Sec 20)

1 Angle control switch 2 Driver/passenger selector switch

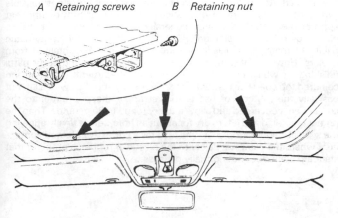

Fig. 13.220 Sunroof lower frame-to-glass screws (Sec 20)

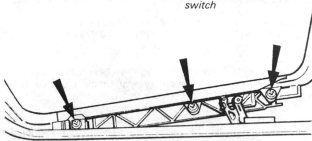

Fig. 13.221 Sunroof gear-to-glass screws (Sec 20)

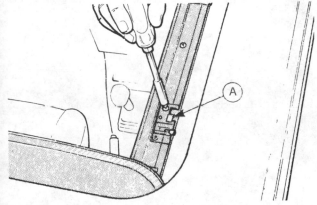

Fig. 13.222 Sunroof guide plate (A) (Sec 20)

44 Remove the instrument cluster, and where fitted, the indicator control unit of the auxiliary warning system and/or the fuel computer.
45 Remove the choke cable.
46 Remove the heater control knobs.
47 Undo the two heater control facia panel screws, pull the panel out and disconnect the wiring multi-plug. Remove the seal.
48 Remove the ashtray.
49 Remove the radio or radio/cassette player.
50 Undo the radio/ashtray facia panel screws, withdraw the panel and disconnect the cigar lighter wiring. Remove the panel.
51 Remove the glove compartment.
52 Undo the nine screws and one nut securing the facia then remove it from the car.
53 The crash padding can be removed after undoing the screws from behind the facia.
54 Refitting is a reversal of removal.

Exterior mirrors – general
55 To adjust the mirror on the passenger side, simply move the glass within the frame. The frame is fixed.
56 On Ghia models, the exterior mirrors are electrically controlled and heated to dispel moisture and frost.
57 The control switch is located on the centre console. To move the mirror on the passenger side, first move the switch to the left-hand side.
58 The mirror is heated at the same time as the heated rear window is switched on.
59 Removal and refitting of the exterior mirrors is as described in Chapter 12, except that before starting work, disconnect the battery negative terminal and as the removal operations proceed, disconnect the mirror wiring plugs.

Sunroof – elimination of wind noise
60 If wind noise is a problem when the sunroof is closed, carry out the following operations.
61 Check that the weatherseal is in good condition. If it is not, renew it.
62 The sunroof panel at its front edge should follow the contour of the roof. If it is not in alignment, slide the panel back to its halfway position and then, working inside the car, grip the panel and pull downwards or push upwards until the metal frame on the glass bends sufficiently to improve the panel to roof alignment.
63 The sunroof panel should be between flush and 2.0 mm below the roof at its front end and flush to 2.0 mm above the roof at its rear end.
64 To adjust the height of the panel, extract the three screws which hold the lower frame to the glass. Slide the frame towards the back of the car.
65 Set the sunroof panel in the tilt position to gain access to the retaining screws (Fig. 13.221).
66 To adjust the front end of the panel, slacken the front and centre screws.
67 To adjust the rear end of the panel, slacken the centre and rear screws.
68 Close the panel and check the alignment. Re-adjust if necessary, then refit the three frame screws.
69 A 2.0 mm thick feeler blade, when inserted between the weatherstrip and the front edge of the roof aperture, should be a light sliding fit with even resistance. Any adjustment required should be carried out with the roof panel in the half-open position. Use a plastic hammer to bend the weatherstrip flange rearwards to relieve any resistance.
70 Where necessary, open the roof panel to expose the guide plates. Release one retaining screw and move the plate forwards or backwards one or two gradations, then check the fit of the feeler blade.

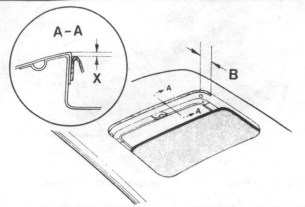

Fig. 13.223 Sunroof supplementary seal fitting diagram (Sec 20)

B   = 7.0 to 13.0 mm   X   = 1.0 to 2.0 mm
     (0.28 to 0.51 in)   (0.039 to 0.079 in)

71   If, after all checks and adjustments have been carried out, wind noise is still evident, a supplementary seal should be fitted in the following way.
72   Slide the sunroof to the half-open position.
73   Using a suitable solvent, clean the front edge of the roof aperture.
74   Cut the length of the new sealing strip to 840.0 mm (33.1 in) and stick it to the front closure face of the roof aperture. Make sure that the seal is positioned as shown in Fig. 13.223.

Plastic components – repair

75   With the use of more and more plastic body components by the vehicle manufacturers (eg bumpers, spoilers, and in some cases major body panels), rectification of more serious damage to such items has become a matter of either entrusting repair work to a specialist in this field, or renewing complete components. Repair of such damage by the DIY owner is not really feasible owing to the cost of the equipment and materials required for effecting such repairs. The basic technique involves making a groove along the line of the crack in the plastic using a rotary burr in a power drill. The damaged part is then welded back together by using a hot air gun to heat up and fuse a plastic filler rod into the groove. Any excess plastic is then removed and the area rubbed down to a smooth finish. It is important that a filler rod of the correct plastic is used, as body components can be made of a variety of different types (eg polycarbonate, ABS, polypropylene).
76   Damage of a less serious nature (abrasions, minor cracks etc) can be repaired by the DIY owner using a two-part epoxy filler repair material like Holts Body + Plus or Holts No Mix which can be used directly from the tube in the case of Holts No Mix), this is used in similar fashion to the bodywork filler used on metal panels. The filler is usually cured in twenty to thirty minutes, ready for sanding and painting.
77   If the owner is renewing a complete component himself, or if he has repaired it with epoxy filler, he will be left with the problem of finding a suitable paint for finishing which is compatible with the type of plastic used. At one time the use of a universal paint was not possible owing to the complex range of plastics encountered in body component applications. Standard paints, generally speaking, will not bond to plastic or rubber satisfactorily, but Holts Professional Spraymatch paints to match any plastic or rubber finish can be obtained from dealers. However, it is now possible to obtain a plastic body parts finishing kit which consists of a pre-primer treatment, a primer and coloured top coat. Full instructions are normally supplied with a kit, but basically the method of use is to first apply the pre-primer to the component concerned and allow it to dry for up to 30 minutes. Then the primer is applied and left to dry for about an hour before finally applying the special coloured top coat. The result is a correctly coloured component where the paint will flex with the plastic or rubber, a property that standard paint does not normally possess.

Conversion factors

Length (distance)
Inches (in)	X	25.4	= Millimetres (mm)	X 0.0394	= Inches (in)
Feet (ft)	X	0.305	= Metres (m)	X 3.281	= Feet (ft)
Miles	X	1.609	= Kilometres (km)	X 0.621	= Miles

Volume (capacity)
Cubic inches (cu in; in³)	X	16.387	= Cubic centimetres (cc; cm³)	X 0.061	= Cubic inches (cu in; in³)
Imperial pints (Imp pt)	X	0.568	= Litres (l)	X 1.76	= Imperial pints (Imp pt)
Imperial quarts (Imp qt)	X	1.137	= Litres (l)	X 0.88	= Imperial quarts (Imp qt)
Imperial quarts (Imp qt)	X	1.201	= US quarts (US qt)	X 0.833	= Imperial quarts (Imp qt)
US quarts (US qt)	X	0.946	= Litres (l)	X 1.057	= US quarts (US qt)
Imperial gallons (Imp gal)	X	4.546	= Litres (l)	X 0.22	= Imperial gallons (Imp gal)
Imperial gallons (Imp gal)	X	1.201	= US gallons (US gal)	X 0.833	= Imperial gallons (Imp gal)
US gallons (US gal)	X	3.785	= Litres (l)	X 0.264	= US gallons (US gal)

Mass (weight)
Ounces (oz)	X	28.35	= Grams (g)	X 0.035	= Ounces (oz)
Pounds (lb)	X	0.454	= Kilograms (kg)	X 2.205	= Pounds (lb)

Force
Ounces-force (ozf; oz)	X	0.278	= Newtons (N)	X 3.6	= Ounces-force (ozf; oz)
Pounds-force (lbf; lb)	X	4.448	= Newtons (N)	X 0.225	= Pounds-force (lbf; lb)
Newtons (N)	X	0.1	= Kilograms-force (kgf; kg)	X 9.81	= Newtons (N)

Pressure
Pounds-force per square inch (psi; lbf/in²; lb/in²)	X	0.070	= Kilograms-force per square centimetre (kgf/cm²; kg/cm²)	X 14.223	= Pounds-force per square inch (psi; lbf/in²; lb/in²)
Pounds-force per square inch (psi; lbf/in²; lb/in²)	X	0.068	= Atmospheres (atm)	X 14.696	= Pounds-force per square inch (psi; lbf/in²; lb/in²)
Pounds-force per square inch (psi; lbf/in²; lb/in²)	X	0.069	= Bars	X 14.5	= Pounds-force per square inch (psi; lbf/in²; lb/in²)
Pounds-force per square inch (psi; lbf/in²; lb/in²)	X	6.895	= Kilopascals (kPa)	X 0.145	= Pounds-force per square inch (psi; lbf/in²; lb/in²)
Kilopascals (kPa)	X	0.01	= Kilograms-force per square centimetre (kgf/cm²; kg/cm²)	X 98.1	= Kilopascals (kPa)
Millibar (mbar)	X	100	= Pascals (Pa)	X 0.01	= Millibar (mbar)
Millibar (mbar)	X	0.0145	= Pounds-force per square inch (psi; lbf/in²; lb/in²)	X 68.947	= Millibar (mbar)
Millibar (mbar)	X	0.75	= Millimetres of mercury (mmHg)	X 1.333	= Millibar (mbar)
Millibar (mbar)	X	0.401	= Inches of water (inH₂O)	X 2.491	= Millibar (mbar)
Millimetres of mercury (mmHg)	X	0.535	= Inches of water (inH₂O)	X 1.868	= Millimetres of mercury (mmHg)
Inches of water (inH₂O)	X	0.036	= Pounds-force per square inch (psi; lbf/in²; lb/in²)	X 27.68	= Inches of water (inH₂O)

Torque (moment of force)
Pounds-force inches (lbf in; lb in)	X	1.152	= Kilograms-force centimetre (kgf cm; kg cm)	X 0.868	= Pounds-force inches (lbf in; lb in)
Pounds-force inches (lbf in; lb in)	X	0.113	= Newton metres (Nm)	X 8.85	= Pounds-force inches (lbf in; lb in)
Pounds-force inches (lbf in; lb in)	X	0.083	= Pounds-force feet (lbf ft; lb ft)	X 12	= Pounds-force inches (lbf in; lb in)
Pounds-force feet (lbf ft; lb ft)	X	0.138	= Kilograms-force metres (kgf m; kg m)	X 7.233	= Pounds-force feet (lbf ft; lb ft)
Pounds-force feet (lbf ft; lb ft)	X	1.356	= Newton metres (Nm)	X 0.738	= Pounds-force feet (lbf ft; lb ft)
Newton metres (Nm)	X	0.102	= Kilograms-force metres (kgf m; kg m)	X 9.804	= Newton metres (Nm)

Power
Horsepower (hp)	X	745.7	= Watts (W)	X 0.0013	= Horsepower (hp)

Velocity (speed)
Miles per hour (miles/hr; mph)	X	1.609	= Kilometres per hour (km/hr; kph)	X 0.621	= Miles per hour (miles/hr; mph)

Fuel consumption*
Miles per gallon, Imperial (mpg)	X	0.354	= Kilometres per litre (km/l)	X 2.825	= Miles per gallon, Imperial (mpg)
Miles per gallon, US (mpg)	X	0.425	= Kilometres per litre (km/l)	X 2.352	= Miles per gallon, US (mpg)

Temperature

Degrees Fahrenheit = (°C x 1.8) + 32   Degrees Celsius (Degrees Centigrade; °C) = (°F - 32) x 0.56

*It is common practice to convert from miles per gallon (mpg) to litres/100 kilometres (l/100km),
where mpg (Imperial) x l/100 km = 282 and mpg (US) x l/100 km = 235

Index